is volume originally appeared in various issues of
IAL OF WOMEN IN CULTURE AND SOCIETY.
at of the original publication data can be found on the
h essay.

of Chicago Press, Chicago 60637
of Chicago Press, Ltd., London
1983, 1987, 1991, 1992, 1993, 1994, 1995 by the
icago.
d. Published 1995
nited States of America
5   5 4 3 2 1

of Congress Cataloging-in-Publication Data

olitical / edited by Johanna Brenner, Barbara Laslett,
at.

ex.
07397-1. — ISBN 0-226-07399-8 (pbk.)
n politics.   2. Feminism.   3. Women—Government
tizenship.   I. Brenner, Johanna.   II. Laslett, Barbara.
n, 1955—   .
        1995

                                95-7645
                                CIP

RETHINKING THE POLITICAL

RETHINKING

GENDER, RESIST

EDITED BY BARB

JOHANNA BRENN

AND YESIM ARAT

The University of Chicago

Chicago and London

ays

JOU

vledg

ge of

ivers

ivers

, 198

ity of

ts res

in the

97 9

Libra

ing th

'eşim

. cn

ludes i

N 0-2.

Wome

. 4.

rat, Y

236.R4

2—dc2

er used

n Natic

r Printe

CONTENTS

The Editors   **1–8**   Feminists Rethink the Political

GENDER, CITIZENSHIP, AND COLLECTIVITY

Ruth H. Bloch   **11–32**   The Gendered Meanings of Virtue in Revolutionary America

Nancy Fraser and Linda Gordon   **33–60**   A Genealogy of *Dependency:* Tracing a Keyword of the U.S. Welfare State

Trisha Franzen   **61–76**   Differences and Identities: Feminism and the Albuquerque Lesbian Community

Sonia Kruks   **77–98**   Gender and Subjectivity: Simone de Beauvoir and Contemporary Feminism

Iris Marion Young   **99–124**   Gender as Seriality: Thinking about Women as a Social Collective

COLLECTIVE ACTION AND WOMEN'S RESISTANCE

Louise A. Tilly   **127–144**   Paths of Proletarianization: Organization of Production, Sexual Division of Labor, and Women's Collective Action

Temma Kaplan   **145–166**   Female Consciousness and Collective Action: The Case of Barcelona, 1910–1918

Samira Haj   **167–184**   Palestinian Women and Patriarchal Relations

Arlene Elowe MacLeod   **185–209**   Hegemonic Relations and Gender Resistance: The New Veiling as Accommodating Protest in Cairo

Gay W. Seidman   **210–239**   "No Freedom without the Women": Mobilization and Gender in South Africa, 1970–1992

Nancy Saporta Sternbach, Marysa Navarro-Aranguren, Patricia Chuchryk, and Sonia E. Alvarez   **240–281**   Feminisms in Latin America: From Bogotá to San Bernardo

Anne Walthall   **282–312**   Devoted Wives/Unruly Women: Invisible Presence in the History of Japanese Social Protest

GENDER AND THE STATE

Bronwyn Winter   **315–350**   Women, the Law, and Cultural Relativism in France: The Case of Excision

Patricia Stamp   **351–388**   Burying Otieno: The Politics of Gender and Ethnicity in Kenya

Elizabeth Schmidt   **389–413**   Patriarchy, Capitalism, and the Colonial State in Zimbabwe

Muriel Nazzari   **414–431**   The "Woman Question" in Cuba: An Analysis of Material Constraints on Its Solution

Wendy Luttrell   **432–473**   "The Teachers, They All Had Their Pets": Concepts of Gender, Knowledge, and Power

475–480   About the Contributors
481–489   Index

Acknowledgments

We are particularly grateful to Kim Rowe, a *Signs* student intern who very ably assisted us in the initial research for this volume and correspondence with the contributors, and to Jeanne Barker-Nunn, the managing editor of *Signs,* who has coordinated the editing and production of this volume.

The Editors

Feminists Rethink the Political

The Editors

FEMINISTS WITHIN and outside the academy have revised our conceptions of the political and understanding of power by viewing them through the lens of gender. This rethinking of the political has also become more nuanced as historical and national variations have been brought into view. The collection of articles presented here highlights this revitalization of the discourses on the political in feminist examinations of citizenship, women's collective action, and the state.

There are many ways of defining and thinking about the political from a feminist perspective. The choices we have made for this volume flow from our interest in women's collective action, our conviction that understanding such action requires at least historical and comparative perspective, and our theoretical concern with the relationship between social structure and human agency. The articles in this collection are part of feminist challenges to traditional conceptualizations of the political. Feminist scholars, for instance, have contested the ways that the political has been demarcated through a public/private dichotomy; asserted the significance of gender in shaping political institutions such as citizenship and the nation-state that appear to be gender-neutral; made women's collective action visible in both historical and contemporary politics; and exposed the deeply gendered categories of political theory. This volume is also an intervention into debates within feminism itself, particularly over the issues of difference and identity and their implications for both feminist theory and feminist activism.

Each of the articles reprinted here contributes in one way or another to a set of questions that we feel are crucial to feminist rethinkings of the political. Across time and place, the articles consider the circumstances that foster or undermine women's capacities for collective action and resistance. Here we see analyzed the social, economic, cultural, and political conditions that shape not only levels of participation but also the forms that resistance takes. The role played by representations of gender—how gender identities are deployed in political discourses and mobilized by political actors and to what effect—is another theme explored in case studies from different national contexts. Finally, again in a comparative context, the articles offer cautionary tales about and possible strategies for addressing relations of dominance within women's collective action and feminist politics.

We begin with two articles that take up an issue central to the feminist critique of the political: the false universalization of white male practices of citizenship in Western liberal democratic polities. Ruth H. Bloch demonstrates that the emergence of modern notions of citizenship based on reason, justice, and rational "enlightened" calculation of self-interest was accompanied by a redefinition of public virtue and the gendered capacities for exercising it. What had been defined as uniquely male characteristics (courage, benevolence, and self-sacrifice) fitting men for public life were now defined as female character traits associated with service rather than citizenship. While these gendered definitions of virtue justified the exclusion of women from participation in the rights and responsibilities of citizenship, they also provided resources upon which women could and did act, translating their private virtues into the public realm through movements for moral and social reform.

The deeply gendered character of citizenship is further illuminated by Nancy Fraser and Linda Gordon in their analysis of historical shifts in the meaning of the term dependency. Although women eventually may have won formal citizenship rights, their substantive rights in relationship to the welfare state were quite different from those of men, expressed in the gendered opposition of dependence/independence. With the rise of capitalism, participation in public economic and political life came to be structured in terms of individual independence, reserved for the free wage laborer and the citizen. In preindustrial society, dependency was, and was regarded to be, a normal condition for men as well as for women. In industrial society, dependency came to be defined as deviant even as it remained feminized and racialized in the contrast between the (white) free wage laborer and the Black slave and between the independent male breadwinner and the dependent housewife. As the welfare state evolved, the feminization and racialization of dependence became associated with a gendered, two-track system of state provision that stigmatized the predominantly female recipients of public assistance as it mystified the actual economic dependency of other recipients of state aid (such as the elderly, the unemployed, and recipients of agricultural loans and home mortgage assistance).

Although their opportunities for contesting the institutions and practices defining citizenship have been constrained, women also have struggled with some success to reshape the political realm. In this effort, a feminist identity has served as an important basis for political organization. Yet contemporary feminist theory and practice also have highlighted the complicated nature of identity and the cleavages, tensions, and contradictions that divide women as a group. Several articles directly address this issue. In her history of the lesbian community in Albuquerque, Tricia Franzen observes that experience, because it is multidimensional and shaped by class and race as well as gender and sexuality, cannot provide the sole basis for political solidarity. The political identities created by predominantly white, middle-class, and newly out lesbianfeminists excluded older generations of lesbian women, including closeted and out, middle-class and working-class, and women of color. Ironically, it is to the example of this older generation that Franzen turns for an alternative practice of solidarity, arguing that while they were never organized politically, they understood and respected each other's choices without denying each others' subjectivity.

Franzen's vision of a political solidarity that avoids either false universalism or essentialist constructions of identity is explored at a more theoretical level by Iris Marion Young and by Sonia Kruks. Aware of the radical challenge to feminist politics and scholarship raised by the charge that conceptualizing women as a group reduces the diversity of women's experience to a common denominator, they nonetheless also contend that political organization, even feminism itself, requires a notion of women as purposive acting subjects with interests in common. As some poststructuralist feminists have acknowledged, women cannot act collectively—that is, politically—as women without the capacity to define common purposes, interests, or needs. If there is no such thing as Woman, if commonality does not reside in bodies, experiences, or identities, then it will have to be found elsewhere, for unless we conceptualize women as a social collective, "feminist politics evaporates," in Young's words. In an interesting juxtaposition, Young turns to Sartre's concept of a series to provide a nonessentialist basis for women's relationship to each other and their potential to organize as a group, while Kruks draws on de Beauvoir for an account of historically situated gendered subjectivity.

The next section opens up with two now-classic contributions to feminist historical scholarship and feminist redefinitions of the political: articles by Temma Kaplan and by Louise A. Tilly that analyze the conditions under which working-class women have acted collectively. Calling attention to working-class women as political actors and to women's political action outside explicitly feminist movements for citizenship rights, these articles take complementary tacks toward revising assumptions about women's participation in politics. Tilly demonstrates that under conditions approximating those of male skilled workers, women proletarians have been equally capable of sustained organization and contestation. Kaplan, on the other hand, highlights the ways in which working-class women have organized differently from men, drawing on their maternal responsibilities as resources for political action.

These gender similarities and differences in self-organization and mobilization are explored in a number of case studies outside the European-American context that we have included, some providing instances where women have notably limited possibilities for resistance. In addition to providing a comparative perspective, these articles illuminate the political as well as the social, cutural, and economic conditions that shape women's collective action. Compare, for example, Arlene Elowe MacLeod's analysis of the "accommodating protest" by working women in contemporary Cairo where organized feminism is in retreat to the description by Nancy Saporta Sternbach and her coauthors of how working-class women's participation in popular protest, and particularly the *movimientos de mujeres,* has responded to and fundamentally challenged an institutionalized feminist movement. North American feminists can be inspired by their example and learn from it. In Latin America, feminist activists from the *movimientos de mujeres* together with increasingly class- and race-conscious veterans of organized feminism are constructing a vibrant and inclusive feminist politics.

The relationship between movements against dictatorship and for national liberation and women's opportunities for self-organization is further explored by Samira Haj and Gay W. Seidman. At certain points in the Palestinian liberation struggle and in the South African struggle to overthrow apartheid, popular civilian protest and community organization became strategically central. In those moments a space opened up for women's collective action based in their maternal responsibilities. In certain instances, perhaps only short-lived or among younger people, women came to challenge traditional gender relations through their political activism on behalf of their families and communities. Feminists have been both appreciative and critical of women's "traditional place" in the domestic realm, and these studies demonstrate that domestic location can stultify women's capacities for action, can provide resources for action, and can be transcended through action. Placing side by side the article by MacLeod on Egyptian women in Cairo and that by Haj about Palestinian women on the West Bank should also serve to caution against universal assumptions about Islamic cultures or about their impact on women's political action and strategies of resistance.

Once in power, movements for national liberation have often replaced a concern for women's equality articulated during the struggle with a concern for national unity. Writing in 1993, Seidman suggests that grassroots organizing among South African working-class women who framed demands for their equality in autonomous groups empowered women in the African National Congress to take up feminist demands.

Yet politics and political movement do not stand still. A variety of circumstances that both reflected and created increasing township violence during the later protracted transition to democratic government undermined the community-based women's groups that had formed a feminist constituency within the antiapartheid movement. The question, as Seidman now sees it, is whether women who are in key political positions—such as seats in Parliament—in the newly democratized South African state will be able to push feminist demands when they no longer have the same feminist constituency to support a central place for women and women's issues. The challenge facing feminists in the new government, then, is how to rebuild the grassroots women's movement so that newly established legal equality can be translated into changes in women's daily lives.[1]

The importance of women's capacities for self-organization—and how they can grow out of struggles for national liberation even though women's voices and concerns about equality are often submerged in the rhetoric of national liberation—is also evident among Palestinian women in 1994. Assia Habash, an observer of the *Intifada* and a member of its general support system, reports that since the Gulf War and with the onset of the peace process between Palestinians and Israelis, women have begun to articulate their role in the national struggle and their political and social concerns as women. In the West Bank and Gaza, women's institutes not representative of any particular political faction have been conducting research, seminars, and workshops; mobilizing women for elections; and generally providing a space where women's issues can be articulated. The developing women's studies program at Beir-Zeit University is another example of such a space. Women's voices on women's issues are also beginning to be heard in Islamic organizations.[2] The absence of attention to women's issues within liberation struggles at one point in time does not therefore guarantee continued inattention to them.[3]

As feminist scholars have worked to make women's collective action visible, they have also argued for a more expansive definition of political resistance, recognizing the severe constraints under which women have often been forced to struggle. The articles by Anne Walthall and by

[1] Gay W. Seidman, personal communication, November 1994.
[2] Assia Habash, personal communication, October 1994.
[3] Julia Szalai, in "Women and Democratization: Some Notes of Recent Changes in Hungary" (Institute of Sociology, Hungarian Academy of Sciences, Budapest, 1994), makes a related point about the capacities for and the sites of women's self-organization in Hungary. Although women seem to make up a declining percentage of elected officials in that country, they are nonetheless a marked presence in its political life: in newly organized associations, in local groups, and as committee members in local governments.

MacLeod draw attention to instances where women have engaged in protest as individual actors rather than as parts of collectivities. They point out that women have both used and contested familial ideologies and gendered norms to gain access to public space and to secure their conditions of life. Walthall also raises important questions concerning the impact of gender on knowledge about women's political action, especially in the past. Considering the evidence available to her on early modern Japan, Walthall points out that existing histories, scholarly and popular, are male constructions of women's deeds and words. Our ability to excavate the truth of women's public action is inevitably limited by the fact that we are forced to rely on sources produced by men within patriarchal state institutions and beyond them.

The insight that state institutions are deeply gendered is a significant aspect of feminist rethinking of the political. The articles in the final section exemplify this accomplishment in case studies analyzing a range of states and state institutions. Bronwyn Winter draws attention to the dilemmas facing those who attempt to protect or defend women of color through the legal system of the modern French state and how political contests within that context affect different views about how that system should be used. Illuminating the gulf between principles institutionalized in the law and in the courts and the reality of immigrant women's lives, Winter's study brings into sharp relief the fracturing of feminist solidarity across the divide of race/ethnicity and class. Middle-class white feminists in France have approached excision (clitoridectomy) through universalizing notions of the legal and judicial systems. They appear to be ready to sacrifice poor immigrant women of color to prevent harm to immigrant daughters. At the same time, the conditions of immigrant women's daily lives severely limit their capacity to be heard in debates about what should happen to their and their daughters' bodies. Yet, as Winter points out, empathy with women of color does not alleviate the barriers they confront. Reference to universalist norms, deployed in an educational strategy, could allow immigrant women to help themselves, to have a voice in the decisions and policies that so intimately affect them and their daughters.

Winter's analysis demonstrates how the courts become an arena where political actors play out their own agendas on the bodies of women, particularly on those of less powerful women. This argument—that women's sexuality, its control, regulation, and construction, whether directly intended or not, is a central element in state policy as well as often being a screen for other kinds of struggles—is taken up in articles about colonial and postcolonial Africa. In her analysis of Wambui Otieno's struggle to claim her husband's estate in contemporary Kenya, Patricia Stamp provides another example of the actions of the courts in relation to women's rights and women's access to resources. This legal conflict engaged Wambui Otieno not only in a contest over political power but also over "modernity" versus patriarchal "traditions." The opposition between enlightenment universalism and cultural relativism, between the modern and the traditional, is by no means a solely academic question, as this article demonstrates. Strategies and discourses relying on one or the other of these poles remain ongoing sources of political and social conflict.[4]

This invention of "traditions" regarding women and their invocation to legitimate state policy also played an important part in the implantation and perpetuation of colonial rule. In her analysis of the British colonial administration in Southern Rhodesia, Elizabeth Schmidt demonstrates the centrality of gender conflict to the evolution of colonial economic arrangements and governing policies, including the creation of "customary law." In order to maintain its authority and to stabilize access to the labor of younger men, the patriarchal colonial state colluded with chiefs, headmen, and other older men to counter women's resistance to economic and gender oppression and to reinforce men's control over women's resources, wages, children, mobility, and marriages. Going beyond an account rooted entirely in capitalist class interests, Schmidt shows that gender struggles also shaped the colonial economy.

Muriel Nazarri's article on Cuba addresses the other side of the coin, arguing that state policies centered on gender issues are shaped by the dynamics of the political economy. Many feminist critiques of postrevolutionary societies have focused on patriarchal culture and social arrangements carried into the new society from the past in order to explain the failure to institutionalize equality for women. Nazzari expands that analysis to consider how certain key economic policy decisions—to prioritize investment in industrial production, to improve productivity, and to tie individuals' standard of living more closely to the wage—limited the avenues through which traditional gender division of labor and women's "double day" might have been changed.

In addition to the courts and the law, educational systems are central state institutions and, as Wendy Luttrell shows, they are deeply gendered, racialized, and classed. In her study of white working-class women and rural women of color as teachers and students, Luttrell demonstrates how school experiences shape gender, knowledge, and power, how they

[4] For a continuing dialogue about the Otieno case and its importance for understanding women's politics and capacities for self-organization, see April Gordon, "Gender, Ethnicity, and Class in Kenya: 'Burying Otieno' Revisited," *Signs: Journal of Women in Culture and Society,* vol. 20 (Summer 1995).

affect the voices that are heard and spoken, the faces and bodies that are seen and unseen. Schools are not simply neutral spaces for "schoolwise learning." They are sites of political conflict and social action, including conflict between women. Through the stories she collects and analyzes, Luttrell shows, in ways similar to MacLeod's study of working women in Cairo, how seemingly self-defeating actions such as dropping out of school can be instances of resistance and critique.

In conclusion, we hold to the idea that it is necessary and desirable for feminists to both theorize the political and remain sensitive to differences shaped by historical context. Although we accept the postmodern criticisms of theories that essentialize categories of women and universalize women's problems, we nonetheless affirm the need to define women as a group if we are to self-organize and take political action. At the same time, we recognize the need for dynamic formulations that are aware of differences in locations, power, traditions, and histories. If politics is the attempt to shape a common future, we believe as feminists in the need to engage in this endeavor with other women. We hope that this volume will contribute to this goal.

GENDER, CITIZENSHIP,
AND COLLECTIVITY

The Gendered Meanings of Virtue in Revolutionary America

Ruth H. Bloch

In its contemporary colloquial usage, "virtue" is usually a term for female sexual prudence and benevolent activity with old-fashioned connotations. It evokes traits like chastity and altruism and, in a cynical post-sexual-revolution world, prudery and hypocritical do-goodism.

On the one hand, these connotations are very old in Western culture. The sexual meaning of the word dates back to medieval and ancient times when the virtues were symbolized as virgins.[1] The Catholic ideals of celibacy and charity also reinforced the association of Christian virtue with sexual purity and personal sacrifice. On the other hand, the Protestant Reformation placed less emphasis on these qualities, criticizing the monastic ideal of celibacy and denying the spiritual efficacy of church offerings. It stressed other individual virtues—piety, temperance, frugality, and work in a useful calling.

Earlier versions of this paper were presented to the 1985–86 Gender Seminar at the Institute for Advanced Study in Princeton and to the Faculty Research Seminar on Women at the University of California, Los Angeles. Many members of these seminars provided useful criticisms. I am especially grateful to the anonymous readers for *Signs* and to Joyce Appleby, Daniel Walker Howe, Jan Lewis, Phyllis Mack, Debora Silverman, and Kathryn Kish Sklar for their helpful suggestions.
    [1] Morton W. Bloomfield, *The Seven Deadly Sins* (East Lansing: Michigan State University Press, 1952), 64, 137.

[*Signs: Journal of Women in Culture and Society* 1987, vol. 13, no. 1]

The view that women were capable of greater sexual self-control and generosity than men arose later, in the eighteenth and nineteenth centuries, at different times and to different degrees in different places and social groups. This transformation was, at most, only indirectly a consequence of the cultural changes brought on by the Reformation. In middle-class America, where both Calvinism and early evangelical Protestantism were particularly strong, it was not until the end of the eighteenth century that women were commonly idealized as selfless and pure. According to the quintessentially Victorian view, intrinsically feminine traits—traits eventually satirized as "motherhood and apple pie"—lay at the base of the American nation. It is the echo of this nineteenth-century culture that we hear in the colloquial use of the word virtue today.

Among historians identified with the recent interpretation of the American Revolution known as the "Republican synthesis," the word "virtue" has, however, been invested with an older political meaning.[2] Resurrected in its classical and early modern republican forms, the term refers not to female private morality but to male public spirit, that is, to the willingness of citizens to engage actively in civic life and to sacrifice individual interests for the common good. Is virtue, then, to be understood as a word with two different meanings—one personal and female, the other political and male? Or is there a deeper historical and symbolic connection between the two definitions?

An appreciation of the eighteenth-century political use of the term is essential to an understanding of the American Revolution, but it is becoming increasingly clear that such an appreciation must also take into account the history of masculine and feminine symbolism. Conceptions of politics and of gender were tied together in late eighteenth-century America in ways that historians have only begun to unravel. The transition toward the personal and feminine definition of "virtue" was a development already occurring during the Revolutionary period, partly in response to political events and partly in response to changes in gender-based symbols that had already begun.

The experiences and perceptions of women during the American Revolution have attracted considerable scholarly attention from historians of women. So far, most studies point to the importance of women's activity during the Revolution and to the ways in which their social status was

[2] For a useful review of this literature, see Robert Shalhope, "Republicanism and Early American Historiography," *William and Mary Quarterly* 39 (1982): 334–56. The classical republican idea of virtue has also been invoked outside the historical discipline. See, e.g., Sheldon Wolin, *Politics and Vision: Continuity and Innovation in Western Political Thought* (Boston: Little, Brown & Co., 1960); Robert N. Bellah, *The Broken Covenant: American Civil Religion in a Time of Trial* (New York: Seabury Press, 1975); Alasdair MacIntyre, *After Virtue: A Study in Moral Theory* (Notre Dame, Ind.: University of Notre Dame Press, 1981).

affected, for good or ill.[3] Here the relationship of women to the Revolution will be approached from a somewhat different angle. Pursuing insights contained in a few recent writings, I would suggest that conceptions of sexual difference—views that were at once deeply held (often only implicitly) and highly unstable—underlay some of the most basic premises of the Revolution and shaped important ideological changes in the early Republic.[4] However much the meaning of virtue changed over the course of this period, it remained a word laden with assumptions about gender.

The focus of this essay, in other words, is less on the Revolution's impact on women and more on the influence of gender-based symbols in the formation of Revolutionary thought. To trace the late eighteenth-century changes in this symbolism contributes to our understanding of gender as a cultural—and, therefore, historical—construct. The connections between the constructions of gender and politics point to the importance of women's history in exploring the conventional questions of political history.[5]

Some of the most influential recent intellectual historians of Anglo-American political thought have considered individual words—liberty, tyranny, corruption, and especially virtue—as keys that unlock the meaning of the broadly consensual historical "discourse" of classical republicanism.[6] A few others have only just begun to challenge the overly static

---

[3] See esp. Linda K. Kerber, *Women of the Republic: Intellect and Ideology in Revolutionary America* (Chapel Hill: University of North Carolina Press, 1980); Mary Beth Norton, *Liberty's Daughters: The Revolutionary Experience of American Women, 1750–1800* (Boston: Little, Brown & Co., 1980); Joan Hoff-Wilson, "The Illusion of Change: Women and the American Revolution," in *The American Revolution: Explorations in the History of American Radicalism*, ed. Alfred F. Young (Dekalb: Northern Illinois University Press, 1976), 383–445.

[4] A few studies that partly address this question and helped to stimulate this article are: Kerber, *Women of the Republic*, 269–88, and "The Republican Ideology of the Revolutionary Generation," *American Quarterly* 37 (1985): 474–95; Paula Baker, "The Domestication of Politics: Women and American Political Society, 1780–1920," *American Historical Review* 89 (1984): 620–47; Jan Lewis, "The Republican Wife," *William and Mary Quarterly*, 3d ser., vol. 44 (October 1987); J. G. A. Pocock, "Modes of Political and Historical Time in Early Eighteenth-Century England," in his *Virtue, Commerce, and History* (New York: Cambridge University Press, 1985), 98–100; Hanna Fenichel Pitkin, *Fortune Is a Woman* (Berkeley: University of California Press, 1984).

[5] Joan W. Scott calls for this in her "Gender: A Useful Category of Analysis," *American Historical Review* 91 (December 1986): 1053–75.

[6] See esp. J. G. A. Pocock, *The Machiavellian Moment: Florentine Political Thought and the Atlantic Republican Tradition* (Princeton, N.J.: Princeton University Press, 1975), and *Virtue, Commerce, and History;* Bernard Bailyn, *The Ideological Origins of the American Revolution* (Cambridge, Mass.: Harvard University Press, 1967); Caroline Robbins, *The Eighteenth-Century English Commonwealthmen* (Cambridge, Mass.: Harvard University Press, 1959); Gordon S. Wood, *The Creation of the American Republic, 1776–1787* (Chapel Hill: University of North Carolina Press, 1969); Lance Banning, *The Jeffersonian Persuasion: Evolution of a Party Ideology* (Ithaca, N.Y.: Cornell University Press, 1978); Drew R. McCoy,

and holistic conception of culture that this "republican synthesis" implies.[7] I argue here that an examination of the multivalent meanings embedded in the term virtue leads to a more complex and dynamic understanding not only of gender but also of Revolutionary ideology itself.

The work of Caroline Robbins, Bernard Bailyn, Gordon Wood, and J. G. A. Pocock outlines the extent to which American patriots conceptualized the American Revolution within the intellectual framework of classical republicanism. As we now understand this intellectual background, the revival of ancient republican theories—first in the city-states of the Italian Renaissance, then in seventeenth-century England—was kept alive into the eighteenth century by a small, disunified, yet vociferous group of political dissidents in England. The distinctive structural conditions of politics in the colonies, in combination with the values of American Protestantism, led the colonists of the mid-eighteenth century to embrace many of the tenets of classical republicanism.

According to the basic constitutional theory of classical republicanism, the preservation of liberty depended on a mixed and balanced government. Such a government consisted essentially of three parts, each representative of a different social order: the king in the monarchy, the aristocracy in the House of Lords (or the colonial Councils), and the property-holding populace in the elected legislature. The hallmark of a free republic, according to this theory, was the autonomy of a legislature with institutionalized power to tax. The social base necessary to sustain this arrangement, described most fully by James Harrington in the seventeenth century,[8] was a large class of arms-bearing freeholders—fairly equal and independent property owners, able to defend themselves, and sharing a regard for the public good—whose common voice would be expressed in their elected legislature. When in the 1760s and 1770s the British imperial government challenged powers traditionally exercised by the elected colonial legislatures, including the power to tax, colonists interpreted the new policy in the terms of republican theory—as a fundamental assault on their liberty.

Even then, however, the political ideas espoused by the American Revolutionaries were a hybrid mixture. Some of these derived not from the classical republican tradition of Machiavelli and Harrington but from con-

---

The Elusive Republic: Political Economy in Jeffersonian America (Chapel Hill: University of North Carolina Press, 1980).

[7] For example, from the perspective of liberalism, Joyce Appleby, *Capitalism and a New Social Order: The Republic Vision of the 1790s* (New York: New York University Press, 1984); from the perspective of American Protestantism, Ruth H. Bloch, *Visionary Republic: Millennial Themes in American Thought* (New York: Cambridge University Press, 1985).

[8] The key text is James Harrington, *Oceana*, ed. S. B. Liljegren (Heidelberg: Carl Winters Universitätsbuchlung, 1924).

stitutional ideas about individual rights and from Protestant theories about the providential purpose of government. For American Revolutionaries, as for those English opposition writers, such as John Trenchard and William Gordon, who were most widely read in the colonies, the ideas of egalitarian individualism and Nonconforming Protestantism were blended with classical republican notions about the sovereignty of the popular legislature.

Throughout the Revolutionary period, virtue was the most valued quality defining individual commitment to the American republican cause. One reason for its salience was that both the classical republican and the Protestant traditions emphasized the value of public virtue. According to both, virtue reconciled otherwise contradictory commitments to both individual political freedom and the greater public good because virtue would prompt otherwise selfish individuals to actions on behalf of a just and harmonious social order. The main difference between these traditions lay in their assumptions about the source of virtue: within orthodox Protestantism, it was bestowed by Providence or faith; within classical republicanism, it was obtained through independent property holding and mixed government. Each tradition, moreover, had its own way of describing the relation of virtuous citizens, high and low, to the body politic. Within orthodox Protestantism political virtue was primarily a trait of good rulers who, with God, tended the political order. Ordinary members of the covenanted community assumed the more limited responsibility of obeying good rulers and living according to the moral code. Within classical republicanism, also, the few and the many exercised their virtue in dissimilar ways: the titled and the propertied were to rule; the people were to rise against threats of foreign invasion and political corruption. Yet according to each of these traditions, the virtue of both the rulers and the populace was indispensable to preserving the good health of the polity.

The orthodox Protestant and classical republican traditions also fundamentally agreed that public virtue was an inherently masculine trait. Patriarchal analogies pervaded seventeenth-century English and American Protestant political thought, which drew heavily on Old Testament models: a good leader, like a good father, was wise, caring, and firm.[9] In 1637, the New England Puritan governor John Winthrop defended the power of the Massachusetts magistrates against Henry Vane, a supporter of Anne Hutchinson, by insisting on the superior judgment of the "fathers of the commonwealth." The Aristotelian notion of virtue as always "united with a rational principle"—a notion that continued to dominate American

---

[9] Gordon Schochet, *Patriarchalism in Political Thought* (Oxford: Basil Blackwell, 1975). The patriarchal familial imagery within New England Puritan writings about political leadership is well known. For a recent explication, see Melvin Yazawa, *From Colonies to Commonwealth: Familial Ideology and the Beginnings of the American Republic* (Baltimore: Johns Hopkins University Press, 1985).

Puritan ethical theory until the late seventeenth century—by definition favored men since men were deemed more rational than women.[10]

Not that women were ever regarded as incapable of all kinds of virtue. Women were thought to be as rational as men in exercising the private, Christian virtues—temperance, prudence, faith, charity. It was specifically public virtue—active, self-sacrificial service to the state on behalf of the common good—that was an essentially male attribute. While there were a few exceptional early American women who won recognition for their heroic defense of the wider community, these were the kind of exceptions that proved the rule. Public virtue was indeed possible for exceptional women, but it was never an inherently feminine characteristic.

Among the most renowned examples of exceptional women were the New Englanders Hannah Dustin and Mary Rowlandson who bravely withstood Indian attacks.[11] Hannah Dustin, who won her fame by brutally scalping her assailants, demonstrated qualities of physical courage and strength that conformed to a typically male model of virtue. What distinguished her as a heroine was precisely her ability to step out of her femininity. Mary Rowlandson, to the contrary, never overtly violated the Puritan conception of a virtuous woman. Her heroism consisted in her pious adherence to Puritan faith and in her shrewd use of domestic skills to earn the protection of her enemies. Yet it was the very fact that she was an *exceptional* woman—a woman who kept her faith and maintained her wits amid heathens—that largely accounts for the sensational popularity of her captivity narrative. Despite the striking differences between them, Hannah Dustin and Mary Rowlandson won public acclaim precisely because they, as women, went so far beyond typical expectations: they proved themselves neither weaker nor less capable of absorbing and retaining the standards of civilization than men.

In the classical republican tradition, the masculine attributes embedded in the concept of public virtue are even more pronounced than those in American Puritanism. The ancient origins of this highly gendered concept can be traced as far back as the Homeric idea of *aretê* or human excellence

[10] John Winthrop, as quoted in Thomas Hutchinson, ed., *A Collection of Original Papers Relative to the History of the Colony of Massachusetts Bay* (Boston: Thomas & John Fleet, 1769), reprinted in Joyce O. Appleby, ed., *Materialism and Morality in the American Past: Themes and Sources* (Reading, Mass.: Addison-Wesley Publishing Co., 1974), 34, 38. For the Aristotelian notion of virtue, see Norman Fiering, *Moral Philosophy at Seventeenth-Century Harvard* (Chapel Hill: University of North Carolina Press, 1981), 72. The abundant literature documenting the negative cultural evaluation of female reason is summarized briefly in Ruth H. Bloch, "Untangling the Roots of Modern Sex Roles: A Survey of Four Centuries of Change," *Signs: Journal of Women in Culture and Society* 4, no. 2 (Winter 1978): 237–52.

[11] These cases are described in more detail in Laurel Thatcher Ulrich, *Good Wives* (New York: Oxford University Press, 1982), 184–201; Nancy Woloch, *Women and the American Experience* (New York: Alfred A. Knopf, 1984), 1–15.

(later translated as "virtue"), which stressed the physical strength and bravery displayed in athletic contests and in battles. This emphasis on courage remained a basic component of the classical tradition and later fused with Greek and Roman ideas about the intellectual and cooperative virtues (such as judgment, justice, and friendship) that bind men in citizenship within the polis.[12] According to the revitalized Renaissance republicanism of Machiavelli, virtue was, again, best displayed in acts of military heroism and civic activism. Exemplary citizens were above all daring soldiers and inspired orators—those who risked danger and won glory in valiant defense of liberty. As Pocock has defined it, the Machiavellian *virtù* that proved so influential in America consisted in "the skill and courage by which men are enabled to dominate events and fortune."[13] Hannah Pitkin examined the gender implications of the word in her book on Machiavelli's political theory: "Though it can sometimes mean [Christian] virtue, *virtù* tends mostly to connote energy, effectiveness, virtuosity. . . . The word derives from the Latin *virtus*, and thus from *vir*, which means 'man.' *Virtù* is thus manliness, those qualities found in a 'real man.'"[14] The political realm was constituted by the actions of fathers and sons—patriarchal founders and fraternal citizens. Typically, women appeared in this symbolic matrix as the dangerous, unreliable force of *fortuna* (or, later, according to Pocock, public credit), threatening to sabotage the endeavor of virtuous men.[15]

On the face of it, the masculinity embedded in ideas of public virtue appears trivial, the simple reflection of the male domination of political institutions. In fact, property requirements guaranteed that statesmen, soldiers, and enfranchised citizens would be, by definition, men. The intrinsic maleness of the term virtue could be seen, then, as the logical,

[12] For examples of the specialized debate over the various classical meanings of these terms, see MacIntyre (n. 2 above), 114–53; Arthur Madigan, "Plato, Aristotle and Professor MacIntyre," and A. A. Long, "Greek Ethics after MacIntyre and the Stoic Community of Reason," both in *Ancient Philosophy* 3 (1983): 171–83, 184–97. That *virtù* was a fundamentally male quality, associated with courage and involvement in civic life, is a common theme. For the purposes of this essay, what is important is that these elements were revived by Machiavelli and other Renaissance republicans and then transmitted to America.

[13] Pocock, *The Machiavellian Moment*, 92. The traditional idea of virtue as glory is also explicated in Albert O. Hirschman, *The Passions and the Interests: Political Arguments for Capitalism before Its Triumph* (Princeton, N.J.: Princeton University Press, 1977), 7–66.

[14] Pitkin (n. 4 above), 25.

[15] Ibid.; Pocock, "Modes of Political and Historical Time" (n. 4 above), 98–100. Quentin Skinner has taken issue with Pitkin's exclusive emphasis on the negative feminine symbolism in Machiavelli, pointing out that he used feminine Italian nouns (including *virtù* itself) to describe the abstract goals and ideals of the republic. Yet Pitkin herself questions the value of this kind of narrow linguistic analysis (n. 4 above, 131), and even Skinner agrees that Machiavelli's words to describe "the active and shaping features of public life" are masculine (Skinner, "Ms. Machiavelli," *New York Review of Books* [March 14, 1985], 29–30).

even automatic, cultural consequence of male political hegemony. But there is more to it.

These notions of masculinity were fundamental to the concept of public virtue in a way that would change in Revolutionary America without corresponding changes in military recruitments, property holding, or franchise requirements. As ideas about the political order underwent a profound transformation during the Revolutionary period, so did the understanding of virtue. Even as political institutions continued to be essentially male, underlying shifts in the gendered meaning of virtue expressed (even, perhaps, helped to make possible) a new understanding of republican politics.

* * *

In the mid-1770s, with the outbreak of revolution and war, the specifically masculine qualities embedded in conceptions of public virtue received, if anything, still more emphasis. The model patriot was frequently described according to classical republican ideals as a heroic orator or citizen-soldier.[16] In a widely distributed 1775 oration commemorating the Boston Massacre, Joseph Warren envisioned "fathers / looking / . . . with smiling approbation on their sons who boldly stand forth in the cause of virtue."[17] Virtue was above all the mark of "the uncorrupted patriot, the useful citizen, and the invincible soldier."[18] Even as military enthusiasm began to flag in subsequent years, calls to "virtuous Americans" to give "firm and manly support" to the war effort continued.[19] According to a minister preaching before Virginia troops in New Jersey in 1777, virtue was inextricably associated with glory and fame: "Glory is the reward of honourable toils, and public fame is the just retribution for public service; the love of which is so connected to virtue, that it seems scarcely possible to be possessed of the latter without some degree of the former."[20]

If the virtues of heroic courage, glory, and fame were inherently male, the opposites—cowardice, idleness, luxury, dependence—were, not sur-

[16] Isaac Story, *The Love of our Country Recommended and Enforced* (Boston: John Boyle, 1774), 13–16. The association of virtue with military courage during the *"rage militaire"* of 1775 is described in Charles Royster, *A Revolutionary People at War* (Chapel Hill: University of North Carolina Press, 1979), 25–53.

[17] Joseph Warren, *An Oration Delivered March Sixth 1775* (Boston: Edes & Gill, 1775), 21.

[18] John Witherspoon, *The Dominion of Providence over the Passions of Men* (Philadelphia: Aitken, 1776), 60.

[19] Phillips Payson, *A Sermon Preached before the Honourable Council . . . of the State of Massachusetts Bay* (Boston: John Gill, 1778), 32.

[20] John Hurt, *The Love of Our Country* (Philadelphia: Styner & Cist, 1777), 17. Also, see Richard Henry Lee as quoted in Pauline Maier, *The Old Revolutionaries: Political Lives in the Age of Samuel Adams* (New York: Vintage Trade Books, 1980), 198.

prisingly, castigated as the "effeminate" weaknesses of unpatriotic men. Whereas the Americans were "a hardy virtuous set of men," proclaimed a patriot orator in 1776, their corrupt British enemies had succumbed to "that luxury which effeminates the mind and body."[21] But what about women themselves? Was there any model of female public virtue consistent with the glorification of male heroism in the Revolution? The most famous examples were the legendary "Molly Pitcher" of the Battle of Monmouth and Deborah Sampson Gannett, a young woman subsequently glorified for disguising herself as a man in order to enlist in the Revolutionary army.[22] More typical were the women gathered in such organizations as the Daughters of Liberty and the Ladies Association, who abstained from tea drinking, boycotted loyalist shops, made homespun clothing, and raised money in support of the Revolutionary cause.[23] Neither the courage of Gannett nor these women's less heroic—Protestant as well as republican—virtues of industriousness, abstention, charity, and frugality differed markedly from what was expected of patriotic men. Essentially the only distinctively feminine images of Revolutionary virtue during the 1770s were those of a mother passively donating her sons to the struggle or of a helpless virgin physically abused by the enemy.[24]

[21] Peter Thacher, *Oration Delivered March 5, 1776*, as quoted in Wood (n. 6 above), 100. Morally deficient American as well as British men were frequently depicted as feminine. See, e.g., John Witherspoon, *Dominion of Providence*, 57; [Royall Tyler], *The Contrast* (Philadelphia: Prichard & Hall, 1790); Kerber, *Women of the Republic* (n. 3 above), 31; Wood, 110. Within the classical republican tradition, such rhetoric goes back to Machiavelli and beyond (see Pitkin [n. 4 above], 109–10).

[22] Such rare if dramatic examples of female heroism are recounted in Sally Smith Booth, *The Women of '76* (New York: Hastings House, 1973), 173–74, 266–70.

[23] For a full account and analysis of these activities, see Mary Beth Norton (n. 3 above).

[24] Kerber, *Women of the Republic*, 106. For more examples of the maternal imagery, see Royster (n. 16 above), 30, 90; Story (n. 16 above), 16–17. For examples of women physically abused by the enemy, see Jay Fliegelman, *Prodigals and Pilgrims* (New York: Cambridge University Press, 1982), 117, 137–44. A similar religious image was that of America as the woman in the wilderness of the book of Revelation, pursued by minions of Satan: see, e.g., William Foster, *True Fortitude Delineated* (Philadelphia: John Dunlap, 1776), 17; [Wheeler Case], *Poems, Occasioned by Several Circumstances and Occurrences* (New Haven, Conn.: Thomas & Green, 1778), 21. This theme of women as innocent, passively virtuous victims of male vice—tyranny and lust—was an extension of the themes of popular fiction into political discourse. Jan Lewis explores this association in "The Republican Wife" (n. 4 above). For the opposite image of Great Britain as a bad mother, see Edwin G. Burrows and Michael Wallace, "The American Revolution: The Ideology and Psychology of National Liberation," *Perspectives in American History* 6 (1972): 190–214. This theme also had its analogues in fiction about bad mothers (see Fliegelman, 51–52, 118). For examples of the biblical scarlet whore image, see Henry Cumings, *A Sermon Preached in Billerica on the 3rd of November, 1775* (Worcester, Mass.: L. Thomas, 1775), 12; Enoch Huntington, *A Sermon, Delivered at Middletown, July 20th, A.D. 1775* (Hartford, Conn.: Ebenezer Watson, 1775), 21. The rebellious implications of unmasking ignoble political origins are explored in Judith N. Shklar, "Subversive Genealogies," in *Myth, Symbol, and Culture*, ed. Clifford Geertz (New York: W. W. Norton & Co., 1971), 129–53.

It was later, in the 1780s and 1790s, when a significantly separate image of female public spirit began to appear. During the period in which the exigencies of warfare gave way to the politics of state, women were increasingly presented as indispensable and active promoters of patriotism in men. As mothers, young social companions, and wives, women came to be idealized as the source not only of domestic morality but also of civic virtue itself.

Historian Linda Kerber has already drawn attention to the emerging idea of the "republican mother" in the late eighteenth century.[25] It was already a cliché of the age that mothers, not fathers, were particularly responsible for inculcating children with the piety, benevolence, and self-discipline that compose virtue.[26] By the turn of the century, several patriotic commentators had extended this responsibility to include the public virtue deemed necessary to sustain the republic. Women, according to this view, would serve the new nation by making good citizens of their sons despite formal exclusion from institutional political life. A few even justified the education of women on these grounds as a patriotic necessity. A young female graduate of Susanna Rowson's Academy foresaw the day when "future heroes and statesmen," having learned "the love of virtue" as children, "shall exaltingly declare, it is to my mother I owe this elevation."[27] In the words of one minister preaching in 1802, "How should it enflame the desire of the mothers and daughters of our land to be the occasion of so much good to themselves and others! —You will easily see that here is laid the basis of public virtue; of union, peace and happiness in society. . . . Mothers do, in a sense, hold the reins of government and sway the ensigns of national prosperity and glory."[28]

Though they held this responsibility as mothers, women were to instill public virtue in men through courtship and marriage perhaps even more.[29] It was repeatedly claimed, by American and English moralists both, that women's influence over men gave them the power to reform the manners

---

[25] Kerber, *Women of the Republic*, 265–88.

[26] See Ruth Bloch, "American Feminine Ideals in Transition: The Rise of the Moral Mother," *Feminist Studies* 4 (June 1978): 101–26.

[27] As quoted in Kerber (n. 3 above), 229. Also see Benjamin Rush, "Thoughts upon Female Education" (originally published in 1787), in *Essays on Education in the Early Republic*, ed. Frederick Rudolph (Cambridge, Mass.: Harvard University Press, 1965), 25–40; "Oration upon Female Education, Pronounced . . . in Boston, September, 1791," in *The American Preceptor*, ed. Caleb Bingham, 44th ed. (Boston: Manning & Loring, 1813), 47–51.

[28] William Lyman, *A Virtuous Woman the Bond of Domestic Union* (New-London, Conn.: S. Green, 1802), 22.

[29] In this period there was still far more literature on courtship, marriage, and the social utility of female education than on motherhood per se. In her forthcoming article, Jan Lewis (n. 4 above) argues that the image of the "republican wife" was more prevalent than that of the "republican mother."

and morals of society.[30] In the writings of American patriots, this notion took on a distinctively republican coloring. "Love and courtship, it is universally allowed, invest a lady with more authority than in any other situation that falls to the lot of human beings," declared a Columbia College orator in 1795. Describing American women as "patriots and philanthropists," he insisted that it was up to them to withstand "the deluge of vice and luxury, which has well nigh overwhelmed Europe, . . . [and] to save, to aggrandize your country! . . . The solidity and stability of the liberties of your country rest with you; since Liberty is never sure, 'till Virtue reigns triumphant."[31] Another writer similarly insisted that "female virtue," by which he essentially meant chastity, was the key to "national prosperity and the honour and happiness of posterity," because "the profoundest politicians, wisest statesmen, most invincible champions, greatest generals, ingenious artists, and even pulpit orators" spent so much of their time with women.[32] American men were advised that good republican citizenship, as well as personal happiness, would follow ineluctably from true love and marriage.[33]

*   *   *

To understand the origins of this transformation of ideas about public virtue, it is necessary to look not only at Revolutionary political discourse but also at the seemingly nonpolitical ideas about human psychology, education, and women that were current in the eighteenth century. In this broader intellectual history one finds the origins of a long-term redefinition of gender distinctions already well underway by the 1770s and intimately connected to changes in the nonpolitical understanding of virtue. Over the course of the Revolutionary period, particularly as debates surrounding the Constitution formulated a new conception of republican government, these nonpolitical ideas about virtue came to assume political significance. Changes in the gender-based meaning of public virtue in the late eighteenth century owed as much to these earlier intellectual developments as to the influences of Revolutionary politics.

[30] For example, Rush; Jane West, *Letters to a Young Lady* (Troy, N.Y.: O. Penniman, 1806), 27; "Scheme for Encreasing the Power of the Fair Sex," *Baltimore Weekly Magazine* 1 (April 1801): 241–42; *Advice to the Fair Sex; in a Series of Letters on Various Subjects: Chiefly Describing the Graceful Virtues* (Philadelphia: Robert Cochran, 1803), 3–4; Samuel Kennedy Jennings, *The Married Lady's Companion, or Poor Man's Friend* (Richmond, Va.: T. Nicholson, 1804), 5.

[31] "Female Influence," *New York Magazine* (May 1795), 299–305.

[32] Thomas Branagan, *The Excellency of the Female Character Vindicated* (New York: Samuel Wood, 1807), xii.

[33] "Panegyrick on Marriage," *Columbia Magazine and Universal Advertiser* (October 1786), 74; "On Love," *New York Magazine* (June 1791), 311.

It is possible to identify at least three understandings of virtue that emerged in the American colonies during the eighteenth century—not one of which was derived from traditional Protestant or classical republican ideas of public virtue. The first, most pronounced in New England, was essentially religious. It concerned, above all, the relationship between virtue and grace. American Puritans, like Reform theologians in general, had long sought to balance the Calvinist belief in faith as the free gift of God with the view that individuals could voluntarily take certain steps to prepare for salvation. Acts of virtue themselves, the offspring of the human will and the intellect, could never lead to redemption. Yet at the same time a life of virtue would be the likely consequence of a predisposition toward grace.

Recent scholarship emphasizing the emotional, experiential aspects of Puritan piety has pointed to the continuities between developments within seventeenth-century Puritanism and the new forms of eighteenth-century evangelical Protestantism.[34] Even among seventeenth-century Harvard students of moral philosophy, the idea of virtue gradually became inseparable from a positive evaluation of the emotions.[35] In the middle of the eighteenth century, Jonathan Edwards used his formidable intellectual talent to reconcile this increasingly naturalistic conception of virtue with an uncompromising Calvinist belief in the sovereignty of God. An articulate proponent of religious revivalism, Edwards preached that only saving grace, experienced through the affections, could give rise to the real virtue of "disinterested benevolence." Unregenerate self-love could, he acknowledged, give rise to behavior in conformity with a narrowly utilitarian moral law. But "true virtue," as he defined it, consisted in a selfless "love to Being in general."[36]

When Edwards distinguished between sinful self-love and the virtue of "public benevolence," he did not mean public virtue in the classical republican sense.[37] He measured virtue by the disposition of the will and heart rather than by the performance of civic duty. Yet, for all his denial of the importance of external behavior, his ideal individual, like the classical republican one, would disregard narrow self-interest when it conflicted

[margin handwritten notes: Virtue as a felt, private act, not religiously based]

[34] See, e.g., Robert Middlekauff, *The Mathers: Three Generations of Puritan Intellectuals* (New York: Oxford University Press, 1971); Norman Pettit, *The Heart Prepared: Grace and Conversion in Puritan Spiritual Life* (New Haven, Conn.: Yale University Press, 1966); Charles Hambrick-Stowe, *The Practice of Piety* (Chapel Hill: University of North Carolina Press, 1982); Charles Lloyd Cohen, *God's Caress: The Psychology of Puritan Religious Experience* (New York: Oxford University Press, 1986).

[35] Norman Fiering, *Moral Philosophy at Seventeenth-Century Harvard* (n. 10 above), and *Jonathan Edwards's Moral Thought in Its British Context* (Chapel Hill: University of North Carolina Press, 1981).

[36] Jonathan Edwards, "The Nature of True Virtue," in *Jonathan Edwards*, ed. Clarence H. Faust and Thomas H. Johnson, rev. ed. (New York: Hill & Wang, 1962), 351.

[37] Ibid., 365.

with the common good. Not surprisingly, during the American Revolution individuals combined elements of his nonpolitical conception of virtue with classical republicanism. In 1774 a Marblehead minister defined patriotism as "the grand law of love," explaining that "disinterested benevolence" led to "the support of virtue; the controul of vice, and the advancement of the best interests of [the] country." For many Revolutionary clergymen, the words virtue, piety, and righteousness were basically interchangeable.[38]

This type of religious virtue was not, of course, regarded as distinctively feminine. Yet there is, beginning in the late seventeenth century, a steady climb in the number of sermons that celebrate models of female virtue and piety. Women, long regarded as morally encumbered by their supposedly excessive emotionalism, were beginning to be regarded as particularly receptive to grace. The first vigorous proponent of this view was the third generation Puritan pietist Cotton Mather. He explained that the greater tendency of women to experience religious conversion was a response to the distinctively female "difficulties both of *Subjection* and of *Child bearing*."[39] Over the course of the eighteenth century, evangelical and liberal Protestant ministers alike increasingly preached on the theme of female piety.[40]

A second, though related, conception of virtue that emerged in eighteenth-century America came from the psychological theories of John Locke and the Scottish moral philosophers. Medieval faculty psychology, which had survived even the Protestant Reformation, became a subject of controversy in the late seventeenth and in the eighteenth century. Among the many points at issue was the status of the "moral sense": Was it a rational or an emotional faculty? Some figures of the British Enlightenment, including John Locke and Thomas Reid, agreed with the older scholastic position that it was rational. Virtue was the chief object of Locke's educational theory and was, for him, still an essentially masculine trait. He wrote above all for the fathers of sons, emphasizing not only reason, but other qualities culturally associated with men as well: stoicism, self-sufficiency, and physical hardiness.[41]

[38] Story (n. 16 above), 7, 10. This religious use of the word virtue in revolutionary literature is discussed in Bloch, *Visionary Republic* (n. 7 above), esp. 109; Royster (n. 16 above), 17–25.

[39] Cotton Mather, *Ornaments for the Daughters of Zion* (Cambridge: Samuel Phillips, 1692), 45. Also see Cotton Mather, *Elizabeth on Her Holy Retirement* (Boston: B. Green, 1710).

[40] For a few examples of this literature, see Benjamin Colman, *The Honour and Happiness of the Vertuous Woman* (Boston: B. Green, 1716); Chauncy Whittelsey, *A Discourse . . . Mary Clapp* (New Haven, Conn.: Thomas & Samuel Green, 1769); Deborah Prince, *Dying Exercises of Mrs. Deborah Prince; and Devout Meditations of Mrs. Sarah Gill* (Newbury-port, Mass.: John Mycall, 1789); George Strebeck, *A Sermon on the Character of the Virtuous Woman* (New York: n.p., 1800); Samuel Worcester, *Female Love to Christ* (Salem, Mass.: Pool & Palfray, 1809).

[41] Despite one perfunctory remark to a female friend on how the education of the sexes

Another wave of Enlightenment opinion, represented in Scotland by Francis Hutcheson and in England by Lord Shaftesbury, claimed morality for the emotions.[42] It was, argued Hutcheson, not the offspring of reason but an inborn principle of sociability, "an instinct toward happiness."[43] If innate, however, moral sense was dependent, especially in infancy and early childhood, on parental nurturance. In their emphasis on education, if not in their epistemology, Locke and the Scots agreed: they all stressed noncoercive child rearing, saw children as corruptible but not corrupt, and posited innate qualities—whether reason or moral sense—which, if cultivated, would lead to virtue.[44] Although these particular philosophers envisioned men as the principal educators, their ideas about the importance of early childhood education gradually led to a greater emphasis on the motherhood role in didactic and medical literature.[45]

The question of whether reason or emotion was the more important source of virtue was never, of course, fully answered, but it is clear that the eighteenth century was a time of particular confusion and conflict over these basic epistemological issues.[46] Albert O. Hirschman has argued, for example, that avarice, previously regarded as a sinful "passion," was elevated to the status of a rational "interest" in this period.[47] This realignment coincided, more or less explicitly, with a revision of binary gender distinctions: rationality, long associated with men, was linked to interest; the emotions, long associated with women, to morality. Scottish philosophy and evangelical Protestantism, each occupying a kind of middle ground between the atomistic individualism of Locke and Hobbes and the communitarian ethos of classical republicanism, were particularly important in establishing these new connections.

---

should be largely the same, at least "in their younger years," Locke explicitly focused *Some Thoughts concerning Education*—including key passages on virtue—on the upbringing of "young Gentlemen." When women do appear, as mothers, they tend (by their excessive "Fondness") to be an obstacle to good education (*The Educational Writings of John Locke*, ed. James L. Axtell [London: Cambridge University Press, 1968], 117, 117n., 123, 125, 166–67, 170, 344–46).

[42] On differences among Scottish moral philosophers, see Daniel W. Howe, "European Sources of Political Ideas in Jeffersonian America," *Reviews in American History* 10 (1982): 28–44.

[43] As quoted in Fliegelman (n. 24 above), 24.

[44] Fliegelman (23–26) points to this underlying similarity in contrast to the sharp separation drawn between Locke and the Scots by Garry Wills in his *Inventing America: Jefferson's Declaration of Independence* (Garden City, N.Y.: Doubleday & Co., 1978), and *Explaining America: The Federalist* (Garden City, N.Y.: Doubleday & Co., 1981).

[45] Bloch, "American Feminine Ideals in Transition" (n. 26 above).

[46] Fiering, *Moral Philosophy at Seventeenth-Century Harvard* (n. 10 above), and *Jonathan Edwards's Moral Thought in Its British Context* (n. 35 above).

[47] Hirschman (n. 13 above).

Yet a third cultural movement—literary sentimentalism—contributed to this eighteenth-century reassessment of emotional life. Indeed, the intellectual boundaries between British moral philosophy, evangelical Protestantism, and sentimental fiction are impossible to draw clearly. As Norman Fiering has recently emphasized, the new moral philosophy of Hutcheson and Shaftesbury owed its origins to Puritan piety.[48] Edwards, determined to discourage a belief in a natural moral sense, nonetheless shared many of the ideas of the new moral philosophy. Edwards read sentimental fiction, and the Scottish moralists, also known as "sentimental philosophers," influenced those works through the writings of popularizers like Lord Kames.[49]

Yet, despite these historical interconnections, literary sentimentalism had a different orientation, style, and audience than either evangelicalism or moral philosophy. It concentrated on neither salvation nor epistemology, but on the quest for personal happiness through domestic relationships. Like exhortatory evangelical writings, but unlike moral philosophy, sentimental fiction was a relatively popular literary form in America (though largely imported from Britain). And, of all three movements, it was clearly literary sentimentalism that had the most to say specifically to and about women.

According to literary sentimentalism, virtue was above all a feminine quality. In the chain of being, women were the link between men and angels; they "ennoble human nature" by being not only "the fair" but also the "cherishing," "pious," "pacific," "sympathetic," and "reverential" sex.[50] The chief female virtues were "modesty," "tenderness," "delicacy," and "sensibility."[51] Women have a "superior sensibility of their souls," read one piece that appeared in several late eighteenth-century American magazines. "Their feelings are more exquisite than those of men; and their sentiments greater and more refined."[52] Others summed up this idealized impression of women by stressing the female "qualities of the heart."[53]

---

[48] Fiering, *Moral Philosophy at Seventeenth-Century Harvard*, 147–206, 239–94, and *Jonathan Edwards's Moral Thought in Its British Context*, 106.

[49] For example, Henry Home, Lord Kames, *Loose Hints upon Education, Chiefly concerning the Heart* (Edinburgh: John Bell, 1782). See n. 53 below for an example of its use.

[50] "On Woman," *Pennsylvania Magazine* (November 1775), 527; Thomas Branagan (n. 32 above), 111–12.

[51] Marchioness de Lambert, "Reflections on Female Virtues," *Royal American Magazine* (June 1774), 220; "Qualifications Required in a Wife," *American Museum* (December 1788), 578; [Noah Webster], "Address to Ladies," *American Museum* (March 1788), 244; "On Sensibility," *Pennsylvania Magazine* (April 1774), 176.

[52] "Comparison of the Sexes," *American Museum* (January 1789), 59. This piece was reprinted at least twice, in the *Christian Scholar's and Farmer's Magazine* (April and May 1789), 85–87; and in *Lady's Magazine* (August 1792), 111–13.

[53] For example, John Gregory, *A Father's Legacy to His Daughters* (Boston: J. Douglass M'Dougall, 1779), 35; John Bennet, *Letters to a Young Lady* (New York: John Buel, 1796), 68.

According to one American work of didactic fiction, women were best equipped to teach what Lord Kames had taught was "the chief branch" of learning, "the culture of the heart."[54]

If women were idealized for these supposedly innate qualities of emotionalism, tenderness, and delicacy, so too were they valued for a kind of self-discipline. The sentimental conception of female virtue was closely linked to chastity and to the maintenance of simple tastes and manners. Often the word virtue was used simply to mean chastity, and in the didactic literature of the period women were repeatedly enjoined to protect their sexual purity.[55] In the midst of the early Revolutionary fervor a patriot magazine instructed its readers, "What Bravery is in man, Chastity is in Woman." Among the dominant themes in the popular fiction of the period, best exemplified in such works as Samuel Richardson's *Clarissa* and Susanna Rowson's *Charlotte Temple*, was that of the innocent virgin ruined by male lust. Another variation on this theme of seduction was that of the adulterous husband redeemed by his faithful and forgiving wife—also a plot developed by Richardson in *Pamela*.[56]

As Ian Watt stressed many years ago in his *Rise of the Novel*, this literature conveyed a specifically middle-class version of personal morality. Typically, the lustful men were aristocratic rakes, and the women were wholesome commoners. In America, especially after the Revolution, such plots took on an additional patriotic significance. The villains could be seen as representing not only aristocratic but European decadence as well. While the idea that women should abstain from sexual temptations and ornamental refinements was scarcely new in this period—American Protestant teachings had traditionally instructed housewives to be sexually self-restrained, frugal, and industrious—the equation of female virtue with chastity, modest dress, and useful knowledge became more pronounced in the late eighteenth century as women were increasingly deemed the moral instructors of men.[57] The numerous proponents of a practical education for women repeatedly made this point.[58] No longer were the traditional ascetic and self-sacrificial virtues regarded as more easily achieved by men. The older view of women as more closely tied to base physical nature than men

[54] Enos Hitchcock, *Memoirs of the Bloomsgrove Family* (Boston: Thomas & Andrews, 1790), 47–48.

[55] For example, [William Kenrick], *The Whole Duty of Woman . . . Sixth Ed.* (Boston: Hall, 1790), 46; Gregory, 12, 16, 18, 22, 41; "A Letter," *Lady's Magazine* (November 1782), 281; Branagan.

[56] "Reflections on Chastity," *Royal American Magazine* (February 1775), 61. For the popularity of the forgiving-wife plot, see Lewis (n. 4 above).

[57] Lewis; Bloch, "American Feminine Ideals in Transition" (n. 26 above).

[58] For example: Rush (n. 27 above); Thomas Dawes, "Resolves Respecting the Education of Poor Female Children," *American Museum* 6 (September 1789): 213; John Bennet, *Strictures on Female Education* (Philadelphia: W. Spotswood & H. P. Rice, 1793).

had been gradually displaced by an image of women as particularly receptive to moral education. On the one hand, female virtues were themselves
regarded as essentially natural. On the other hand, such virtues in women
needed cultivation, and still more important, women were needed to
cultivate virtue in men. In these respects, the late eighteenth century can
be seen as a time in Western history when the nearly universal association
of women with nature, and men with culture, was disrupted.[59]

*   *   *

Each in a different way, then, American Protestantism, Scottish moral
philosophy, and literary sentimentalism opened the way for the feminization of ideas about public virtue. During the course of the Revolutionary
period, these seemingly nonpolitical ideas began to displace the earlier
idea of public virtue as military courage and civic glory. Royall Tyler's *The
Contrast*, a popular play of the late 1780s, publicized as the first dramatic
work by a "Citizen of the United States," conveniently marks the transition. The hero, appropriately named Colonel Manly, combines the new
and old ideals of virtue. On the one hand, he is depicted as an old-fashioned
New Englander and former Revolutionary War officer, who believes, in
classical republican fashion, that the reason for the decline of ancient
Greece was that "the common good was lost in the pursuit of private
interest." His heroic manliness stands in contrast to the foppish and
self-indulgent effeminacy of the English villain. Yet, the virtuous Manly
himself, like the woman he loves, exudes "tenderness" and speaks "the
language of sentiment."[60]

The changing meaning of virtue at once facilitated and reflected a
transformation within American political thought. Several historians of
political culture have noted that American Revolutionaries gradually revised their conceptions of public virtue. Earlier classical republican ideas
increasingly competed with a more instrumental theory of government in
which virtue played a much less conspicuous part.[61] Already in 1776
Thomas Paine's *Common Sense* argued that human cooperation and happiness were rooted in "society," not "government." Far from being the arena
for the expression of virtue, a minimal state was necessary only because of

[59] For the argument that this female-nature/male-culture dichotomy is universal, see esp.
Sherry Ortner, "Is Female to Male as Nature Is to Culture?" in *Women, Culture, and Society*,
ed. Michelle Rosaldo and Louise Lamphere (Stanford, Calif.: Stanford University Press,
1974), 67–88. For another work on the eighteenth century that qualifies this perspective, see
L. J. Jordanova, "Natural Facts: A Historical Perspective on Science and Sexuality," in
Nature, Culture, and Gender, ed. C. MacCormack and M. Strathern (New York: Cambridge
University Press, 1980).

[60] [Tyler] (n. 21 above), 48–49, 55.

[61] For example, Wood (n. 6 above); most recently, Yazawa (n. 9 above).

the "inability of moral virtue to govern the world."[62] By the late 1780s, in the argument for the U.S. Constitution in the *Federalist Papers*, the maintenance of the Republic no longer depended on a conception of goodness within collective social life. Instead, the most realistic and necessary conditions of liberty were the competition of conflicting factional interests and the balance of governmental powers. Such conditions ideally would encourage the rise of a "virtuous" elite of political representatives, but the conception of virtue implied here was not the classical republican one.[63] The word virtue itself scarcely appeared in the *Federalist Papers*. Instead of being based in a self-sacrificial public spirit, the moral underpinnings of good government were reason, justice, and enlightenment—all qualities presumably embodied in the "natural aristocracy" that would emerge to lead the Republic. Good leadership was in this view fully compatible with "true" or "enlightened" self-interest.[64]

Not that the republican belief in disinterested public virtue altogether vanished with the creation and ratification of the Constitution. This classical idea continued to find expression in opposition movements well into the nineteenth century.[65] Moreover, even in the late eighteenth-century ideological mainstream, a revised notion of republican virtue remained very much alive on the periphery of political debate. The demise of classical conceptions of virtue did not simply give rise to purely individual and utilitarian standards of morality devoid of reference to the common good.[66] Unlike the early Revolutionary virtue, the public virtue that remained was for the most part located outside rather than inside the state—the virtue of a diffuse, patriotic public whose allegiance was not to particular rulers or to the common interest of a homogeneous property-holding social order but to a large and impersonal republican nation. The

---

[62] Thomas Paine, *Common Sense*, ed. Isaac Kramnick (New York: Viking Penguin, Inc., 1976), 68.

[63] For example, [James Madison], "Federalist Paper Number 57," in *The Federalist Papers*, ed. Clinton Rossiter (New York: New American Library, 1961), 350. On virtue in the *Federalist Papers*, see Wood (n. 6 above), 610; and Garry Wills, *Explaining America* (n. 44 above). The distinction between these meanings of virtue is clarified in Daniel W. Howe, "The Political Psychology of *The Federalist*," *William and Mary Quarterly*, 3d ser., vol. 4 (1987).

[64] Howe, "The Political Psychology of *The Federalist*."

[65] Lance Banning, *The Jeffersonian Persuasion: Evolution of a Party* (Ithaca, N.Y.: Cornell University Press, 1978); Drew R. McCoy, *The Elusive Republic: Political Economy in Jeffersonian America* (Chapel Hill: University of North Carolina Press, 1980); Sean Wilentz, *Chants Democratic: New York City and the Rise of the American Working Class* (New York: Oxford University Press, 1984); Dorothy Ross, "The Liberal Tradition Revisited and the Republican Tradition Addressed," in *New Directions in American Intellectual History*, ed. John Higham and Paul K. Conkin (Baltimore: Johns Hopkins University Press, 1979); and a special issue on republicanism, ed. Joyce Appleby, *American Quarterly*, vol. 37 (Fall 1985).

[66] Compare MacIntyre (n. 2 above).

institutional basis of this collective identification was to be found not in the military or in participatory government but in churches, schools, and families. Women—as social companions, wives, and mothers—assumed a major role in instructing men to be virtuous.

This transition can be seen in part as a response to political events between the 1770s and 1790s. By the late 1780s, Revolutionaries had generally given up the quest for heroic mastery associated with the early war effort and had taken on the task of political reform involved in the process of state building. The early ethic of public service called on the presumably voluntary participation of free and independent (male) individuals. It was, at bottom, deeply anti-institutional—hostile to established churches, to government bureaucracy, to standing armies, to banks. The movement toward a more personal, domestic, and feminized definition of morality in the 1780s and 1790s was linked to a greater acceptance of institutionalized public order. A similar transformation, also expressed in the substitution of female for male Revolutionary symbolism, has been recently traced in the French Revolution by historian Lynn Hunt.[67] In America, this transitional phase in the Revolution coincided with the creation and establishment of the American Constitution in the late 1780s.

The *Federalist Papers* insisted on strengthening national government—giving it, in Alexander Hamilton's words, the "energy" the decentralized Confederation had previously lacked—while at the same time denying that the government had the power to interfere with natural rights or to eliminate inevitable factional conflict. Gone was the assumption that citizens would unite around a common conception of the public good. This false hope had only given rise to the specter of "majority tyranny" under the state constitutions of the 1770s and 1780s. In the words of an especially hard-bitten Federalist newspaper polemicist, "*virtue*, patriotism, or love of country, never was nor never will be till men's natures are changed, a fixed, permanent principle and support of government."[68]

The political order produced by the Constitution was designed more to protect private virtue than to be the arena for the expression of manly *virtù*. Despite the increased power of the national government in relation to that of the states, a continuing hostility to formal political institutions remained a major theme in American reform efforts well into the nineteenth century. The Constitution's provision of stable, limited government opened the way for the proliferation of voluntary associations that enlisted significant numbers of women as well as men. These associations,

[67] In France, however, prior to the ascendency of the conservative images of Marianne and Liberty in the late 1790s, a militant version of Marianne competed with that of the male radical symbol Hercules (see Lynn Hunt, *Politics, Culture, and Class in the French Revolution* [Berkeley and Los Angeles: University of California Press, 1984], 87–119).

[68] *Providence Gazette*, December 29, 1787, as quoted in Wood (n. 6 above), 610.

often formed for the "benevolent" purposes of moral and social reform, were repeatedly justified on patriotic grounds as vital to the preservation of the liberty and harmony of the American nation.

The Revolution had in effect accelerated a long-term cultural process that began well before the outbreak of the imperial conflicts with Britain. A transition in the meanings of virtue associated with changes in ideas about sex difference meant that women and the emotions became increasingly associated with moral activity, while men and reason became more exclusively associated with the utilitarian pursuit of self-interest. By the end of the eighteenth century, most people were beginning to believe that these were complementary contributions to the common good.[69]

These changes in themselves owed little to the American Revolution or to republican thought. The underlying cultural transformation was already underway by the 1770s, and it was, from the beginning, transatlantic in scope. What did change as a specific consequence of the American Revolutionary experience was that the feminine notion of virtue took on a political significance it had previously lacked. Americans never altogether abandoned the idea that the populace of the republic should be virtuous. Instead, they relegated the production and maintenance of public virtue to a new realm, one presided over largely by women. Women, as Lester Cohen and Linda Kerber have observed about the Revolutionary writer Mercy Otis Warren, continued to embody the collectivist values of classical republicanism after they had ceased to resonate in national politics.[70] The transformation in conceptions of femininity and masculinity, the emotions, and self-interest that had occurred in the eighteenth century made it possible to preserve the notion of public virtue while at the same time divesting it of its former constitutional significance. Virtue, if still regarded as essential to the public good in a republican state, became ever more difficult to distinguish from private benevolence, personal manners, and female sexual propriety.[71]

Subsequent developments among the early nineteenth-century middle and upper classes deepened these symbolic associations.[72] The declining

[69] Hirschman (n. 13 above); Appleby (n. 7 above); Howe, "The Political Psychology of *The Federalist*"; Michael Zuckerman, "A Different Thermidor: The Revolution beyond the American Revolution" (paper presented to the Philadelphia Center for Early American Studies, May 1986).

[70] Lester Cohen, "Explaining the Revolution: Ideology and Ethics in Mercy Otis Warren's Historical Theory," *William and Mary Quarterly*, 3d ser., 37 (1980): 200–218, and "Mercy Otis Warren: The Politics of Language and the Aesthetics of Self," *American Quarterly* 35 (1983): 481–98; Kerber, "The Republican Ideology of the Revolutionary Generation" (n. 4 above), 483.

[71] Pocock has pointed similarly to a shift from virtue to manners, although he misses the gender symbolism involved in this change and associates it only with elite English culture (Pocock, *Virtue, Commerce, and History* [n. 4 above], 49–50).

[72] This historical overview is especially indebted to the interpretation in Nancy F. Cott,

birth rate in the nineteenth century may have been a result of the growing ability of women to discipline male sexuality.[73] As the American polity became more democratic and expansionist, women, as teachers in the school system, played an increasingly important role in service to the republican nation—a role often seen as an extension of the practice of maternal virtue.[74] The fervent religious revivalism of the Second Great Awakening along with the birth of romantic literature furthered the connections between morality and the emotions already perceived by evangelicals, moral philosophers, and sentimental writers in the previous century. As eager supporters and occasional leaders, women were active participants in both the revivalist and the romantic cultural movements.[75]

From the late eighteenth century onward, the conflation of the virtuous with the feminine produced tensions. Looking back over the Revolutionary period with characteristic pessimism, John Adams once commented, "The people are Clarissa."[76] Public virtue had, for him, become associated with the passive virtues of female chastity—destined to be deceived and violated by unscrupulous men in power. Indeed, the representation of public virtue as a feminine trait hinged on the exclusion of women from institutional public life. If virtue was regarded as outside politics, what better way to conceive of it than as feminine? In an increasingly competitive male political system, the distinction faded between virtuous men committed to public service and unvirtuous men pursuing narrow self-interest. The new distinction between feminine virtue and masculine self-interest eased the process by which all white men (whether rich or

---

The Bonds of Womanhood: Woman's Sphere in New England, 1780–1835 (New Haven, Conn.: Yale University Press, 1977).

[73] Daniel Scott Smith, "Family Limitation, Sexual Control, and Domestic Feminism in Victorian America," *Feminist Studies* 1 (Winter–Spring 1973): 40–57; Carl Degler, *At Odds: Women and the Family in America from the Revolution to the Present* (New York: Oxford University Press, 1980), 144–278.

[74] Katherine Kish Sklar, *Catherine Beecher: A Study in American Domesticity* (New Haven, Conn: Yale University Press, 1973); Keith Melder, "Woman's High Calling: The Teaching Profession in America, 1830–1860," *American Studies* 13 (Fall 1972): 19–32; Nancy Hoffman, *Women's 'True' Profession* (Old Westbury, N.Y.: Feminist Press, 1981); Anne Firor Scott, "What, Then, Is This American: This New Woman?" *Journal of American History* 65 (December 1978): 679–703.

[75] Keith Melder, *The Beginnings of Sisterhood: The American Women's Rights Movement, 1800–1850* (New York: Schocken Books, 1977); Barbara Leslie Epstein, *The Power of Domesticity: Women, Evangelism, and Temperance in Nineteenth-Century America* (Middletown, Conn.: Wesleyan University Press, 1981); Mary P. Ryan, "The Power of Women's Networks: A Case Study of Female Moral Reform in Antebellum America," *Feminist Studies* 5 (Spring 1979): 66–86; Ann Douglas, *The Feminization of American Culture* (New York: Alfred A. Knopf, 1977); Susan P. Conrad, *Perish the Thought: Intellectual Women in Romantic America, 1830–1860* (New York: Oxford University Press, 1976).

[76] As quoted in Fliegelman (n. 24 above), 89.

poor, individually "virtuous" or not) could become political actors and all women could not.[77] That the ideal of female virtue was typically extended to upper- and middle-class women but not to poor women—who, as Christine Stansell has shown, continued to be characterized in the new nation in blatantly misogynist terms—reveals the extent to which the older republican emphasis on both virtue and social rank remained particularly strong within conceptions about women.[78]

The transformation in the meaning of virtue during the Revolutionary period sharpened the social boundaries between the sexes in ways that continue to deny power to all classes of women. The deep cultural connections between American patriotism and female middle-class domesticity persist to the present day, most conspicuously among conservative evangelical groups. Yet the increasing participation of early nineteenth-century women in the teaching profession, religious benevolent associations, and voluntary reform societies—activities that led directly to the early women's rights movement—suggests another side to the story. Virtue, even if domesticated, still contained residues of *virtù*, which for a long time helped to legitimate women's activities in American public life.

Department of History
University of California, Los Angeles

---

[77] This sexual asymmetry is stressed in Gerda Lerner, "The Lady and the Mill Girl: Changes in the Status of Women in the Age of Jackson, 1800–1840," in *A Heritage of Her Own*, ed. Nancy F. Cott and Elizabeth H. Pleck (New York: Simon & Schuster, 1979), 182–96.

[78] Christine Stansell, *City of Women: Sex and Class in New York, 1789–1860* (New York: Alfred A. Knopf, 1986), 19–37.

A Genealogy of *Dependency:* Tracing a Keyword of the U.S. Welfare State

Nancy Fraser and Linda Gordon

EPENDENCY HAS BECOME a keyword of U.S. politics. Politicians of diverse views regularly criticize what they term *welfare dependency.* Supreme Court Justice Clarence Thomas spoke for many conservatives in 1980 when he vilified his sister: "She gets mad when the mailman is late with her welfare check. That's how dependent she is. What's worse is that now her kids feel entitled to the check, too. They have no motivation for doing better or getting out of that situation" (quoted in Tumulty 1991). Liberals usually blame the victim less, but they, too, decry welfare dependency. Democratic Senator Daniel P. Moynihan prefigured today's discourse when he began his 1973 book by claiming that "the issue of welfare is the issue of dependency. It is different from poverty. To be poor is an objective condition; to be dependent, a subjective one as well. . . . Being poor is often associated with considerable personal qualities; being dependent rarely so. [Dependency] is an incomplete state in life: normal in the child, abnormal in the adult. In a world where completed men and women stand on their own feet, persons who are dependent—as the buried imagery of the word denotes—hang" (Moynihan 1973, 17). Today, "policy experts" from both major parties agree "that [welfare] dependency is bad for people, that it undermines their motivation to support themselves, and isolates and stigmatizes welfare recipients in a way that over a long period feeds into and accentuates the underclass mindset and condition" (Nathan 1986, 248).

Nancy Fraser is grateful for research support from the Center for Urban Affairs, Northwestern University; the Newberry Library/National Endowment for the Humanities; and the American Council of Learned Societies. Linda Gordon thanks the University of Wisconsin Graduate School, Vilas Trust, and the Institute for Research on Poverty. We both thank the Rockefeller Foundation Research and Study Center, Bellagio, Italy. We are also grateful for helpful comments from Lisa Brush, Robert Entman, Joel Handler, Dirk Hartog, Barbara Hobson, Allen Hunter, Eva Kittay, Felicia Kornbluh, Jenny Mansbridge, Linda Nicholson, Erik Wright, Eli Zaretsky, and the *Signs* reviewers and editors.

[*Signs: Journal of Women in Culture and Society* 1994, vol. 19, no. 2]

If we can step back from this discourse, however, we can interrogate some of its underlying presuppositions. Why are debates about poverty and inequality in the United States now being framed in terms of welfare dependency? How did the receipt of public assistance become associated with dependency, and why are the connotations of that word in this context so negative? What are the gender and racial subtexts of this discourse, and what tacit assumptions underlie it?

We propose to shed some light on these issues by examining welfare-related meanings of the word *dependency*.[1] We will analyze *dependency* as a keyword of the U.S. welfare state and reconstruct its genealogy. By charting some major historical shifts in the usage of this term, we will excavate some of the tacit assumptions and connotations that it still carries today but that usually go without saying.

Our approach is inspired in part by the English cultural-materialist critic, Raymond Williams (1976). Following Williams and others, we assume that the terms that are used to describe social life are also active forces shaping it.[2] A crucial element of politics, then, is the struggle to define social reality and to interpret people's inchoate aspirations and needs (Fraser 1990). Particular words and expressions often become focal in such struggles, functioning as keywords, sites at which the meaning of social experience is negotiated and contested (Williams 1976). Keywords typically carry unspoken assumptions and connotations that can power-fully influence the discourses they permeate—in part by constituting a body of *doxa*, or taken-for-granted commonsense belief that escapes critical scrutiny (Bourdieu 1977).

We seek to dispel the *doxa* surrounding current U.S. discussions of dependency by reconstructing that term's genealogy. Modifying an approach associated with Michel Foucault (1984), we will excavate broad historical shifts in linguistic usage that can rarely be attributed to specific agents. We do *not* present a causal analysis. Rather, by contrasting present meanings of dependency with past meanings, we aim to defamil-

---

[1] Another part of the story, of course, concerns the word *welfare*. In this article, our focus is U.S. political culture and thus North American English usage. Our findings should be of more general interest, however, as some other languages have similar meanings embedded in analogous words. In this article we have of necessity used British sources for the early stages of our genealogy, which spans the sixteenth and seventeenth centuries. We assume that these meanings of *dependency* were brought to "the New World" and were formative for the early stages of U.S. political culture.

[2] This stress on the performative, as opposed to the representational, dimension of language is a hallmark of the pragmatics tradition in the philosophy of language. It has been fruitfully adapted for sociocultural analysis by several writers in addition to Williams. See, e.g., Bourdieu 1977, 1990a, 1990b; Scott 1988; Fraser 1989, 1990, 1992; and Butler 1990.

iarize taken-for-granted beliefs in order to render them susceptible to critique and to illuminate present-day conflicts.

Our approach differs from Foucault's, however, in two crucial respects: we seek to contextualize discursive shifts in relation to broad institutional and social-structural shifts, and we welcome normative political reflection.[3] Our article is a collaboration between a philosopher and a historian. We combine historical analysis of linguistic and social-structural changes with conceptual analysis of the discursive construction of social problems, and we leaven the mix with a feminist interest in envisioning emancipatory alternatives.

In what follows, then, we provide a genealogy of *dependency*. We sketch the history of this term and explicate the assumptions and connotations it carries today in U.S. debates about welfare—especially assumptions about human nature, gender roles, the causes of poverty, the nature of citizenship, the sources of entitlement, and what counts as work and as a contribution to society. We contend that unreflective uses of this keyword serve to enshrine certain interpretations of social life as authoritative and to delegitimate or obscure others, generally to the advantage of dominant groups in society and to the disadvantage of subordinate ones. All told, we provide a critique of ideology in the form of a critical political semantics.

Dependency, we argue, is an ideological term. In current U.S. policy discourse it usually refers to the condition of poor women with children who maintain their families with neither a male breadwinner nor an adequate wage and who rely for economic support on a stingy and politically unpopular government program called Aid to Families with Dependent Children (AFDC). Participation in this highly stigmatized program may be demoralizing in many cases, even though it may enable women to leave abusive or unsatisfying relationships without having to give up their children. Still, naming the problems of poor, solo-mother families as *dependency* tends to make them appear to be individual problems, as much moral or psychological as economic. The term carries strong emotive and visual associations and a powerful pejorative charge. In current debates, the expression *welfare dependency* evokes the image of "the welfare mother," often figured as a young, unmarried black woman (perhaps even a teenager) of uncontrolled sexuality. The power of this image is overdetermined, we contend, since it condenses multiple and often contradictory meanings of dependency. Only by disaggregating those different strands, by unpacking the tacit assumptions and evaluative

---

[3] The critical literature on Foucault is enormous. For feminist assessments, see Butler 1987; Weedon 1987; the essays in Diamond and Quinby 1988; Alcoff 1990; and Hartsock 1990. For balanced discussions of Foucault's strengths and weaknesses, see Fraser 1989; McCarthy 1991; and Honneth 1992.

connotations that underlie them, can we begin to understand, and to dislodge, the force of the stereotype.

Registers of meaning

In its root meaning, the verb *to depend* refers to a physical relationship in which one thing hangs from another. The more abstract meanings — social, economic, psychological, and political — were originally metaphorical. In current usage, we find four registers in which the meanings of dependency reverberate. The first is an economic register, in which one depends on some other person(s) or institution for subsistence. In a second register, the term denotes a sociolegal status, the lack of a separate legal or public identity, as in the status of married women created by coverture. The third register is political: here dependency means subjection to an external ruling power and may be predicated of a colony or of a subject caste of noncitizen residents. The fourth register we call the moral/psychological; dependency in this sense is an individual character trait like lack of will power or excessive emotional neediness.

To be sure, not every use of *dependency* fits neatly into one and only one of these registers. Still, by distinguishing them analytically we present a matrix on which to plot the historical adventures of the term. In what follows, we shall trace the shift from a patriarchal preindustrial usage in which women, however subordinate, shared a condition of dependency with many men to a modern, industrial, male-supremacist usage that constructed a specifically feminine sense of dependency. That usage is now giving way, we contend, to a postindustrial usage in which growing numbers of relatively prosperous women claim the same kind of independence that men do while a more stigmatized but still feminized sense of dependency attaches to groups considered deviant and superfluous. Not just gender but also racializing practices play a major role in these shifts, as do changes in the organization and meaning of labor.

Preindustrial *dependency*

In preindustrial English usage, the most common meaning of *dependency* was subordination. The economic, sociolegal, and political registers were relatively undifferentiated, reflecting the fusion of various forms of hierarchy in state and society, and the moral/psychological use of the term barely existed. The earliest social definition of the verb *to depend* (*on*) in the *Oxford English Dictionary* (*OED*) is "to be connected within a relation of subordination." A *dependent*, from at least 1588, was one "who depends on another for support, position, etc.; a retainer, attendant, subordinate, servant." A *dependency* was either a retinue or body of servants or a foreign territorial possession or colony. This family of terms applied widely in a hierarchical social context in which nearly everyone was subordinate to someone else but did not incur individual stigma thereby (Gundersen 1987).

We can appreciate just how common dependency was in preindustrial society by examining its opposite. The term *independence* at first applied primarily to aggregate entities, not to individuals; thus in the seventeenth century a nation or a church congregation could be independent. By the eighteenth century, however, an individual could be said to have an *independency,* meaning an ownership of property, a fortune that made it possible to live without laboring. (This sense of the term, which we would today call economic, survives in our expressions *to be independently wealthy* and *a person of independent means.*) To be dependent, in contrast, was to gain one's livelihood by working for someone else. This of course was the condition of most people, of wage laborers as well as serfs and slaves, of most men as well as most women.[4]

Dependency, therefore, was a normal, as opposed to a deviant, condition, a social relation, as opposed to an individual, trait. Thus, it did not carry any moral opprobrium. Neither English nor U.S. dictionaries report any pejorative uses of the term before the early twentieth century. In fact, some leading preindustrial definitions were explicitly positive, implying trusting, relying on, counting on another, the predecessors of today's *dependable.*

Nevertheless, *dependency* did mean status inferiority and legal coverture, being a part of a unit headed by someone else who had legal standing. In a world of status hierarchies dominated by great landowners and their retainers, all members of a household other than its "head" were dependents, as were free or servile peasants on an estate. They were, as Peter Laslett put it, "caught up, so to speak, 'subsumed' . . . into the personalities of their fathers and masters" (1971, 21).

Dependency also had what we would today call political consequences. While the term did not mean precisely *unfree,* its context was a social order in which subjection, not citizenship, was the norm. *Independence* connoted unusual privilege and superiority, as in freedom from labor. Thus, throughout most of the European development of representative government, independence in the sense of property ownership was a prerequisite for political rights. When dependents began to claim rights and liberty, they perforce became revolutionaries.

---

[4] In preindustrial society, moreover, the reverse dependence of the master upon his men was widely recognized. The historian Christopher Hill evoked that understanding when he characterized the "essence" of feudal society as "the bond of loyalty and dependence between lord and man" (1972, 32). Here *dependence* means interdependence.

Dependency was not then applied uniquely to characterize the relation of a wife to her husband. Women's dependency, like children's, meant being on a lower rung in a long social ladder; their husbands and fathers were above them but below others. For the agrarian majority, moreover, there was no implication of unilateral economic dependency, because women's and children's labor was recognized as essential to the family economy; the women were economic dependents only in the sense that the men of their class were as well. In general, women's dependency in preindustrial society was less gender-specific than it later became; it was similar in kind to that of subordinate men, only multiplied. But so too were the lives of children, servants, and the elderly overlaid with multiple layers of dependency.

In practice, of course, these preindustrial arrangements did not always provide satisfactorily for the poor. In the fourteenth century new, stronger states began to limit the freedom of movement of the destitute and to codify older informal distinctions between those worthy and unworthy of assistance. When the English Poor Law of 1601 confirmed this latter distinction, it was already shameful to ask for public help. But the culture neither disapproved of dependency nor valorized individual independence. Rather, the aim of the statutes was to return the mobile, uprooted, and excessively "independent" poor to their local parishes or communities and, hence, to enforce their traditional dependencies.

Nevertheless, dependency was not universally approved or uncontested. It was subject, rather, to principled challenges from at least the seventeenth century on, when liberal-individualist political arguments became common. The terms *dependence* and *independence* often figured centrally in political debates in this period, as they did, for example, in the Putney Debates of the English Civil War. Sometimes they even became key signifiers of social crisis, as in the seventeenth century English controversy about "out-of-doors" servants, hired help who did not reside in the homes of their masters and who were not bound by indentures or similar legal understandings. In the discourse of the time, the anomalous "independence" of these men served as a general figure for social disorder, a lightning rod focusing diffuse cultural anxieties—much as the anomalous "dependence" of "welfare mothers" does today.

Industrial *dependency:* The worker and his negatives

With the rise of industrial capitalism, the semantic geography of dependency shifted significantly. In the eighteenth and nineteenth centuries, *independence,* not *dependence,* figured centrally in political and economic discourse; and its meanings were radically democratized. But if we read the discourse about independence carefully, we see the shadow of a powerful anxiety about dependency.

What in preindustrial society had been a normal and unstigmatized condition became deviant and stigmatized. More precisely, certain dependencies became shameful while others were deemed natural and proper. In particular, as eighteenth and nineteenth century political culture intensified gender difference, new, specifically gendered senses of dependency appeared—states considered proper for women but degrading for men. Likewise, emergent racial constructions made some forms of dependency appropriate for the "dark races" but intolerable for "whites." Such differentiated valuations became possible as the term's preindustrial unity fractured. No longer designating only generalized subordination, *dependency* in the industrial era could be sociolegal or political or economic. With these distinctions came another major semantic shift: now *dependency* need not always refer to a social relation; it could also designate an individual character trait. Thus, the moral/psychological register was born.

These redefinitions were greatly influenced by Radical Protestantism. It elaborated a new positive image of individual independence and a critique of sociolegal and political dependency. In the Catholic and the early Protestant traditions, dependence on a master had been modeled on dependence on God. In contrast, to the radicals of the English Civil War, or to Puritans, Quakers, and Congregationalists in the United States, rejecting dependence on a master was akin to rejecting blasphemy and false gods (Hill 1961). From this perspective, status hierarchies no longer appeared natural or just. Political subjection and sociolegal subsumption were offenses against human dignity, defensible only under special conditions, if supportable at all. These beliefs informed a variety of radical movements throughout the industrial era, including abolition, feminism, and labor organizing, with substantial successes. In the nineteenth century these movements abolished slavery and some of the legal disabilities of women. More thoroughgoing victories were won by white male workers who, in the eighteenth and nineteenth centuries, threw off their sociolegal and political dependency and won civil and electoral rights. In the age of democratic revolutions, the developing new concept of citizenship rested on independence; dependency was deemed antithetical to citizenship.

Changes in the civil and political landscape of dependence and independence were accompanied by even more dramatic changes in the economic register. When white workingmen demanded civil and electoral rights, they claimed to be independent. This entailed reinterpreting the meaning of wage labor so as to divest it of the association with dependency. That in turn required a shift in focus—from the experience or means of labor (e.g., ownership of tools or land, control of skills, and the organization of work) to its remuneration and how that was spent. Radical workingmen, who had earlier rejected wage labor as "wage slavery," claimed a new form of manly independence within it. Their collective pride drew on another aspect of Protestantism, its work ethic, that valorized discipline and labor. Workers sought to reclaim these values within the victorious wage labor system; many of them—women as well as men—created and exercised a new kind of independence in their militance and boldness toward employers. Through their struggles, economic independence came eventually to encompass the ideal of earning a family wage, a wage sufficient to maintain a household and to support a dependent wife and children. Thus, workingmen expanded the meaning of economic independence to include a form of wage labor in addition to property ownership and self-employment.[5]

This shift in the meaning of independence also transformed the meanings of dependency. As wage labor became increasingly normative—and increasingly definitive of independence—it was precisely those excluded from wage labor who appeared to personify dependency. In the new industrial semantics, there emerged three principal icons of dependency, all effectively negatives of the dominant image of "the worker" and each embodying a different aspect of nonindependence.

The first icon of industrial dependency was "the pauper," who lived not on wages but on poor relief.[6] In the strenuous new culture of emergent capitalism, the figure of the pauper was like a bad double of the upstanding workingman, threatening the latter should he lag. The image of the pauper was elaborated largely in an emerging new register of dependency discourse—the moral/psychological register. Paupers were not simply poor but degraded, their character corrupted and their will sapped through reliance on charity. To be sure, the moral/psychological condition of pauperism was related to the economic condition of poverty, but the relationship was not simple, but complex. While nineteenth-century charity experts acknowledged that poverty could contribute to pauperization, they also held that character defects could cause poverty (Gordon 1992). Toward the end of the century, as hereditarian (eugenic) thought caught on, the pauper's character defects were given a basis in

---

[5] One might say that this redefinition foregrounded wage labor *as* a new form of property, namely, property in one's own labor power. This conception was premised on what Macpherson 1962 called "possessive individualism," the assumption of an individual's property in his [*sic*] own person. Leading to the construction of wages as an entitlement, this approach was overwhelmingly male. Allen Hunter (personal communication, 1992) describes it as a loss of systemic critique, a sense of independence gained by narrowing the focus to the individual worker and leaving behind aspirations for collective independence from capital.

[6] In the sixteenth century the term *pauper* had meant simply a poor person and, in law, one who was allowed to sue or defend in a court without paying costs (*OED*). Two centuries later, it took on a more restricted definition, denoting a new class of persons who subsisted on poor relief instead of wages and who were held to be deviant and blameworthy.

biology. The pauper's dependency was figured as unlike the serf's in that it was unilateral, not reciprocal. To be a pauper was not to be subordinate within a system of productive labor; it was to be outside such a system altogether.

A second icon of industrial dependency was embodied alternately in the figures of "the colonial native" and "the slave." They, of course, were very much inside the economic system, their labor often fundamental to the development of capital and industry. Whereas the pauper represented the characterological distillation of economic dependency, natives and slaves personified political subjection.[7] Their images as "savage," "child-like," and "submissive" became salient as the old, territorial sense of dependency as a colony became intertwined with a new, racist discourse developed to justify colonialism and slavery.[8] There emerged a drift from an older sense of dependency as a relation of subjection imposed by an imperial power on an indigenous population to a newer sense of dependency as an inherent property or character trait of the people so subjected. In earlier usage, colonials were dependent because they had been conquered; in nineteenth-century imperialist culture, they were conquered because they were dependent. In this new conception, it was the intrinsic, essential dependency of natives and slaves that justified their colonization and enslavement.

The dependency of the native and the slave, like that of the pauper, was elaborated largely in the moral/psychological register. The character traits adduced to justify imperialism and slavery, however, arose less from individual temperament than from the supposed nature of human groups. Racialist thought was the linchpin for this reasoning. By licensing a view of "the Negro" as fundamentally *other*, it provided the extraordinary justificatory power required to rationalize subjection at a time when liberty and equality were being proclaimed inalienable "rights of man"—for example, in that classic rejection of colonial status, the United States' "Declaration of Independence." Thus racism helped transform dependency as political subjection into dependency as psychology and forged enduring links between the discourse of dependency and racial oppression.

[7] Actually, there are many variants within the family of images that personify subjection in the industrial era. Among these are related but not identical stereotypes of the Russian serf, the Caribbean slave, the slave in the United States, and the American Indian. Moreover, there are distinct male and female stereotypes within each of those categories. We simplify here in order to highlight the features that are common to all these images, notably the idea of natural subjection rooted in race. We focus especially on stereotypes that portray African-Americans as personifications of dependency because of their historic importance and contemporary resonance in the U.S. language of social welfare.

[8] The evolution of the term *native* neatly encapsulates this process. Its original meaning in English, dating from about 1450, was tied to dependency: "one born in bondage; a born thrall," but without racial meaning. Two centuries later it carried the additional meaning of colored or black (*OED*).

Like the pauper, the native and the slave were excluded from wage labor and thus were negatives of the image of the worker. They shared that characteristic, if little else, with the third major icon of dependency in the industrial era: the newly invented figure of "the housewife." As we saw, the independence of the white workingman presupposed the ideal of the family wage, a wage sufficient to maintain a household and to support a nonemployed wife and children. Thus, for wage labor to create (white male) independence, (white) female economic dependence was required. Women were thus transformed "from partners to parasites" (Land 1980, 57; Boydston 1991). But this transformation was by no means universal. In the United States, for example, the family wage ideal held greater sway among whites than among blacks and was at variance with actual practice for all of the poor and the working class. Moreover, both employed and nonemployed wives continued to perform work once considered crucial to a family economy. Since few husbands actually were able to support a family singlehandedly, most families continued to depend on the labor of women and children. Nevertheless, the family wage norm commanded great loyalty in the United States, partly because it was used by the organized working class as an argument for higher wages (Hughes 1925; Breckinridge 1928; Pruette 1934; Gordon 1992).

Several different registers of dependency converged in the figure of the housewife. This figure melded woman's traditional sociolegal and political dependency with her more recent economic dependency in the industrial order. Continuing from preindustrial usage was the assumption that fathers headed households and that other household members were represented by them, as codified in the legal doctrine of coverture. The sociolegal and political dependency of wives enforced their new economic dependency, since under coverture even married women who were wage workers could not legally control their wages. But the connotations of female dependency were altered. Although erstwhile dependent white men gained political rights, most white women remained legally and politically dependent. The result was to feminize—and stigmatize—sociolegal and political dependency, making coverture appear increasingly obnoxious and stimulating agitation for the statutes and court decisions that eventually dismantled it.

Together, then, a series of new personifications of dependency combined to constitute the underside of the workingman's independence. Henceforth, those who aspired to full membership in society would have to distinguish themselves from the pauper, the native, the slave, and the housewife in order to construct their independence. In a social order in which wage labor was becoming hegemonic, it was possible to encapsulate all these distinctions simultaneously in the ideal of the family wage. On the one hand, and most overtly, the ideal of the family wage premised the white workingman's independence on his wife's subordination and economic dependence. But on the other hand, it simultaneously contrasted with counterimages of dependent men—first with degraded male paupers on poor relief and later with racist stereotypes of Negro men unable to dominate Negro women. The family wage, therefore, was a vehicle for elaborating meanings of dependence and independence that were deeply inflected by gender, race, and class.

In this new industrial semantics, white workingmen appeared to be economically independent, but their independence was largely illusory and ideological. Since few actually earned enough to support a family singlehandedly, most depended in fact—if not in word—on their wives' and children's contributions. Equally important, the language of wage labor in capitalism denied workers' dependence on their employers, thereby veiling their status as subordinates in a unit headed by someone else. Thus, hierarchy that had been relatively explicit and visible in the peasant-landlord relation was mystified in the relationship of factory operative to factory owner. There was a sense, then, in which the economic dependency of the white workingman was spirited away through linguistic sleight of hand—somewhat like reducing the number of poor people by lowering the official poverty demarcating line.

By definition, then, economic inequality among white men no longer created dependency. But noneconomic hierarchy among white men was considered unacceptable in the United States. Thus, *dependency* was redefined to refer exclusively to those noneconomic relations of subordination deemed suitable only for people of color and for white women. The result was to differentiate dimensions of dependency that had been fused in preindustrial usage. Whereas all relations of subordination had previously counted as dependency relations, now capital-labor relations were exempted. Sociolegal and political hierarchy appeared to diverge from economic hierarchy, and only the former seemed incompatible with hegemonic views of society. It seemed to follow, moreover, that were sociolegal dependency and political dependency ever to be formally abolished, no social-structural dependency would remain. Any dependency that did persist could only be moral or psychological.

The rise of American *welfare dependency:* 1890–1945

Informed by these general features of industrial-era semantics, a distinctive welfare-related use of *dependency* developed in the United States. Originating in the late nineteenth-century discourse of pauperism, modified in the Progressive Era, and stabilized in the period of the New Deal, this use of the term was fundamentally ambiguous, slipping easily, and repeatedly, from an economic meaning to a moral/psychological meaning.

The United States was especially hospitable to elaborating dependency as a defect of individual character. Because the country lacked a strong legacy of feudalism or aristocracy and thus a strong popular sense of reciprocal obligations between lord and man, the older, preindustrial meanings of dependency—as an ordinary, majority condition—were weak and the pejorative meanings were stronger. In the colonial period, dependency was seen mainly as a voluntary condition, as in indentured servitude. But the American Revolution so valorized independence that it stripped dependency of its voluntarism, emphasized its powerlessness, and imbued it with stigma. One result was to change the meaning of women's social and legal dependency, making it distinctly inferior (Gundersen 1987).

The long American love affair with independence was politically double-edged. On the one hand, it helped nurture powerful labor and women's movements. On the other hand, the absence of a hierarchical social tradition in which subordination was understood to be structural, not characterological, facilitated hostility to public support for the poor. Also influential was the very nature of the American state, weak and decentralized in comparison to European states throughout the nineteenth century. All told, the United States proved fertile soil for the moral/psychological discourse of dependency.

As discussed earlier, the most general definition of economic dependency in this era was simply non-wage-earning. By the end of the nineteenth century, however, that definition had divided into two: a "good," household dependency, predicated of children and wives, and an increasingly "bad" (or at least dubious) charity dependency, predicated of recipients of relief. Both senses had as their reference point the ideal of the family wage, and both were eventually incorporated into the discourse of the national state. The good, household sense was elaborated via the census (Folbre 1991) and by the Internal Revenue Service, which installed the category of dependent as the norm for wives. The already problematic charity sense became even more pejorative with the development of public assistance. The old distinction between the deserving and the undeserving poor intensified in the late nineteenth century's Gilded Age. Theoretically, the undeserving should not be receiving aid, but constant vigilance was required to ensure they did not slip in, disguising themselves as deserving. Dependence on assistance became increasingly stigmatized, and it was harder and harder to rely on relief without being branded a pauper.

Ironically, reformers in the 1890s introduced the word *dependent* into relief discourse as a substitute for *pauper* precisely in order to destigmatize the receipt of help. They first applied the word to children, the paradigmatic "innocent" victims of poverty.[9] Then, in the early twentieth century, Progressive-era reformers began to apply the term to adults, again to rid them of stigma. Only after World War II did *dependent* become the hegemonic word for a recipient of aid.[10] By then, however, the term's pejorative connotations were fixed.

The attempt to get rid of stigma by replacing *pauperism* with *dependency* failed. Talk about economic dependency repeatedly slid into condemnation of moral/psychological dependency. Even during the Depression of the 1930s, experts worried that receipt of relief would create "habits of dependence" or, as one charity leader put it, "a belligerent dependency, an attitude of having a right and title to relief" (Brandt 1932, 23–24; Gibbons 1933; Vaile 1934, 26). Because the hard times lasted so long and created so many newly poor people, there was a slight improvement in the status of recipients of aid. But attacks on "chiseling" and "corruption" continued to embarrass those receiving assistance, and many of the neediest welfare beneficiaries accepted public aid only after much hesitation and with great shame, so strong was the stigma of dependency (Bakke 1940a, 1940b).

Most important, the New Deal intensified the dishonor of receiving help by consolidating a two-track welfare system. First-track programs like unemployment and old age insurance offered aid as an entitlement, without stigma or supervision and hence without dependency. Such programs were constructed to create the misleading appearance that beneficiaries merely got back what they put in. They constructed an honorable status for recipients and are not called welfare even today. Intended at least partially to replace the white workingman's family wage, first-track programs excluded most minorities and white women. In contrast, second-track public assistance programs, among which Aid to Dependent Children (ADC), later Aid to Families with Dependent Children (AFDC), became the biggest and most well-known, continued the private charity tradition of searching out the deserving few among the many chiselers. Funded from general tax revenues instead of from earmarked wage deductions, these programs created the appearance that claimants were

[9] For example, Warner 1894–1930 uses *dependent* only for children. The same is true of Abbott and Breckinridge (1921, 7) and National Conference of Charities and Correction (1890s–1920s). This usage produced some curious effects because of its intersection with the dependency produced by the normative family. For example, charity experts debated the propriety of "keeping dependent children in their own homes." The children in question were considered dependent because their parent(s) could not support them; yet other children were deemed dependent precisely because their parents did support them.

[10] Studies of welfare done in the 1940s still used the word *dependents* only in the sense of those supported by family heads; see, e.g., Brown 1940; Howard 1943; Bruno 1948.

getting something for nothing (Fraser and Gordon 1992). They established entirely different conditions for receiving aid: means-testing; morals-testing; moral and household supervision; home visits; extremely low stipends—in short, all the conditions associated with welfare dependency today (Fraser 1987; Gordon 1990; Nelson 1990).[11]

The racial and sexual exclusions of the first-track programs were not accidental. They were designed to win the support of Southern legislators who wanted to keep blacks dependent in another sense, namely, on low wages or sharecropping (Quadagno 1988). Equally deliberate was the construction of the differential in legitimacy between the two tracks of the welfare system. The Social Security Board propagandized for Social Security Old Age Insurance (the program today called just "Social Security") precisely because, at first, it did not seem more earned or more dignified than public assistance. To make Social Security more acceptable, the board worked to stigmatize public assistance, even pressuring states to keep stipends low (Cates 1983).

Most Americans today still distinguish between "welfare" and "nonwelfare" forms of public provision and see only the former as creating dependency. The assumptions underlying these distinctions, however, had to be constructed politically. Old people became privileged (nonwelfare) recipients only through decades of militant organization and lobbying. All programs of public provision, whether they are called welfare or not, shore up some dependencies and discourage others. Social Security subverted adults' sense of responsibility for their parents, for example. Public assistance programs, by contrast, aimed to buttress the dependence of the poor on low-wage labor, of wives on husbands, of children on their parents.

The conditions of second-track assistance made recipients view their dependence on public assistance as inferior to the supposed independence of wage labor (Milwaukee County Welfare Rights Organization 1972; West 1981; Pope 1989; 73, 144). Wage labor, meanwhile, had become so naturalized that its own inherent supervision could be overlooked; thus one ADC recipient complained, "Welfare life is a difficult experience. . . . When you work, you don't have to report to anyone" (Barnes 1987, vi). Yet the designers of ADC did not initially intend to drive white solo mothers into paid employment. Rather, they wanted to protect the norm of the family wage by making dependence on a male breadwinner con-

---

[11] Starting in the 1960s increasing numbers of black women were able to claim AFDC, but prior to that they were largely excluded. At first, the language of the New Deal followed the precedent of earlier programs in applying the term *dependent* to children. De facto, however, the recipients of ADC were virtually exclusively solo mothers. Between the 1940s and 1960s the term's reference gradually shifted from the children to their mothers.

tinue to seem preferable to dependence on the state (Gordon 1992). Aid to Dependent Children occupied the strategic semantic space where the good, household sense of dependency and the bad, relief sense of dependency intersected. It enforced at once the positive connotations of the first and the negative connotations of the second.

Thus, the poor solo mother was enshrined as the quintessential *welfare dependent*.[12] That designation has thus become significant not only for what it includes but also for what it excludes and occludes. Although it appears to mean relying on the government for economic support, not all recipients of public funds are equally considered dependent. Hardly anyone today calls recipients of Social Security retirement insurance *dependents*. Similarly, persons receiving unemployment insurance, agricultural loans, and home mortgage assistance are excluded from that categorization, as indeed are defense contractors and the beneficiaries of corporate bailouts and regressive taxation.

Postindustrial society and the disappearance of "good" dependency

With the transition to a postindustrial phase of capitalism, the semantic map of dependency is being redrawn yet again. Whereas industrial usage had cast some forms of dependency as natural and proper, postindustrial usage figures all forms as avoidable and blameworthy. No longer moderated by any positive countercurrents, the term's pejorative connotations are being strengthened. Industrial usage had recognized some forms of dependency to be rooted in relations of subordination; postindustrial usage, in contrast, focuses more intensely on the traits of individuals. The moral/psychological register is expanding, therefore, and its qualitative character is changing, with new psychological and therapeutic idioms displacing the explicitly racist and misogynous idioms of the industrial era. Yet dependency nonetheless remains feminized and racialized; the new psychological meanings have strong feminine associations, while currents once associated with the native and the slave are increasingly inflecting the discourse about welfare.

One major influence here is the formal abolition of much of the legal and political dependency that was endemic to industrial society. Housewives, paupers, natives, and the descendants of slaves are no longer formally excluded from most civil and political rights; neither their subsumption nor their subjection is viewed as legitimate. Thus, major forms of dependency deemed proper in industrial usage are now considered

[12] Men on "general relief" are sometimes also included in that designation; their treatment by the welfare system is usually as bad or worse.

objectionable, and postindustrial uses of the term carry a stronger negative charge.

A second major shift in the geography of postindustrial dependency is
affecting the economic register. This is the decentering of the ideal of the
family wage, which had been the gravitational center of industrial usage.
The relative deindustrialization of the United States is restructuring the
political economy, making the single-earner family far less viable. The
loss of higher paid "male" manufacturing jobs and the massive entry of
women into low-wage service work is meanwhile altering the gender
composition of employment (Smith 1984). At the same time, divorce is
common and, thanks in large part to the feminist and gay and lesbian
liberation movements, changing gender norms are helping to proliferate
new family forms, making the male breadwinner/female homemaker
model less attractive to many (Stacey 1987, 1990; Weston 1991). Thus,
the family wage ideal is no longer hegemonic but competes with alternative gender norms, family forms, and economic arrangements. It no
longer goes without saying that a woman should rely on a man for
economic support, nor that mothers should not also be "workers." Thus,
another major form of dependency that was positively inflected in industrial semantics has become contested if not simply negative.

The combined result of these developments is to increase the stigma of
dependency. With all legal and political dependency now illegitimate, and
with wives' economic dependency now contested, there is no longer any
self-evidently good adult dependency in postindustrial society. Rather, all
dependency is suspect, and independence is enjoined upon everyone. Independence, however, remains identified with wage labor. That identification seems even to increase in a context where there is no longer any
"good" adult personification of dependency who can be counterposed to
"the worker." In this context, the worker tends to become the universal
social subject: everyone is expected to "work" and to be "self-supporting."
Any adult not perceived as a worker shoulders a heavier burden of self-
justification. Thus, a norm previously restricted to white workingmen
applied increasingly to everyone. Yet this norm still carries a racial and
gender subtext, as it supposes that the worker has access to a job paying
a decent wage and is not also a primary parent.

If one result of these developments is an increase in dependency's
negative connotations, another is its increased individualization. As we saw,
talk of dependency as a character trait of individuals was already widespread in the industrial period, diminishing the preindustrial emphasis on
relations of subordination. The importance of individualized dependency
tends to be heightened, however, now that sociolegal and political dependency are officially ended. Absent coverture and Jim Crow, it has
become possible to claim that equality of opportunity exists and that

individual merit determines outcomes. As we saw, the groundwork for that view was laid by industrial usage, which redefined dependency so as to exclude capitalist relations of subordination. With capitalist economic dependency already abolished by definition, and with legal and political dependency now abolished by law, postindustrial society appears to some conservatives and liberals to have eliminated every social-structural basis of dependency. Whatever dependency remains, therefore, can be interpreted as the fault of individuals. That interpretation does not go uncontested, to be sure, but the burden of argument has shifted. Now those who would deny that the fault lies in themselves must swim upstream against the prevailing semantic currents. Postindustrial dependency, thus, is increasingly individualized.

Welfare dependency as postindustrial pathology

The worsening connotations of *welfare dependency* have been nourished by several streams from outside the field of welfare. New postindustrial medical and psychological discourses have associated dependency with pathology. In articles with titles such as "Pharmacist Involvement in a Chemical-Dependency Rehabilitation Program" (Haynes 1988), social scientists began in the 1980s to write about *chemical, alcohol,* and *drug dependency,* all euphemisms for addiction. Because welfare claimants are often—falsely—assumed to be addicts, the pathological connotations of *drug dependency* tend also to infect *welfare dependency,* increasing stigmatization.

A second important postindustrial current is the rise of new psychological meanings of dependency with very strong feminine associations. In the 1950s, social workers influenced by psychiatry began to diagnose dependence as a form of immaturity common among women, particularly among solo mothers (who were often, of course, welfare claimants). "Dependent, irresponsible, and unstable, they respond like small children to the immediate moment," declared the author of a 1954 discussion of out-of-wedlock pregnancy (Young 1954, 87). The problem was that women were supposed to be just dependent enough, and it was easy to tip over into excess in either direction. The norm, moreover, was racially marked, as white women were usually portrayed as erring on the side of excessive dependence, while black women were typically charged with excessive independence.

Psychologized dependency became the target of some of the earliest second-wave feminism. Betty Friedan's 1963 classic, *The Feminine Mystique,* provided a phenomenological account of the housewife's psychological dependency and drew from it a political critique of her social subordination. More recently, however, a burgeoning cultural-feminist, postfeminist, and antifeminist self-help and pop-psychology literature has obfuscated the link between the psychological and the political. In Colette Dowling's 1981 book, *The Cinderella Complex,* women's dependency was hypostatized as a depth-psychological gender structure: "women's hidden fear of independence" or the "wish to be saved." The late 1980s saw a spate of books about "codependency," a supposedly prototypically female syndrome of supporting or "enabling" the dependency of someone else. In a metaphor that reflects the drug hysteria of the period, dependency here, too, is an addiction. Apparently, even if a woman manages herself to escape her gender's predilection to dependency, she is still liable to incur the blame for facilitating the dependency of her husband or children. This completes the vicious circle: the increased stigmatizing of dependency in the culture at large has also deepened contempt for those who care for dependents, reinforcing the traditionally low status of the female helping professions, such as nursing and social work (Sapiro 1990).

The 1980s saw a cultural panic about dependency. In 1980, the American Psychiatric Association codified "Dependent Personality Disorder" (DPD) as an official psychopathology. According to the 1987 edition of the *Diagnostic and Statistical Manual of Mental Disorders* (DSM-III-R), "The essential feature of this disorder is a pervasive pattern of dependent and submissive behavior beginning by early childhood. . . . People with this disorder are unable to make everyday decisions without an excessive amount of advice and reassurance from others, and will even allow others to make most of their important decisions. . . . The disorder is apparently common and is diagnosed more frequently in females" (American Psychiatric Association 1987, 353–54).

The codification of DPD as an official psychopathology represents a new stage in the history of the moral/psychological register. Here the social relations of dependency disappear entirely into the personality of the dependent. Overt moralism also disappears in the apparently neutral, scientific, medicalized formulation. Thus, although the defining traits of the dependent personality match point for point the traits traditionally ascribed to housewives, paupers, natives, and slaves, all links to subordination have vanished. The only remaining trace of those themes is the flat, categorical, and uninterpreted observation that DPD is "diagnosed more frequently in females."

If psychological discourse has further feminized and individualized dependency, other postindustrial developments have further racialized it. The increased stigmatization of welfare dependency followed a general increase in public provision in the United States, the removal of some discriminatory practices that had previously excluded minority women from participation in AFDC, especially in the South, and the transfer of many white women to first-track programs as social-insurance coverage expanded. By the 1970s the figure of the black solo mother had come to epitomize welfare dependency. As a result, the new discourse about welfare draws on older symbolic currents that linked dependency with racist ideologies.

The ground was laid by a long, somewhat contradictory stream of discourse about "the black family," in which African-American gender and kinship relations were measured against white middle-class norms and deemed pathological. One supposedly pathological element was "the excessive independence" of black women, an ideologically distorted allusion to long traditions of wage work, educational achievement, and community activism. The 1960s and 1970s discourse about poverty recapitulated traditions of misogyny toward African-American women; in Daniel Moynihan's diagnosis, for example, "matriarchal" families had "emasculated" black men and created a "culture of poverty" based on a "tangle of [family] pathology" (Rainwater and Yancey 1967). This discourse placed black AFDC claimants in a double-bind: they were pathologically independent with respect to men and pathologically dependent with respect to government.

By the 1980s, however, the racial imagery of dependency had shifted. The black welfare mother that haunted the white imagination ceased to be the powerful matriarch. Now the preeminent stereotype is the unmarried teenage mother caught in the "welfare trap" and rendered dronelike and passive. This new icon of welfare dependency is younger and weaker than the matriarch. She is often evoked in the phrase *children having children,* which can express feminist sympathy or antifeminist contempt, black appeals for parental control or white-racist eugenic anxieties.

Many of these postindustrial discourses coalesced in early 1990s. Then–Vice President Dan Quayle brought together the pathologized, feminized, and racialized currents in his comment on the May 1992 Los Angeles riot: "Our inner cities are filled with children having children . . . with people who are dependent on drugs and on the narcotic of welfare" (Quayle 1992).

Thus postindustrial culture has called up a new personification of dependency: the black, unmarried, teenaged, welfare-dependent mother. This image has usurped the symbolic space previously occupied by the housewife, the pauper, the native, and the slave, while absorbing and condensing their connotations. Black, female, a pauper, not a worker, a housewife and mother, yet practically a child herself—the new stereotype partakes of virtually every quality that has been coded historically as antithetical to independence. Condensing multiple, often contradictory meanings of dependency, it is a powerful ideological trope that simultaneously organizes diffuse cultural anxieties and dissimulates their social bases.

Postindustrial policy and the politics of dependency

Despite the worsening economic outlook for many Americans in the last few decades, there has been no cultural revaluation of welfare. Families working harder for less often resent those who appear to them not to be working at all. Apparently lost, at least for now, are the struggles of the 1960s that aimed to recast AFDC as an entitlement in order to promote recipients' independence. Instead, the honorific term *independent* remains firmly centered on wage labor, no matter how impoverished the worker. Welfare dependency, in contrast, has been inflated into a behavioral syndrome and made to seem more contemptible.

Contemporary policy discourse about welfare dependency is thoroughly inflected by these assumptions. It divides into two major streams. The first continues the rhetoric of pauperism and the culture of poverty. It is used in both conservative and liberal, victim-blaming or non-victim-blaming ways, depending on the causal structure of the argument. The contention is that poor, dependent people have something more than lack of money wrong with them. The flaws can be located in biology, psychology, upbringing, neighborhood influence; they can be cast as cause or as effect of poverty, or even as both simultaneously. Conservatives, such as George Gilder (1981) and Lawrence Mead (1986), argue that welfare causes moral/psychological dependency. Liberals, such as William Julius Wilson (1987) and Christopher Jencks (1992), blame social and economic influences but often agree that claimants' culture and behavior are problematic.

A second stream of thought begins from neoclassical economic premises. It assumes a "rational man" facing choices in which welfare and work are both options. For these policy analysts, the moral/psychological meanings of dependency are present but uninterrogated, assumed to be undesirable. Liberals of this school, such as many of the social scientists associated with the Institute for Research on Poverty at the University of Wisconsin, grant that welfare inevitably has some bad, dependency-creating effects but claim that these are outweighed by other, good effects like improved conditions for children, increased societal stability, and relief of suffering. Conservatives of this school, such as Charles Murray (1984), disagree. The two camps argue above all about the question of incentives. Do AFDC stipends encourage women to have more out-of-wedlock children? Do they discourage them from accepting jobs? Can reducing or withholding stipends serve as a stick to encourage recipients to stay in school, keep their children in school, get married?

Certainly, there are real and significant differences here, but there are also important similarities. Liberals and conservatives of both schools rarely situate the notion of dependency in its historical or economic context; nor do they interrogate its presuppositions. Neither group questions the assumption that independence is an unmitigated good nor its identification with wage labor. Many poverty and welfare analysts equivocate between an official position that *dependency* is a value-neutral term for receipt of (or need for) welfare and a usage that makes it a synonym for *pauperism*.

These assumptions permeate the public sphere. In the current round of alarums about welfare dependency, it is increasingly claimed that "welfare mothers ought to work," a usage that tacitly defines work as wage earning and child raising as nonwork. Here we run up against contradictions in the discourse of dependency: when the subject under consideration is teenage pregnancy, these mothers are cast as children; when the subject is welfare, they become adults who should be self-supporting. It is only in the last decade that welfare experts have reached a consensus on the view that AFDC recipients should be employed. The older view, which underlay the original passage of ADC, was that children need a mother at home—although in practice there was always a class double standard, since full-time maternal domesticity was a privilege that had to be purchased, not an entitlement poor women could claim. However, as wage work among mothers of young children has become more widespread and normative, the last defenders of a welfare program that permitted recipients to concentrate full-time on child raising were silenced.

None of the negative imagery about welfare dependency has gone uncontested, of course. From the 1950s through the 1970s, many of these presuppositions were challenged, most directly in the mid-1960s by an organization of women welfare claimants, the National Welfare Rights Organization (NWRO). The women of NWRO cast their relation with the welfare system as active rather than passive, a matter of claiming rights rather than receiving charity. They also insisted that their domestic labor was socially necessary and praiseworthy. Their perspective helped reconstruct the arguments for welfare, spurring poverty lawyers and radical intellectuals to develop a legal and political-theoretical basis for welfare as an entitlement and right. Edward Sparer, a legal strategist for the welfare rights movement, challenged the usual understanding of dependency: "The charge of antiwelfare politicians is that welfare makes the recipient 'dependent.' What this means is that the recipient depends on the welfare check for his [*sic*] material subsistence rather than upon some other source . . . whether that is good or bad depends on whether a better source of income is available. . . . The real problem . . . is something entirely different. The recipient and the applicant traditionally have been dependent on the whim of the caseworker" (Sparer 1970–71, 71). The cure for welfare dependency, then, was welfare rights. Had the NWRO not been greatly weakened by the late 1970s, the revived discourse of pauperism in the 1980s could not have become hegemonic.

Even in the absence of a powerful National Welfare Rights Organization, many AFDC recipients maintained their own oppositional interpretation of welfare dependency. They complained not only of stingy allowances but also of infantilization due to supervision, loss of privacy, and a maze of bureaucratic rules that constrained their decisions about housing, jobs, and even (until the 1960s) sexual relations. In the claimants' view, welfare dependency is a social condition, not a psychological state, a condition they analyze in terms of power relations. It is what a left-wing English dictionary of social welfare calls *enforced dependency,* "the creation of a dependent class" as a result of "enforced reliance . . . for necessary psychological or material resources" (Timms and Timms 1982, 55–56).

This idea of enforced dependency was central to another, related challenge to the dominant discourse. During the period in which NWRO activism was at its height, New Left revisionist historians developed an interpretation of the welfare state as an apparatus of social control. They argued that what apologists portrayed as helping practices were actually modes of domination that created enforced dependency. The New Left critique bore some resemblance to the NWRO critique, but the overlap was only partial. The historians of social control told their story mainly from the perspective of the "helpers" and cast recipients as almost entirely passive. They thereby occluded the agency of actual or potential welfare claimants in articulating needs, demanding rights, and making claims.[13]

Still another contemporary challenge to mainstream uses of *dependency* arose from a New Left school of international political economy. The context was the realization, after the first heady days of postwar decolonization, that politically independent former colonies remained economically dependent. In *dependency theory,* radical theorists of "underdevelopment" used the concept of dependency to analyze the global neocolonial economic order from an antiracist and anti-imperialist perspective. In so doing, they resurrected the old preindustrial meaning of dependency as a subjected territory, seeking thereby to divest the term of its newer moral/psychological accretions and to retrieve the occluded dimensions of subjection and subordination. This usage remains strong in Latin America as well as in U.S. social-scientific literature, where we find articles such as "Institutionalizing Dependency: The Impact of Two Decades of Planned Agricultural Modernization" (Gates 1988).

What all these oppositional discourses share is a rejection of the dominant emphasis on dependency as an individual trait. They seek to shift the focus back to the social relations of subordination. But they do not have

---

[13] For a fuller discussion of the social control critique, see Gordon 1990. On needs claims, see Fraser 1990 and Nelson 1990.

much impact on mainstream talk about welfare in the United States today. On the contrary, with economic dependency now a synonym for poverty, and with moral/psychological dependency now a personality disorder, talk of dependency as a social relation of subordination has become increasingly rare. Power and domination tend to disappear.[14]

Conclusion

Dependency, once a general-purpose term for all social relations of subordination, is now differentiated into several analytically distinct registers. In the economic register, its meaning has shifted from gaining one's livelihood by working for someone else to relying for support on charity or welfare; wage labor now confers independence. In the sociolegal register, the meaning of dependency as subsumption is unchanged, but its scope of reference and connotations have altered: once a socially approved majority condition, it first became a group-based status deemed proper for some classes of persons but not others and then shifted again to designate (except in the case of children) an anomalous, highly stigmatized status of deviant and incompetent individuals. Likewise, in the political register, dependency's meaning as subjection to an external governing power has remained relatively constant, but its evaluative connotations worsened as individual political rights and national sovereignty became normative. Meanwhile, with the emergence of a newer moral/psychological register, properties once ascribed to social relations came to be posited instead as inherent character traits of individuals or groups, and the connotations here, too, have worsened. This last register now claims an increasingly large proportion of the discourse, as if the social relations of dependency were being absorbed into personality. Symptomatically, erstwhile relational understandings have been hypostatized in a veritable portrait gallery of dependent personalities: first, housewives, paupers, natives, and slaves; then poor, solo, black teenage mothers.

These shifts in the semantics of dependency reflect some major sociohistorical developments. One is the progressive differentiation of the official economy—that which is counted in the domestic national product—as a seemingly autonomous system that dominates social life. Before the rise of capitalism, all forms of work were woven into a net of dependencies, which constituted a single, continuous fabric of social hierarchies. The whole set of relations was constrained by moral understandings, as in the preindustrial idea of a moral economy. In the patriarchal families and communities that characterized the preindustrial period, women

---

[14] For an argument that Clinton's recent neoliberal discourse continues to individualize dependency, see Fraser 1993.

were subordinated and their labor often controlled by others, but their labor was visible, understood, and valued. With the emergence of religious and secular individualism, on the one hand, and of industrial capitalism, on the other, a sharp, new dichotomy was constructed in which economic dependency and economic independence were unalterably opposed to one another. A crucial corollary of this dependence/independence dichotomy, and of the hegemony of wage labor in general, was the occlusion and devaluation of women's unwaged domestic and parenting labor.

The genealogy of dependency also expresses the modern emphasis on individual personality. This is the deepest meaning of the spectacular rise of the moral/psychological register, which constructs yet another version of the independence/dependence dichotomy. In the moral/psychological version, social relations are hypostatized as properties of individuals or groups. Fear of dependency, both explicit and implicit, posits an ideal, independent personality in contrast to which those considered dependent are deviant. This contrast bears traces of a sexual division of labor that assigns men primary responsibility as providers or breadwinners and women primary responsibility as caretakers and nurturers and then treats the derivative personality patterns as fundamental. It is as if male breadwinners absorbed into their personalities the independence associated with their ideologically interpreted economic role, whereas the persons of female nurturers became saturated with the dependency of those for whom they care. In this way, the opposition between the independent personality and the dependent personality maps onto a whole series of hierarchical oppositions and dichotomies that are central in modern culture: masculine/feminine, public/private, work/care, success/love, individual/community, economy/family, and competitive/self-sacrificing.

A genealogy cannot tell us how to respond politically to today's discourse about welfare dependency. It does suggest, however, the limits of any response that presupposes rather than challenges the definition of the problem that is implicit in that expression. An adequate response would need to question our received valuations and definitions of dependence and independence in order to allow new, emancipatory social visions to emerge. Some contemporary welfare-rights activists adopt this strategy, continuing the NWRO tradition. Pat Gowens, for example, elaborates a feminist reinterpretation of dependency:

> The vast majority of mothers of *all classes and all educational levels* "depends" on another income. It may come from child support . . . or from a husband who earns $20,000 while she averages $7,000. But "dependence" more accurately defines dads who count on women's unwaged labor to raise children and care for the home.

Surely, "dependence" doesn't define the single mom who does it all: child-rearing, homemaking, and bringing in the money (one way or another). When caregiving is valued and paid, when dependence is not a dirty word, and interdependence is the norm—only then will we make a dent in poverty. [Gowens 1991, 90–91]

Department of Philosophy and Center for Urban Affairs
and Policy Research
Northwestern University (Fraser)
Department of History
University of Wisconsin—Madison (Gordon)

References

Abbott, Edith, and Sophonisba P. Breckinridge. 1921. *The Administration of the Aid-to-Mothers Law in Illinois.* Publication no. 82. Washington, D.C.: U.S. Children's Bureau.

Alcoff, Linda. 1990. "Feminist Politics and Foucault: The Limits to a Collaboration." In *Crisis in Continental Philosophy,* ed. Arleen B. Dallery and Charles E. Scott, 69–86. Albany: SUNY Press.

American Psychiatric Association. 1987. *Diagnostic and Statistical Manual of Mental Disorders,* 3d ed. revised. Washington, D.C.: American Psychiatric Association.

Bakke, E. Wight. 1940a. *Citizens without Work: A Study of the Effects of Unemployment upon Workers' Social Relations and Practices.* New Haven, Conn.: Yale University Press.

———. 1940b. *The Unemployed Worker: A Study of the Task of Making a Living without a Job.* New Haven, Conn.: Yale University Press.

Barnes, Annie S. 1987. *Single Parents in Black America: A Study in Culture and Legitimacy.* Bristol, Conn.: Wyndham Hall.

Bourdieu, Pierre. 1977. *Outline of a Theory of Practice.* Cambridge: Cambridge University Press.

———. 1990a. *In Other Words,* trans. Matthew Adamson. Oxford: Polity.

———. 1990b. *The Logic of Practice,* trans. Richard Nice. Stanford, Calif.: Stanford University Press.

Boydston, Jeanne. 1991. *Home and Work: Housework, Wages, and the Ideology of Labor in the Early Republic.* New York: Oxford.

Brandt, Lilian. 1932. *An Impressionistic View of the Winter of 1930–31 in New York City.* New York: Welfare Council of New York City.

Breckinridge, Sophonisba P. 1928. "The House Responsibilities of Women Workers and the 'Equal Wage.' " *Journal of Political Economy* 31:521–43.

Brown, Josephine Chapin. 1940. *Public Relief, 1929–1939.* New York: Henry Holt.

Bruno, Frank J. 1948. *Trends in Social Work.* New York: Columbia University Press.

Butler, Judith. 1987. "Variations on Sex and Gender: Beauvoir, Wittig and Foucault." In *Feminism as Critique,* ed. Seyla Benhabib and Drucilla Cornell, 128–42. Minneapolis: University of Minnesota Press.

———. 1990. *Gender Trouble: Feminism and the Subversion of Identity.* New York: Routledge.

Cates, Jerry R. 1983. *Insuring Inequality: Administrative Leadership in Social Security, 1935–54.* Ann Arbor: University of Michigan Press.

Diamond, Irene, and Lee Quinby, eds. 1988. *Foucault and Feminism: Reflections on Resistance.* Boston: Northeastern University Press.

Dowling, Colette. 1981. *The Cinderella Complex: Women's Hidden Fear of Independence.* New York: Summit.

Folbre, Nancy. 1991. "The Unproductive Housewife: Her Evolution in Nineteenth-Century Economic Thought." *Signs: Journal of Women in Culture and Society* 16(3):463–84.

Foucault, Michel. 1984. "Nietzsche, Genealogy, History." In *The Foucault Reader,* ed. Paul Rabinow, 76–100. New York: Pantheon.

Fraser, Nancy. 1987. "Women, Welfare, and the Politics of Need Interpretation." *Hypatia: A Journal of Feminist Philosophy* 2(1):103–21.

———. 1989. *Unruly Practices: Power, Discourse and Gender in Contemporary Social Theory.* Minneapolis: University of Minnesota Press.

———. 1990. "Struggle over Needs: Outline of a Socialist-Feminist Critical Theory of Late-Capitalist Political Culture." In *Women, the State, and Welfare,* ed. Linda Gordon, 199–225. Madison: University of Wisconsin Press.

———. 1992. "The Uses and Abuses of French Discourse Theories for Feminist Politics." In *Revaluing French Feminism: Critical Essays on Difference, Agency, and Culture,* ed. Nancy Fraser and Sandra Bartky, 177–94. Bloomington: Indiana University Press.

———. 1993. "Clintonism, Welfare and the Antisocial Wage: The Emergence of a Neoliberal Political Imaginary." *Rethinking Marxism* 6(1):1–15.

Fraser, Nancy, and Linda Gordon. 1992. "Contract versus Charity: Why Is There No Social Citizenship in the United States?" *Socialist Review* 22(3):45–68.

Friedan, Betty. 1963. *The Feminine Mystique.* New York: Norton.

Gates, M. 1988. "Institutionalizing Dependency: The Impact of Two Decades of Planned Agricultural Modernization." *Journal of Developing Areas* 22(3):293–320.

Gibbons, Mary L. 1933. "Family Life Today and Tomorrow." *Proceedings, National Conference of Catholic Charities* 19:133–68.

Gilder, George. 1981. *Wealth and Poverty.* New York: Basic.

Gordon, Linda. 1990. "The New Feminist Scholarship on the Welfare State." In *Women, the State, and Welfare,* ed. Linda Gordon, 9–35. Madison: University of Wisconsin Press.

———. 1992. "Social Insurance and Public Assistance: The Influence of Gender in Welfare Thought in the United States, 1890–1935." *American Historical Review* 97(1):19–54.

Gowens, Pat. 1991. "Welfare, Learnfare—Unfair! A Letter to My Governor." *Ms.* (September–October), 90–91.

Gundersen, Joan R. 1987. "Independence, Citizenship, and the American Revolution." *Signs* 13(1):59–77.

Hartsock, Nancy. 1990. "Foucault on Power: A Theory for Women?" In *Feminism/ Postmodernism*, ed. Linda J. Nicholson, 157–75. New York: Routledge.

Haynes, M. 1988. "Pharmacist Involvement in a Chemical-Dependency Rehabilitation Program." *American Journal of Hospital Pharmacy* 45(10):2099–2101.

Hill, Christopher. 1972. *The World Turned Upside Down: Radical Ideas during the English Revolution*. New York: Viking.

Honneth, Axel. 1992. *The Critique of Power: Reflective Stages in a Critical Social Theory*. Cambridge, Mass.: MIT Press.

Howard, Donald S. 1943. *The WPA and Federal Relief Policy*. New York: Russell Sage.

Hughes, Gwendolyn S. 1925. *Mothers in Industry*. New York: New Republic.

Jencks, Christopher. 1992. *Rethinking Social Policy: Race, Poverty, and the Underclass*. Cambridge, Mass.: Harvard University Press.

Land, Hilary. 1980. "The Family Wage." *Feminist Review* 6:55–77.

Laslett, Peter. 1971. *The World We Have Lost: England before the Industrial Age*. New York: Scribner.

McCarthy, Thomas. 1991. *Ideals and Illusions: On Reconstruction and Deconstruction in Contemporary Critical Theory*. Cambridge, Mass.: MIT Press.

Macpherson, C. B. 1962. *The Political Theory of Possessive Individualism: Hobbes to Locke*. Oxford: Oxford University Press.

Mead, Lawrence. 1986. *Beyond Entitlement: The Social Obligations of Citizenship*. New York: Free Press.

Milwaukee County Welfare Rights Organization. 1972. *Welfare Mothers Speak Out*. New York: Norton.

Moynihan, Daniel P. 1973. *The Politics of a Guaranteed Income: The Nixon Administration and the Family Assistance Plan*. New York: Random House.

Murray, Charles. 1984. *Losing Ground: American Social Policy, 1950–1980*. New York: Basic.

Nathan, Richard P. 1986. "The Underclass—Will It Always Be with Us?" Unpublished paper, quoted by William Julius Wilson, "Social Policy and Minority Groups: What Might Have Been and What Might We See in the Future." In *Divided Opportunities: Minorities, Poverty, and Social Policy*, ed. Gary D. Sandefur and Marta Tienda, 231–52. New York: Plenum.

National Conference of Charities and Correction. 1890s–1920s. *Proceedings*.

Nelson, Barbara J. 1990. "The Origins of the Two-Channel Welfare State: Workmen's Compensation and Mothers' Aid." In *Women, the State, and Welfare*, ed. Linda Gordon, 123–51. Madison: University of Wisconsin Press.

Pope, Jacqueline. 1989. *Biting the Hand That Feeds Them: Organizing Women on Welfare at the Grass Roots Level*. New York: Praeger.

Pruette, Lorine, ed. 1934. *Women Workers through the Depression: A Study of White Collar Employment Made by the American Woman's Association*. New York: Macmillan.

Quadagno, Jill. 1988. "From Old-Age Assistance to Supplemental Social Security Income: The Political Economy of Relief in the South, 1935–1972." In *The Politics of Social Policy in the United States*, ed. Margaret Weir, Ann Shola Orloff, and Theda Skocpol, 235–63. Princeton, N.J.: Princeton University Press.

Quayle, Dan. 1992. "Excerpts from Vice President's Speech on Cities and Poverty." *New York Times,* May 20.

Rainwater, Lee, and William L. Yancey. 1967. *The Moynihan Report and the Politics of Controversy.* Cambridge, Mass.: MIT Press.

Sapiro, Virginia. 1990. "The Gender Basis of American Social Policy." In *Women, the State, and Welfare,* ed. Linda Gordon, 36–54. Madison: University of Wisconsin Press.

Scott, Joan Wallach. 1988. *Gender and the Politics of History.* New York: Columbia University Press.

Smith, Joan. 1984. "The Paradox of Women's Poverty: Wage-earning Women and Economic Transformation." *Signs* 10(2):291–310.

Sparer, Edward V. 1971 (c. 1970). "The Right to Welfare." In *The Rights of Americans: What They Are—What They Should Be,* ed. Norman Dorsen, 65–93. New York: Pantheon.

Stacey, Judith. 1987. "Sexism by a Subtler Name? Postindustrial Conditions and Postfeminist Consciousness in the Silicon Valley." *Socialist Review* 96:7–28.

——— . 1990. *Brave New Families: Stories of Domestic Upheaval in Late Twentieth Century America.* New York: Basic.

Timms, Noel, and Rita Timms. 1982. *Dictionary of Social Welfare.* London: Routledge & Kegan Paul.

Tumulty, Karen. 1991. *Los Angeles Times,* July 5.

Vaile, Gertrude. 1934. "Public Relief." In *College Women and the Social Sciences,* ed. Herbert Elmer Mills, 19–40. New York: John Day.

Warner, Amos Griswold. 1894–1930. *American Charities and Social Work.* New York: Thomas Y. Crowell.

Weedon, Chris. 1987. *Feminist Practice and Poststructuralist Theory.* Oxford: Basil Blackwell.

West, Guida. 1981. *The National Welfare Rights Movement: The Social Protest of Poor Women.* New York: Praeger.

Weston, Kath. 1991. *Families We Choose: Lesbians, Gays, Kinship.* New York: Columbia University Press.

Williams, Raymond. 1976. *Keywords: A Vocabulary of Culture and Society.* Oxford: Oxford University Press.

Wilson, William Julius. 1987. *The Truly Disadvantaged: The Inner City, the Underclass, and Public Policy.* Chicago: University of Chicago Press.

Young, Leontine. 1954. *Out of Wedlock.* New York: McGraw Hill.

Differences and Identities: Feminism and the Albuquerque Lesbian Community

Trisha Franzen

THIS ARTICLE is about the politicization of the Albuquerque, New Mexico, lesbian community. It is also very much about race, class, sexuality, and difference. It traces how three subcommunities of lesbians in this southwestern city defined themselves and each other during the period 1965–80, the years when feminism became a significant influence among them.

I came out in Buffalo, New York, in a lesbian community where I perceived continuity between members of the older lesbian community, gay liberation activists, and lesbians active in the women's movement. In that environment, many of us "new" lesbians learned the social and political lessons of lesbian culture from our "elders," that is, from those women who had lived as lesbians before the emergence of contemporary feminism and the articulation of lesbian theory. Among our core lessons was to listen to women's life stories and not to privilege the written word over the lived experience. Feminist and lesbian theory were accepted only if validated by lesbians' own lives. Issues of race and class were raised and debated as they connected with our lives. The process was, to use Cherríe Moraga and Gloria Anzaldúa's term, "theory in the flesh" (1981, 23).

When I moved to Albuquerque in 1980, I did not find analogous connections within its lesbian community. I soon became part of a feminist lesbian network, the core of which was overwhelmingly Anglo in a

I wish to thank those women who contributed to this research: the women of the Albuquerque lesbian community who shared their histories with me; Liz Lapovsky Kennedy, whose work with Madeline Davis inspired and guided my work and who supported this project in many ways; Jane Slaughter, who read this article in its early stages, offered constructive criticism, and always encouraged my efforts; Louise Lamphere, who made important suggestions for clarifying my argument; Chris Ruggiero, whose enthusiasm sustained me through numerous revisions; and Kristine Long, whose suggestions in the final stages of editing strengthened the article.

[*Signs: Journal of Women in Culture and Society* 1993, vol. 18, no. 4]

city where Anglos are barely the majority. Most of the women I met had moved to New Mexico as adults and had come to their lesbian identities within the women's movement. There did not seem to be much connection between this part of the Albuquerque lesbian community and an indigenous pre–women's movement one. There were no elders within the feminist lesbian circles, no women who had been active in the public bar community and were now involved in the feminist lesbian activities.

I found the absence of women of color and lesbian elders startling. The stratification I found between newly out feminist lesbians and native-born Albuquerque lesbians challenged my personal experience and my understanding of the emerging works in lesbian and gay history that suggested that politicization follows a sense of shared identity and community consciousness (see, e.g., D'Emilio 1983). The lack of racial integration was disturbing in light of the increasingly strong challenges being made to feminist theory and activism by poor and working-class women and women of color.[1] Within lesbian studies, the invisibility of less-privileged lesbians was being countered by writers, activists, and scholars who were demanding that lesbians too examine the assumption that "all women's issues are the same" (Gibbs and Bennett 1980, 49).

Concurrent with these discussions were the feminist sexuality debates that asked, among other questions, who rightfully could claim lesbian and feminist identities and whether there are politically correct and incorrect sexual behaviors.[2] The relevance of this last controversy to issues of diversity and interconnections within the lesbian community was not immediately clear. What was clear was that it was not easy to talk about sex within feminist lesbian circles in Albuquerque. Even discussions concerning sexual behavior, roles, and S/M were suspect and were often met with silencing sarcasm and ridicule. An attempt to hold a public forum at the feminist bookstore on what was termed at the time "the sexual fringe" deteriorated into a battle between two hostile camps and a years-long public silence on these issues.

All these issues made me want to know why the Albuquerque lesbian community had split the way it had. This curiosity led to a formal research project based on interviews with lesbians who were involved with this community between 1965 and 1980. The interviews were open-ended and semistructured, focusing on each woman's experience as a lesbian in this southwestern city. Throughout this project I attempted to balance my sample on the factors of race/ethnicity and class as well as

---

[1] Some of the early works include Bethel and Smith 1979; Davis 1981; Moraga and Anzaldúa 1981.

[2] See, e.g., Cook 1977, 42–61; Rich 1980, 62–91; Faderman 1981; Samois 1981; Ferguson, Zita, and Addelson 1982, 147–88; Linden et al. 1982; Snitow, Stansell, and Thompson 1983; and Vance 1984.

between lesbians who were born and raised in New Mexico and those who settled there as adults. Therefore, when I refer to native New Mexicans I am talking not about Native Americans but women of all races from New Mexico. The result provided diversity though it does not completely match the racial/ethnic composition of the city. I supplemented this data with newspaper articles, findings from a 1981 community survey, and records from the National Lesbian Feminist Organization and Siren, an early women's music production and education group.

While the questions for this research originated in my personal experiences in this community, I myself did not move to Albuquerque until 1980 and was not a participant in the community during the period I studied. I was, by the time I was doing this research, part of what I am terming the feminist lesbian network. I was publicly out, working for a lesbian-owned business, active in lesbian and gay organizations, and associated with a lesbian softball team. I was also involved in other feminist institutions and organizations and through that work built connections with lesbians who had played important roles in this community in other than the feminist lesbian network. When my research became more systematic, these women were key, sharing their stories with me in interviews and acting as brokers by contacting old friends and convincing women who did not know me that I could be trusted. Nevertheless, throughout this project it was easier to find feminist lesbians willing to be interviewed, as working-class and older lesbians and lesbians of color were far more reluctant to talk with me. During the years I worked on this project I presented various drafts of this article at public forums in Albuquerque.

For the purpose of this article I have had to impose a static framework on what were dynamic divisions within a complex community. The three groups I compare are defined only on the basis of their public lesbian activities: women who were socially and politically active as lesbians within feminism; women who were socially active as lesbians, usually through the bars, but were not politically active or were not politically active as lesbians; and closeted women who were not socially or politically active as lesbians. What is important to remember is that there were active feminists in all three groups. The differentiating identifications for women in this article are not their feminist identities but, again, their public lesbian activities or "outness." Some women from all three groups, for example, were associated with the Women's Center at the University of New Mexico, but many more of the women from the first group than from the second or third. I did not ask any of the feminists in my sample to define themselves by any particular theoretical position—radical feminist, liberal feminist, socialist feminist, etc.—nor did I delve into the sexual attitudes or behaviors of any of the women in this study.

As background, some sense of New Mexican history is helpful. The state's history is one of repeated colonizations, military, civil, and cultural. It is also a history of resistance. This resistance, along with the state's geographical position, has resulted in the survival of various Native American cultures and the evolution of a uniquely New Mexican Hispanic tradition. Anglos arrived in significant numbers only in the second half of the nineteenth century, along with a small number of African Americans. New Mexico was a territory of the United States after the Treaty of Guadalupe-Hidalgo in 1846 but did not become a state until 1912.

Since World War II, Albuquerque has seen a tremendous growth in population as part of the general migration to Sunbelt regions and the increase in U.S. Department of Defense bases and laboratories. Between 1960 and 1980, this city's population increased 65 percent. Most of these new Albuquerqueans are Anglo (U.S. Census 1960, 1980). Given New Mexican history, this population growth has produced concerns about outsiders and the preservation of what is special about New Mexico generally.

Politically, during the 1960s New Mexico was the site of a civil rights struggle that was regionally focused while also influenced by and part of the national civil rights movement. As with the larger movement, demands for civil rights were followed by the eruption of racial and cultural tensions that heightened the political consciousness of people of color throughout the region and underscored the gaps between those not privileged in this society and those who are.

The long and complex history of racial/cultural conflict and assimilation contrasts with what little we know of lesbians and gay men in Albuquerque. This is the first systematic research done on the Albuquerque lesbian and gay community, although lesbian and gay historians have begun to document the growth of sexuality-based communities on other urban areas (see, e.g., Kennedy and Davis 1993). These histories have begun to identify the factors contributing to the development of such communities that led to gay liberation and the emergence of lesbian activism within feminism. Relevant to this time period and region are two World War II–related phenomena: the urban growth fostered by wartime mobilization and job opportunities and the relatively laissez-faire attitude toward sexuality of the military during the war (Berube 1989). While the subsequent repression of the McCarthy era certainly scarred these young communities, such crackdowns did not break them. In fact, this period may have broadened gay self-consciousness of oppression. In spite of the vagaries of public opinion and policy during these years, lesbian and gay communities continued to grow. In Albuquerque this growth is documented by the increase in public spaces where gay men and lesbians could gather in relative safety during the 1960s and 1970s. The earliest gay bar remembered by my narrators was the Newsroom, which later became Duke's Cave. According to Paula: "It was pretty awful looking. Very small, very smoky. It was down under [a straight bar]. The bathroom leaked into the . . . I mean I don't know what was leaking exactly, but the bathroom was above and it never worked right. It wasn't scary, but a horrible dump. But I had a lot of fun there." The Newsroom fits the stereotype of early gay bars: smoky, dark, and a little sleazy. The police came regularly, sometimes stopping action throughout the bar to check IDs. To add to the risk and excitement, there were occasional fights. According to my informants, however, the limits of this bar were far over-shadowed by the relief patrons felt in finding a lesbian/gay community.

During this period, gay men also gathered at the coffee houses that served the Albuquerque "beat" crowd; although comfortable and ac-cepted in these public places, they made up only a small percentage of the clientele. For their part, Albuquerque lesbians frequented a jazz bar in Santa Fe, sixty miles to the north. This establishment was owned and managed by a French woman named Claude, who set the tone for non-conforming gender behavior by appearing some evenings in a flamboyant evening gown and full makeup and other nights in a tuxedo and slicked-back hair. This bar attracted a mature, mixed crowd—women and men, gay and straight—and was a favorite of middle-class lesbians.[3]

These gathering places were followed by what came to be called the Old Heights, the first of several bars run by a gay couple, Bill and Larry. One woman remembered it as opening in 1958. While their first bar was not a great improvement over the Newsroom, the New Heights, which opened several years later, was. It was attached to one of the most elegant restaurants in the city, which employed a number of gay men. Bill and Larry are remembered with great fondness as being, according to Bar-bara, "extremely gracious": "I felt real safe in the New Heights. With them I always felt safe. If people got tossed in jail, they'd go and do your bail."

The number of bars continued to grow. By the mid-1960s, lesbians could choose from the Wellington, a relatively fancy bar and restaurant; the Limelight, a large, rustic establishment located in the mountains east of the city; Mildred's, an in-town bar; the Upstairs Lounge, an after-hours club; and Crickets, a women's private club. Part of a family bar in the town north of Albuquerque also served as a gay bar for a short period of time.

Except for Crickets, these were all mixed bars (i.e., serving lesbians and gay men) with full liquor licenses. Crickets, owned by a Native

---

[3] Many of the women I interviewed spoke of knowing of a separate Santa Fe lesbian network of older wealthy women who had settled in Santa Fe or Taos and participated in the artistic circles of those cities.

American woman, operated under a private club liquor license, as does a lesbian bar that opened later. There was no agreement among my interviewees about the reasons for this difference in liquor licenses. One bar owner stated that the private club license was the only legal means to have an all-women's bar. But those who patronized these "clubs" argued that such licenses were cheaper and easier to obtain. There was speculation that family connections had helped the bar owners obtain their licenses.

Many of the bars were located along a section of Central Avenue, the old U.S. Route 66, about two miles east of downtown Albuquerque and just east of the University of New Mexico. This area is currently undergoing gentrification, but historically it has been dominated by small commercial operations, stores, motels, and a few shopping centers. The surrounding residential areas are predominantly Anglo middle-class neighborhoods and are considered nice places to live. While there is no "gay ghetto" in Albuquerque, many lesbians and gay men do live in these neighborhoods. The Metropolitan Community Church and Common Bond, the city's largest gay organization, are housed in this relatively uptown section.

For the lesbians of this earlier era, finding the bars was often synonymous with finding a named identity and a community. Robin, an Anglo born and raised in Albuquerque, had always had a sense of herself as different and had always been attracted to women. She was introduced to her first gay bar when she was in college in Albuquerque and became part of a circle of women who were also attracted to other women.

> We would all go to the Caravan (a straight bar) for happy hour. But we [Robin and her girlfriend] kept being left behind. They'd say, "Well, we're going home now," or make up something. We'd sit there . . . and it's eight o'clock, thinking what's wrong with these people. So one time I got pissed at Sue in the parking lot. I said, "Goddamn it, what's going on here? You ride with me and we're supposed to spend the evening doing something and then you take off with those folks." She got out of the car, went over to those others, talked to them and came back. And she just said, I'll never forget it, "Get in." On the way . . . she said, "Remember when I said there was a place I would never take you?" I said, "Yeah?" She said, "We're going there now." And I said, "Damn. Alright. It's about time."

Albuquerque lesbians remember the late sixties and early seventies as good times. While the bars ranged from plush to sleazy, lesbians felt they had choices about where to socialize, and they recall harassment as minimal. Public lesbian culture in Albuquerque, according to the women who frequented the bars, shared many of the features identified by other lesbian historians (Nestle 1987; Kennedy and Davis 1993). One's social and sexual lives involved butch-femme roles with the accompanying dating etiquette and dress codes. Private parties supplemented nights at the bars. At these parties, the lesbians who did go to the bars socialized with their more closeted friends. Softball was a very important lesbian activity and teams drew women of all races and classes from across the city. This sport provided another opportunity for closeted women to interact with more public lesbians and for lesbians in general to meet and socialize with each other outside of the bars. Among the memorable teams were the Dukettes (Albuquerque is the Duke City, named for the Duke of Albuquerque, Spain), also known as the "Dykettes," a team of older butches. One woman recalled, "You could hardly tell their gender."

Across the board, lesbians active in the bars and the closeted networks in the 1960s emphasize the solidarity they felt among themselves and between lesbians and gay men. The lesbians not only shared the public bar space with gay men but also considered them their friends. For some lesbians these men provided compatible dates for those occasions that called for a heterosexual cover.

While the bars were the centers of gay life in Albuquerque as elsewhere, many lesbians who frequented the bars were also in contact with closeted lesbians. As my research progressed, I became increasingly conscious of the interconnections and overlappings among the various lesbian social networks through friendships, school, softball, and parties, convincing me that the closeted lesbians were important players in the history of the public community and the growth of feminism.

My research suggests that in this community during this period, the bar-going lesbians and the lesbians who did not socialize at the bars defined themselves in part against each other, but in an opposition free of hostility. They saw in each other two ways to be lesbian, one based on safety and passing and one based on risk and an identity that was articulated and affirmed by a community. While one group's identity was centered at the bars, the closeted women kept theirs private within their homes and the homes of their closest friends.

To understand how these two subgroups related to each other, it is important to recognize that within each were individuals who had known each other often from childhood on. They had gone to school together, played sports with each other, and worked with each other. From these shared histories they could identify with each other. It also was not unusual for women to move back and forth between these two groups. Robin frequented the bars far less when she became involved with Alice, who was completely closeted. Conversely, Gloria had never gone to the bars and was part of a closeted circle until she gained more job security, when she celebrated by going to the bar for the first time. In these ways these two groups were in flux.

When asked, most closeted women gave concerns about their jobs as their reason for avoiding public lesbian spaces. They felt they had to struggle hard enough as women to achieve economic self-sufficiency and accepted remaining in the closet as the price they had to pay for it. Only a few of the women mentioned that they did not like the bars or could not identify with the women in them.

It appears therefore that the decisions of the closeted women served as constant reminders to the public/bar lesbians of the dangers involved in participating in public gay life as well as demonstrating another, less risky way to be gay. Nevertheless, the lesbians I interviewed who were part of these social networks before the reemergence of the women's movement did not convey any sense of resentment or judgment toward each others' choices about the bars. In several cases, younger lesbians mentioned older, closeted lesbians who had served as on-the-job mentors, passing on survival strategies and warnings about the dangers of not being discreet. Although the lessons were not always appreciated immediately, they were respected in retrospect. Several quite out lesbians strongly stated their support for the decisions of closeted women, especially those in educa-tion. As one Chicana stated, there was a "live and let live attitude" within the community.

The respectful acceptance of different choices and different ways to be lesbian was strongest among women who had grown up and gone to school together, regardless of differences in race and class. On the other hand, the closeted networks of women who were not native Albuquer-queans conveyed a sense of distance from bar lesbians. Nor did the "natives' " sense of solidarity extend to the feminists who became part of the Albuquerque lesbian scene in the late sixties and early seventies. The bar lesbians were confused and put off by their actions and ideas. The extent to which the bar lesbians viewed feminism as foreign is best cap-tured by the name given the women most frequently credited with intro-ducing feminist lesbianism to Albuquerque. Consistently this group is referred to as the "Boston crazies." What was clear about these feminists, according to one bar lesbian, was that they were "not us."

If one group of lesbians discussed in this article centered their lesbian identities at the bars and the other in their homes, this third group built their identities around the Women's Center at the University of New Mexico. While straight women and lesbians from the other categories were important in the development of the center, according to my infor-mants, feminist lesbianism was centered there. The women in this third network connected with each other on the basis of their feminism and lesbianism. Many of them were students at the University of New Mexico as undergraduates, graduate students, and law students. Joan, for example, an Anglo from a middle-class family, was introduced to feminism and lesbianism at the university. She became involved in consciousness-raising groups and came out as a lesbian about the same time she became one of the first staff members at the Rape Crisis Center and a founder of a women's concert production company.

Although feminist lesbianism was centered at the university, tensions between feminist lesbians and other lesbians were clearest at the bars. Several of the feminist lesbians remember the arrangements in the early 1970s as "old gays on one side, new gays on the other." When asked if there was much interaction, one feminist stated, "Very little between old gay and new gay. Very little. Only old gays we saw were those at the bar. And I think they viewed us as interlopers into their space. That we were dilettantes and eating pussy just to see what it tasted like and would go home to our hubbies. I mean they felt their area was being invaded." This informant also discussed what had happened when she had attended a "jock" party several years earlier with women who were part of Robin's circle. She saw women disappearing two-by-two into the bedrooms but found that no one was willing to discuss the fact that they were lesbians. She concluded, "Seeing lesbians dealing with each other in such a dishonest way sent me back into the closet, though a different closet from the one I had known when I was thirteen." This woman did not claim her lesbian identity until lesbian feminism was an option.

The split between these two sectors of the community can also be seen around specific issues. As I mentioned earlier, bar lesbians had often socialized with gay men and felt a sense of solidarity with them. Barbara, for example, stated that she preferred mixed bars. When her friends started going to the lesbian bar in the 1970s, she went with them but missed the guys. In contrast, Joan, a feminist lesbian, does not recall knowing any gay men. "We hated all men. Just hated them because the political rhetoric was that gays got together with other men because they hated women."

This difference may have more complex roots than separatist rhetoric. The differing histories of the individuals in these groups suggest that the extent of their earlier relationships with men influenced their acceptance of and interaction with gay men. Few of the bar or closeted lesbians I interviewed had ever been seriously involved with men in romantic or sexual ways. The males in their lives, besides family and work colleagues, had been these gay men with whom they shared public gay spaces and a sense of refuge from straight society. In contrast, many of the feminist lesbians had been married or recently involved in heterosexual relationships. For example, one feminist recalls that at its inception all of the women in her consciousness-raising group identified themselves as heterosexual and several were married. Looking back, she realizes that all these women eventually came out. In short, while the older lesbians tended to confront sexism and their lack of heterosexual privilege in the public sphere—in school, on the job, when trying to get a mortgage—the feminist lesbians had struggled over gender issues in intimate relationships with husbands and boyfriends.

Feminist lesbians also had a disdain for butch/femme roles and the dress and etiquette codes associated with them. On the other side, bar lesbians saw the feminist uniform of Levis, flannel shirts, work boots, and short hair as unattractive, even sloppy. Interestingly, while the feminist lesbians were reacting strongly against such roles, among the bar lesbians there was some sense that the importance and rigidity of these roles had diminished by this time. One woman told this story to illustrate that point:

> I think when our age group came out I think it was that we saw this whole butch/femme thing as a game. Like some people really took this seriously. The fem would never touch the butch in bed. The butch would always make love to the fem. I think we saw it as more of a game, and if you needed to play the game you did, depending on who you went out with. I remember this scene in my apartment with this woman. And it was the first time we were going to give a hug. I went here [around the waist] and she went here [around the waist]. And we had a collision. And she said, "Ah we're going to have to work something out here. This isn't going to work." I said, "Okay." And I went up here [around the shoulders].

After 1978 the divisions within the lesbian community became even more pronounced with the opening of a second lesbian bar. While the first exclusively lesbian bar originally had been downtown, it soon moved and remained for the rest of its existence on the predominantly Hispanic, working-class west side. In the late 1970s a native New Mexican Chicana who had worked in the first lesbian bar opened a new bar in the predominantly Anglo Northeast Heights. The owner of this new bar stated that she opened her establishment to "provide women with a nicer place." What resulted was a self-segregation based on class and race, with middle-class and Anglo women going to the new bar and the older bar's clientele becoming increasingly working-class or poor women and women of color.

Not surprisingly, the feminist lesbians generally abandoned the older bar and patronized the newer one. But this arrangement did not have a long honeymoon. As stated earlier, both of these "women's" bars were run under private club licenses that made the clubs nonprofit organizations in which individuals bought memberships. These "members" theoretically had some say in the management of "their club." This situation appears to have produced higher expectations for these clubs than for gay bars generally, and even higher ones for the new bar and its owner. The feminists assumed that the owner of the new bar would run it more democratically and expected what was to the owner's mind a private business to be run according to feminist principles. Not long after the bar opened, a group of feminist lesbians asked for a meeting with the owner and confronted the owner about certain of her management decisions, claiming that they were frustrated by the owner's lack of support for their activities and their politics. On her part, the owner claims that "they wanted a share of the profits." Whatever happened, whatever the motives, these differences were not resolved amicably, and to this day the owner identifies the feminists as "trouble-making radicals."

Another example of the difficulties between these groups can be seen in a story I first heard as part of the oral history of the feminist lesbian community. I had been told about a great party that had been held, the highlight of which was two popular women appearing dressed only in cowboy boots, hats, and guns and holsters. This story was passed on as hilarious, a celebration of the outrageous behavior that was part of the early days of feminist lesbianism. I had no reason to doubt this analysis until I heard a very different version from the woman whose home was the site of the party. This Anglo, native New Mexican lesbian had only recently discovered feminism and had become part of a central feminist lesbian circle. She ran her business, which involved giving lessons mostly to children, out of her home. Her feminist friends had wanted to have a party at her house but she resisted because she was afraid it would hurt her business. They held the party anyway when she was away on a business trip. She only found out about the party when women she barely knew came up to her at the bar and said how much they liked her house. When she finally figured out the connection between the drop in her business and the people who claimed to have been in her home, she tried to confront her feminist friends about the party. They refused to hear her and shunned her afterward as being too bourgeois and closeted.

But these particular instances of suspicion and overt hostility needed to be contextualized within a greater sense of separation between the two networks sharing the public lesbian space. Although the feminist lesbians frequented the bars, they did so with other feminists, straight, gay, and undecided. This group was very much caught up in the excitement of the women's liberation movement. Their activism centered around the University of New Mexico, and they were instrumental in founding and maintaining the U.N.M. Women's Center and Women Studies Program, the Albuquerque Rape Crisis Center, and the Shelter for Victims of Domestic Violence. As lesbians, they had to struggle for recognition of their lives and lesbian issues within these organizations as well as in others such as the National Organization for Women and the New Mexico chapter of the National Women's Political Caucus. They were an important presence at a left-feminist sit-in at the campus newspaper in the early 1970s and at the state hearings for the Equal Rights Amendment. In 1976 an out lesbian was elected homecoming queen at the University of New Mexico (although the governor refused to crown her).

It was often in the political arena that the third category of lesbians, the women in the closeted networks, came into contact with the feminist lesbians. A significant number of closeted lesbians became leaders in women's political organizations and worked alongside the out feminist lesbians, though they themselves remained closeted. In spite of this shared work, women from each group had suspicions about the other. The closeted lesbians did not feel that the open lesbians understood and respected their decisions to remain closeted. They also felt that the feminist lesbians were interested only in the sexuality issue, the lesbian perspective, and would not support them in their struggles around less specifically lesbian concerns, especially those based on class and race. On their part, the feminist lesbians felt betrayed by the closeted lesbians' less-than-wholehearted support of their position, support that frequently would have necessitated abandoning their closets. The feminist lesbians interpreted the closeted lesbians' personal and political decisions as internalized oppression.

Significantly, no specifically lesbian formal organization was founded in Albuquerque until a chapter of the National Lesbian Feminist Organization was begun in 1978. The gay student organization at the University of New Mexico, founded in 1970, has been and remains a predominantly male group.

*   *   *

As far as the indigenous lesbian community was concerned, feminist lesbianism as political theory and practice might just as well have dropped from a spaceship. That is how alien these new lesbians, these new ways of being lesbians were to the women who made up the early public community and closeted networks. The more important question, however, is why this combination of political philosophy and personal identification was greeted with suspicion and resistance and perceived of as imposed and invasive in Albuquerque. When there appeared a group of lesbians articulating an analysis of lesbian oppression, why was this group rejected by the native community? And what does this history of the lesbian community in Albuquerque have to contribute to lesbian history and theory?

In Albuquerque, neither shared lesbian identities nor shared feminist identities were sufficient bases for solidarity across the lesbian community. Why? This research suggests that sexuality is at the core of all the issues involved and that sexuality is a problematic basis for political solidarity among women. The feminist sexuality debates made this point clear. Among other complications, women have been divided into good and bad, esteemed or despised, protected or exploited, all on the basis of sexuality. And in the dominant culture's portrayals of female sexuality, that very sexual Other that all women should fear becoming has often been the poor woman, the woman of color, and the lesbian.

Did lesbian theory and practice take these issues into account when lesbians were confronting each other in Albuquerque? In a limited way, yes. Feminists knew how calling women lesbians was a threat used to divide women and keep women in their places, but there was no recognition of how sexuality interacted with racism and classism to separate women from each other within lesbian communities. Albuquerque feminist lesbians could not talk about sex, but without talking about sex they could not really talk about being lesbians. Only now is the diversity of lesbian voices being heard, and it has taken time for lesbians to research and reveal the history needed to build theory and examine how race and class differences are entwined with sexuality and issues of trust and power. Now lesbians are asking if we feared identifying with each other because in that identity would be claiming a sexuality that was threatening.

What does it mean that for lesbians claiming one's sexuality makes us sexual outlaws? Joan Nestle (1987) describes the struggle against this labeling and speaks of how feminism appeared to offer a comforting respectability to lesbians. Lesbians could be the best feminists, but only if we discarded all in lesbianism that might be seen as tainted by heterosexuality. In Albuquerque there was certainly that sense that feminist lesbians wanted other lesbians to "clean up their acts." This included, for example, discarding both the behavior and appearances associated with butch/femme roles. Feminist lesbians in Albuquerque interpreted these roles as pseudo-heterosexuality rather than what Elizabeth Lapovsky Kennedy and Madeline Davis, from their study of the Buffalo lesbian community, see as an authentically lesbian-developed set of sexual norms (1993). Feminist lesbians in Albuquerque also wanted to rid lesbianism of its overt sexuality, of sexual desire based on difference seen clearly in roles but also associated with working-class lesbians and lesbians of color.

On the other side of this hostility were the bar lesbians' views of feminist lesbians. In a state where civil rights struggles had produced a heightened awareness of race and class privilege and where longtime New Mexicans felt their material and cultural lives threatened by a rapid influx of newcomers, having a group of newly out, newly New Mexican, middle-class, educated, Anglo women start telling them how to be lesbians understandably might antagonize the women who had made up the public lesbian community in Albuquerque, many of whom were lesbians of color and from poor and working-class backgrounds.

In mutual suspicion, these groups confronted each other over who defined "real" lesbians. The feminist lesbians came informed, and in their eyes validated, by feminist and lesbian-feminist theory that viewed lesbians as superior feminists. Yet few of them had much experience living as lesbians, negotiating the realities of being self-supporting women while finding a positive sexual identity in a society that condemned lesbians. The public and the closeted lesbians had that practice, had "theory in the flesh," but little articulated analysis of their lives and their oppression. There were few links between these two groups to foster a dialogue.

Such a dialogue might have been possible if there had been any other organized group within the gay/lesbian community. The lack of any community-based homophile or Gay Liberation activities is important here. There was no gay civil rights activism in Albuquerque up to the emergence of feminism: no Mattachine chapter, no Daughters of Bilitis, or any other group that might have provided a base for a shared political consciousness or even a sense of an organized political community. This absence of a grass-roots, sexuality-based movement kept Albuquerque from following the pattern of politicization historians have identified in cities in which there was greater continuity between the public gay/lesbian communities and gay/lesbian political activism. The consequence was the splits I saw when I entered this community.

But such tensions were not all that existed in the Albuquerque lesbian community. It seems equally important that differences based on race and class had always existed, and yet solidarity within the sexuality-based community had been possible before lesbian feminism was introduced. This appears to be due to the long history lesbians in Albuquerque had had with each other before feminism. The women who had grown up, gone to school, and played ball together knew each other well enough across class and racial lines that even when they made different choices on how to live as lesbians, those choices could be understood and respected without denying each others' subjectivity. To me, what existed between these two groups is an example of what Marilyn Frye (1983) and Maria Lugones (1990) termed "loving perception," as opposed to the "arrogant perception" that existed between them and the feminist lesbians.

Although this brief history of the Albuquerque lesbian community demonstrates how race, class, and other power issues interconnect with sexuality in our lives, it also warns of the limitations of theory. Trying to be both activists and theorists, the feminist lesbians of Albuquerque proceeded in the best way they knew how, given both their reliance on theory and the state of lesbian and feminist theory at that point in time. Today, unfortunately, those roles are becoming increasingly separate, and, if anything, academically based feminists are even more dependent upon theory as the means to gain status within their professional lives. All feminists need to heed the critiques of our dependence on theory and to keep our theory connected with the realities of women's lives. (See, e.g., Christian 1990 and Rebolledo 1990.)

In Albuquerque, many of the early feminist lesbian leaders left, a couple became important theorists, one helped found Olivia Records (a lesbian-owned recording company), another headed a national gay organization, a few are again living straight lives. The lesbians who remained in Albuquerque found that the city is too small and the need for one another too great for lesbians to ignore each other. Additionally, the Albuquerque lesbian community has been too dynamic a scene for these earlier divisions to solidify. With new leaders and the time for trust to grow through continuing interaction and dialogue, lesbians in Albuquerque are perhaps in the vanguard in building a multicultural feminist lesbian community.

Anna Howard Shaw Women's Center
Albion College

References

Bérubé, Allan. 1989. *Coming Out under Fire: Lesbian and Gay Americans and the Military during World War II*. New York: Free Press.

Bethel, Lorraine, and Barbara Smith, eds. 1979. *Conditions: five*, the black women's issue.

Christian, Barbara. 1990. "The Race for Theory." In *Making Faces, Making Soul—Haciendo Caras: Creative and Critical Perspectives by Women of Color*, ed. Gloria Anzaldúa, 335–45. San Francisco: Aunt Lute.

Cook, Blanche Weisen. 1977. "Female Support Networks and Political Activism: Lillian Wald, Crystal Eastman, and Emma Goldman." *Chrysalis* 3:43–61.

Davis, Angela Y. 1981. *Women, Race and Class*. New York: Vintage.

D'Emilio, John. 1983. *Sexual Politics, Sexual Communities: The Making of a Homosexual Minority in the United States*. Chicago: University of Chicago Press.

Faderman, Lillian. 1981. *Surpassing the Love of Men*. New York: Morrow.

Ferguson, Ann, Jacquelyn Zita, and Kathryn Pyne Addelson. 1982. "On 'Compulsory Heterosexuality and Lesbian Existence': Defining Terms." In *Feminist Theory: A Critique of Ideology*, ed. Nannerl O. Keohane, Michelle Z. Rosaldo, and Barbara C. Gelpi, 147–88. Chicago: University of Chicago Press.

Frye, Marilyn. 1983. *The Politics of Reality: Essays in Feminist Theory.* Trumansburg, N.Y.: Crossing.

Gibbs, Joan, and Sara Bennett, eds. 1980. *Top Ranking: A Collection of Articles on Racism and Classism in the Lesbian Community.* Brooklyn, N.Y.: February Third Press.

Kennedy, Elizabeth Lapovsky, and Madeline Davis. 1993. *Boots of Leather, Slippers of Gold: The History of a Lesbian Community.* New York: Routledge & Kegan Paul.

Linden, Robin Ruth, Darlene R. Pagano, Diana E. H. Russell, and Susan Leigh Star, eds. 1982. *Against Sadomasochism: A Radical Feminist Analysis.* East Palo Alto, Calif.: Frog in the Well.

Lugones, Maria. 1990. "Playfulness, 'World'-Travelling and Loving Perception." In *Making Faces, Making Soul/Haciendo Caras,* ed. Gloria Anzaldúa. San Francisco: Aunt Lute.

Moraga, Cherríe, and Gloria Anzaldúa, eds. 1981. *This Bridge Called My Back: Writings by Radical Women of Color.* Watertown, Mass.: Persephone.

Nestle, Joan. 1987. *A Restricted Country.* Ithaca, N.Y.: Firebrand.

Rebolledo, Tey Diana. 1990. "The Politics of Poetics: Or, What Am I, a Critic, Doing in This Text Anyhow?" In *Making Faces, Making Soul—Haciendo Caras: Creative and Critical Perspectives by Women of Color,* ed. Gloria Anzaldúa, 346–55. San Francisco: Aunt Lute.

Rich, Adrienne. 1980. "Compulsory Heterosexuality and Lesbian Existence." *Signs* 5(4):631–60.

Samois, ed. 1981. *Coming to Power: Writings and Graphics on Lesbian S-M.* Boston: Alyson.

Snitow, Ann, Christine Stansell, and Sharon Thompson, eds. 1983. *Powers of Desire: The Politics of Sexuality.* New York: Monthly Review.

U.S. *Census of Population: 1960, Final Report.* PHC(1)-4, 1–54. Washington, D.C.: Government Printing Office.

U.S. *Census of Population and Housing: 1980.* PHC 80-2-62, Census Tracts. Washington, D.C.: Government Printing Office.

Vance, Carole, ed. 1984. *Pleasure and Danger: Exploring Female Sexuality.* Boston: Routledge & Kegan Paul.

Gender and Subjectivity: Simone de Beauvoir and Contemporary Feminism

Sonia Kruks

THEORETICAL DEBATE among North American feminists in the last decade has been widely influenced by postmodernism. Indeed, some have gone so far as to claim that feminist theory is inherently postmodern, its very project necessarily challenging such "Enlightenment myths" as the existence of a stable self or subject and the possibility of attaining objective truth about the world through the use of reason. They argue that feminist theory, with its deconstruction of what appears natural in our society, its focus on difference, and its subversion of the stable phallocentric norms of Western thought, "properly belongs in the terrain of postmodern philosophy" and that "feminist notions of the self, knowledge, and truth are too contradictory to those of the Enlightenment to be contained within its categories" (Flax 1987, 625).

I am not convinced, however, that such claims can be substantiated. For one thing, they presuppose a binary opposition, Enlightenment/postmodern, that is itself both historically and conceptually questionable. For another, we do not have a sufficiently clear consensus on what we might mean by "feminist" notions of "the self, knowledge, and truth" to permit us to be able to claim that they "properly" belong anywhere in particular. Most important, feminism is much more than a field of scholarship, and it is when we come to the terrain of feminist politics that postmodernism arguably presents the greatest difficulties.

In a spate of recent articles, authors such as Wendy Brown (1987), Nancy Hartsock (1987), and Linda Alcoff (1988) claim that postmod-

Thanks go to Eleanore Holveck, Patricia Jagentowicz Mills, Marion Smiley, and Christine Di Stefano for comments on earlier versions of this article. Thanks also to Debra Bergoffen, Hester Eisenstein, Joan Tronto, and Linda Zerilli for conversations that helped me to form my ideas.

[*Signs: Journal of Women in Culture and Society* 1992, vol. 18, no. 1]

ernism depoliticizes feminism and urge feminists to have virtually no truck with it.[1] Such authors argue that the problems that postmodernism presents for feminist practice, its radical nominalism or constructivism (including a constructivist account of the body) and its discourse-boundedness, preclude a grasp of the objective conditions of women's lives. Most significantly, they hold, the postmodern refusal to conceive of the self or subject as a knowing and volitional agent—a conception of agency that has underpinned most prior feminist visions of political action—implies an unacceptable passivity: women are reduced to no more than the effects of discursive practices, products of the play of signifiers, victims of a "discourse determinism."[2] No place, they charge, is left in the postmodern account of social change for the organized and conscious struggle of groups or individuals. For postmodernists erroneously claim that change takes place through a suprahuman play of discourses over which we can have little or no influence.

Though such writers portray postmodernism as irremediably flawed and inimical to effective feminist politics, others who share some of their concerns also believe that it is still worth attempting to work toward a rapprochement with postmodernism. Sandra Harding, for example, has recently argued that feminist epistemology needs both Enlightenment and postmodern agendas and that neither agenda can be constructed to the total exclusion of the other (1990). Mary Poovey has neatly summed up the problem this way: "The challenge for those of us who are convinced both that real historical women do exist and share certain experiences *and* that deconstruction's demystifying of presence makes theoretical sense is to work out some way to think both women and 'woman.' It isn't an easy task" (1988, 52–53).[3]

My own view, while critical of the more grandiose claims sometimes made in the name of postmodernism—including those for the "death of the subject," for the impossibility of any totalizing or continuous account of history, and for the irrelevance of biology to sexuality (let alone

---

[1] The following passage from Wendy Brown's article well sums up the general concerns and sentiments of these authors: "What woman needs to be deconstructed, to know herself as a field of discourse, a 'fiction,' a 'text,' a play of 'free-floating signifiers'? These are the very things woman has been; indeed they constitute a marvelous, if parodied, shorthand for the history of women's oppression. Deconstructive politics may indeed be a remedy for a disease afflicting men—an inflated sense of self as *sui generis* individuals, as inventors, as systematizers, and as capable of godlike omnipotence. . . . But women will deconstruct only at the peril of sustaining their exclusion from history, losing the 'narrative' that is essential to their emergence into visible history, shying from power and the discovery of their own voices. Women can only emerge into the world as subjects and as claimants of power" (1987, 15).

[2] The phrase is Wendy Holloway's, cited by Teresa de Lauretis (1987, 15).

[3] Two recent anthologies that encapsulate much of the debate about feminism and postmodernism are edited by Irene Diamond and Lee Quinby (1988) and Linda J. Nicholson (1990).

gender)—is that, at a more modest theoretical altitude than that to which its adherents usually aspire, postmodernism offers valuable tools and techniques to feminism. The best of what postmodern feminism has developed so far is not "high theory" so much as a series of radical glosses on the now classic starting point proposed by Simone de Beauvoir: "one is not born a woman, one becomes one." Postmodern deconstructive techniques and genealogical methods, like the work of Beauvoir, may help us to de-essentialize and de-naturalize the concept of "woman."

What we have learned (or perhaps re-learned) from postmodern theories is the very real power of discourse and the lack of transparency of language: there is no returning to a simple realism today. Yet I share with Poovey a concern that we remain able to talk about "real historical women" and that we do not embrace a kind of postmodern hyperconstructivism[4] in which the very category of "women" can disappear (as, e.g., in Riley [1988]).

we must be careful how postmodern we get

Similarly, what we have learned from the postmodern critique of the Enlightenment subject is that we should not attribute to consciousness the absolute power to constitute its own world: subjectivity is never "pure" or fully autonomous but inheres in selves that are shaped by cultural discourses and that are always embodied—selves that thus are also gendered. Yet to acknowledge all of this does not mean that we are obliged to proclaim definitively "the death of the subject." It is important for feminist politics (as Alcoff and others have argued) that we remain able to grant a role to individual consciousness and agency, to insist even on a notion of individual responsibility for our actions. But we must do so while also acknowledging the ways in which subjectivity is discursively and socially constructed. In particular, we need to be able to account for gender as an aspect of subjectivity, but to do so without either essentializing or dehistoricizing it.

As a contribution to such an attempt to re-construct the subject, this article sets out to re-examine the work of an earlier thinker: Simone de Beauvoir. For it is not the case that before postmodernism there was only the Enlightenment or modernity. Indeed, if ever there was a binary op-

---

[4] I have in mind here what Donna Haraway (1988) has critically referred to also as "strong constructivism." Alcoff (1988) refers to this position as "nominalism." However, this does not seem to me the appropriate term to use as it is quite possible to be at one and the same time a realist (in the sense of claiming that things have a substantial existence independence of our consciousness) and a nominalist (in the sense of denying that universal or general concepts describe anything more than a collection of discrete entities). Hume, e.g., subscribes to such a position and can be described as both a realist and a nominalist. Postmodern thinkers generally reject the claim that things have an existence independent of the human discourses (if not consciousnesses) that construct them. They do not, however, necessarily reject the claim that general concepts refer to something more than a collection of discrete entities. They are, in other words, antirealists who are not necessarily committed to nominalism in its classical sense.

position that needs deconstructing, it is that between modernity and postmodernity. Fortunately, we do not have to choose between the unhappy alternatives of an Enlightenment subject (i.e., an autonomous or self-constituting consciousness) on the one hand and the attempt, as Michel Foucault pithily put it, "to get rid of the subject itself" on the other ([1977] 1980, 117).[5] In the work of Beauvoir, I want to argue, we find a nuanced conception of the subject that cannot be characterized as either Enlightenment or postmodern: rather, it is a conception of the subject as situated.

In her account of women as subjects "in situation," Beauvoir can both acknowledge the weight of social construction, including gender, in the formation of the self and yet refuse to reduce the self to an "effect." She can grant a degree of autonomy to the self—as is necessary in order to retain such key notions as political action, responsibility, and the oppression of the self—while also acknowledging the real constraints on autonomous subjectivity produced by oppressive situations. As I suggest later, Beauvoir's account of situated subjectivity is one from which we could begin to develop an account of the gendering of subjectivity that can avoid both essentialism and hyperconstructivism.

It will perhaps be helpful to return to Beauvoir through a brief overview of recent intellectual history, recalling that, like the main proponents of postmodernism, Beauvoir wrote in a distinctly French intellectual milieu. Postmodernism and the existential phenomenology that shaped Beauvoir's thought form (to write old-fashioned narrative) part of the same history. Although the postmodern critique of modernity can be traced back to Nietzsche or to the later work of Heidegger, what has been imported into American feminist theory in the last decade under the rubric of postmodernism is a cluster of ideas formulated primarily in France from the late 1960s onward.[6] I would argue, however, that these ideas do not constitute the profound epistemic or epistemological break their authors frequently claim for them but, rather, are both absorptions of and reactions against the work of earlier generations of French thinkers.

Postmodernism emerged in France above all as a radicalizing critique of 1960s structuralism, as "poststructuralism." In spite of its objectivist stance and claims to scientificity, structuralism easily passed into poststructuralism through their shared hostility to the classical notion of the subject. What links structuralism and poststructuralism in France is what

---

[5] In another essay Foucault writes that if we are to talk of "the subject" at all, it "must be stripped of its creative role—thus analyzed as an effect only" ([1969] 1977a, 138). See also, for a "feminist" version, Julia Kristeva's formulation: "The subject never is. The subject is only the signifying process and he appears only as a *signifying practice,* that is, only when he is absent *within the position* out of which social, historical and signifying activity unfolds" (1984, 215).

[6] See Poovey (1988) for an excellent brief overview of this process of importation.

may be summed up as their antihumanism. From the insistence of Claude Lévi-Strauss that the aim of the human sciences is "to dissolve man" and the claims of Jacques Lacan and Louis Althusser that "the subject" is a mere "effect," to Jacques Derrida's attacks on the metaphysics of "presence" and Foucault's arguments that subjects are "constituted" as a function of discourse, what has been under attack are those notions of autonomous subjectivity and agency that have indeed been central to philosophy since the Enlightenment.

Although this attack can, if one so chooses, be located in the broad historical sweep from modernity to postmodernity, the emergence of French antihumanism was in its origins also a far more parochial phenomenon: a Parisian-based reaction against the hegemony exercised by humanistic existential phenomenology and Marxism in postwar France. It was, above all, against Jean-Paul Sartre that the battle was waged. Indeed, the "dissolution of man" was first proclaimed by Lévi-Strauss in 1962 in the context of a chapter-length attack on Sartre's *Critique of Dialectical Reason* ([1962] 1968, chap. 9, esp. 247). In the late 1970s, Foucault still bluntly stated his agenda as the attempt to use genealogy to displace not only Marxism but also the phenomenology of his student days: the phenomenological subject, in any form, had to be destroyed, he insisted. Long after we might have thought phenomenology dead in France, Foucault felt it necessary to insist on killing it yet again:

> I don't believe the problem can be resolved by historicizing the subject, as posited by the phenomenologists, fabricating a subject that evolves through the course of history. One has to dispense with the constituent subject, to get rid of the subject itself, that's to say, to arrive at an analysis which can account for the constitution of the subject within a historical framework . . . [Genealogy] is a form of history which can account for the constitution of knowledges, discourses, domains of objects etc., without having to make reference to a subject which is either transcendental in relation to the field of events or runs in its empty sameness throughout the course of history. [(1977) 1980, 117]

This statement opposes as stark alternatives a conception of the subject as "constituent" (or constituting) and as "transcendental" to history, on the one hand, and a conception of the subject as constituted and to be analyzed as an "effect" of its historical framework, on the other. In it we find posed those oversimple choices between humanism and antihumanism, between Enlightenment or modernity and postmodernity that postmodernists frequently tend to present us with because of the dichotomizing lenses through which they view the history of philosophy. In order to account for the weight of social structures, discourses, and practices in the shaping of subjectivity and yet still to acknowledge that an element of freedom is intrinsic to subjectivity—an element that allows us to talk, as I think we must, of individual human agency and responsibility—we need a far more complex, indeed dialectical, account of the subject than Foucault's work would grant us.[7] Ironically, such an account is be found in the work of some of the very French phenomenologists Foucault dismissed, including Beauvoir and Maurice Merleau-Ponty.[8] It is also to be found in Sartre's later works, such as *Critique of Dialectical Reason* ([1960] 1976) and his monumental study of Flaubert ([1971] 1981, [1971] 1987, and [1971] 1989). As I have argued elsewhere (1990a, 1990b), however, it was not yet present in his 1940s "existentialism," of which *Being and Nothingness* (1943) was the fullest formulation: a work that still asserted (albeit paradoxically) a version of the classic Enlightenment subject.[9]

Simone de Beauvoir, the "Mother" of second wave feminism (Ascher 1987), was, of course, closely associated with Sartre personally and philosophically. When *The Second Sex* (1949) was adopted by American feminists in the late 1960s, its insight that one is not born but becomes a woman, that femininity is a social construct and not an unchangeable essence or a biological destiny, seemed a revelation. But although this insight remains central to postmodern feminism, by the late 1970s *The Second Sex* began to seem rather passé. It was not only that Beauvoir's descriptions of women's experiences increasingly applied to a bygone age and to women of a narrow social stratum. Her solutions—the book ended with a call for a "fraternal" collaboration of men and women in establishing "the reign of liberty in the midst of the world of the given"[10]—seemed to deny the female difference that many feminists now valorized. Her notion of liberation arguably implied making women conform to a male ideal. Her persistent use of sexist language (the Sartrean

---

[7] This is the case at least until Foucault's very last years. There are some intriguing indications in one of his last interviews, e.g., that he was beginning to shift his ground on the question of the subject (see Foucault 1984, 381–90).

[8] It was above all Merleau-Ponty (1908–61) who developed such a dialectical account of the subject. Merleau-Ponty worked closely with Beauvoir and Sartre on the journal *Les Temps Modernes* in the late 1940s and early 1950s, and Beauvoir had a deep familiarity with his work. I have argued elsewhere that in many ways her conception of subjectivity is closer to his than to Sartre's (see Kruks 1991, 285–300).

[9] There are, of course, serious disagreements among Sartre scholars over what Sartre's early conception of subjectivity was and whether he altered it significantly in his later works. I have argued for this reading, that Sartre shifted his conception of subjectivity over time, in Kruks (1990a, esp. chap. 5, 146–79).

[10] Beauvoir ([1949] 1974, 814). Unless otherwise indicated, all subsequent page references citing Beauvoir are to *The Second Sex*.

language of "man" and "his" world) demonstrated how insensitive she had been to male dominance in her own intellectual milieu.

Moreover, since Beauvoir was said to share with Sartre not only a misogynist dislike of the female body but the entire philosophical baggage of "existentialism," including the Sartrean conception of the subject, postmodern feminism has come to dismiss her as methodologically naive.[11] Today Beauvoir is generally treated as a venerable ancestor, but she is no longer regarded as having anything of significance to contribute to the on-going development of feminist theory. Rather than consigning her to ancestor worship, however, I want to argue that Beauvoir remains highly relevant to current theoretical concerns. In particular she still speaks to the problem of developing an adequate feminist theory of the gendering of subjectivity.

Both in her ethical essays of the 1940s and in *The Second Sex*, Beauvoir developed a somewhat submerged account of "being-in-situation," or situated subjectivity, that was radically different from Sartre's.[12] To claim that Beauvoir departs significantly from the notion of the autonomous subject is also, of course, to say that Beauvoir was far more philosophically independent from Sartre than has generally been recognized. I will begin from this last point, to show that Beauvoir's work is not as consistently rooted in Sartrean philosophy as has been commonly supposed and that it departs from Sartre's identification of subjectivity with an inviolable, autonomous consciousness. I will then suggest, in the final section, what it is about Beauvoir's conception of the subject that makes it of enduring significance for the project of reconstructing our account of the gendering of subjectivity.

* * *

It was Beauvoir herself who insisted that her work was philosophically derivative of Sartre's. Repeatedly, and until the last years of her life,

---

[11] For criticisms of her attitude to the female body see, e.g., McCall (1979, 209–23); Evans (1980, 395–404). For a discussion of Sartre's horror of the female sex in *Being and Nothingness,* see Collins and Pierce (1976, 112–27). For critiques of Beauvoir's adherence to existentialism and allegations of her ensuing philosophical naïveté, see McCall (1979); Le Doeuff (1980, 277–89); Elshtain (1981, 306–10); O'Brien (1981, 65–76); Evans (1985); and Okely (1986). For a discussion of some of these criticisms in their original French context, see Kaufmann (1986, 121–31).

[12] For Sartre the subject always constitutes the meaning of a situation, even if its facticities are beyond choice. See, esp., *Being and Nothingness* ([1943] 1956, esp. pt. 4, chap. 1, sec. 2, "Freedom and Facticity: The Situation," 481–553). For Beauvoir, however, situations can become conditions that impose their meaning on the subject and that, as we will see, may even permeate subjectivity to the point where self-reflection and thus freedom cease to be possible.

Beauvoir said that she lacked originality and was merely Sartre's disciple in matters philosophical. She was willing to claim originality for herself in the field of literature, but in the more hallowed field of philosophy she could not compete but only follow. "On the philosophical level," she insisted, "I adhered completely to *Being and Nothingness* and later to *Critique of Dialectical Reason.*"[13] Too many scholars and commentators have taken Beauvoir at her word. Most assume that, as one author recently put it, she simply uses Sartre's concepts as "coat-hangers" on which to hang her own material, even to the point where it can be said that "Sartre's intellectual history becomes her own" (Okely 1986, 122).[14] Yet such a view, even though embraced by Beauvoir herself, is misleading. For although Beauvoir doubtless tried to work within a Sartrean framework (i.e., the framework of *Being and Nothingness*), she did not wholly succeed. Many of the leaps and inconsistencies one can find in her work reflect, I believe, a tension between her formal adherence to Sartrean categories and the fact that the philosophical implications of her work are in large measure incompatible with Sartreanism.

For Sartre, subjectivity or "being-for-itself" is wholly autonomous and, because unconditioned, free. Man is an "absolute subject." Each subject, although existing "in situation" and thus encountering the facticity of the world of things (or "being-in-itself"), always freely and autonomously constitutes the meaning of its own situation through the capacity for transcendence. Moreover, in relations between human beings, which Sartre characterizes as the fundamentally conflictual relation of Self and Other, this absolute autonomy of the subject always remains intact. Thus, for Sartre, relations of unequal power have no bearing on the autonomy of the subject. "The slave in chains is as free as his master," Sartre tells us ([1943] 1956, 550), because each is equally free to choose

---

[13] Beauvoir makes this statement in an interview with Sicard (1979, 325). In Schwarzer (1984), Beauvoir makes a similar point: "In philosophical terms, he was creative and I am not . . . I always recognized his superiority in that area. So where Sartre's philosophy is concerned, it is fair to say that I took my cue from him because I also embraced existentialism myself" (109). The account of Beauvoir's intellectual relationship to Sartre that emerges from Bair's recent biography (1990) also paints her as deferential to Sartre on philosophic matters.

[14] This standard view of the relation of Sartre and Beauvoir has begun to be challenged, most systematically by Margaret A. Simons (1981, 25–42; and 1986, 165–79). See also Butler (1986, 35–49, esp. 48) for the suggestion that Beauvoir sought to "exorcise" Sartre's Cartesianism long before he tried to do so himself. Tong (1989) has also briefly remarked that Beauvoir should be read as philosophically independent of Sartre (196). Le Doeuff ([1989] 1991) is also extensively concerned with the Beauvoir-Sartre philosophic relationship. Even so, much more work remains to be done on this question. While I cannot develop the argument here, it seems to me that many themes in Sartre's *Cahiers pour une morale,* written in the late 1940s and posthumously published in 1983, draw from insights in Beauvoir's earliest ethical writings. A case could also be made that the concept of "destiny" in the *Critique of Dialectical Reason* has it roots in Beauvoir's account of "woman's destiny" in pt. 1 of *The Second Sex.*

the meaning he gives his own situation. The question of material or political inequality between master and slave is simply irrelevant to their relation as two freedoms, as two absolute subjects. In the same vein, Sartre is able to write—in the middle of World War II!—that the Jew remains free in the face of the anti-Semite because he can choose his own attitude toward his persecutor.

unrealistic breakdown of power constructions

In his delineation of the absolute subject, Sartre remains within what many feminists have suggested is a typically male conception of the subject. He presents a version of what Nancy Hartsock has characterized as the "walled city" view of the self, which conceives of the self as not only radically separate from others but also as always potentially hostile. As Hartsock has observed, Hegel's account of the emergence of self-consciousness in the "master-slave dialectic," the struggle in which each consciousness "seeks the death of the other"—an account that Sartre appropriates as the relation of self and other in *Being and Nothingness*—restates a common masculine experience: "The construction of a self in opposition to another who threatens one's very being reverberates throughout the construction of both class society and the masculinist world view and results in a deep-going and hierarchical dualism" (Hartsock 1985, 241).[15] Moreover, Sartre's notion of the subject shares the abstract universalism that others have suggested comes with a specifically male notion of reason (see, e.g., Lloyd [1984] and Harding [1986]). To be master or slave, anti-Semite or Jew—or male or female—has, for Sartre, no bearing on the absolute and inviolable subjectivity of which each of us is the bearer.

Given these arguably masculinist elements of the Sartrean notion of the subject, his philosophy would not seem to provide a hospitable framework within which to develop feminist theory. Insofar as Beauvoir tries to remain within it, she does appeal to a predominantly male notion of abstract, universal freedom as the goal for the liberated woman. Existing in unhappy antagonism with the Sartrean framework, however, is a significantly different notion of the self from which Beauvoir operates. This is a less dualistic and more relational notion of the self, such as Hartsock and others have argued often emerges from the particularities

Beauvoir

[15] Hartsock is careful to point out that she is elaborating what Weber called an "ideal type." This point needs to be emphasized, for it is important to avoid essentializing or dehistoricizing conceptions of "abstract masculinity" or the walled city subject. There is a danger of oversimplistically opposing them to conceptions of the "feminine" as concrete and relational. Few individuals correspond exactly to ideal types, and the Western philosophic tradition itself is far more untidy than some feminist readings of it might suggest. There is, e.g., an ethical socialist tradition, exemplified in the work of William Morris, that cuts across the abstract/relational dichotomy. Or, for a blistering attack on the abstract self, but one that functions as an unapologetic defense of patriarchalism, one need look no further than Edmund Burke.

of women's life experience (Hartsock 1985, 242 ff.).[16] It involves, contra the early Sartre, a tacit rejection of the notion of the "absolute subject" for a situated subject: a subject that is intrinsically intersubjective and embodied, thus always "interdependent" and permeable rather than walled.[17]

Beauvoir had already begun to develop a notion of the subject different from Sartre's well before she wrote *The Second Sex*. This is apparent in the summary in her autobiographical volume, *The Prime of Life,* of a series of conversations she had with Sartre in the spring of 1940. In these conversations, Sartre set out for her the main lines of the argument of what was to become *Being and Nothingness*. Their discussions, Beauvoir recalled in 1960, centered above all on the problem of "the relation of situation to freedom." On this point they disagreed:

> I maintained that, from the point of view of freedom, as Sartre defined it—not as a stoical resignation but as an active transcendence of the given—not every situation is equal: what transcendence is possible for a woman locked up in a harem? Even such a cloistered existence could be lived in several different ways, Sartre said. I clung to my opinion for a long time and then made only a token submission. Basically I was right. But to have been able to defend my position, I would have had to abandon the terrain of individualist, thus idealist, morality, where we stood. [(1960) 1962, 34]

Beauvoir was right that her "submission" was no more than "token." Although she was never willing to challenge head-on Sartre's conception of freedom, or the notion of the impermeable "walled city subject" that it implied, she quietly subverted them. This becomes clearer in two essays

[16] The argument that women experience the self as relational has now been made on a number of different grounds. It has been argued from a psychoanalytic viewpoint by Nancy Chodorow (1978) and others and from the evidence of social psychology by Carol Gilligan (1982). It has also been argued from the specificities of women's daily practical life by, among others, Sara Ruddick (1989). There now seems to be a clear, if minimal, consensus on what we might call the phenomenological evidence: most women in the West today do experience themselves more relationally than most men do. But it is important not to transform such phenomenological evidence into stronger claims for an essentially different female self.

[17] It is one of the paradoxes of Sartre's work in the immediate postwar period that he defends such a radically individualistic and detotalized account of subjectivity while trying also to argue the case for socialist solidarity and a collective revolutionary project. His inability to bring these two dimensions of his thought into adequate relation with each other arguably accounts for his failure to complete the ethics that he attempted to write as a sequel to *Being and Nothingness*. I have argued this more fully in Kruks (1990b).

on ethics she wrote prior to *The Second Sex: Pyrrhus et Cinéas* (1944) and *The Ethics of Ambiguity* ([1947] 1967). In *Pyrrhus et Cinéas*, written while *Being and Nothingness* was in press, Beauvoir begins from the Sartrean autonomous subject but ends by putting in question the theory of fundamentally conflictual social relations that Sartre develops from it. Although Beauvoir presents freedoms as separate, she argues that, paradoxically, they are also intrinsically interdependent.[18] If one tries to imagine a world in which one is the only person, the image is horrifying, she insists. For everything one does would be pointless unless there were other subjects to valorize it: "A man [*sic*] alone in the world would be paralysed by the self-evident vanity of all his goals; he could not bear to live" (1944, 65).[19]

Moreover, for others to valorize one's project, Beauvoir argues, it is not enough that they are free merely in Sartre's sense; it is not sufficient for them to be subjects each of whom constitutes, like the master and the slave, the meaning of his or her own discrete situation. Freedom for Beauvoir, far more than for Sartre, involves a practical subjectivity: the ability of each of us to act in the world so that we can take up each other's projects and give them a future meaning.[20] And for this to be possible, we also require an equal degree of practical freedom:

> The other's freedom can do nothing for me unless my own goals can serve as his point of departure; it is by using the tool which I have invented that the other prolongs its existence; the scholar can only talk with men who have arrived at the same level of knowledge as himself . . . I must therefore endeavour to create for all men situations which will enable them to accompany and surpass my transcendence. I need their freedom to be available to use me, to preserve me in surpassing me. I require for men health, knowledge, well being, leisure, so that their freedom does not consume itself in fighting sickness, ignorance, misery. [1944, 113–14]

[18] Sartre does, of course, discuss what he calls "being-for-others" in *Being and Nothingness*. However, for Sartre, unlike Beauvoir, being-for-others cannot be an ontological structure of the for-itself (see Sartre [1943] 1956, 282).

[19] In all her works, *The Second Sex* included, Beauvoir repeatedly uses "man" to refer to all human beings and lapses into masculine forms for any discussion that does not positively require feminine ones. I have decided to keep such male-oriented language in my text where I either cite or paraphrase her. *Pyrrhus et Cinéas* (as well as many of Beauvoir's early political essays) remains unavailable in English. However, a few extracts have been translated (Miskowiec 1987, 135–42).

[20] Sartre also emphasizes practical subjectivity in his later attempt to synthesize Marxism and existentialism, in the *Critique of Dialectical Reason* ([1960] 1976); yet again the question of the extent to which Sartre was intellectually influenced by Beauvoir is raised.

Already, then, Beauvoir is aware of the interdependence of subjectivities and, in ways that Sartre is not, of the permeability of the subject. She arguably takes the first step here toward adequately linking Sartre's individualistic existentialism with their shared commitment to the solidaristic and communal values of socialism. In *The Ethics of Ambiguity,* she went a step further. There she suggests that oppression can permeate subjectivity to the point where consciousness itself becomes no more than a product of the oppressive situation. The freedom that Sartre had associated with subjectivity can, in a situation of extreme oppression, be wholly suppressed, even though it cannot be definitively eliminated. In such a situation, the oppressed become incapable of the project of resistance, unable to maintain the reflective distance necessary to be aware that they are oppressed. In such a situation, "living is only not dying, and human existence is indistinguishable from an absurd vegetation" ([1947] 1967, 82–83). The oppressed—and this is a point Beauvoir will later return to in her analysis of woman's situation—live in an "infantile world" of immediacy, with no sense of alternative futures. Freedom is no longer the capacity to choose how to live even the most constrained of situations, which Sartre had claimed it to be. Freedom is here seen as reducible to no more than a suppressed potentiality. It is made "immanent," unrealizable. Yet, for all this, freedom, is still not a "fiction" or an "imaginary" for Beauvoir. For should oppression start to weaken, freedom can always reerupt.

In *The Second Sex,* Beauvoir's break from Sartre's version of the walled city subject becomes even more marked. She begins *The Second Sex* on what appears to be firmly Sartrean ground. "What is a woman?" she asks, and answers initially that woman is defined as that which is not man—as Other: "She is determined and differentiated with reference to man and not he with reference to her; she is the inessential as opposed to the essential. He is the subject, he is the Absolute: she is the Other" (xix).[21]

Some commentators have used this and other similar passages to accuse Beauvoir of taking on board the Sartrean (and Hegelian) notion of the self-construction of subjectivity through conflict.[22] Very early in the book, however, Beauvoir relativizes the notion of otherness by introducing a distinction not found in *Being and Nothingness,* and whose originality needs emphasizing. We can, she argues, distinguish two significantly different kinds of relations of otherness: those between social equals and

---

[21] Translation altered. There are numerous difficulties with the only published translation of *The Second Sex,* by H. M. Parshley. In what follows I have retranslated many passages, although I still give page references to his standard English version.

[22] See, e.g., Lloyd (1984, esp. 93–102); also Hartsock (1985, app. 2, 286–92). O'Brien (1981) has an interesting discussion of the ways in which she thinks Beauvoir misapplies Hegel's "master-slave dialectic" to women (69–72).

those that involve social inequality. Where the relation is one of equality, she suggests that otherness is "relativized" by a kind of "reciprocity": each, as she had said in *Pyrrhus et Cinéas*, recognizes that the Other is an equal freedom. Where, however, otherness exists through relations of inequality, there reciprocity is to a greater or lesser extent abolished, replaced by relations of oppression and subjection. When one of the two parties in a conflict is privileged by having some material or physical advantage, then, "this one prevails over the other and undertakes to keep it in subjection" (1944, 69). It is not, then, woman's otherness per se but her subjection—the nonreciprocal objectification of woman by man—that Beauvoir sets out to explain. It is not only that woman is the Other; she is the unequal Other. The question is, if this inequality is not inscribed in nature, how does it occur?

B/c she is unequal she is constantly oppressed

The short answer for Beauvoir is, of course, that "being a woman" is a socially constructed experience; it is to live a social situation that men have, for their own advantage, attempted to impose on women. Beauvoir's discussion of the varying degrees to which women choose or are forced to accept this imposition suggests a continuum of different possible responses. Some—the "independent" women she describes in the last part of the book—consistently, if unsuccessfully, attempt to resist it. Some choose to accept it in what Sartre termed "bad faith" (a strategy to evade the pain and responsibility that come with freedom) because of the security and privilege it brings. Others, unable to conceive of real alternatives, accept it while engaging in forms of passive resistance and resentment. For yet others, as for the oppressed whom Beauvoir had described in *The Ethics of Ambiguity*, freedom is suppressed to the point where they cease to be capable of choice or resistance. What is of interest here is that in describing the most oppressed end of the continuum Beauvoir departs even more sharply from the Sartrean notion of the subject than in her earlier essays. In so doing, she also breaks free of any kind of Enlightenment notion of the subject, although (as we will see) she certainly does not thereby intend to "get rid of the subject itself."[23]

as absolute & deciding his own fate

Once again Beauvoir relativizes Sartre's ideas in ways that significantly transform them. She begins by appearing to agree with Sartre that there

[23] Judith Butler (1986) has argued that for Beauvoir gender is always actively chosen. For Beauvoir, to "*become* a woman" is, according to Butler, "a purposive and appropriative set of acts, the acquisition of a skill, a 'project', to use Sartrian [*sic*] terms, to assume a certain corporeal style and significance" (36). Butler draws from this reading the claim that there is "an absolute difference" between gender and sex and that gender could thus be completely remade. Certainly such a liberatory message could be drawn from Beauvoir's text, but only by ignoring the other end of the continuum: the point where Beauvoir breaks with Sartre in arguing that, for the oppressed, a "project" can cease to be possible.

is a radical disjuncture between the human and the natural realms, with freedom and subjectivity characterizing the human. Indeed, this claim is the basis for her rejection of deterministic biological explanations of the female condition. However, yet again, Sartre's dualistic ontology rapidly becomes transmuted in her hands. While biology is not itself "destiny," the oppressive situation that men across the ages have imposed on women and justified in large part on the grounds of real biological difference can function analogously to a natural force. Women can have a man-made destiny; indeed, she says at one point, "the whole of feminine history has been man made" (144). If a woman is oppressed to the point where her subjectivity is suppressed, then her situation is de facto her "destiny" and she ceases to be an effective or morally responsible agent. "Every subject," she writes,

♀ becomes so oppressed & suppressed that she loses her role as a moral agent

> continually affirms himself through his projects as a transcendence; he realizes his freedom only through his continual transcendence toward other freedoms; there is no other justification for present existence than its expansion towards an endlessly open future. Each time that transcendence falls back into immanence there is a degradation of existence into the 'in-itself,' of freedom into facticity; this fall is a moral fault if the subject agrees to it; it takes the form of a frustration and an oppression if it is inflicted upon him. [xxxiii]

♀ then not responsible for what she does

Woman, then, is locked in immanence by the situation man inflicts *existing only in the mind* upon her—and she is not necessarily responsible for that condition. Although the language in the passage is Sartrean, the argument is not. A consistent Sartrean position would make woman responsible for herself, no matter how constrained her situation. But for Beauvoir, women are not the primary source of the problem even though some comply with their oppressors in "bad faith." For many, there is no moral fault because there simply is no possibility of choice. In the notion that freedom can "fall back into the 'in-itself,' " that the "for-itself" can be turned through the action of other (i.e., male) freedoms into its very opposite, Beauvoir has radically departed from the Sartrean notion of the absolute subject. For Sartre, there can be no middle ground. Either the for-itself, the uncaused upsurge of freedom, the "absolute subject," exists whatever the facticities of its situation, or else it does not exist at all. In the latter case, one is dealing with the realm of nature or inert being. Insofar as Beauvoir's account of woman's situation as one of immanence involves the claim that freedom, the for-itself, can be penetrated and modified by the in-itself, it implies another notion of the subject than Sartre's. Beauvoir is trying to describe human existence as a synthesis of freedom and constraint, of consciousness and materiality that, finally, is incompatible with Sartre's version of the walled city subject.

Indeed, so far has Beauvoir moved that one might even be tempted to formulate her position, albeit only at this extreme end of the spectrum, in Foucault's terms: woman is a historically constituted, not a constituting, subject. For not only does woman fail freely to choose her situation, according to Beauvoir, she is in the most extreme situation its product: "When . . . a group of individuals is kept in a situation of inferiority, the fact is they are inferior . . . yes, women on the whole *are* today inferior to men, which is to say that their situation gives them less possibilities" (xxviii).

Yet unlike Sartre's postmodern critics, Beauvoir never wholly discards a notion of free subjectivity. Even when it is suppressed, reduced to immanence, subjectivity remains a distinctly human potentiality. Thus, for example, while much of her painstaking and detailed account of the young girl's *formation*[24] could be retold in the Foucauldian mode of "the political technology of the body" and of "discipline," Beauvoir would never have agreed to abandon the notion of a repression of freedom. However suppressed, however disciplined, it is still freedom-made-immanent that distinguishes even the most constituted human subject from a trained animal. For Beauvoir, a real repression or oppression of this subject is also always possible, unlike for Foucault. However socially constructed its identities may be, for Beauvoir the subject is still something other than the "effect" of its conditionings. Although she avoids the essentialism of the subject as, for example, a Cartesian cogito, she also rejects the hyperconstructivism of the Foucauldian account, which presents the subject as discursively produced, to be "stripped of its creative role and analysed as a complex and variable function of discourse" (Foucault [1969] 1977a, 138).

* * *

How then does Beauvoir develop this account of a situated subject that can be characterized neither as an autonomous walled city nor as uniquely a construct of discursive practices? Two fundamental insights orient the development of her account of situated subjectivity. The first is her recognition of what I will call the intersubjectivity of the subject. By this is meant something more than the interconnectedness of subjects. What is meant is the impossibility of a subjective self-constitution that is not always socially and culturally permeated. If all that took place be-

---

[24] Among numerous other problems of translation, Parshley renders Beauvoir's chapter heading *Formation* as "The Formative Years," thus weakening the notion of an active production of the self implied by the French term.

tween an individual man and woman was a struggle of consciousnesses between two human beings, one of whom happened to be male and one female, then we could not anticipate in advance which of them would objectify the other. If, however, we examine the relations of a husband and a wife, then it is very different. For the social institution of marriage in all its aspects—legal, economic, sexual, cultural, etc.—has formed in advance for the protagonists their own relation of inequality. As Beauvoir points out in a strikingly unSartrean passage, "*It is not as single individuals that human beings are to be defined in the first place;* men and women have never stood opposed to each other in single combat; the couple is an original *Mitsein;* and as such it always appears as a permanent element in a larger collectivity" (39, emphasis added).

Although subjectivity is individually lived, it is never, then, simply an individual constitution of existence. Rather, according to Beauvoir, it is both constituting and constituted. It is, to use Sartre's later terminology, "singular universal" (Sartre [1972] 1983, 141–69). Thus it follows (as Beauvoir had already made clear in her ethical essays) that oppression of any kind affects more than its immediate victims and that liberatory struggles cannot be other than collective. That Beauvoir herself did not apparently see at the time she wrote *The Second Sex* that she should explicitly apply these conclusions to women (as she was already doing in the late 1940s to colonial peoples) is an indication of the isolation in which she wrote her book and of the limits to her own political imagination.[25] But this failure should not blind us to the implications of her argument.

Beauvoir's later assessment of *The Second Sex* was that it was not a "militant" book (1972, 623). Insofar as it presents no call for a concerted resistance by women to their oppression, she was justified in this judgment. But if not militant, the book is in its implications deeply political—and it is here that much of its continuing relevance lies. For in her insistence that freedoms are interdependent and that freedom, however suppressed, however immanent, is an enduring potentiality, Beauvoir affirms that women's oppression is real and that political struggle is indeed possible. While eschewing the naive assumptions of individual free agency and responsibility that are central to the Enlightenment conception of subjectivity, she also insists that subjectivity cannot be accounted for solely in terms of the effect of the apparently autonomous power of structures, technologies, or discourses.

---

[25] It should be noted, however, that it would have called for remarkable powers of imagination to envision an active women's movement in postwar France. France was still a primarily agrarian, Catholic country, in which women had only just obtained the vote. The early defeat and occupation of France by the Germans meant that, unlike in the United States or Britain, few women were pushed out of their traditional domestic roles by the war.

I turn now to Beauvoir's second insight. This concerns the inherence of subjectivity in the body: the idea, which she borrows from Merleau-Ponty, that the subject is always properly called a "body-subject."[26] It is toward the specificities of embodied subjectivities that Beauvoir orients us to grasp the oppression of women. If the couple is an "original *Mitsein*" (Heidegger's term, meaning a fundamental "being with"),[27] this is because of its reproductive significance. By stressing that reproduction and sexuality are socially and culturally constituted phenomena, Beauvoir avoids the essentialism of biological reductionism. But she also avoids hyperconstructivism by arguing that reproduction is ontologically fundamental. If (as she had argued in *Pyrrhus et Cinéas*) we need others to take up our projects and overcome our finitude, then each individual freedom requires "the perpetuation of the species." Thus, she now argues, "we can regard the phenomenon of reproduction as ontologically founded" (8).[28] In an argument that is neither realist nor constructivist but dialectical, Beauvoir insists that although biological "facts" have no significance outside the values that human beings give them, they do still have an objective reality: there are real limits to the significations we can choose. It is helpful to contrast Beauvoir with Foucault here. According to Foucault, "nothing in man—not even his body—is sufficiently stable to serve as the basis for . . . self-recognition" ([1971] 1977b, 153). For Beauvoir, however, although the body is not a stable essence, it still is encountered by the self as an objective given. And whether or not a woman decides to procreate, it is an inescapable fact that of the two biological sexes her physiology is geared to the more extended and physiologically demanding role in perpetuating the species. Although a woman's body "is not itself sufficient to define her as woman," it is, Beauvoir argues, "an essential element of the situation she occupies in the world" (41).[29]

---

[26] "Woman, like man, *is* her body," she writes, and then cites Merleau-Ponty in a note: "So I am my body, in so far, at least, as my experience goes, and conversely my body is as a life model, or as a preliminary sketch for my total being" (33).

[27] In *Being and Nothingness* Sartre had explicitly rejected the concept, arguing against Heidegger that there can be no fundamental ground of shared being and that all human relations are intrinsically conflictual ([1943] 1956, 300 ff.). Beauvoir's use of Heidegger's concept here represents a startling departure from Sartre's thinking.

[28] There is a certain privileging of heterosexual relations implicit in this claim insofar as they are the only sexual relations that permit the continuance of the human species. However, given Beauvoir's insistence that biology is not destiny, that "the facts of biology take on the values the existent bestows upon them" (41), this privileging is in no way definitive. In her chapter on lesbianism Beauvoir suggests that, although not guaranteed, greater reciprocity may in fact be more possible in lesbian relations than in heterosexual ones: "Between women . . . there is no struggle, no victory, no defeat; in exact reciprocity each is at once subject and object, sovereign and slave; duality becomes mutuality" (465).

[29] Thus I do not think that Beauvoir would have accepted the argument for the possibility of totally delinking sex and gender that Judith Butler claims to find implied in

But the only important thing is reason/freedom

Beauvoir has been criticized, with considerable justification, for her horror of the female body and its functions. There are indeed many passages in *The Second Sex* where women's bodily functions are identified with animality, passivity, and lack of freedom and are denigrated from the masculinist standpoint of an apparently disembodied reason and freedom. There is, however, another reading of woman's body to be found in Beauvoir's text as well. This reading, which I intend to pursue here as the more fruitful one for feminism, tells us that it is as body that human subjectivity both encounters and gives meaning to its own inescapable rootedness in objective reality. In Beauvoir's account, women encounter this in a particularly intense form, one whose alienating aspects she most emphasizes: "Woman, like man, *is* her body," she says, but immediately adds, "but her body is something other than herself" (33).

The important point that is lodged here against Enlightenment or walled city conceptions of the subject is that subjectivity is not given in closed contradistinction to a realm of objective entities that it oversees or contemplates in detachment. Rather, it is through the body that we each inhere in one and the same world. Moreover, this common inherence may form the basis for an overlapping or for an even fuller sharing of experience on which common action may be based.[30] Beauvoir's woman is not, then, a Sartrean for-itself for whom the body is merely a facticity. But neither, contra Foucault, is she merely a "soul . . . produced permanently around, on, the body, by the functioning of a power that is exercised on . . . those one supervises, trains, corrects" ([1975] 1977c, 30). Rather, for Beauvoir, we need to explore what she calls "the strange ambiguity of existence made body" (810). For "to be present in the world

---

her work (see Butler 1986, esp. 45–46; and 1987). Although anatomy is not destiny for Beauvoir, its connection to gender cannot be viewed as wholly contingent, either. If, as Monique Wittig observed (cited in Butler 1987, 135), we do not ask about the shape of the earlobes of a newborn baby whereas we do ask about its sex, this is surely because sex is, as Beauvoir argues, ontologically significant in a way that earlobes are not. To be born of a particular sex is to be born with or without the capacity to bear and to nourish the next generation of our species: i.e., to be born with or without significantly different options (however we may choose, or be forced, to use them) with regard to an activity that is intrinsic to human existence as we know it.

[30] It is intriguing to note that in "Situated Knowledges" (1988) Donna Haraway also stresses the connection between the existence of embodied selves and the possibility of an objective (or sharable) knowledge. Calling for "a doctrine of embodied objectivity," she observes that "objectivity turns out to be about particular and specific embodiment and definitely not about false vision promising transcendence of all limits and responsibilities. The moral is simple: only partial perspective promises objective vision" (582–83). While I doubt whether Haraway would want to identify her own work with the phenomenological tradition, there are striking resonances between what she is saying and the views of both Beauvoir and, above all, Merleau-Ponty, on whose critique of "high-altitude thinking" Beauvoir drew.

implies strictly that there exists a body which is *at the same time* a thing) ✗
in the world and a point of view on this world" (7, emphasis added).)

For Beauvoir, subjectivity is corporally constituted; it is coextensive
with the body, while being simultaneously "a point of view." This account is significantly different from Sartre's, for whom "my body for-
me" and "my body for-others"—that is, the body as object—are on
"different and incommunicable levels of being" ([1943] 1956, 374). She
holds that biological difference itself, as well as the socially constructed
significations that adhere to that difference, permeates subjectivity, but it
is not reducible to their effect. Thus, rather than accepting either a realism of the kind that posits an inevitable feminine essence grounded in the
body and in mothering or the position of much postmodern theory in
which the body itself becomes no more than a discursive construct, Beauvoir suggests a less dichotomized account of subjectivity. Such an account
allows us to acknowledge the sameness of women as biologically sexed
and socially constructed females without pinning an immutable essence
of womanhood onto "real historical women" whose lives may also be
radically divergent, shaped also by class, race, ethnicity, age, sexual orientation, and many other factors. Biological sex is always present as a
given in the "lived experience" of the body.[31] Yet our lived experience of
the body is never "natural." It is, for Beauvoir, one of the always socially
mediated experiences we have of the objective givens of our lives. Thus
Beauvoir would, I think, approve of postmodern feminist projects to
contest the discursive constructions of gender, even though she would
reject the hyperconstructivist epistemology upon which they generally
rest.

Thus, against the hyperconstructivism incipient in postmodernism, in
which subjectivity itself can become but a fiction and everything, including the category of woman, can cease to be real, Beauvoir sketches an
account of the gendering of subjectivity that can best be characterized as
a dialectical realism. By this I mean an account in which not only discourse but also a discursively mediated "beyond" of discourse is acknowledged. This "beyond" of discourse includes, on the one hand, the
existence of objective parameters to human life, such as sex, birth, disease, malnutrition, and death and, on the other hand, an always-present
potentiality for that margin of autonomous thought and action in situation that Beauvoir calls "freedom." For unless we grant that real historical women live and die, that they do decide and act, and that they can in
varying degrees be oppressed or free, we risk becoming our own grave
diggers. If we need to seek a way between hyperconstructivism and es-

[handwritten margin note: B manages to link hyper-constructivism + essentialism — by not falling into Sartre's absolute subject]

[31] *L'expérience vécue* is the title Beauvoir gave to the second volume of *The Second
Sex*. It is unfortunately rendered in the English translation as "Woman's Life Today,"
which fails to capture Beauvoir's phenomenological intent.

[handwritten note: she allows others as well as the self to construct herself.]

sentialism, Beauvoir's work remains richly suggestive as to how we might set about it.

Department of Politics
Oberlin College

References

Alcoff, Linda. 1988. "Cultural Feminism versus Post-Structuralism: The Identity Crisis in Feminist Theory." *Signs: Journal of Women in Culture and Society* 13(3):405–36.

Ascher, Carol. 1987. "Simone de Beauvoir—Mother of Us All." *Social Text* 17(Fall): 107–9.

Bair, Deirdre. 1990. *Simone de Beauvoir: A Biography.* New York: Summit Books.

Beauvoir, Simone de. 1944. *Pyrrhus et Cinéas.* Paris: Gallimard.

———. (1960) 1962. *The Prime of Life,* trans. Peter Green. Cleveland: World Publishing.

———. (1947) 1967. *The Ethics of Ambiguity,* trans. Bernard Frechtman. New York: Citadel.

———. 1972. *Tout compte fait.* Paris: Gallimard.

———. (1949) 1974. *The Second Sex,* ed. and trans. H. M. Parshley. New York: Vintage Books.

Brown, Wendy. 1987. "Where Is the Sex in Political Theory?" *Women and Politics* 7(1):3–23.

Butler, Judith. 1986. "Sex and Gender in Simone de Beauvoir's *Second Sex.*" In "Simone de Beauvoir: Witness to a Century," ed. Hélène Vivienne Wenzel, special issue of *Yale French Studies* 72:35–49.

———. 1987. "Variations on Sex and Gender: Beauvoir, Wittig and Foucault." In *Feminism as Critique,* ed. Seyla Benhabib and Drucilla Cornell, 128–42. Minneapolis: University of Minnesota Press.

Chodorow, Nancy. 1978. *The Reproduction of Mothering: Psychoanalysis and the Sociology of Gender.* Berkeley and Los Angeles: University of California Press.

Collins, Margery L., and Christine Pierce. 1976. "Holes and Slime: Sexism in Sartre's Psychoanalysis." In *Women and Philosophy: Toward a Theory of Liberation,* ed. Carol C. Gould and Marx W. Wartofsky, 112–27. New York: Capricorn.

de Lauretis, Teresa. 1987. *Technologies of Gender.* Bloomington: Indiana University Press.

Diamond, Irene, and Lee Quinby, eds. 1988. *Feminism and Foucault: Reflections on Resistance.* Boston: Northeastern University Press.

Elshtain, Jean. 1981. *Public Man, Private Woman.* Princeton, N.J.: Princeton University Press.

Evans, Mary. 1980. "Views of Women and Men in the Work of Simone de Beauvoir." *Women's Studies International Quarterly* 3:395–404.

———. 1985. *Simone de Beauvoir: A Feminist Mandarin.* London: Tavistock.

Flax, Jane. 1987. "Postmodernism and Gender Relations in Feminist Theory." *Signs* 12(4):621–43.

Foucault, Michel. (1969) 1977a. "What Is an Author?" In *Language, Counter-Memory, Practice,* ed. Don Bouchard, 113–38. Ithaca, N.Y.: Cornell University Press.

———. (1971) 1977b. "Nietzsche, Genealogy, History." In *Language, Counter-Memory, Practice,* ed. Don Bouchard, 139–64. Ithaca, N.Y.: Cornell University Press.

———. (1975) 1977c. *Discipline and Punish: The Birth of the Prison,* trans. Alan Sheridan. London: Penguin.

———. (1977) 1980. "Truth and Power." In *Power/Knowledge,* ed. Colin Gordon, 108–33. New York: Pantheon.

———. 1984. "Polemics, Politics, and Problemizations," interview by Paul Rabinow. In *The Foucault Reader,* ed. Paul Rabinow, 381–90. New York: Pantheon.

Gilligan, Carol. 1982. *In a Different Voice: Psychological Theory and Women's Development.* Cambridge, Mass.: Harvard University Press.

Haraway, Donna. 1988. "Situated Knowledges: The Science Question in Feminism and the Privilege of Partial Perspective." *Feminist Studies* 14(3):575–89.

Harding, Sandra. 1986. *The Science Question in Feminism.* Ithaca, N.Y.: Cornell University Press.

———. 1990. "Feminism, Science, and the Anti-Enlightenment Critiques." In *Feminism/Postmodernism,* ed. Linda J. Nicholson, 83–106. New York: Routledge.

Hartsock, Nancy. 1985. *Money, Sex, and Power: Toward a Feminist Historical Materialism.* Boston: Northeastern University Press.

———. 1987. "Rethinking Modernism: Minority vs. Majority Theories." *Cultural Critique* 7:187–206.

Kaufmann, Dorothy. 1986. "Simone de Beauvoir: Questions of Difference and Generation." In "Simone de Beauvoir: Witness to a Century," ed. Hélène Vivienne Wenzel, special issue of *Yale French Studies* 72:121–31.

Kristeva, Julia. 1984. *Revolution in Poetic Language,* trans. Margaret Waller. New York: Columbia University Press.

Kruks, Sonia. 1990a. "Sartre's 'First Ethics' and the Future of Ethics." In *The Future of Difference,* ed. David Wood, 181–91. New York: Routledge.

———. 1990b. *Situation and Human Existence: Freedom, Subjectivity and Society.* New York: Routledge.

———. 1991. "Simone de Beauvoir: Teaching Sartre about Freedom." In *Sartre Alive,* ed. Ronald Aronson and Adrien van den Hoven, 285–300. Detroit: Wayne State University Press.

Le Doeuff, Michèle. 1980. "Simone de Beauvoir and Existentialism." *Feminist Studies* 6(2):277–89.

———. (1989) 1991. *Hipparchia's Choice,* trans. Trista Selous. Cambridge, Mass.: Blackwell.

Lévi-Strauss, Claude. (1962) 1968. *The Savage Mind.* Chicago: University of Chicago Press.

Lloyd, Genevieve. 1984. *The Man of Reason: "Male" and "Female" in Western Philosophy.* Minneapolis: University of Minnesota Press.

McCall, Dorothy Kaufmann. 1979. "Simone de Beauvoir, *The Second Sex,* and Jean-Paul Sartre." *Signs* 5(2):209–23.

Miskowiec, Jay. 1987. "Selections from *Towards a Morals of Ambiguity, According to Pyrrhus and Cinéas*" (translation of extracts from Beauvoir's *Pyrrhus et Cinéas*). *Social Text* 17:135–42.

Nicholson, Linda J., ed. 1990. *Feminism/Postmodernism.* New York: Routledge.

O'Brien, Mary. 1981. *The Politics of Reproduction.* Boston: Routledge & Kegan Paul.

Okely, Judith. 1986. *Simone de Beauvoir.* London: Virago.

Poovey, Mary. 1988. "Feminism and Deconstruction." *Feminist Studies* 14(1): 51–65.

Riley, Denise. 1988. *"Am I That Name?" Feminism and the Category of Women in History.* Minneapolis: University of Minnesota Press.

Ruddick, Sara. 1989. *Maternal Thinking.* Boston: Beacon.

Sartre, Jean-Paul. (1943) 1956. *Being and Nothingness,* trans. Hazel E. Barnes. New York: Philosophical Library.

——— . (1960) 1976. *Critique of Dialectical Reason,* trans. Alan Sheridan-Smith, ed. Jonathan Rée. London: New Left Books.

——— . (1971) 1981. *The Family Idiot,* vol. 1, trans. Carol Cosman. Chicago: University of Chicago Press.

——— . (1972) 1983. "Kierkegaard: The Singular Universal." In *Between Existentialism and Marxism,* trans. John Matthews, 141–69. London: Verso.

——— . (1971) 1987. *The Family Idiot,* vol. 2, trans. Carol Cosman. Chicago: University of Chicago Press.

——— . (1971) 1989. *The Family Idiot,* vol. 3, trans. Carol Cosman. Chicago: University of Chicago Press.

Schwarzer, Alice. 1984. *After "The Second Sex": Conversations with Simone de Beauvoir,* trans. Marianne Howarth. New York: Pantheon.

Sicard, Michel. 1979. "Interférences" (interview with Simone de Beauvoir and Jean-Paul Sartre). *Obliques* 18–19:325–29.

Simons, Margaret A. 1981. "Beauvoir and Sartre: The Question of Influence." *Eros* 8(1):25–42.

——— . 1986. "Beauvoir and Sartre: The Philosophical Relationship." In "Simone de Beauvoir: Witness to a Century," ed. Hélène Vivienne Wenzel, special issue of *Yale French Studies* 72:165–79.

Tong, Rosemary. 1989. *Feminist Thought: A Comprehensive Introduction.* Boulder, Colo.: Westview.

Gender as Seriality: Thinking about Women as a Social Collective

Iris Marion Young

I N THE SUMMER of 1989 I worked in Shirley Wright's campaign for a seat on the Worcester School Committee. Shirley is African American in a city where about 5–7 percent of the population are African American, and 7–10 percent are Hispanic. As in many other cities, however, more than 35 percent of the children in the public schools are black, Hispanic, or Asian, and the proportion of children of color is growing rapidly. For more than ten years all six of the school committee seats have been held by white people, and only one woman has served, for about two years. In her announcement speech Shirley Wright pledged to represent all the people of Worcester. But she noted the particular need to represent minorities, and she also emphasized the importance of having a woman's voice on the committee.

A few weeks later a friend and I distributed Shirley Wright flyers outside a grocery store. The flyers displayed a photo of Shirley and some basics about her qualifications and issues. In the course of the morning at least two women, both white, exclaimed to me, "I'm so glad to see a woman running for school committee!" This African American woman claimed to speak for women in Worcester, and some white women noticed and felt affinity with her as a woman.

This seemed to me at the time an unremarkable, easily understandable affinity. Recent discussions among feminists about the difficulties and dangers of talking about women as a single group, however, make such incidents appear at least puzzling. These discussions have cast doubt on the project of conceptualizing women as a group, arguing that the search for the common characteristics of women or of women's oppression leads to normalizations and exclusions. While I agree with such critiques, I also agree with those who argue that there are pragmatic

I am grateful to Linda Alcoff, David Alexander, Sandra Bartky, Sonia Kruks, Lynda Lange, Bill McBride, Uma Narayan, Linda Nicholson, Vicki Spelman, and anonymous reviewers for *Signs* for comments on earlier versions of this article.

[*Signs: Journal of Women in Culture and Society* 1994, vol. 19, no. 3]

political reasons for insisting on the possibility of thinking about women as some kind of group.

Clearly, these two positions pose a dilemma for feminist theory. On the one hand, without some sense in which "woman" is the name of a social collective, there is nothing specific to feminist politics. On the other hand, any effort to identify the attributes of that collective appears to undermine feminist politics by leaving out some women whom feminists ought to include. To solve this dilemma I argue for reconceptualizing social collectivity or the meaning of social groups as what Sartre describes as a phenomenon of serial collectivity in his *Critique of Dialectical Reason* (1976). Such a way of thinking about women, I will argue, allows us to see women as a collective without identifying common attributes that all women have or implying that all women have a common identity.

I

Doubts about the possibility of saying that women can be thought of as one social collective arose from challenges to a generalized conception of gender and women's oppression by women of color, in both the northern and southern hemispheres, and by lesbians. Black, Latina, Asian, and indigenous women demonstrated that white feminist theory and rhetoric tended to be ethnocentric in its analysis of gender experience and oppression. Lesbians, furthermore, persistently argued that much of this analysis relied on the experience of heterosexual women. The influence of philosophical deconstruction completed the suspension of the category of "women" begun by this process of political differentiation. Exciting theorizing has shown (not for the first time) the logical problems in efforts to define clear, essential categories of being. Let me review some of the most articulate recent statements of the claim that feminists should abandon or be very suspicious of a general category of woman or female gender.

Elizabeth Spelman (1988) shows definitively the mistake in any attempt to isolate gender from identities such as race, class, age, sexuality, and ethnicity to uncover the attributes, experiences, or oppressions that women have in common. To be sure, we have no trouble identifying ourselves as women, white, middle class, Jewish, American, and so on. But knowing the "right" labels to call ourselves and others does not imply the existence of any checklist of attributes that all those with the same label have in common. The absurdity of trying to isolate gender identity from race or class identity becomes apparent if you ask of any individual woman whether she can distinguish the "woman part" of herself from the "white part" or the "Jewish part." Feminist theorists nevertheless have often assumed that the distinctive and specific attributes of gender can be identified by holding race and class constant or by examining the lives of women who suffer only sexist oppression and not also oppressions of race, class, age, or sexuality.

The categories according to which people are identified as the same or different, Spelman suggests, are social constructs that reflect no natures or essences. They carry and express relations of privilege and subordination, the power of some to determine for others how they will be named, what differences are important for what purposes. Because it has assumed that women form a single group with common experiences, attributes, or oppressions, much feminist theorizing has exhibited privileged points of view by unwittingly taking the experience of white middle-class heterosexual women as representative for all women. Even when feminists attempt to take account of differences among women, moreover, they often manifest such biases because they fail to notice the race or class specificity of white middle-class women and how these also modify our gender. Much feminist talk about paying attention to differences among women, Spelman points out, tends to label only women of color or old women or disabled women as "different."

Chandra Mohanty believes that the "assumption of women as an already constituted, coherent group with identical interests and desires, regardless of class, ethnic or racial location, or contradictions, implies a notion of gender or sexual difference or even patriarchy which can be applied universally or even cross-culturally" (1991, 55). She believes that this category of "woman" as designating a single, coherent, already constituted group influences feminists to regard all women as equally powerless and oppressed victims. Rather than developing questions about how and whether women in a particular time and place suffer discrimination and limitation on their action and desires, questions that can then be empirically investigated, the assumption of universal gender categories bypasses such empirical investigation by finding oppression a priori. This tendency is especially damaging in the way European and American feminists think and write about women in the southern and eastern hemispheres. Assumptions about a homogeneous category of women helps create a homogeneous category of Third World women who stand as the Other to western feminists, who define Third World women as powerless victims of patriarchy.

Judith Butler draws more explicitly on postmodern theories to argue against the viability of the category of "woman" and of gender (1990). In a Foucauldian mode, Butler argues that the idea of gender identity and the attempt to describe it has a normalizing power. The very act of defining a gender identity excludes or devalues some bodies, practices, and discourses at the same time that it obscures the constructed, and thus contestable, character of that gender identity.

Feminism has assumed that it can be neither theoretical nor political without a subject. Female gender identity and experience delineate that subject. Feminist politics, it is assumed, speaks for or in the name of someone, the group women, who are defined by this female gender identity.

The category of gender was promoted by feminism precisely to criticize and reject traditional efforts to define women's nature through "biological" sex. In its own way, however, according to Butler, gender discourse tends to reify the fluid and shifting social processes in which people relate, communicate, play, work, and struggle with one another over the means of production and interpretation. The insistence on a subject for feminism obscures the social and discursive production of identities.

In one of the most important arguments of her book, Butler shows that the feminist effort to distinguish sex and gender itself contributes to such obscuring by ignoring the centrality of enforced heterosexuality in the social construction of gender. However variable its content is understood to be, the form of gender differentiation is always a binary opposition between the masculine and the feminine. Inasmuch as sexual difference is classified only as man and woman, then, gender always mirrors sex. The binary complementarity of this sex/gender system is required and makes sense, however, only with the assumption of heterosexual complementarity. Gender identification thus turns out not to be a culturally variable overlay on a given biological sex; rather, the categories of gender construct sexual difference itself. "Gender can delineate a *unity* of experience, of sex, gender and desire, only when sex can be understood in some sense to necessitate gender. The internal coherence or unity of either gender, man or woman, thereby requires both a stable and oppositional heterosexuality. Thus we see the political reasons for substantializing gender" (Butler 1990, 23).

This mutual reinforcement of (hetero)sex and gender as fixed categories suppresses any ambiguities and incoherences among heterosexual, homosexual, and bisexual practices. This unity of sex and gender organizes the variability of desiring practices along a single scale of normal and deviant behavior. Butler concludes that feminism's attempt to construct or speak for a subject, to forge the unity of coalition from the diversities of history and practice, will always lead to such ossifications. The primary task for feminist theory and politics is critical: to formulate genealogies that show how a given category of practice is socially constructed. Feminist discourse and practice should become and remain open, its totality permanently deferred, accepting and affirming the flows and shifts in the contingent relations of social practices and institutions.

These analyses are powerful and accurate. They identify ways that essentializing assumptions and the point of view of privileged women dominate much feminist discourse, even when it tries to avoid such hegemonic moves. They draw important lessons for any future feminist theorizing that wishes to avoid excluding some women from its theories or freezing contingent social relations into a false necessity. But I find the exclusively critical orientation of such arguments rather paralyzing. Do these arguments imply that it makes no sense and is morally wrong ever to talk about women as a group or, in fact, to talk about social groups at all? It is not clear that these writers claim this. If not, then what can it mean to use the term *woman*? More important, in the light of these critiques, what sort of positive claims can feminists make about the way social life is and ought to be? I find questions like these unaddressed by these critiques of feminist essentialism.

[margin handwritten: some Qs are unanswered in aggressive feminist anti-collective talk.]

II

What is the genealogy of the essentializing discourse that established a normative feminist subject, woman, that excluded, devalued, or found deviant the lives and practices of many women? Like most discursive constructs, this one is overdetermined. But I suggest that one important source of the oppressive and paradoxical consequences of conceptualizing women as a group is the adoption of a *theoretical* stance. In large part feminist discourse about gender was motivated by the desire to establish a countertheory to Marxism, to develop a feminist theory that would conceive sex or gender as a category with as much theoretical weight as class. This desire employs a totalizing impulse. What *is* a woman? What *is* woman's social position such that it is not reducible to class? Are all societies structured by male domination, and of the same form or of variable forms? What are the origins and causes of this male domination?

These are all general and rather abstract theoretical questions. By "theory" I mean a kind of discourse that aims to be comprehensive, to give a systematic account and explanation of social relations as a whole. A theory tries to tell the way things are in some universal sense. From it one can derive particular instances or at least one can apply the theoretical propositions to particular facts that the theory's generalities are supposed to cover. A social theory is self-enclosed, in the sense that it offers no particular purpose other than to understand, to reveal the way things are.

Despite much work in the last twenty years to make such theories, feminists do not need and should not want theory in this sense. Instead, we should take a more pragmatic orientation to our intellectual discourse. By being pragmatic I mean categorizing, explaining, developing accounts and arguments that are tied to specific practical and political problems, where the purpose of this theoretical activity is clearly related

[margin handwritten: we should specifically personally engage in discourse]

to those problems (see, e.g., Bordo 1989). Pragmatic theorizing in this sense is not necessarily any less complex or sophisticated than totalizing theory, but rather it is driven by some problem that has ultimate practical importance and is not concerned to give an account of a whole. In this article I take the pragmatic problem to be a political dilemma generated by feminist critiques of the concept of "woman," and I aim to solve it by articulating some concepts without claiming to provide an entire social theory.

From this pragmatic point of view, I wish to ask, why does it matter whether we even consider conceptualizing women as a group? One reason to conceptualize women as a collective, I think, is to maintain a point of view outside of liberal individualism. The discourse of liberal individualism denies the reality of groups. According to liberal individualism, categorizing people in groups by race, gender, religion, and sexuality and acting as though these ascriptions say something significant about the person, his or her experience, capacities and possibilities, is invidious and oppressive. The only liberatory approach is to think of and treat people as individuals, variable and unique. This individualist ideology, however, in fact obscures oppression. Without conceptualizing women as a group in some sense, it is not possible to conceptualize oppression as a systematic, structured, institutional process. If we obey the injunction to think of people only as individuals, then the disadvantages and exclusions we call oppressions reduce to individuals in one of two ways. Either we blame the victims and say that disadvantaged people's choices and capacities render them less competitive, or we attribute their disadvantage to the attitudes of other individuals, who for whatever reason don't "like" the disadvantaged ones. In either case structural and political ways to address and rectify the disadvantage are written out of the discourse, leaving individuals to wrestle with their bootstraps. The importance of being able to talk about disadvantage and oppression in terms of groups exists just as much for those oppressed through race, class, sexuality, ethnicity, and the like as through gender (cf. Young 1990, chap. 2).

The naming of women as a specific and distinct social collective, moreover, is a difficult achievement and one that gives feminism its specificity as a political movement. The possibility of conceptualizing ethnic, religious, cultural, or national groups, for example, rarely comes into question because their social existence itself usually involves some common traditions—language, or rituals, or songs and stories, or dwelling place. Women, however, are dispersed among all these groups. The operations of most marriage and kinship forms bring women under the identity of men in each and all of these groups, in the privacy of household and bed. The exclusions, oppressions, and disadvantages that women often suffer can hardly be thought of at all without a structural conception of women as a collective social position. The first step in feminist resistance to such oppressions is the affirmation of women as a group, so that women can cease to be divided and to believe that their sufferings are natural or merely personal. Denial of the reality of a social collective termed *women* reinforces the privilege of those who benefit from keeping women divided (Lange 1991).

Feminist politics evaporates, that is, without some conception of women as a social collective. Radical politics may remain as a commitment to social justice for all people, among them those called women. Yet the claim that feminism expresses a distinct politics allied with anti-imperialism, antiracism, and gay liberation but asking a unique set of enlightening questions about a distinct axis of social oppression cannot be sustained without some means of conceptualizing women and gender as social structures.

The logical and political difficulties inherent in the attempt to conceptualize women as a single group with a set of common attributes and shared identity appear to be insurmountable. Yet if we cannot conceptualize women as a group, feminist politics appears to lose any meaning. Is there a way out of this dilemma? Recent feminist discussions of this problem have presented two strategies for solving it: the attempt to theorize gender identity as multiple rather than binary and the argument that women constitute a group only in the politicized context of feminist struggle. I shall argue now that both of these strategies fail.

Spelman herself explores the strategy of multiple genders. She does not dispense with the category of gender but, instead, suggests that a women's gender identity and gender attributes are different according to what race, class, religion, and the like she belongs to. Gender, she argues, is a relational concept, not the naming of an essence. One finds the specific characteristics and attributes of the gender identity of women by comparing their situation with that of men. But if one wishes to locate the gender-based oppression of women, it is wrong to compare all women with all men. For some women are definitely privileged when compared to some men. To find the gender-specific attributes of a woman's experience, Spelman suggests, one must restrict the comparison to men and women of the same race or class or nationality. Women of different races or classes, moreover, often have opposing gender attributes. In this reasoning, women as such cannot be said to be a group. Properly designated groups are "white women," "black women," "Jewish women," "working-class women," "Brazilian woman," each with specific gender characteristics (Spelman 1988, 170–78).

In a recent paper Ann Ferguson proposes a similar solution to the contradictions and quandaries that arise when feminists assume that all women share a common identity and set of gendered attributes. "Instead of a concept of sisterhood based on a shared gender identity," she suggests, "it may be more helpful to posit different racial gender positions, and possibly different class gender positions. Processes of racialization in U.S. history have created at least ten gender identities informed with racial difference if we consider the various subordinate races: black, Latino, Native American, and Asian, as well as the dominant white race" (1991, 114–15).

There is much to recommend this concept of multiple genders as a way of describing the differentiations and contradictions in the social experience of gender. The idea of multiple genders highlights the fact that not all men are equally privileged by gender. It also makes clear that some women are privileged in relation to some men, a privilege that derives partly from their gender. It allows the theorist to look for race or class in specific gender interactions and expectations without essentializing them. Multiple gender conceptualization may also address the problems of binarism and heterosexism that Butler finds in gender theory. According to a concept of multiple genders, the gender identity of lesbians, for example, can be conceptualized as different from that of straight women.

Despite its promising virtues, the strategy of multiplying gender also has some dangers. First, it is just not true, as Spelman suggests, that gender relations are structured primarily within a class, race, nationality, and so on. A working-class woman's gendered experience and oppression is not properly identified only by comparing her situation to working-class men. Much of her gendered experience is conditioned by her relation to middle-class or ruling-class men. If she experiences sexual harassment at work, for example, her harasser is at least as likely to be a middle-class professional man as a working-class assembler or delivery man. Examples of such cross-class or cross-race relations between men and women can be multiplied. In such relations it would be false to say that the class or race difference is not as important as the gender difference, but it would be equally false to say that the cross-class or cross-race relations between men and women are not gendered relations. But if we conceive of an African American feminine gender, for example, as having one set of attributes in relation to African American men and another in relation to white men, one of two things results: either we need to multiply genders further or we need to draw back and ask what makes both of these genders womanly.

Second, the idea of multiple genders presumes a stability and unity to the categories of race, class, religion, and ethnicity that divide women. To conceptualize "American Indian woman" as a single identity different from "white woman," we must implicitly assume "American Indian" or "white" as stable categories. As Susan Bordo points out, feminist arguments against conceptualizing women as a single group often privilege categories of race or class, failing to challenge the appropriateness of these group categories (Bordo 1989). But the same arguments against considering these categories as unities can be used as the arguments against thinking about women as a unity. American Indians are divided by class, region, religion, sexuality, and ethnicity as well as by gender. Working-class people are divided by race, ethnicity, region, religion, and sexuality as well as by gender. The idea of multiple genders can solve the problems and paradoxes involved in conceptualizing women as a group only by presuming categorical unities to class and race.

This last point leads to my final objection to the idea of multiple genders. This strategy can generate an infinite regress that dissolves groups into individuals. Any category can be considered an arbitrary unity. Why claim that Black women, for example, have a distinct and unified gender identity? Black women are American, Haitian, Jamaican, African, Northern, Southern, poor, working class, lesbian, or old. Each of these divisions may be important to a particular woman's gender identity. But then we are back to the question of what it means to call her a woman. The strategy of multiple genders, then, while useful in directing attention to the social specificities of gender differentiation and gender interaction, does not resolve the dilemma I have posed. Instead, it seems to swing back and forth between the two poles of that dilemma.

Some feminist theorists propose "identity politics" as a different answer to the criticism of essentializing gender while retaining a conception of women as a group. According to this view, an identity *woman* that unites subjects into a group is not a natural or social given but rather the fluid construct of a political movement, feminism. Thus Diana Fuss agrees that *woman* cannot name a set of attributes that a group of individuals has in common, that there is not a single female gender identity that defines the social experience of womanhood. Instead, she holds, feminist politics itself creates an identity *woman* out of a coalition of diverse female persons dispersed across the world. "Coalition politics precedes class and determines its limits and boundaries; we cannot identify a group of women until various social, historical, political conditions construct the conditions and possibilities for membership. Many anti-essentialists fear that positing a political coalition of *women* risks presuming that there must first be a natural class of women, but this belief only makes the fact that it is coalition politics which constructs the category of women (and men) in the first place" (Fuss 1989, 36).

Interpreting the theoretical writings of several Black feminist writers, Nancie Caraway proposes a similar understanding of women as a group. She argues that unity and solidarity among women is a product of political discussion and struggle among people of diverse backgrounds, experiences, and interests who are differently situated in matrices of power and privilege. The process of discussion and disagreement among feminists forges a common commitment to a politics against oppression that produces the identity "woman" as a coalition. Thus, says Caraway, "identity politics advances a space for political action, praxis, justified by the critical *positioning* of the marginalized subjects against hierarchies of power—the Enlightenment promise of transcendence. . . . These emerging theories are codes about the fluid construction of identity. They are not racially specific; they speak to both white and Black feminists about the shared and differentiated faces of female oppression" (1989, 9).

The identity politics position has some important virtues. It rightly recognizes that the perception of a common identity among persons must be the product of social or political process that brings them together around a purpose. It retains a conception of women as a group that it believes feminist politics needs, at the same time clearly rejecting an essentialist or substantive conception of gender identity. There are, however, at least two problems with identity politics as a way to get out of the dilemma I have articulated.

Judith Butler points out the first. Even though identity politics' coalition politics and deconstructive discourse avoids the substantialization of gender, the dangers of normalization are not thereby also avoided. The feminist politics that produces a coalition of mutually identifying women nevertheless privileges some norms or experiences over others. Thus Butler suggests that feminist politics should be suspicious of settling into a unified coalition. The question of solidarity should never be settled, and identities should shift and be deconstructed in a play of possibilities that exclude no one.

My second objection to the idea that women are a group only as the construction of feminist politics is that it seems to make feminist politics arbitrary. Some women choose to come together in a political movement, to form themselves as a group of mutually identifying agents. But on the basis of what do they come together? What are the social conditions that have motivated the politics? Perhaps even more important, do feminist politics leave out women who do not identify as feminists? These questions all point to the need for some conception of women as a group prior to the formation of self-conscious feminist politics, as designating a certain set of relations or positions that motivate the particular politics of feminism.

III

Stories like Shirley Wright's race for school committee remind us that everyday language seems to be able to talk about women as a collective in some sense, even though women's experiences vary considerably by class, race, sexuality, age, or society. But Spelman, Mohanty, Butler, and others are right to criticize the exclusionary and normalizing implications of most attempts to theorize this everyday experience. We want and need to describe women as a group, yet it appears that we cannot do so without being normalizing and essentialist.

I propose a way out of this dilemma through a use of the concept of seriality that Sartre develops in his *Critique of Dialectical Reason*. I propose that we understand gender as referring to a social series, a specific kind of social collectivity that Sartre distinguishes from groups. Understanding gender as seriality, I suggest, has several virtues. It provides a way of thinking about women as a social collective without requiring that all women have common attributes or a common situation. Gender as seriality, moreover, does not rely on identity or self-identity for understanding the social production and meaning of membership in collectives.

One might well question any project that appropriates Sartrian philosophy positively for feminist theory (see Murphy 1989). Much of Sartre's writing is hopelessly sexist and male biased. This is certainly manifest in his theorization and functionalization of heterosexual relations. Perhaps more fundamentally, Sartre's early existentialist ontology presumes human relations as oppositional, egoistical, and basically violent. While his later philosophy on which I will draw is less individualistic than his early philosophy, the later thinking retains the assumption of human relations as latently violent. In it, boxing is a paradigm of the relation of self and other as mediated by a third.

Although Sartre's writing is sexist and his ontological assumptions about human relations tend to derive from masculine experience, I nevertheless have found the idea of seriality in particular, and its distinction from other kinds of social collective, of use in thinking about women as a collective. Linda Singer has talked about the feminist philosopher as a "Bandita," an intellectual outlaw who raids the texts of male philosophers and steals from them what she finds pretty or useful, leaving the rest behind (1992). I aim to approach Sartre's texts with the spirit of this Bandita, taking and rearticulating for my purposes the concepts I think will help resolve the dilemma I have posed. In doing so I need not drag all of Sartre with me, and I may be "disloyal" to him.

In the *Critique of Dialectical Reason*, Sartre distinguishes several levels of social collectivity by their order of internal complexity and reflexivity. For the purposes of addressing the problem of thinking about women as a social collective, the important distinction is between a group and a series. A group is a collection of persons who recognize themselves and one another as in a unified relation with one another. Members of the group mutually acknowledge that together they undertake a common project. Members of the group, that is, are united by action that they undertake together. In acknowledging oneself as a member of the group, an individual acknowledges oneself as oriented toward the same goals as the others; each individual thereby assumes the common project as a project for his or her individual action. What makes the project shared, however, is the mutual acknowledgment among the members of the group that they are engaged in the project together; this acknowledgment usually becomes explicit at some point in a pledge, contract, constitution, set of by-laws, or statement of purpose. The project of the group is a collective project, moreover, insofar as the members of the group mutually acknowledge that it can only be or is best undertaken by a group— storming the Bastille, staging an international women's conference, achieving women's suffrage, building an amphitheater (Sartre 1976, bk. 2, secs. 1, 2, and 3).[1]

So far in this article I have used the term *group* loosely, as does ordinary language, to designate any collection of people. Since my theorizing about women depends on Sartre's distinction between group and series, however, from now on in this article I shall reserve the term *group* for the self-consciously, mutually acknowledging collective with a self-conscious purpose. Much of an individual's life and action takes place in and is structured by a multitude of groups in this sense. Not all structured social action occurs in groups, however. As Sartre explains it, groups arise from and often fall back into a less organized and unself-conscious collective unity, which he calls a series.

Within Sartre's conception of human freedom, all social relations must be understood as the production of action. Unlike a group, which forms around actively shared objectives, a series is a social collective whose members are unified passively by the objects around which their actions are oriented or by the objectified results of the material effects of the actions of the others. In everyday life we often experience ourselves and others impersonally, as participating in amorphous collectives defined by routine practices and habits. The unity of the series derives from the way that individuals pursue their own individual ends with respect to the same objects conditioned by a continuous material environment, in response to structures that have been created by the unintended collective result of past actions.

Sartre describes people waiting for a bus as such a series. They are a collective insofar as they minimally relate to one another and follow the

---

[1] Sartre in fact distinguishes several levels of group: the group in fusion, the statutory group, the organization, and the institution. Each is less spontaneous, more organized and rule bound, and more materialized than the last. All come under the more general definition I am offering here, which is all that is necessary to develop my argument. Although my summaries of Sartre throughout this article leave out a great deal of detail, I believe they are nevertheless adequate to the text and sufficient for developing my argument.

rules of bus waiting. As a collective they are brought together by their relation to a material object, the bus, and the social practices of public transportation. Their actions and goals may be different, and they have nothing necessarily in common in their histories, experiences, or identity. They are united only by their desire to ride on that route. Though they are in this way a social collective, they do not identify with one another, do not affirm themselves as engaged in a shared enterprise, or identify themselves with common experiences. The latent potential of this series to organize itself as a group will become manifest, however, if the bus fails to come; they will complain to one another about the lousy bus service, share horror stories of lateness and breakdowns, perhaps assign one of their number to go call the company, or discuss sharing a taxi.

Such serial collectivity, according to Sartre, is precisely the obverse of the mutual identification typical of the group. Each goes about his or her own business. But each is also aware of the serialized context of that activity in a social collective whose structure constitutes them within certain limits and constraints. In seriality, a person not only experiences others but also himself or herself as an Other, that is, as an anonymous someone: "Everyone is the same as the other insofar as he is Other than himself" (p. 260). Individuals in the series are interchangeable; while not identical, from the point of view of the social practices and objects that generate the series, the individuals could be in one another's place. It is contingent that I am third in line for the bus today. Thus in the series individuals are isolated but not alone. They understand themselves as constituted as a collective, as serialized, by the objects and practices through which they aim to accomplish their individual purposes. Often their actions take into account their expectations of the behavior of others in the series whom they nevertheless do not encounter. For example, I ask for a later schedule at work so that I will miss the crowd of bus riders at the rush hour.

Sartre uses the example of radio listening to illustrate some of the characteristics of seriality. The collective of radio listeners is constituted by their individual orientation toward objects, in this case radios and their material possibilities of sound transmission. As listeners they are isolated, but nevertheless they are aware of being part of a series of radio listeners, of others listening simultaneously linked to them indirectly through broadcasting. One's experience of radio listening is partly conditioned by the awareness of being linked to others from whom one is separated and of serving as Other for them. Frequently the radio announcer explicitly refers to the serialized being of the listeners.

Sartre calls the series a practico-inert reality. The series is structured by actions linked to practico-inert objects. Social objects and their effects are the results of human action; they are practical. But as material they also constitute constraints on and resistances to action that make them experienced as inert. The built environment is a practico-inert reality. The products of human decision and action daily used by and dwelt in by people, the streets and buildings, are inert. Their material qualities enable and constrain many aspects of action.

Sartre calls the system of practico-inert objects and the material results of actions in relation to them that generate and are reproduced by serial collectives the milieu of action. The milieu is the already-there set of material things and collectivized habits against the background of which any particular action occurs. Thus for the series, commuters, for example, the milieu is the totality of the structured relations of the physical space of streets and rail lines, together with the predictable traffic patterns that emerge from the confluence of individual actions, together with the rules, habits, and cultural idiosyncracies of driving, riding, and walking.

Serialized action within the milieu results in *counterfinalities*: the confluence of individual intentional actions to produce a result that is counter to some purposes and that no one intended. Within a certain kind of milieu the series commuters will produce a gridlock; each individual driver pursues his or her own individual ends under material conditions that eventually makes a large cluster of them unable to move.

The collective otherness of serialized existence is thus often experienced as constraint, as felt necessities that often are experienced as given or natural. Members of the series experience themselves as powerless to alter this material milieu, and they understand that the others in the series are equally constrained. "A series reveals itself to everyone when they perceive in themselves and Others their common inability to eliminate their material differences" (277). At the same time, the material milieu and objects are conditions of enablement for action. Objectives can be realized only through the mediation of already there things, practices, and structures. A market is paradigmatic of such structured relations of alienation and anonymity that are felt as constraints on everyone. I take my corn to market in hopes of getting a good price, knowing that some people are trading on its price in a futures market and that other farmers bring their corn as well. We know that by bringing our large quantity of corn that we contribute to a fall in its price, and we might each play the futures market ourselves. But we are all equally as individuals unable to alter the collective results of these individual choices, choices that themselves have been made partly because of our expectations of what is happening to market prices.

Membership in serial collectives define an individual's being, in a sense—one "is" a farmer, or a commuter, or a radio listener, and so on, together in series with others similarly positioned. But the definition is anonymous, and the unity of the series is amorphous, without determinate limits, attributes, or intentions. Sartre calls it a unity "in flight," a collective gathering that slips away at the edges, whose qualities and characteristics are impossible to pin down because they are an inert result of the confluence of actions. There is no concept of the series, no specific set of attributes that form the sufficient conditions for membership in it. Who belongs to the series of bus riders? Only those riding today? Those who regularly ride? Occasionally? Who may ride buses and know the social practices of bus riding? While serial membership delimits and constrains an individual's possible actions, it does not define the person's identity in the sense of forming his or her individual purposes, projects, and sense of self in relation to others.

[margin note: hard to pin down the collective b/c it's constantly ~~changing~~ changing]

Thus far the examples of seriality have been rather simple and one-dimensional. Sartre's theoretical purpose in developing the concept, however, is to describe the meaning of social class. Most of the time what it means to be a member of the working class or the capitalist class is to live in series with others in that class through a complex interlocking set of objects, structures, and practices in relation to work, exchange, and consumption.

[margin note: but not just w/ others of your class—the system is interlocking—how you relate w/ other classes?]

Class being does not define a person's identity, however, because one is a class member in a mode of otherness, otherness to oneself in one's subjectivity. If one says, "I am a worker," in naming serialized class being, this does not designate for one a felt and internalized identity but a social facticity about the material conditions of one's life. (To be sure, one can and many do say, "I am a worker," as a badge of pride and identity. But when this happens the class being is not experienced in seriality; rather, one has formed a *group* with other workers with whom one has established self-conscious bonds of solidarity.) As serialized, class lies as a historical and materialized background to individual lives. A person is born into a class in the sense that a history of class relations precedes one, and the characteristics of the work that one will do or not do are already inscribed in machines, the physical structure of factories and offices, the geographic relations of city and suburb. An individual encounters other members of the class as alienated others, separated from one through the materiality of the things that define and delimit his or her class being— the factory with its machines, the physical movements and demands of the production process, the residential districts, buses, and highways that bring the workers into contact. As class members the individuals are relatively interchangeable, and nothing defines them as workers but the practico-inert constraints on their actions that they find themselves powerless to change. "If you want to eat, then you have to get a job," expresses the anonymous constraints on anyone who lacks independent means of support.

Let me now summarize the major elements in the concept of seriality. A series is a collective whose members are unified passively by the relation their actions have to material objects and practico-inert histories. The practico-inert milieu, within which and by means of whose structures individuals realize their aims, is experienced as constraints on the mode and limits of action. To be said to be part of the same series it is not necessary to identify a set of common attributes that every member has, because their membership is defined not by something they are but rather by the fact that in their diverse existences and actions they are oriented around the same objects or practico-inert structures. Membership in the series does not define one's identity. Each member of the series is isolated, Other to the Others, and as a member of the series Other than themselves. Finally, there is no concept of the series within attributes that clearly demarcate what about individuals makes them belong. The series is a blurry, shifting unity, an amorphous collective.

Seriality designates a level of social life and action, the level of habit and the unreflective reproduction of ongoing historical social structures. Self-conscious groups arise from and on the basis of serialized existence, as a reaction to it and an active reversal of its anonymous and isolating conditions. Next I shall examine how gender is seriality and then explain the relationship between groups of women and the series, women.

IV

Applying the concept of seriality to gender, I suggest, makes theoretical sense out of saying that "women" is a reasonable social category expressing a certain kind of social unity. At the same time, conceptualizing gender as a serial collectivity avoids the problems that emerge from saying that women are a single group.

As I explained earlier, seriality designates a certain *level* of social existence and relations with others, the level of routine, habitual action, which is rule-bound and socially structured but serves as a prereflective background to action. Seriality is lived as medium or as milieu, where action is directed at particular ends that presuppose the series without taking them up self-consciously.

Thus, as a series *woman* is the name of a structural relation to material objects as they have been produced and organized by a prior history. But the series *women* is not as simple and one-dimensional as bus riders or radio listeners. Gender, like class, is a vast, multifaceted, layered, complex, and overlapping set of structures and objects. *Women* are the individuals who are positioned as feminine by the activities surrounding those structures and objects.

The loose unity of the series, I have said, derives from the fact that individuals' actions are oriented toward the same or similarly structured objects. What are the practico-inert realities that construct gender?

Clearly female bodies have something to do with the constitution of the series *women*, but it is not merely the physical facts of these female bodies themselves—attributes of breasts, vaginas, clitoris, and so on—that constructs female gender. Social objects are not merely physical but also inscribed by and the products of past practices. The female body as a practico-inert object toward which action is oriented is a rule-bound body, a body with understood meanings and possibilities. Menstruation, for example, is a regular biological event occurring in most female bodies within a certain age range. It is not this biological process alone, however, that locates individuals in the series of women. Rather, the social rules of menstruation, along with the material objects associated with menstrual practices, constitute the activity within which the women live as serialized. One can say the same about biological events like pregnancy, childbirth, and lactation.

The structure of the social body defining these bodily practices, however, is enforced heterosexuality. The meanings, rules, practices, and assumptions of institutionalized heterosexuality constitute the series, women, as in a relation of potential appropriation by men. Likewise the series *men* appears in the structures of enforced heterosexuality. The assumptions and practices of heterosexuality define the meaning of bodies—vaginas, clitorises, penises—not as mere physical objects but as practico-inert.

Even one so anti-essentialist as Gayatri Spivak locates heterosexuality as a set of material-ideological facts that constitute women cross-culturally. The material practices of enforced heterosexuality serialize women as objects of exchange and appropriation by men, with a consequent repression of autonomous active female desire. In Spivak's terms, "In legally defining woman as object of exchange, passage, or possession in terms of reproduction, it is not only the womb that is literally 'appropriated'; it is the clitoris and signifier of the sexed object that is effaced. All historical theoretical investigation into the definition of women as legal object—in or out of marriage; or as politico-economic passageway for property and legitimacy would fall within the investigation of the varieties of the effacement of the clitoris" (1987, 151).

Bodies, however, are only one of the practico-inert objects that position individuals in the gender series. A vast complex of other objects and materialized historical products condition women's lives as gendered. Pronouns locate individual people, along with animals and other objects, in a gender system. Verbal and visual representations more generally create and reproduce gender meanings that condition a person's action and her interpretation of the actions of others. A multitude of artifacts and social spaces in which people act are flooded with gender codes. Clothes are the primary example, but there are also cosmetics, tools, even in some cases furniture and spaces that materially inscribe the norms of gender. (I may discover myself "as a woman" by being on the "wrong" dorm floor.)

What usually structures the gendered relation of these practico-inert objects is a sexual division of labor. Though their content varies with each social system, a division of at least some tasks and activities by sex appears as a felt necessity. The division between caring for babies and bodies, and not doing so, is the most common sexual division of labor, over which many other labor divisions are layered in social specific ways. Other sexual divisions of tasks and activities are more arbitrary but, in practice, also felt as natural. (Think, e.g., about the genderization of football and field hockey in most American colleges.) The context of the sexual division of labor varies enormously across history, culture, and institutions. Where the division appears, however, it usually produces a multitude of practico-inert objects that constitute the gendered series. The offices, workstations, locker rooms, uniforms, and instruments of a particular activity presuppose a certain sex. The language, gestures, and rituals of exclusion or inclusion of persons in activities reproduce the divisions by attracting people to or repelling people from those activities.

In short, then, bodies and objects constitute the gendered series women through structures like enforced heterosexuality and the sexual division of labor. As I have interpreted Sartre's concept, being positioned by these structures in the series women does not itself designate attributes that attach to the person in the series, nor does it define her identity. Individuals move and act in relation to practico-inert objects that position them as women. The practico-inert structures that generate the milieu of gendered serialized existence both enable and constrain action, but they do not determine or define it. The individuals pursue their own ends; they get a living for themselves in order to have some pleasures of eating and relaxation. The sexual division of labor both enables them to gain that living and constrains their manner of doing so by ruling out or making difficult some possibilities of action. The bathroom enables me to relieve myself, and its gender-marked door constrains the space in which I do it and next to whom.

The practico-inert structures of the gender series are abstract in relation to individuals and to groups of individuals. They are possibilities and orientations for concrete actions that give them content.[2] The gender structures are not defining attributes of individuals but are material social

[2] In terms of Sartre's early work, I am here interpreting seriality as a condition of facticity that helps constitute a situation but in no way determines action. Action, the having of projects and goals, the realizing of ends, I am saying here, is what constitutes the identities and experiences of persons. Action is situated against a background of serialized existence, which means that it is constrained but neither general nor determined.

facts that each individual must relate to and deal with. The subjective experiential relation that each person has, and sometimes groups have, to the gender structure, are infinitely variable. In a heterosexist society, for example, everyone must deal with and act in relation to structures of enforced heterosexuality. But there are many attitudes a particular individual can take toward that necessity: she can internalize norms of feminine masochism, she can try to avoid sexual interaction, she can affirmatively take up her sexual role as a tool for her own ends, she can reject heterosexual requirements and love other women, to name just a few.

In seriality, I have said above, the individual experiences herself as anonymous, as Other to herself and Other to the others, contingently interchangeable with them. Sometimes when I become aware of myself "as a woman" I experience this serial anonymous facticity. The serialized experience of being gendered is precisely the obverse of mutual recognition and positive identification of oneself as in a group. "I am a woman" at this level is an anonymous fact that does not define me in my active individuality. It means that I check one box rather than another on my driver's license application, that I use maxipads, wear pumps, and sometimes find myself in situations in which I anticipate deprecation or humiliation from a man. As I utter the phrase, I experience a serial interchangeability between myself and others. In the newspaper I read about a woman who was raped, and I empathize with her because I recognize that in my serialized existence I am rapeable, the potential object of male appropriation. But this awareness depersonalizes me, constructs me as Other to her and Other to myself in a serial interchangeability rather than defining my sense of identity. I do not here mean to deny that many women have a sense of identity as women, an issue I will discuss in the next section. Here I only claim that the level of gender as series is a background to rather than constitutive of personal or group identity.

Sartre's main purpose in developing the concept of seriality is to describe unorganized class existence, the positioning of individuals in relations of production and consumption. Race or nationality can also be fruitfully conceptualized as seriality.[3] At the level of seriality racial position is constructed by a relation of persons to a materialized racist history that has constructed

---

[3] While Sartre does not thematize race as such, I think he provides grounds for understanding race positioning as seriality. He describes being Jewish as initially belonging to a series. As a social fact or social label, being Jewish in a society that marks or devalues Jews does not name some concept, a set of specific attributes a person must be identified as having in order to be classed as Jewish. In the social relation of being Jewish, there is no separate substance that Jews have in common that makes them Jews. The group label is never real, specific limited, here; it always names an alien otherness coming from elsewhere, from the facticity of "them," the anonymous others who say things about the Jews, who "know" what the Jews are: "In fact, the being-Jewish of every Jew in a hostile society, which persecutes and insults them, and opens itself to them only to

racially separated spaces, a racial division of labor, racist language and discourse, and so on. A person can and often does construct a positive racial identity along with others from out of these serialized positionings. But such racial identification is an active taking up of a serialized situation. Which, if any, of a person's serial memberships become salient or meaningful at any time is a variable matter.

Like gender structures, class or race structures do not primarily name attributes of individuals or aspects of their identity but practico-inert necessities that condition their lives and with which they must deal. Individuals may take up varying attitudes toward these structures, including forming a sense of class or racial identity and forming groups with others they identify with.

Thus the concept of seriality provides a useful way of thinking about the relationship of race, class, gender, and other collective structures, to the individual person. If these are each forms of seriality, then they do not necessarily define the identity of individuals and do not necessarily name attributes they share with others. They are material structures arising from people's historically congealed institutionalized actions and expectations that position and limit individuals in determinate ways that they must deal with. An individual's position in each of the series means that they have differing experiences and perceptions from those differently

[margin handwriting: We these structures affect them differently depending on who they are]

---

reject them again, cannot be the only relation between the individual Jew and the antisemitic, racist society which surrounds him; it is this relation insofar as it is lived by every Jew in his direct or indirect relations with all the other Jews, and in so far as it constitutes him, through them all, an Other and threatens him in and through the Others. To the extent that, for the conscious, lived Jews, being-Jewish (which is his status to *non-Jews*) is interiorized as his responsibility in relation to all other Jews and his being-in-danger, out there, owing to some possible carelessness caused by Others who mean nothing to him, over whom he has no power and every one of whom is himself like Others (in so far as he makes them exist as such in spite of himself,) the *Jew,* far from being *the type* common to each separate instance, represents *on the contrary* the perpetual being *outside-themselves-in-the-other* of members of this practico-inert grouping" (268). Sartre also discusses colonialism as a serial social relation, mediated by an anonymous public opinion that constitutes racist discourse. He says that the most important thing about racist ideas and utterances is that they are not *thoughts*. Racism as operative in everyday life and as a medium of works and beliefs for reproducing practically congealed social relations of oppression and privilege is not a *system* of beliefs, thought through and deliberated. On the contrary, the racist language is unconsidered, uttered as the obvious, and spoken and heard always as the words of an Other. Everyday repeated stereotypes such as that Blacks are lazy or more prone to be aggressive, or that they prefer to stay with their own kind, "have never been anything more than this system itself producing itself as a determination of the language of the colonists in the milieu of alterity. And, for this point of view, they must be seen as material exigencies of language (the *verbal milieu* of all practico-inert apparatuses) addressed to colonialists both in their eyes and in those of others, in the unity of a gathering. . . . The sentence which is uttered, as a reference to the common interest, is not presented as the determination of language by the individual himself, but as his *other* opinion, that is to say, the claims to get it from and give it to others, insofar as their unity is based purely on alternity" (301).

situated. But individuals can relate to these social positionings in different ways; the same person may relate to them in different ways in different social contexts or at different times in their lives.

A person can choose to make none of her serial memberships important for her sense of identity. Or she can find that her family, neighborhood, and church network makes the serial facts of race, for example, important for her identity and development of a group solidarity. Or she can develop a sense of herself and membership in group affiliations that makes different serial structures important to her in different respects or salient in different kinds of circumstances.

V

The purpose of saying that *women* names a series thus resolves the dilemma that has developed in feminist theory: that we must be able to describe women as a social collective yet apparently cannot do so without falling into a false essentialism. An essentialist approach to conceiving women as a social collective treats women as a substance, as a kind of entity in which some specific attributes inhere. One classifies a person as a woman according to whether that person has the essential attributes of womanness, characteristics all women share: something about their bodies, their behavior or dispositions as persons, or their experience of oppression. The problem with this approach to conceptualizing women as a collective is that any effort to locate those essential attributes has one of two consequences. Either it empties the category *woman* of social meaning by reducing it to the attributes of biological female, or in the effort to locate essential social attributes it founders on the variability and diversity of women's actual lives. Thus, the effort to locate particular social attributes that all women share is likely to leave out some persons called women or to distort their lives to fit the categories.

Conceptualizing gender as seriality avoids this problem because it does not claim to identify specific attributes that all women have. There is a unity to the series of women, but it is a passive unity, one that does not arise from the individuals called women but rather positions them through the material organization of social relations as enabled and constrained by the structural relations of enforced heterosexuality and the sexual division of labor. The content of these structures varies enormously from one social context to the next. Saying that a person is a woman may predict something about the general constraints and expectations she must deal with. But it predicts nothing in particular about who she is, what she does, how she takes up her social positioning.

Thinking of gender as seriality also avoids the problem of identity. At least since Nancy Chodorow developed her theory of the psychodynamics of mother-infant relations, gender has been understood as a mode of personal identity (1978). By identity, I mean one of two conceptions, which sometimes appear together. First, identity designates something about who persons are in a deep psychological sense. This is the primary meaning of identity in Chodorow's theory of gender identity. She argues that feminine gender identity gives women more permeable ego boundaries than men, thus making relations with other persons important for their self-conception. Many recent moral and epistemological theories have been influenced by this notion of gender identity and suggest that theories, modes of reasoning, and ways of acting tend to be structured by those feminine and masculine identities.

Second, identity can mean self-ascription as belonging to a group with others who similarly identify themselves, who affirm or are committed together to a set of values, practices, and meanings. This is the sense of identity expressed by theorists of identity politics. Identity here means a self-consciously shared set of meanings interpreting conditions and commitments of being a woman.

Criticisms of gender as identity in either of these senses are similar to criticisms of gender essentialism. This approach either leaves out or distorts the experience of some individuals who call themselves or are called women. Many women regard their womanness as an accidental or contingent aspect of their lives and conceive other social group relations—ethnic or national relations, for example—as more important in defining their identity. Many women resist efforts to theorize shared values and experiences specific to a feminine gender identity—in a caring orientation to relationships, for example—claiming that such theories privilege the identities of particular classes of women in particular social contexts. Even among women who do take their womanhood as an important aspect of their identity, the meaning of that identity will vary a great deal (cf. Ferguson 1991).

Thinking about gender as seriality disconnects gender from identity. On the one hand, as Elizabeth Spelman argues, at the level of individual personal identity there is no way to distinguish the "gender part" of the person from her "race part" or "class part." It may be appropriate, as Butler argues, to think of subjects or personal identities as constituted rather than as some transcendental origin of consciousness or action. It nevertheless would be misleading to think of individual persons as mixtures of gender, race, class, and national attributes. Each person's identity is unique—the history and meaning she makes and develops from her dealings with other people, her communicative interactions through media, and her manner of taking up the particular serialized structures whose prior history position her. No individual woman's identity, then, will escape the markings of gender, but how gender marks her life is her own.

Conceptions of gender as an identity, however, more often seek to name women as a group—that is, a self-conscious social collective with common experiences, perspectives, or values—than to describe individual identity. Conceiving gender as seriality becomes especially important for addressing this mistake. In Sartre's conceptualization, a group is a collection of persons who do mutually identify, who recognize one another as belonging to the group with a common project that defines their collective action. A series, on the other hand, is not a mutually acknowledging identity with any common project or shared experience. Women need have nothing in common in their individual lives to be serialized as women.

A relationship between series and groups does exist, however. As self-conscious collectives of persons with a common objective that they pursue together, groups arise on the basis of and in response to a serialized condition. The group in fusion is a spontaneous group formation out of seriality. When those who have waited for the bus too long begin complaining to each other and discussing possible courses of action, they are a group in fusion. Once groups form and take action, they either institutionalize themselves by establishing meetings, leaders, decision-making structures, methods of acquiring and expending resources, and so on, or they disperse back into seriality. Social life consists of constant ebbs and flows of groupings out of series; some groups remain and grow into institutions that produce new serialities, others disperse soon after they are born.

At its most unreflective and universal level, being a women is a serial fact. But women often do form groups, that is, self-conscious collectives that mutually acknowledge one another as having common purposes or shared experiences. Let me give an example of a movement from women as a serial collective to a group of women. In her novel, *Rivington Street*, Meredith Tax vividly portrays the lives of Russian Jewish immigrant women in the Lower East Side of Manhattan at the turn of the century (1982). In one episode of the novel, some women in the neighborhood discover that a local merchant has manipulated the chicken market in order to make more profits. They talk with one another with anger and then go about their business. One of them, however, thinks a bit more in her anger and decides to act. She calls her three or four women friends together and tells them that they should boycott the butcher. The women organize a boycott by going from apartment to apartment talking to women. Gradually these neighborhood women, formerly serialized only as shoppers, come to understand themselves as a group, with some shared experiences and the power of collective action. When the boycott succeeds, they hold a street celebration and honor their leader, but then they quickly disperse back into the passive unity of the series.

The gendered being of women's groups arises from the serial being of women, as taking up actively and reconstituting the gendered structures that have passively unified them. The chicken boycott arises from the serialized condition of these women defined by the sexual division of labor as purchasers and preparers of food. While the gendered series *women* refers to the structured social relations positioning all biologically sexed females, groups of women are always partial in relation to the series—they bring together only some women for some purposes involving their gender serialized experience. Groups of women are usually more socially, historically, and culturally specified than simply women—they are from the same neighborhood or university, they have the same religion or occupation. Groups of women, that is, will likely, though not necessarily, emerge from the serialities of race and class as well as gender. The chicken boycotters live in the same neighborhood, speak the same Russian-Yiddish, and are passively united in a marginal working-class series in the class structure of Manhattan. All of these serialized facts are relevant to their story and partially explain their grouping.

The chicken boycott example shows a case of women grouping self-consciously as women and on the basis of their gendered condition, but the boycott is not feminist. There can be many groupings of women as women that are not feminist, and indeed some are explicitly antifeminist. Feminism is a particularly reflexive impulse of women grouping, women grouping as women in order to change or eliminate the structures that serialize them as women.

In order to clarify and elaborate the relation of series and group in understanding women as a collective, let me return to my story of Shirley Wright. In her announcement of her candidacy for school committee, when Shirley Wright says that she intends to represent women, she is referring to a gender series defined primarily by the sexual division of labor. *Women* names a position in the division of labor that tends to be specifically related to schools, the primary parent to deal with schools, at the same time that it names a position outside authority structures. In that speech Wright is not claiming a group solidarity among the women of Worcester, either around her candidacy or in any other respect, but is referring to, gesturing toward, a serial structure that conditions her own position and that she aims to politicize. To the degree that Shirley Wright aims to politicize gender structures in her campaign and on the school committee, she invites or invokes the positive grouping of women out of the gender series, but her candidacy speech neither names a group nor generates it. Her claiming to represent "minorities" is also a reference to a serial structure of race and racism that she claims conditions her position and that she aims to politicize.

The women who responded to my handing them a flyer with satisfaction at seeing a woman running are also serialized, as women, as voters. Their identification with Shirley Wright as a woman, however, makes for a proto-group. If some women are motivated to come together to form a "Women for Shirley Wright" committee, they have constituted an active grouping. In relation to the series women, or even to the series "the women of Worcester," the group is necessarily partial—it will probably attract only certain kinds of women, with only some kinds of experiences, and it will focus only on some issues.

In summary, then, I propose that using the concept of seriality and its distinction from the concept of a group can help solve the conundrums about talking about women as a group in which feminist theory has recently found itself. *Woman* is a serial collective defined neither by any common identity nor by a common set of attributes that all the individuals in the series share, but, rather, it names a set of structural constraints and relations to practio-inert objects that condition action and its meaning. I am inclined to say that the series includes all female human beings in the world, and others of the past, but how and where we draw the historical lines is an open question. We can also claim that there are also social and historical subseries. Since the series is not a concept but a more practical-material mode of the social construction of individuals, one need not think of it in terms of genus and species, but as vectors of action and meaning.

Unlike most groups of women, feminist groups take something about women's condition as the explicit aim of their action, and thus feminist groups at least implicitly refer to the series of women that lies beyond the group. Feminist politics and theory refers to or gestures toward this serial reality. Feminist reflection and explicit theorizing draw on the experience of serialized gender, which has multiple layers and aspects. Feminism itself is not a grouping of women; rather, there are many feminisms, many groupings of women whose purpose is to politicize gender and change the power relations between women and men in some respect. When women group, their womanliness will not be the only thing that brings them together; there are other concrete details of their lives that give them affinity, such as their class or race position, their nationality, their neighborhood, their religious affiliation, or their role as teachers of philosophy. For this reason groupings of women will always be partial in relation to the series. Women's groups will be partial in relation to the series also because a group will have particular objectives or purposes that cannot encompass or even refer to the totality of the condition of women as a series. This is why feminist politics must be coalition politics. Feminist organizing and theorizing always refers beyond itself to conditions and experiences that have not been reflected on, and to women whose lives are conditioned by enforced heterosexuality and a sexual division of labor who are not feminist and are not part of feminist groups. We should maintain our humility by recognizing that partiality and by remaining open to inquiring about the facts of the series beyond us.

Graduate School of Public and International Affairs
University of Pittsburgh

References

Allen, Jeffner, and Iris Marion Young, eds. 1989. *Thinking Muse: Feminism and Modern French Philosophy.* Bloomington: Indiana University Press.

Bordo, Susan. 1989. "Feminism, Postmodernism, and Gender-Scepticism." In *Feminism/Postmodernism,* ed. Linda Nicholson. New York: Routledge.

Butler, Judith. 1990. *Gender Trouble.* New York: Routledge.

Caraway, Nancy. 1989. "Identity Politics and Shifting Selves: Black Feminist Coalition Theory." Paper presented at American Political Science Association.

Chodorow, Nancy. 1978. *Reproduction of Mothering: Psychoanalysis and the Sociology of Gender.* Berkeley: University of California Press.

Ferguson, Ann. 1991. "Is There a Lesbian Culture?" In *Lesbian Philosophies and Cultures,* ed. Jeffner Allen, 63–88. Albany: State University of New York Press.

Fuss, Diana. 1989. *Essentially Speaking.* New York: Routledge.

Lange, Lynda. 1991. "Arguing for Democratic Feminism: Postmodern Doubts and Political Amnesia." Paper presented to the meeting of the American Philosophical Association, Midwest Division, Chicago.

Mohanty, Chandra Talpade. 1991. "Under Western Eyes: Feminist Scholarship and Colonial Discourses." In *Third World Women and the Politics of Feminism,* ed. Chandra Talpade Mohanty, Ann Russo, and Lourdes Torres, 51–80. Bloomington: Indiana University Press.

Murphy, Julien. 1989. "The Look in Sartre and Rich." In Allen and Young 1989.

Sartre, Jean-Paul. 1976. *Critique of Dialectical Reason,* trans. Alan Sheridan Smith, ed. Jonathan Ree. London: New Left Books.

Singer, Linda. 1992. *Erotic Welfare.* New York: Routledge.

Spelman, Elizabeth. 1988. *Inessential Woman.* Boston: Beacon.

Spivak, Gayatri Chakravorty. 1987. "French Feminism in an International Frame." In *In Other Worlds: Essays in Cultural Politics.* New York: Methuen.

Tax, Meredith. 1982. *Rivington Street.* New York: Morrow.

Young, Iris Marion. 1990. *Justice and the Politics of Difference.* Princeton, N.J.: Princeton University Press.

COLLECTIVE ACTION AND

WOMEN'S RESISTANCE

Paths of Proletarianization:
Organization of Production,
Sexual Division of Labor,
and Women's Collective Action

Louise A. Tilly

On October 25, 1880, the women cigar makers in the government monopoly tobacco factory in Lyon, France, sat down at their work with their arms folded. The factory manager, along with the prefect of the department, met with a delegation of strikers and proposed a compromise. The workers refused and continued their strike. Their agitation increased until, finally, the police forcefully evacuated the courtyard of the factory where the workers had gathered to demonstrate.

The manager and the prefect then requested that the government send an inspector-engineer from Paris with full authorization to bargain, and this was done. In another negotiating session, the Paris delegate agreed that no new measures would be taken that directly or indirectly reduced workers' salaries. Nor would the striking women's delegates be punished for their role. The cigar makers then agreed to return to work.[1]

Charles Mannheim, a French scholar who wrote his 1902 thesis on the condition of workers in the state tobacco factories, remarked further that the Lyon plant was in a state of "incessant agitation" throughout the period from 1880 to 1883.[2] In fact, a large section of his study is devoted to descriptions of strikes in the tobacco industry—twenty-seven of them—between 1870 and 1900. In all of the strikes, women workers played a dominant part. Michelle Perrot notes in her magisterial study of French strikes that "although they accounted for only .5 percent of the female labor force [in the period from 1870 to 1890] they [tobacco workers] supplied 16 percent of the female strikers."[3]

1. Charles Mannheim, *De la condition des ouvriers dans les manufactures de l'etat (tabacs-allumettes)* (Paris: Giard & Brière, 1902), pp. 420–22.

2. Ibid., p. 420.

3. Michelle Perrot, *Les Ouvriers en grève: France, 1871–1890* (Paris: Mouton, 1974), p. 329.

[*Signs: Journal of Women in Culture and Society* 1981, vol. 7, no. 2]

What a contrast to the often-assumed passivity of women workers!
Although her chief concerns are elsewhere, Perrot is very evenhanded in
her evaluation of women as strikers. Nevertheless, she concludes that
women were characterized by "timidity and lack of resolution" when it
came to striking.[4]

Why were the women tobacco workers such an exception to the
common rule that women, relative to men, were unlikely to strike? What
does the case of the tobacco workers suggest about the conditions which
promote female strikes?

This paper focuses on women's collective action in response to the
multifaceted process of proletarianization in France and the new organizations of production and household division of labor that accompanied
it. It focuses exclusively on urban working-class women and primarily,
but not exclusively, on workplace-based collective action. The argument
is developed by a systematic comparison of contrasting situations, in
which variations in the organization of production and in the household
division of labor provide part of the answer to the central question,
Under what conditions will women's participation in collective action be
more or less likely? The paper begins with a brief discussion of the
concept of "collective action" and its usefulness for understanding wom-
en's class-based action. The French economic-historical context for proletarianization and women's economic activity is the topic of the next
section. Brief case studies of typical proletarian situations follow, each
involving a different "mix" of organization of production and household
division of labor. The cases proceed along a continuum from household
organization of production, that setting least likely to promote women's
collective action, to individual wage earning in industrial production, in
which certain circumstances facilitated it. Typical forms of female collective action and different participation patterns are identified in each
setting. The conclusion lays out some generalizations about the connections among organization of production, the household division of
labor, women's propensity to act, and the form of that action.

Collective Action

Many political historians ignore women—and men—who had no
formal role in political structures. They focus on the power center of a
polity, the capital, and confine their analyses to formal politics: legislation, day-to-day administration of government activity, officials, and

---

4. Ibid., p. 322. See Kate Purcell, "Militancy and Acquiescence among Women Workers," in *Fit Work for Women*, ed. Sandra Burman (New York: St. Martin's Press, 1979), pp.
112–33, for comparable conclusions in present-day England but a model that explains low
female strike participation rates in terms of situational factors rather than personal
characteristics.

policy and its enforcement. Those without a role are marginal from this perspective; if they appear at all, it is only incidentally, when they come into intermittent contact with formal politics. Historically, the political activity of women has been most often outside this central arena, for they have had no formal rights or duties as citizens. To observe women's politics, then, it is necessary to look beyond the formal arena and seek out a more comprehensive method of analysis. The concept of "collective action" as a struggle over control of resources among groups is the theoretical framework used here. (One of these groups may be government and members of the polity; others may be classes; still others part of a class, an interest group, a community, a region, or a religious sect.)

Collective action is defined as a group's application of pooled resources to common ends. Acting in their own interests, groups apply their resources to other groups or to authorities at any level of government. Political power, then, is the return from the application of resources to governments. Violence occurs when governments or other groups resist the collective action of a mobilizing group, or when a mobilizing group deliberately chooses violent means.[5]

Economic Change, Proletarianization, and Women's Productive Role in France

The eighteenth- and nineteenth-century Industrial Revolution initiated an enormous shift of labor and resources away from primary production—agriculture, fishing, forestry—toward manufacturing and commercial and service activities. The scale of production increased, and the factory eventually replaced the household as the most common unit of productive activity. In France, the pace of industrialization was very gradual; it affected groups and geographic areas at different rates and times. The decline of small units of production was generally accompanied by a declining number of propertied peasants and artisans. The growth of industrial capitalism meant an increase of propertyless proletarians working for wages in city or country. Dependence on a labor market and on markets for subsistence needs—markets managed by others—increased the proletarians' lack of control over their own work.

For ordinary people witnessing the growth of industrial capitalism, proletarianization was the central social experience. *Proletarianization* is defined here as the process of increase in the number of "people whose survival depended on the sale of labor power."[6] Although pro-

5. Charles Tilly, *From Mobilization to Revolution* (Reading, Mass.: Addison-Wesley Publishing Co., 1978), pp. 52–59.

6. Charles Tilly, "Did the Cake of Custom Break?" in *Consciousness and Class Experience in Nineteenth-Century Europe*, ed. John M. Merriman (New York: Holmes & Meier, 1979), p. 29.

letarianization was a common experience, how it occurred in given populations varied markedly, as did the timing of the process. The paths or patterns of proletarianization were linked systematically to patterns of collective action.

The entire nineteenth century saw French agriculture, in sharp contrast to that of Britain, dominated by the small, family-run peasant farm. There were regional variations, to be sure. The tendency toward "an increase in the number of small owners whose assets consisted of no more than a house, a garden and one or two fields" continued throughout the period.[7] The peasantry was an important section of the French population that escaped proletarianization. Unlike the British farmer, the French peasant continued to depend on the labor of his family; thus wives and daughters living on small peasant holdings were an important part of France's agricultural work force. Individually, however, members of peasant households became proletarians if they left holdings to seek work or if the holdings were inadequate and wage labor had to be sought to supplement income.

This is not to suggest that rural proletarianization, which preceded urban industrial proletarianization in almost all European nation-states, did not occur in France. Absolutely and proportionately, the French agricultural proletariat was less important than that of Britain. But part of the agricultural work force in France consisted of day laborers and of live-in servants and hands. Sometimes these workers were the sons and daughters of propertied peasant families who had no chance to inherit land; sometimes they were offspring of landless workers. Both were, in a classic Marxian sense, proletarians. Although rural, agricultural proletarianization was an integral part of the process, it is not discussed in the primarily urban case studies that follow.

Urbanization occurred in nineteenth-century France as the proportion of population in cities increased, but even at the end of the century, much manufacturing took place in the households of part-time peasants, craftsmen, and rural workers in domestic industry or in small-scale workshops. Because of the particular character of French industrialization, operating alongside continuing peasant agriculture, France's manufacturing population was scattered throughout the country in rural as well as urban areas; thus "the distinction between industrial and agricultural work is often artificial."[8] Protoindustrialization—cottage industry, or the putting-out system, as it was called by the classic economic historians—had begun as a stratagem of merchant capitalists to tap underemployed labor power in needy rural households to produce cheap goods for distant markets. It lingered in France, in small towns

7. Roger Thabault, *Education and Change in a Village Community: Mazières-en-Gâtine, 1848–1914* (New York: Schocken Books, 1971), p. 21.

8. Claude Fohlen, "The Industrial Revolution in France, 1700–1914," in *The Emergence of Industrial Societies*, ed. Carlo Cippola (London: Fontana Books, 1973), p. 26.

and villages, even in the late nineteenth century, because it allowed high-quality craftsmanship and quick changeover of styles to match fashions, not to mention low wages. By the late nineteenth century, families working as cottage production units owned their tools, usually looms, and sometimes they hired an assistant or two. Despite these anomalies they were all proletarians, parents and children alike, selling their labor power with little control over their joint wage except putting additional family members to work or laboring longer hours.

Urban industrial growth had created new kinds of cities in France by the 1870s. The textile cities of the Nord, and mining and metalworking cities of the Nord and Pas-de-Calais (or of the Stephannois region of the Center-South), are examples. These cities, all products of industrial capitalist concentration, had very different labor force characteristics. In the textile city, there was heavy labor force participation by girls and women, including some married women. In the mining town, most jobs were men's jobs. Girls did some auxiliary work around the mines and shops or were servants; married women were seamstresses or store or cafe keepers, if they were wage earners. The division of labor by sex in the coal miners' or metalworkers' families was especially sharp. Men and boys worked in heavy labor removed from the household. Married women generally stayed in the home and were responsible for housework, childbearing, and child care.

Most French cities did not have the peculiar labor force characteristics of the textile city or the mining town. In other towns and cities, public administration, commerce, and small businesses that produced directly for consumers were common. In these cities women worked primarily in domestic service, the garment industry (young women in shops, married women in their homes), food processing, and paper and tobacco plants. Throughout the century there were also many urban women in informal, casual labor as carters, petty traders, street hawkers, and laundresses. Although consumer production and merchandising became large scale in the nineteenth century, the specialization of sectors of these urban economies changed little. Unmarried women in cities usually earned wages for their work. The decline of the household organization of production in the urban sector meant that even if they worked at home—and the late nineteenth century was a heyday of sweated home industry—women were unlikely to be part of a family productive unit. Instead they labored as isolated individuals for employers who paid them a wage. Married women in the working class often worked intermittently doing laundry, cleaning, and the like, for they had heavy home responsibilities too. Women's work, then, had changed rather little: The majority of working women had low-skilled jobs in areas considered women's work for centuries.

The economic life of the manufacturing classes can be characterized by organization of production. First, household organization did not disappear in nineteenth-century France; craftshops continued household-organized production. Second, other household production units, particularly in handloom weaving and small metal production, were composed of proletarian wage earners. Third, individual wage earning was the predominant mode in urban industry. Hence, a distinctive characteristic of French economic production in the second half of the nineteenth century was that the household organization of production was preserved in some proletarianized production. That is the economic context for the first case in the typology of organization of production and women's class-based collective action.[9]

The cases to be examined next are those of household manufacture in the Cambrésis, the silk industry of Lyon and the Lyonnais, the large-scale textile industry of the Nord, the mining and metalworking industry, and the tobacco industry.

Household Manufacture in the Cambrésis

The linen handloom weavers of the Cambrésis in northern France seemed an anachronism even to their contemporaries. Here is an ethnographic account of these weavers' work and family life written at the turn of the century:

> The father of the family groups the community of workers, of whom he is the natural head, in the workshop, at the looms. He himself works too, giving each of his family the joint responsibility of working in the enterprise. All the family members collaborate to varying degrees, without exception, in the production of cloth.
>
> From an early age, the children of both sexes help their father do his job by producing the *trames*. This task consists of winding the linen thread on a bobbin, which is then placed in the hollow of the weaver's shuttle. Once they are thirteen, the children are rapidly taught how to weave by their own family and assigned to their own loom. . . .
>
> The mother is concerned above all with house work, aided in her many tasks by her daughters. The rest of the time, often rising before dawn, she also prepares the bobbins for the weavers' shuttles; if there is an idle loom, she hurries to replace a sick or absent worker.
>
> [In the family workshop] each person finds the task appropriate for his or her strength and intelligence. The children, far from being a burden for their parents, become very real resources for the family. Raised to be weavers, they become weavers.[10]

9. The economic change described above is more fully discussed in Louise A. Tilly and Joan W. Scott, *Women, Work and Family* (New York: Holt, Rinehart & Winston, 1978).

10. Charles Blaise, *Le Tissage à la main du Cambrésis: Etude d'industrie à domicile* (Lille: Bigot, 1899), pp. 36–37.

Without the unpaid labor of his wife and the wages of his children, it would have been impossible for the male weaver to support a family. Wages were very low in the industry, reflecting its marginal relationship to the industrialized textile industry, located in the same area of France. Furthermore, there were sharp cycles in the trade, and in any ordinary year there were likely to be several periods of unemployment.[11] In response, all family members were pressed to accept familial goals, even if this meant sacrifice of individual hopes. Children were not schooled; they went to work very young. Their marriages could be delayed, or they could be sent out to find work elsewhere as their younger siblings took their places at the looms.[12] The weavers' chief solutions to poverty, short of migration, were working longer hours and having children who could work, too.

As their conditions degenerated, the weavers did act collectively in large strikes in 1889, 1895, and 1906. The strikes of the handloom weavers were largely male events; those who dealt with the bosses and paraded their demands through the small towns of the Cambrésis were the male heads of weaving households. They were accompanied by their sons but not by their wives and daughters. There was a strict division of labor in these households; the shop, even though located in the weaver's cottage cellar, was the male weaver's preserve. He was the boss, the person who carried on family contacts with the public world of the labor market. Although the children of these families earned individual wages, the wives did not. Children's wages were given to the mother to spend on household needs, as were the father's wages. The organization of production promoted familial orientations among the handloom weavers. Workers in the small, separate, household production units were slow to mobilize and strike. When they did, the women's role was minimal.[13]

The Silk Industry of Lyon and the Lyonnais

There were some similar characteristics in the organization of production in the silk industry of Lyon. There the once proud and independent artisan silk handweavers were undergoing slow, painful proletarianization. For a time, the defense of their jobs met with some success, for the merchant capitalists benefited from the concentration of weavers in the city. Just as the linen entrepreneurs of the Cambrésis, these merchants were hampered by the cyclical demand for their prod-

11. Ibid., pp. 53–55.

12. Serge Grafteaux, *Mémé Santerre: Une vie* (Verviers: Marabout, 1975), passim.

13. See Louise A. Tilly, "Linen Was Their Life: Family Survival Strategies and Parent-Child Relations in a French Handloom Weaving Village" (paper prepared for Round Table II: History and Anthropology, sponsored by the Max Planck Institut für Geschichte, Göttingen, and the Maison des Sciences de l'Homme, Paris, 1980).

ucts, based on trends in fashion, which made them hesitate to invest in factories or big inventories.[14]

An economic journalist, writing in 1860, noted the continuing importance of the household as productive unit: "One fact is striking, right off; that is family life. The stable workers, owners of one or more looms, are almost all married. Since the assistance of a wife is indispensable for the multitude of tasks auxiliary to weaving, they marry young. By the nature of his work, the weaver stays in his home."[15] Recent research shows that by this period, however, the household economy had been considerably modified. Between 1847 and 1866, there had been "a reduction in the proportion of residents in the household not related to the head of the household or to his spouse, and in the proportion of nonresident workers needed to weave the active looms ('familialization'), and a reduction in the proportion of males, both kinfolk of the head or spouse and nonkin, residing in the same household ('feminization')."[16] Women workers—kin of the master weavers or live-in wage earners who were part textile workers and part servants—performed the various tasks of preparing and winding the warp, and they did the weaving. George Sheridan concludes "that women played an especially important role in preserving the traditional household economy."[17]

A second kind of productive unit, in addition to the household-organized silk workshop, was the convent weaving shop, located in the suburbs of Lyon. There nuns supervised women weavers and managed the business, which was financed by Lyon entrepreneurs.[18] A third productive unit was the silk *internat,* sometimes metaphorically called a convent factory. At these institutions, girls and young women boarded in dormitories attached to silk spinning and reeling mills, their work and personal lives strictly supervised, often by nuns.[19] In both cases, women were greatly limited in their freedom of action because of supervision and threats of dismissal on the job and of lost wages and fines if they quit. At the same time, there were a growing number of large-scale mills, mostly in small towns but also in Lyon, where silk reeling, throwing, and the various spinning and twisting operations were done by local women and girls hired on a daily basis.

14. George J. Sheridan, Jr., "Household and Craft in an Industrializing Economy: The Case of the Silk Weavers of Lyon," in Merriam, ed., pp. 120–23.

15. Armand Audiganne, *Les Populations ouvrières et les industries de la France: Etudes comparatives* (Paris: Capelle, 1860), p. 44.

16. Sheridan, p. 111; see also Laura S. Strumingher, *Women and the Making of the Working Class: Lyon, 1830–1870* (Montreal: Eden Press Women's Publications, 1979), pp. 1–16.

17. Sheridan, p. 113.

18. Strumingher, pp. 8–9.

19. See Dominique Vanoli, "Les Ouvrières enfermées: Les couvents soyeux," *Les Révoltes logiques* 2 (1976): 19–39; Paul LeRoy-Beaulieu, *Le Travail des femmes au XIXe siècle* (Paris: Charpentier, 1873), pp. 410–25; Perrot, p. 328.

By the 1860s the repressive regime of the Second Empire and hard times in the silk industry had greatly reduced the level of Lyonnais *canut* ("silk weaver") mobilization and action. It was only when new labor laws, which relaxed prohibitions on association, were passed in the last years of the Second Empire that a large strike of the *Fabrique* (the Lyonnais handweaving system) brought out urban *canuts*, rural domestic weavers, *and* women factory workers. The largest group of women who struck in the city were some 600 *ovalistes*, who performed a special twisting operation on the silk thread, usually in medium-sized shops. It was in the "revolutionary fervor" of 1869, in response to an organizing effort by the Lyonnais affiliates of the First International, that "for the first time, we witness large strikes of women workers, who held meetings, discussed issues, set up committees and organized unions."[20] The petition of the *ovalistes*, which one historian calls an illustration of their "naiveté and inexperience," asked the prefect to arbitrate between them and their employers. The bosses pointed out that they were competing with lower-paid Italian workers and refused any concession. Some *ovalistes* who received room and board from their employer were evicted. The women gathered in menacing groups around his house, breaking windows and threatening to burn the building down. Several of the women were arrested, and the strike was broken by police action.[21] Given their circumscribed lives, such women ordinarily would not be expected to strike. The contemporaneous large waves of strikes made theirs more thinkable and offered them models of collective action.

Generally, neither the girls and women working in the proletarianized household production of silk nor those in the *internats* were often involved in collective action, even when male weavers were. The *internats* were set up such that they preserved women's social ties—frequent home visits were allowed—while isolating them from other workers.[22] Parents could be fined if their daughters left their jobs. The women were so closely supervised and overworked that it was hard for them to develop any solidarity. Lucie Baud, a silk union activist around 1900, was one who decried the effects of the *internats* on women workers' solidarity.[23]

Later, in the 1870s and 1880s, however, there were women's committees among factory silk workers in Lyon and the surrounding region that affiliated with local union confederations (*chambres syndicales*). Most of the southeastern strikes in that period were led by such groups. In the

20. Sreten Maritch, *Histoire du mouvement social sous le Second Empire à Lyon* (Paris: Rousseau, 1930), p. 253; see also Maurice Moissonier, *La Première Internationale et la commune à Lyon (1865–1871)* (Paris: Editions Sociales, 1972).

21. Maritch, pp. 221–22; Moissonier, pp. 81–83.

22. Michael Hanagan, "Artisans and Industrial Workers: Work Structure, Technological Change and Worker Militancy in Three French Towns: 1870–1914" (Ph.D. diss., University of Michigan, 1976), p. 276.

23. Michelle Perrot, ed., "Document: Le témoignage de Lucie Baud, ouvrière en soie," *Le Mouvement social* 105 (1978): 139–46.

period from 1871 to 1890, one-third of the all-female strikes in France were in the textile and garment sector, and one-third were in the silk industry.[24] When women workers organized with men, they struck with them as well. By the end of the nineteenth century, then, women engaged in industrial production. They earned independent wages, and though both their husbands and their parents often had a claim on these wages, the women mobilized and acted collectively in strikes.

The Textile Industry of the Nord

Women constituted a large minority, sometimes even a majority, of millworkers in the classic cotton and wool textile cities of the Nord. By the 1870s the industry was mechanized and located in large-scale shops. Michelle Perrot describes a favorite photographic study at the turn of the century—men and women flooding through the textile factory gates together at the end of the day *(sortée d'usine)*: "[There were] crowds of workers of both sexes, young, gaunt, wrung out, underfed, but clowning crudely nevertheless, as if emboldened by their number, by the 'collective being' of which they were a part. . . ."[25] Although men and women were both employed in these mills, the type of work done by each sex was usually quite different. Women and children did preparatory work; they were piecers and helpers. Proportionately fewer women did the central tasks of textile production—spinning and weaving. Those who did weave were more likely to work in a mixed setting. Women who worked in the mills were primarily young and unmarried, though toward the end of the period there was a clear tendency for more married women to work.[26]

Women in the northern textile mills did strike with other workers. The published statistics did not always report numbers of women in strikes that involved both women and men prior to 1890; nevertheless, newspaper and police accounts placed women in demonstrations and processions on the occasion of strikes. In the weavers' strike of 1867 in Roubaix, a strike directed against an employer speedup that required each worker to watch two looms instead of one, two of the ninety-eight persons arrested were women.[27] Later the same year a woman, along with two men, was arrested for beating up a male weaver who had accepted the two-loom regime.[28] In an 1880 city-wide strike in Roubaix, the commanding officer of the gendarmerie reported to Paris that all of the male and female workers, some 12,000–15,000 strong, were on strike

24. Perrot, pp. 326–27.

25. Ibid., p. 352.

26. Louise A. Tilly, "The Family Wage Economy of a French Textile City, Roubaix, 1872–1906," *Journal of Family History* 4 (1979): 381–94.

27. Prefect of the Nord to Paris, March 30, 1867, F¹² 4562, Archives nationales de France, Paris (hereafter cited as AN).

28. Prefect of the Nord to Paris, July 10, 1867, F¹² 4652, AN.

in the spinning and weaving mills. He noted large groups of strikers clustering in the streets and parading about.[29] Nevertheless, women did not strike in proportion to their numbers in the industry.[30]

Women workers were in a difficult position in the northern mills. Male workers accused women of competing, at low wages, for men's jobs. Contemporaries, both workers and authorities, believed women were less likely to strike. In 1886, for example, striking Roubaix weavers demanded that their employer fire one of the women workers who would not strike with them over a wage issue.[31] The boss refused to fire the woman. The police reports for a series of textile strikes during the fall and winter of 1899 in Roubaix and Tourcoing further illustrate male/female discord. The women did not strike often, but they were put out of work by the strikes. In only one of the strikes reported did women weavers join male workers—thirty-five women accompanied seventy men in the initial walkout on November 20, 1899. In Wattrelos on December 4, 1899, there were taunting serenades outside the homes of families whose daughters did not join the strike at the Motte wool-combing establishment in Roubaix. The parents were blamed for their daughters' lack of solidarity, an accusation that may have been justified in some cases; one of the fathers involved was himself a dissident from the strike.[32]

Male workers were ambivalent about women workers. A song written by a militant socialist accused the bosses of hiring women to undercut male wages and the women of collaborating with this policy.[33] Women generally were not welcomed in the northern textile unions. They were seldom chosen to be leaders. Of the ten national congresses of the textile unions whose proceedings Madeleine Guilbert was able to locate, only three had a single female delegate. At eight of the ten congresses, the question of women workers was not discussed.[34]

Women textile workers were also especially vulnerable because there were many young women seeking work. In a strike of women bobbin winders in December 1880, fourteen women protested the dismissal of one of their co-workers. Their employer promptly gave them their papers and replaced them with no difficulty.[35] Moreover, most women workers, single or married, lived with families. Their families claimed their wages and loyalty and could influence, particularly among

29. Report, May 5, 1880, F[12] 4660, piece 711, AN.

30. Perrot, Les Ouvriers en grève, pp. 318–19.

31. Report of the Conseiller de Préfecture délégué to Paris, January 28, 1886, F[12] 4661, AN.

32. Police report to Prefect, Roubaix, November 23, 1899; police report, Wattrelos, December 4, 1899, M 625/106, Archives départementales du Nord (hereafter cited as ADN).

33. Song, M 625/106, ADN.

34. Madeleine Guilbert, Les Femmes et l'Organisation syndicale avant 1914 (Paris: Editions du CNRS, 1966), pp. 117–23.

35. December 22, 1880, F[12] 4660, piece 719, AN.

young women, their decisions about striking. That women were proletarian wage earners was not sufficient to promote their participation in collective action parallel to that of men. This was due less to personal characteristics, such as the female passivity so often invoked by contemporaries, than to situational factors. Young single women, in particular, were less likely to strike because of their economically vulnerable position, their relatively brief commitment to industrial employment, their lack of opportunity to develop solidarity on or off the job, and, finally, their reliance on the family for personal well-being. The situation was different for married women. Although relatively few of them worked at any time, even in the textile industry, it is likely that over the years an individual woman worked often enough to develop connections and a kind of solidarity with other workers, as well as lore about strikes, which could serve her when the occasion to strike arose. At this time, I have no evidence of differential participation rates in strikes by married women, but statistics indicate that there were more women strikers, proportionately, as the female textile work force came to include proportionately more married women after 1900.

The Mining and Metalworking Industry

The metalworking and mining town, another prototypical industrial city, was characterized by quite a different industrial organization and household division of labor. Men and boys were the primary wage earners, and wives were concerned with the home, children, and food purchase and preparation. Young women could be coal sorters at the mine, or perhaps servants, but few other jobs existed for women.

The coal miner's wife was noted among workers' wives in her active role in work-related struggles. She had often been employed at the mine as a girl; she knew the work of the mine. As a married woman, she had to deal with the company as landlord, as owner of the store, as distributor of health services, and sometimes, even, as school board. Michelle Perrot writes that the mine strike was an "affair of the tribe: committed, the women demonstrated unequaled tenacity, seeking contributions for aid to strikers, organizing their slim resources, boosting the flagging morale of the men, involving themselves with the policing of the strike. At the time the workers' shifts changed, they stood across the roads, [and] blocked access of scabs to the pits. . . ."[36]

An incident illustrative of women's collective action occurred in April 1906, in Billy-Montigny, a mining town in the Pas-de-Calais. A month earlier, a disaster had shaken the pits of nearby Courrières. More than 1,000 miners were trapped and died. A strike followed; the miners demanded that the companies attend to their workers' safety. The action was bitter and violent and included a dynamite attack on an employer's home.

36. Perrot, *Les Ouvriers en grève,* p. 405.

On April 10, a group of 500 women carrying red and tricolored flags trimmed with black crepe went to the train station in Billy-Montigny to meet a woman believed to be on the train from Bethune. Madame Ringard was returning from the *chef-lieu* ("county seat"), where she had given testimony to a judge against three accused bombers. She was not on the train, but the crowd searched the platforms, assembled to sing the "Internationale," and marched off down the street. The same day another group of women carrying black flags marched to petition the mine administration to hasten rescue efforts in the flooded pits, as some survivors had been found. The two groups joined. When police and soldiers tried to hasten the procession, "a great number of rocks were thrown at the soldiers."[37]

The women who met the train at Billy-Montigny were seeking to discipline the woman who, they believed, had betrayed the striking workers. The second women's demonstration indicates the utter dependence of the wife on her husband's wages. The death of a husband was devastating to the miner's wife, who lived in a community where it was very difficult for a woman to support herself. The women were not wage earners; they could not strike, but they expressed their solidarity with striking workers through a demonstration.

Another homemakers' protest, a version of the food riot, was launched in 1911 in Ferrière-la-Grande, a metalworking city in the northern industrial belt near Maubeuge. Women from a nearby town dumped a merchant's goods when he refused to lower his prices. In Maubeuge itself, on August 25, a crowd broke the windows of a butter merchant. On Saturday, August 26, no butter or eggs were available in the market. A small group of women wearing red insignia marched into the marketplace. As they marched, they sang, to the tune of the "Internationale,"

> Rise, each mother of a family
> Arise and let us unite
> Let's march to fight the misery
> That the farmers have brought down on the country.
> And if one day we are victorious
> We'll show our dear husbands
> That all women have fought
> For the lives of their poor little ones.
>
> Forward comrades,
> Friends, rise with us,
> No fear, no riot
> We want butter at fifteen sous![38]

37. *Le Temps* (Paris) (April 11, 1906).

38. *Le Figaro* (Paris) (August 27, 1911), quoted in Paul R. Hanson, "The 'Vie chère' Protests in France, 1911," photocopy (Berkeley: University of California, 1976); and in Jean-Marie Flonneau, "Crise de vie chère et mouvement syndical, 1910–1914," *Le Mouvement social* 72 (1970): 49–81.

A wave of protest about food prices swept over the industrial departments, including a violent incident at Billy-Montigny on August 30. There a crowd of women and men attacked a baker's wagon. The baker shot one of the demonstrators, and the crowd turned on him in fury. When he hid in a house, the crowd smashed the windows, looted the chicken coop, and set a wagon on fire before they were dispersed by gendarmes.[39]

Both the protest over food prices and the strike-related collective action originated among women in households with a strict division of labor. The miners and metallurgists left housework and child rearing to their wives. The women, in turn, were expected to use male wages to purchase a comfortable living. The worker's home, like the bourgeois home, was a haven from work—a haven for which the wife was primarily responsible. With this household division of labor, the wife's role as wise consumer was salient.

This consumer interest recalls the role of women in the eighteenth-century grain and bread riot. Yet there are differences. The 1911 food protest began in industrial areas, not in agricultural marketing or administrative cities.[40] The object was less often the basic diet items of bread and grain and more often butter, milk, and eggs. The protesters were often connected with unions or parties—witness the red insignia and the "Internationale of Butter." Indeed, the unions soon took over the movement and began formal, nationwide demonstrations. The early demonstrators tried to police prices, just as coal miners' wives policed the strike. Those who resisted their demands, who tried to elude the set price, were attacked. The reporter for *Le Figaro* who filed the report from Maubeuge on August 27, 1911, employed the strike metaphor when he wrote that the protest was "more than a strike but not quite a crusade."[41]

Still other aspects of the 1911 collective action clearly distinguished it from the earlier grain and bread riot. The women's food demonstration, which had an elected committee and a designated chair, was organized in a more formal and almost bureaucratic fashion than was the food riot, a protest held together by the rioters' shared sense of justice and communal rights. It was the consumer interest of working-class wives which led them to protest in 1911, but the form of their action had more in common with other collective actions of the period than with the food riot of the Old Regime.

The Tobacco Industry

We have seen women as purposeful actors in strikes and demonstrations in late nineteenth-century France. Whether, when, and how

39. *Le Temps* (August 31, 1911), quoted in Hanson.
40. Hanson; Flonneau, pp. 60–62; Perrot, *Les Ouvriers en grève,* pp. 130–34.
41. *Le Figaro* (August 27, 1911), quoted in Hanson.

they acted was determined by their familial position as well as by the organization of production. Their interests were often familial, whether they were supporting striking husbands, protesting high consumer prices, or striking (or choosing not to strike) on their own behalf. We return now to the tobacco workers, whose work situation pulled them away from family interest and placed them in a different relationship to their work.

The factories of the tobacco monopoly—which produced cigarettes, cigars, loose tobacco, and matches—employed thousands of people in one institution, the majority of them women. Women in the tobacco industry worked in shops far removed from their households each day. Although they were generally unmarried, as were most women workers, a disproportionate number were married women, as the jobs in the tobacco industry were relatively secure and skilled. Cigar makers in France apprenticed and trained for several years, and, unlike the comparable labor force in the United States, the majority of French cigar makers were women.[42] The privileges these skilled workers won were often passed on to their co-workers. A tobacco worker's daughter often sought a position in the same shop as her mother; working conditions and wages were superior to those of most female jobs.[43] Apprenticeship, parent-to-child continuity in the same occupation, and lifetime commitment to one job provided opportunities for the development of solidarity and association among women tobacco workers not unlike the opportunities of male craftsmen and skilled workers.

In fact, the tobacco workers founded mutual aid or friendly societies and then formed unions, just as did male skilled workers and artisans. In the Lyon strike described in the introduction of this paper, a mutual club preceded the strike, and its leaders represented the women.[44] The first union was set up two days after a successful strike in January 1887, in Marseille. The tobacco workers organized in their interests as workers, to improve conditions of work and to claim benefits such as paid maternity leave. The particularities of their work situation accounted for the assertiveness of these women in defining and acting in their interests. In addition, their average pay was closer to men's salaries than was the pay of other women workers. The tobacco workers' earning power continued to increase over most of their working lives because of their long-term work commitment. (To be sure, these factors could have been a result as well as a cause of their activism.)

The organization and scale of the tobacco industry also promoted association by grouping many women together and possibly even by segregating women in certain positions; teams of workers were paid as

42. Mannheim (n. 1 above), p. 22.
43. Ibid., p. 63; see also Perrot, *Les Ouvriers en grève*, pp. 329–30; and Guilbert, pp. 93–99.
44. Mannheim, p. 421.

teams. It is not surprising, then, that tobacco workers organized in female or predominantly female groups. Theirs was one of the few unions in which women played a significant leadership role. Their activism was an ongoing affair, not tied to temporary mobilization and strikes. It led a male supervisor to complain, "Neither the privileges which the state worker enjoys nor the generosity and concessions which they have received have led them to moderate their demands."[45] These women knew what they wanted and were ready to fight for it.

Conclusion

The cases examined here, focusing on working-class women's collective action in different proletarianized situations—household manufacture in the Cambrésis, the silk industry of Lyon and the Lyonnais, the large-scale textile industry of the Nord, the mining and metalworking industry, and the tobacco industry—illustrate the conditions under which such collective action was more or less common. They do not address the questions of women organizing and acting on women's issues but, rather, the ways in which industrial capitalism changed and shaped wage labor and households, men's and women's relations to each, and patterns of collective action.

Characteristics of the organization of production and the household division of labor were critical variables in women's participation in collective action. Women working in household production were isolated from other workers except family members. The chief of the household productive organization was also head of the family. Hence, in the strikes in domestic industry, the heads of household acted for the family as they did in other relationships with the state or with employers.

Some women in the large-scale silk industry of Lyon were isolated from their families when they were at work because they lived in dormitories at their place of employment. But these women were frequently working for their families or to save for marriage, which made them extremely vulnerable to possible employer retaliation if they complained or acted collectively. In the face of a massive class mobilization, however, such women did join a strike movement. As time went on, more women who worked in silk factories were older, "permanent" workers; that is, they worked for more of their lives, though not necessarily continuously. This gave them the opportunity to build networks of solidarity and association and, I speculate, a higher propensity to class-based workplace actions. Furthermore, the silk industry unions facilitated women's organization through women's committees.

45. Quoted in Marie-Hélène Zylberberg-Hocquard, "Les Ouvrières d'etat (tabacs-allumettes) dans les dernières années du XIXe siècle," *Le Mouvement social* 105 (1978): 87–107.

In the Nord, women workers in the early years of the cotton and wool textile industry were more likely to be young and single. In the workplace their work differed from that of men, and they were less skilled. If employers tried to substitute women for male workers, the men blamed the women and perceived the only way out of the problem as eliminating or limiting women's work. Compared with men, women were shut out of workers' organizations. Their family connections also tended to isolate single women from other workers with similar class interests. Sometimes they were pressed to strike (or pressed not to strike) by family as well as class interest, or by personal inclination, but they lacked independent associations or opportunity to build solidarity. Thus it is no surprise to find uncertainty and lower levels of strike participation among young women. The sexual division of labor in the household could act as a deterrent for married women workers, for they were obliged to do housework as well as wage work. There were also cases of husbands who intervened to prevent their wives' striking. Nevertheless, as the cotton and wool industry, like the silk industry, hired more married women, their lifetime commitment to wage work and the opportunity to build association gave women more chances to participate in collective action.

Paradoxically, perhaps, a very strict division of labor in the household, such as that in the homes of metal and mining workers, seems to have encouraged wives to participate actively in workplace struggles because of their dependence on the wages of the male head of the household. The community of work in these industries included women, even if women were not themselves wage laborers. Women in this setting, and other wives whose major concern was managing household consumption, also acted out of consumer interests.

Only in the case of the tobacco industry was there strong participation of women in class-based workplace collective action, which grew out of the special characteristics of their work, the organization of production, and their lifetime commitments.

This historical evidence, then, suggests that proletarian women will tend to act collectively more often when *as workers*

(1) they associate with others with similar interests;
(2) they can translate these interests into structured association;
(3) they have resources they can mobilize and deploy;
(4) their employers are dependent on their regular supply of labor;
(5) there is a favorable economic climate, which means that withdrawal of labor represents a real burden for the employer and, potentially, a real gain for the workers;
(6) their position is not extremely vulnerable; and
(7) there is a general climate of economic claims; and

(8) their position in the household division of labor gives them the opportunity to act autonomously.

Furthermore, women will tend to act collectively more often *as members of households* when

(9) the household itself is mobilized in defense of interests that can be generalized as those of the household as well as of individual members.

These conclusions do not differ very markedly from those that predict higher participation rates by men. The chief difference is in the case of defense of household consumer interest. Women were much more likely than men to participate in such collective action. Responsibility for household consumption was rarely a primary concern of men in an industrial economy. A general theory about comparative propensity to participate in working-class collective action, whether strikes or food protest, informs about women, too. No special psychological or gender-attribute explanation is needed to understand women's proportionately lower participation rates. Certain women, in positions and situations that promoted their readiness to act, did act. The paths of proletarianization shaped women's wage labor and their family responsibility and, consequently, determined both their propensity to act collectively and the form of action they chose.

Department of History
University of Michigan

Female Consciousness and Collective Action: The Case of Barcelona, 1910–1918

Temma Kaplan

Female Consciousness and Collective Action

Female consciousness, recognition of what a particular class, culture, and historical period expect from women, creates a sense of rights and obligations that provides motive force for actions different from those Marxist or feminist theory generally try to explain. Female consciousness centers upon the rights of gender, on social concerns, on survival. Those with female consciousness accept the gender system of their society; indeed, such consciousness emerges from the division of labor by sex, which assigns women the responsibility of preserving life. But, accepting this task, women with female consciousness demand the rights that their obligations entail. The collective drive to secure those rights that result from the division of labor sometimes has revolutionary consequences insofar as it politicizes the networks of everyday life.

Various people sparked ideas they may not wish to endorse. I am especially grateful to Renate Bridenthal, Nancy Cott, Estelle Freedman, Linda Gordon, Claudia Koonz, Charles Maier, David Montgomery, Rayna Rapp, Ellen Ross, Gavin Smith, Meredith Tax, Gaye Tuchman, Daniel Walkowitz, Annette Weiner, and John Womack, Jr.

EDITORS' NOTE: *By looking from a historical perspective at definitions of gender and class consciousness, Temma Kaplan's essay brings forward aspects of consciousness raising that may be added to those set forth by Catharine MacKinnon. Women, Kaplan maintains, do have a unique consciousness; it is not precisely the kind of gender consciousness that we tend to consider feminist, but centered as it is on the maintenance of life, it may have more truly radical implications than any other revolutionary ideology.*

[*Signs: Journal of Women in Culture and Society* 1982, vol. 7, no. 3]

As part of being female, women learn to nurture, a task with social as well as psychological effects.[1] Women of the popular classes perform work associated with the obligation to preserve life; such jobs range from shopping for necessities to securing fuel and to guarding their neighbors, children, and mates against danger. The lives of women in the lower classes revolve around their work as gatherers and distributors of social resources in the community, whether or not they also work for wages outside their households. Women who have money simply hire other women to do for them the work of sustaining life that they do not want to do themselves. (Thus before refrigeration and running water, urban women went to fountains and markets every day, while those who could afford servants sent them.) But all classes of women understand what their society's division of labor by sex requires of them: the bedrock of women's consciousness is the need to preserve life. Now as in the past, women judge themselves and one another on how well they do work associated with being female.

Recognition of the existence of female consciousness necessitates reorientation of political theory: by placing human need above other social and political requirements and human life above property, profit, and even individual rights, female consciousness creates the vision of a society that has not yet appeared. Social cohesion rises above individual rights and quality of life over access to institutional power. Thus female consciousness has political implications, as women's collective actions have shown, although women themselves along with historians of their movements have remained ignorant about the motivations for female mass action.

Theories of consciousness attempt to explain causality in history. Modern theories of consciousness began with G. W. F. Hegel's *Philosophy of History,* which analysts such as Karl Marx attempted to rescue from abstraction. Whereas Hegel viewed consciousness as the effect of transcendent Reason operating inexorably through history, Marx restored human consciousness and intentional action as central objects of inquiry.[2] Feminist consciousness, understood from this Marxist perspec-

1. Nancy Chodorow explores the psychological dimensions of the fact that women nurture and men do not in her book, *The Reproduction of Mothering: Psychoanalysis and the Sociology of Gender* (Berkeley and Los Angeles: University of California Press, 1978). Although she does not stress the social requirements for women to nurture, Dolores Hayden examines women's work and describes the efforts of a group she calls "materialist feminists" to transform physical space by collectivizing laundries and kitchens, thereby making women's work more efficient. See Hayden, *The Grand Domestic Revolution: A History of Feminist Designs for American Homes, Neighborhoods, and Cities* (Cambridge, Mass.: MIT Press, 1981).

2. Even the leading early twentieth-century work on consciousness, George Lukács's *History and Class Consciousness* (Cambridge, Mass.: MIT Press, 1971), dwells on ideas rather than movements.

tive, is about power relationships and access to institutions. Feminism attempts to win for women full rights and powers both in the context of class and in the dominant political system. There may be differences among feminists by virtue of the priorities they give to different forms of oppression: radical feminists oppose the gender system solidified in the division of labor by sex; socialist feminists oppose gender and class systems and all power relations based on sexual differences or forms of work.[3] However, all feminists attack the division of labor by sex because roles limit freedom, and to mark distinctions is to imply superiority and inferiority.

The study of female mass movements calls attention to female consciousness. It is possible to examine a range of motivation in the everyday lives of women that might lead them to act collectively in pursuit of goals they could not attain as individuals. Women's movements follow common patterns; they focus on consumer and peace issues and they oppose outside aggressors. Accepting and enforcing the division of labor by sex, therefore, can bring women into conflict with authorities. Women may even attack their rulers when food prices rise too high for suspicious reasons, when sexual harassment brings women's dignity into question, or when the community of women appears to be under attack.

A sense of community that emerges from shared routines binds women to one another within their class and within their neighborhoods. The degree to which women carry out their work in community settings that bring them into contact with each other also influences what and how they think. Physical proximity—such as occurs in plazas, wash houses, markets, church entries, beauty parlors, and even female jails—contributes to the power of female community. These loose networks facilitate the tight bonds that exhibit their strength in times of collective action.

Female solidarity, a manifestation of consciousness, clearly changes in relationship to improvements in women's household working conditions. Thus middle-class women who work for a wage and who pay another woman to perform their housekeeping tasks do not have to go to public laundries or markets. Unlike women in the popular classes, middle-class women have more time for other activities. But they see fewer women on a daily basis. The sense of shared work as women that contributes to female communal consciousness is diminished. The com-

3. Most recent attention to the class implications of the division of labor can be found in feminist work about the impoverishment of welfare systems under late capitalism. It considers how the work women and minority men do in the public sector resembles the service work women do in their households and communities. See Laura Balbo, "The Servicing Work of Women and the Welfare State," mimeographed (Milan: University of Milan, Department of Sociology, 1980); and Temma Kaplan, "A Marxist Analysis of Women and Capitalism," in *Women and Politics*, ed. Jane Jaquette (New York: John Wiley & Sons, 1974), pp. 257–66.

munal work women do influences the way they think, especially about government obligation to regulate necessary resources.

Gossip exchanged during shared work, for example, provides an opportunity for women to think out loud.[4] It may be the means by which women enforce the division of labor upon one another, but it is also the means by which they explore their obligation to sustain life in the midst of difficult conditions. Through gossip, women both express and find reinforcement for their thoughts, which then influence what they do.

When social disorder breaks or endangers daily routines, women of the popular classes sometimes work to reestablish them, even by attempting to seize power themselves. But it is impossible to prove their motivations, as they seldom leave evidence in their own words about the reasons for their actions. This paucity of evidence has caused many who study crowd behavior to focus on acts rather than thoughts. It has led others to associate irrationality and spontaneity with collective action. In the case of female collective action, the thesis that women of the popular classes fight to preserve the sexual division of labor invites a reductionist view that what women do determines what they think. But women reflect upon their lives; they do not act mechanistically.[5]

Still other views of consciousness, those that stress strikes and the development of unions, either leave women out or focus on female worker militance without considering the ways in which women of the popular classes either supported or rejected such efforts.[6] The advantage of relating rise in consciousness with propensity to unionize is that such analysis stresses the importance of self-generating organizations developed by the working class. But these analyses imply that unions alone are the agencies of the working class; they ignore other forms of associational life in the family, the church, workers' circles, cooperatives, and women's groups. Mass support, particularly from women, comes precisely from such organizations. Preserving the networks that connect their associations galvanizes women to act in mining and textile strikes when community survival is at stake.

4. Susan Harding studies the relationship between gossip and female gender identity in "Women and Words in a Spanish Village," in *Toward an Anthropology of Women,* ed. Rayna Reiter [Rapp] (New York: Monthly Review Press, 1975), pp. 283–308.

5. There is no totally convincing explanation of the relationship between consciousness and action. In *The German Ideology* of 1844, Karl Marx presented three contradictory notions of consciousness. The first was that "as individuals express their life, so they are. What they are therefore coincides with their production, both with *what* they produce and with *how* they produce." He amplified this argument when he said that "consciousness can never be anything else than conscious existence, and the existence of men is their actual life-process." Yet he also claimed that humans develop "ideological reflexes and echoes of this life-process." See Karl Marx, *The German Ideology* (New York: International Publishers, 1966), pp. 7, 14.

6. Among the best treatments of strikes are Michelle Perrot, *Les Ouvriers en grève: France 1871–1890,* 2 vols. (Paris: Mouton, 1974); and Rolande Trempé, *Les Mineurs de Carmaux, 1848–1914,* 2 vols. (Paris: Editions Ouvriers, 1971).

The problem associated with viewing female consciousness from the perspective of women's participation in strikes is that it does not explain why men dominate even textile strikes, though the majority of textile workers are women; and why women strike less frequently than men when the issues emphasize working conditions rather than communal survival. Such a perspective cannot explain why so many strikes in which women engage expand into mass strikes that absorb people from the larger community. Even when exploitation at work and drives for unionization precipitate struggles in which women engage, female participants broaden demands to include social reforms.

Another approach considers political parties to be the measure of political consciousness and uses the number of women in leadership positions as an index of women's consciousness. According to this view, great women in male-dominated parties contribute to the general effort and thereby demonstrate class consciousness. Leaders instill consciousness into the popular class and direct its struggles for state power. Women who do not participate in such parties but act according to female consciousness often pursue the same goals as the parties that act in their names. They simply do not follow the dictates of leaders or a previously established program. The teleological view that consciousness exists only if it leads to the seizure of power telescopes all other forms of collective action and associational life into a single "prepolitical" stage, which cannot reveal the changes that arise out of developing consciousness. Most women appear as unconscious auxiliaries who act without thought even when they do precipitate movements such as the Russian Revolution of February 1917.[7]

By viewing consciousness as the creation of party leaders, who are seldom women with female consciousness, this party-centered view underestimates mass organization and self-generating class struggle.[8] It overlooks the contributions made by militants and others who are not party members but who, like women, struggle in the larger community around social issues of food supply, health, and pacifism. The party-centered view brands all nonparty political organization—neighborhood committees, for example—as prepolitical. It cannot explain how women's consciousness develops in the course of struggle; consciousness is seen as a quantum of matter rather than a process.

There are approaches, however, that view consciousness as just another word for women's culture as it extends itself through networks. Thus far, most studies of women's culture have focused upon middle-

---

7. Paolo Spriano takes consciousness to be nearly synonymous with party formation. See Spriano, *Socialismo e classe operaia a Torino dal 1892 al 1913* (Turin: Einaudi, 1958), and *Storia del Partito Comunista Italiano*, 4 vols. (Turin: Einaudi, 1967–76).

8. For a preliminary study of communalism and its political expression, see Temma Kaplan, "Class Consciousness and Community in Nineteenth-Century Andalusia," *Political Power and Social Theory* 2 (1981): 21–57.

class women because they have left evidence of their activity in letters and in contributions to printed literature.[9] But cultural traditions, with their own networks and institutions, also enable women of the popular classes to mobilize against oppressors and work toward an alternative society, the conception of which is well articulated and widely shared. Consciousness appears as the expression of communal traditions altered in response to economic developments and political conflict. Culture, in this case, emerges as solidarity built around networks—a form of solidarity that carries out the division of labor by sex. Communal rituals, regularized processions, songs, and stories passed on through oral tradition constitute a cultural world for women of the popular classes. Consciousness emerges as women reflect upon culture and work—two aspects of the division of labor.

During periods of social mobilization, as in the mass strikes that occurred throughout the world from the 1880s through the 1920s, women's neighborhood networks galvanized into political action groups. Women participated in public meetings and began to organize their own. They demonstrated with men and without them. They transformed their physical neighborhoods, particularly the public squares, in political ways. They moved beyond their neighborhoods, where they carried out women's work, to the seats of power in other sections of the city. They took a message they had developed schematically, a message that assumed even deeper meaning as they continued to make their demands. Thus, a historically rooted analysis that moves from action to thought must work inductively and examine a variety of movements in which women participated.[10]

This paper is a study of one such movement. It describes three kinds

9. See the general debate, "Politics and Culture in Women's History: A Symposium," *Feminist Studies* 6, no. 1 (Spring 1980): 26–64, in which Ellen DuBois, Mari Jo Buhle, Temma Kaplan, Gerda Lerner, and Carroll Smith-Rosenberg refine arguments about women's culture.

10. Charles Tilly uses the phrase "collective action" to describe social movements at incipient stages, long before anyone would consider them revolutionary. See Tilly, *From Mobilization to Revolution* (Reading, Mass.: Addison-Wesley Publishing Co., 1978). The new social history has examined group behavior, radical ideology, religious commitments, and popular culture, among other topics. Its leading practitioners and their pivotal works are Natalie Z. Davis, *Culture and Society in Early Modern France* (Stanford, Calif.: Stanford University Press, 1975); Eric J. Hobsbawm, *Primitive Rebels* (New York: W. W. Norton Co., 1959), and *Labouring Men: Studies in the History of Labour*, 3d ed. (London: Weidenfeld & Nicolson, 1966); and E. P. Thompson, *The Making of the English Working Class* (New York: Vintage Books, 1963). The best argument for the use of inductive reasoning appears in the work of the Italian cultural historian, Carlo Ginzburg. See Ginzburg, *The Cheese and the Worms: The Cosmos of a Sixteenth-Century Miller* (Baltimore: Johns Hopkins University Press, 1980), "Clues: Roots of a Scientific Paradigm," *Theory and Society* 7 (1979): 273–88, and "Morelli, Freud, and Sherlock Holmes: Clues and Scientific Methods," trans. Anna Davin, *History Workshop* 9 (Spring 1980): 5–36. This branch of social history attempts to explain motivation and discover the causes of collective action.

of female mobilization in Barcelona between 1910 and 1918. The events that occurred there show that women's defense of the rights accorded them by the sexual division of labor, although fundamentally conservative, had revolutionary consequences. Conscious that their government was not aiding them to fulfill their role as nurturers, women in Barcelona and elsewhere confronted the state to demand their rights as mothers and potential mothers.

Mass strikes (actually locally rooted, popular insurrections) engaged tens of thousands of women in Spain and elsewhere until the 1920s. Following waves of strikes and rebellions that began with the Barcelona General Strike of 1902, the women's networks in the popular quarters acquired a political character. Networks devoted to preserving life by providing food, clothing, and medical care to households became instruments used to transform social life. Examination of female collective action in 1910 following a case of child molestation, in the 1913 Constancy textile strike, and in the 1918 Barcelona women's war demonstrates how women's consciousness of broader political issues emerged in their defense of rights due them according to the division of labor.

Collective Action: Barcelona, 1910

Community solidarity forms in opposition to a ruling class whose power is supported by army and police. Common antagonism, even more than shared values, welds people together, and consciousness among women that they constitute a community often appears when they share outrage. When they perceive some violation of the norms they uphold according to the sexual division of labor, they gain consciousness of themselves as a community.

Against the background of a long metallurgist and machinist strike, a scandal gripped Barcelona's female working-class community in October 1910. Male workers were fighting for the nine-hour day and against forced layoffs and unemployment. These were obviously matters of concern for their female relatives and for the few females who shared their particular trades. But there seems to have been a sexual division of concern. Male workers preoccupied themselves with the labor situation. Women were outraged by child molestation.[11]

The widow of a police inspector and mother of six children who were all ill in some way had placed the two youngest girls, aged seven and four, in a convent orphanage. On October 10, 1910, she received a letter from the Mother Superior telling her that her seven-year-old was ill and should return home. The child suffered excruciating pain in her

11. Information about this incident appeared in Barcelona's republican newspaper, *El diluvio* (October 18, 1910), pp. 8–9 (morning ed.).

genital area due to internal and external lesions. The nuns said she had a contagious disease. After some delay, the physicians from the clinic admitted that she had venereal disease, the result of rape by a strange man who had promised to bathe her.

The female community of Barcelona took the victim as their own. On October 17, a local festival on the vigil before Saint Luke's Day, large numbers of humble women, described as "mujeres del pueblo," and market women from the Borne and Barceloneta markets of the old city gathered in front of the little girl's house. They bypassed the church; few of them engaged in the anticlerical demonstrations that the men organized. What seems to have been at issue for the women was solidarity with the mother and her sick child rather than rancor at the church. Throughout the marketplaces women talked of nothing else. The female neighbors lamented with the mother as it gradually dawned on all of them that the child had been sexually molested. When the police put pressure on the mother and child, the neighbors carried on a vigil and acted as chorus. The police tried to persuade the mother that her child engaged in immoral acts outside the convent school, but the women became as outraged as the mother, who proclaimed her child's innocence. Despite the far-flung publicity and talk, however, women did not participate in demonstrations beyond the confines of their neighborhood, the physical embodiment of their communal consciousness. They did not leave their neighborhood to attack the convent as the men did. They solidified their bonds as women, as mothers, and as neighbors through talk, support, and small financial contributions to the impoverished family of the victim.

Only when the case went to court for an official inquiry, thereby moving out of the neighborhood into the public realm, did the women act politically. They planned demonstrations at the Plaza of Bishop Urquinaona (a square just down from the central Plaza of Catalonia) and at a big park in the victim's neighborhood. When the women attempted to unite as women, they alarmed authorities, and the governor banned the meeting.[12] An increasing consciousness that officials, not they, would determine how the victim and her family were treated outraged the women. The officials' response amounted to a violation of women's rights to protect children and other women. For, apart from the violence itself, sexual harassment indeed challenges women's authority over other women and over their collective sexuality, the norms of which they enforce through gossip. The use of force against any woman brings into focus contradictions between the rights women believe are theirs according to the division of labor and their inability to enforce those rights against male encroachment.

12. Ibid. (October 30, 1910), p. 15 (morning ed.).

Collective Action: Barcelona, 1913

Political consciousness among women sometimes emerges from female consciousness, as it did in 1913 in Barcelona during the Constancy textile strike. In that action women of the popular classes took their grievances to the governor rather than to their bosses. The fortunes of the textile industry and working conditions in it affected almost all the women in Barcelona's working class. In 1913, 16–18 percent of all women over fourteen in and immediately around Barcelona labored in textile factories and related industries. These figures do not include women who did garment work, embroidery, and whitework in cottage industries. The spinning and weaving factories were often workshops, and they generally employed fewer than forty women. The women worked an eleven- or twelve-hour day, although male laborers usually worked only ten hours. In 1913, the average male wage in textiles was between 3 pesetas and 3 pesetas 75 céntimos a day; the average female wage was between 1 peseta 75 céntimos and 2 pesetas 50 céntimos. Few women, however, earned more than 2 pesetas a day. A shirtmaker, who worked at home, earned about 2 pesetas 50 céntimos for a dozen men's shirts, which took her twelve hours to complete.

For many of the anonymous women who did work at home manufacturing corsets, paper boxes, artificial flowers, shoes, and garments, only a community-wide strike offered the opportunity to attack their oppressors—the jobbers who provided them with piecework. Women organized by neighborhood, not by trade. In their neighborhoods they experienced the power of networks created through years of shared tasks.[13] There was a good reason for female factory workers and women in the community, most of whom earned a living in cottage industry at some time in their life, to unite as they did in 1913.[14]

Many of these women who were mothers watched their children die in the first part of the twentieth century in Barcelona. Dead fetuses and foundlings near starvation were left on the streets of the working-class districts almost every day in the winter and spring of 1913. During that year a family of four, eating three meals a day, consumed coffee and bread in the morning, salt cod and rice at midday dinner, and potatoes and salt pork at night. On the average, this cost 1 peseta 54 céntimos a day, of which 76 céntimos went for bread alone. (The rising cost of

13. A provocative treatment of urban space and consciousness appears in Henri Lefèvre, *La Production de l'éspace* (Paris: Anthropos, 1974).

14. The only detailed description of the Constancy strike of 1913 and its social background appears in Albert Balcells, "La mujer obrera en la industria catalana durante el primer cuarto del siglo XX," *Trabajo industrial y organización obrera en la Cataluña contemporánea (1900–1936)* (Barcelona: Editorial Laia, 1974), pp. 9–121. José Elías Molins, *La obrera en Cataluña, en la ciudad y en el campo. Orientaciones sociales* (Barcelona: Imprenta Barcelonesa, 1915), reported on the oppression of women from a Catholic perspective.

living, due to the intensification of Spain's war against Moroccan guerillas and to bad grain harvests throughout the world between 1904 and 1912, contributed to high bread prices.) With the immigration of peasants to the city following the wine blight, rent in the poorest working-class districts of Barcelona had skyrocketed. The cost of an apartment in these districts was 50 céntimos a day or 14 pesetas a month. In 1910, clothing, blankets, and soap came to 25 céntimos a day, and fuel came to another 20 céntimos.[15] Women helped nurse one another's children, thereby forming tight bonds. When the government raised hopes for cheap housing, working-class women demonstrated in favor of such projects, but few new apartments were built.

In Spain, as elsewhere, housewives had sometimes organized sections of strong political parties in their villages or districts. Female anarchists did the same throughout Spain.[16] Male leftists had long recognized that women—through neighborhood organization of laundries, clinics, and food kitchens—supported men during strikes. But little had been done to win better wages for female workers. In October 1912, the Constancy Union was formed to organize unskilled men, women, and children in the textile industry. Organizers called a general meeting of Constancy on February 17, 1913, and two thousand people, mostly women, showed up. Only one woman spoke, a textile worker and socialist from Madrid named María García. Those who shared the platform and chaired the meeting were generally union activists. Speakers from the floor included anarcho-syndicalists and some socialists from a variety of trades. Few were women. The speakers discussed the need to end the unbearable workdays women suffered in factories, but they never discussed cottage industry or life in the neighborhoods; the Constancy Union, while leading the strike in the name of female workers, was as slow as contemporary historians to recognize the noneconomic

15. Molins, p. 23; and "Sucessos," *La publicidad* (Barcelona) (January 28–30, February 5, and April 21, 1913), gave just a few examples of how many foundlings and dead fetuses appeared in the streets of working-class neighborhoods. The labor situation was covered in "Vida sindicalista," *La voz del pueblo* (Tarràsa) (February 22, 1913); "La vida obrera en Barcelona," *El socialista* (Madrid) (April 18, 1913); and "Contra el trabajo nocturno," *El socialista* (July 19, 1913). A. López Baeza, "Acción social: El trabajo en Barcelona," *El socialista* (November 25, 1913), discussed the statistical unreliability of *Anuari d'estatística social de Catalunya,* edited by the Museo Social de Barcelona. Most Spanish statistics should be regarded as approximations. The prices come from the report of a seamstress who testified before the Bishop of Barcelona. Dolors Moncerdá de Maciá, a leading Catalan Catholic feminist, reported on conditions in the garment trades on March 16, 1910, in an address to a Catholic group called Popular Social Action. It was reprinted as a pamphlet, "Conferencia sobre L'Acció Católica social femenina" (Barcelona: L'Acció Católica, 1910), pp. 13–14.

16. See Temma Kaplan, "Spanish Anarchism and Women's Liberation," *Journal of Contemporary History* 7, no. 2 (1971): 101–10, and "Women and Spanish Anarchism," in *Becoming Visible: Women in European History,* ed. Renate Bridenthal and Claudia Koonz (Boston: Houghton Mifflin Co., 1977), pp. 400–421.

aspects of the strike. The organizers agreed to boycott the biggest companies in the districts of Sans, San Andrés, San Martín, Pueblo Nuevo,
and Clot, new working-class suburbs immediately contiguous to the
factories and to the old city.

There is no way to document how the women's networks grew out
of female consciousness and helped intensify that consciousness as the
situation deteriorated during the spring of 1913, but the networks had
just that effect. Women carried on support work and established food
kitchens for female strikers in the silk industry, who were striking
against piece rates and fines. The local dairies, where women bought
milk or simply congregated, served as information centers. Neighborhood women in Clot and San Andrés and San Martín targeted the
company of Fábregas y Jordá, which conveniently had factories in all
three districts. They carried on demonstrations in the main squares of
each of those neighborhoods to publicize their demands.

The summer of 1913 approached, and prices continued their steady
rise. Women, whether they worked outside the home or not, found it
difficult to put food on the table. Despite widespread unemployment in
the region—an estimated eighty thousand people were out of work—
women pushed for a strike in the textile industry.[17] Apart from demands
for a nine-hour day and an eight-hour night shift, Constancy called for a
40 percent increase in piece rates and a 25 percent hike in day wages.
From the beginning, the governor sought one group among the owners
to bargain with workers, but he was unsuccessful. The workers gave
employers one month to decide.

In the meantime, women activated their networks in the working-
class community. In a general meeting in San Martín, under the auspices
of Constancy, women from throughout the city discussed strategies to
spread their demands and to organize the strike they knew would come.
They decided to send representatives to all the major food markets to
talk with women who gathered there daily. Many of the people at this
meeting had undoubtedly been involved in the anti–Moroccan War
demonstrations of mid-June 1913, which had led to the arrest of socialist
leaders.

On the night of July 27, people from throughout the popular
neighborhoods of Barcelona and the surrounding textile towns gathered
at the Socialist House of the People, on Aragon Street in the Clot district
of Barcelona, to discuss the employers' failure to act on their demands.
More than a thousand women attended the meeting. By all accounts,
they led the demand to strike. On July 30, almost twenty thousand
workers in Barcelona, of whom thirteen thousand were women and
children, went out on strike. Countless others, including garment work-

17. "Las huelgas," *El socialista* (July 26, 1913); "De la Vaga textil. El Seny," *La campana
de Gracia* (Barcelona) (August 9, 1913).

ers, seem to have joined them in street demonstrations. As a liberal journalist explained, "The spirit of women has spoken with enough eloquence to launch the entire working population and, as in other campaigns for social justice, the women excite the exaltation. It will be necessary to negotiate with them, because they will never accept a settlement short of their goals."[18] The goals had emerged in the course of struggle; action promoted new levels of consciousness among ordinary women.

Mass activity centered in the Sans area on the southwest edge of the old city, and in the San Martín, San Andrés, Clot, and Pueblo Nuevo areas throughout the industrialized northern sections. The women of these neighborhoods were particularly suited to lead the struggle. Sans, a village absorbed into Barcelona along with San Martín and San Andrés at the end of the nineteenth century, had its own distinct plazas and daily markets. All the "new" districts were linked to the downtown area by coach and trolley lines. By the time they officially joined Barcelona, they had become popular districts of the old city. But women generally went at least once a week to one of the old markets. When the open street market of the Plaza of Padró, near the first cotton mills of the old city, moved to the covered iron-work market of San Antonio in 1879, the women of Sans and of District V of the old town met there either daily or weekly. The Plaza of Padró was contiguous to the streets where the first steam-driven factories were established in 1835. Many of the new spinning mills grew up just twenty blocks away in Sans. The young women and children of old Barcelona and Sans provided the labor power for these mills into the twentieth century. These first mills grew up in the old, settled working-class districts whose squares became rallying places during subsequent demonstrations.[19]

The women of the Sans factories began the strike by demanding that a 1900 law about night work be enforced. Their employers had locked them out. With their female neighbors, the workers began to frequent the leftist centers, but they preferred the Plaza of Catalonia, the city's civic center. Four or five hundred met in groups at the large plaza. Not all the women were factory workers, an issue that later caused much controversy among authorities. On August 5, they began what was to become a daily female community ritual. Instead of gathering at the San José market along the Ramblas, the promenade to the sea, they marched from the Plaza of Catalonia, down the Ramblas, across Columbus Way,

18. "Las huelgas de Barcelona," *El imparcial* (Madrid) (July 30·and August 1, 1913); "El conflicto del Arte Fabril en Cataluña," *El socialista* (July 31, 1913); "Contra la violencia," *El imparcial* (August 2, 1913).

19. Tomás Cabellé y Clos, *Costumbres y usos de Barcelona. Narraciones populares* (Barcelona: Casa Editorial Seguí, 1947), p. 416; Jacques Valdour, *La Vie ouvrière. L'ouvrière espagnol. Observations vécues par Jacques Valdour*, vol. 1, *Catalogne* (Paris: Arthur Roussea, 1919), pp. 21–22.

and on to the governor's office at the Plaza of the Palace.[20] It is significant that the female community went to the governor rather than to their employers to voice their general grievances and that they did not attempt to build the strength of the Constancy Union. They seem to have been conscious more of communal than of trade union goals.[21]

For four days, the women carried on the same procession, which took about fifteen minutes. They marched at three o'clock in the afternoon, just as the normal crowds swelled the Ramblas after the dinner break. It was hard to distinguish these women from other poor women who frequented the Ramblas. There was a comic element to the scene as the number of undercover police increased; the government was growing nervous about street agitation. On August 8, as the women began their daily march, police stopped them and ordered them to disperse. The women sent the men, who sometimes accompanied them, away to avoid violence. They tried to outsmart the police by regrouping along the predetermined path. Approximately two hundred women reached the governor's office, but the police prevented them from entering. The governor sent word that he had already presented their union representatives with proposals to end the strike. The committee had one day to consider the plan.[22]

Constancy called an assembly to discuss the proposals, scheduling the meeting for seven o'clock at a downtown theater the next evening, August 10. The women, instead of meeting in the Plaza of Catalonia, gathered at the theater at three o'clock that afternoon. Their assembly included women from throughout the city, not just textile workers. They remained until the night meeting began. Luis Serra, who acted as chair, announced that the meeting was an assembly of the community rather than a union meeting; all were welcome and could speak as equals. Debate about the accords ensued, but the assembly voted overwhelmingly to continue the strike. Railroad workers were among those who attended, and they agreed to discuss calling a sympathy strike. Foundry workers in the city had been agitating since mid-July, and they continued their strike. By the night of the tenth, the general strike had begun.[23]

20. "Huelga en el Arte Fabril," *Diario de Barcelona* (Barcelona) (August 5, 1913), pp. 10, 603 (night ed.).

21. "Gobierno Civil. Cuestiones obreras," *La publicidad* (April 12, 1913); "Las operarias en seda. En Barcelona. Las batallas del proletariado. Ecos de la lucha," *El socialista* (April 10, 1913); and "Las obreras triunfan," ibid. (April 11, 1913).

22. "De la Vaga textil. El Seny," *La campana de Gracia* (August 9, 1913); *Diario de Barcelona* (August 4, 1913), pp. 10, 532–34; (August 7, 1913), pp. 10, 653; (August 8, 1913), pp. 10, 712; (August 9, 1913), pp. 10, 796.

23. T. Herros, "Feminismo en actividad," *Almanaque de "Tierra y Libertad" para 1914* (Barcelona: Imprenta 'Germinal,' 1913), pp. 98–99; *Diario de Barcelona* (August 11, 1913), pp. 10, 837–38 (morning ed.); (August 12, 1913), pp. 10, 873 (morning ed.).

Through street demonstrations, women activated female consciousness about the relationship between social life and economic reforms. Some male leaders of Constancy begged them to stop their street
action, but the women answered with catcalls. On the afternoon of August 11, a massive demonstration of about fifteen hundred women and
eight hundred men gathered in the Plaza of Catalonia and marched
down the Ramblas and Columbus Way to the governor's offices. As they
approached the Plaza of the Palace, they sent a sixteen-woman committee ahead to meet the governor and explain that they would not return
to work. They retraced their steps up Columbus Way. As they reached
the Gate of Peace, below the statue of Columbus at the mouth of the
Ramblas, the police charged and tried to disperse them. Some strikers
broke through to the Ramblas of Santa Mónica and regrouped. Others
fought the police. They all reassembled at the Plaza of Catalonia.[24]

On August 12, the women began their march from the Plaza of
Catalonia an hour earlier than usual, at two o'clock. But police clearly
had orders to stop them without using direct force. The women re-
treated through the neighboring streets to Pelayo, to the Plaza of Bishop
Urquinaona, and to the Plaza of the University in order to approach the
Ramblas by the back streets. Most headed down toward the Royal Plaza
where mounted police drove them off. The police, with some experience
in riot control, blocked all streets that opened onto the Ramblas, and
drove them to the nearest back streets. The women and police spent the
afternoon battling for control of the Ramblas. Meanwhile the railroad
workers, who met nearby, voted three to one to join the battle and
extend the general strike.[25]

Throughout the rest of the strike—which was not completely over
until September 15—the women continued to hold their demonstrations
on the Ramblas. They also held daily meetings throughout the streets
and markets of the old city, especially those of Sans, San Andrés, San
Martín, Pueblo Nuevo, and Clot. The main focus shifted to the Plaza of
Spain, where the old city meets Sans. The women and the new strike
committee that had been elected at the August 10 assembly were not
cordial. Even the militant labor leaders disapproved of the unruly wom-
en's demonstrations. They opposed the tactics women used against
female scabs—cutting their hair to mark them as traitors. Female strikers
warned the scabs to think of their beauty rather than their stomachs next
time. They suggested selling the hair to wigmakers to raise money for
the food kitchens. Constancy denounced the women as a mob, and tried
to persuade them to stop demonstrating. The women assembled at the
Plaza of Spain on August 20 and attempted to march from there down

24. *Diario de Barcelona* (August 12, 1913), pp. 10, 904 (night ed.).
25. Ibid., pp. 10, 905.

the Paralelo, the main street leading from the Plaza of Spain to the harbor where the governor's offices were, to explain that they would not abide by agreements made by the strike committee. The police persuaded them not to march. The women then went to the strike committee offices on Vista Alegre 12, in the heart of District V. They insisted that it was they and not the strike leadership who spoke for the community, and that they would not agree to end the strike.[26]

The governor published the Royal Decree early. It included the sixty-hour week, or a maximum of three thousand hours of work per year in the textile industry. Women could arrange their work day, so long as they managed to work sixty hours a week. The flexibility was meant to permit them a half-day of five hours on Saturdays, so that they could catch up with their housework.[27] In the end, the Royal Decree accomplished nothing for the strikers. Employers refused to abide by a law that interfered with their right to run their factories as they chose.

Nevertheless, the strike had important positive consequences for the women of the city. The street demonstration, especially that which proceeded down the Ramblas to the governor's office, gave physical evidence of their political consciousness; it amounted to a political theory in motion. As the critic John Berger has written: "A mass demonstration can be interpreted as the symbolic capturing of a capital. . . . The demonstrators interrupt the regular life of the streets they march through or of the open spaces they fill. They 'cut off' these areas, and, not yet having the power to occupy them permanently, they transform them into a temporary stage on which they dramatise the power they still lack."[28]

Mass strikes are more than labor struggles over wages and working conditions. What distinguishes them from other strikes is that they carry struggle over into the normal activity of society. They demonstrate the power of those who produce goods and services over those who manage them. During such struggles, daily life becomes a problem that the entire community must solve. Feeding people becomes more than the responsibility of individual women. Providing medical care for wounded strikers becomes a political act. General strikes close down cafes and restaurants where unmarried male workers congregate. The Barcelona community in struggle in 1913 had to create alternative places for them. All mass strikes invariably affect living conditions because privatized "women's work" becomes a public responsibility. Women become increasingly aware of the essential though invisible services they perform. But they also learn that the power they allegedly wield in their own sphere requires struggle if it is to become theirs in practice.

26. Ibid. (August 20, 1913), pp. 11, 238 (night ed.).
27. Ibid. (August 21, 1913), pp. 11, 245 (morning ed.).
28. John Berger, "The Nature of Mass Demonstrations," *New Society* (May 23, 1968), pp. 754–55.

Collective Action: Barcelona, 1918

The effect of subsistence issues upon the development of female consciousness became only too obvious during World War I when Spain was a nonbelligerent. Inflation and war shortages afflicted civilian populations in Barcelona in 1917 and 1918 and exacerbated the normal difficulties working-class women experienced in providing food, fuel, and shelter for their communities. The inability of Spanish authorities to regulate necessities caused women to use direct action in placing social need above political order. A government that fails to guarantee women their right to provide for their communities according to the sexual division of labor cannot claim their loyalty. Experiencing reciprocity among themselves and competence in preserving life instills women with a sense of their collective right to administer everyday life, even if they must confront authority to do so.

Under normal circumstances, women's networks allocate resources ranging from goods and fuel to consciousness and culture. During wartime, food and fuel are removed from women's control to become matters of state concern. So long as authorities regulate supplies, housing, and fuel when they are in short supply or when prices rise above the limitations of normal budgets, women will accept reduced provisions and governmental regulation, as they did in England during World War I. In other situations they may oppose authority, as they did between 1917 and 1923 in Russia, Italy, and Mexico.

The women's insurrection in Barcelona began in early January 1918, during one of the coldest winters on record. Lack of gas and electric power due to coal shortages had forced more than ten thousand workers out of the factories. Bread prices had been inching upward since October 1917. Rumors circulated in early January that they would rise another 5 céntimos. The city established a price board to investigate fuel and food prices. Bakers complained that they needed price hikes to break even, and coal merchants complained that they could not stay in business if they sold coal at prices the board suggested. The shortage and high price of coal used to heat houses triggered the Barcelona movement. By January 9, more than five hundred women began to attack coal trucks throughout the five major districts of Barcelona. About a thousand women attacked a big coal retailer on Parliament Street in the old downtown section of the city and auctioned off the coal at the lowest stipulated price.[29]

The second phase of the growing movement began on January 10,

29. Here, as in the coverage of the 1913 Constancy strike, I have attempted to include accounts from as many different newspapers as possible in order to accumulate detailed evidence about the events. *La Veu de Catalunya* (Barcelona) (January 2–12, 1918); *Diario de Barcelona* (January 10, 1918), p. 459 (night ed.).

when a crowd of about two hundred housewives from the old working-class districts of Barceloneta circulated through the city to the textile factories, where the work force was largely female. They called women workers out. They carried signs that read: "Down with the high cost of living. Throw out the speculators. Women into the streets to defend ourselves against hunger! Right the wrongs! In the name of humanity, all women take to the streets." Have women the right to speak for humanity? These women believed they did, so long as they acted to preserve the division of labor, to do what women do—that is, to act female.

Gathering their forces, housewives and female workers marched down to the governor's offices at the Plaza of the Palace. As the crowd shouted, "Long live this" and "Down with that," a delegation of six young women, led by Amalia Alegre and Amparo Montoliu, climbed the stairs to present the women's grievances to the governor. They asked that coal prices be regulated along with the prices of bread, olive oil, meat, and potatoes.[30] Elsewhere in the city, women continued to attack coal yards, and the mayor dispatched police to guard coal transports. In Gracia, with its well-developed radical political culture, women marched on the slaughterhouse and tried to auction meat. Near Tetuan Plaza, where new metallurgical factories had gone up, women urged men to go on strike.[31]

In an apparent effort to reduce fuel consumption, women from the harbor districts marched on the music halls. The splendor of these palaces of leisure attracted attention throughout Europe; Barcelona had become known as the "Paris of the South." Up and down the streets of pleasure, in from the avenue of the Marquis of Duero, popularly known as the Paralelo, women with sticks broke down doors, smashed mirrors, and sometimes succeeded in persuading bar girls and cabaret dancers to join them. When necessary, as in the Eden Palace, women and owners engaged in physical fights over women's assumed right to control the use of electricity in the music halls.

Women's consciousness became apparent in the patterns of mobilization they chose and the way they defined their movement. They wandered from coal yard to coal yard to gather supporters. Throughout the six-week-long mobilization, women revealed a female urban network. They began with the lines in front of coal dealers and moved later to the San José, Santa Catalina, San Antonio, Sans, Gracia, and Clot markets. Processions and consciousness of community were closely associated in Catholic life. The secular networks of women adopted this old connection, but the markets substituted for shrines and churches along the processional route.

30. *Diario de Barcelona* (January 11, 1918), pp. 467–68 (night ed.); *El diluvio* (January 11, 1918), p. 7 (morning ed.), and (January 11, 1918), p. 2 (afternoon ed.); *La Veu de Catalunya* (January 12, 1918).

31. *Diario de Barcelona* (January 12, 1918), p. 505 (night ed.).

Naming things, including oneself, promotes consciousness. The meaning of the term "vecindaria" was transformed in the course of the uprising. The masculine "vecino" simultaneously means "inhabitant," "head of household," and "citizen." But the feminine correlate is "hembra," or simply, "female." "Vecindaria" is a village term, which denotes a member of a tightly knit community. It is as close to a kinship term as the contemporary language could muster for a civic relationship. It roughly translates as "female comrade" or "sister." The term did not transcend the period of the uprising, but its use during the uprising indicates a sense of female self-awareness and solidarity that grew throughout January and February of 1918. On January 10, in the harbor section, a woman affixed a wall poster that called upon the "vecindaria" to protest the increased cost of living.

Female neighborhood commissions sent informal delegates to one another. On January 12, two separate women's delegations visited the exasperated governor. The group, which seems to have been dominated by younger women, told the governor that they hoped "to stop all work of women in Barcelona until the authorities rolled back prices on all primary necessities."[32] Women excluded men from their daily activities, including visits to the governor.

The delegation that approached him on January 14 demanded that no food or fuel leave the province. By six o'clock that evening, another women's delegation called for a rollback on all prices to pre–World War I levels. Moderate women demurred, visited the governor's office at midnight, and claimed they would be satisfied with more reductions of food and fuel costs.[33] The governor complained that with all the visits from women's delegations, he could not get any work done. A crowd of about a thousand women had gathered at the Plaza of Catalonia and had marched to the governor's office with the regular delegation of women at their head. When the women heard the governor's exasperated comment, they grew angry. They attempted to surge up the stairs, but the police cut them off, panicked, and shot nineteen women.[34]

Female consciousness, which may lack predetermined doctrine and structure, develops rather quickly when rulers resort to force. The shooting on the stairwell seems to have marked the governor's decision to repress rather than receive delegations of women. When women attempted to hold a demonstration on the afternoon of January 15 in the Plaza of Catalonia, the police dissolved the meeting. They shot into the air as women congregated in the nearby Ramblas. They cordoned off the Royal Plaza, another public area that had become a regular gather-

32. *El diluvio* (January 13, 1918) (night ed.).

33. *Diario de Barcelona* (January 14, 1918), p. 516 (morning ed.), and p. 573 (night ed.).

34. Ibid. (January 14, 1918), pp. 573–74 (night ed.), (January 15, 1918), p. 586 (morning ed.), and pp. 621–22 (night ed.); *El diluvio* (January 15, 1918), p. 7 (morning ed.); *La hormiga de oro:Ilustración católica* (Barcelona) (January 19, 1918), p. 31.

ing place for female dissidents. The women grew angry and began to whistle and jeer. A journalist remarked that "repressive action of the police exacerbated the women's rebellious spirit."[35]

Female consciousness united housewives in the working-class districts with female factory workers. From January 15 on, most of the female workers went on strike and forced shops to close, while about seventeen hundred male laborers also refused to work.[36] Women of the popular classes continued to interrupt daily routines. They marched on El Siglo, Barcelona's first department store, where they called saleswomen to join their demonstration. By mobilizing around the sexual division of labor and the common female obligation to distribute resources through their networks, women of the popular class were united, whether or not they worked for a wage.

Women's networks had assumed leadership of a social struggle they pursued in the name of the entire female community. Their attacks on food stores throughout the city increased, as did periodic attempts by police to repress them through armed force. They adopted a committee structure, not unlike the soviets developed in Russia in 1917, to regulate attacks on grocery stores. In the process of solidifying their networks, they formulated new programs for action. These in turn brought the women to new levels of political consciousness about their rights to act according to the division of labor by sex.

Despite official opposition, thousands of Barcelona's women gathered at the Globe Theater for a public meeting. A female weaver presided. The women called for rollbacks on prices of all basic commodities to pre–World War I levels. They demanded rent reductions and lower railroad costs, which they believed were a major element in the general increase in the cost of living, and they demanded that six thousand male railroad workers be rehired. Large numbers of women participated in the general discussion.[37]

Officials in Madrid, though unfamiliar with female networks, were always wary about social strife in Barcelona. Irregular food supplies and fuel shortages, the causes of the struggle, promoted lockouts at those factories that still remained open. The governor tried to reestablish order by calling workers back to their jobs, but he lacked the cooperation of employers. Women sought to air their grievances at the governor's offices on January 21, but they were intercepted by the police.

Fearing civil war, authorities in Madrid recalled the governor. Women continued to attack commercial property in an effort to win control over food distribution. On January 25, the new military governor declared a state of siege and suspended civil rights. Nevertheless, strikes in the textile industry continued until February. Despite military

35. *El diluvio* (January 16, 1918), pp. 7–8 (morning ed.).
36. *Diario de Barcelona* (January 18, 1918), p. 769 (morning ed.).
37. *El diluvio* (January 18, 1918), p. 9 (morning ed.).

repression, women refused to acquiesce to the greed of speculators and the irregularities of the market. As late as February 15, price increases for salted cod at the Gracia market led to political mobilizations.[38]

Conclusion

The 1918 women's war reveals how closely social welfare and female consciousness are linked. The insurrection was a revolution of direct democracy in which everyday life became a political process, and through that process women's awareness grew. Disorders of war brought into view networks responsible for daily distribution of social resources. Breaks in routine raised questions about the quality of life women achieved through the networks they had formed to carry out the division of labor by sex. Women recreated these networks in political ways when merchants, governors, and states impeded their efforts to provide for their community. Women's growing familiarity with government offices, where they went to present proposals, brought them to physical spaces in the city where working-class women had seldom previously appeared. Their own movement through space, from the popular neighborhoods where housewives worked to the buildings where the men of power ruled, represented a flight in consciousness that revealed how the sexual division of labor fit into a larger political schema.

The capacity of local female networks to transcend the purposes for which they were originally formed appeared as women moved further and further away from their own neighborhoods and into the spaces occupied by the government and commercial groups. In 1910, women made forays out of their neighborhoods only at the time of the inquest to show their outrage about the molested child. Otherwise they remained in their own neighborhoods. By 1913, what appeared to be a labor struggle became a ritualized battle over social policy between the popular community, led by women, and the authorities. The street became the stage for this conflict, proof that female consciousness moves women to take radical action in defense of the division of labor.

The logic of female collective action in early twentieth-century Barcelona demonstrates an implicit language of social rights that emerges from commitment to the sexual division of labor. In defending the notion of separate rights based on separate work, women violated the selfsame notion. They beseeched and then confronted government officials in the urban plazas and offices that were symbolic of the political and commercial power men wield. Ideas about how daily life and social stability dovetail propelled women to collective action to preserve their routines. They disrupted what was left of orderly life in their neigh-

38. *El sol* (Madrid) (January 9–February 2, 1918); *Almanaque de el Diario de Barcelona para el año 1919* (Barcelona: Imprenta de Diario de Barcelona, 1918), pp. 24–25.

borhoods and, in the course of movement, shocked police and authorities. Dramatization of their place in society wakened female consciousness as well as government fears.

By taking action, women of the popular classes promoted further thought. Shared sensibilities about rights and obligations took political shape in large assemblies of women, in processions, and in visits to the governor's offices. These shared goals, largely unformed until the experience of collective action created understanding, entailed supplying social need in spite of the requirements of war and statecraft. Networks defined themselves more sharply when solidarity found expression in words like "vecindaria" and in physical contact outside familiar neighborhood centers in new physical spaces. Consciousness about the syncopation between power and social need dawned upon female activists because it reproduced in the political arena the division of labor that governed female consciousness in the community. Welfare and inflation shattered social order even in nonbelligerent countries. Preoccupied with providing for themselves and their neighbors, women assumed revolutionary positions in order to defend everyday life and the female rights they needed in order to carry out their obligations.

To understand female consciousness in the popular classes one must comprehend the degree to which working-class women uphold the sexual division of labor because it defines what women do and therefore provides a sense of who they are in society and culture. The women incorporate social expectations with their particular notions of femininity. Their attempts to act according to notions held by their class and in their historical period about what women do sometimes leads them to a reactionary stance, as in the French Vendée and in Salvador Allende's Chile. But whether they act to serve the left or the right, women's disruptive behavior in the public arena appears incompatible with stereotypes of women as docile victims. The common social thread is their consistent defense of their right to feed and protect their communities either with the support of government or without it. Their conviction grows from their acceptance of the sexual division of labor as a means of survival.

Insofar as some feminist theory stresses the need to transform society so that men as well as women attribute high value to nurturance, such theory incorporates female consciousness into feminism. The degree to which women in political parties tend to find themselves channeled toward areas of health, education, and welfare also represents unconscious recognition that women have special prerogatives and socialized skills in these areas. But the insights of female consciousness, which place life above all other political goals, have never found expression in a major state or even a political party. Consider the implications of this for political programs, especially feminism: women's most conservative self-image could potentially convince them to demand that states place life above other goals.

Although the content of the division of labor varies enormously, the process of marking the differences it entails has cultural as well as material and psychological implications. In the course of struggling to do what women in their society and class were expected to do, women in Barcelona became outlaws. To fulfill women's obligations, they rebelled against the state. Their double duty as defenders of community rights and as law-abiding citizens became a double bind, which they forcibly ruptured through direct action.

Female consciousness, though conservative, promotes a social vision embodying profoundly radical political implications that feminist theorists have scarcely recognized. To do the work society assigns them, women have pursued social rather than narrowly political goals. When it appears that the survival of the community is at stake, women activate their networks to fight anyone—left or right, male or female—whom they think interferes with their ability to preserve life as they know it.

The nature of the sexual division of labor into which women are socialized predisposes them to political arguments about social issues. Reactionary political groups have often appealed to women on these grounds. Feminists, who value women's work, seldom argue that a just society would allocate its major spiritual and material resources to the tasks all women have learned to do. Pessimistic in the face of legislation like the Family Protection Act, which threatens the rights women have won in the past decade, feminists may abandon discussion of feminism's social vision to focus on more limited political defense of past gains that are now in jeopardy. That would be a mistake. Incorporating female consciousness into feminist arguments about programs for future economic and social democracy may be the only way to keep the content and spirit of what we have won and could promote a more broadly based social movement than any feminists have previously achieved.

Department of History
University of California, Los Angeles

Palestinian Women and
Patriarchal Relations

Samira Haj

I N THIS ARTICLE, I will analyze how patriarchal relations are
both reproduced and contested in the occupied territories of the
West Bank and Gaza strip as the economic transformation experienced under Israeli occupation has forced the massive proletarianization of the Palestinian population. Contrary to developmentalist theorists who equate a market economy with economic development and
economic progress, I will argue that a market economy (or wage labor)
is not a uniformly liberating force.[1] In the case of Palestinian rural
women, proletarianization under Israeli colonization guaranteed neither
economic freedom nor the breakdown of patriarchal structures. The Israeli occupation did contribute to the contestation of traditional gender
relations by provoking a popular Palestinian national movement in
which women play a crucial role. During my field research with Palestinian women, I observed that this national movement opened channels,
especially for the younger generation of women, to challenge and undermine patriarchal structures.[2]

In discussing the Palestinian case, I also wish to contribute to the
ongoing development of an informed analysis of women's experiences
outside the Western context. The available literature on women, rich as

[handwritten marginal note: inadvertently / Israeli / occupation / helped]

I wish to thank Johanna Brenner for reading this text and offering criticisms and
suggestions. I am especially grateful to Norman Finkelstein for carefully editing it.

[1] I am also against the notion that the market economy is uniformly negative for
women. The effects of the market vary and can affect women differently depending on
the particular circumstances and conditions of women under study. To determine the
effects of the market, one has to consider class and gender, cultural and regional differences, and national and international circumstances. For further information on this issue, see Maria Mies, *Patriarchy and Accumulation on a World Scale: Women in the International Division of Labour* (London: Zed, 1986).

[2] The field research for this article was conducted over two summers in 1988 and
1989. Interviews with women activists from the villages, camps, and towns were facilitated by the various women's factions and through personal connections. The women
were interviewed first in groups and then as individuals.

[*Signs: Journal of Women in Culture and Society* 1992, vol. 17, no. 4]

it is, focuses mostly on the experiences and struggles of women in Western industrialized societies. As a result, the overarching assumptions of feminist theory have generally been Eurocentric and ethnocentric. These limitations are especially apparent in the generally reductive and ahistorical scholarship on Middle Eastern women, which commonly centers on the harem, the veil, gender segregation, arranged marriages, clitoridectomies, and other presumed pathologies of Islamic culture.

Increasingly, feminists are realizing that patriarchy and the ways in which it is reproduced can be grasped only within cultural and historical contexts. Patriarchy and the subordination of women cannot be explained simply as a universal need of men to dominate women, as somehow fixed and immutable. Rather, Western anthropologists, Marxist feminists, and feminists of the Third World[3] have demonstrated that this universal conception of male dominance tends to obscure rather than to reveal the differences in the nature of patriarchal relations by ignoring the distinct inner workings and gender organizations of particular historical and cultural forms of patriarchy.

Deniz Kandiyoti, for instance, contrasts two systems of patriarchy—the less corporate, relatively autonomous mother-child units in sub-Saharan polygyny and the more corporate, male-headed extended family households under classic patriarchy—to illustrate how different forms of male dominance provide very different contexts within which women contest, accommodate, and negotiate their relationships with men; she shows that these contexts are fluid and are susceptible to historical changes that can open up new grounds for contestation and negotiation in the relations between the genders.[4] In another study, she demonstrates how such different forms of male dominance and gender arrangements also provide radically different cultural frameworks for the internalization and reproduction of a woman's subjective identity. Taking the case of Turkish

---

[3] I agree with Chandra Mohanty that the term "Third World" has to be used critically; it is used here with qualification and for lack of a better alternative. Categories such as first and third worlds are problematic because they (*a*) imply a linear and a hierarchical interpretation of historical development, and (*b*) pose differences in essentialist, binary, and oppositional terms: e.g., the First World reads development, modernity, progress, and rationality, while the Third World reads underdevelopment, tradition, backwardness, religiosity, irrationality, etc.; Chandra Mohanty, "Under Western Eyes: Feminist Scholarship and Colonial Discourse," *Feminist Review,* no. 30 (Autumn 1988), 333–58.

[4] According to Kandiyoti, the central feature of classic patriarchy is the patrilineal/patrilocal extended household, which is commonly associated with the reproduction of the peasantry. Classic patriarchy may be found in what is considered the "patriarchal belt," which includes North Africa, the Middle East (including Turkey, Iran, and Pakistan), and India and China. As Kandiyoti points out, the implications of the patrilineal system for women are remarkably similar and involve modes of control that can transcend cultural and religious differences (e.g., Islam, Hinduism, and Confucianism). Deniz Kandiyoti, "Bargaining with Patriarchy," *Gender and Society* 2, no. 3 (September 1988): 274–89.

women, she points out that in Middle Eastern societies the cultural framework for the internalization of unequal gender relations is not the nuclear family with its gender arrangement of male breadwinner and female dependent but rather the patrilineal extended household. This household is organized through corporate control over female sexuality, links female sexual purity to male honor, and is marked by sex-segregated institutions and a particular female life cycle.[5] As Kandiyoti argues, recognizing variations in the content and form of patriarchy and gender arrangements can help us grasp more fully the different processes involved in the internalization and reproduction of women's subordination and their implications for women's consciousness and struggles.

In the predominantly agrarian Palestinian society, it is not the nuclear family but the patrilineal family complex of classic patriarchy that provides the cultural framework for internalizing and reproducing female subordination. To be sure, this form of patriarchy is less common in the urban areas, especially among middle-class professionals. But despite the nuclearization of urban families, kinship ties are still crucial for their survival as individual units; female relatives such as mother, sister, and aunt continue to serve as a backup resource to share household tasks, especially the care of preschool children.

In contrast, the common family form among the rural population is the extended household, where (in Kandiyoti's words) "corporate control over female sexuality, sex-segregated networks of sociability with their extensive support systems, and a life-cycle involving a continued valuation of women's maternal roles, combine to produce a specific experience of one's gender."[6] In this system, the female life cycle is crucial in shaping gender identity. Power is acquired through seniority and by bearing male heirs. A young bride enters her husband's household at an extreme disadvantage as she will be subordinate not only to all men in the family but also to senior women, especially the mother-in-law. She first begins to wield power only after giving birth to a son.[7] Once her sons reach manhood and take brides, her power and influence come to full bloom. Because a woman's authority derives so exclusively from the male heirs she has borne, mother-son relationships tend to be very intimate

---

[5] It is important to note that corporate patriarchy is common to many other societies outside the Western context (e.g., China and India).

[6] Deniz Kandiyoti, "Emancipated but Unliberated? Reflections on the Turkish Case," *Feminist Studies* 13, no. 2 (1987): 317–35.

[7] Young brides have little power because they enter their husband's household practically propertyless despite the fact that they are entitled to their inherited property and their dowry price under Qur'anic provision. In practice, however, women in the rural areas rarely claim their inherited property rights for fear of land fragmentation and the impoverishment of their kin and also for fear of losing the protection and support of their *hamula* in cases of marital hardship.

and indulgent, even after the son has taken a wife. Indeed, a bitter rivalry between mothers and daughters-in-law within this household is not uncommon. In sum, then, for a woman in the extended household, the crucial realities are devaluation of the daughter against the son, early marriage, membership in the male-headed household of one's spouse, and the birth of a male heir and the acquisition of power that eventually attends it.

The woman's maternal role is reinforced by the manner in which female sexuality is viewed.[8] As Kandiyoti points out, female sexuality in Middle Eastern societies is defined and controlled by the corporate body of the clan or *hamula*—that is, the extended family ranging from parents and siblings to close and distant relatives and sometimes even including other members of the community. Women are taught early that their sexuality does not belong to them, is not theirs to give or to withhold; it is the inalienable, permanent property of the *hamula*. As a result, sexual purity and lineage honor are seen as inseparable. One way to ensure lineage honor is early arranged marriage; sex segregation is another. The effects of the latter practice are twofold. On the one hand, a sex-segregated society perpetuates female subordination and leaves intact prevailing male prerogatives. On the other hand, it allows women to be less dependent on men for their self-definition. It enables women to foster and maintain their own networks of sociability outside those of men and their marriages. Leila Ahmed observes that, in contrast to Western societies "where women live dispersed and isolated among men," these networks in Middle Eastern societies offer women more control over their own world and protect them against emotional and social isolation.[9]

---

[8] Female sexuality is arguably related to Islamic ideas and practices. Fatima Mernissi, a Moroccan radical feminist, contends that Islam and Moslem patriarchal structures are accountable for "neutralizing" women and their sexuality. Moslem traditions, she contends, consider female sexuality to be in essence powerful, potent, and subversive to the Moslem social order. To protect the Moslem *Umma* (community) from *fitna* (chaos) and *Keid* (disorder), female power and female sexuality have to be contained and neutralized through legal and other institutional measures (sex segregation, veiling). See Fatima Mernissi, *Beyond the Veil* (New York: Schenkman, 1975), and Fatna Sabbah, *Woman in the Muslim Unconscious* (New York: Pergamon, 1984). In a more convincing manner, Riffat Hassan, a Moslem feminist theologian, states that it is not the Qur'an (which represents the Words of Allah) but the rigidly patriarchal Islamic tradition (including the Sunnah, the Hadith literature, and Fiqh), which interpreted the Qur'an, that contributed to the oppression of Moslem women. It is hardly surprising, Hassan goes on to argue, that "these sources on which Islamic tradition has been primarily based, have been interpreted by Moslem men who have assigned to themselves the task of defining the ontological, theological, sociological and eschatological status of Moslem women"; R. Hassan, "Woman-Man Equality in the Islamic Tradition," *Harvard Divinity Bulletin* (Harvard Divinity School) (January–May 1987), 2–4.

[9] Leila Ahmed, "Western Ethnocentrism and Perceptions of the Harem," *Feminist Studies* 8, no. 3 (Fall 1982): 528; see also Lila Abu Lughod, "A Community of Secrets:

Patriarchal relations in the Palestinian case must be further situated in the context of Israel's colonization policies and their impact on Palestinian national, class, and gender relations (including the redistribution of power). Under these particular circumstances, two crucial points need to be kept in mind: (1) Palestinian men are also exploited, oppressed, and barred from positions of power, and therefore (2) it is not just gender but gender as a social relation and its interaction with other social relations and activities that defines the perspectives, self-definitions, and mutual interactions of Palestinian men and women.

Since the occupation of 1967, Israel has consistently pursued an annexationist policy, extending Jewish control over what remains of the "land of Israel"—that is, the West Bank and Gaza Strip.[10] Through military orders, it put in place a series of regulations that governed every aspect of the social, economic, and political lives of the newly disenfranchised Palestinian population. Israel confiscated much of the territories' resources, especially land and water. So-called security zones were established over vast areas of land that Palestinians could no longer use. Restrictions were put on water consumption and on the cultivation of crops. Palestinian agriculture naturally suffered, especially the output of certain key crops such as citrus. Restrictions were also put on local manufacturing, trade, commercial transactions, and loans. Local employment opportunities dried up as the destruction of the indigenous economy proceeded apace.[11]

These regulations led inextricably to the distortion and destruction of the agricultural and manufacturing sectors. Under Jordanian rule, the West Bank economy was largely agrarian, with a diversity of crops under cultivation. Over 50 percent of the labor force was employed in the agricultural sector. Between 1968 and 1983, agricultural production fell from 36.3 percent to 26.9 percent of the GDP, forcing a large portion of the peasantry out of agriculture and into wage labor. According to one source, employment in agriculture as a percentage of total employment declined from 44.8 percent in 1969 to 18.7 percent in 1985 in the West Bank, and from 33.1 percent to 9.7 percent in Gaza. Industrial produc-

---

The Separate World of Bedouin Women," *Signs: Journal of Women in Culture and Society* 10, no. 4 (1985): 637–57; and C. Makhlouf-Obermeyer, *Changing Veils: A Study of Women in South Arabia* (Austin: University of Texas Press, 1979).

[10] The West Bank includes East Jerusalem, which was openly annexed by Israel in 1980. Though I am not discussing the Golan Heights in this article, the Golan was also incorporated into the "land of Israel" in 1981.

[11] For the best overview of the Palestinian economy under occupation, see George Abed, ed., *Palestinian Economy: Studies in Development under Perpetual Occupation* (London: Routledge, 1988); and Meron Benvenisti, *The West Bank Handbook: A Political Lexicon* (Jerusalem: Jerusalem Post Press, 1986).

tion also declined from 8.3 percent in 1968 to 6.9 percent of the GDP in 1983.[12] The exploitation of the occupied territories can be seen in other contexts as well: high taxes without services; the deduction of social service taxes from the income of the West Bank and Gaza workers without the provision of these services; and high returns on Israeli investments there, especially from subcontracting firms in garment and construction industries.

Meron Benvenisti has concluded that Israeli policies have dealt a death blow to the economic viability of the Palestinians as a community. The West Bank and Gaza are now simply a captured market for Israeli products and a source of cheap Palestinian labor for the Israeli economy. The occupied territories are, after the United States, Israel's second most important export market with "export sales of about $600 million per year according to the military government."[13]

There are over 120,000 Palestinians working inside Israel, bringing home a sizable proportion (roughly 30 percent) of the West Bank/Gaza national income. A labor survey revealed that, in the construction industry, there is a 50–60 percent differential in hourly wages between Palestinians and Israeli Jewish workers with the same skills.[14] Day workers are typically forced to leave their villages and camps in the occupied territories in the early hours of the morning and journey to the closest Israeli town, where contractors bid for their labor. Israelis themselves refer to this informal arrangement as the *shuk avadim,* the slave market. For example, Abu Muhammad, who is fifty years old, lives in a small village on the main road, al-Sawiya. Five days each week, he leaves home around 3 A.M. and returns around 5 P.M. Usually, he does construction work in the Bnei Brak area near Ramat Gan in Israel, earning on the average 4 JDs ($12) per day. Abu Fatah is a seventeen-year-old Palestinian day laborer from the village of Sa'air, near Hebron. He leaves his home at 4:30 every morning except Saturday. In Jerusalem, he joins hundreds of other West Bank workers waiting at the city's Musrara quarter, where Israeli employers or contractors drive by to pick up however many workers they need that day.[15] Such capriciousness and long hours are typical of the experience of Palestinian males dependent upon Israeli employment.

As is often the case, however, rural Palestinian women make out the worst in the system of labor exploitation in the occupied territories. Female labor has always served the important function for capital accu-

[12] Abed, ed., 85.

[13] Noam Chomsky, *The Fateful Triangle* (Boston: West End Press, 1983), 46.

[14] This survey was conducted by the Histadrut in 1982 and published in *Ha'aretz* (August 17, 1982).

[15] Joost Hiltermann, "Before the Uprising: The Organization and Mobilization of Palestinian Workers and Women in the Israeli-occupied West Bank and Gaza Strip" (Ph.D. diss., University of California, Santa Cruz, 1988), 176–80.

mulation of depressing wages and increasing profits. In the Palestinian instance, the labor market has incorporated the traditional structures and ideology of patriarchy for its own ends. In a word, capitalism has not eroded but, rather, has reinforced patriarchy.[16]

Palestinian women wage workers are concentrated in seasonal agriculture (mainly tobacco and citrus harvests), textiles, and food processing. They constitute an estimated 12 percent of the total Palestinian Arab labor force working for Israel. The exact percentage is unknown because these women are generally undocumented, both in Israel and in the occupied territories. According to a female trade unionist interviewed by Joost Hiltermann, "Women find work usually through social contacts in their village, not through the Israeli Labor Exchange. Many of them do not have a permit." Because of cultural restrictions on female mobility, women agricultural workers are picked up either by a contractor in a van or by Israeli Egged or Leshka buses. They leave around five or six in the morning and return twelve hours later. The hours spent in transportation are not included in their monthly wage, which is only about 30–40 dinars ($90–$100).[17]

Because the Palestinian woman wage laborer is undocumented and is dependent on social contacts, she has very little leverage in the labor market. Often either her father or brother serves as the contracting agent. In Gaza, for instance, "fathers and brothers tend to arrange for daughters or sisters to be picked up by an Arab agent [*simsar*], who then takes them to work in more distant factories like processing industries and seasonal food industries like citrus and ice-cream packaging."[18] Consequently, the female wage laborer has little or no control over her income and continues to be dominated by the male members of her family.

The age at which women join the labor force is closely connected to their reproductive cycle. Women working outside the home (in seasonal agricultural or in unskilled industrial labor) are usually single and between the ages of fifteen and twenty-five or past the age of forty. Young married women with child care responsibilities form part of the

---

[16] The patrilineage both totally appropriates women's labor and renders their work and contribution to production invisible. The institution of sex segregation and other status symbols such as veiling further reinforce women's subordination and their economic dependence on men. The observance of restrictive practices is such a crucial element in the reproduction of family status that women will resist breaking the rules even when it means further economic hardship. As Kandiyoti points out, women under classical patriarchy often "adhere as far and as long as they possibly can to rules that result in the unfailing devaluation of their labor. The cyclical fluctuations of their power position, combined with status consideration, result in their active participation in their own subordination"; Kandiyoti, "Bargaining with Patriarchy," esp. 280–82.

[17] Hiltermann, 132.

[18] Susan Rockwell, "Palestinian Women Workers in the Israeli Occupied Gaza Strip," *Journal of Palestine Studies* 14, no. 2 (1985): 115–36, esp. 123.

*young mothers
do home
slave labor*

"invisible"—that is, unaccounted for—labor force, as they work at home for sewing and embroidery firms that subcontract out at substandard wages. Economic need has forced most of these women to join the labor force. Such is the case, for example, of Amina and her sisters. Amina is a forty-two-year-old single woman from the village of Ya'bud who lives with her widowed mother and works inside Israel a few months each year during the walnut harvest. Her two sisters, Khadija and Aisha, were recruited through Amina. Khadija, forty-five years old, is married and has no children. Aisha is fifty-seven and a widow. Hired by a Palestinian contractor, they work eight hours each day under the supervision of an Israeli manager. They earn between one half and one dinar ($1.3 and $2.5) a day. In contrast, the Palestinian contractor makes forty dinar on each woman he contracts and the Israeli supervisor even more.[19]

The most exploitative conditions take place in the garment industry, where national, class, and gender oppression combine to produce a flagrantly oppressive working environment. Globally, subcontracting through small local firms or piecework at home allows for very low labor costs and flexibility of production. In the Israeli case, garment firms are able to reduce production costs and extract high profit rates by exploiting Palestinian female domestic labor, thus saving on capital investment and on the social and health benefit payments required under Israeli labor law.[20] The Palestinian agent is one more beneficiary of this system of exploitation of the pauperized rural Palestinian population.

The garment industry in the West Bank is organized into small workshops that hire no more than twenty workers at a time. A UNIDO study conducted in 1984 estimated that sewing and garment workshops constitute 13.4 percent of the total industrial sector and employ about 20.5 percent of the total labor force. In Tulkarem (a West Bank town), more than 65.4 percent of the labor force is employed by this industry; in Nablus (the largest West Bank city), the percentage is 29.9.[21]

Such exploitation by Israeli subcontractors compels the small indigenous Palestinian manufacturers to follow suit. For example, Israeli firms subcontract to small and medium Palestinian workshops without written contracts, which means substandard wages for workers. To survive in this highly competitive market, the small local firms must also keep

[19] Hiltermann, 205–7.
[20] For more details, see Brian Van Arkadi, *Benefits and Burdens: A Report on the West Bank and Gaza Strip Economies since 1967* (Washington, D.C., and New York: Carnegie Endowment for International Peace, 1977); and Hillel Frisch, *Stagnation and Frontier: Arab and Jewish Industry in the West Bank* (Jerusalem: West Bank Data Base Project, 1983).
[21] United Nations International Development Organization, *Survey of Manufacturing Industry in the West Bank and Gaza* (New York: United Nations, 1981).

wages low by hiring female labor. According to a study by Flavia Pesa, the average monthly wage of a woman in these workshops rarely exceeds 45 dinars ($135), as compared to a Palestinian man working in Israel at the same job who earns 110 dinars ($300).[22]

Here as elsewhere, subcontracting is closely related to the feminization of the labor force. Palestinian rural women, as the cheapest form of labor available in the territories, have been targeted for jobs in the garment industry. Once again, it is difficult to guess the number of women so employed because they are contracted not just in workshops scattered all over the camps, villages, and towns, but at home as well. As Flavia Pesa concludes, "It is impossible to know or even estimate how many Palestinian women are involved in this form of home labor. The women's only contact is with the Arab hustler who delivers the cut material, picks up the work, sets pay rates, and is the middleman with the Tel Aviv manufacturers. His cut is anywhere between 10–50 percent of the amount of the subcontract."[23] One study found that women constituted 95 percent of the labor force employed in this industry. Perhaps as much as half of the West Bank female labor force is employed in it.[24] An employer I interviewed estimated that 25,000 to 30,000 women are employed in the garment industry in Gaza alone.

Research shows that employees in these firms come from the rural areas and represent the poorest strata of Palestinian society—including the dispossessed, declassed peasantry living in refugee camps. Annelies Moors, who has studied the Nablus garment industry, observes that "in the Jordanian period, girls from middle class families went to learn sewing from skilled female tailors, while girls from very poor families would more likely work as cleaners, or in the countryside as agricultural laborers. . . . [Now, however,] sewing has increasingly become a non-urban trade. . . . At present most of the women employed in the [ready-to-wear] workshops in Nablus are from outside the city."[25] Women are especially vulnerable to exploitation, not only because of their relative poverty but also because of the value Palestinian society attaches to female sexual purity and the practice of sex segregation.[26] For example, employers

[22] Flavia Pesa, "Women's Work and Women's Pay: Super Exploitation in the Sewing Industry," *Al-Fajr Jerusalem Palestinian Weekly* (April 19, 1985).

[23] Ibid.

[24] Hiltermann, 133.

[25] Annelies Moors, "Restructuring and Gender Garment Production in Nablus," occasional paper, no. 3 (Middle East Research Associates, Amsterdam, 1989), 14–15.

[26] The circumstances and conditions of Palestinian home workers remind me of Maria Mies's study of the Indian women lace makers of Narsapur, where lace making offered these women the opportunity to combine their roles as housewives and workers. The prevailing ideology that they are respectable housewives using their leisure time in a profitable manner makes these women particularly vulnerable to exploitation. Rather than resist such rules and status symbols, these women abide by them even when it re-

supply daily transportation for the women because their virtue might be compromised. In practice, this provision gives employers extra leverage over their female workers. They can restrict the mobility of female workers, guaranteeing their abstention from trade union activity and controlling the workers' arrival and departure times, thus enabling employers to prolong working hours. This is apparently a common practice. There are reports of women working up to fourteen hours a day without overtime pay.[27]

Work conditions in this sector are notorious. Women are constantly under pressure to increase production through speed-up work, long hours, and no breaks. Employees are closely supervised and work in complete isolation from one another. A field report conducted by a women's committee in the Ramallah district revealed that the majority of women in this sector work without a contract, and only half of them receive the benefits entitled to them by law (e.g., paid sick leave, paid vacation, maternity leave, and compensation). Very few have been unionized.[28]

The informal method of recruitment is another mechanism used to exploit and control female workers. Women workers are not hired as free agents or through a formal arrangement as with a labor exchange office. Rather, they are hired informally through social contacts, usually female friends and relatives employed in these workshops. Some are even relatives of the Palestinian employers. In most of the cases, the employer establishes an informal relationship with the family of the worker and promises to protect and take care of her. In effect, he assumes the paternalistic and authoritarian role of a patriarch. Consequently, patriarchal relations at home and in the workplace are mutually reinforcing. In the words of Seniora, this form of "employment combined with the existence of an informal social relationship between the employer and the workers' heads of families strengthens the employers' hold over the workforce. At the slightest disobedience or misbehavior, employers will directly inform the worker's male supporters. . . . Women are forced by their families to behave, since their misbehavior will bring disrespect to their families."[29] Thus, the capitalist market in the occupied territories has not acted as the progressive force it is often touted to be for women. Just the contrary, the capitalist market has made use of patriarchal relations to depress female wages and control the female labor force.

---

sults in economic hardships and the devaluation of their labor. Maria Mies, *The Lace Makers of Narsapur* (London: Zed, 1982).

[27] Randa Seniora, "Palestinian Labour in a Dependent Economy: The Case of Women in the Sub-contracting Clothing Industry in the West Bank" (M.A. thesis, American University of Cairo, 1987), 83–91.

[28] Hiltermann, 134.

[29] Seniora, 83.

Israeli occupying forces also use sexuality as a weapon of political intimidation and domination. As stated earlier, sexuality in Arab cultures is ascribed to the woman by the *hamula* or clan; violation of sexual mores is considered not only a personal disgrace but also a disgrace upon the *hamula's* honor. Cognizant of the powerful cultural implications of female sexuality for Palestinians, the Israelis have not shied away from using it as a tool of intimidation. Since the *Intifada,* women's committees as well as human rights activists (both Israeli and Palestinian) have been recording cases of sexual harassment and attempted rapes by Israeli soldiers and interrogators intended to pressure and neutralize Palestinian activists. As of last summer, there had been an alarming number of reports of "fallen women" who had turned collaborators; women who had been sexually assaulted were then threatened with exposure, forcing them to cooperate with and report to Israeli intelligence on political activists in their communities.

To be sure, this form of intimidation was practiced since the occupation and before the *Intifada* of 1988. As Sayigh pointed out in a study done in the early 1980s, "Where girls and women are concerned they are vulnerable as females, not just as Palestinians, because the Israeli reading of Arab psychology leads to sexual aggression or threat being used against them as a means of intimidating the population as a whole. Apart from what women have suffered on their account as activists, perhaps three times as many have been tortured or threatened to put pressure on husbands, brothers or sons. Many threats were made against their sisters. Rasmiyeh Odeh's father was forcibly involved in his daughter's sexual violation in a complex attempt to shame both of them. All possible combinations of family-bound male/female feelings—love, fear, shame, protectiveness—are employed to shock and break down resistance."[30] Sayigh noted, however, that even then the increasing politicization of women was helping to challenge these cultural norms and to neutralize Israel's strategy. The most striking example is the recent adoption by young women activists of the slogan *al-ard qabla al-'ard* ("land before honor"), which reverses the traditional popular slogan of "honor before land."

As one would expect, women's politicization in the national struggle could not but include a struggle against patriarchal authority and cultural modes of female control. Although, as we shall see presently, women have been mobilized into the national struggle through their traditional roles, the process of their politicization has entailed a genuine challenge to patriarchal structures. The contestation of patriarchal authority, how-

---

[30] Rosemary Sayigh, "Encounters with Palestinian Women under Occupation," *Journal of Palestine Studies* 10, no. 4 (Summer 1981): 3–26, esp. 7.

ever, has been generational in form and is closely related to the cyclical nature of women's relative power position in the household.

As in the case of reproduction of patriarchal structures, contestation of gender roles must also be considered within the framework of the overarching power structures. The family cannot be considered, in all times and all places, as just a site of female oppression. In the context of Israeli occupation, the Palestinian family household has come to play two contradictory roles: a site of oppression (as I observed earlier) and a source of support and resistance. In the face of a larger insecure and dehumanizing world, it is only natural that the family will come to provide security, dignity, and hope. It is also inclined to become the vehicle for political mobilization and resistance, especially for women. Palestinian women were initially politicized through their roles in the family—as mothers, protectors, and nurturers. Yet, as we shall see, they learned through their struggle that gender and national struggles are inseparable and that patriarchal structures must be challenged.

The participation of women in the struggle has been a central force in sustaining the Palestinian *Intifada.* Their involvement has included not only middle-class or urban women but also ordinary working rural women from the most destitute classes. In their struggle to end the Israeli occupation, Palestinian women have not shied away from joining street demonstrations, hurling stones and shouting at Israeli soldiers, or using their bodies as barricades to block the beatings and to stop the arrests of their children. Still, it would be wrong to assume that the role of Palestinian women has been limited to confrontations and to the protection of their children and families from the brutality of the Israeli forces. They also have played an essential and vital part in the popular and neighborhood support committees that effectively replaced the institutions of civil administration in the towns, villages, and camps.

The *Intifada,* while sharing certain features of national liberation struggles in general, is in many ways unique. In my view, it is these differences that account for its success in mobilizing women. Generally speaking, armed liberation struggles (such as the FLN in Algeria) have tended to reinforce rather than challenge patriarchal structures and traditional relations of domination. As armed freedom-fighting organizations, these movements have been inclined to draw on one segment of the society—young men. Even in, say, the Nicaraguan case, where women were recruited into the ranks of the Sandinistas and relations between male and female fighters were somewhat equal, the scale of female recruitment remained very modest, and the experiences of women fighters had little impact on the masses of women in the society at large. The success of armed struggle also is dependent on maintaining structures of authority and hierarchy within the fighting ranks. Traditional power relations—including patriarchal relations—tend, then, to be upheld, not undermined. This is not to deny the importance of armed struggle—particularly in the final stages of the revolution—but, rather, to emphasize that national liberation struggles have typically tended to rely on military, not civilian, mobilization.

The *Intifada,* as an unarmed liberation struggle, depends exclusively on its ability to reach out and mobilize all segments of society—rural and urban, men and women, young and old, regardless of class or social background. Three related points are worth stressing. The social and economic dislocation of the Israeli occupation undermined the traditional leadership that was closely connected with the Jordanian regime and the landed class. Israel's repressive policies toward Palestinian nationalists and activists—such as deportations and imprisonment—also served to eliminate and silence most of the older, traditional, political leadership. Thus, in many ways, Israel's policies have backfired because they created the conditions for the emergence of a much younger leadership organically connected to its popular roots. This factor has helped to democratize the movement: the nonhierarchical, decentralized character of the *Intifada* also was preceded by a grass-roots movement. Under occupation, the various political factions within the Palestinian movement could not openly organize, especially on the central issue of national liberation. Political militants were compelled to focus their attention on "bread and butter" issues. From the mid-seventies, political activists began to organize around the daily social, economic, and legal problems that Palestinians encountered under occupation. By making health, education, trade unions, and the violation of human rights their primary concerns, the political factions were much more successful in reaching out to segments of the Palestinian society that would have been otherwise unreachable, including women.

As one type of grass-roots organization, women's committees set their tasks as mobilizing women around issues of family and work: creating and maintaining day-care centers, after-school activities, clinics and health education programs, literacy classes, and vocational training; unionizing women workers; and establishing women's industrial collectives. As a result, they came into contact with and drew in women from remote towns, villages, and camps.[31] From their experiences in these grass-roots movements, women activists gradually became aware of

[31] Charitable or social welfare organizations are the older women's organizations run primarily by middle-class women who are older and socially well connected. These organizations, based on volunteer work, provide a wide range of services, such as embroidery cooperatives, orphanages, literary classes, etc. These organizations include the Arab Orphan's Society of Tulkarem (founded in 1961), the Arab Women's union of al Bireh (1955), Hebron Women's Charitable Organization (1956), Dar al-Tifl al-Arabi (1949), and In'ash al-Usra (1965), among others.

the difficulty of separating the national struggle from the women's struggle. By the testimony of their activists, it was not their original intention to establish a separate women's movement with its own infrastructure. Their goal was—like that of Palestinian women activists in Lebanon and other Arab countries—to build a women's movement inside the existing institutions. As one of these activists recalls, "We started building a women's movement in 1978. . . . Our purpose was to create a new mass-based movement as an alternative to the charitable societies, which have a limited membership: we were filling a gap . . . our aim was to create leaders everywhere and [build] an integrated national movement. . . . Our aim was not to replace trade unions but to organize women inside the trade unions. But there was opposition from inside the unions. So we set up a Tailoring [garment] Workers Union in Ramallah. . . . We began to initiate them in trade union organizing. But we found that they also face social oppression in the family."[32]

Since the 1980s, Palestinian women have begun to articulate the idea of the inseparability of the two struggles and the importance of organizing women not only around national rights but also around issues of family and work. For example, the Union of Palestinian Women's Committees (PWC) has emphasized the need to struggle against social as well as national oppression. In an interview, one PWC activist from Hebron explained the position of her committee as follows: "We place the women's question before the national question. We focus all our activities on bringing women out of their homes to make them more self confident and independent. Once they believe in themselves, they will know that they can become leaders in any field they choose . . . if a woman first gains her own rights by breaking down her internal barriers—in her house and then in society at large, only then will she be able to deal with the occupation. It depends completely on the woman herself, not her father or brothers. A woman cannot fight the occupation if she is not even convinced that she has rights, for example, the right to leave her house, for whatever reason."[33] Likewise, the Union of Women's Work Committees (UWWC) (later to be called Federation of Palestinian Women's Actions Committees) has also stressed the importance of organizing housewives and women wage workers as they constitute the majority of women in the occupied territories and face triple oppression: as workers, as women, and as Palestinians. One of the founders of the UWWC, a union activist, observed that "the struggle for our rights as workers and as women should start now or we'll end up with another bourgeois state

[32] Hiltermann, 429–30.
[33] Ibid., 486–87.

and another kind of regime that will oppress women and the working class. It all has to go side by side."[34]

Thus the feminist consciousness of these Palestinian women was in fact the outcome of their own experiences as activists. Once they began to focus on women's rights, they came to realize the importance of developing a separate women's movement. For example, the Palestinian Working Women's Committee was established after several of their founding members split from the Nablus Seamsters Union to create their own independent unit in 1981. According to these women, the split was the result of their inability to work in a union controlled by men who had no understanding of and were unwilling to take into account the particular problems facing women workers at home and at work. Their ambivalence toward a male-governed union, combined with their direct experiences with women workers, drove these women activists to develop their own independent union and independent committee.[35]

Nonetheless, the process of political participation of women has differed according to class status, geographical location, and age. Most interesting is the difference in the politicization process between the young and the old. The generational distinction, in my view, is closely related to the female life cycle and the woman's power position within the household. The entry of the older generation of activists into the political struggle is a natural extension of their relatively powerful status as mothers within the extended family household, earned through seniority and bearing sons. Since they are part of the power structure, their political mobilization does not lead them to question patriarchal relations or the prevailing forms of gender inequalities. Simply put, they have an investment in protecting patriarchal relations. One such activist, Um Khalil, the founder of one of the largest charitable societies in the Territories, In'ash al-Usra (The Family Rehabilitation Society in al-Bireh), is known among

---

[34] Ibid., 478.

[35] It is perhaps fair to say that women activists in the occupied territories have developed a much higher level of feminist consciousness than Palestinian women activists elsewhere. Women militants in Lebanon could not and did not challenge gender relations in the same way. They did not form an autonomous women's movement nor raise the issue of the inseparability of the two struggles. This is not to say that Palestinian activists in Lebanon have not organized around women's concerns but that these issues were almost always subordinated to the larger question—the national struggle. In the words of Julie Peteet, who studies Palestinian women in Lebanon, "Women's activism may have awakened the stirrings of a feminist consciousness. . . . Yet this newly awakened consciousness did not prompt the formation of a women's movement ready to confront patriarchy. The level of crisis, the protracted nature of the national struggle, and the communal bases of resistance clearly militated against such trends. This coincided with a history of national movements incorporating the women's movement"; Julie Peteet, "No Going Back: Women and the Palestinian Movement," *Middle East Report,* no. 138 (January–February 1986), 20–24.

young activists to be "conservative" on the question of women and feminism. Often called a matriarch, she is "still loved because she symbolizes defiance to the occupation. Her social work has spilled over into demonstrations and sit-ins; she has been imprisoned six times." She is not a feminist, however, but known among young women activists as an "enforcer" of patriarchal authority. She has said, for instance, that "when a girl begins to earn money she may begin to impose conditions on her family. We don't encourage such a spirit in our girls. To open the door too wide would cause a bad reaction."[36]

The case is quite different among the younger generation of women activists. The *Intifada* has marked off a new period in their political and social development. (This is true of the younger men as well.) Their politicization has led them to defy not just Israeli occupation but traditional authority and patriarchal structures. The stories of two rural women, W. and M., show how in the process of their politicization they learned to question and defy their ascribed traditional roles. W. is the wife of the *mukhtar* (head) in the village of H. outside the city of Jerusalem. The village of H. exemplifies the general conditions in agriculture. Most of its population, including the *mukhtar*'s family, has been forced to abandon agriculture to work as day laborers, building Jewish settlements on the confiscated lands in and around the village. W. had only finished elementary grade school when she was married off to the *mukhtar*. Since she could not bear children, the *mukhtar* took a second wife. W. was recruited along with other women from the same village by one of the women's committees to start a preschool nursery for village children. After six months' training in the Early Childhood Resource Center's outreach program, W. began her new life as an activist and a teacher's aid. In the process, W. earned freedom of mobility, control over her income, and legitimacy within the household. Her husband, threatened by her newly acquired freedom, tried to force her to quit her job but she, in turn, threatened to divorce him. M. is a young widow, heading a separate household and raising four children alone. Since her father-in-law took over her late husband's share of the land, she has been forced to earn a meager income by contracting work at home, mainly doing embroidery. Today she is politically active and is part of a women's food-processing collective in the village of Sa'air. She has freedom of mobility, but she has lost her property. She is considering a court challenge to her father-in-law's right to the land. It is clear from these examples that these women, through their experiences within the women's

---

[36] Sayigh, 12.

movement, came to defy in their own ways patriarchal authority and unequal gender relations.

Generational and gender-related conflicts are common features of the struggle today. As women activists predicted, once the young learn to stand up against the powerful Israeli state, its laws, and its organized army, they become less afraid to challenge the authority of their parents, brothers, husbands, and other corporate modes of control. There are many cases of young women from the refugee camps and villages who, through the politicizing process of the *Intifada,* gained rights previously forbidden to them, including interaction with men, unrestricted mobility, and employment outside the home. They all see their defiance of traditional relations as resulting from their mobilization as political subjects. Of course, the presence of women's committees with experience in organizing women around specific women's issues is an important factor in encouraging young women activists to question traditional prescriptions.[37] It is not uncommon, for example, for women committees to intervene in support of active women who are facing difficulties at home. What makes the defiance of patriarchal structures more viable is the fact that it is not carried out as an individual act but in the context of a movement. As part of the *Intifada,* it is much easier to question the marriage of young girls and dowry or the bride price. In addition, activists are championing the legitimate rights of women, especially in regard to property rights (e.g., legal title to the land) and personal rights (e.g., the right to divorce).

But can we conclude from all this that the Palestinian women's movement is a "feminist" movement? Clearly, the Palestinian women's movement is not just "activating" women; it is also taking on certain gender relations. It is a movement that encourages self-organization and the empowerment of women. Most important, it is not led by men. Thus, although Palestinian women activists do not challenge unequal gender

---

[37] A Palestinian female journalist, Majeda al-Batash, reports in *Ha'aretz* (December 5, 1989) on the erosion of patriarchal relations during the *Intifada.* She reports that women, neighborhood, and youth committees have been able to usurp authority, both formal and informal. They have, e.g., replaced local police, municipalities, and even the Qadis in the Islamic courts on the formal level and the sheikhs and the elders on the informal level. In cases of theft, damage to property, and other criminal acts, it is the members of the local committees who rule on these issues. On the impact of the *Intifada* on the Arab family, she says, "Once, when a woman would complain to the sheikhs and the village elders that she does not want to live with her husband in her mother-in-law's home, they would try to convince her not to dismantle the extended family framework. The ruling of the young committees is different: they do not adhere at any price to the traditional patterns of the extended family and there are many cases in which they will advise the husband and wife to move into their own home—and will assist them financially for this purpose."

relations in the same manner or use the same rhetoric as Western feminists, they are challenging male domination both in the family and in society at large. In this central sense, the Palestinian women's movement is a feminist movement.

To make this claim, however, is to remind us once again of the importance of analyzing family and gender relations inside their cultural and historical contexts and recognizing the impact of other structures of domination on women's political consciousness and self-organization. Some debates that have so occupied Western feminism—for instance over separatist strategy—are unimaginable in the context of the national liberation struggle. Some theoretical positions—for example, the family as the principal site of women's oppression—have no resonance among women whose families and communities are under assault by an occupying power. The case of the Palestinian women's movement underscores many of the critiques of Western feminist analysis put forward by those non-Western feminists and feminist women of color writing within Western industrial societies who have pointed to the inadequacy of defining the female subject exclusively in terms of gender identity, bypassing class and ethnic identities. The Palestinian case also points to the limitations of a feminist theory built around an assumed male breadwinner/dependent female nuclear family.[38] As many feminists of color have pointed out, this model has little relevance to the experiences and the struggles of women of color and working-class women, forced to join the labor market early either as primary breadwinners in single-headed households or as part-timers to subsidize family income.[39] The example of the Palestinian women's movement offers a direction for a more diversified feminist theory and for feminist movements that incorporate the experiences of all women.

Kevorkian Center
New York University

---

[38] See Michèle Barrett, *Women's Oppression Today,* rev. ed. (London: Verso, 1989); Henrietta Moore, *Feminism and Anthropology* (Minneapolis: University of Minnesota Press, 1988); Jane Flax, "Postmodernism and Gender Relations in Feminist Theory," in *Feminism/Postmodernism,* ed. Nancy Fraser and Linda J. Nicholson (New York and London: Routledge, 1990).

[39] Barbara Laslett and Johanna Brenner, "Gender and Social Reproduction: Historical Perspective," *Annual Review of Sociology* 15 (1989): 381–404; Evelyn Glenn, "Racial Ethnic Women's Labor: The Intersection of Race, Gender and Class Oppression," *Review of Radical Political Economy* 17, no. 3 (1985): 86–108; Valerie Amos and Praibha Parmar, "Challenging Imperial Feminism," *Feminist Review,* no. 17 (Autumn 1984).

Hegemonic Relations and Gender Resistance: The New Veiling as Accommodating Protest in Cairo

Arlene Elowe MacLeod

Power invests [the dominated], passes through them and with the help of them, relying on them just as they, in their struggle against power, rely on the hold it exerts on them. [MICHEL FOUCAULT][1]

THE PERSISTENCE OF women's subordination throughout history and across many cultures presents a difficult puzzle; although women are clearly assertive actors who struggle for better conditions for themselves and for their families, their efforts often seem to produce limited or ephemeral results. The recent widening of opportunities for some women is unusual, and when placed in historical and cross-cultural perspective, its future seems uncertain.[2] In

I am pleased to acknowledge the helpful advice of Jim Scott, Fred Shorter, Barbara Ibrahim, Homa Hoodfar, Diane Singerman, and Bruce MacLeod on earlier manifestations of the ideas expressed in this article. I also thank the *Signs* editors and reviewers for their thorough and challenging comments. Earlier versions of this article were presented at the Northeastern Political Science Association meeting in 1986 and at the National Women's Studies Association meeting in 1989; I would like to thank panelists and discussants for their helpful thoughts as well. The students of my "Power and Protest" seminar criticized many of the ideas presented here; I thank them for their comments and also thank Kankana Das and Jason Baker for help in producing this manuscript. Finally, I gratefully acknowledge the financial support of the American Research Center in Cairo, which administered my USIA grant in 1983–84, and Bates College for providing travel funds to Cairo in 1988. My greatest debt is to the women who are the subjects of this study; they have my deepest respect and gratitude for letting me temporarily enter their lives.

[1] Michel Foucault, quoted in Gilles Deleuze, *Foucault* (Minneapolis: University of Minnesota Press, 1988), 27–28.

[2] There is a large anthropological literature countering the idea that women are oppressed in every society; for a recent example see the essays in Peggy Reeves Sanday and Ruth Gallagher Goodenough, eds., *Beyond the Second Sex: New Directions in the Anthropology of Gender* (Philadelphia: University of Pennsylvania Press, 1990). These

[*Signs: Journal of Women in Culture and Society* 1992, vol. 17, no. 3]

this article, I explore the puzzle of women's persistent efforts toward change and the equally persistent presence of gender inequality—the puzzle of the resilience of power in gender relations. Part of the problem, I argue, is located in a style of struggle women employ to resist the constraints of power, a style I have called "accommodating protest."

Feminist theorists have long been interested in the part women play within relations of power. They have often cast women as victims, accepting the inevitability of domination.[3] Others have portrayed women as consenting subordinates, relatively satisfied with a deferential role. More recently, to counter these images of passive victimization and active acceptance, feminists have depicted women as powerful wielders of hidden, informal influence. This latter view begins to deal with the nuances of power relations by detailing various forms of power and by arguing that women are both active subjects and subjects of domination. To continue this effort of detailing the complexities of women's part in power relations, I argue that women, even as subordinate players, always play an active part that goes beyond the dichotomy of victimization/acceptance, a dichotomy that flattens out a complex and ambiguous agency in which women accept, accommodate, ignore, resist, or protest— sometimes all at the same time. Power relationships should be viewed as an ongoing relationship of struggle, a struggle complicated by women's own contradictory subjectivity and ambiguous purposes.[4] Such a perspective on power relations builds on the work of Antonio Gramsci, the Italian Marxist who tried to comprehend the puzzles of class consciousness and lower-class consent in modernizing societies. Here I extend his arguments on the complexity of consent to consider the problem of hegemonic relations and gender resistance.

The case of Middle Eastern women is particularly interesting with reference to this issue. From a Western vantage point, women in the Middle East are often pitied as the victims of an especially oppressive

---

counterexamples are intriguing as they push us away from thinking of women solely as victims and ask us to reconsider the different forms power relations may take; nonetheless, they remain exceptions, which forces us, without falling into essentialism, to think about the ways women's inequality is perpetuated in various cultural, class, ethnic, and national settings.

[3] For an intriguing discussion on recent Western discourse casting Third World women as victim, see Chandra Talpade Mohanty, "Under Western Eyes," and Rey Chow, "Violence in the Other Country," both in *Third World Women and the Politics of Feminism,* ed. Chandra Mohanty, Ann Russo, and Lourdes Torres (Bloomington: Indiana University Press, 1991), 51–80, 81–100.

[4] This view of power is derived principally from the works of Antonio Gramsci and Michel Foucault. See, e.g., Antonio Gramsci, *Selections from the Prison Notebooks,* ed. Quinton Hoare and Geoffrey Nowell Smith (New York: International Publishers, 1971); and Michel Foucault, *Power/Knowledge* (New York: Pantheon, 1980), *The History of Sexuality* (New York: Vintage, 1980), *Discipline and Punish* (New York: Pantheon, 1977), and *Madness and Civilization* (New York: Vintage, 1973).

culture, generally equated with Islamic religion. Women are depicted as bound to the harem, downtrodden and constrained; the ultimate symbol of their oppression and their acceptance of inferiority is the veil. Yet this picture cannot be reconciled with the assertive behavior and influential position of women in many Middle Eastern settings. In Cairo, for instance, many women manage the household budget, conduct important marriage arrangements, and coordinate extensive socioeconomic networks.[5] They are more than deferential partners, playing effective roles in their homes and the wider community, as demonstrated by the recent literature examining women's networks and the informal powers, bargaining tactics, or hidden strategies exercised by Middle Eastern women.[6] By implication, although these women definitely struggle to widen their options, they also play a real part in maintaining the social context, including power relations, that limit women's opportunities. The dichotomization in the literature on Middle Eastern women between women-of-the-harem victimization and behind-the-scenes-but-truly-powerful agency tends to produce arguments which flatten out the subtleties of women's subjectivity under power. Lost in either of these views, which stem in part from postcolonial discourses embedded within feminist theory, is the much more ambiguous reality of women's attempts to understand and act.[7] Using the new veiling movement as an example, I want to draw attention to these ambiguities of women's simultaneous attempts to alter and to maintain, to protest and to accommodate.

My argument is based on a study of working women in lower-middle-class Cairo.[8] These women form part of a new class in Egyptian society, one created in part by the revolution of 1952 that removed a British-supported monarchy and established a new state. The revolution, a military coup led by a group of army officers, evolved into an attempt to wed Arab nationalism with socialism under the leadership of Gamal Abdul Nasser, Egypt's new president and the Arab world's new popular leader. Nasser's authoritarian populism stressed social welfare programs, self-

---

[5] For a recent example from Cairo, see Diane Singerman, "Avenues of Participation: Family and Politics in Popular Quarters of Cairo" (paper presented at the Middle East Studies Association meeting, Baltimore, 1986).

[6] For example, see Susan Carol Rogers, "Female Forms of Power and the Myth of Male Dominance," *American Ethnologist* 2, no. 4 (November 1975): 727–56; or Lawrence Rosen, *Bargaining for Reality* (Chicago: University of Chicago Press, 1984).

[7] For an insightful discussion of the difficulties of cross-cultural feminist discourse, see Marnia Lazreg, "Feminism and Difference: The Perils of Writing as a Woman on Women in Algeria," in *Conflicts in Feminism*, ed. Marianne Hirsch and Evelyn Fox Keller (New York: Routledge, 1990), 326–48.

[8] The field research on which this article is based was conducted in Cairo, Egypt, from September 1983 to December 1984 and in follow-up visits in February 1986 and June–July 1988. For a full account of this research, see Arlene Elowe MacLeod, *Accommodating Protest: Working Women, the New Veiling, and Change in Cairo* (New York: Columbia University Press, 1991).

determination in foreign policy, and pan-Arabic regional unity. His policies propelled Egypt into political leadership in the Arab world but also
into a top-heavy and relatively unproductive bureaucratic regime.[9] The
new middle class that emerged from the peasantry through free education
and guaranteed jobs in government offices is increasingly squeezed economically by the government's attempt to maintain a welfare state with
relatively meager resources. The economic and social struggles of this new
middle class frame the circumstances of women working as low-ranking
clerks in the government bureaucracy. Indeed, the values and living standards of middle-class life assume a magnified importance for these women
and their families in marking family position and individual identity. Although they have the example of upper-class women who hold political
power or important jobs in the business and bureaucratic worlds, these
women face the novel experience of being the first in their families' recent
histories to pursue formal education and jobs outside the home.[10]

In recent years, many of these women have embraced the controversial
new veiling, a voluntary women's movement to abandon Western clothes
in favor of some form of covered Islamic dress. My interpretation of the
politics of this dress centers on its expression of a contradictory message
of both protest and accommodation. While this ambiguous symbolic
politics takes on the distinctive and dramatic form of veiled dress in
Cairo, the argument it raises about women's part in power relations is
suggestive for women elsewhere as well.[11] For the new veiling in Cairo
takes place not as a remnant of traditional culture or a reactionary return
to traditional patterns, but as a form of hegemonic politics in a modernizing environment, making its meaning relevant to women in other such
settings as well—settings in which, as Foucault reminds us, power and

---

[9] For general background on modern Egypt, see, e.g., John Waterbury, *The Egypt of
Nasser and Sadat* (Princeton, N.J.: Princeton University Press, 1983); or Raymond Hin-
nesbusch, *Egyptian Politics under Sadat* (New York: Cambridge University Press, 1985).
[10] Actually, women's work outside the home has varied considerably, and families of
this level might have had women workers in earlier generations, although not recently.
On the realities of women's work in historical context, see Judith Tucker, *Women in
Nineteenth Century Egypt* (New York: Cambridge University Press, 1985).
[11] Two examples, in the interest of exploration, can be mentioned here. The use of
the arts to embody new ideas of women's role and identity can be a form of resistance,
located in uniquely "feminine" places. For instance, see Judith Lynne Hanna, "Dance,
Protest, and Women's 'Wars': Cases from Nigeria and the United States," in *Women and
Social Protest*, ed. Guida West and Rhoda Lois Blumberg (New York: Oxford University
Press, 1990), 333–45. Yet, as with the new veils, arts such as embroidery or dance may
also contribute to traditional stereotypes. Another example is women's important presence in religious movements; the African-American church and gospel singing, funda-
mentalist Christianity, or resurgent Islam all offer a place for women to express their
ideas within a traditional and therefore safe space; yet this can serve to reinforce rather
than alter women's inequality.

resistance both reveal themselves in transformed and ever more subtle arrangements.[12]

Choosing to look at women's use of the veil in an urban center in the Middle East and using that case study to reflect on women's part in power relations also illustrates some of the unresolved methodological dilemmas of writing about women and power in the Third World. The veil has been an obsession of Western writers from early travelogues to more recent television docudramas, serving as the symbol par excellence of women as oppressed in the Middle East, an image that ignores indigenous cultural constructions of the veil's meanings and reduces a complex and ever-changing symbolism into an ahistorical reification. Although a more recent literature on women's informal powers has revised this image, it has tended to so contextualize women's situation that the larger issues of women's subordination are sometimes left untouched. The polemics of global feminist discourse create a context in which it becomes difficult to talk about women's subordination at all without contributing to earlier

women's subordination creates a
t loses its foundation for ethical
lize the use of the veil for these
agency; however, I also examine
f the new veils, raising questions
resistances more generally.
lation with twenty-eight lower-
ding about eighty-five women.
gh participant observation and
ig long visits with women and
n the workplaces. In later stages
men were selected for informal
l on working and veiling. Cer-
ld research and writing consid-
other is from Maine. I went to
ld research for my dissertation;
is both Arabic and American,
wn purposes in different social
s a married woman and even-

[handwritten margin note: in discussing veils we must contextualize them + emphasize their agency]

e and its "erasure of 'other'
Western feminism dispense with an
' women?" (340); Lazreg argues
"intersubjectivity" in cross-cultural
rcher and researched, a complicated
; ourselves to "difference," which

tually a mother, for example, or as a political scientist, also shaped the nature of our encounters and thus the ideas expressed here. Throughout this study, women's words and my reflections on their meaning are interwoven. Recounting women's words is common in feminist texts, but the status of these words is often unclear;[14] here, they are meant to illustrate the range of thinking women offered in my presence and those aspects of our encounter which led to my thinking about the new veils and women's resistance in terms of accommodating protest. In this context, it is important to note that a case study such as this has both benefits and limitations. Its strength lies in the ability to illuminate the distinctive details of a local situation and use these details to think beyond the boundaries of the specific case. Yet this ability to interpret and reflect on the meaning of the case could also be seen as its primary weakness, for the case does not "prove" in the same way as large-scale surveys or statistical analyses; nonetheless, it offers insight into the dynamics of women's lives that larger studies often cannot provide.

The politics of veiled dress   VeILINB:

While to many Westerners veiling symbolizes the coercive manipulation of female behavior, within the Middle East it serves indigenous symbolic purposes that extend well beyond such stereotypes. Veiling is employed in a wide variety of situations, with social, economic, and nationalistic as well as sexual connotations. Indeed, the wide range of styles and social meanings is perhaps the most striking feature of veiled dress, demonstrating the variety of political relationships that may be reinforced or challenged by such clothing.[15]

The Quran and Islamic doctrine are usually blamed by Westerners for initiating the covering and seclusion of women. However, veiling existed in many of the Arab tribes before the beginning of Islam. The Quran itself

---

[14] For discussion of the methodological issues involved in letting Third World women "speak" in feminist texts, see Gayatri Spivak, "Can the Subaltern Speak?" in *Marxism and the Interpretation of Culture,* ed. Cary Nelson and Lawrence Grossberg (Urbana: University of Illinois Press, 1988), 271–313; also see Elsbeth Probyn, "Travels in the Postmodern: Making Sense of the Local," in *Feminism/Postmodernism,* ed. Linda Nicholson (New York: Routledge, 1990), 176–89; and Rosalind O'Hanlon, "Recovering the Subject: Subaltern Studies and Histories of Resistance in Colonial South Asia," *Modern Asian Studies* 22, no. 1 (February 1988): 189–224.

[15] A wide literature exists on veiling, both within and outside the Middle Eastern context; see, e.g., Richard Antoun, "On the Modesty of Women in Arab Muslim Villages," *American Anthropologist* 70, no. 4 (August 1968): 671–98; Carroll McC. Pastner, "A Social, Structural and Historical Analysis of Honor, Shame and Purdah," *Anthropological Quarterly* 45, no. 4 (October 1972): 248–62; Hannah Papanek, "Separate Worlds and Symbolic Shelter," *Comparative Studies in Society and History* 15 (1973): 289–325; and Jane Schneider, "Of Vigilance and Virgins: Honor, Shame and Access to Resources in Mediterranean Societies," *Ethnology* 10, no. 1 (January 1971): 1–24.

advocates the covering of the hair, shoulders, and upper arms and se-
cluding oneself from inappropriate viewers; this advice refers, however,
to the wives of the Prophet, who had both the religious and social status
of an elite group and the special problem of being permanently in the
public eye.[16] The implications for other women are unclear and have
been interpreted in a wide variety of ways depending on local needs, class
interests, kinship structures, and women's endeavors.

Although the widespread concern with women's dress does indicate a
cultural focus on modest behavior, veiling is a subtle and evocative symbol with multiple meanings that cultural participants articulate, read, and
manipulate. Veiling may, for example, function to emphasize appropriate
relations of familiarity and distance within the web of kinship bonds.[17]
Women may draw their covering dress closer about them or cover their
face when in the presence of strangers, and then leave their face uncov-
ered within the home or in front of certain male relatives. Indeed, as
many families make the transition from village to urban settings, veiling
may be extended as women are more often in the range of strangers'
vision. Veiling can also be tied to class; often less feasible for poorer
women laboring in the fields or outside the home, veiling tends to increase as class standing rises and families can afford the "luxury" of more
seclusion for women.[18] Thus, covered dress may signal higher prestige
and status, making it more desirable to families moving to a higher class
standing. Further, veiling may present overt political statements centered
on cultural authenticity or political and religious affiliations.[19] Finally,
veiling may function as a mode of communication between the wearer
and viewer, a public way of sending social or economic messages, perhaps about marital status, education, or village origin. The subtle alter-
ations of how the veil is worn, what material it is made from, and which
small decorations complement an outfit highlight the fact that veiling is
a two-way mode of communication, not merely a form of dress imposed
on women against their will. Women, to some extent, use veiling for their

Qu'ran does not overtly instruct f to veil (like Judaism)

tied to strangers

to class

political/rel. statements

---

[16] Nesta Ramazani, "The Veil—Piety or Protest?" *Journal of South Asian and Middle Eastern Studies* 7, no. 2 (Winter 1983): 20–36.

[17] For instance, see Robert Murphy, "Social Distance and the Veil," in *Peoples and
Cultures of the Middle East,* ed. Louise Sweet (New York: Natural History Press, 1970),
290–315; and Carla Makhlouf, *Changing Veils: Women and Modernization in North
Yemen* (Austin: University of Texas Press, 1979). Also, for an account of modesty codes
centered on another group in the Egyptian setting, see Lila Abu-Lughod, *Veiled Sentiments* (Berkeley and Los Angeles: University of California Press, 1986).

[18] See Lois Beck and Nikki Keddie, *Women in the Muslim World* (Cambridge, Mass.:
Harvard University Press, 1978), esp. 8–9.

[19] See, e.g., Adele K. Ferdows, "Women and the Islamic Revolution," *International
Journal of Middle East Studies* 15, no. 2 (May 1983): 283–98; or Nahid Yeganeh and
Nikki R. Keddie, "Sexuality and Shi'i Social Protest in Iran," in *Shi'ism and Social Protest,* ed. Juan Cole and Nikki Keddie (New Haven, Conn.: Yale University Press, 1986),
108–36.

own purposes—as attraction, as warning, as a reminder of kin and social obligations.[20] Veiling emerges as an evocative sign of the intersection of domination and resistance, highlighting interpretive struggles over women's identity and role.

The importance of veiling as a symbol of power relations in Middle Eastern society is underlined by the history of veiling in Cairo. In 1923 Huda Shaarawi, an upper-class woman involved in the nationalistic struggles against British colonial power, launched a movement to abandon the face veil.[21] This movement eventually triumphed and until fairly recently upper-middle- and upper-class women in Cairo have worn Western-style dress. On the other hand, lower-class women, both of rural and traditional-urban origins, have continued to wear various traditional outfits, which generally include long colorful dresses and a black outer garment and gauzy headscarf.[22]

Yet, in the last fifteen years, many middle- and upper-class women are re-veiling—or more accurately, adopting new versions of Islamic dress ranging from fashionable turbans and silky gowns to austere head-to-toe coverings.[23] The most interesting aspect of this changed dress centers on its emergence as a women's movement, a voluntary veiling initiated primarily by women. Not confined to Cairo, but a widespread movement with varying popularity throughout the Islamic world, the new veiling clearly has symbolic significance for many. However, its meaning varies from country to country, class to class, even individual to individual; it has been used to signal identification within political disputes, as in Iran before and after the revolution; to signal membership in Islamic revivalist groups, as in the universities in Egypt in the late 1970s or in Istanbul today; and to signal anti-Western or nationalistic sentiment, as in the occupied territories in the Palestinian *intifada*. The popularity of the new veiling movement among lower-middle-class working women in Cairo in the mid-1980s has its own specific and local meanings as well, to which we can now turn.

[20] See Unni Wikan, *Behind the Veil in Arabia* (Baltimore: Johns Hopkins University Press, 1982); or Hannah Papanek's discussion of "mobile curtains" in "Purdah: Separate Worlds and Symbolic Shelter," *Comparative Studies in Society and History* 15 (1973): 289–325.

[21] See Huda Shaarawi, *Harem Years: Memoirs of an Egyptian Feminist,* trans. Margot Badran (New York: Feminist Press, 1987).

[22] For a detailed description of the variations on these outfits, see Andrea Rugh, *Reveal and Conceal: Dress in Contemporary Egypt* (New York: Syracuse University Press, 1986).

[23] See Fadwa El Guindi, "Veiling Infitah with Muslim Ethic: Egypt's Contemporary Islamic Movement," *Social Problems* 28, no. 4 (April 1981): 465–87, and "Veiled Activism: Egyptian Women in the Contemporary Islamic Movement," *Femmes de la Mediterranee, Peuples Mediteraneens* 22, 23 (1983): 79–89; John Alden Williams, "A Return to the Veil in Egypt," *Middle East Review* 11, no. 3 (Spring 1979): 49–54. In addition, the film by Elizabeth Fernea and Marilyn Gaunt, *A Veiled Revolution* (1982), offers an interesting view of voluntary veiling in this period.

Lower-middle-class working women and the new veiling

Cairo has grown in population in the last generation from about 2 million to about 12 million, swelled in part by an influx of rural families in search of work and a "more modern" life. These families, the foundation of the lower middle class, struggle to overcome poverty and reach for middle-class security. The women I knew generally grew up in families with about eight living children in cramped apartments of two or three tiny rooms in the traditional quarters of the city. Their mothers are housewives who may raise ducks or chickens for extra income, and their fathers work as construction laborers, drivers, mechanics, or small shopkeepers. These families are the beneficiaries of the socialist programs of the Nasser era, especially the educational reforms that allowed children to attend school and guaranteed jobs to all graduates in the government bureaucracy. These jobs offer respectable working conditions for families very concerned with female members's reputations and the secure, if small, incomes.

Additionally, these jobs offer the prestige of middle-class status to families seeking to differentiate themselves from more recent migrants or from manual laborers, domestics, or street peddlers. Lower-middle-class women distinguish themselves from the "poor," the "peasants" of the lower classes, who follow "uncivilized" and "not modern" life-styles. With household incomes barely rising above the levels of lower-class families, who often follow less prestigious but more lucrative occupations, women from these families are hard pressed to pay for rent, food, commuting, and clothes.[24] Yet they emphasize the status and prestige of class differences, however subtle, which separate them from lower-class families and exaggerate their similarities to families with more resources. In these families, women's working not only affects their individual standing but also moves the entire family from the lower class to the bottom rungs of the middle class.

These women—educated, working, modernizing—have started to veil, abandoning the modest versions of Western dress that are the badge of their hoped-for class position and turning to the long dresses and headscarfs of the *muhaggaba*, the covered woman. This movement initiated as a political and religious statement in the universities after the 1967 and 1973 wars with Israel[25] and has over the years been transformed into a new movement with different adherents and reasoning. Women's stories

---

[24] Two interesting accounts of the lives of lower-class women, from whom lower-middle-class women seek to differentiate themselves, are Unni Wikan, *Life among the Poor in Cairo* (London: Tavistock, 1980); and Nayra Atiya, *Khul-Khaal: Five Egyptian Women Tell Their Stories* (New York: Syracuse University Press, 1982).

[25] See the articles by El Guindi.

illustrate some of the controversies which are provoked by this increasingly common pattern in lower-middle-class Cairo.[26]

Mervat graduated from a two-year institute with a degree in business three years ago; she works as a typist in a government office. She and her four officemates are all single and enjoy the chance to be out of the home which working affords. Since their duties are light, they tend to spend their day chatting over cups of sweet tea about family affairs, the clothes and furnishings they are saving to buy, or the men in the nearby offices. Like many of her friends, Mervat wears Western dress. She has most of her clothes made by her sister-in-law, which is less expensive than buying them ready-made, and she saves carefully to buy shoes on credit to match her skirts and blouses. She explains this effort as marriage strategy: "Men like women to look beautiful of course! So, if I wish to find a husband, I wear this kind of clothes." When asked about the *higab,* she expresses a typical sentiment: "I hope to wear the *higab* some day. Not right now, but I respect the women who have made this decision and perhaps I will feel in my heart that this is right too, God willing. Not everyone can make this decision at the same time; I don't think about these things very much now, but maybe I will in the future. It will be important to me, like it is for my sister. She has just decided to become covered and perhaps this decision will come to me too." On the other hand, Mervat's older neighbor, Sanayya, who is married with teenage children and also wears Western clothes, is quite adamant about never putting on the *higab:* "Some women wear this scarf over their hair, and that is alright for them, but for me, no. I will never put on those clothes. It's important to wear modern clothes and go to work and educate your children, not to cover yourself up. Clothes don't matter anyway, it is a fad for younger girls."

Aida is engaged, and she lives with her family in a traditional quarter in central Cairo. Aida's father is a migrant laborer who works as a driver in the Gulf states and has been away for many years; her mother is illiterate and a *sitt al-bayt,* a housewife, who has never worked outside the home. Some time ago, Aida broke off her engagement because her fiance refused to consider Aida's working after their marriage. But Aida definitely wants to continue in her job; her reasons include the income she can earn, security, and the chance to socialize. Most important, however, is the need to be challenged: "I need to keep busy, and have something to think about and be doing all day. I can't just sit in the home and chat with neighbors and cook the meals; I know how to do all these

---

[26] Numbers on women's status in the Middle East are notoriously difficult to acquire; I estimate that, in 1984, about one-third of the working women from Cairo's lower middle class actually veiled, and another third stated that they intended to veil at some undefined time in the future. These numbers increased to about two-thirds of the women by the summer of 1988.

things but I like to be out with people and working hard to accomplish something. Then, when my husband will come home at night, even though he says 'cook my dinner,' we are equal, we stand together, and this will make a marriage work better." In time, Aida was again engaged, this time to a man who agreed that she could continue working after the wedding. One day, while discussing her plans for the ceremony and the future, she mentioned her intention to become a *muhaggaba,* a covered woman. She planned to change her colorful Western outfits for a long modest skirt and a headscarf wrapping over her hair and shoulders. "See this beautiful hair," she laughed, "you won't see it anymore. Well, maybe you will see a little peeking out here and there, but I will wear the *higab.*" When asked when she would put on this garb, she was vague: "Not right after the wedding, no, maybe a year, maybe two. I am not sure." About a year after the wedding, after giving birth to a son and resuming her work at the office, and despite her husband's objections, Aida indeed put on covering dress.

Husnayya is married and has three small children; she and her husband both work in government offices. Husnayya has been wearing the *higab* for several years now; family photos show her earlier Western dress now changed to ankle-length skirts, long sleeved jackets, and a scarf wrapped securely around her hair and shoulders. She explained the change this way: "Here in Cairo, we are Muslim women, and so we dress this way, with long sleeves and covering our hair and shoulders. Sometimes no kohl on the eyes even! But I wear kohl, just a little. No lipstick though, only for my husband in the evening in our house! Before we dressed differently, I don't really know why. But this dress is better, when I wear these clothes I feel secure, I know I am a good mother and a good wife. And men know not to laugh and flirt with me. So it is no problem to go out to work, or to shop, or anything. This is a good way to dress, it solves many problems."

From such accounts it is clear that women have many different reasons for the dress they wear, including religion, fashion, harassment, and family responsibilities; indeed women, families, friends, and co-workers spend long hours in amiable or contentious debate about what women should be wearing. Husbands and wives may not always agree, and sometimes men prefer women to wear Western dress, promoting their "modern" status. Women's dress, always symbolic in this society, provokes intriguing controversy.

Hegemony and resistance

Why would these women, who are educated, dedicated to working, and relatively successful symbols of modernization, return to a traditional symbol like the veil? Why agree to, or even encourage, what seems to be a return to an inferior status? These questions confront us with one of the central issues of any study of subordinates within relations of power: why do subordinate groups seem to aid the reproduction of power relations which function to their disadvantage?

In his *Prison Notebooks,* Gramsci considers the problem of the endurance of power relations and the puzzle of obedience within relations of class inequality: Why do people consent? Why do people seldom rebel? Why do people actually aid their own subordination? He develops the concept of hegemony as a characterization of power relations within modern societies where consent operates more obviously than force, eventually using the term to convey several different approaches to this web of problems. One interpretation portrays hegemonic interaction as the shaping of beliefs and behavior of a subordinate class by a dominant group. Consent is achieved by the instrumental molding of the common sense of subordinates, directed toward the interests of the upper class. This interpretation of hegemony essentially argues that the ruling class is able to structure a situation in which the lower classes are unable to perceive the ways they are subordinated. Certainly, the new veiling in Cairo initially appears a classic example of hegemony so defined, for in deciding to veil, women seem to reproduce their own inequality. Hegemonic relations, conceived in this manner, indicate that these women must be deluded about their true interests and duped into behavior which reinforces their own subordination; they are victims of a "false consciousness."

Yet more recent studies of class relations encourage a more encompassing reading of Gramsci's ideas and of subordinate's behavior, viewing hegemony as ideological struggle rather than ideological domination.[27] Focusing on an examination of what "consent" really amounts to in specific situations, scholars have discovered that the role of subordinate groups is a great deal more complex than the "false consciousness" model of hegemonic relations suggests. Consent, or the lack of overt and organized political opposition, is actually a blanket term that can cover a range of possible consciousness and political activity, from active support to passive acceptance to submerged resis-

[27] Gramsci uses the term "hegemony" to convey several different approaches to this web of problems; see Gramsci (n. 4 above), as well as Nicholas Abercrombie, Stephan Hill, and Bryan Turner, eds., *The Dominant Ideology Thesis* (London: Allen & Unwin, 1980); Joseph Femia, "Hegemony and Consciousness in the Thought of Antonio Gramsci," *Political Studies* 23, no. 1 (March 1975): 29–48; Ernesto LaClau and Chantal Mouffe, *Hegemony and Socialist Strategy* (Thetford, Norfolk: Thetford Press, 1985); and Anne Showstack Sassoon, ed., *Approaches to Gramsci* (London: Writers and Readers, 1982).

tance.[28] Consent emerges as a more complicated interaction than it first appears, highlighting the need to rethink the question of such ideological struggle in cases of gender inequality as well.

In the case of lower-middle-class women in Cairo, two important signs reinforce the need to think of hegemony as a mode of political struggle rather than a process of top-down domination. First, these veils are a new kind of covering clothing. In Cairo, lower-middle-class women have been wearing Western clothes for some years now; Western dress signified modernity and women's ability to be equal partners in aiding Egypt's recovery and growth. Women are not simply clinging to the past; covering clothes have not been their normal dress for many years. Indeed, the dress these women are putting on is not even the traditional dress of their mothers or grandmothers but a quite distinct and new style, clearly distinguished from the traditional garb of lower-class women. The second sign of struggle is that this is a movement initiated by women themselves. Women have the right, which they exercise, to decide what dress they will wear; covering dress is considered a personal decision a woman makes in her heart and not a matter her husband can decide for her. So the new veiling cannot be explained as the maintenance of traditional ways or as the revival of a traditional symbol at men's insistence. The controversies over voluntary veiling in lower-middle-class Cairo alert us to the complexity of women's "consent" and lead to the question of what this new dress signifies as part of a hegemonic struggle.

Women's dilemma and the new veiling

Although lower-middle-class women now leave the household for outside work, we cannot assume that this produces greater opportunities; in fact, many women complain that working carries considerable burdens

---

[28] For example, looking at peasants in Malaysia, Scott argues that consent is actually not present among the lower class in the village to any appreciable degree; a range of resistance can be discovered in which peasants act against the upper class to present their own view of justice. Peasants' "little tradition" offers an alternative interpretation of the great tradition, and its existence argues that a surface situation of obedience can be achieved despite ongoing submerged conflict. See James C. Scott, "Protest and Profanation: Agrarian Revolt and the Little Tradition," *Theory and Society* 4, nos. 1, 2 (January, March 1977): 1–38, 211–46, *Weapons of the Weak* (New Haven, Conn.: Yale University Press, 1985), and *Domination and the Arts of Resistance* (New Haven, Conn.: Yale University Press, 1990). In an influential study of working-class boys, Willis argues that they do not believe in promises of social mobility and therefore they do not strive to better their situation. Instead they participate in the working-class counterculture of opposition to school values, ultimately guaranteeing that they will end up in working-class jobs. The existing class inequalities endure not through the boy's active belief in the system, but through a very different kind of "consent" which partially penetrates the situation to see the impossibility of success. See Paul Willis, *Learning to Labour* (Westmead: Saxon House, 1977).

along with limited benefits. As one married woman with two young children complained: "Of course it is good now that we can go out of the house and go everywhere to work, but it is also hard. Each day I must go to work, ride the bus, shop for food, pick up my children, cook the meals, and clean the house. There is never enough time and I am always very tired." This comment was echoed by many others who cited responsibilities that make working outside the home especially burdensome. The double load of working inside and outside the home is aggravated by women's feeling that men do not, and indeed, could not, be expected to help with household labor in any significant way. In addition, everyone complained that the salaries they earn are far too low: "I spend each day here from nine until two [normal work hours], and look how little I earn, I should have more money for the work I do here!" Women complain that the government has encouraged their education and promised a good living, yet today their salaries are hardly meeting rising costs.

As for the work in the offices, women called their duties "boring and unchallenging" and "useless." The government policy of hiring all graduates has produced a civil service that provides some economic security, but at the cost of overcrowding, inadequate equipment, and lack of productivity. A typical work day for one energetic woman named Hoda, for instance, involves making the appointments for a manager down the hall. Since two other women in her office are also responsible for the same task, they can easily cover for each other while one slips out to shop for vegetables, visit a sick friend, or pray. Each day, two or three appointments are recorded in a worn book, and the hours are filled by chatting and drinking tea. Some women stated that this lack of responsibility is an advantage, as they can save their energy for the work that awaits them at home, while others were frustrated. Clearly, this is not the kind of work that would offer women the skills or sense of accomplishment that might create a new, positive identity as worker or professional, even though it compares favorably with the work lower-class women must do as domestics, factory laborers, or street peddlers. Even ambitious and energetic lower-middle-class women have very few options for other jobs outside the public sector. Since the *infitah* period (the opening) initiated by Anwar Sadat, the growth of a dual economy with a privileged private sector alongside the public has widened class inequities. As one woman noted, "I would love to have a job typing or being a receptionist in a private travel agency. There I would make a salary which is three times the amount I make here. But I do not know how to get such a job, I think you must have connections to work there and also you must know English and even French. But I don't think it is right that I make so little money, after all I need to buy the same things for my family that those women do." Even equivalent secretarial positions in the private sector are generally available only to upper-middle-class women with foreign language abilities, appropriate social skills, and family connections. On balance, working is generally portrayed by these women as a progressive step for the increased mobility it provides but also as troublesome and tiring; it is not surprising that many women claim they would quit their jobs if they could.[29]

These complaints point to an important problem women are experiencing as they move into the intersection of the two worlds of household and workplace; they face a deep dilemma of identity and role. Although many husbands maintain (at least in public) that they want a wife who stays at home, most women quickly state that this is impossible. "It is ridiculous! Today all wives have to work to help the family, it is not possible to pay for children, and rent and food without a wife working." Women see their work as a trade-off for the necessities of middle-class status—a two room apartment, an electric fan, a refrigerator, and tutors for children. The economic pressures that push women into the workplace are reinforced by the ideological requirements of class standing. These are ambitious families with high expectations for a better life, expectations promoted by the policies of a welfare state that encouraged education, government jobs, and an increased standard of living. These values were fueled in the late 1970s and early 1980s with the consumerism accompanying the *infitah* policies of the Sadat years. Families of this level have very high hopes for a better standard of living and are willing to work hard to gain their goals, which appear in enticing television advertisements of modern kitchens, labor-saving appliances, and ready-made clothes. In overwhelming numbers, these families choose to have female members enter the formal work force to gain the extra income.

Yet the economic ideology which pushes women into the workplace is countered by a gender ideology which frames women's place within the home as mother and wife. Members of this class believe that women and men embody different natures that make them suited to quite different tasks and responsibilities. According to both women and men, women belong in the home, where their nature is fulfilled by caring for husband and children and managing the household.[30] One unhappy husband complained, "Before I used to get a hot dinner every night, my mother had it ready for me and my father as soon as we walked in the door. Now

[29] In fact, few will have this opportunity due to economic realities, and more women than ever are attempting to enter the work force. Yet the government bureaucracy cannot absorb more employees, and women are being squeezed out by policies promoting women's leaves and emphasizing women's family roles.

[30] For discussion of women's nature in other Middle Eastern settings, see Fatna Ait Sabbah, *Women in the Muslim Unconscious* (New York: Pergamon, 1984); in Cairo, see Sawsan al-Messiri, *Ibn al-Balad: A Concept of Egyptian Identity* (Leiden: Brill, 1978).

I have to wait and wait while Samira cooks the dinner." This recollection of life before women left the home was echoed by his wife, busy cooking in the hot kitchen after the same long day in a government office and on the overcrowded city buses. "Before, my mother would have the whole day to go to the market and select the very best vegetables. Look at these awful things, they're terrible, bad! But I only have time to shop on the way home from work, and to cook in a rush like this. I hardly ever have time to make good meals. I used to be a good cook, but now we eat macaroni all the time." These comments are interesting, not only for the generalized belief that life in Cairo is getting more difficult, but also for the underlying assumption that women really should be at home, that families would be better off if this were possible. The clash of gender beliefs with economic realities and ideology creates a compromising dilemma for these women: "I work because my income is necessary, look at this budget, how could we live here and eat and send my sons to school if I didn't work? But I miss my sons very much, I know they are happy here with my mother every day, and I visit each afternoon. Still, a mother should be with her children. I want the hours to play with them and cook for them." Women working outside the home feel they are neglecting their husbands and children despite the fact that they work, in good part, for their families rather than for personal satisfaction.[31] This dilemma is reinforced by the intractibility of the economic situation, which is worsening as high inflation eats away at income and raises the price of household goods. Rents especially have become an extremely difficult expense to meet, yet a middle-class apartment is considered a necessity for marriage and establishing a family.

Women's double bind is intensified by the seeming immutability of gender roles. Since male and female natures are perceived as set, there is little hope of enticing men into helping with household work. Indeed, while some women wished their husbands would help out at home, many expressed the idea that the home was their domain and seemed unwilling to have it invaded. As one young wife emphasized: "Women are in charge in the home, yes, of course we do alot of work, but on the other hand men don't know how to do these things. You know, men can make tea perhaps or something small like that. But cooking a good meal, or arranging things properly, these are women's matters. I am tired at the end of the day, but I want my husband to know what a good wife I am." Individual men may more or less fit the qualities of male nature, but in general men act in certain ways and are responsible for certain tasks, as

[31] Of course, stating that one is working for one's own satisfaction would violate the norms of family life, which put the group above the individual. Nonetheless, the importance of family makes the goals of these women different than those of many Western feminists, who often stress self-actualization and autonomy as appropriate goals.

are women. "Men will not change, they are rough and hard; they are not suited for doing things in the home. That takes a woman who is soft and feels things in her heart."

Caught in a double bind of economic and gender ideologies, women face a loss of respect and resources despite small economic gains. It is in this context that many women have started to wear the new veils. When asked why they wear this dress, women overwhelmingly responded, "This is what Muslim women wear." Over time, as I came to know certain women better, they expanded on their original answer. "Now we have realized the need, where before we were in the dark," answered one woman, a thought that suggested an awakening of insight inspired by a return to religious and cultural values. Beauty and dignity were common adjectives for the woman who veils: "I think a woman who wears the *higab* is very beautiful, she shows her inner strength. I hope that I will feel in my heart the urge to wear this dress soon," said one young woman wearing Western dress, with sincere admiration of her co-workers who were dressed in covering garb. Others felt it decreased attractiveness and stressed that a woman had better find a husband before putting on this dress. "I don't wear the *higab* because I want to look good, and show off a little, how else will I find a good husband after all!" The claim that this dress is a trend, "it's what everyone does these days," also emerged in many women's comments. Fashions come and go, they suggested, and no one really knows why; some of the more thoughtful stressed that economic hard times and a sense of cultural crisis create a need to return to cultural roots in the face of an onslaught of Western consumer goods and television values. Overt religious sentiment was remarkable in its relative absence in women's accounts; only a very few emphasized increased religious feeling as a reason for altering their dress, and affiliation with Islamic groups was rare. Neither did this dress seem associated with a given time of life; women cited "after I marry," "after I have children," "when I get a little older," "when I feel the need in my heart" as times in the future when they would consider changing their dress, but no one said it was required in any way at particular stages of a woman's life.

With no simple or settled answers about the meaning of this symbol, and with the controversy expressed in the media and in daily conversations, it seems unlikely that the meaning of this symbol is entirely regulated by political or religious groups (although both do try to control and manipulate its meaning). Women take veiling seriously as an important decision they must make about who they are and what women should be. One point women repeatedly made is that the dress makes a statement about their identity as wives and mothers. "This dress says to everyone that I am a Muslim woman, and that I am here working because my family needs me to. Not for myself! I am here because I love my family and we need some things for our home." While individual women put on the new veils for many reasons, the new veiling seems to serve as a symbolic mediator for many women, expressing and ameliorating women's concerns arising at the intersection of work and family. Aida, mentioned earlier, explained her desire to veil at some time after her marriage: "Life is like an account book, with columns of numbers on the credit and debit sides. Good and bad actions are weighed at the end. If I work after I am married, this is very bad, so I need to do something very good to make up for it." Working, Aida maintains, is forbidden for women by religion and the Quran.[32] However, working before marriage is not so terrible as working afterward, for then she would be neglecting her real duties as wife and mother to a far greater extent. To counteract this problem and still keep her job, she has made the personal decision to veil; her covering clothes will serve as compensation, righting the balance of her compromising behavior. Aida's account illuminates a dilemma many women feel, that they violate their duties as wife and mother by working outside the home despite their families' need for their income. Her recognition of this double bind is acute: "I want to be able to buy nice things for my home. You see this refrigerator? I bought this for my mother after I started working, we never had one in the house when I was small. It is necessary to have one, for the food, and water. It saves work because we can cook a big meal and store the rest in there to eat for several more days. My mother could not do these things. She waits for my father to give her money, this is not secure. But she was always home with us as children, our home was a warm place. This is also very important." Many women expressed the idea that the veil in some way compensates for and even alleviates the dilemma they experience. "When I wear this dress, men will respect me," commented a young woman in her early twenties, who is hoping to marry a government employee like herself. "The *higab* is a protection from annoying people on the street," mentioned a married woman who had a long walk to her office building; "I don't have to worry that men in the cafe or on the street are talking about me every day as I pass." In another vein, a married woman with three children commented, "This dress looks beautiful and shows people that I am a woman even though I am working. My neighbors feel that a real woman stays at home, but now their tongues are silent about me." In a sentiment echoed by many women, one woman said, "This *higab* says I am a good Muslim woman, I can go out on the streets and to the

---

[32] The question of whether women may work outside the home is a matter of great controversy among these women. In general, there is confusion (which can be very useful for women) about what Islamic texts actually state, and reliance on custom is common. In times of changing norms and behavior, interpreting the tradition, and the question of who is allowed to interpret, become crucial.

office and no one can say I am not a good woman and mother." Women's answers, while stressing individual needs met by this dress, converge in their expressions of the need to make a statement about identity in a time of shifting norms.

As the veil has emerged as a mass-employed symbol rather than the outfit of relatively elite political actors as in the 1970s, its meaning has altered to suit differing political needs. These women object to the loss of their traditional identity, their valued and respected roles as mother and wife—crucial roles considering the extreme importance of the family in Egyptian society. "I don't know why my husband thinks I can cook meals and clean the house the way he would like when I am at work all day. It is not possible! Every night he is hard on me and upset." Another woman claimed, "These days men are not polite on the streets, before men left women alone, now they are always bothering women. I wear these clothes so they will know they should respect me." Through the veil, these women express their distress with their double bind; they want to reinstate their position as valued centers of the family but without losing their new ability to leave the home. Many agreed with the comment made by one woman: "It's wonderful now how women can go out visiting or to work. I would not want to return to the days of sitting in the house. I like to visit my sister in Imbaba and my cousin in Sayyida Zeinab and these days I can do this. With this dress it is easier." By emphasizing the dignity traditionally due to women for their valued part within the household, a respect eroded by women's current compromising behavior of working outside the home, the veil expresses women's concerns and makes a host of symbolic demands.

Accommodating protest

Women's accounts signal a much more complex story underlying what first appears as reactionary behavior. The assessment of voluntary veiling as an example of hegemony, narrowly defined as ideological domination, is misguided. Veiling involves a struggle over women's identity and role in society, a negotiation of symbolic meaning that women initiate. While hegemony is typically discussed as what dominant groups do to subordinates, it is evident in this case that women are hardly active consenters to their domination, nor even passive acceptors of societal arrangements. Instead, they attempt to control meaning on their own, advancing demands which revolve around transforming identity and widening opportunity in a changing Cairo. Although more familiar examples of protest such as strikes, demonstrations, riots, or revolutions are less equivocal statements, recent studies identify many less easily codified behaviors as forms of resistance and stress the submerged and subtle ways subordinates may advance political demands, significantly widening definitions of protest and suggesting that the categories we use to think about consent, resistance, and protest may need to be reworked.[33]

Although the veil is employed as a form of protest, it is also true that women's intentions in Cairo are more ambivalent; indeed, I argue that the veil conveys women's desire to accommodate as well as resist. This accommodation could be read as subterfuge, a useful technique in power struggles often employed by subordinate groups, but women's use of the new veils goes beyond disguise to a more intertwining and inseparable linkage of protest with accommodation. The dress of the *muhaggaba* expresses both a demand for renewed dignity and compliance. One accommodating aspect of the new veil, for instance, is the fact that this dress is often impractical. While covering clothes can be less expensive than numerous Western outfits, women also complained that they are awkward, heavy, and stifling in the summer. More significant are the ways in which veiling conveys women's adjustment to and acceptance of existing conceptions of appropriate female behavior. One example is women's expectation that veiling will help lessen the sexual teasing and harassment they receive on the streets and in the offices. As one woman stated, "I wear these clothes to show the kind of woman I am, and now these men on the street should respect me." Another commented, "In the workplace men used to comment on my hair, and face and clothes, now they see that they should not discuss these things about me." Rather than charging men with the responsibility for changing their unwelcome behavior, women accommodate by altering their dress to fit the prevailing norm that men cannot help responding to women as temptations. While this may be a helpful short-term policy for individual women, veiling thus reinforces the belief that women invade men's world when they leave the home to work.

Veiling presents a double face; it both symbolizes women's protest against a situation that threatens valued identity and status, and it signals women's acceptance of a view of women as sexually suspect and naturally bound to the home. Protest is firmly bound to accommodation in a resonant public symbol, creating an ambiguous resistance, an accommo-

---

[33] For example, Richard Cloward and Frances Fox Piven discuss suicide and other forms of deviance in "Hidden Protest: The Channeling of Female Innovation and Resistance," *Signs: Journal of Women in Culture and Society* 4, no. 4 (Summer 1979): 651–69; conversational strategies are considered by Rosen (n. 6 above); disbelief as resistance is discussed by Elizabeth Janeway in *Powers of the Weak* (New York: Knopf, 1980); Vaclav Havel in *The Power of the Powerless* (Armonk, N.Y.: Sharpe, 1985) discusses "living authentically" as resistance; walking in city streets as everyday protest is discussed by Michel de Certeau in *The Practice of Everyday Life* (Berkeley and Los Angeles: University of California Press, 1984); and various forms of "everyday resistance" are portrayed by Scott in *Domination and the Arts of Resistance*.

dating protest. Although women clearly struggle to shape their identity and future status, and are not simply ideologically manipulated by dominant groups, the bare fact that such struggle exists is not in itself sufficient reason for optimism.[34] Why would women mount their protest in what seems an ambivalent and compromised form? Numerous studies citing women's active manipulation within difficult circumstances refute the possible conclusions that women are more constrained or more susceptible to ideological domination than other groups and thus more likely to "consent." The recent focus on the complexities of consent in class analysis pushes us to reconsider what such "complicity" might mean in gender relations as well. It has been argued that for some subordinate groups such accommodations can be tactics, a disguise to mask the reality of hidden struggles;[35] yet this implies a straightforward and unambiguous subjectivity which does not seem to characterize women's situation particularly well. In his *Prison Notebooks,* Gramsci discusses the "fragmentation" and "contradictory consciousness" of the working class as evidence of the need for a vanguard party and political leadership,[36] but perhaps we could draw on these ideas to think about ambiguous subjectivity—and the necessarily ambiguous agency such consciousness would generate—without concluding that this implies a distorted or undeveloped consciousness. Ambiguity can, after all, be productive and not simply undirected.

The linkage of accommodation with protest signals something of importance about the power relations in which women are enmeshed, as opposed to those of other subordinate groups. From the numerous possible reasons why women's resistance might take this form, I raise three here for the purposes of exploration. The first centers on the distinctive situation that women occupy with respect to the relations of power that constrain their lives. For women, there is no clear-cut other to confront directly. Facing a layered and overlapping round of oppressors, women do not have the relative luxury of knowing their enemy. Relations with men, class relations, and the more distant realm of global inequalities all affect lower-middle-class women in Cairo, yet none is exclusively responsible for women's subordination. Women see a web of cross-cutting power relations, and an ambiguous symbolic solution like the veil that speaks on different political levels suits the nature of these overlapping power constraints.

[marginalia: an ambiguous symbol like the veil is the only way to accommodate / resist domination or harassment]

[34] Lila Abu-Lughod argues against the "romance of resistance," tracing power relations in a Bedouin community; she says that young people seem oblivious to ways their resistance to elders within the community backs them into more complex subordination to world economic and political powers. See Lila Abu-Lughod, "The Romance of Resistance: Tracing the Transformations of Power through Bedouin Women," *American Ethnologist* 17, no. 1 (February 1990): 41–56.

[35] See Scott, *Domination and the Arts of Resistance.*

[36] Gramsci, *Selections from the Prison Notebooks* (n. 4 above), esp. 326–27, 333.

Another factor influencing women's style of protest centers on women's attempt to pursue different goals than other subordinate groups when resisting domination. For women's power relations are often entwined with other kinds of ties, such as romantic love or family bonds. Although a peasant may wish to be a landlord or a worker might wish to be a capitalist owner, the majority of women do not wish to become men, nor even to rid the world of men. Ideologies of opposition and inversion are less attractive when the end goal centers on creating a new relationship of cooperation or equality rather than eliminating the other.[37] In Cairo, for example, most husbands and wives consider themselves partners in the family structure, and neither wishes to switch roles nor to dissolve the differences between male and female character. In such a context, the ambitions of women in power struggles necessarily become more complex. Further, women daily inhabit the worlds of their oppressors rather than only occasionally intersecting the lives of the dominant group. Women live with, among, and in some ways, as one of, the dominant group; the everyday interaction, for example, of husbands and wives insures that women will often identify with their husbands, despite the times when these husbands act as oppressors. This identification should not be confused with simple ideological domination. Women truly do inhabit a unique position; accommodation is involved because women are part of both the dominant culture and the subordinate subculture.

A final reason women's struggles may take the form of accommodating protest centers on the constrained nature of choice. Working women of lower-middle-class Cairo have few viable ideological alternatives; any action they might take must be a choice which fits within their cultural tradition. Women's struggle is limited by the constraints of existing social discourse. For instance, women's descriptions of male character, which include the adjectives "hard," "rough," "stubborn," and "stupid," are interesting not only for their assertion that men are in many ways imperfect and even inferior to women, but for the underlying assumption that male character is set by nature and therefore unalterable. While these adjectives implicitly convey women's criticisms of male nature, and perhaps the potential of an alternative perspective which might motivate protest, women interpret their own adjectives within the constraints of existing discourse.

Of course there are other images available, but they do not attain the compelling state of the natural, remaining alternatives, but only in the

---

[37] See Diane Margolis, "Considering Women's Experience: A Reformulation of Power Theory," *Theory and Society* 18, no. 3 (May 1989): 387–416. Margolis argues that the cooperative aspects of power have been ignored and that bringing in women's experiences will widen our understanding of power from purely oppositional forms to include other categories.

sense of oddities. For instance, the Western woman is imagined according to the images available on television, including the women portrayed in imported shows such as *Dallas* and *Flamingo Road;* the glamorous women in commercials advertising cars, perfumes, and cosmetics; and the scantily clad singers featured in European nightclub shows. None of these images, focused as they are on women as sexual object and glamorous consumer, fit the lives of these women or offer an attractive alternative image. Further, in a postcolonial context, any images derived from the West are politically and culturally suspect.[38] Images from within the Islamic tradition, such as stories about the active lives of Fatima or Aisha, are much more attractive and useful, but subject to the same ambiguities of interpretation the veil itself embodies.[39]

Such limiting of discourse lies at the center of hegemonic politics, and it differs from the narrowed idea of hegemony as the obscuring of reality from subordinate participants. Hegemony can be understood as a symbolic struggle, a negotiation over meaning that involves constraints on imagination, where ideology is not so much a tool in the hands of a dominant class as an enveloping version of reality in which all social encounters are necessarily conducted. Such hegemonic struggles, and the accompanying constraints on political imagination, may be an especially common pattern in modern and modernizing cultures. Further, the constraints on imagination may tighten as local cultures are overtaken by mass-manufactured and Western popular culture.[40] In Cairo, despite the opportunity opened by economic changes in everyday routines and habits, women and men remain enveloped in traditional ideas about male and female character, roles, rights, and responsibilities, enmeshed in a struggle where oppositional imagination cannot effectively engage reality.

In this context, women's veiling calls on the Muslim tradition, not as an indiscriminate recollection of all traditional values, but as a highly selective attempt to revitalize and emphasize some of the old ideals. Yet

---

[38] For a discussion of how Westernization and a history of colonialism act within national movements to complicate feminist discourses in the Middle East, see Evelyne-Accad, *Sexuality and War: Literary Masks in the Middle East* (New York: New York University Press, 1990), esp. the introduction; also see Julie Peteet, *Gender in Crisis: Women and the Palestinian Resistance Movement* (New York: Columbia University Press, 1991).

[39] There are strong feminist groups in Egypt, but often their goals seem distant to women of this class, and indeed their knowledge of such women's organizations is generally slight. On Egyptian feminism, see Akram Khater and Cynthia Nelson, "Al-Harakah al-Nissa'iyah: The Women's Movement and Political Participation in Modern Egypt," *Women's Studies International Forum* 11, no. 5 (1988): 465–83; Margot Badran, "Dual Liberation: Feminism and Nationalism in Egypt," *Feminist Issues* 8, no. 1 (Spring 1988): 15–34; and Beth Baron, "Unveiling in Early Twentieth Century Egypt," *Middle Eastern Studies* 25, no. 3 (July 1989): 370–86.

[40] See Abu-Lughod, "The Romance of Resistance," for a fascinating example of this tendency in the Egyptian context.

there is always the danger of recalling not only the desired dignity which women hope to replant in the modern environment, but the accompanying emphasis on seclusion and constraint. Particularly for those who seek to recall the past not as holders of power, but as those constrained by power, the dangers need to be considered as well. The example of women's veiling recalls the Bakhtinian idea of the immense difficulties of appropriating language for new and oppositional uses. Women may choose to veil for their own reasons; yet the symbol maintains a somewhat separate life of its own, carrying both intended and unintended messages. The acquiescing and accommodating aspects of women's mode of hegemonic negotiation open the gates to possible co-optation.

Indeed, there are signs in Cairo that this co-optation is beginning to take place. For example, the character of this movement as women's personal decision is starting to be threatened; as husbands try to browbeat wives into veiled dress, or neighbors argue that a woman should be more modest, or religious leaders sermonize on women's clothes and role as mother, the choice of dress may become the province of men, the family, or the state, and less the decision of women. In the end, the *higab* operates as a symbol within a system where women's relations of inequality tend, more often than not, to be reproduced. The resilience of power relations can be explained, not as something which happens behind women's backs, but as the result, in part, of the way women struggle. Women's creative use of the new veils in lower-middle-class Cairo exemplifies the ambiguities which are the strength and the weakness of this style of resistance.

The idea that women's power relations may take the form of accommodating protest requires us to rethink our understanding of women's agency, rather than trying to fit women's actions within constraining categories or assuming a linear progression of consciousness from acquiescence to resistance to conscious protest. Once again, Gramsci's idea of hegemony can be useful, for he argues for the possibility of creating a counterhegemony, a working or popular class worldview which would combat, on the cultural front, the dominant class and create an alternative vision of social relations.[41] While alternatives can emerge from outside the hegemonic discourse, such imported ideologies seldom answer local needs nor attain viability in their new environment. The crucial and difficult question is exactly how alternative visions might emerge from within a culture to engage belief in a way which allows alternative discourse and ultimately effective political actions. For women, then, the

[41] For an interesting discussion of the difficulties involved, see Chantal Mouffe, "Hegemony and Ideology in Gramsci," in *Gramsci and Marxist Theory*, ed. Chantal Mouffe (Boston: Routledge & Kegan Paul, 1979), esp. 185–98. Also see LaClau and Mouffe (n. 27 above), esp. chap. 3 on antagonisms and hegemonic politics.

idea of accommodating protest does not imply that women will always be victims despite their struggles, but encourages us instead to think beyond the dichotomies of victim/actor or passive/powerful toward the more complicated ways that consciousness is structured and agency embodied in power relations. Suggesting that part of women's continued subordination results from women's actions may be uncomfortable, but examining carefully the ambiguities of women's accommodating protests in different contexts may offer a clarity about women's subjectivity under domination that we need to address questions of gender inequalities and political change.

Political Science Department
Bates College

"No Freedom without the Women": Mobilization and Gender in South Africa, 1970–1992

Gay W. Seidman

SINCE AT LEAST the turn of the century, nationalist movements have regularly promised to improve the status of women: before taking power, they have pledged to end gender-based subordination. Just as regularly, however, most of these promises have gone unfulfilled. In general, although feminist activists have occasionally won some changes in women's legal status, basic household structures have remained intact, including men's control over women and property and elders' control over children.

Why is this pattern so frequent? Although each case differs, explanations generally revolve around a fear on the part of (mainly male) leaders that the attempt to change women's options could divide the "imagined community" on which nationalist ideologies are built, creating conflicts among their supporters. Some authors suggest that in anticolonial, or anti-Western, struggles, nationalist leaders have avoided explicit challenges to gender subordination because they viewed the domestic arena as the source of an autonomous national identity that must be protected (Chatterjee 1989; Tohidi 1991). In other cases, external threats may persuade nationalist leaders to emphasize preserving national unity instead of gender equality. In Mozambique, for example, the postindependence government backed away from gender subordination in order to strengthen its popular base: "Women's concerns have been taken off the

I am grateful to Barbara Laslett, Kate Tyler, Iris Berger, several unnamed reviewers for *Signs,* and participants at a 1990 sociology department seminar at Northwestern University and at the 1990 African Studies Association meeting in Baltimore for comments on earlier versions of this article.

[*Signs: Journal of Women in Culture and Society* 1993, vol. 18, no. 2]

immediate agenda, and replaced by the concerns of the nation as a whole" (Urdang 1989, 218).[1]

Nationalist leaders, as sociologist Judith Stacey points out, have regularly faced a conundrum: even when they sincerely hope to challenge the subordination of women, their effort to maintain a popular base requires them to respond to supporters' demands, articulated primarily by men who generally have little immediate interest in challenging gender subordination. These demands frequently involve the reconstruction of beleaguered peasant households, even when that means reconstructing gender inequality (Stacey 1983, esp. 248–67). Women have often been active in nationalist movements but have rarely achieved visible leadership roles, and, rather than challenge gender subordination, they have frequently stressed pragmatic efforts to give women access to the resources required for fulfilling traditionally defined domestic roles (Molyneux 1986). In Nicaragua and Zimbabwe as well as in China, reinforcing existing household relations has meant women have generally remained in, or even returned to, a subordinate position.

South Africa, however, may prove different. As it moves from a situation of white-minority rule to some kind of democracy in which the black majority is fully represented, a postapartheid government is likely to face demands articulated by an urban popular movement, not a movement based in the peasantry. In this article, I suggest that industrialization and urbanization have affected black men and women differently; new patterns of daily life have altered the context in which popular goals are elaborated.[2] Changes in the organization of work and family, coupled with changing forms of political organization, mean that a postapartheid state is likely to face gender-specific demands, articulated by women who may not explicitly accept feminist labels but who may refuse to subsume questions of gender subordination under appeals to national unity.

Although African women have remained concentrated in less skilled, low-paid work, they have been integrated into an industrial labor force

---

[1] Urdang 1989 points out that the Mozambican liberation movement (FRELIMO), which claimed to be both nationalist and socialist, was somewhat contradictory in its attitude toward a national consensus: "While class struggle is called for as a constructive force, women's struggle is seen as divisive." Kruks and Wisner 1989 offer a slightly different explanation, suggesting that, in addition to the external threat, FRELIMO tended to "dwell on women's ideological backwardness and passivity, [and] to identify women's problems primarily as those of traditional family relations." A "male-dominated (and urban-biased) FRELIMO" in the 1980s generally limited its discussion of gender issues to "exhortations to involve women in socialized production"—exhortations that ignored the extent to which women were already involved in peasant production.

[2] In lieu of a better alternative, I have followed a practice common among South Africans opposed in principle to apartheid's racial classification, using the term "African" when discussing people classified "African" and "black" when referring to people classified "African," "Colored," or "Indian."

and have an unusual degree of economic independence. South Africa's migrant labor system has eroded the peasant economy almost beyond recognition; the conditions of social reproduction—the circumstances in which workers and their families live from day to day—have undermined the male-dominant household patterns that other nationalist movements have reinforced. During the 1980s, in the context of broad political mobilization, changes in women's labor force participation rates and in household patterns have led black working women to question assumptions of domestic subordination. Especially in the labor movement and within community groups, there is clear evidence that many black women believe a postapartheid state should respond to gender-specific concerns. Women activists, often organized in semiautonomous women's groups and supported by the international spread of feminist ideas and assistance, have increasingly raised what Maxine Molyneux (1986) calls "strategic" gender issues, questioning gender inequality within political organizations, within workplaces, and even within the domestic arena (Molyneux 1986).

This shift from "pragmatic" to "strategic" gender concerns is not unique to South African women's groups. Recent studies describe the way structural changes in Latin American households and work, in the context of women's political mobilization, have prompted new attention to gender inequalities (Alvarez 1990; Jelin 1990; Chinchilla 1991). Similarly, in the United States, changes in work and social reproduction—especially when women could draw on organizational resources of their own—play a crucial role in explaining why women activists began to frame gendered demands on the state in terms of women's autonomy, rather than in terms of a family wage (Brenner and Laslett 1991).

The South African case is unusual, however, for the extent to which feminist demands are beginning to reshape the agenda of a broad nationalist movement. During the past decade, as South African women have increasingly engaged in political activity, they have inserted gender issues into debates around the transition to majority rule. Gender-specific demands articulated by women who are already economically independent and who draw on their own organizational resources may not be ignored as easily as the histories of other nationalist movements would imply. Discussions of the popular movement in South Africa that ignore the degree of black women's participation in both the labor movement and the nationalist struggle generally overlook the extent to which class and nationalist consciousness have been shaped by a markedly gendered movement, in which women activists articulate gender-specific demands and reject gender subordination. In South Africa, we have the opportunity to observe in a contemporary setting a process that feminist historians claim has been overlooked in historical discussions of the making of

European and North American working classes: a gendered construction of what it means to be a worker and citizen, and a gendered understanding of what working-class and political organizations should demand (Scott 1988, esp. 53–67).

Beginning with an analysis of the antiapartheid movement's historical approach to gender issues, I will describe how two decades of structural change have altered basic household patterns for many South Africans; how the emergence of semiautonomous women's groups has provided a forum in which women activists could raise gender-specific concerns within the popular antiapartheid movement; and how debates within the newly legal African National Congress (ANC), within the South African labor movement, and within women's groups indicate growing support for gendered demands. Drawing on activists' articles in South African community publications and on a participant-observation study involving attendance at meetings and unstructured discussions with a range of male and female activists, mainly in 1990–91, I will explore the reasons why gendered demands appear to have become so visible.[3]

Gendered migrant streams

South Africa's migrant labor system has long been considered fundamental to the apartheid system: for most of this century, most black South Africans have been legally allowed into white-designated areas only when employed in white-owned enterprises. The effects of this system can be seen in virtually all social relationships among people classified "African." Sociologists increasingly recognize that families can respond very differently to gendered migrant streams, depending on who goes, what reinvestment and income-earning opportunities exist, and how families respond to long separations (Russell 1986; Pedraza 1991). But in South Africa and the surrounding region, nearly all migrants have historically been male. Most discussions stress the way a gendered migrant labor system has left African women behind, socially as well as geographically: women have been expected to remain working in subsistence agriculture, waiting for male migrants to send their wages home (Murray 1981).

Since the early twentieth century, some African women have considered urban employment an attractive alternative to a subordinate position in homestead production, but state policies intervened to keep women and other Africans not employed by whites from moving to town,

---

[3] Unless I had explicit permission to quote interviewees by name, I have preferred to identify them only by position or occupation.

often backed by rural African authorities who sought to preserve existing household relationships (Walker 1990, 196). Both the South African authorities and neoclassical economists have often suggested that rural households receiving migrants' remittances could do better economically than those without wage workers, because migrants' wages could provide investment capital (Lucas 1987). But in South Africa's bantustans— the areas set aside for the country's African majority, where 57 percent of South Africa's African women legally resided in the early 1980s (Simkins 1984, 6)—legal restrictions and overcrowding undermined peasant agriculture. Since the 1930s, few rural African households have been able to expand land or cattle-holdings (Beinart 1987; Bonner 1990). Remittances might help families survive, but migrants' wages could only rarely increase productive capacity (Keenan and Sarakinsky 1987). With few exceptions, women remaining in rural areas have experienced grinding poverty, increased agricultural labor, and persistent dependence on migrant remittances. By 1970, many rural African families relied on remittances for over half their monthly income; on its own, peasant agriculture rarely offered any hope of adequate family maintenance (Murray 1987).

In the context of declining family production, rural South African women's paid labor has often been essential for family survival. In the words of one African farm worker, "If the women and children don't work, we don't eat" (Comaroff 1985, 161; Marcus 1989, 100). Only a handful of African women could gain access to the education required for jobs in nursing, teaching, or social work, and few industrial jobs were open to women before the mid-1970s. In 1970, 3 percent of employed African women were professional workers, and 4 percent were industrial workers; 81 percent worked in agriculture or in service (Lawson 1986, 17–19). A strictly sex- and race-segregated labor market meant that most African women seeking work were limited to low-paid domestic or farm labor, to low-earning informal-sector activities such as food preparation, or to the better-paid but illegal and dangerous activities of beer brewing and prostitution.

Given the migrant labor system, the erosion of peasant agriculture, and the nature of jobs historically available to African women in South Africa, it is hardly surprising that discussions of apartheid's impact on black women have tended to emphasize the destabilization of African households rather than gender-based inequality within those households. Discussions of the problems confronting African women have tended to focus on how the collapse of rural households has left women impoverished and isolated, lacking either support from men or income-earning opportunities for themselves. Through most of this century, researchers pointed to marital breakdown, female-headed households, and high illegitimacy rates—sometimes estimated at 60 percent of births in urban areas—as demonstrating the threat to family life posed by enforced separation and low male wages (Horrell 1968; Duncan 1983, 38).[4]

In this context, it is hardly surprising that South African social reformers have historically stressed the need for family reconstruction; the household has been treated as an unproblematic unit. While gender ideologies in southern Africa are somewhat confusing, mixing together Western ideals of female domesticity with the assumption that women should contribute to family survival (Cock 1990; Meintjies 1990), political leaders have rarely questioned family patterns that treat women as providers of child care and housework and that assume men retain authority within the family despite long absences.

Antiapartheid women's organizations have tended to take the same approach, using "women" interchangeably with "wives" and "mothers" for most of this century (Walker 1982, 264). South Africa's employment, property, and tax laws have systematically discriminated against women, abortion remains illegal, and violence against women is endemic, yet few nationalist organizations have questioned domestic patterns. Until the late 1980s, nationalist organizations placed national liberation ahead of challenges to gender ideologies, an approach that had the added political advantage of avoiding a direct challenge to male household heads. From its founding in 1954, the ANC-affiliated Federation of South African Women (FSAW) called on the national liberation movement to address issues of special concern to women, but most of these concerns appeared directly linked to women's domestic roles. The organization as a whole "never doubted that its first responsibility was to the general liberation struggle, by blacks, against the white supremacist state" (Walker 1982, 263).[5] That tradition persisted when antiapartheid groups were outlawed in 1960. In 1979, speaking for the ANC women's secretariat, Mavis Nhlapo said, "In our society women have never made a call for the recognition of their rights as women, but always put the aspirations of the whole African and other oppressed people of our country first" (Kim-

---

[4] Figures on the increase in the formation of families outside marriage are complicated by the somewhat confused definition of "ever-married"; some unmarried couples behave as if they were married, even if no marriage has been legally recorded because bridewealth has not been paid to the woman's family.

[5] In 1954, some 137 delegates to FSAW's first meeting approved a "Women's Charter" listing demands that "staked a claim to full equality between the sexes and began the search for answers to the questions about how best that could be achieved." This charter, however, was drawn up by a rather small group of leaders and received relatively little discussion within the liberation movement as a whole. Walker concludes, "Many of the women involved in the Federation of South African Women and the ANC Women League [before the ANC's banning in 1960] accepted that women were, in some way, subordinate to men, their responsibilities primarily domestic, and their political contribution supportive rather than innovative" (Walker 1982, esp. 156, 182, 264).

ble and Unterhalter 1982, 13). In 1985, an ANC spokeswoman told the Nairobi Women's Conference, "It would be suicide for us to adopt feminist ideas. Our enemy is the system and we cannot exhaust our energies on women's issues" (*Work in Progress* 1985, 31). In 1986, ANC activist Frene Ginwala slightly revised the theme but echoed its basic thrust: "Women's liberation in South Africa cannot be achieved outside of the context of the liberation struggle" (Ginwala 1986, 13). Until 1987, the exiled ANC Women's Section avoided discussing feminism, only setting up a commission on "women's emancipation" in 1987 — a commission that apparently never met (Daniels 1991, 36).[6]

By the mid-1980s, the nationalist organization's leaders began to recognize, at least rhetorically, that working-class black women confronted gender-specific problems. But even when the ANC called for equal wages, for day-care facilities, or for job opportunities for women, discussions of what is still regularly called "the woman question" rarely addressed male dominance in the household. In 1989, a woman writing in the South African Communist party's journal insisted, "Our immediate task is the liberation of the black people," not raising gender-specific demands ("Clara" 1989, 39). Viewing attempts to politicize gender or family relationships as arising from "bourgeois" or "Western" feminism, spokespeople for any of the major organizations struggling against white-minority rule tended to suggest that "the woman question" was best left unasked (but see Kgotsisile 1990).

Increased labor force participation

Had this story ended in the 1970s, South Africa would almost certainly have followed the path of other newly independent African states: even if a democratically elected government had instituted land reform or minimum wage laws, persistent gender-based discrimination in employment, in property laws, and in politics probably would have reinforced gender ideologies in which men remained dominant in households. Certainly the ANC leadership, which will almost certainly form the first elected government, had expressed little interest in changing those patterns, and the antiapartheid movement seemed destined to repeat the pattern followed elsewhere.

A postapartheid government in the 1990s, however, may face demands that challenge traditional household structures. Paradoxically, over the past twenty years, state policies designed to promote industrialization and to slow African urbanization have also created new urban informal

---

[6] At that 1987 meeting, the ANC Women's Section also suggested for the first time that the ANC should discipline members who battered their wives.

settlements while increasing African women's labor force participation outside agriculture. In the 1980s, segregated African townships became the center of widespread community activism: as women were mobilized into unions and community groups, and especially as independent women's groups were created, working women and community activists increasingly articulated demands outside the framework of the male-dominant household. Structural changes altered the conditions of social reproduction in ways that increased the possibility that some women might pursue gender-specific demands more vigorously and strengthened their capacity to do so.

Probably the most important structural shift affecting African families since the 1970s has been the increased labor force participation of women, in both urban and rural settings. Rapid industrial expansion through the 1960s increased employers' demand for African labor: by the early 1970s, government officials had effectively acquiesced in the shift to a black industrial labor force, allowing employers to hire Africans in skilled positions previously restricted to whites. In the 1960s, the government had tightened legal controls on unemployed Africans' movements, hoping to slow urbanization; but in the 1970s, as African workers were incorporated into the long-term industrial work force, their families often joined them in urban areas, legally or not (Greenberg 1987). By 1986, when the pass laws blocking unemployed Africans from moving into white-designated areas were officially removed, at least half of South Africa's African population lived in urban or peri-urban areas (Hindson 1987; Mabin 1989, 2).

Obviously, urbanization does not by itself eliminate gender hierarchies. In South Africa, moving to town can reinforce gender subordination; women illegally in cities may become completely dependent on, and vulnerable to demands of, men who hold legal residence rights (Ramphele 1989). But in the 1970s, families moving illegally to urban areas often joined informal settlements near major industrial centers; few could find space to rent in government-owned housing. Workers and their families lived in the interstices of apartheid's urban plans, without legal residence permits, without infrastructure or services, and under constant threat of pass raids and forced removals. Especially in informal settlements, women and men had equally precarious legal rights and equally inadequate resources.

Urbanization in the 1970s increased pressures on African women to find paid work, given that subsistence agriculture was impossible: here, the struggle was for land on which to build shacks, not to farm. Most black women had to find paid work. In the retail and clothing trades, 43 percent of married women reported receiving no economic support from their husbands, who were unemployed, lived elsewhere, and sent no money or simply did not contribute to family upkeep; even those receiving support from their husbands said they could not raise their families on a single worker's wage (Barrett et al. 1985, 138). Although relatively few household-level studies of urban South Africa exist—an understandable lacuna, given the dangers facing would-be researchers in townships in the 1980s—the evidence that women remain largely responsible for household maintenance is incontrovertible. Many women live alone with children and receive little support from their children's fathers, but even women in stable relationships are likely to take financial responsibility for important aspects of household maintenance. Out of twenty-two households, for example, Caroline White found that only two of six female household heads received any financial assistance. In households that included two working adults, arrangements varied, but all the women White interviewed clearly considered their financial contributions as well as their domestic work essential to family reproduction (White 1991).

By 1980, over a third of African women in South Africa were formally registered in the work force, certainly an understatement of actual labor force participation (Pillay 1985, 22). Generally, work available to African women was low paid and low skilled: in a labor market segregated by both race and sex, African women had few options. Many black South African women were employed as domestic workers or earned cash through unregistered activities, usually hawking. But through the 1970s, somewhat better-paid, more stable jobs became available, especially to women with some education. As employers sought to cut labor costs, African women could find jobs in the commercial sector, usually as retail clerks or in low-skilled manufacturing jobs. By 1980, women made up 24.5 percent of the labor force in manufacturing and 38.6 percent of the labor force in commerce (Pillay 1985, 25). For employers, African women seemed to represent a labor pool that could be paid less than, and that was believed to be more docile than, men; for many women, even low-paid industrial or commercial work was more secure and better paid than domestic or informal sector work. Even in heavy industries, some activities—usually relatively unskilled, often involving assembly, machine-operating, sewing, and cleaning—were increasingly defined as women's work: in 1989, about 10 percent, or 34,000, of 330,000 metalworkers were women, most of them African (National Union of Metal Workers of South Africa [NUMSA] 1989, 14).

Patterns of African women's employment also changed in rural areas during the 1980s. Two aspects of government policy in the 1970s increased the chances for women living in bantustans to find paid work near or inside bantustan borders. First, government-aided mechanization of white agriculture reduced the numbers of farm laborers overall but coincided with an increase in women working on farms, generally as seasonal workers at the harvest period.[7] Women's share of the total labor force in commercial agriculture doubled, reaching 24 percent. In 1980, about 17 percent of employed African women worked on commercial farms (Barrett et al. 1985, 20; Marcus 1989, esp. 100–112).

State policies also created new possibilities for industrial employment for African women living outside urban centers. Through the 1970s and especially after 1982, the government began providing new incentives to industries willing to relocate, as part of the effort to slow black urbanization. By the mid–1980s, about 20 percent of South Africa's industrial production was located in nonmetropolitan areas (Wellings and Black 1987, 190). Heavier, more capital-intensive industries, such as metalworking, were unlikely to abandon the infrastructure, access to markets, and skilled labor forces of primary urban centers. But although labor-intensive industries such as textiles complained of the inconvenience, they tended to be attracted by low labor costs: workers in bantustan industrial sites received less than half the wages paid in white-designated urban centers, and labor costs were further cut by government incentive schemes paying as much as 95 percent of the total wage bill (Glaser 1987, 41; Keenan and Sarakinsky 1987, 595; Wellings and Black 1987, 191).

As they moved to semirural areas, employers also developed new attitudes toward employing African women in industrial jobs. The textile industry, which had previously employed mainly non-African women or African men, generally considered African women to be the best potential labor pool in the new industrial sites. Although initially cautious about the shift—in at least one case, hiring psychologists to study the motivation and aptitude of prospective African women workers—a 1970 report by textile industry researchers announced "the suitability of African women for industrial labor" (Mager 1989, 51). By the mid-1980s, African women over twenty were as likely as men to have completed elementary school, while more widespread use of birth control reduced the threat of what one factory supervisor called "the pregnancy factor" (Maconachie 1989, 91; Mager 1989, 51).[8] Employers also recognized that

---

[7] This pattern is not unique to South Africa. Agricultural mechanization reduces total labor requirements but tends to increase seasonal labor demands. In South Africa, even more than elsewhere, poor rural women provide a flexible labor pool, working in family subsistence plots most of the year but remaining available to commercial farmers as wage laborers during peak periods, such as harvesting.

[8] This is a highly controversial issue; a history of racist efforts to reduce African birth rates has made it difficult to find reliable data regarding actual rates of voluntary contraceptive use. Nevertheless, contraceptive use has almost certainly increased over the past decades. In 1982, the Human Sciences Research Council found 57 percent of African women, 78 percent of women classified Indian, and 72 percent of women classified

African women would send their children to be raised by relatives rather than lose their jobs, so that family responsibilities seemed less likely to keep women from working steadily. By 1989, 27 percent of employed black women worked in clothing or leather manufacturing, making up more than two-thirds of the industry's labor force (NUMSA 1989, 14).

Changing labor force participation rates alone clearly do not alter attitudes toward gender ideologies; jobs available to most black South African women remain low paid, backbreaking, insecure, and unrewarding. Until 1981, South African law permitted employers to pay women 20 percent less than men in the same job category; men and women now have equal minimum wages, but pay scales vary, and black women generally remain segregated in low paid occupational categories (Lawson 1986, 57). In industries that employed black semiskilled and skilled workers, black women tended to remain concentrated in less-skilled sections of the factory (NUMSA 1989, 16).

Not surprisingly, many working women say they would prefer to stay at home: long hours and low pay combine with household chores to create a double shift in South Africa as elsewhere, and women often echo a single mother who insisted that the best change a new government could bring women was "to make sure men are paid enough to support their families."[9] Given women's domestic responsibilities and limited options in a labor market shaped by class, race, and gender, many, perhaps most, women may aspire to an idealized nuclear family, in which family members live together, and the husband's wage supports them all.

Nevertheless, a surprising number of working African women comment on the benefits they perceive in working—even when that labor is as backbreaking, low paid, and insecure as seasonal farm work. For women left alone with child-rearing responsibilities, wage labor means both income and greater control over their lives. Given the extraordinary fluidity and insecurity of household structures affected by gendered migration, many women say they prefer working to waiting (Barrett et al. 1985, 138). The links between work and autonomy are often explicit. A domestic worker with six children said she prefers to stay unmarried because "I can be my own boss."[10] A single farm worker feared anything preventing her from working would erode her independence: "I don't have a husband, many women's husbands are migrants, and we must

---

Coloured between the ages of fifteen and forty-nine were using birth control (South African Institute of Race Relations 1986, 3).

[9] Interview conducted by the author with a diamond polisher, Johannesburg, July 11, 1991.

[10] Interview conducted by the author with a domestic worker, Johannesburg, July 13, 1991.

have the ability to speak for ourselves" (Ritchken 1989, 443). Women who have already experienced marriage as an arena of subordination may view staying single as a preferable alternative, even if they have children to raise—as long as they can work (Mullins 1983, 39).[11]

Gender-specific demands

That some women find wage labor grants them greater autonomy both outside and inside the household hardly implies a broad challenge to male domination: similar attitudes were voiced by many nineteenth-century American factory women, and yet the family wage, with attendant dependence on male wage earners, became a standard goal in labor campaigns (May 1985). In a context of political mobilization, however, increased labor force participation and new resources available to semi-autonomous women's groups have changed the way many activists discuss their aspirations. Women involved in the labor movement and in community groups have begun to articulate their political demands as independent citizens with specific needs: instead of asking a postapartheid state to respond to their needs as wives and mothers, they increasingly call for policies that will support women's autonomy while also responding to gender-specific needs.

Since the late 1970s, waves of urban popular mobilization—strikes, demonstrations, boycotts, and worker stay-aways—have placed intermittent pressure on employers and the South African state. Beginning in 1973 when African workers began to organize semilegal unions, the labor movement became a key component of resistance against the state. While some women workers have been active in unions since the 1950s, in the mid-1970s most analysts assumed that black South African women would be more compliant than semiskilled men. By the mid-1970s, however, labor conflicts often involved women workers. Describing strikes in South Africa's textile and garment industry in the 1970s, Iris Berger (1986) concluded that women industrial workers had participated fully in recent labor campaigns, although their specific grievances as women rarely were voiced.

Women workers in South Africa have been directly involved in collective action far more regularly than is usually recognized—in part because, as Joan Scott points out, the language of class tends to be universalist, and universal categories tend to assume male subjects (Scott 1988, 64). A

[11] Even for women with husbands living at home, relatively steady employment can alter the balance of power within the household. A textile worker said, "I like shift work. It gives me time to myself so that I have time away from my husband at home. I don't have to work so hard in the house and attend to my husband. . . . We don't quarrel so much when I work shift" (Mager 1989, 51–52).

1976 metalworkers' strike at Heinemann's, for example, is famous in South African labor history because fired workers successfully challenged employers and police in court. The strike involved over a hundred women workers, but descriptions of the strike, using the gender-neutral term "worker," have tended to obscure that fact.[12] Similarly, in the mid-1980s, the retail workers' union mounted one of the longest national strikes in South African history, yet reports on the strike generally failed to mention that the membership was almost entirely female (*Work in Progress* 1987).

Especially after unions were more or less legalized starting in 1979, women workers could hardly be described as docile. By the mid-1980s, labor organizers increasingly acknowledged that despite their relatively insecure position on the labor market, and despite domestic responsibilities, women workers in urban areas had often participated actively in the unions of the 1970s.[13] Speaking in a slightly different context, Frances Baard, a veteran trade unionist and leading community activist, put it succinctly: "We know that there is no freedom [for] the men without the women" (Baard 1986, 89).

Two tendencies help explain the surprising degree of activism by women workers, each related to women's subordination at home and at work. As real wages declined in the 1970s, black workers—always poorly paid—found wages could no longer stretch to cover family needs. Thus, "the massive strike actions of 1973–74 over low wages might [be] interpreted as addressing the mounting problems of adequate reproduction for urban dwellers" whose low wages were unlikely to be supplemented by family agriculture in rural areas (Mabin 1989, 7). Women workers, especially single women with children to feed, were especially vulnerable, relegated as they generally were to low-paid jobs, yet left with primary responsibility for child maintenance. June Rose Nala, a Natal metalworkers' organizer in the 1970s, concluded, "The sense of responsibility of women to the family often contributed to their strength. Most of the women were single mothers. . . . Since [their wage] was their only source of income, the need to improve it increased their determination to fight for better wages and working conditions" (Beall, Hassim, and Todes 1989, 46). Moreover, a labor market strictly divided along racial and gender lines, in which few African women could expect to move into semiskilled or skilled jobs, meant that most women industrial workers could not hope to be given better jobs within the factory hierarchy. Thus, collective action offered the only real possibility of improved wages;

---

[12] Interview conducted by the author with Lydia Kompe, community organizer, Johannesburg, May 1987. (See also *South African Labour Bulletin* 1977.)

[13] Interview conducted by the author with a Paper, Wood and Allied Workers' Union organizer, Johannesburg, July 1984.

individual mobility within a workplace was unlikely. A member of the Congress of South African Trade Unions (COSATU) women's committee said, "Women's problems are the same at work and at home—low wages and low skills. They have to organize to overcome them."[14]

But in South Africa as in much of the world, most visible labor and community leaders were men. In the labor movement, with some notable exceptions (Lydia Kompe, Emma Mashinini, June Rose Nala), most paid organizers were male, even in industries with largely female work forces. Until the early 1980s, union activists generally echoed the nationalist movement as a whole: challenges to gender subordination were considered a threat to the labor movement's unity. Some gender-specific demands—maternity leave, equal pay, day-care centers, health care facilities, and protection for pregnant women—were included in union negotiations beginning in 1983 (Jaffee 1987), but until the late 1980s the labor movement generally subsumed women workers' needs under the needs of all workers.

It is conceivable that women workers raised issues of domestic subordination but that these were overlooked or repressed by organizers who were threatened personally by them or who feared division within the movement. In questioning labor and community activists, however, I could find no clear examples of this kind of squelching before the late 1980s. A more likely explanation is that few women felt comfortable raising such issues in mixed groups until after political mobilization and women's self-organization had changed the prevailing climate. Whatever the reason, gender relations within the working class were generally only mentioned when household responsibilities were blamed for women workers' failure to attend union meetings. Although COSATU's 1985 "Resolution on Women" recognized the "equal right of men and women to work," the sex-segregation of the labor market, and the dangers of sexual harassment on the job (COSATU 1985), COSATU's education officer, Chris Seopesenge, acknowledged three years later that this had remained "a paper resolution," because "there is little sympathy for women's problems" within the labor federation's leadership (COSATU, 1988).

Organizational resources

By the early 1990s, however, few community or labor activists would openly dismiss gender-specific concerns or suggest postponing discussions of "women's problems." Indeed, the oft-repeated description of the

---

[14] Interview conducted by the author with a COSATU women's committee member, Johannesburg, July 7, 1991.

goals of the antiapartheid movement expanded from "a nonracial, democratic South Africa" to "a nonracial, democratic, nonsexist South Africa"—a rhetorical shift reflecting growing awareness and acceptance of gender concerns. What gave rise to the increased visibility of gender-specific demands? From the mid-1980s, in communities and within unions, women activists took up new forms of organization, creating forums in which women could articulate their own demands and drawing on new resources available for women's organizations. With increased institutional support for a gendered perspective, women activists began to raise issues in broader organizations, and these issues were gradually incorporated into the broad political agenda of the antiapartheid movement.

Participation of large numbers of working women in community groups became especially visible beginning in the early 1980s, as segregated black communities began to organize around local issues such as bus fare and rent increases, education, and the legalization of squatter communities. Emphasizing problems of urban social reproduction—especially the absence or cost of basic urban social services—community organizations often grew out of family concerns: parents concerned about the growing education crisis or adults unable to stretch low wages to cover family maintenance.

The leadership of most civic associations remained largely male, and these groups rarely addressed issues of social reproduction in gendered terms.[15] But because most local issues were related to the domestic sphere, focusing on the state's failure to provide basic resources to African households, these groups were especially likely to attract women participants. While no black worker could easily overlook the close relation between low wages and the low living standards of black townships, women workers—given primary responsibility for family maintenance under both Western and African gender ideologies—were especially likely to view domestic issues in political terms. In the mid-1980s, as community mobilization was beginning to escalate into what would become a full-scale uprising, a member of the Vaal Women's Organization said, "The problem is that people . . . get low wages and can't afford [high] rent. . . . As mothers we can't afford the rent. When a child is hungry the mother is affected, and she can't afford to educate her children because the rent is high" (Barrett et al. 1985, 252). Some groups

---

[15] Emphasizing the lack of women leaders, Seekings 1991 suggests that women's roles in the uprising were shaped by patriarchal gender ideologies and the division of household labor. However, his description completely ignores most women's organizations, and his focus on violent confrontations and arrest figures may lead him to underestimate the role of women activists in less confrontational forms of political mobilization.

were explicitly oriented toward women, such as cooperatives formed to provide alternative income-generating projects for women unemployed in the worsening recession (Beall et al. 1987).

As political organization spread and mobilization intensified, women began increasingly to organize their own groups. By 1986, separate women's organizations had been formed in most of South Africa. The United Women's Organization, for example, was formed in Cape Town in 1979; the Vaal Women's Organization was formed in 1983; the Lamontville women's group was formed in 1983; and the Federation of South African Women, first founded in 1954, was revived in the early 1980s. By the late 1980s, many of these groups had begun to articulate a visible gendered perspective within the nationalist movement.

Black South African women have a long tradition of organizing separately, and many of the new women's organizations in the 1980s explicitly drew on the women's neighborhood groups and savings clubs through which many urban African women have coped with poverty and local community problems (Barrett et al. 1985, esp. 214–23). It would not have been surprising if these new women's organizations, most of which were affiliated to broader political groups, had subsumed gender-specific issues under the banner of national liberation, avoiding discussions of gender subordination that might split the popular movement. Often led by women who sought to improve women's condition without challenging male control, these groups could, and sometimes did, see themselves as "ladies' auxiliaries" to local civic associations, not as groups planning to articulate feminist demands.

But through the uprising of the late 1980s, women activists increasingly discussed domestic issues in terms of gender relations as well as in terms of racial and class oppression. In a highly politicized environment, discussions of income-generating opportunities for women, day-care facilities, or the political basis of problems of household maintenance could lead to discussions of family relationships, as women explored the causes of their problems together. For black women, it has been argued, involvement in political campaigns sometimes served as a kind of consciousness-raising process: as more women felt a new degree of political efficacy, some activists began to distinguish gender subordination from the struggle against racial domination (Beall, Hassim, and Todes 1989). Moreover, so many women worked outside the home and participated actively in the labor movement as well as in community organizations that many groups began to challenge the assumption that women's activities were or should be restricted to the household.

Perhaps the most vivid illustration of the way political mobilization could lead to discussions of gender relations within townships was the 1986 stay-away organized by the Port Alfred Women's Organization. Shortly after its founding at the height of the 1985–87 uprising, the organization learned that police had released a known rapist shortly after he had viciously attacked a fifty-nine-year-old African woman. The following day, virtually every working African woman in the township stayed away from work; the stay-away—a tactic that capitalized on women's high labor force participation—lasted a week. Sexual harassment appears to have been discussed openly and explicitly as a form of oppression of women, and the women's organization refused to allow the civic association's male leaders to participate in negotiations with the local white authorities. A leading activist said, "We did not want men involved in organizing or negotiating around the stayaway. Men are not victims of rape" (Forrest and Jochelson 1986). Although the alleged rapist, who was black, was protected by white police, his house was burned down, and he was eventually charged with assault. Since then, debates around the political aspects of rape and violence against women (Vogelman 1990; van Zyl 1991) reflect a growing awareness, at least among political activists, that problematizing gender issues involves moving beyond questions of equal pay to consider the links among sexuality, reproduction, and gender inequality.[16]

As community-based women's organizations grew in strength and visibility, activists in the labor movement also began to stress gender-specific issues. For women unionists, community issues appear to have been particularly salient, often taking priority over workplace organization; metalworker Lydia Kompe, for example, left her union in the early 1980s because of what she called a "reformist" emphasis on the shop floor and her union's refusal to address broader community problems.[17] Emma Mashinini, former retail workers' organizer, has written, "The trade unions have got to follow the workers in all their travels—to get them home, and to school, in the education and welfare of their children, everywhere. The whole life of a worker needs trade union involvement" (Mashinini 1991, 119). Berger found that garment workers "saw their economic grievances as central to fulfilling their roles as women" and referred constantly to "the necessity to feed, clothe and educate their children" (Berger 1986, 232–33).

Women workers were not alone in asking unions to take up issues of social reproduction as well as issues from the workplace; male unionists also raised issues like rents and transportation, viewing these costs as

---

[16] During late 1989 and 1990, a broad public discussion among community activists in Soweto and other townships focused on gangs involved in what was called "jack-rolling," or gang rape. Because policing in black communities for normal crimes is practically nonexistent, however, and because rape is generally underreported, it is impossible to be sure whether the increased discussion is due to an actual increase in the incidence of rape, or whether it is due to increased reporting linked to politicization of issues around gender and sexuality. Both factors may be involved.

[17] Interview conducted by the author with Lydia Kompe, community organizer, Johannesburg, May 1987.

reducing their wages.[18] But women's responsibilities for most domestic maintenance may have prompted them to view labor and community issues as inextricably interlocked. Berger (1989) suggests that the emergence of a broadly defined "class consciousness," where labor movements take up issues beyond the workplace, may be a gendered process, in which women workers' domestic responsibilities have made them more likely to raise community issues than their male co-workers.

Certainly this was true of the broad working-class movement that swept South Africa in the mid-1980s, which encompassed rural workers and their families as well as industrial workers and which expressed its goals in terms of all workers rather than union members alone. Clearly linked to the rise of community activism, the labor movement reflected members' understanding of the links between work and family life and made demands on the state that reflected the sphere of reproduction as well as production. The extent to which women workers differed from their male counterparts in the formulation of demands remains relatively unexplored, but as the broad labor movement spread, women workers certainly began to argue that their domestic roles gave them a special set of concerns about child care, family health, family maintenance, and reproductive rights.

To many activists, women's separate organization appeared a key first step toward ensuring that those concerns would be expressed in public debates. In 1988, when the labor federation COSATU held its first "women's conference," the debate around gender-specific demands had moved past maternity benefits and equal pay to focus more directly on how to organize women workers separately so that they could formulate and articulate their needs in an atmosphere less dominated by male unionists. Although many of the conference resolutions expressed demands that had been raised in the past—equal pay, maternity leave, health care, day care, and an end to sexual harassment by supervisors— all resolutions were worded to stress men's and women's equal responsibility for, and control within, families. The conference insisted that COSATU should help challenge gender ideologies, suggesting that it sponsor workshops on family violence and sexual harassment and on "progressive methods of equalizing relationships between men and women" and that it educate members about "the role of women as breadwinners and about the need to share childcare and housework."

[18] See, e.g., Minutes of Raleigh Cycles (Nutfield) Management/Works Committee Meetings 60 and 61, n.d., and September 9, 1979, Federation of South African Trade Unions (FOSATU) archives. Topics discussed included management refusals to allow trade union meetings on premises; protective clothing and toilet facilities; overfull buses to townships; transportation for late shifts; and the possibilities of employer intervention to assist with tax refunds. FOSATU later merged with other union groups to become COSATU.

Finally, the conference called on the labor movement to campaign for free and legal abortions, address unequal property rights for women, and challenge church teachings and gender ideologies that "propagat[e] women's domestic inferior role" (COSATU 1988, esp. 17–36).

Left on paper, these resolutions might not have been particularly influential. But the conference proposed that, instead of blaming women for failing to attend meetings, the federation should seek to increase women's participation in leadership by creating separate women's groups in each union. Despite objections that such structures might divide the unions and split working women from women in communities and despite fears that women's forums would only attract women already active in unions rather than generate new participation, these structures were in place in several unions within four years.[19] Organizers believed the groups helped women overcome cultural patterns that prevent women from speaking out in front of men. Shop steward Elizabeth Thabethe told an interviewer, "We have found that some of the women are more open and prepared to talk when they attend the Women's Forum than when they participate in [branch meetings] or in the congresses. They build confidence in the Women's Forum and then are able to attend and participate in other structures. They begin to understand why they are involved and that women can be leaders too. . . . From there they are able to move to other positions" (Thabethe 1991, 92). And organizer Lucy Nyembe said, "The fact of the matter is, so long as there are not women's structures, women's issues are marginalized to the extent that they are not even put on any agenda" (Shefer 1991, 55).

Forum organizers claim that the creation of a separate space in which women workers can discuss issues such as maternity rights or day-care facilities makes it more likely these issues will be elaborated, brought forward to the general union, and raised in negotiations with employers. In 1991, despite objections from unionists who feared separate women's groups would marginalize women's concerns from mainstream union activities, COSATU agreed to employ a full-time women's coordinator, responsible for organizing women's forums and conducting research into problems facing women workers.[20] A parallel process occurred within the broader antiapartheid movement: women activists, often representing separate women's groups, increasingly raised gender-specific issues within the broader movement, challenging nationalist organizations to take these issues more seriously and to incorporate them into a broader political agenda.

[19] *COSATU News*, no. 1 (February 1989), 13; *COSATU News*, no. 2 (March 1989), 13. (See also Klugman 1989.)
[20] Resolution passed at the Fourth COSATU Congress, July 1991.

The spread of women's organizations and the increased visibility of gender-specific issues were certainly assisted by a growing awareness of international feminist perspectives. National debates take place within an international context, which in turn helps shape dynamics in internal discussions. South African women activists, both in exile and inside the country, were influenced by international feminist debates. There have also been more direct interventions, as international groups offered opinions and resources supporting gendered organizations and demands. Outside agencies often promoted a gendered perspective of nationalist goals. Sometimes, outside organizations raised awareness of gender-specific problems just by asking questions. A COSATU officer offered this example: "When the Canadian unions sent a delegation here, they sent mainly women, because of debates in their own unions. In addition to their regular work, they wanted to meet COSATU women, and talked to them about women's issues. It made us think more seriously about those issues than we might have otherwise."[21] Because international donors were ready to fund programs geared primarily to women, he said, it was easier for COSATU to adopt new programs. "It made us more amenable than we might otherwise have been" to attempts to increase women's representation within union discussions and to creating separate women's forums. Other union organizers similarly acknowledge that union decisions to emphasize recruitment of women workers were sometimes designed to appeal to foreign donors, rather than simply reflecting internal demand.[22]

South African activists knew that international donors, aware by the 1980s of how international aid programs have tended to neglect women's needs, were willing to support programs aimed at women; the availability of these resources almost certainly gave gender issues greater institutional support than they might otherwise have received. From the mid-1980s, several books and journals raising gender-related issues were published with external assistance, and community groups found funding for projects geared specifically to women relatively available from international church, labor, and antiapartheid groups. In 1982, for example, a Johannesburg women's group embarked on a study of apartheid's effects on working African women initiated and funded by the Catholic Institute for International Relief.[23] *Speak,* a women's magazine aimed at working women that seeks to popularize issues of women's health, family issues,

---

[21] Interview conducted by the author with a COSATU official, Johannesburg, May 1991.

[22] Interview conducted by the author with an organizer for the Commercial, Catering Workers' Union, Durban, June 1990.

[23] Interview conducted by the author with a member of the group that wrote *Vukani Mahkhosikazi,* Johannesburg, 1983.

and gender-specific labor issues, was funded by overseas church groups as well as by street sales.[24] But perhaps the most obvious example of how outside interventions could change political discourse in the antiapartheid movement occurred when Dutch antiapartheid activists brought several hundred South African women to Holland in early 1990 to discuss the incorporation of gender issues into the antiapartheid agenda. The papers presented at this conference have been criticized for a tendency to correlate "women" with motherhood, but debates at the conference and the views of Dutch feminists clearly affected the way many South African participants viewed gender issues (Charman, de Swart, and Simons 1991). A Durban community activist said, "I had already thought women had special issues; but the Dutch feminists, and some of the South African exiles we met in Holland, made us rethink the relation between those issues and the anti-apartheid struggle" — especially the importance of raising gender issues during the process of social transformation, rather than waiting until after attaining national liberation.[25]

There seems to be widespread agreement among activists that foreign interest has helped strengthen the institutional framework in which gender-specific issues have been raised. This tendency, however, does not imply that gender-specific issues are a foreign import. Indeed, the Cape Town's United Women's Organization specifically voted to reject international donations for organizational work in order to avoid unnecessary dependence — although, even in this unusual case, funds were accepted for "special projects" such as a day-care center. But international donors' interest in gender issues clearly helped make gender-specific programs more acceptable. As one community activist concluded, "Access to that kind of money does affect the way people think about issues."[26]

The extent to which gender-related issues had been incorporated in debates within the popular nationalist movement became clear in January 1991 when an academic conference in Durban designed to bring together gender-related research provoked controversy, not from those who wished to postpone discussion of divisive feminist issues but instead from those who believed conference organizers should have focused on community concerns rather than on academic research. In the heat of the debate, few commented on how surprising it would have been a decade earlier if any community activists had been willing to attend such a meeting (e.g., *Agenda* 1991; Horn 1991). Activists who almost certainly

[24] Interview conducted by the author with a member of the *Speak* editorial board, March 1987.

[25] Interview conducted by the author with a Malibongwe participant, Durban, July 1990.

[26] Interview conducted by the author with an FSAW activist, Johannesburg, August 9, 1991.

once would have considered gender issues divisive were remarkably insistent that these issues now had a grass-roots constituency and could no longer be postponed. While community activists warned that academic interventions could distract from issues of immediate importance to women in the nationalist movement, their concern was more about whether community women's voices would be heard in the feminist discussion than whether any discussion of feminism at all would distract from the struggle against white supremacy.

Gender on the national agenda?

Since early 1990, when the South African government removed its bans on political parties, released most political prisoners, and allowed exiles to return, debates about the transition to majority rule and about the system of governance to follow apartheid have been heated—and have included questions about how gender issues will be addressed. Few South African women easily accept the label "feminist" even now, but the problematization of gender relations and the household has increasingly been included in broader debates within the antiapartheid movement. Within the urban popular movement, support has clearly emerged for demands that in another context would be labeled feminist: equal access to work, shared family resources and responsibilities, and challenges to male political and social domination, even in the private sphere. No one could claim that gender-specific demands are fully incorporated into the agenda of either the ANC or the labor movement, nor can one be sure how far these discussions are carried into personal relationships. Nevertheless, at least in the public arena, debates in the early 1990s indicated that gender relations and ideologies were questioned more and more within important working-class and political organizations.

Within the ANC's Women's League—an organization that previously insisted on postponing discussion of gender until after liberation—activists have insisted on raising gender issues during negotiations toward majority rule. Officially launched inside South Africa in early 1991, the league has been marked by a far more assertive feminist approach than had been expected by most of its organizers, mainly returned exiles. A returned exile said after the launch meeting that she had been "stunned" by the extent to which "ordinary delegates wanted to raise feminist issues"—from a gendered job market and the double day to sexual harassment and male attitudes within political organizations.[27] Another delegate said, "The grassroots delegates knew what their problems are,

---

[27] Interview conducted by the author with an ANC Women's Section officer, Johannesburg, May 1991.

and could describe them in great detail; the leadership has to learn to listen."[28] League officials claimed that even activists who still draw on traditional images of women as wives and mothers have recognized the changing terms of the debate: "The older women speak a different language but they are not resisting the changes" (Daniels 1991).

After its launch, league officials planned both to continue to encourage women's participation in national antiapartheid campaigns and to continue a campaign to draw up a new "women's charter" to be included in the constitutional arrangements for a future government. Unlike an earlier document with the same name, this charter was to be created through consultation with local women's groups across the political spectrum, in a process designed to encourage debate among women about their needs.[29] By holding public meetings about what would be included in the charter, the Women's League hoped to develop broad consensus among women about issues such as maternity and child-care rights, gender oppression within family units, unpaid labor within the household, control over fertility, violence against women, and property rights (Maurice 1991). While recognizing that differences of race, age, class, education, and political perspective divide South African women, the Women's League hoped to explore common themes by focusing on gender relations within the household and on social relations that perpetuate gender subordination.

But perhaps the Women's League's most controversial proposal was that the ANC adopt a quota to ensure that women were included in its national leadership—a proposal illustrating the Women's League's growing insistence that women's voices be included in negotiations. In July 1991, fifty new members were to be elected to the ANC national executive committee. The Women's League asked that 30 percent, or fifteen positions, be given to women, arguing that unrestricted elections would merely perpetuate a long history of gender-based discrimination in which women activists worked within organizations but were rarely given leadership positions.[30] The Women's League's insistence on a quota stood in direct contrast to its long history as a ladies' auxiliary organization; delegates asked "that the organization honor its commitment to women,"

[28] Interview conducted by the author with a United Women's Organization executive committee member and Women's League member, Cape Town, July 1991.

[29] While the new Women's Charter will certainly include new issues—reflecting both the broader process through which it is being drawn up, and the way that circumstances and language have changed since the 1950s—the process probably has greater legitimacy in the eyes of many ANC activists than it might have had if the earlier charter had not existed.

[30] The proposal was somewhat confusing. The Women's League's initial proposal had apparently been to ask that 30 percent of nominees be women, leaving delegates to vote freely. At the ANC's national congress, however, the proposal was presented in terms of elected positions, not candidates.

arguing that women were already active participants at the grass-roots level and that only affirmative action could overcome institutionalized gender oppression (Turok 1991, 9).

If it had been accepted, the quota "would have gone a long way in giving a practical demonstration of the ANC's expressed support of affirmative action" (Serote 1991). The debate nearly derailed the entire ANC conference: supporters of the motion, both male and female, insisted that only a quota would avoid the familiar pattern restricting women activists to mid-level leadership, while opponents argued that a quota would limit delegates' free choice. Although the national leadership appeared to support the proposal, ordinary delegates—83 percent of whom were men—rejected the principle. More controversial than any other issue at the week-long meeting, the proposal never came to a vote; after three hours of heated debate, the Women's League withdrew the resolution, replacing it with a vaguer resolution in support of affirmative action (Turok 1991, 9). Ultimately, only nine women were elected to the national executive committee, and of these, as Women's League activists pointed out, nearly all had remained relatively silent during the quota discussion.[31] Several women activists who had been expected to win election to the national executive believed they had been penalized for their vocal support of a quota.[32]

As this quota debate revealed, demands that directly challenged male control of popular organizations were still likely to meet a great deal of resistance in organizations dominated by male activists. In 1989, a COSATU congress had similarly tabled resolutions condemning sexual harassment of women workers by union organizers and calling for conscious efforts to elect women leaders. As in the ANC, national union leaders' support for feminist demands was outweighed by objections from rank-and-file male delegates (Obery 1989). Recognizing the pattern, a furious ANC activist commented, "Backward attitudes of male superiority and female inferiority need to be changed in both men and women. Nelson Mandela told the racist court in 1962 that he felt he was a black man in a white man's court. Women should not feel in the ANC and other democratic organizations that they are women in a men's movement. A genuine commitment to end discrimination against women is needed, in practice and not just in declared policy" (Mayibuye Correspondent 1991).

Strong opposition to challenges to traditional gender ideologies should hardly come as a surprise; such opposition is hardly limited to nationalist movements. Far more surprising is the extent to which activists within the

[31] The actual number of women on the ANC's national executive is greater, because several women are among the thirty-two ex-officio members.

[32] Interview conducted by the author with a Women's League officer, Johannesburg, July 20, 1991.

ANC have begun to insist that the nationalist movement address gender concerns directly. Shireen Hassim warned, "We need to maintain a healthy scepticism about the ability of the post-apartheid state to meet the demands of women, or to anticipate policies which will empower women. . . . Unless the Women's League begins to intervene actively in these debates, the possibility grows that women's concerns will be marginalized yet again" (Hassim 1991).

These debates illustrate the extent to which gender issues have been problematized, at least in public debates. Without household-level research, it is hard to draw any conclusions about whether personal relationships are changing; at least at the level of public discussions within the nationalist movement, however, gender issues have clearly gained new prominence. Indeed, in early 1992, the Women's League created a special committee to work with the ANC's negotiating team to ensure that all proposals for new government structures included some consideration of gender issues,[33] and the league joined thirty-nine other women's organizations from across the political spectrum to discuss possible constitutional proposals (Baker 1992).

While it would be foolhardy to predict what will happen during the process of transition, it seems undeniable that feminist demands within the South African nationalist movement emanate not from a few educated women or the national leadership but from within precisely the popular base from which the ANC draws its support. To a far greater extent than other nationalist movements attaining power, the postapartheid state will certainly face popular pressure to give women equal access to resources, jobs, training, and property, as well as pressure to question male control within the household. That pressure will come from women who are already economically independent, who have organized in independent and semi-independent women's groups, and who clearly insist that gender-specific issues must be addressed in the transition to a democratic society.

Conclusion

Until the mid-1980s, a postapartheid South African state seemed likely to mirror the experience of other nationalist movements, where male activists would seek to recreate households that assumed male dominance. In the 1990s, however, such reconstruction seems far less likely, in part because the peasant economy has been undermined, but also because women, initially mobilized against the state, have increasingly incorporated gender issues into their understanding of the problems they confront.

---

[33] Personal communication to the author from Jacklyn Cock, April 1992.

Three distinct, though related, processes have created a social basis for popular feminist demands in South Africa—demands that challenge gender subordination and male-dominant gender relations within the popular movement. First, the gender-specific effects of the migrant labor system have undermined the peasant economy; once in power, the nationalist movement is less likely to seek to reconstruct peasant households, a goal that seems repeatedly to have subverted feminist goals in more agrarian-based movements. Second, the high labor force participation of African women in South Africa has created an unusual degree of economic independence among women, increasing the likelihood that women could participate in unions and community groups and strengthening the recognition that women's activities are not confined to the domestic sphere. Third, the involvement of significant numbers of women in community and labor organizations—especially in separate women's forums—has allowed the articulation of gender-specific demands, not for a family wage for male earners but for increased equality for women both inside and outside the home. In an international context that provides support and resources for raising gender-specific issues, South African activists have begun to place gendered demands on the national agenda.

Historically, nationalist movements have tended to respond to demands articulated by male household heads, overlooking the ways in which women have sought to restructure society. Similarly, the demands of working-class women have repeatedly been subsumed by demands for a family wage, reinforcing male authority within the household. In South Africa, we can watch in a contemporary setting the formation of a nationalist and working-class consciousness and observe the extent to which women activists articulate a somewhat different agenda than do their male counterparts. As women activists organize a broad constituency for gender-specific demands, it seems increasingly probable that the demands they make on the postapartheid state will seek to create an unusual degree of support for women's economic independence and personal autonomy.

Department of Sociology
University of Wisconsin—Madison

References

Agenda. 1991. "Impressions: Conference on 'Women and Gender in Southern Africa.'" *Agenda: A Journal about Women and Gender* 9:20–23.

Alvarez, Sonia E. 1990. *Engendering Democracy in Brazil: Women's Movements in Transition Politics.* Princeton, N.J.: Princeton University Press.

Baard, Frances. 1986. *My Spirit Is Not Banned.* As told to Barbie Schreiner. Harare: Zimbabwe Publishing House.

Baker, Beathur. 1992. "Sisters Are Doing It for Themselves." *Weekly Mail* (March 13–19).

Barrett, Jane, Aneene Dawber, Barbara Klugman, Ingrid Obery, Jennifer Shindler, and Joanne Yawitch. 1985. *Vukhani Makhosikazi: South African Women Speak.* London: Catholic Institute for International Relief.

Beall, Jo, Michelle Friedmann, Shireen Hassim, Ros Posel, Lindy Steibel, and Alison Todes. 1987. "African Women in the Durban Struggle, 1985–1986: Towards a Transformation of Roles?" In *South African Review Four,* 93–103. Johannesburg: Ravan Press.

Beall, Jo, Shireen Hassim, and Alison Todes. 1989. " 'A Bit on the Side?' Gender Struggles in the Politics of Transformation in South Africa." *Feminist Review* 33:30–56.

Beinart, William. 1987. "Amafelandawonye (the Die-hards)." In *Hidden Struggles in Rural South Africa,* by W. Beinart and C. Bundy, 222–70. London: James Currey.

Berger, Iris. 1986. "Sources of Class Consciousness: South African Women in Recent Labor Struggles." In *Women and Class in Africa,* ed. Claire Robertson and Iris Berger, 216–36. New York: Africana Publishing.

———. 1989. "Gender and Working-Class History: South Africa in Comparative Perspective." *Journal of Women's History* 1(2):117–33.

Bonner, Philip. 1990. " 'Desirable or Undesirable Basotho Women?' Liquor, Prostitution and the Migration of Basotho Women to the Rand, 1920–1945." In *Women and Gender in Southern Africa to 1945,* ed. Cherryl Walker, 221–50. Cape Town: David Philip.

Brenner, Johanna, and Barbara Laslett. 1991. "Gender, Social Reproduction and Women's Self-Organization: Considering the U.S. Welfare State." *Gender and Society* 5(3):311–33.

Charman, A., C. de Swart, and M. Simons. 1991. "The Politics of Gender: Negotiating Liberation." *Transformation* 15:40–64.

Chatterjee, Partha. 1989. "Colonialism, Nationalism, and Colonized Women: The Contest in India." *American Ethnologist* 16(4): 622–33.

Chinchilla, Norma Stoltz. 1991. "Marxism, Feminism and the Struggle for Democracy in Latin America." *Gender and Society* 5(3):291–310.

"Clara, writing from the underground." 1989. "Feminism and the Struggle for National Liberation." *African Communist* 118:38–43.

Cock, Jacklyn. 1990. "Domestic Service and Education for Domesticity." In *Women and Gender in Southern Africa to 1945,* ed. Cherryl Walker, 76–96. Cape Town: David Philip.

Comaroff, Jean. 1985. *Body of Power, Spirit of Resistance: The Culture and History of a South African People.* Chicago: University of Chicago Press.

Congress of South African Trade Unions. 1985. "Resolution on Women." Johannesburg: COSATU.

———. 1988. *COSATU Women's Conference.* Johannesburg: COSATU.

Daniels, Glenda. 1991. "ANC's Women's League: Breaking Out of the Mold?" *Work in Progress,* no. 75, 36.

Duncan, Sheena. 1983. "Aspects of Family Breakdown." *Work in Progress,* no. 27, 36–38.

Forrest, Kally, and Karen Jochelson. 1986. "The Port Alfred Women's Stayaway: Uniting against Rape." *Work in Progress,* no. 43, 25–28.

Ginwala, Frene. 1986. "ANC Women: Their Strength in the Struggle." *Work in Progress,* no. 45, 10–14.

Glaser, Daryl. 1987. "A Periodisation of South Africa's Industrial Dispersal Policies." In *Regional Restructuring under Apartheid: Urban and Regional Policies in Contemporary South Africa,* ed. Richard Tomlinson and Mark Addleson, 28–54. Johannesburg: Ravan Press.

Greenberg, Stanley. 1987. *Legitimating the Illegitimate: State, Markets and Resistance in South Africa.* Berkeley and Los Angeles: University of California Press.

Hassim, Shireen. 1991. "Gender, Social Location and Feminist Politics in South Africa." *Transformation* 15:79–81.

Hindson, Doug, 1987. *Pass Controls and the Urban African Proletariat in South Africa.* Johannesburg: Ravan Press.

Horn, Patricia. 1991. "Conference on Women and Gender in Southern Africa: Another View of the Dynamics." *Transformation* 15:83–88.

Horrell, Muriel. 1968. *The Rights of African Women: Some Suggested Reforms.* Johannesburg: South African Institute of Race Relations.

Jaffee, Georgina. 1987. "Women in Trade Unions and the Community." In *South African Review Four,* 75–92. Johannesburg: Ravan Press.

Jelin, Elizabeth, ed. 1990. *Women and Social Change in Latin America,* trans. J. Ann Zammit and M. Thomson. London: Zed Press and UN Research Institute for Social Development.

Keenan, Jeremy, and Mike Sarakinsky. 1987. "Reaping the Benefits: Working Conditions in Agriculture and the Bantustans." In *South African Review Four,* 581–99. Johannesburg: Ravan Press.

Kgositsile, Baleka. 1990. "The Woman Question: Are the Chains Breaking?" *African Communist* 120:52–59.

Kimble, Judy, and Elaine Unterhalter, 1982. "ANC Women's Struggles, 1912–1982." *Feminist Review* 12:11–35.

Klugman, Barbara. 1989. "Women Workers in the Unions." *South African Labour Bulletin* 14(4):13–36.

Kruks, Sonia, and Ben Wisner. 1989. "Ambiguous Transformations: Women, Politics and Production in Mozambique." In *Promissory Notes: Women in the Transition to Socialism,* ed. Sonia Kruks, Rayna Rapp, and Marilyn B. Young, 148–71. New York: Monthly Review Press.

Lawson, Lesley, for the SACHED Trust. 1986. *Working Women in South Africa.* London: Pluto Press.

Lucas, Robert E. B. 1987. "Emigration to South Africa's Mines." *American Economic Review* 77(3):313–30.

Mabin, Alan. 1989. "Struggle for the City: Urbanisation and Political Strategies of the South African State." *Social Dynamics* 155(1):1–28.

Maconachie, Moira. 1989. "Looking for Patterns of Women's Employment and Educational Achievements in the 1985 Census." *Agenda: Journal about Women and Gender* 5:89–95.

Mager, Ann. 1989. "Moving the Fence: Gender in the Ciskei and Border Textile Industry, 1945–1986." *Social Dynamics* 15(2):46–62.

Marcus, Tessa, 1989. *Modernizing Super-exploitation: Restructuring South African Agriculture.* London: Zed Press.

Mashinini, Emma. 1991. *Strikes Have Followed Me All My Life.* New York: Routledge, Chapman, Hall.

Maurice, Portia. 1991. "Protecting the Rights of SA's Women." *Weekly Mail* (August 9–15).

May, Martha. 1985. "Bread before Roses: American Workingmen, Labor Unions and the Family Wage." In *Women, Work and Protest,* ed. Ruth Milkman, 1–21. New York: Routledge & Kegan Paul.

Mayibuye Correspondent. 1991. "Affirmative Action." *Mayibuye: Journal of the African National Congress* 2(7):28.

Meintjes, Sheila. 1990. "Family and Gender in the Christian Community at Edendale, Natal, in Colonial Times." In *Women and Gender in Southern Africa to 1945,* ed. Cherryl Walker, 125–45. Cape Town: David Philip.

Molyneux, Maxine. 1986. "Mobilization without Emancipation? Women's Interests, State, and Revolution." In *Transition and Development: Problems of Third World Socialism,* ed. Richard R. Fagen, Carmen Diana Deere, and Jose Luis Coraggio, 280–302. New York: Monthly Review Press.

Mullins, Anne. 1983. "Working Women Speak," *Work in Progress,* no. 27, 38–40.

Murray, Colin. 1981. *Families Divided: The Impact of Migrant Labour in Lesotho.* Johannesburg: Ravan Press.

———. 1987. "Class, Gender and the Household: The Development Cycle in Southern Africa." *Development and Change* 18:235–49.

National Union of Metalworkers of South Africa. 1989. *NUMSA Women Organise!* Johannesburg: COSATU.

Obery, Ingrid. 1989. "Challenging Sexual Exploitation." *Work in Progress,* no. 61, 30–33.

Pedraza, Silvia. 1991. "Women and Migration: The Social Consequences of Gender." *Annual Review of Sociology* 17:303–25.

Pillay, Pundy. 1985. "Women in Employment: Some Important Trends and Issues." *Social Dynamics* 11(2):20–37.

Ramphele, Mamphela. 1989. "The Dynamics of Gender Politics in the Hostels of Cape Town: Another Legacy of the South African Migrant System." *Journal of Southern African Studies* 15(3):393–414.

Ritchken, Edwin. 1989. "The KwaNdebele Struggle against Independence," *South African Review Five,* 391–402. Johannesburg: Ravan Press.

Russell, Sharon Stanton. 1986. "Remittances from International Migration: A Review in Perspective." *World Development* 14(6):677–96.

Scott, Joan. 1988. *Gender and the Politics of History.* New York: Columbia University Press.

Seekings, Jeremy. 1991. "Gender Ideology and Township Politics in the 1980s." *Agenda: A Journal about Women and Society* 10:77–88.

Serote, Pethu. 1991. "National Liberation Equals Women's Emancipation: A Myth Totally Exploded." *Agenda: A Journal about Women and Society* 11:5–6.

Shefer, Tammy. 1991. "COSATU Women's Forums: Separate to Get Strong." *Agenda: A Journal about Women and Society* 9:53–59.

Simkins, Charles. 1984. "The Distribution of the African Population of South Africa by Age, Sex and Region Type, 1950–1980." In *Studies in Urbanisation in South Africa.* Johannesburg: South African Institute of Race Relations.

South African Institute of Race Relations. 1986. *Race Relations Survey, 1985.* Johannesburg: South African Institute of Race Relations.

South African Labour Bulletin. 1977. "Workers under the Baton: An Examination of the Labour Dispute at Heinemann Electric Company," *South African Labour Bulletin* 3(7):49–59.

Stacey, Judith. 1983. *Patriarchy and Socialist Revolution in China.* Berkeley and Los Angeles: University of California Press.

Thabethe, Elizabeth. 1991. "Showing the Way for Women in the Unions." *South African Labour Bulletin* 15(7):91–93.

Tohidi, Nayereh. 1991. "Gender and Islamic Fundamentalism: Feminist Politics in Iran." In *Third World Women and the Politics of Feminism,* ed. Chandra Mohanty, Ann Russo, and Lourdes Torres, 251–70. Bloomington: Indiana University Press.

Turok, Mary. 1991. "The Women's Quota Debate: Building Non-Sexism." *Work in Progress,* no. 76, 7–9.

Urdang, Stephanie. 1989. *And Still They Dance: Women, War, and the Struggle for Change in Mozambique.* New York: Monthly Review Press.

Van Zyl, Mikki. 1991. "Invitation to Debate: Towards an Explanation of Violence against Women." *Agenda: A Journal about Women and Society* 11:66–77.

Vogelman, Lloyd. 1990. *The Sexual Face of Violence: Rapists on Rape.* Johannesburg: Ravan Press.

Walker, Cherryl. 1982. *Women and Resistance in South Africa.* London: Onyx Press.

———. 1990. "Gender and the Development of the Migrant Labour System c. 1850–1930: An Overview." In *Women and Gender in Southern Africa to 1945,* ed. Cherryl Walker, 168–96. Cape Town: David Philip.

Wellings, Paul, and Anthony Black. 1987. "Industrial Decentralization under Apartheid: An Empirical Assessment." In *Regional Restructuring under Apartheid: Urban and Regional Policies in Contemporary South Africa,* ed. Richard Tomlinson and Mark Addleson, 181–206. Johannesburg: Ravan Press.

White, Caroline. 1991. " 'Close to Home' in Johannesburg: Oppression in Township Houses." *Agenda: A Journal about Women and Society* 11:78–89.

Work in Progress. 1985. "The Nairobi Conference." *Work in Progress,* no. 38, 29–32.

———. 1967. "Striking OK Workers in Class War." *Work in Progress,* no. 46, 1–6.

Feminisms in Latin America: From Bogotá to San Bernardo

Nancy Saporta Sternbach, Marysa Navarro-Aranguren, Patricia Chuchryk, and Sonia E. Alvarez

I. Introduction

IN THE LAST DECADE, North American and Western European feminist scholars have become increasingly aware of Latin American women and their political activism. Yet this awareness has by no means dispelled the once prevalent notion in the United States that Latin American women do not consider themselves feminists, a notion that has been reinforced recently by texts that fall within the domain of "testimonial" literature and by research focusing on women's participation in grassroots movements and in national liberation struggles, rather than on feminism.[1] Additionally, North American feminists

We have listed our names in reverse alphabetical order. This order in no way reflects the magnitude of individual contributions. We would like to acknowledge the assistance of the following: Tinker Foundation, Kirkland Endowment, and Picker Fellowship (Sternbach); Darmouth Faculty Research Fund and the John Sloan Dickey Endowment for International Understanding (Navarro-Aranguren); University of Lethbridge Faculty Research Fund and the Social Sciences and Humanities Research Council of Canada Isolation Fund (Chuchryk); and the UC-MEXUS Travel Fund (Alvarez). Alvarez and Navarro would like to thank Pat Sanders and Gail Vernazza, respectively, for their assistance in the preparation of the manuscript. Alvarez would also like to thank Judit Moschkovich for her helpful suggestions. In addition, the authors are most grateful to the anonymous *Signs* readers for their comments.

[1] For examples of testimonial literature, see Domitilia Barrios de Chungara (with Moerna Viezzer), *Let Me Speak!* (New York: Monthly Review Press, 1978); Elizabeth Burgos-Debray, ed., Ann Wright, trans., *I, Rigoberta Menchú: An Indian Woman in Guatemala* (London: Verso, 1984); and Margaret Randall and Lynda Yanz, eds., *Sandino's Daughters* (Vancouver: New Star, 1981).

[*Signs: Journal of Women in Culture and Society* 1992, vol. 17, no. 2]

are frequently heard to comment that "feminism is not appropriate for Latin America," a comment that in our view reflects unfamiliarity with the contemporary reality of Latin American women.[2] As recent research has shown and as we shall argue in this article, not only is feminism appropriate for Latin America, but it also is the kind of thriving, broad-based social movement that many other feminist movements are still aspiring to become.

The assumption that Latin American women do not define themselves as feminists ironically mirrors the stance adopted by much of the Latin American Left in the mid-seventies when the first stirrings of second-wave feminist voices were heard. At that time, Latin American feminists were dismissed as upper middle-class women who were concerned with issues that were irrelevant to the vast majority of women throughout the region. Some Latin Americans, both women and men, contended that the absence of a movement of continental proportions was not surprising because feminism was the product of contradictions existing in highly industrialized countries but not in underdeveloped societies. Others argued that a movement for women's liberation was unnecessary because liberation could be achieved only through socialism, and once firmly established, it would eliminate women's oppression. And all agreed with the widely held notion that Latin American feminists were small groups of misguided petites bourgeoises, disconnected from the reality of the continent, women who had thoughtlessly adopted a fashion, as others had done with jeans or the miniskirt, without realizing that in so doing, "le hacían el juego al imperialismo yanqui" (they were tools of Yankee imperialism). In Chile, some sectors of the Left have even asserted that El Poder Femenino, a right-wing women's organization that participated in the downfall of the democratic government of Salvador Allende, was a feminist movement.[3]

In the last decade, however, Latin American feminist movements, or "feminisms," have grown steadily and undergone profound transformations, emerging today at the very center of international feminist debates. In some cases, their movements have continually challenged oppressive regimes (e.g., Chile); in others, they have achieved recognition from their governments (e.g., Nicaragua, Brazil). In still others, the concurrent battles of women's and people's liberation (e.g., Honduras, El Salvador, and Guatemala) give us new definitions of what it is to be a feminist.

[2] Jayne Bloch, "The Women Outside the Gates," *Progressive* 49, no. 12 (December 1985): 18.

[3] See, e.g., the arguments suggested in Michele Mattelart, "Chile: The Feminine Version of the Coup d'état," in *Sex and Class in Latin America,* ed. June Nash and Helen Safa, (Brooklyn: Bergin, 1980), 279–301; and Maria Crummett, "El Poder Femenino: The Mobilization of Women against Socialism in Chile," *Latin American Perspectives* 4 no. 4 (Fall 1977): 103–13.

In this article, we sketch a general picture of the political trajectory of Latin American feminisms during the 1970s and 1980s.[4] It is, of course, difficult, if not dangerous, to generalize across countries in a region as diverse as Latin America when discussing any sociopolitical phenomenon. But here, for heuristic and analytical purposes, we will view feminist development in Latin America and the Caribbean as a whole by examining the regionwide feminist *Encuentros* convened biannually since 1981.[5] Held in Bogotá, Colombia (1981), Lima, Peru (1983), Bertioga, Brazil (1985), Taxco, Mexico (1987), and San Bernardo, Argentina (1990), these meetings can serve as historical markers, highlighting the key strategic, organizational, and theoretical debates that have characterized the political trajectory of contemporary Latin American feminisms.

Attended by grassroots and professional feminist activists alike from throughout Latin America and the Caribbean, the *Encuentros* have provided critical forums in which participants could share experiences as well as measure their respective countries' progress in relation to a continental movement. A close look at the principal issues and debates manifest during each of these *Encuentros* will enable us to view the landscape of contemporary feminisms in the Latin American region, albeit very broadly.

Latin American nations are plagued by chronic economic and political crises. In all countries feminist groups must make heroic efforts to stay afloat organizationally amid staggering national debts, painful austerity plans, and dramatic political changes. In this context, the *Encuentros* provide feminist activists with periodic forums wherein they can gain theoretical and strategic insights as well as sisterly support from feminists in other nations struggling to overcome analogous organizational and theoretical predicaments. Moreover, the core issues debated at each of the *Encuentros* have had significant repercussions within movement

---

[4] We use the word *feminisms*—as do Latin American feminists themselves—because Latin America and the Caribbean are composed of many discrete nations, races, and classes, and therefore many interpretations of reality. Within the Latin American and Caribbean context, feminism varies from country to country. When we speak of those diverse interpretations of feminism we shall refer to them as "feminisms."

[5] *Encuentro* (from the Spanish *encontrar*—to meet or to find oneself or another, to confront oneself or another. Also used in the reflexive, *encontrarse*—to find oneself, or to meet each other, as in coming together, to share). A meeting place where one exchanges ideas, expresses feelings, thoughts and emotions; listens and is listened to, agrees and disagrees, affirms and contradicts" (cited in Eliana Ortega and Nancy Saporta Sternbach, "Gracias a la vida: Recounting the Third Latin American Feminist Meeting in Bertioga, Brazil, July 31–August 4, 1985," *off our backs* 16, no. 1 [January 1986]: 1). Throughout this article, we have maintained the original Spanish in terminology that would get either lost or confused in translation. In addition to *Encuentro*, readers will also find terms such as *movimientos de mujeres* (women's grassroots organizations), *históricas* and *veteranas* (veterans of the feminist movement), and *militantes* or *políticas* (left-wing political activists).

groups in individual countries, sometimes foregrounding and even defusing potential areas of ideological and organizational conflict before these have fully played themselves out in a particular national setting. The decision to center our analysis on the *Encuentros*, then, stems from the belief, shared by many feminists in Latin America, that these regional meetings have been crucial to the development of Latin American feminist theory and practice. *Encuentro* documents have been widely disseminated among feminists throughout the region. Although not all the issues raised and ideological struggles waged at the *Encuentros* have precise counterparts in every national context, the *Encuentros* nonetheless have served as springboards for the development of a common Latin American feminist political language and as staging grounds for often contentious political battles over what would constitute the most efficacious strategies for achieving gender equality in dependent, capitalist, and patriarchal states.

The analysis presented in this article also draws on our own experiences as Latin Americanists and feminists who have done research on women's movements in at least six Latin American countries. We have all been involved in at least two Latin American feminist *Encuentros;* two of us have participated in three, and one of us has attended all five. We are one U.S. woman, one Vasca/Española/Latinoamericana, one Canadian woman, and one Latina/Cubana. While each of us feels she has experienced the richness and diversity of Latin American feminism individually, the scope of our collective experience motivated us to write this article. In it, we also try to include some of the perspectives of the hundreds of Latin American women with whom we have talked and worked over these years—women who define themselves as feminists. Collectively, we represent the humanities and the social sciences, a collaboration that provides a uniquely interdisciplinary approach to our understanding and discussion of Latin American feminisms. Among us, we teach literature, history, sociology, political science, Latin American studies, and women's studies. All of us teach and write about Latin American women on a regular basis.

The purpose of this article is not only to trace the growth of Latin American feminisms in the last decade but also to dispel the myth that Latin American women do not define themselves as feminists. From our observation, not only is the Latin American model unique in its organization of women, but it has also garnered a political base which could, and most certainly should, be the envy of feminists everywhere.[6]

[6] The very uniqueness of Latin American feminisms as social phenomena may further be evidenced by the coinage of a terminology appropriate to the region's circumstances. Although we have given English equivalents to all these terms, we prefer to refer to them in their original Spanish in order to maintain their integrity.

The questions we address are: What is distinctive about Latin American feminisms? And what can we learn from them? To contextualize our discussion of the *Encuentros* themselves, we begin with a brief overview of the emergence and early development of feminisms in Latin America. We then discuss the first four *Encuentros,* emphasizing their significance for the theory and practice of feminism in the region. We closely examine what transpired at the Fourth *Encuentro,* in Taxco in October 1987, as a turning point in the movement, so as to delve more deeply into the contemporary political conjuncture—the principal organizational and strategic issues and dilemmas faced by Latin American feminisms in the late 1980s and early 1990s. Finally, we present a brief discussion of the most recent *Encuentro,* held in San Bernardo in November 1990, and end with our conclusions about feminisms in Latin America.

II. The genesis of late twentieth-century feminisms in Latin America

Paradoxically, feminism emerged during one of the most somber decades in Latin American history. During the 1970s (as, in some cases, in the 1960s), military regimes and nominal democracies alike crushed progressive movements of all sorts, "disappeared" thousands of people, and unleashed the repressive apparatus of the state upon civil society—all in the name of national security. Contemporary feminisms in Latin America were therefore born as intrinsically oppositional movements.

From the moment the first feminist groups appeared in the mid-1970s, many Latin American feminists therefore not only challenged patriarchy and its paradigm of male domination—the militaristic or counterinsurgency state—but also joined forces with other opposition currents in denouncing social, economic, and political oppression and exploitation. Thus, the realities of both state repression and class warfare were instrumental in shaping a Latin American feminist praxis distinct from that of feminist movements elsewhere. For example, from the beginning, feminists in countries ruled by military regimes unveiled the patriarchal foundations of state repression, militarism, and institutionalized violence, a stance that was gradually adopted more generally by Latin American feminists.

Whereas male analysts stressed the cultural or economic determinants of the militarization of civilian rule and the entrenchment of modern military dictatorships in the 1970s,[7] feminists argued that such politics

[7] For a comprehensive discussion of the mainstream theoretical debates surrounding the origins and the dynamics of military authoritarian regimes in Latin America during the 1960s and 1970s, see David Collier, ed., *The New Authoritarianism in Latin America* (Princeton, N.J.: Princeton University Press, 1979).

are also rooted in the authoritarian foundations of patriarchal relations in the so-called private sphere: the family, male-female relations, and the sexual oppression of women.[8] Authoritarianism, feminists proclaimed, represented the "highest form" of patriarchal oppression. As one Latin American feminist, referring to Chile, has declared: "The Junta, with a very clear sense of its interests, has understood that it must reinforce the traditional family, and the dependent role of women, which is reduced to that of mother. The dictatorship, which institutionalizes social inequality, is founded on inequality in the family."[9]

Under both civilian and military rule, traditional conceptions of women's roles and impassioned appeals to "Western Christian family values" were, indeed, at the core of national security ideology, counterinsurgency, and regressive social policies. But a wide gap separated the state's discourse on gender and the family from the reality of women's lives. While official discourse extolled the virtues of traditional womanhood, regressive economic policies thrust millions of women into the

[8] The most sophisticated theoretical treament of this aspect of military rule can be found in the work of Julieta Kirkwood; see esp. her "La formación de la conciencia feminista en Chile" (The formation of a feminist consciousness in Chile), Materia de Discusión, no. 7 (Santiago: Programa de Facultad Latinoamericano de Ciencias Sociales [FLACSO], 1980), "Chile: La mujer en la formulación política" (Chile: Women in political formulation), Documento de Trabajo, no. 109 (Santiago: Programa FLACSO, 1981), "El feminismo como negación del autoritarismo" (Feminism as negation of authoritarianism), Materia de Discusión, no. 52 (Santiago: Programa FLASCO, 1983), Ser política en Chile: Las feministas y los partidos (Being political/political being in Chile) (Santiago: Facultad Latinoamericana de Ciencias Sociales, 1986), and Feminarios (Feminars) (Santiago: Ediciones Documentos, 1987); and Patricia Crispi, Tejiendo rebeldías: Escritos feministas de Julieta Kirkwood (Weaving rebellions: Julieta Kirkwood's feminist writings) (Santiago: Centro de Estudios de la Mujer and La Morada, 1987). María Inacia d'Avila Neto explores some of the psychosocial dimensions of the relationship between authoritarianism and the subordination of women in her O autoritarismo e a mulher: O jogo da dominação macho-fêmea no Brasil (The male-female domination game in Brazil) (Rio de Janeiro: Achiame, 1980). For an analysis of gender ideology and policies of militaristic states in different national contexts, see Carmen Tornaria, "Women's Involvement in the Democratic Process in Uruguay," in The Latin American Women's Movement: Reflections and Actions, ed. ISIS International (Rome and Santiago: ISIS International, 1986); Ximena Bunster-Burotto, "Watch Out for the Little Nazi Man That All of Us Have Inside: The Mobilization and Demobilization of Women in Militarized Chile," Women's Studies International Forum 2, no. 5 (Summer 1988): 485–91; María Elena Valenzuela, Todas íbamos a ser reinas: La mujer en Chile militar (We were all going to be queens: Women in military Chile) (Santiago: Ediciones Chile y América, 1987); and Patricia Chuchryk, "Protest, Politics and Personal Life: The Emergence of Feminism in a Military Dictatorship, Chile 1973–1983" (Ph.D. diss., York University, 1984), esp. chaps. 3 and 4.

[9] Cited in Chuchryk, "Protest, Politics and Personal Life," 320. See also María Elena Valenzuela, "El fundamento militar de la dominación patriarcal en Chile" (paper presented at the Second Chilean Sociology Conference, Santiago, August 1986). In this paper, Valenzuela argues that the Chilean military state is the quintessential expression of patriarchy. She draws similarities between the military's control over civil society and male domination over women.

work force. Furthermore, female victims of state repression were brutalized, sexually violated and humiliated, and subjected to abuse that was hardly consonant with the military's ideological exaltation of femininity and its quintessential incarnation, motherhood.[10] By the late 1970s, in countries ruled by civilians and military men alike, reactionary social and political policies sparked widespread opposition movements; women of all social classes defied their historical exclusion from things political and joined the opposition in unprecedented numbers. In Peru in the early 1980s, for example, working-class women were in the vanguard of grassroots survival struggles that increasingly challenged the social and economic policies of the conservative civilian Belaúnde Terry administration.[11] Similarly, during the 1970s in military-ruled Argentina, Chile, Uruguay, and Brazil, women enlisted massively in the opposition's struggle for democracy and became known internationally for their participation in human rights struggles.[12]

[10] See esp. Ximena Bunster-Burotto, "Surviving beyond Fear: Women and Torture in Latin America," in *Women and Change in Latin America,* ed. June Nash and Helen Safa (South Hadley, Mass.: Bergin & Garvey, 1985), 297–325.

[11] On Peruvian women's movements, see Maruja Barrig, "The Difficult Equilibrium between Bread and Roses: Women's Organizations and the Transition from Dictatorship to Democracy in Peru," in *The Women's Movement in Latin America: Feminism and the Transition to Democracy,* ed. Jane S. Jaquette (Boston: Unwin Hyman, 1989), 114–48; Virginia Vargas, "Movimiento feminista en el Perú: Balance y perpectivas" (Feminist movement in Peru: Balance and perspectives), in *Década de la Mujer: Conversatorio sobre Nairobi* (The decade on women: Conversation about Nairobi) (Lima: Centro Flora Tristán, 1985), and her "El aporte a la rebeldía de las mujeres" (Contribution to women's rebellion), in *Jornadas feministas: Feminismo y sectores populares en América Latina* (Feminist workshops: Feminism and the popular classes of Latin America), ed. Coordinación de Grupos de las Jornadas Feministas (México, D.F.: Ed. Electrocomp, 1987), 213–39; J. Anderson Velasco, "The U.N. Decade for Women in Peru," *Women's Studies International Forum* 8, no. 2 (1985): 107–9; Susan C. Bourque, "Urban Activists: Paths to Political Consciousness in Peru," in *Women Living Change,* ed. Susan C. Bourque and Donna C. Divine (Philadelphia: Temple University Press, 1985), 25–56; and Carol Andreas, *When Women Rebel: The Rise of Popular Feminism in Peru* (Westport, Conn.: Lawrence Hill, 1985).

[12] On Uruguay, see Carina Perelli, "Putting Conservatism to Good Use: Women and Unorthodox Politics in Uruguay, from Breakdown to Transition," in Jaquette, 95–113; Silvia Rodríguez Villamil and Graciela Sapriza, "Mulher e estado no Uruguay do seculo XX" (Women and state in the Uruguay of the twentieth century), *Revista das Ciencias Sociais* 1, no. 2 (1987): 209–19; Tornaría, "Women's Involvement in the Democratic Process in Uruguay," and "Uruguay," in Coordinación de Grupos Organizadores de las Jornadas Feministas, eds., 241–48. On Argentina, see María del Carmen Feijóo, "El movimiento de mujeres," in *Los nuevos movimientos sociales,* ed. Elizabeth Jelín (Buenos Aires: Centro Editor de América Latina, 1985), and "The Challenge of Constructing Civilian Peace: Women and Democracy in Argentina," in Jaquette, ed., 72–94; and Silvia Chester, "The Women's Movement in Argentina: Balance and Strategies," in ISIS International, eds. On Chilean women's movements, see Patricia M. Chuchryk, "Feminist Anti-authoritarian Politics: The Role of Women's Organizations in the Chilean Transition to Democracy," in Jaquette, ed., 149–84; Kirkwood, *Ser política en Chile,* and *Feminarios.* On Brazil, see the discussion of the Bertioga *Encuentro* below.

In the early part of the 1970s, at least, much of the opposition to oligarchical democracy and military authoritarianism came from the Left of the political spectrum. As in North America (Canada and the United States) and Western Europe, then, second-wave feminism in Latin America was born of the "New Left."[13] But, because the progressive opposition was male-dominated and its practice sexist, women and "their issues" were invariably relegated to a secondary position within Latin American progressive and revolutionary movements. Feminist consciousness was thus fueled by multiple contradictions experienced by women active in guerrilla movements or militant organizations, forced to go into exile, and involved in student movements, politicized academic organizations, and progressive political parties.[14] The prototypical early Latin American feminist activist in many countries was a former radical student militant or *guerrillera* and hardly a self-obsessed bourgeois "lady," as many of the Left would have us believe. However, unlike North American radical feminists, Latin American feminists retained a commitment to radical change in social relations of production—as well as reproduction—while continuing to struggle against sexism within the Left. That is, although feminism in many countries broke with the Left organizationally, it did not fully do so ideologically.

The alliance with progressive sectors of the opposition, though uneasy at best, was essential to the viability of the feminist project. In countries ruled by exclusionary and repressive regimes (hardly disposed to grant concessions to movements pursuing progressive change of any kind) feminists could find political space only within the larger opposition struggle. Many early feminist groups functioned clandestinely; some were formed as "front" groups for the left-wing opposition; others avoided the term "feminist," forming "women's associations" and taking refuge in the age-old belief that anything women do is "by nature" apolitical and therefore less threatening to "national security." As economic crises and cuts in social welfare threatened the very survival of Latin America's "popular" classes,[15] many feminists joined the Left in seeking solutions to the absolute impoverishment of the vast majority of the region's people.

---

[13] The Argentine case stands as the exception that proves the rule. There, feminism emerged primarily from professional women and not necessarily from women who had been involved with the Left.

[14] For a comparative discussion of the emergence and development of women's movements in Peru, Chile, Argentina, Uruguay, and Brazil, see Jaquette, ed. See also Cornelia Butler Flora, "Socialist Feminism in Latin America," *Women and Politics* 4, no. 1 (Winter 1984): 69–93. On the contradictions experienced by women active in militant organizations, see Angela Neves-Xavier de Brito, "Brazilian Women in Exile: The Quest for an Identity," *Latin American Perspectives* 13, no. 2 (Spring 1986): 58–80.

[15] We take the word "popular" in English from the Spanish *popular*, which means "of the people," and use it accordingly. Throughout this article, we shall use it in this context to refer to everyone who is not of a professional or owning class: workers, campesinos, shopkeepers, people who are working class or lower middle class, etc.

They got caught up in Marxist philosophy + tried to make gender issues secondary (or maybe they were secondary)

The legacy of the Left weighed heavily on Latin American feminism during the early years of the movement, an inheritance that led early feminists to privilege class over gender struggle and, in the Marxist tradition, to focus on women's work and on women's integration or incorporation into the public world of politics and production. The Guevarist/Leninist legacy also led early feminists to view themselves as the vanguard of what was to become a mass-based, cross-class, revolutionary women's movement.

The "rearguard," in this view, was to be made up of the hundreds of working-class women's groups then proliferating throughout much of Latin America.[16] Economic crises impelled working-class women to devise creative, collective survival strategies. Often under the tutelage of the Catholic Church and the male Left, women's groups formed at the neighborhood level to provide the basic necessities of life, a responsibility consistent with women's traditionally defined roles. In keeping with their socially ascribed responsibilities as wives, mothers, and nurturers of family and community, women have taken the lead in the day-to-day resistance strategies of Latin America's popular classes. In every country in the region, women have participated disproportionately in movements to secure better urban services, to protest the rising cost of living, and to secure health care and education for their children. Torture, disappearances, and other forms of political repression also have united women of all social classes to organize human rights movements.[17]

In Latin America, both of these types of movements are commonly referred to as *movimientos de mujeres* (women's movements) or *movimientos femeninos* (feminine movements).[18] Contemporary Latin American feminists, then, form but one part of a larger, multifaceted, socially and politically heterogeneous women's movement. And in most Latin

[16] For the most comprehensive comparative treatment of the *movimiento de mujeres,* see Elizabeth Jelín, ed., *Women and Social Change in Latin America* (Geneva: United Nations Research Institute for Social Development [UNRISD]; London: Zed Books, 1990).

[17] On the important role of human rights organizations in the Argentine transition from authoritarian rule, see María Sonderéguer, "Aparición con vida: El movimiento de los Derechos Humanos en la Argentina" (Appearing with life: The human rights movement in Argentina), in Jelín, ed., *Los nuevos movimientos sociales* (New social movements), 7–32; Marysa Navarro, "The Personal Is Political: Las Madres de Plaza de Mayo," in *Power and Popular Protest: Latin American Social Movements,* ed. Susan Eckstein (Berkeley and Los Angeles: University of California Press, 1989), 241–58. On Chile, see Patricia M. Chuchryk, "Subversive Mothers: The Women's Opposition to the Military Regime in Chile," in *Women, the State, and Development,* ed. Sue Ellen M. Charlton, Jane Everett, and Kathleen Staudt (Albany: SUNY Press, 1989), 130–51.

[18] A distinction between "feminine" and "feminist" women's movement organizations is commonly made by both movement participants and social scientists in Latin America. Paul Singer clarifies the usage of these concepts: "The struggles against the rising cost of living or for schools, day-care centers, etc., as well as specific measures to protect women who work interest women closely and it is possible then to consider them *feminine* revindications. But they are not *feminist* to the extent that they do not

American countries, feminists initially gave higher priority to working with poor and working-class women active in that larger movement, helping women organize community survival struggles while fostering consciousness of how gender roles shaped their political activism.

For fear of alienating this potential mass base, many early feminists shunned doing political work on, or even discussing, "classic" feminist issues such as sexuality, reproduction, violence against women, or power relations in the family. An additional deterrent was the fear of losing legitimacy in the eyes of their "macho-Leninist" comrades-in-struggle. In the view of these comrades, only two kinds of feminism existed: a good one, which privileged the class struggle and could therefore assume its "rightful" place within the ranks of the revolutionary opposition; and a bad one, which supposedly was "one more instance of ideological imperialism"—an imported, bourgeois, man-hating feminism that had no place in Latin America.[19]

Still today, in many popular women's organizations linked to the progressive Catholic Church or the secular Left, women are continually admonished against adopting "bad" feminist beliefs, such as abortion rights and the right to sexual self-determination, as these are seen as intrinsically bourgeois and likely to "divide" the united struggle of the working class. It is significant, then, that many grassroots women's groups are sponsored or controlled by the Church or the Left as, together with the mainstream media, male religious and secular activists have tergiversated and misrepresented the meaning and character of feminism, often deliberately blocking the development of a critical gender consciousness among the participants of the *movimientos de mujeres*. This, in many cases, explains the reticence of women in "popular" organizations to embrace the feminist label even when they espouse feminist

---

question the way in which women are inserted into the social context" ("O feminino e o feminismo," in *Sao Paulo: O povo em movimento,* ed. P. Singer and V. C. Brant [Sao Paulo: The people in movement] [Petropolis: Vozes, 1980], 116–17). On "feminine" movements or the *movimientos de mujeres,* see Andreas (n. 11 above); and Marianna Schmink, "Women in Brazilian Abertura Politics," *Signs: Journal of Women in Culture and Society* 7, no. 1 (Autumn 1981): 115–34; and Elizabeth Jelín, ed., *Cuidadanía e identidad: La mujeres en los movimientos sociales Latino-americanos* (Citizenship and identity: Women in Latin American social movements) (Geneva: UNRISD, 1987).

[19] This distinction between "good" and "bad" feminisms is elaborated in Anette Goldberg, "Feminismo em Regime Autoritario: A Experiencia do Movimento de Mulheres no Rio de Janeiro" (Feminism in authoritarian regime: The women's movement experience in Rio de Janeiro) (paper presented at the twelfth Congresso Mundial da Associação Internacional de Ciencia Politica, Rio de Janeiro, August 9–14, 1982), 10–11. Portions of the ensuing discussion draw on Sonia E. Alvarez, *Engendering Democracy in Brazil: Women's Movements in Transition Politics* (Princeton, N.J.: Princeton University Press, 1990), esp. chaps. 3–5.

beliefs. That is, this reluctance is not a "natural" outcome of their class position.

Partly in response to their leftist interlocutors, feminists in the region were careful to emphasize the specifically Latin American dimension of their banners. The problem of women's health, for example, is not only a question of controlling one's body; Latin American feminists insist that it also includes an understanding of how international organizations and multinational corporations determine national health and population policies in their countries. As for the campaign against sexual violence, it must have a different dimension in Latin America because in many countries women political prisoners have been systematically subjected to sexual torture.[20]

Moreover, many Latin American feminists see their movement as part of the continent's struggle against imperialism. As one feminist explained, imperialism controls "biological reproduction which favors [imperialism's] economic and political interests in Latin America through its need to retain domestic work for material reproduction and for the survival of the whole system."[21] Yet not all groups enthusiastically espouse the anti-imperialist stand, nor do members make a point of calling themselves socialist-feminists.

In Latin America as elsewhere, feminism has taken a wide variety of organizational forms and has combated women's oppression in the full range of political, economic, and cultural arenas in which patriarchal domination is embedded. But again, the distinctive Latin American context of economic dependence, exploitation, and political repression gave rise to feminist political projects centered at the intersection of gender oppression and other more local forms of exploitation and domination. In Brazil, for example, the first contemporary feminist organizations paid only minimal attention to the "inward-oriented" activities—such as consciousness-raising—so central to early feminists in the United States and Europe. During much of the 1970s, Brazilian feminists instead focused their energies on "outward-oriented" activities in an effort to spread the feminist message to women of the popular classes, to link feminism to other progressive forces, and to relate women's struggles to the society's struggle against military rule. Feminists published women's newspapers that were made available to working-class women's groups in the urban

[20] See Alicia Partnoy, *The Little School: Tales of Disappearance and Survival in Argentina* (San Francisco: Cleis Press, 1986); *Nunca Más: A Report by Argentina's National Commission on Disappeared People* (London: Faber & Faber, 1986); and Bunster-Burotto, "Surviving beyond Fear" (n. 10 above).

[21] The textual quotations in this article are based on interviews conducted by all four coauthors. When no citation appears, readers should assume that these remarks are from one of the *Encuentros*.

periphery; they collaborated closely with women in the human rights movement and in the community survival struggles; they organized women's congresses to recruit ever larger numbers of women to the feminist cause; and they actively promoted the organization of women of the popular classes.

Over time, feminists found at least two reasons to challenge the Left's notion of good and bad feminisms. First, in working with women of the popular classes, feminists learned that so-called taboo issues such as sexuality, reproduction, or violence against women were interesting and important to working-class women—as crucial to their survival as the bread-and-butter issues emphasized by the male opposition. In fact, as will become amply evident from our discussion of the *Encuentros,* many working-class, black, and Indian women in Latin America have reclaimed the feminist label—refusing to accept the male Left's tergiversation of its meaning as another form of colonialist oppression—and are now insistent that feminism is neither inherently bourgeois or Western nor instrincally divisive of the people's struggle. In so doing, they have expanded the parameters of feminist theory and practice.

As the ranks of feminism grew larger and the movement developed a political identity distinct from that of the male-dominated revolutionary Left, feminists undertook increasingly more focused or specialized activities, centered not only on working with the *movimiento de mujeres* but also on deepening a specifically gendered vision of politics, culture, and society. The number of feminist magazines, film and video collectives, centers for battered women and rape victims, feminist health collectives, lesbian rights groups, and other gendered feminist projects steadily expanded throughout the 1980s.

As parties attempted to manipulate women's organizations by imposing their political agendas on the movements, and the male Left continued to insist that sexism would "wither away after the revolution," feminists in many countries found a second reason to contest the notion that gender struggle was inherently divisive. Arguing that male-dominated parties sought to instrumentalize and direct women's struggles, feminists' critique of the Left became ever more pointed.

Latin American feminists began redefining and expanding the prevailing notion of revolutionary struggle, calling for a revolution in daily life, asserting that a radical social transformation must encompass changes not only in class but in patriarchal power relations as well. Some feminists increasingly denounced the hierarchical, Leninist or Trotskyist styles of "doing politics" typical of male-dominated revolutionary groups in most countries, and insisted on more participatory, democratic forms of pursuing radical social change.

In this context, the regional *Encuentros* have provided critical forums for movement debates about evolving feminist politics and the movements' relationship to the overall struggle for social justice in Latin America. But the feminists who attended the first *Encuentro* in Bogotá could hardly have known that would occur. Rather, it was the feeling of political isolation in their country, coupled with the desire to chart an autonomous political path, that led Colombian women to call a regionwide meeting of feminist activists.

III. The Latin American and Caribbean feminist *Encuentros*

Bogotá

In July 1981, more than two hundred Latin American feminists, representing some fifty organizations, convened for four days in Bogotá, Colombia, in the first continental meeting of its kind since the early years of the century. Instantly, the Latin American feminist map was extended, both literally and metaphorically. By the end of the first day, walls were covered with poems, proclamations, information about organizations, announcements, posters describing women's conditions in various countries, and a large map of Latin America on which participants wrote the names of feminist organizations in their countries.[22] According to the announcement Latin American feminists made at the United Nations Mid-Decade Conference in Copenhagen (July 1980), the purpose of the Bogotá *Encuentro* was to offer Latin American women "engaged in feminist practice" the opportunity "to exchange experiences and opinions, identify problems and evaluate different practices, as well as plan tasks and projects for the future." While such a definition has served to characterize all five *Encuentros*, the principal axis of discussions at the Bogotá meeting was the historical conflict with the male Left.

Word of the Bogotá *Encuentro* spread through emerging international feminist networks, primarily reaching white, middle-class, university-educated women. Women from the *movimiento de mujeres* were largely absent from the critical debates that ensued about the proper relationship of feminism to the revolutionary struggle, as the spheres of feminisms and the *movimientos* were yet to coalesce politically on a regional scale. The following countries were represented: Mexico, Dominican Republic, Puerto Rico, Panamá, Curaçao, Venezuela, Ecuador, Perú, Chile, Brazil, Argentina, and of course, Colombia. Some participants were young university students; others were older, working-class organizers. There were

[22] Marysa Navarro, "First Feminist Meeting of Latin America and the Caribbean," *Signs* 8, no. 1 (Autumn 1982): 154–57.

homemakers, medical doctors, professors, lawyers, government employees and agricultural workers, poets, and filmmakers. They came from
centers for battered women, peasant organizations, research groups,
women working in the slums of Latin America's large cities, movie collectives, and feminist magazines. Some had been active in feminist movements since the early seventies; one Colombian woman had even taken
part in her country's 1954 campaign for women's suffrage; others had
only recently encountered feminism and had never attended a feminist
meeting before; many had been members of left-wing political parties but
had abandoned them when they discovered feminism; and a substantial
number, though not the majority, were feminists who were still active
members of left-wing parties.

Except for the Colombians, who had representatives from Bogotá and
several other cities, the largest delegation—sixteen women—came from
the Dominican Republic. The registration fee, US$50 for Latin Ameri-
cans and US$80 for all others, included expenses for the four days. While
the conference was conceived for Latin American women, a few "foreigners" were admitted: two from Canada, three from the United States,
and a dozen from Europe (Spain, Italy, France, Switzerland, Holland, and
Germany). A few women, forced into exile by repressive governments
(Brazil, Uruguay, Argentina, and Chile) also attended.

This historic regionwide gathering was itself the outcome of a pro-
longed and conflicted organizing process, characterized by dissension and
acrimonious debates among a physically heterogeneous—if socially relatively homogeneous—group of middle-class, educated, Colombian
women.[23] These discussions and confrontations have been echoed in other
countries and in planning for subsequent regional meetings, so a detailed
consideration of the organization of this First *Encuentro* will provide a
broad map of the debates that have demarcated radically differing conceptions of gender struggle in Latin America and the Caribbean in the last
decade.

In major Colombian cities where feminists were active, collectives
were formed to undertake the planning of the *Encuentro*. In Bogotá, one
such collective emerged, comprising *independientes* (women who did not
belong to any particular group), members of feminist organizations (the
(Círculo de Mujeres, Mujeres en la Lucha, and El Grupo), as well as
feminists who belonged to political parties—the Partido Socialista de los
Trabajadores (PST, Socialist) and the Partido Socialista Revolucionario
(PSR, Trotskyist). All the collectives met April 19–20, 1980, in Sopó,
Cundinamarca, to coordinate their efforts, and they resolved that the

---

[23] Actually, it was a group of Venezuelan feminists, La Conjura, who first thought
about organizing an *Encuentro*, in August 1979. Only after it was clear that they could
not do it did the Colombian feminists take up the challenge.

Encuentro would take place in December 1980. In addition to being open to feminists, it would also be *amplio* (broad-based). The topics to be discussed would be feminism and political struggle; sexuality and daily life; women and work; and women, communication, and culture.[24]

Despite these early agreements, the definition of the conference, which had already provoked long and heated discussions between *militantes* or *políticas* (left-wing party activists) and independent or "autonomous" feminists in the various collectives, was far from settled: the debate regarding who should attend the meeting persisted among the various constituencies. Should it be open to women belonging to all kinds of women's groups (*amplio*) or should it be restricted to self-proclaimed feminists? Should participants be asked to attend the meeting on an individual basis or should they take part in it as representatives of organizations or political parties? These questions were vital ones given ongoing conflicts with nonfeminist women and men on the Left. "Independent" or nonpartisan feminists eschewed what they considered to be false representational stances while women affiliated with traditional parties and unions preferred a more structured, formal "congress." Independent feminists also feared that "party women" would impose their sectarian agendas on the meeting, insist on discussing women's role in "the revolution," and divert participants from discussions of issues that a nonfeminist revolution would not encompass—issues central to feminist organizing such as reproductive rights or domestic violence. Since the disagreements were paralyzing the preparation of the *Encuentro,* the Cali *coordinadora* (coordinating committee), made up mostly of *militantes,* or *políticas,* called a national meeting to settle the issues, it was hoped, once and for all.

Before attending the national meeting, however, the Bogotá collective met on August 21, 1980, and decided to sponsor a conference for Latin American women engaged in feminist practice; moreover, they decided that participants would attend as individuals, representing themselves, rather than organizations or parties. The agreement was even supported by the three PSR (Trotskyist) members of the collective who were also members of the *coordinadora.*

In Cali, the assembly voted to open the meeting to all women "engaged in the struggle for their liberation" and to make representation of organizations and political parties the basis for participation. The votes taken in Cali broke down the precarious alliance between the *políticas* and *feministas.* The *coordinadoras* from Medellín and Bogotá (with the exception of the three PSR members) refused to honor the decision.

[24] See Marysa Navarro, "El primer encuentro de Latinoamérica y el Caribe" (The first Latin American and Caribbean feminist *encuentro*), in *Sociedad, subordinación y feminismo* (Society, subordination and feminism), ed. Magdalena León (Bogotá: Asociación Colombiano de Estudios Populares, 1982), 309–18.

Accusations and recriminations ensued while the *Encuentro*, still to be held in December, remained unprepared. In October, the Cali *coordinadora* called another meeting, attended by representatives of only four cities, and decided to cancel the conference. At that point, the Bogotá *coordinadora* resolved to proceed and organize a feminist *Encuentro* to take place July 16–19, 1981.

The divisions between *militantes* and *feministas* were exacerbated when a group of *políticas* was denied entry to the actual *Encuentro*, a denial they refused to accept. While the first morning was spent listening to both versions of the confrontation, sectarianism and recriminations were eventually set aside. An extraordinary spirit of conciliation prevailed throughout the four days: the fact that the *Encuentro* was finally taking place overshadowed everything else.

In the most widely attended session, "Feminism and Political Struggle," participants agreed to discuss the three topics considered to be most relevant for Latin American feminists: the autonomy (ideological and organizational political independence) of the feminist movement; *doble militancia* (double militancy, or concurrent participation in, and dual commitment to, a political party and to feminism); and feminism and imperialism. Discussion questions ranged from how to widen, strengthen, and deepen the organized participation of women from the popular sectors, to the actual shape an *Encuentro* should take and the specific conditions of feminist political practice in Latin America. The chaotic and frequently heated debate centered on two of the three points: autonomy and *doble militancia*. While participants agreed on some basic principles, for example, the existence of gender inequality, they differed greatly as to the strategies feminists should adopt to end women's oppression.

All participants concurred that women suffer a specific oppression that becomes particularly acute in the most exploited classes. Women, therefore, need to articulate and struggle for their specific demands: the end of the double burden, equal pay for equal work, the right to work, the right to have an abortion, and "maternidad libre y voluntaria."[25] Furthermore, participants agreed that these demands had heretofore not been included in political party platforms.

Beyond these points of agreement, two recognizable positions emerged, which divided women's movement activists irrespective of their country of origin, class, or educational status. Each national "delegation" included women who adhered to one or the other position.

---

[25] In Spanish "maternidad libre y voluntaria" essentially means "every child a wanted child."

2 positions emerge:

Independence of pol. issues

The first position held that neither capitalism nor socialism alone could eliminate women's oppression and that, consequently, women's specific demands must be articulated in a movement outside and independent of all existing political parties. For those who defended this position, feminism represented a new revolutionary project, the first real alternative for the total transformation of oppressive social relations in Latin America. As for the issue of *la doble militancia,* these feminists *+ dual commitment* began by redefining the conventional dichotomy between feminism and *militancia política,* political activism. They rejected the use of the name *militantes* or *políticas* in opposition to *feministas,* because they viewed feminism as a legitimate and comprehensive political praxis. Therefore, feminists should focus their political work primarily, if not exclusively, in their own feminist organizations: the sexist structures of political parties, as well as the conflicts that emerge within those structures when feminist issues are raised, make *doble militancia* extremely difficult in practice. These women were disenchanted with the manipulative strategies of the Left and decried its androcentric conceptions of the privileged revolutionary agent, the (male) working class. Nevertheless, some did defend the possibility of establishing alliances with political parties in pursuit of specific goals.

Those who held the second position advanced at the Bogotá *Encuentro* insisted that feminism in and of itself could not be a revolutionary project. Because of their primary commitment to socialism, they argued that feminism should not be separated from the party but that it should have an organic autonomy within that structure. Feminists' objectives, in this view, could not be separated from those of the working class and its struggle to end class oppression. They saw *doble militancia* as a false problem and, while not denying that being a feminist within a political party presented practical difficulties, they believed that such difficulties were not insurmountable.

On the final day of the *Encuentro,* the plenary session heard reports from the various sessions and adopted numerous resolutions. These ranged from concrete expressions of solidarity with women in specific countries (including Chile, Colombia, Guatemala, and the Madres de Plaza de Mayo of Argentina) and with specific national struggles (Nicaragua and El Salvador) to more general issues such as equal pay for equal work, reproductive rights, day care, improved education, and the right to work. In a resolution to end violence against women, participants declared November 25 as the International Day of Nonviolence against Women, in memory of three Dominican women, the Miraval sisters, who were killed in 1960 by Trujillo's henchmen. Following a resounding vote of thanks to the *Encuentro*'s organizers, a final resolution to meet again in two years in Lima, Peru, was adopted amid tears and enthusiastic expressions of international feminist solidarity.

Indeed, despite the sometimes acrimonious debates, it was this joyful enthusiasm and spirit of solidarity that made the Bogotá *Encuentro* an unforgettable experience for most of the participants. For four days, there was a nonstop exchange and sharing of ideas and experiences. The dialogue followed the workshops into the central patio, surrounded by laughter, singing, poetry, and dancing. This, more than anything else, represented the sense of feminist collectivity that was to become Bogotá's legacy to future *Encuentros*.

One of the most important consequences of the Bogotá meeting was that it bore witness to the existence of a feminist movement of continental proportions, though still uneven in its composition, and revealed a broad process of mobilization among Latin American women. However, as subsequent *Encuentros* demonstrated, such mobilization was informed and guided by two distinct approaches to gender struggle. The dialogue and confrontation between the *feministas* and the *políticas* manifest at Bogotá was replete with all the conflict and contradictions that characterized most Latin American feminist practice in the 1970s and the 1980s.

Lima

No one was quite prepared for the growth that the Latin American feminist movement had experienced in the two years since Bogotá when six hundred women arrived in Lima in July 1983 to participate in the Second *Encuentro*. Least prepared of all was the Comisión Organizadora, which had to find a new site for the *Encuentro* close to the meeting date because the one originally chosen was washed out by floods.

In an effort to further a specifically feminist, autonomous, or nonpartisan women's politics, the Lima Comisión Organizadora decided that the Second *Encuentro* was to center on "patriarchy," a bold and ultimately controversial theme still associated with "bad," imperialist feminism by many nonfeminist women and men on the Left. Following the position adopted by the Bogotá *coordinadora,* it also decided that participation in the *Encuentro* should be on an individual basis as opposed to consisting of delegated representatives of groups and organizations. Participants became aware politically and strategically that being a feminist and working with women were not necessarily the same thing. The distinction that grew between the feminist movement and the *movimientos de mujeres* would prove to be acutely concretized and problematized at later *Encuentros*. Organizers were concerned that a *feministómetro*—a feminist yardstick—not be used to invalidate all the different kinds of

Not to invalidate work of f, but

work done by, for, and with women.[26] At the same time, they wanted to preserve a uniquely feminist "space" for feminist activists. Indeed, many *veteranas* or *históricas* (veteran or historic feminists, those present at Bogotá) lamented the absence of an intimate feminist space or *espacio feminista* with less theory and more *convivencia* (sharing). Those who had been at Bogotá were especially nostalgic for what had occurred there, claiming that it was impossible to feel and live closeness and solidarity with six hundred women. In spite of this discontent, one of the most important consequences of the Lima *Encuentro* was the involvement in feminism of large numbers of women who would become identified with the feminist movement as a result of their *Encuentro* participation, thus establishing a pattern that would be repeated in subsequent meetings.

Women from all over Latin America came to El Bosque (an enclosed vacation spot for middle-class families approximately forty kilometers outside of Lima) to share their experiences as feminists, researchers, grassroots activists, health workers, university students, union organizers, political exiles, party militants, filmmakers, and writers. Although throughout Latin America, and Peru in particular, the grassroots *movimientos de mujeres* had grown massively in the late 1970s and early 1980s, noticeably underrepresented were Indian women, working-class activists, and women from Central American countries; their low representation reflected either the prohibitive registration fee (US$50) or the state of the feminist movement in their respective countries. A large proportion of those who attended were, like the members of the organizing commission, nonpartisan, academic, and professional *feministas*; their presence was reflected in the organization and atmosphere of the entire four-day *Encuentro*.

Nineteen workshops (*talleres*) had been organized, all of which were prefaced with "Patriarchy and . . ."; among the wide-ranging topics were health, Church, power, sexuality, violence against women, and feminist research. Each workshop had an expert facilitator or *encargada de taller,* usually an academic, who was responsible for coordinating the discussion and, in many cases, for coordinating the "papers" that would be presented.[27] Predictably, this structure smacked of hierarchy and elitism to many participants and yet again raised issues regarding the form and expression of Latin American feminisms. Where was the "space" for

[26] The term *feministómetro* was first encountered in the report on the Lima *Encuentro.* See *Il Encuentro Feminista Latinoamericano y del Caribe* (Santiago, Chile: ISIS International, special issue of *Revista de las Mujeres,* no. 1, June 1984), 7–8.

[27] A document published about the Lima *Encuentro* listed sixty-three papers that had been presented. See ibid., 140–44. Until San Bernardo, the formal presentation of papers tended to be minimized. Rather, each *taller* or workshop becomes a working group that comes together to address a single issue.

less-structured discussion and for spontaneity? Where was the "space" for nonintellectuals who came to share their experiences in the *poblaciones, barriadas,* and *favelas* (shantytowns)? Where were all of the women from the *sectores populares* (poor and working-class sectors)? Heated debates ensued about whether the Second *Encuentro*'s focus on patriarchy was indeed too academic or too theoretical and whether the workshop format prevented a *verdadera convivencia* (true coming together).

In spite of some resistance to so much emphasis on patriarchy, Lima did represent an advance over the central political debates that had been formulated and articulated in Bogotá. Most important, the discussions in Lima, informed by a need to establish a theoretical understanding of Latin American patriarchy in all of its material, ideological, cultural, linguistic, institutional, and sexual expressions, deepened and advanced the movement's analysis of gender power relations and how these intersected with other relations of power in Latin American societies. The debates in Bogotá that centered on *doble militancia* as a political strategy and on the role of the (male-dominant) political party in feminism were reformulated in an analysis of the political party as an example of a patriarchal institution. For some Latin American feminists, then, an analysis of the role of the party moved from a debate about strategy to a debate about structure. Moreover, the focus on patriarchy allowed some Latin American feminists to further distinguish their socialist feminism from the way in which the Left had traditionally defined the "woman question." That is, by the Second *Encuentro,* many feminists, from a wide range of countries, had begun to insist that sexism was not the "outcome" of capitalism and imperialism but rather was shaped by a relatively autonomous, patriarchal sex-gender system.

There were several workshops, not part of the original program, that represented a significant departure from conventional Marxist understandings of the "woman question" and signaled the growing complexity and diversity of struggles considered "feminist." For example, "mini-workshops" on lesbianism and racism were held, neither of which had an expert facilitator. With an estimated three hundred women in attendance, the mini-workshop on lesbianism had to be moved from a small room to one of the larger halls. For the first time, there was a public response to the demands of lesbians that their presence within Latin American feminism be recognized. Historically, this workshop signaled the emergence of lesbian visibility within the movement and challenged heterosexual feminists to confront their homophobia. For many, this was one of the most significant accomplishments of the Lima meeting.

Similarly, the mini-*taller* on racism, although not as massively attended or as publicly visible, provided a forum in which to criticize the lack of "space" in the *Encuentro* to confront racism. This workshop, in which primarily black and Indian women participated, challenged the Lima and subsequent *Encuentros* to address racism, not only in the context of the lived experiences of women in their various social, cultural, and national contexts but also within the feminist movement itself.

At Lima, *feministas* and *militantes* also continued to do battle over who represented the "true" interests of women of the popular classes. Both women from the *movimiento de mujeres* and women who considered themselves feminists, though active in parties of the Left, were among the participants. As in Bogotá, class and ideological differences were expressed in discussions about the structure, content, and cost of the *Encuentro*. Many of the participants insisted that conference organizers had not done enough outreach to women within Peru's *movimiento de mujeres* and that issues central to those women's lives were not being discussed. Still others pointed out that the organizers had assumed all feminists were middle class and would be able to afford the registration fee.

While the Lima *Encuentro* represented important advances in the articulation of Latin American feminisms, at the same time it established a framework within which some difficult issues could later resurface. An analysis of patriarchy and gender power relations, for example, gave a new context to the dialogue between *feministas* and *militantes* as well as the discussion of feminist strategy. The participation of those who worked with women but did not necessarily define themselves as feminists set the stage for the future conceptualization, within the feminist movement, of the *movimientos de mujeres*. The final plenary produced an often tearful and emotional dialogue regarding the relationship between *feministas* and *militantes,* which in some women evoked a nostalgic longing for the solidarity with which the Bogotá *Encuentro* concluded. Essentially, participants at Lima felt that the issue was not to repeat Bogotá but, rather, to question why the *históricas* felt it so necessary to reproduce what had occurred there. In retrospect, the discontent with and critique of the structure of the Lima *Encuentro* was a fitting precursor to the next *Encuentro,* at Bertioga, which, although well organized, was based not on structure but, rather, on *auto-gestión.*[28]

Bertioga

The third time Latin American feminists met (in July 1985, just as the U.N. Decade was winding down in Nairobi) there was a special air of

[28] *Auto-gestión* literally means "self-gestating"; i.e., a free form or spontaneous structure that would permit participants to organize and create their own *talleres* on the spur of the moment. It should be pointed out that in spite of its emphasis on *auto-gestión,* the Bertioga *Encuentro* was, nonetheless, structured and organized.

anticipation as women arrived. Nearly nine hundred women came to the *Encuentro* in Bertioga, at a little-known, union-owned *colonia de vacaciones* (vacation resort club) on the Brazilian coast. The number of participants once again surprised and delighted all those involved. The Brazilian organizers had procured a physical space that most participants had visited only in dreams—with palm trees, open breezeways, and a beach—and that had many places for spontaneous, unstructured meetings. It seemed as if nothing could go wrong. And as participants looked at themselves and at each other, they saw among Latin American feminists an extraordinary cultural, ethnic, and political diversity that they had, until then, only imagined.

Indeed, by the time of the Brazil *Encuentro*, Latin American feminism had truly come into its own, politically and culturally. Feminists were pursuing their goals in a wide variety of institutional and extrainstitutional arenas—from government ministries to trade unions to alternative health centers to lesbian-feminist collectives.

The nearly four hundred Brazilians present embodied the broad range of ideologies and activities among self-proclaimed feminists in the mid-1980s. The Brazilians had created what was perhaps the largest, most radical, most diverse, and most politically influential of Latin America's feminist movements. Their national and regional *Encuentros,* their experience with elections and political parties, and their visibility in national politics had made the Brazilian movement both the envy of and, to some extent, the model for Latin American feminist movements.[29] Perhaps for this reason what ensued at the Brazil meeting not only left many participants perplexed but, more important, also exacerbated existing tensions between *militantes* and *feministas*, and between feminisms and the *movimiento de mujeres*.

On the first day, a busload of women from the shantytowns (*favelas*) of Rio de Janeiro arrived at the Bertioga conference site, their bus compliments of the Rio Lion's Club (known for its ties to the state's dominant

---

[29] On the Brazilian feminist movement and the issues it has politicized, see Alvarez, *Engendering Democracy in Brazil* (n. 19 above). See also Cynthia Sarti, "The Panorama of Brazilian Feminism," *New Left Review* 173 (January–February 1989): 75–90; Maria Lygia Quartim de Moraes, *Mulheres em Movimento* (Women in movement) (São Paulo: Nobel and CECF (Conselho Estadua da Condicão Feminina), 1985); Anette Goldberg, "Os movimentos de liberaçío de Mulher na França e na Italia (1970–1980): Primeiros elementos para um estudo comparativo do novo femenismo na Europa e no Brasil" (Women's liberation movements in France and Italy [1970–1980]: First elements of a comparative study of the new feminism in Europe and Brazil), in *O lugar de mulher* (Woman's place), ed. M. T. Luz (Rio de Janeiro: Graal, 1982); and Ana Alice Costa Pinheiro, "Avances y definiciones del movimiento feminista en el Brasil" (Advances and definitions of the feminist movement in Brazil) (master's thesis, Colegio de Mexico, 1981); and Branca Moreira Alves and Jacqueline Pitanguy, *O que é o feminismo?* (What is feminism?) (São Paulo: Brasilense, 1981).

political party); the women asked to be admitted to the *Encuentro* although they lacked the money to pay the registration fees. Consistent with the previous *Encuentro,* the US$60 registration fee was prohibitive for the vast majority of Latin American women.[30] Most of the women on the bus were black and all were poor, and Brazilian participants suspected them all of being manipulated by political leaders in Rio who had undermined the feminist movement on previous occasions. Proponents of another hypothesis declared that the Lion's Club was attempting to garner the *favela* vote by providing the bus. Some *feministas* insisted that sectarian parties of the Left had orchestrated the arrival of the *favela* women in an attempt to discredit the feminist movement as elitist, bourgeois, and hence divisive to the working-class struggle.[31]

Participants' opinions about admitting the *faveladas* became greatly polarized. The organizing committee (Brazilians) took the position that everyone would play by the same rules; that is, nobody could enter without paying the registration fee. They tried to assure the participants from other countries that their position was formulated in relation to suspected party manipulation rather than as a response to the women on the bus, with whom they empathized.

The organizers insisted that anyone who was not Brazilian would have difficulty understanding the complexities of Brazilian politics. Sectarian political parties had repeatedly disrupted national and regional feminist meetings in Brazil during the early 1980s. The bus incident, many Brazilians present maintained, was but another manifestation of the relentless and insidious partisan efforts to manipulate, discredit, and distort feminist politics. They pointed out that the *Encuentro* organizers had secured one hundred scholarships for Brazilian women unable to pay the registration fee and that the group now clamoring at the gate had received five of those scholarships. Many among the hundreds of poor and working-class participants from Brazil's *movimiento de mujeres* argued that their groups had raised funds to attend and had applied for scholarships. Most agreed that it was improper and politically manipulative for the women on the bus to insist on being admitted at that late date. Yet, here were twenty-three women, camped outside the gates of the *Encuentro,* refusing to leave when not admitted as a group, and thereby creating a separate and distinct space for those who wished to talk to them. Many participants did.

---

[30] For a more detailed account of this polarizing series of events, see Ortega and Sternbach, "Gracias a la Vida" (n. 5 above); and Judit N. Moschkovich, Maria Cora, and Sonia E. Alvarez, "Our Feminisms," *Connexions: An International Women's Quarterly,* no. 19 (Winter 1986), 16–18.

[31] For a background to the long-standing conflicts between the Brazilian feminist movement and the sectarian Left, see Sonia E. Alvarez, "Women's Movements and Gender Politics in the Brazilian Transition," in Jacquette, ed. (n. 11 above), 28–71.

Immediately, it seemed as if the battle lines were drawn: those who supported the organizers' decision and those who opposed it. The first position held that allowing the women to participate would constitute a capitulation to partisan manipulation, tantamount to admitting that feminism was indeed an elitist movement and that the organizers had made no effort to include working-class women in the *Encuentro*—even though poor and working-class women were present in far greater numbers than at either Bogotá or Lima, and many among them were proudly proclaiming themselves *feministas*. Those who did not support the organizers' decision were a politically heterogeneous group. Some were *militantes* who saw the bus incident as an opportunity to fan the flames of the decade-long debate about whether gender or class was most important for Latin American women. Others were members of Brazil's recently created black feminist collectives who argued that barring the *favela* women from the *Encuentro* was emblematic of the racism that pervaded Brazilian feminism. Still others, black, white, and *mestizas*, working class and middle class, insisted that the women on the bus should be allowed to participate in the *Encuentro*, if only to counteract the negative press coverage that it immediately generated and to get on with the meeting as planned.

The implications of these political divisions among participants informed much of the discussion for the next days. While some argued that the organizers "showed great courage in their decision," others questioned whether it was really courageous to deny entry to the *faveladas;* still others thought that doing so constituted feminist political suicide and would cause a great scandal with the media, most particularly the press, always looking to malign feminism and thereby discredit the movement. Some women swore they would never participate in another *Encuentro;* others spent sleepless nights drafting documents or press releases in solidarity with either the *faveladas* or the organizing committee. Aside from the fact that the *faveladas* were denied entry, the most unfortunate aspect of the incident was that discussions centered on the bus (who had sent it for what reasons?) and on admission of its passengers, rather than on the race and class implications for the movement raised by its presence. By the end of the *Encuentro* the issue was still not resolved.

Nevertheless, the *Encuentro* continued. For one thing, not all participants were equally disturbed by the bus issue. They had come for an *Encuentro*, and an *Encuentro* was what they planned to get. The physical space itself fostered spontaneity among the participants, providing both privacy (for sharing secrets) and openness (to encourage wandering). Everyone present was injected with the Brazilian style of feminism, which seemed to infuse a certain flair and panache into everything. In retrospect, many Latin American feminists, especially if they had not attended

Bogotá, recall Bertioga as the most imaginative and creative *Encuentro,* the most relaxed, and the one with the perfect number of participants and the most ideal setting. Here, the two Nicaraguans in attendance helped to focus attention on the political significance of the intersection of feminism and revolutionary struggles. Significant as well was that lesbians, made visible at the Lima *Encuentro,* now chose to meet on their own in closed session, when only two years earlier discussing lesbianism had been practically taboo. Instead of having to explain their existence to heterosexual women, lesbians were now able to politicize a lesbian identity. Not only did women meet by sexual preference, but also by country, by profession, by years of involvement in the movement, by class, by race, by age, by religion, and by any other characteristic that seemed to identify a group. Repeatedly, feminists discovered that they had counterparts in other countries. The Bertioga *Encuentro* made participants keenly aware of the growth of the movement and the concomitant diversity that it had created; few suspected that Bertioga was only a prelude to the next *Encuentro,* in Mexico.

Taxco

To this day, nobody is quite sure to what to attribute the presence of over 1,500 women at the Fourth *Encuentro* held in Taxco, Guerrero, Mexico, in October 1987: the perfection of the region's feminist network; Mexico's strategic geographical location; unprecedented advertising in the feminist press; the more finely developed organizational skills of women from more distant countries; or, more simply, the geometric expansion of feminist activism throughout the region since the mid-1980s. For the first time, women from all the countries of Central and South America and the Spanish-speaking Caribbean were present. Despite the enormous distances and disastrous economies of their nations, it was surprising that over 150 women came from the Southern Cone alone (Argentina, Chile, Paraguay, and Uruguay). While the significant presence of women from countries with the longest history of feminist struggle (Peru and Brazil) was expected, the unprecedented participation of hundreds of Central Americans, mostly from the *movimientos de mujeres,* was remarkable.[32] And the enthusiastic participation of over

[32] On the development of revolutionary feminism in Sandinista Nicaragua, see Norma Stoltz Chinchilla, "Revolutionary Popular Feminism in Nicaragua: Articulating Class, Gender, and National Sovereignty," *Gender and Society* 4, no. 3 (September 1990): 370–97; Maxine Molineux, "Mobilization without Emancipation? Women's Interests, State and Revolution," in *Transition and Development: Problems of Third World Socialism,* ed. Richard Fagen, Carmen Diana Deere, and José Juis Coraggio (New York: Monthly Review Press and Center for the Study of the Americas, 1986), 280–302, and "The Politics of Abortion in Nicaragua: Revolutionary Pragmatism or Feminism in the Realm of Necessity?" *Feminist Review,* no. 29 (Spring 1988), 114–32.

fifty Nicaraguan women truly caused a stir. Unprecedented as well was the presence of four representatives from the Federation of Cuban Women, an organization that had been reluctant to identify ideologically with the feminist cause. The very interest of the Cubans in participating signals their recognition of feminism as a force in Latin America that can no longer be ignored by progressive and/or revolutionary forces. *recognition of feminism*

Participants were engaged in every conceivable type of political, cultural, and educational feminist activity. There were women who worked for the state, in recently established commissions or ministries on the status of women; "party women" who may or may not have considered themselves feminists; union women (both urban and rural); and of course, women from the *movimientos de mujeres*.[33] Also present were "cultural workers"—women who worked in the arts, including film and video workers, writers, and poets. Other participants included those who worked with specifically feminist projects—battered women's support groups, women's health centers, and feminist documentation centers—and, for the first time, a significant number of Catholic feminist activists. This time lesbian feminists not only participated in the *Encuentro*, but also held their own *Encuentro* immediately prior to Taxco, attended by over 250 women.

Following the Brazilian example of securing funding from outside sources, the Mexican organizing commission provided dozens of scholarships, enabling poor and working-class women from Mexico and other nations to participate in the *Encuentro* in great numbers. Nevertheless, fewer black and Indian women attended than in Brazil, and neither Latin American Jewish women nor Latin American Asian women were visible. The cost of attending the Fourth *Encuentro*—US$100—remained prohibitive by Latin American standards, making it extremely difficult even for middle-class women to participate. While economic issues did not erupt into overt conflict as they had at Bertioga, questions of outreach and economic accessibility were once again a central focus of discussions and pointed to the need to devise alternative organizational schemes. In this respect the financing of the *Encuentros* has remained a point of contention.

How the Latin American feminist revolution is to be financed is a problem confronted by feminist organizations in every country and at

---

[33] For example, some of the groups represented included mothers' clubs, housewives' associations, *ollas comunes, comedores populares,* Mexico City's *damnificadas,* and rural women's organizations. (*Ollas comunes* and *comedores populares* are economic survival strategies designed by shantytown women to provide basic necessities of life; the *damnificadas* are likewise shantytown women's organizations to assist the victims of natural disasters such as floods or earthquakes.)

every *Encuentro;* women systematically raised questions about appropriate funding sources. Some have always protested the reliance on outside funds (such as those provided by the Ford Foundation). Yet other potential sources of financial assistance have been problematical. For example, the long-standing insistence on absolute autonomy among some sectors of the movement has thus far discouraged organizers from accepting subsidies from national governments and/or political parties. Alternatively, as suggested by some in Bertioga, the infrastructure work of the *Encuentro* has not been modified in ways that might reduce the overall cost (i.e., sliding scales, work exchange, use of public or government facilities). While participation in the *Encuentros* has increased dramatically over the years, the financial and organizational burdens are still shouldered exclusively, and perhaps unfairly, by a small group of organizers in the host country.

At Bertioga, many Latinas—and others sympathetic to their position— had hoped that the Mexico *Encuentro* would provide the ideal forum for a long-overdue dialogue between Latinas in the United States (some of whom had been consistent *Encuentro* participants) and their feminist counterparts in Latin America. However, there were few U.S. Latinas among the participants.[34] The small numbers are, in part, attributable to the fact that the Mexican organizing commission only reluctantly and belatedly accepted that such a dialogue was necessary or even desirable. In setting a quota of one hundred "foreign" participants, in which they included Latinas, organizers effectively discouraged many Chicanas and those Latin Americans living abroad from attending the *Encuentro*. Despite the steady participation of Latinas at *Encuentros* since Lima, and their repeated efforts to bring Latina issues to the attention of Latin American feminists, vital links between the two movements have yet to be consolidated.

On a more positive note, Taxco provided ample evidence that Latin American feminism was confronting a new political conjuncture. The absolute increase in numbers, in spite of economic inaccessibility and distance, signaled the quantitative expansion of feminist movements in the region. More important, Taxco demonstrated that there had been qualitative improvements as well. Women witnessed the increased diver-

---

[34] A Latina is a "woman of Latin American heritage or descent permanently residing in the U.S." (Eliana Ortega and Nancy Saporta Sternbach, "At the Threshold of the Unnamed: Latina Literary Discourse in the Eighties," in *Breaking Boundaries: Latina Writing and Critical Readings,* ed. Asunción Horno-Delgado, Eliana Ortega, Nina M. Scott, and Nancy Saporta Sternbach [Amherst: University of Massachusetts Press, 1989], 2–23, esp. n. 15). This definition is adapted from Juan Bruce-Novoa's definition of "Chicano," in *Chicano Authors: Inquiry by Interview* (Austin: University of Texas Press, 1980), 3.

sity of spheres of feminist activism and a movement that had grown and been enriched by that diversity. Feminists now seemed to pervade all walks of life and were no longer a fringe or marginal group.

At Taxco, it seemed that Latin American feminism had finally accomplished what it originally set out to do: foster a mass movement of women. But it had done so almost in spite of itself and not without complaints from veteran feminists (*las históricas*), who saw their own feminist space being usurped by women from the *movimientos de mujeres*. Yet, feminist discourse and practice clearly had had a critical and significant impact on a wide variety of social and political movements— from unions to peasant organizations, to urban squatters, to traditional and progressive political parties, to the state.

The *movimientos de mujeres* had themselves become quite diverse. Included within this vast category, for example, were women's groups that explicitly identified with feminism, whose work in communities centered not only on gender-related issues—such as urban services that would facilitate women's domestic work and thus were crucial to poor and working-class women—but also on gender-specific issues such as women's health, reproductive rights, and violence against women. In many working-class communities, women had organized consciousness-raising groups dealing with unequal power relations in their marriages and families, with contraception, abortion, and sexuality. In others, women's health centers and battered women's support groups had been established. In the process of organizing around "survival issues," many women participants in the *movimientos de mujeres* were empowered both as citizens and as women and consequently often had begun to articulate demands for sexual equality in their homes and communities. Because the Catholic Church, the Left, and conventional political parties had deliberately blocked this process of women's empowerment, the spread of feminist ideas among women of the popular classes was in no small measure due to the persistent grassroots organizing efforts of feminists in many countries.[35] What was confirmed at Taxco was that feminist ideas and projects were not the exclusive preserve of women of the bourgeoisie.

The massive presence of poor and working-class women at Taxco, then, was not merely the consequence of the availability of scholarships. Rather, many were there because they had been politicized through their participation in community struggles and were beginning to grapple with the status of women in those communities. Some, among the hundreds of working-class women present, still rejected the label *feminist*, sometimes

[35] See Sonia E. Alvarez, "Women's Participation in the Brazilian 'People's Church': A Critical Appraisal," *Feminist Studies* 16, no. 2 (Summer 1990): 381–408.

because they formed part of groups controlled by the Church or anti-feminist political parties. But many others had been exposed to feminism through direct contact with feminist organizations or indirectly through feminist electoral campaigns or the media. In countries such as Brazil, Peru, and Mexico, feminists had succeeded in deploying an alternative discourse on gender and the family that had influenced everything from the evening soap opera to government policy pronouncements.

These quantitative and qualitative changes in Latin American feminisms, however, also increased the complexity of feminist politics and presented new challenges for feminists in the region. "Just who is a feminist?" became a key axis of discussion at Taxco. "Just what is a feminist politics?" participants asked. "If all of the types of political work represented here are feminist, then what does that mean?" Some sarcastically reinvoked the *feministómetro* (feminist yardstick) as the "measure" to gauge a woman's "degree" of feminist commitment and consciousness.

Some of the organizers of the *Encuentro* and other veteran feminists insisted they knew the answers to these difficult questions. They mistrusted women who "still" engaged in what they perceived to be ill-informed and ultimately ill-fated double militancy, their version of false consciousness. The same *históricas* emphasized that the movement needed to advance on specifically feminist political projects, to delve more deeply into the many long-standing problems that plagued feminist organizations and confounded feminist political practice. Yet at the final plenary, Central American women and women from unions, parties, and popular movements were all chanting "Todas somos feministas" (we are all feminists), demanding that veteran feminists acknowledge the growth and diversification of the feminist cause.

These divergent positions obscure the fact that at least two new political developments were manifest at Taxco. Whereas feminism was a dirty word even as late as 1981 in Bogotá, feminism definitely had become much more acceptable in public discourse by 1987. Perhaps this can be attributed to the United Nation's Decade for Women, which validated portions of the feminist agenda and/or feminism's newfound legitimacy in leftist circles via the Nicaraguan revolution.

Because in some countries the feminist movement has had a political impact and garnered a significant mass base (e.g., Brazil, Chile, and Nicaragua), male-dominated parties, unions, and governments have jumped on the "pro-woman" bandwagon—at least rhetorically—as never before in an attempt to reap the benefits of feminism's new political respectability. Partisan antifeminist manipulators unquestionably had sent "their women" to Taxco to foment debate and discord about the priority of class versus gender struggle. The manipulation, co-optation, and tergiversation of feminism clearly continued—not only by that "unacceptable" Left but now also by the political Center and Center-Right (representatives from the new "democratic" governments). Feminism, indeed, now provided liberal-democratic legitimacy for new civilian regimes and a fertile recruitment ground and new slogans for political parties.

But a second and much more encouraging phenomenon was evidenced at Taxco: the growth, expansion, and diversification of women's struggles, imbued with and informed by the region's feminisms. Some of the party or rural women who had never before participated in a feminist event of any sort appeared nevertheless to have been reached by feminist ideas and influenced by feminist actions. They were not all mere "dupes" of the manipulative Left, as some *históricas* claimed, and seemed sincere in proclaiming themselves to be legitimate advocates of feminist goals, even as they insisted on the need to broaden and redefine those goals.

IV. Taxco as a reflection of Latin American feminisms today: New issues, old debates

Despite—or perhaps even because of—some of the problematic issues that (re)emerged at the Fourth *Encuentro,* most Taxco participants recognized that something different, indeed unique, was happening there: that, in fact, Taxco represented a transition from the small group of dedicated feminists to a large, broad-based, politically heterogeneous, multiracial movement. Yet, not all Taxco participants (especially the *históricas*) were necessarily pleased with this transition. For within the rubric of a large-scale, continental, multiclass movement were women at differing stages of feminist thought, a frustration for those who wanted to pick up where they had left off at the last *Encuentro.*

The *Encuentro* participants met in Mexico City and piled up in a caravan of rented buses. Enroute to Taxco, they stopped at a cave, La Gruta, for a surprise ceremony that had been planned by the organizing committee. The confused and dramatically differing reactions to this opening ritual, a mystical celebration of women's (magical) power and culture, seemed not to bode well for things to come. Advocates of "cultural feminism," which invokes the Great Mother and celebrates the caves of the earth as her womb, were enthralled by this event. Cultural feminism had only recently gained currency in some Latin American nations. "Socialist" and "professional" feminists as well as *militantes,* anxious to get down to the work of the *Encuentro,* expressed their consternation at the unannounced detour. Finally, at the Taxco town site, participants were dispersed in five hotels, the two largest of which were host to the major events. Because the event sites were located at different ends of the city, two separate, or parallel, *Encuentros* appeared to be taking place. Furthermore, some participants perceived that the lodging arrangements reflected an altogether not inadvertent segregation along national and class lines, with many of *las históricas* concentrated in one hotel while activists in the *movimientos de mujeres* and the *centroamericanas* were lodged in the others.

These space and structural difficulties, in addition to effectively inhibiting dialogue, complicated the organizers' intention to facilitate an *Encuentro* based on a strategy of *auto-gestión*. An often confusing array of hastily composed posters announcing workshops was plastered over the walls of hotel lobbies (by those who could find, beg, or borrow appropriately sized paper and the necessary markers). A recurring comment was that some of the workshops were wonderful—if one could only find them. Clear to most of the participants was that *auto-gestión* did not work well with 1,500 people and that the space limitations could neither accommodate nor facilitate the spontaneity *auto-gestión* required.

Tensions surfaced between feminists and women active in the *movimientos de mujeres*. Many veteran feminists thought the presence of "neophyte" feminists (or of women who did not yet call themselves feminist) rendered the "level" of discourse "too elementary." They expressed fatigue at having to explain basic feminist stances and, particularly, at having to teach women how to speak without using sexist language. Hundreds of feminists had been doing this work on a daily basis among working-class women for years and, as one woman put it, "we need the *Encuentro* to recharge our batteries." They attended *Encuentros* to nourish themselves, to get sustenance for the feminist battles of the next few years, and to find others who shared their point of view. Tired of having to "reinvent the wheel" each time a new woman became interested in feminism, veteran feminists wanted their own *Encuentro*. What they got, in the sentiments of some, was an "invasion," especially from Central America.

Few women from Central America had attended previous *Encuentros* because of distance, the state of their economies, and the omnipresent life/death struggles in most Central American countries. The massive presence in Taxco of women from all over Central America—including combatants, Indian women, and campesinas—altered the complexion of the entire *Encuentro*, and not just because (unlike other *Encuentro* events) the workshops on women in Central America were meticulously planned and publicized.[36] For the Central American women, issues that

---

[36] For a discussion of the interface of revolutionary struggles and gender struggles in contemporary Central and South America, see Norma Stoltz Chinchilla, "Marxism, Feminism, and the Struggle for Democracy in Latin America," in *The Making of Contemporary Social Movements in Latin America,* ed. Arturo Escobar V. and Sonia Alvarez (Boulder, Colo.: Westview, 1992), in press.

were considered key for feminists elsewhere appeared less important. Those very circumstances that had prevented Central American women from attending previous *Encuentros* now seemed to have politicized them. Women made positive associations between their political situation in the state with their private situation at home, evidenced by one woman's remark: "I was as sick of my husband's regime as I was of Somoza's." At the same time, statements such as "It's hard to argue about who's going to do the dishes when your compañero is going into battle" implied a distrust of feminism. Likewise, it highlighted one of the most critical issues facing Latin American feminists: how to promote and advance a more ideological, theoretical, and cultural critique of dependent capitalist patriarchy while maintaining vital links either with poor and working-class women organizing around survival struggles or with revolutionary women organized around national liberation struggles. Yet, *veteranas* and *históricas* responded to the Central American women and those from other *movimientos de mujeres* with some impatience, as this *veterana*'s remark reveals:

We have to find a way to organize ourselves and be self-financed. I think we need much smaller *Encuentros*. There's a history behind these *Encuentros* and we can't deny it, nor can we start from zero every time. In Latin America the *movimientos de mujeres* are growing. We're calling this a feminist *Encuentro* and it turns out to be an *Encuentro de mujeres*. The feminist movement can't remain stagnated. We have to move forward. Our *Encuentros* helped to revitalize us and now they're not doing that anymore. We're tired of being the "compañeras agitadoras, activistas" who have to explain why we're feminists, lesbians who have to explain why they're lesbians. I'm tired of feeling guilty. In Latin America we need two spaces, one for feminists and one for the *movimientos*. We can't mix those two spaces. Bertioga showed us that they could be mixed, but that we also need to have some order. There are two spaces here and each one needs to be respected. The problem with this *Encuentro* is that they wanted to do it all, to have one big beautiful event with *the participation of every country and, therefore, of every problem*. But we can't resolve it all here. We can't sit down and talk about countries, I want to talk as *María, not Ecuador*. It's not that I don't think there's a need to talk about Ecuador, but this *Encuentro* was created to talk about María, Cecilia, María Rosa, etc. Each *Encuentro* gives us one of these injections. So it's time to rethink the *Encuentros*. If we don't have money, we need smaller spaces. And of course we must still keep meeting, but [the organization] shouldn't depend on the efforts of just one country, but various countries.[37]

The tension that emerged in Taxco reflected the contradiction— emerging since Lima—between Latin American feminists' commitment to a movement that was broad-based, multiracial, and multiclass, and their tacit assumption that the Central American reality is not quite "feminist" enough and their frustration with the *movimientos de mujeres'* lack of feminist discourse. This tension was exacerbated by the absence of a "space" at the *Encuentro* to discuss country- or region-specific problems.

For many *históricas* and *mujeres* alike, Taxco represented a new conjuncture in feminist politics, calling for new feminist political strategies. Some *históricas* argued that the *feministas* should pull out of the women's movement (*movimientos de mujeres*), create something "new," and leave this watered-down version of feminism to the parties, the unions, the governments, the manipulators, and the "mujeres." Other participants maintained that in the future two *Encuentros* should be held—one for the feminist movement, another for the *movimientos de mujeres*.

Critics of these proposals argued that the male manipulators might absorb or preempt feminist mobilizations entirely if the *feministas* retreat and that it would be impossible to establish an objective criterion to determine who is and who is not a "true" feminist.

Perhaps the most extreme example of all the attempts at Taxco to impose a restricted proprietary stance over the "true" definition of feminism was the small group of feminists who spent the entire *Encuentro,* divorced from the entire event, in a closed room drafting a statement on the state of "the movement" that was delivered at the final plenary session. The fact that they had not really participated in the *Encuentro,* but offered critiques of it, flared some tempers. In other instances, some *históricas* argued that merely organizing other women irrespective of issue content did not constitute feminist practice. They insisted that the movement's energies should not be consumed by the *mujeres'* efforts to secure running water or adequate sewage for working-class women, for instance. Instead, feminism must promote an alternative "women's culture" and concern itself with those issues that community groups and progressive parties are never going to address—such as abortion, domestic violence, and sexual and reproductive freedom. Only women who make these gender-specific issues and concerns a priority could be considered "true" feminists, from this perspective.

---

[37] Speech by a *veterana* at a workshop titled "Visions for the Future" (Fourth *Encuentro,* Taxco, October 1987).

Many feminists, both middle and working class, stressed that gender oppression takes different forms among women of different classes and racial/ethnic groups. In this view, organizing for running water could be seen as a feminist undertaking given that women were held socially responsible for the care and nurture of their families and that, in poor communities, the lack of basic services imposed further burdens on women's work. A feminist-inspired community organizing effort, unlike those led by nonfeminist or antifeminist forces, would promote a critical consciousness among local women, emphasizing how and why gender shapes their particular organizing efforts. Black and Indian feminists in. Latin America argued that race, like class, is constitutive of gender consciousness and oppression and that their interests as women were not identical to those of white or mestiza Latin American women; that is, that one's *lived* experience of gender encompasses class- and/or race-specific dimensions. For instance, in pointing to the representation of the *muluta,* marketed to tourists and the ultimate symbol of Brazilian sensuality, black feminists in Brazil stressed the ways in which racism shapes black women's gendered oppression.

Most women insisted that the diversification of arenas of feminist struggle represented an advance for the movement. They seemed to be developing a revised conception of double militancy: instead of carrying her party line into a feminist organization, a woman would carry her feminist line into her party, her union, her neighborhood organization, or her job. This reformulation of feminist practice, they argued, would be more appropriate in an era of democratizing regimes and extensive popular political mobilization. A grassroots feminist movement responding to new democracies would develop new critiques, new ideas, and newer ways of "doing politics," thus ensuring that feminists working in parties and in government remain honest and accountable to a movement constituency. A suggested strategy entailed questioning, criticizing, and watching the "manipulators" carefully and relentlessly. At the same time they would continue to promote feminist consciousness among women from all social sectors, preempting co-optation by male movements, parties, and institutions such as the alleged mobilization of the women on the bus in Bertioga.

V. The San Bernardo *Encuentro*

After meeting for almost two years, an organizing committee issued a bulletin in March 1990 announcing that the Fifth *Encuentro* would take place in San Bernardo, Argentina, a newly developed resort town on the Atlantic coast, 400 kilometers south of Buenos Aires. It would begin on November 18 and would conclude with a march in downtown Buenos

Aires on November 25, the day feminists throughout Latin America take to the streets to denounce violence against women, in accordance with the declaration adopted at the Bogotá *Encuentro.* The Fifth *Encuentro* theme, Feminism as a Transformational Movement: Evaluation and Perspectives in Latin America, was chosen purposely to celebrate "almost a decade of historic *Encuentros* which have allowed us to follow step by step the development and growth of feminism in our countries." The organizers also set aside time for collective reflection on the obstacles, achievements, or discoveries of Latin American and Caribbean feminisms during the last decade. They invited participants to write papers or otherwise to prepare to discuss topics such as feminism and the *movimientos de mujeres,* feminism and the state, public policy and political parties, sexuality, and violence against women. As the *Encuentro* approached, the organizers received enough responses from potential participants to propose morning discussion sessions and afternoon *talleres* centered on four subthemes: the construction of collective identities and conflicting values; organizational variants and development spaces; relations between feminism and other social areas; and political proposals, perspectives, and strategies. Each of these would take one day and the conclusions would be read in a plenary.

Despite the uneasy political situation and disastrous economic crisis in Argentina, a group of thirty-two women from five different Argentine cities and from Uruguay's capital, Montevideo, had organized the Fifth *Encuentro* and obtained unprecedented financial support—a total of $280,000.[38] San Bernardo was chosen as the *Encuentro* site because it had a big hotel with eight hundred rooms, numerous meeting areas, and eating facilities for 1,600 people. Unfortunately, in the month of July, as the organizers were ready to sign a contract with the Perónist union that owns the hotel, they were told that inflation had resulted in a ten-dollar increase per person. Unable to meet the new price, and having already prepaid several other hotels, the organizers decided to remain in San Bernardo and, if necessary, put the overflow in the next town—a decision that ultimately compromised space for meetings and workshops.

[38] The problem of financing the *Encuentro* at a time of deep economic crisis, including the questions of alternative financing and use of public facilities, has been central to all organizing committees. After a heated debate, the Argentine group decided to forsake government support (though they received it from a Dutch government agency) and seek foreign funding. They received funds from several foundations, including the Global Fund for Women, the Ford Foundation, the World Council of Churches, Match and CIDA-Canada and Aktionsgeminschaft Solidarische. The funds allowed the organizers to cover 60 percent of the costs of the *Encuentro* and subsidize attendance. Argentines and Uruguayans paid 25 percent of the real cost and women from other Latin American and Caribbean countries paid 50 percent. First World women paid US$100.

Coordination began to go astray on the very first day when the computer system broke down and between 2,500 and 3,000 women, most of whom had not preregistered, had to be processed by hand. In an operation that required much goodwill on the part of the travelers and tireless efforts on the part of the organizers, participants were finally placed in twenty-one hotels situated in San Bernardo and Mar de Ajó, an area covering roughly some forty blocks. Participants came from thirty-eight countries, including Haiti, Ethiopia, Turkey, and once again, Cuba. The largest single foreign group was composed of 650 Brazilians, many of whom had traveled by bus. Although the Mexicans were also numerous, some three hundred, Central American representation was comparatively small this time; in contrast, there were unusually large numbers of Spaniards.

On the first evening participants found themselves celebrating the inauguration of the *Encuentro* in the middle of a central plaza, divided by countries as if they were delegations to a political congress. They were surrounded by astonished San Bernardinos who, as they would for the rest of the week, stared at the renowned exuberance of the Brazilians, the uninhibited expressions of affection among many women, and the performances on the makeshift stage.

All the problems attendant with crowd control seemed to emerge at once. Participants spent the next four days, including one very stormy one, standing in line, waiting for their shift to eat in a cavernous and loud gymnasium, wandering in search of friends, seeking a solution for the lack of day care, acquiring information about the supposedly free buses that ran between the two towns, and most often, looking for the commercial galleries, coffee shops, restaurants, movie houses, and even sidewalks where the workshops were scheduled to take place. Despite the apologies of the organizers, their willingness to provide these spaces, and their efforts to improve the situation—they even published a daily schedule of events—they could not overcome everyone's frustration. By the second day, the Fifth *Encuentro* had become *El Encuentro del Des/Encuentro*[39] or *El Encuentro de la Búsqueda* (the *Encuentro* of the Search).

However, after complaining bitterly about the prevailing chaos, participants decided to make the best of it. Undeterred by distances, electricity blackouts caused by the storm, closed workshops, or lack of available meeting rooms, they attended widely scheduled and spontaneous video sessions, movies, and performances (including a repeat performance of the feminist mass created, composed, and performed by a group of feminists from Rio de Janeiro) and celebrations on the beach in honor

[39] The name in Spanish is deeply ironic. It conveys the idea that while an *Encuentro* is a place to meet people and come together, San Bernardo was actually an *Encuentro* where people missed each other.

of the earth mother. They managed to find the space to listen to formal papers and to hold new workshops and discussion sessions on topics such as: "The Anniversary of the Five Hundred Years," "Feminism and Socialism," "Women and Aids," "Feminist Theology," "Pornography," "The Environment," and many others. On two consecutive days the number of scheduled workshops surpassed eighty.

At one such gathering, Indian women meeting separately to discuss the celebration of the so-called 1492 discovery expressed their repudiation of the anniversary, and proposed that October 11 be declared Indigenous Women Day. Thirty-eight journalists from mainstream or alternative publications attended a workshop where they discussed their profession and their relationships with the *movimientos de mujeres* and feminism. Lesbian issues were the subject of at least four very well-attended sessions, whose topics included homophobia among feminists and the planning of an *Encuentro* of Latin American and Caribbean lesbians in the near future. Two human rights organizations—Familiares de Desaparecidos y Prisioneros por Razones Políticas (Relatives of disappeared and imprisoned for political reasons) and Madres de Plaza de Mayo—Linea Fundadora (Mothers of the Plaza de Mayo—founding group)—sponsored video presentations and discussions of human rights abuses in Argentina. They also sought support from participants for their campaign against granting pardon to the military for atrocities committed in the seventies and eighties.

In several instances, the *talleres* resulted in the creation of new organizations. A group of black women met separately, formed a network they called Red de Mujeres Negras de Latinoamérica y el Caribe (The Latin American and Caribbean black women network), and agreed to meet again to prepare an *Encuentro* in Uruguay sometime in 1992. Some forty mental health organizations founded a mental health network whose activities will be publicized by ISIS International. After holding several meetings, a large group of women—some feminists and others belonging to the *movimientos de mujeres*—organized the Latin American and Caribbean Coordinating Committee for Mobilization in Support of the Right to Have an Abortion. They drafted a document stating that the right to have a "legal abortion, and the right to access to safe and efficient contraceptives are human rights, regardless of our social and economic conditions, our ethnic origin, our religion or the country to which we belong. The states must guarantee these rights." It also called for the creation of national commissions on abortion and the participation of women throughout the region in the campaign to legalize abortion, and declared September 28 the day to celebrate the cause of abortion rights in Latin American and Caribbean countries (a date chosen in memory of the 1871 Brazilian law that declared free all children born of a slave mother).

The presence in San Bernardo of legislators from Uruguay, Argentina, and as far north as Venezuela underscored the importance that Latin American and Caribbean feminism had assumed; it also demonstrated that women engaged in Establishment politics now also viewed an *Encuentro* as a place to meet. Though many had never been in contact with feminists prior to their trip to San Bernardo—and several remained only for a few hours—their participation in a *taller* became a significant event. One of the outcomes of their discussions was the creation of a network to sponsor a meeting in Brazil for women in politics.

Established networks used the *Encuentro* to meet for the first time—except of course for the writers of mujer/fempress, the feminist alternative press founded in 1981, who have met at every *Encuentro* since Lima. Católicas por el Derecho a Decidir (a recent Latin American offshoot of Catholics for Free Choice), held an open meeting to explain its activities and publicize its collectively produced book analyzing abortion from the perspective of Latin American Catholics.[40] The Southern Cone Domestic Violence Network also sponsored four meetings and decided to widen its structure and scope to become the Latin American and Caribbean Network against Sexual and Domestic Violence, which will be coordinated by ISIS International. Latin American members of DAWN (Development Alternatives for Women in the New Dawn) sponsored a three-day workshop attended by some one hundred women on "El feminismo de los 90: Desafíos y propuestas" (Feminism in the 90s: Challenges and proposals). The discussion was based on topics agreed upon at two previous DAWN meetings and resulted in a document that was probably the only real attempt to evaluate Latin American and Caribbean feminism during the Fifth *Encuentro*.

The DAWN document began by acknowledging the rapid and visible growth of feminism over the past ten years:

[Although feminism] has not always found smooth outlets for its expression, which has been more quantitative than qualitative; which has, at times, diluted our subversive character by being diverted into other movements and challenges, which is presently raising problems of internal democracy, of leadership, of structures within the movement, of creating new knowledge, of better channels of communication, of projection into the future, and which challenges us to re-think our movement in order to transform quantitative richness into political vitality and quality. Accordingly, as we enter the 1990s, the movement needs to recapture some of its

[40] See Ana María Portugal, ed., *Mujer e iglesia: Sexualidad y aborto en América Latina* (Women and the church: Sexuality and abortion in Latin America) (Washington, D.C.: Catholics for Free Choice, 1987).

original spark and develop actions that will allow us to shape our proposals in the face of the new demands and the needs of the women of our countries and our continent; directions that will help us to consolidate a democratic, effective, efficient, nurturing, and daring feminist movement in which we all feel expressed.[41]

The *Encuentro* ended with passionate declarations of feminist faith, and some 5,000 women marched along the streets of Buenos Aires on the final day. However, organizationally, from the perspective of an *histórica*—of whom there were noticeably fewer—the Fifth *Encuentro* was a disaster.[42] For one thing, there was no respect for, or commitment to, the longstanding promise to meet in Chile as soon as the Pinochet dictatorship ended. At previous *Encuentros,* the *históricas'* widespread admiration for the courageous actions of Chilean women in general and the Chilean feminists in particular had led them to favor Chile as the site of a future *Encuentro.* Yet in San Bernardo, when Chile was proposed as the next site and explicitly discarded in favor of Cuba, many *históricas* experienced a painful moment, for the commitment they had shared in 1981 at the First *Encuentro* held little currency with the thrust of a movement that now appeared dominated by the *movimientos de mujeres.* Nevertheless, Cuba, too, was discarded after a Cuban participant said it would be impossible to hold the *Encuentro* there; the final choice was "somewhere in Central America."

It was ironic that the selection of Central America, where feminism has only recently re/emerged, should have been felt as a disappointment by many *feministas históricas,* when in fact it was also a measure of the movement's growth and vitality. Additionally, holding the *Encuentro* in Central America will surely strengthen the movement, as has been the case elsewhere. It was also ironic that insofar as San Bernardo demonstrated the existence of numerous networks in the region and their need to hold specialized gatherings, the *feministas* found themselves as one more constituency of groups free to meet separately. Therefore, while *feministas históricas* will undoubtedly attend the Sixth *Encuentro,* along with the other networks, they will also undoubtedly now meet alone as well—probably in Chile—to discuss challenges and elaborate proposals for *el feminismo de los 90.*

---

[41] DAWN, "El feminismo de los 90: Desafíos y Propuestas," *mujer/fempress,* no. 111 (January 1991), 4. The authors define the feminist movement as a social movement that needs to transform itself into a political movement, committed to democracy and diversity. Although they do not elaborate how this is to be accomplished, they discuss two important issues for the movement: the reluctance of feminists to deal with leadership and the funding some women receive from research centers.

[42] At this point, it is impossible to draw conclusions from the small number of *históricas* in attendance at the Fifth *Encuentro;* we would be reluctant to conclude at this date whether their absence was significant or coincidental.

San Bernardo was unmistakably the culmination of a process that had begun in 1981 in Bogotá and which is no longer viable in the conditions of the nineties. Nobody would deny that today's movement differs radically from that of the relatively small group of women who met in Bogotá ten years ago. Now, it is the task of Latin American and Caribbean feminists to elaborate the appropriate structures for the articulation of an ever larger and ever more diverse movement of truly continental proportions.

V. Conclusion

The ideological and strategic debates characteristic of contemporary Latin American feminisms have revolved around two central axes: the relationship between feminism and the revolutionary struggle for justice, and the relationship between what was a predominantly middle-class feminist movement and the growing popular-based *movimientos de mujeres.* As the five *Encuentros* demonstrated, these debates have been repeatedly recast and are far from resolved.

But political and ideological polarization has not stunted the growth of Latin American feminisms. Instead, Latin American feminism today is a politically and socially heterogeneous movement composed of women who identify with feminism but who retain an unwavering commitment to socioeconomic justice and popular empowerment. In a supposedly "postfeminist" era, Latin American feminism is clearly a powerful, vibrant, energetic, creative, and exuberant political force, if still fraught with tensions. Women from all social sectors, and with wide-ranging personal and political trajectories, now call the movement their own. The movement's new visibility and legitimacy have enabled feminists in many countries to proclaim proudly a distinctive political identity. That identity has in turn empowered women to have an impact on public policies, political and social organizations, and revolutionary theory in ways that were unthinkable when feminists first met in Bogotá. Even Chilean feminists, in the face of one of the continent's most nefarious military dictatorships, have remained undaunted, and they have been strengthened by a flourishing women's movement that has become increasingly feminist.

While some old debates have not been resolved, many of them are currently being reformulated. Such is the case with the never-ending, strategic conflict over *doble militancia.* In Bogotá the debate revolved around participation in political parties versus feminist organizations, but today many feminists find that their energies are split between their activism in feminist groups and in the growing *movimientos de mujeres.* The feminist movement and the *movimientos de mujeres,* though too often perceived as diametrically opposed, have, in Chile and elsewhere, reinforced, strengthened, and supported each another. In Central America, this interaction has led the Central American Women's Permanent Assembly for Peace "to begin to articulate and aggressively push for an explicitly feminist perspective."[43] In Argentina, since 1990, the campaign to legalize abortion has been led by a committee composed of feminists and women belonging to the *movimientos de mujeres*. Also in Argentina, members of the human rights group Madres de Plaza de Mayo—Línea Fundadora participate in national *Encuentros* and often coordinate specific actions with one feminist group in particular, Asociación de Trabajo y Estudios de la Mujer, 25 de Noviembre (ATEM 25 de Noviembre [Work and study association on women, November 25]).

However, as women learned in the case of Taxco, mutual support between *veteranas* and *movimientos de mujeres* will be solidified only if the feminist agenda can be expanded to include the specific concerns of women of the popular classes. Incorporating the demands of an increasingly feminist *movimiento de mujeres* for the construction of a more inclusive, racially aware, and class-conscious feminist transformational project is the biggest challenge facing Latin American and Caribbean feminisms in the 1990s.

Though the tensions between *militantes* and *feministas* remain in evidence, they are mostly in the background. Many women of both groups now insist that they must organize around issues of class and race insofar as these shape the way gender oppression is manifest in the lives of women of varied classes and racial/ethnic groups. And it is now recognized by many that participation in male-dominated institutions, parties, and unions is not intrinsically antithetical to feminist political practice— that feminist activists committed to radical change must struggle for gender equality in a wide variety of contexts.

Contrary to the belief of many North American feminists, Latin American and Caribbean feminism is thriving. Not only that, but Latin American feminisms hold lessons for feminists in industrialized countries. We North American and Western European feminists could revitalize our own movements if we tapped the enormous creative energies embodied in our own *movimientos de mujeres*. The present vitality of Third World feminisms within the industrialized world is indicative of this potential. Regressive economic policies and right-wing governments in the "First World" have also created conditions ripe for the mobilization of poor and working-class women and women of color; witness, for example, the recent expansion of organizing efforts concerning welfare rights and publicly funded day care. Just as North American or European feminism

[43] Personal correspondence from Norma Stoltz Chinchilla to Sonia Alvarez, August 21, 1990.

once provided crucial insights for the second wave of feminism in Latin America, perhaps now Latin American feminisms can enrich and inspire our own movements.

Department of Spanish and Portuguese
Smith College (Sternbach)
Department of History
Dartmouth College (Navarro-Aranguren)
Department of Sociology
University of Lethbridge (Chuchryk)
Politics Board
University of California, Santa Cruz (Alvarez)

Devoted Wives/Unruly Women: Invisible Presence in the History of Japanese Social Protest

Anne Walthall

T HOUSANDS OF PEOPLE joined rice riots and peasant uprisings in early modern Japan (1600–1868), but it seems that few of them were women. Books in English on the subject scarcely mention women or question their roles and representations.[1] Until recently, the issue of women in peasant protest in the Japanese literature has been raised only in histories of women, and there only in the most negative terms. Harada Tomohiko makes a commonsense assumption when he states that "it is of course natural that men appeared in the public eye during uprisings, but women must have actively offered their support in the shadows" (1965, 176).[2] In contrast, Morosawa Yōko points to the constructedness of gender roles: the lack of female participation in the repertoire of contention is just one indication of how in this society they could not be called to account for their actions nor were they treated as complete human beings (1969, 127). Despite the difficulties in uncovering women's roles in Japan, comparisons with other early modern societies suggest that the analytic tools developed in those contexts may, with profit, be used to widen the scope of historical inquiry to encompass deeds done by women as well as men.

This article owes its inspiration to two sources, one a request by Majid Siddiqi to participate in a conference on peasant culture and consciousness in Bellagio, Italy, and the second an article by Hosaka Satoru on women and peasant uprisings in Japan. I wish to thank Professor Siddiqi and the other conference participants for their comments on my paper and Professor Hosaka for sharing with me his library on this subject. I am also grateful for the comments and suggestions I received when I presented earlier versions of this article at the Western Conference of the Association for Asian Studies in Long Beach, the Rocky/Mountain/Southwest Japan Seminar in Austin, and Harvard and Columbia. Anand Yang, Peggy Pascoe, and Robert Moeller, who read and commented on this article, deserve more than gratitude for encouraging me to persevere.
[1] In my first book (Walthall 1986) I mention women only once, on p. 146. Other works by Vlastos 1986, Bix 1986, Kelly 1985, and White 1992 mention women not at all.
[2] Following customary practice, Japanese names are given with the surname first.

[*Signs: Journal of Women in Culture and Society* 1994, vol. 20, no. 1]

With the increased visibility of women's issues surrounding the passage of Japan's Equal Employment Opportunity Law in 1986, some historians with a long-standing commitment to the study of resistance to the state began to disaggregate the participants in collective action.[3] Asami Takashi has argued that the presence of women in these events after 1750 suggests that the relations between the household and the village were changing; the community of interests characteristic of earlier times had broken down as the development of commerce brought differential opportunities for getting ahead. The village no longer functioned to maintain households over time, different branches of a lineage pursued their own profit instead of aiding each other, and poor peasants unable to afford lawsuits were forced to abide by informal settlements that might pervert the meaning of justice. Thus men and women, old and young, began to join uprisings to rescue themselves from the crisis of survival and to seek a new world permeated by justice in which the family unit could survive (Asami 1987, 68–72).

In his detailed survey of when and where women appear in various types of records for peasant protest, Hosaka Satoru takes these arguments a step further. He points to the use of gender as a symbolic order in the legends about peasant uprisings, compiled sometimes a hundred years or more after the event, in which women expressed their feelings within the privacy of the home while men marched off to make demands. His analysis of official documents generated in the course of such events suggests that two principles governed whether women actually participated in contention. One was the need for someone to represent a household after the menfolk had been arrested and imprisoned. The other had to do with the social division of labor. Women joined protests against government policies when those policies included the expropriation of their earnings. In addition, he claims that women often played an important role in instigating rice riots because they were in charge of the kitchen, making them keenly conscious of fluctuations in the price of rice (Hosaka 1989, 1–14). I would argue that this last point reads present-day assumptions regarding the place of women back into the past. In his study of English riots, in contrast, John Bohstedt asserts that "women were significant partners to men as bread rioters partly because they were essential partners as bread-winners in the household economies of pre-industrial society" (1988, 90). The same holds true for Japan; indeed, according to Kathleen Uno, both men and women did shopping and housework; neither had a monopoly on productive or reproductive roles (1991, 33–35).

To examine the place of women in Japanese peasant protest, it is necessary to consider the structure of the state that defined what it meant

[3] See, e.g., Saitō 1985, 150–51.

to be a peasant. The Tokugawa shoguns conquered Japan by military force in 1600. They carefully segregated the samurai who constituted the ruling class in castle towns, where they served their lords at a distinct remove from the vast bulk of the commoners, and divided the population into four statuses, ranked in descending order of distinction as samurai, peasant, artisan, merchant. Disarmed by governmental fiat and subjected to surveys to fix who belonged in what village, every peasant, rich or poor, had to be attached to a household whose head represented its members in dealing with the outside world. Households differed greatly in size and in the economic and political resources at their command, but in all cases the preferred household head was male and all members of the household were specified in the population registers according to their relationship to him (Cornell and Hayami 1986, 316–19). All property belonging to the household was inherited patrilineally and administered by the household head; women owned only their clothing and the goods they brought with them at their marriage. Under ordinary circumstances, no woman put her name to records seen by the authorities; indeed, commonsense notions regarding feminine modesty required that she not do so.[4] This system of rule marginalized women within their communities and kept them out of the historical record.

Under such a system of domination, the village headman conducted all official business, often in consultation with assemblies of household heads. In some regions, landless peasants and even widows with no adult men in their households might be allowed at the assemblies; in others they were not (Walthall 1991a, 68). When problems arose, the headman or an assembly might petition higher authorities for redress. In fact, petitions constitute the most common marker of contention in the early modern period. The petition had to conform to an exacting format that severely restricted spontaneous quotidian expressions, and it could go only to an official in charge of rural affairs. Any attempt by the peasants to leapfrog the chain of command by petitioning a high-ranking official directly was ipso facto a heinous crime punishable by death. The Tokugawa shoguns so disliked contention that they tried to suppress all mention of it. Thus the documentary evidence for protest is scanty. In those instances where mention of women does appear, it is tantalizingly fragmentary.

My approach to the study of women and social protest in Japan in this article draws on the work of Japanese scholars, feminist theory, and

---

[4] A rural school near Okayama prided itself on not keeping records of its female students to preserve their modesty (Walthall 1991a, 46). The names of criminal women appeared in the "Record of Punishments for women" for crimes such as adultery, robbery, arson, murder, unfiliality, and assuming a male identity (Ishii 1974; and Robertson 1991, 92). The names of other women occasionally appeared on the lists of peasants punished for their part in protest, but in no way were they there singled out for being women. (See n. 24 below.)

women's history. I begin by analyzing how storytellers constructed the category of woman in legends of peasant uprisings in such a way as to limit her to domestic space. This construction fixed its categories of representation as immutable identities, but it did not tell the whole story. For that I go to petitions and eyewitness reports that blurred when they did not undercut the gendered distinctions between men and women reinforced in legends. I am interested in how gender functions in a specific historical context and how changes in gendered roles interact with other kinds of historical change. I also want to demonstrate how gendered domains might become the site of contestation over the appropriate roles to be filled by women and to raise the possibility that over time the difference between what men and women did in public space might become attenuated. Finally, to expand the possibilities for constructing women as historical subjects, I want to focus on those documents in which a handful of women took advantage of their position in a system of domination that marginalized them politically and economically to raise their own concerns, speak to their own needs, and assert their presence as women in public space.[5]

Imagining women in legends of peasant uprisings

Let us begin with how legends of peasant uprisings represented women. These have come down to us in manuscripts compiled by the rural elite—local intellectuals including former samurai, shrine priests, and wealthy peasant entrepreneurs whose concern for the particularity of local experience led them to construct histories of their regions. Unlike official documents filed away in government offices, written versions of these legends might circulate widely if clandestinely. Most remained un-dated and unsigned, but internal evidence suggests that they were pro-duced mainly in the nineteenth century, often long after the events they purported to relate (Walthall 1991b, 14–28). These legends shared au-dience, authorship, and a sense of crisis with other genres, such as agronomy manuals (Robertson 1984, 170), but because they dealt with political issues the censorship apparatus of the state banned their publi-cation. Some legends depicted the exploits of seventeenth-century heroes who acted alone to redress wrongs; others painted allegorical scenes of battle from the eighteenth and nineteenth centuries. With few exceptions, however, women usually remained in the shadows in guises that spoke to the social conventions of properly feminine behavior as depicted by the men who wrote the texts. They grieved over the sacrifices made by men,

---

[5] I use the term *public* with some trepidation. I do not mean the modern bourgeois public sphere that Joan Landes 1988 has so brilliantly analyzed, though like it this space in Japan also excluded women. I use the term to define a space not family, not village, not state, in which representatives from all three negotiated demands.

but, as Joan Landes has pointed out in another context, grieving women are "merely there to suffer; they represent the consequences of political deeds, not the deed itself" (1988, 155). Their representation suggests certain predispositions concerning the proper role for women, and I will argue that the increasing frequency of their presence in nineteenth-century texts suggests a concern on the part of their authors to reinforce the norms controlling what women did.

In analyzing the range of representations of women in the legends that have come down to us, we need to keep in mind not only when the legends were constructed but also the class position of the men who compiled them. It is significant, I think, that many of the women they described were the wives of village headmen, themselves members of the rural elite. In all cases the women were subordinated to action taken by their husbands; they appeared in stories told to commemorate his deeds. We know the story of O-San, for example, only because her husband was Sakura Sōgorō, headman of a village not far from Tokyo and the most famous of the peasant martyrs. He dominates accounts of how he agreed to risk his life to petition the shogun for tax relief on behalf of over two hundred villages in the mid-seventeenth century. O-San, identified by name only in a minority of the texts, appears once the domanial lord has ordered the execution not solely of Sōgorō but of her and their children as well. From the cross O-San shouted, "I will kill to avenge my children" (Walthall 1991b, 66). In legends and in woodblock prints and Kabuki performances from the 1850s and 1860s, she and Sōgorō came back as angry spirits to haunt the lord who had so cruelly deprived them of their posterity.[6] These accounts make it clear that O-San took revenge on the lord not for what he had done to the villagers, to her husband, or to herself. As a woman, her concerns remained restricted to the threat to her family.

In legends about peasant martyrs, the representation of women's concerns focused solely on the domestic side of family life. But the category of family itself varied much more over time and according to status than these accounts admitted. For the samurai, the house (*ie*) was something akin to the House of Windsor. It had an identity and an income determined by the service performed by its male members to their lord, both inherited by each successive generation of household heads. In these houses, the official role of the wife was to supervise domestic matters, provide an heir, remain ignorant of political issues, and stay indoors as much as possible.[7] Thus the gender ideology that supported the samurai model of household relations assigned distinctly different roles to men

---

[6] Walthall 1991b, 36–40. For a graphic depiction of O-San as an angry spirit, see the woodblock print in Addis 1985, 53.

[7] For an excellent description of what life was like for samurai women, see Yamakawa 1992.

and women. For the commoners of both town and country, status distinctions passed down from father to son structured participation in local political affairs, but a household's economic standing depended on contributions made by everyone in it. Depending on the region, household composition among the wealthy might tend more toward an extended family or a stem family, with a greater or fewer number of servants, though over time stem families came to predominate in most rural areas. By the early nineteenth century, these families too approached the conception of the *ie* enshrined in the 1898 Civil Code in their quest for intergenerational continuity. To say that the poor shared these concerns is problematic.[8] In any case, commoners of whatever stripe never completely conformed to the samurai model of household relations, and the differences were particularly striking when it came to women. Peasant women spent a great deal of time out of doors, whether working in the fields, going to market, or traveling to visit friends and relatives. In smoothing out these differences in social practice, the men who compiled the legends presented as reality a dichotomy between men and public life versus women and domestic life that was in fact an ideological construct.

In many legends of peasant uprisings, a woman's identity was so completely subsumed in that of her father or husband that she was not even dignified with a personal name. She functioned as a kind of alter ego, expressing sentiments that the portrayal of men disallowed. When Takanashi Riemon announced that he was going to sacrifice himself for his village in the 1660s, his wife wept all night (Komuro [1883] 1957, 259–60).[9] In the context of these stories, it was a woman's place to weep, to express the human entanglements that made the man's resolution to die all the more poignant, and to contrast his steadfast determination with her weakness. This is not to say that men never wept, but whereas Riemon might weep at the indignities suffered by the villagers, his wife weeps at the thought of the disaster facing her family. Another woman went further in expressing the ambivalence many peasants felt when faced with the threat of self-sacrifice. Before the 1853 Sanhei uprising in northern Japan, the wife of Magokichi said, at least in legend, "this resolve of yours is completely useless. . . . If you are arrested, you will be severely punished, causing your children endless grief. I beg you please to give up your plans if you have any thought for the future" (Hosaka 1989, 9). According to Hosaka, this statement expresses a woman's true

---

[8] Laurel L. Cornell has challenged assumptions about the prevalence of the stem family household in recent research that examines architectural and religious evidence along with population registers (Cornell 1990a).

[9] In a history of the 1764 riot over the corvée that spread across three provinces, the wife of the ringleader emphasized conjugal affection in a speech made at her husband's arrest (Shōji et al. 1970, 232). For a translation of the entire text see Walthall 1991b, 129–67.

feelings (*honne*) instead of the conventional stoic acceptance of a husband's resolve to sacrifice all on behalf of the community. It might also be a way for the legend writers to highlight the leaders' heroism in contrast to the fears expressed by ordinary people or a way of representing the opposition that the leaders had to overcome when they tried to mobilize the peasants, using a feminine voice to express transgressive language that contradicts commonly held assumptions about community solidarity.

In legends like these, the representations of women served several functions. First, they said what men could not, but they said it only within the confines of the home. Second, they supplemented the text's focus on conflict between peasants and the authorities with portraits of individuals less concerned with community than with family. Drawing on the social conventions of the time, these texts depicted women whose response to their husbands' predicaments sprang from the deep wells of human feeling, an imperative that at moments of crisis could complicate the standards of conduct for public behavior. The distinction made between the male concern for the community as a whole versus the female focus on family survival in these legends differentiates them from the more sophisticated urban literature that allowed both men and women to experience the conflict between social obligation (*giri*) and human feeling (*ninjō*).[10] By denying these feelings to men, the legends established gendered categories that fixed a male identity as well.

Most legends of peasant uprisings that included some mention of women placed them at the end, after the serious business of protest was finished. In these leftover spaces women acted in ways that reinforced the gendered distinction between men and women. Even when they exhibited courage by aspiring to male standards of self-sacrifice, the text continued to emphasize that it was a woman who acted and, for that reason, she could not be expected to achieve the same degree of success as a man. For example, hearing that her father was to be executed for leading an uprising in the early 1820s, O-Tsuta from the Nanbu domain dressed in white clothes with a white headband to demonstrate her determination to die in his place, but she arrived at the execution ground just as the axe fell on his neck (Sekiguchi 1980, 117). This woman was not brave in the same way that men were brave, for she never confronted the authorities face-to-face with demands that could be construed as political nor did she take a leadership role like, say, Jeanne d'Arc. Never did a woman's willingness to die lead, as it did for men, to death. Furthermore, women who were willing to sacrifice themselves for their menfolk did so at the level of the family—not for them was the masculine role of self-sacrifice for the community.

---

[10] Here I have in mind the puppet plays of Chikamatsu Monzaemon, especially those that ended in double suicides, and books like Ihara Saikaku's *Five Women Who Loved Love* (1956), which revolve around the dire consequences of falling in love with someone not one's spouse.

Placing stories about women who aspired to self-sacrifice at the end of the histories of peasant uprisings effectively marginalized even the most laudatory depictions of heroic women. Most anecdotes, however, can be read as a series of meditations on what it meant to be a devoted wife. For example, after Kokichi's arrest for his part in the 1811–12 uprising, his wife spread her sleeping mat in the garden. She refused to change her clothes or comb her hair, claiming that it would not do for her to live a normal life while her husband could not. Word of her virtue soon spread to the authorities, who rewarded her with a cash prize and graciously commuted her husband's sentence from death to life imprisonment.[11] For other women, the final opportunity to serve a husband came with his death. Several women refused to allow the heads of their menfolk to remain exposed like the skulls of common criminals.[12] After Shinnojo had been executed for the Kurakawa riot in Shikoku in 1770, his wife brought his head home every night for seven nights to perform Buddhist services for it; then each morning before dawn she would return it to the execution ground (Ono 1941, 529). Other women took more drastic action, stealing their husbands' heads in order to give them a proper burial (Komuro [1883] 1957, 292; Aoki 1982, 81).

In these cases women were described as defying the authorities, either secretly or overtly, driven by the dictates of family honor and wifely commitment. Human feeling triumphed over legal statutes, but in such a way as to maintain the primacy of household interests. The extraordinary devotion to husbands exhibited by these women was ordinarily unnecessary, but it exemplified the principle of conjugal reciprocity that undergirded the peasant household economy, in contrast to the concubinage practiced by the samurai. At the same time, these stories were didactic. For the rural elite who wrote them long after the actual events, they conjured models of the publicly silent but privately devoted woman that they could use to instruct their wives, daughters, and neighbors.

Legends and histories of peasant uprisings treated women in culturally defined ways. In what is almost a universal constant, "the dominant images of femininity are male fantasies" in which women "conform to the patriarchal standards imposed on them" (Moi 1985, 57). Lords and wealthy commoners alike were involved in a complicity to guide women in the path of righteousness by invoking examples of devoted wives, nurturing mothers, and filial daughters. Yet women were not portrayed with the same variety and depth as men (who at least got to fight for what they believed to be right), a lack that precluded their acting in public space and exposed the invisible sexual politics of this literature. When they appeared at all, their deeds were usually reserved for specific arenas

---

[11] Aoki 1982, 82. For a similar story see Nomura 1932, 179–80.
[12] See, e.g., Matsumoto 1967, 570.

where they reinforced, not undercut, social mores. What gives these depictions of women interest is less a focus on the social problems found in official documents than the use of women to say things about family continuity that men could not.

The legends of peasant uprisings say nothing about what women did when not called to reflect on men's deeds. The later we go into the nineteenth century with the stories of Magoshichi's wife, O-Tsuta, and Kokichi's wife, the more narrowly do they focus on the feminine virtues of devotion and filial piety. Yet as we will see in the next sections, it was precisely during this time that commercialized farming was compromising normative gender roles at the level of the household economy. Even though the income women earned in cottage industries cannot be said to have enhanced their autonomy within the family, it brought them increased opportunities for travel. Certainly peasant women were notorious for their outspokenness and their freedom of movement, especially in comparison with the restricted existence expected of samurai women. In fact, these legends created a model of female submissiveness to the patriarchal code of womanly honor at the moment when peasant women became increasingly active as participants in social protest.[13]

The nineteenth-century authors of the texts in which the legends of peasant uprisings have come down to us rewrote the events in the light of the material and ideological conditions that prevailed during their own time. This has a number of consequences for the structure of the narrative itself; for example, any lingering controversies, especially those that involved the poor after the incident was officially deemed closed, were carefully expunged from the record. What is important here, however, is how women figured in these accounts. We have seen that women could be used metaphorically to express sentiments inappropriate to men within the context of the story; we have seen how the narrative constructed categories of gendered behavior that both concealed what peasant women did on a daily basis and resonated with the social conventions of the time. Yet the legends must be read with care. They ignored the relationship between gender and class, especially when these were implicated in variations in household composition. They reconstituted and absorbed some of women's experiences but disqualified most. While opening a window on family life, they closed the door on women's activities outside the home. For a different perspective on women and protest, let us turn now to documents that named women as actors rather than as observers, recognizing that these too were socially constructed texts.

---

[13] In a parallel development, Jennifer Robertson has pointed out that the intellectual preoccupation with women's roles in the Shingaku religious movement can be read as a response to the destabilization of the social system through the rapid expansion of a market economy (Robertson 1991, 88, 91).

To speak and act in public space

Texts constructed during and through the course of protest, particularly petitions and eyewitness accounts, carry their own ideological burden in their concern not with shaping the totality of an event but in detailing fragments, some of them produced by the participants. In search of a way to retrieve experience as a significant category of analysis, I do not want to place experience and the language used to describe it into a binary opposition, for they both construct each other.[14] The experience of women participating in uprisings could only be expressed in the same language and rhetoric regarding women's proper roles found in legends. Like legends, official records are socially constructed, but they derive their meaning by being fixed in time and space. Legends pretend to both but are in fact bound by neither; they are meaningful no matter how or when they are read. Having examined the representations of social practice found in them, let us now survey the documents produced when women replicated the deeds done by men or acted as surrogates for men, remembering always that the documents were again produced by men; women did not have the training to write official documents, and even when they did make their own statements the reports in which these were encoded included only what the ruling authorities of their time were willing to hear.

The question of why and when women began to appear in the records constructed during and through peasant protest requires a consideration of trends in both economic and demographic history. Scholars agree that during the early modern period, a rise in agricultural output gradually spreading throughout Japan, the diffusion of a monetary economy, and the growth of cottage industry led to what can be called proto-industrialization. Its beginnings were decisively present by the 1780s, and its effects expanded rapidly in the early nineteenth century. But its benefits were distributed unequally and the consequences for women were uneven. Saitō Osamu has argued that the specialization of labor took place not between regions, as in Europe, but within the household, with women working in the home on textile production while men worked in the fields (1983, 40). Other evidence suggests that women worked in both places, but it is nonetheless clear that the impact of commercialization on peasant households increased the types of work thought suitable for women, and in some villages women earned more than men from nonagricultural employment (Fukaya and Kawanabe 1988, 72–74). As long as the male head of household managed the family budget and represented its interests to the outside world, working harder at a greater variety of tasks still rendered women invisible in official documents.

[14] Here I draw on Canning 1993, 106.

What happened when a household lacked a male to represent its interests? Opportunities for migration, either forced through hardship or sought for gain along with a relatively low fertility rate, meant that the incidence of female heads of households increased over time.[15] Households headed by women were vulnerable in ways that those headed by men were not. Laurel Cornell has argued that, given the combination of reproductive and productive work within the peasant family economy, wives and husbands were "absolutely interdependent," but whereas widowers might find a new wife if need be, a widow past childbearing age faced a more problematic future. Women became household heads only when no man, no matter how young, was present; thus female headship marked the beginning of the end for a family (Cornell 1981, 206; 1990b, 719). This helps explains why in a few petitions, women might speak on behalf of the family economy. In pleas for the pardon of their menfolk, they even tried to force the government to take their welfare into consideration, an issue marked by its absence in legends. "We hesitated to make this appeal, but we are all so weak that we cannot maintain our livelihood," said four women after their men had been exiled in 1764 (Saitama kenshi hensan iinkai 1982, 282). In other petitions from Shimōsa in 1814, the women admitted that their men had done wrong but that it mattered less than their families' need for labor: "If they are punished severely, it will cause us extreme hardships."[16] It is quite possible that the authorities pardoned these men because they wanted an excuse not to banish able-bodied taxpayers, but whatever their rationale, they accepted the women's pleas for clemency and respected the principle that a viable household had to include both men and women.

Historians have paid little attention to appeals for clemency, perhaps because they ill fit a chronology determined by what men did. As Yvonne Knibliehler has pointed out, "feminine sequences of events are not synchronous with the masculine," and for women, an uprising did not end until the life of the family had been restored (1992, 36). Like stories centered on women in the legends of peasant uprisings, appeals for clemency came after the serious business of making demands on the ruler and accepting punishment was seemingly over. Like the pardon tales of sixteenth-century France, they constituted a "mixed genre," being a "judicial supplication" aimed at persuasion, "a historical account of past actions, and a story" (Davis 1987, 4). Whether because they were so brief as to add little to an understanding of the socioeconomic dynamic of

[15] The rate of female headships could vary dramatically from one village to another. Cornell found a rate of 9 percent in Yokouchi whereas Hayami found 23 percent in Nishijo (Cornell 1983, 58; Hayami 1983, 15).

[16] Aoki 1982, 487–89. It was said that after eight men were imprisoned for having petitioned to have their taxes paid in silver instead of rice in 1652, all were executed except for Heizaemon, whose wife had appealed for clemency (Ehime-ken nōkai 1943, 149).

contention itself or because they concerned the ever-present and hence banal issue of survival for women and children, issues of authorship, context, and effect have eluded explanation. For that reason, it is hard to say what kinds of interests were concealed by the rhetoric. Perhaps the other households in the village encouraged the wives to petition in order to strengthen the village as a functioning production unit, or perhaps the wives found themselves so marginalized in village affairs or even so threatened by aggressive neighbors out to grab their lands that they turned to the ruling authorities out of desperation.

Two appeals for clemency are of special interest, however, because in them women challenged conventional restrictions on what they were allowed to know about politics, and in bringing their demands to the attention of the authorities they invaded public space. In fact, these women ignored intervening officials to appeal directly to one of the shogun's senior councillors, the highest-ranking position in government next to the shogun himself. In neither case were they punished as a man would have been had he dared appeal to so mighty a lord, perhaps because as women it was assumed that they could not be expected to know better. Although male scribes must have composed the petitions, the narrative voice throughout is that of these women. I would suggest that the women who spoke through this medium appropriated the conventions of the devoted wife but took advantage of their subordinate position to demand a justice their menfolk had been unable to obtain.

In these appeals for clemency, the women used a strategy of self-denial to make their cases and emphasized their subordination to the larger concerns of family and authority. They justified their deeds not by their own survival but by the wrongs suffered by men. In 1772, Soyo, the wife of Sanai, headman of Kanaodani village on the peninsula northeast of Edo, complained that although three villages had petitioned for government loans of seed rice, her husband alone was executed; her younger brother, the headman of another village, was imprisoned; and the officials from the third village went unpunished. "Because I am a woman, I do not know the law," she claimed in a disingenuous proclamation of her own innocence, but men from the third village must have conspired with government officials to manufacture evidence that her husband and brother had led the conspiracy. This she knew "without a doubt." She asked for an investigation of her charges and permission for Sanai's mother and children to continue his family line.[17] In a petition written in

[17] Kyonan chōshi hensan iinkai 1983, 300–302, 384–85. See also Chiba-ken 1962, 142. Soyo died before she made her appeal. Despite being blind and over eighty, her mother-in-law and her stepdaughters managed to reach the ear of the senior councillor. The malfeasance of the local administration was exposed, the evil retainers were banished, her house was restored, and the fields were farmed by the villagers for the benefit of the daughters.

1850, Mie and Sei discussed every charge and countercharge between their husbands and other households in Maki village west of Edo regarding the qualifications for the position for elder in a quarrel that had been going on for fourteen years, showing a remarkable knowledge of village politics and the tortured path followed by the dispute in government courts (Ōtsuki shishi hensanshitsu 1976, 380–92).

It is possible to read these petitions not only for the way the discourse positioned women, but also for the ways they talked back.[18] These women demanded justice for their husbands, and they filled their petition with the details of legal problems, but at the end they incorporated their own experiences, making them into an official issue as well. Soyo wrote, "Myself, my aged mother-in-law of over eighty, two children by a former wife, his mentally deficient younger sister, and two infant girls have been thrown out on the road where we have suffered hardships beyond description. . . . I think it is terrible that not knowing which way to turn, all eight of us will suffer from cold and thirst, and who knows when we will starve to death. . . . There is no one among my relatives whom I could ask to make an appeal for me, so in fear and trembling I am forced to make this appeal myself" (Kyonan chōshi hensan iinkai 1983, 302). With Mie's husband in prison and her father in ill health, the burden of supporting the family had become too much for her. To raise the money to pay her husband's expenses, she had indentured herself to another peasant. "Sei has suffered the same hardships, and she has two young children. At this point I really do not see how she is going to survive another day," Mie reported. "Since the downfall of our families is clearly before our eyes, and we have suffered the most unimaginable hardships, in fear and trembling we make this appeal to you" (Ōtsuki shishi hensanshitsu 1976, 391–92).

The petitionary format restricted the kinds of grievances that these women could raise. Even the language replicated that used by men; no quotidian expressions used solely by women appeared in the text.[19] Except for a brief mention of their own problems, most of the petition gave the history of the political events in which their husbands had become entrapped. Had these women simply been making an appeal on their husbands' behalf, however, their own hardships would have been irrelevant. Instead they used their role as surrogates for their husbands to speak to a female experience, forcing it as well as themselves into public space. These texts can be read in terms of male interests in that the

---

[18] This follows a suggestion made by Canning 1993, 108.

[19] In Japan's early modern period, women dotted their writing with euphemistic feminine terms that set it apart from masculine speech. These consisted chiefly of an honorific, a syllable, then the noun meaning *word*. For example, sushi became *o-su-moji*, the honorable "s" word. See Sugimoto 1985, 156–72.

women asserted that they were trying to maintain the patrilineal family. When they made their appeals, however, these families were composed entirely of women, the survival of women was the issue, and an oblique expression of women's interests underlay statements asserting the importance of the family succession.

The narratives constructed in these two appeals for clemency absolved the women who presented them from participation in the events that led to their husbands' arrests. As part of their rhetorical strategy, the implication was that these women had followed the model for feminine behavior constructed in legends of peasant uprisings by remaining in their proper place inside while the men acted. But whereas this model denied women knowledge of the political entanglements that claimed their husbands, Mie and Soyo admitted to an understanding of what had happened. Their possession of this knowledge undercut representations of social practice found in legends and enabled them to make public statements. The petitions discussed in the following paragraphs suggest that after the middle of the eighteenth century, some women played a more active role in protest.

It might be assumed that when women were heads of households, they had to sign the same official documents that men did. There are indeed cases where every household in the village expressed solidarity by signing a petition, including widows.[20] We find their names even in petitions dealing with village shrine associations (miyaza), from which women were in principle excluded (Aoki 1979, 56; 1983a, 356). But all of these examples come after the 1750s, although census documents indicate some female-headed households much earlier, and by no means do all petitions include their signatures. To a certain extent these petitions reflect an increasing tendency for households to end up without a male head, but they also may have reflected change in the village. As opportunities for commercial gain eroded the older bonds of dependency that had once tied subordinate families to officially designated village leaders, the community could no longer be counted on to present a unified front to the outside world. That unity now had to be constructed, and one way to do it was to have a representative from every household sign the petition, even when it meant ignoring the culturally determined patterns of gendered behavior that had previously kept women out of public space.

The case described below demonstrates a blurring of the line between what men and women did in that public space where demands emanating

---

[20] See, e.g., a petition from 1746 (Yamanashi kenritsu toshokan 1973, 389) a petition from 1750 (Kashiwa shishi hensan iinkai 1971, 51), a petition arising from a village disturbance in 1763 (Yorii-chō kyōiku iinkai chōshi hensan shitsu 1983, 282), a petition from 1802 (Takatsuki shishi hensan iinkai 1979, 360), and a petition from 1822 (Aoki 1983a, 356).

from the village were negotiated with the state. The targets of attack were officials in close contact with members of the village, close enough to make divided loyalties a problem and thus requiring an extraordinary assertion of village solidarity. Beginning in 1840, the twenty households of Oyamada in northern Japan complained that the rear vassals living in the village took advantage of their position to extort money and labor, pay lower taxes than they should, and generally disrupt village affairs. As they said in 1848, "if you continue to employ Chūbei and Sen'emon, we peasants will be forced to desert our wives and children and wander aimlessly on the roads until we collapse and die" (Miyako-shi kyōiku iinkai 1988, 474). Most of the petitions in this dispute were signed "all the peasants" (*sōbyakushō*), but when every household was represented by a signature, the names of several women invariably appeared. For one petition, the peasants signed their names in a circle to disguise their leaders and to demonstrate their shared responsibility for daring to protest. Among the fifteen names was that of the woman Tsue (Miyako-shi kyōiku iinkai 1988, 478). When the dispute was finally resolved in 1848, each household head signed a pledge in blood promising to ostracize Chūbei and his descendants. At the end, as befitted their lowly position, were the names of three women.[21] The appearance of women in this dispute suggests that at the micro level of the village, the peasants had to be pragmatic in assigning gender roles; when no one else was available to represent the household, women appropriated an official role for themselves.

In the kind of issues raised in the petitions that constitute this case, we can see a subversion of the allocation between men and women of the public and domestic spheres. In 1846, one petition accused Sen'emon's wife of stealing radishes from one field and millet from another. An 1840 petition accused Chūbei's sister of disrupting the village with her loud voice. "Although she is a woman, she is always meddling in all sorts of matters, and she says more than she should even at the government office" (Miyako-shi kyōiku iinkai 1988, 439–40, 451–53). Offensive though her behavior was to the writer of this document, it provides readers of today a refreshing contrast to the silent wives depicted in legends of peasant uprisings. Nevertheless, complaints against women so seldom appeared in petitions that one might suspect these alleged misdeeds of having been raised to reinforce the case brought against the men. That even women had done wrong can be said to have constituted the most telling evidence of how profoundly the village social order had been disrupted.

[21] Miyako-shi kyōiku iinkai 1988, 484. One reader wondered whether the women's names actually referred to women. The petition was generated by the village at a time when it was in the village's interest to make sure that the appropriate signatures were collected because if the authorities discovered anyone using a false name, it would have jeopardized the entire enterprise.

For the purposes of my argument here, the presence of some women as signatories to the petitions is more significant than the complaints against other women. The peasants themselves commonly meted out punishment for stealing food or dealt with loudmouthed women without bothering to inform the authorities; indeed, a certain amount of outspokenness, especially on the part of elderly women, was generally tolerated.[22] But for women to sign a complaint signals a profound change in the construction of the village social order. Not only did women head households, their responsibility as such to participate in village affairs had come to be publicly recognized.

The early nineteenth century saw woman invade public space in a number of different ways. Women signed petitions, they figured in complaints, and they contributed issues that concerned them to lists of grievances. In the Oyamada dispute, villagers claimed that the woman Yasu had expected to be appointed Ibei's successor but that government officials had confiscated his property for their own use and placed her in her relatives' custody (Miyako-shi kyōiku iinkai 1988, 448, 467, 476). (Neither she nor her relatives ever signed any of the petitions, suggesting that their status was too low for them to be considered full-fledged members of the village.) Peasants in the 1811 uprising in Bungo accused the authorities of interfering in marriages. Women marched with men in this incident, but unfortunately all that remains today is a summary of the petition that provides no further information (Harada 1965, 176). For the most part, the women's issues concerned economic matters. In principle the government expropriated only the labor of adult males and thus only the problems faced by men were permissible in petitions, but in fact the ruling authorities sometimes tried to take the profit from nonagricultural production as well, and this included the money earned by women.[23] In 1825 in Hizen, women who had been employed to work in government kitchens resisted being forced to pick the *benihana* used to make red dye (Aoki 1983b, 113). In the 1790s, peasants fled Yamashirodani in what is now western Tokushima prefecture to protest the amount of labor they had to perform in the copper mines. "Men and women both begin the corvée from the time they are 18, 19, or 20 for ten years. . . . These long years interfere with the women's ability to get married, some remain single their entire lives, and this causes hardships" (Aoki 1980b, 42–44). The Takatō uprising of 1822 erupted because the ruling authorities imposed a tax of one pair of straw sandals a day per man and one roll of cloth a month per woman (Nagano-ken kōtōgakkō

---

[22] Suzuki Bokushi, a rural entrepreneur from what is now Niigata prefecture wrote in 1837 that "unless from time to time [a wife] speaks up in place of her husband, family affairs will be a mess" 1986, 50).

[23] Women traveling beyond the area of normal Japanese residence in Hokkaidō were required to provide straw mats to the authorities as tribute (Howell 1989, 75).

kyōiku bunka kaigi shakaika kyōiku kenkyūkai 1989, 144–46; and Aoki 1983a, 405, 417).

By the nineteenth century, economic and demographic changes along with changes in patterns of gendered behavior meant that more women had more opportunities to earn money for their household but also faced more threats to their income, and women without men more often represented their households than they had in the past. Beginning in the 1780s, women began to join men not just in signing petitions, but also in marching en masse on the authorities to force them to accept petitions, a process known as *gōso*. Again there is the problem that few records mention women. To say that women joined men's marches ten times between 1782 and 1869 may seriously underrate their presence, but no evidence exists either way for other incidents.[24] One document from the Tottori domain along the Sea of Japan states that when in 1817 women joined a crowd going to make a direct appeal for a tax reduction, like the men they tied towels around their heads, wore straw raincoats, and dressed themselves as beggars (Aoki 1983a, 59). At these times and places, women ignored the common sense of gender-coded propriety imposed on them by the rural elite. By appearing where they were not supposed to, they challenged the social norms of correct behavior that governed their lives.[25] Despite the scantiness of the historical record, it is clear that they had begun to leave their homes and their villages to join men in confrontations with the authorities.

The end of the early modern period was characterized not only by widespread social disorder but by a publicly prominent role taken by the poor, among them unruly women who shocked and revolted the observers. According to one report of the Bushū outburst of 1866, for example, the leaders were masterless warriors, peasants, clerks, porters, and two women, O-Washi, who "frightened everyone," and O-Toi, "a truly ugly woman" (Hayashi 1977, 246). Also in 1866, a group of tenants from Hatori organized appeals for rent reductions to their lord's headquarters in Edo. Rumors flew that all the men would be arrested. A report made by local officials stated, "Not knowing what would happen were everyone ordered to be punished, the innocent wives went crazy. . . . They made an appeal directly to a shogunal official who was passing through Fujisawa, surrounding his palanquin in such a frenzy that they prevented his passage. . . . The post station officials were all shocked. We tried to placate the women, but they refused to listen to us at all. . . . Since this is

[24] In 1782, Tome was arrested for her part in a *goso* in Omi; in 1811 Tsune was arrested for the same crime in Shinano; in 1813 Take was arrested in northern Japan. In addition, records show that women marched with men in 1811 in Kyushu, in 1822 in Shinano, and in 1869 in Hiroshima (Hosaka 1989, 3).

[25] When peasants in Wakayama in 1823 wanted tax relief following a drought, women joined the discussion to decide what to do (Aoki 1983a, 551). In other instances, women served as a channel of communications between villages (Aoki Kōji 1981, 482).

something that concerns women, it is difficult to predict what sort of crazy things they will do."[26] This action, spontaneous though it appeared at the time to the officials, suggested if even for a moment the possibility of a world turned upside down. According to Aoki Michio, when the poor rose up to censure the injustices of village officials in an effort to break out of their poverty, the struggle involved the entire family. At that point it contained the potential for a millenarian movement (*yonaoshi*) to transform the social order (1981, 149).

The descriptions of O-Washi, O-Toi, and the women from Hatori clearly indicate that for the officials who saw them, their bodies served as an object of revulsion. By acting in ways normally monopolized by men and causing trouble in public space, O-Washi and O-Toi made themselves into beings who were not proper women at all. What is an ugly, frightening woman, after all, but a demon or a witch (*onibaba*)? The only way to comprehend, excuse, and belittle the women from Hatori was to claim that they were insane. When people seemingly had committed serious crimes, madness might be considered as a mitigating factor and also served as a culturally coded term for social deviance.[27] Men in positions of power might also have used this term to stigmatize women in such a way that they need not be held responsible for their actions. Dismissing them as merely mad thus denied the implications of the Hatori women's refusal to conform to the relations of order and submission. Instead it made them into objects of pity and trivialized the political import of their demands.

Women in rice riots

In official documents—either those produced by the ruling authorities or fit to be seen by them—women are depicted infrequently and only when they act in a manner unbefitting the conventions of gender-coded propriety by refusing to suffer their lot in silence, by representing their household, or by joining a march on a castle. All too often reference is made merely to a genderless "crowd" or the "poverty-stricken people," a tendency particularly prevalent in reports of rice riots. For these events, which left no lists of names, a different methodology must be employed, one that includes a consideration of historical change and defines these events as broadly as possible, as taking place from the initial complaints until everyone had gone back home. Bohstedt has suggested that women were most likely to appear in English bread riots when they already participated with their husbands in domestic manufacturing for a market

[26] A number of sources exist for this incident. See Fujisawa shishi hensan iinkai 1973, 384–85, 389–90, 1974, 941–47; and Aoki Kōji 1981, 149–50.

[27] Vivien W. Ng makes this point in her study, *Madness in Late Imperial China: From Illness to Deviance* (1990, 138).

capitalist. This kind of productive role gave women the "economic citizenship and hence standing in community politics" that they lacked in either a purely agricultural society or an industrial society (Bohstedt 1988, 94–96). His argument fits with what we know about the spread of cottage industry in the latter half of Japan's early modern period, but it needs to be supplemented with a consideration of the kinds of changes in community relations and household structure that also contributed to their presence in the political conflict described above.

The rice riots of the 1780s mark the point at which conflict became increasingly both a social phenomenon and a mode of contention participated in by women. Rice riots had erupted earlier, of course, but they were few in number and small in scale compared with the political conflict that had centered on relations between commoners and rulers. In his recent book on sociopolitical conflict in Japan, James W. White has argued that the growth of agricultural productivity and the spread of cottage industries in the eighteenth century "created new, increasingly differentiated and at least potentially incompatible class and stratal formations, interests, resources and associational patterns within the commoner class" (1992, 49). He links these changes to the increasing magnitude of contention and the change in its character as people on the margin of subsistence began to turn less to the government and more to their betters within the commoner class for assistance. Taking his argument to its logical conclusion suggests that these changes also brought new actors—women—into the public arena.

Most records regarding rice riots and most essays that analyze them rely on a sequence of events that focuses on men's actions: how much destruction was done and who did it. During these events, called *uchikowashi*, the crowd tried to punish merchants who had done wrong by destroying their property—trashing houses, spilling sake down the gutter, and trampling rice in the mud. The participants never deliberately killed or even injured people, nor did they force merchants to sell food at a "just price," as in Europe. By emphasizing the destructive climax to riots, however, historians have ignored the activities of women. After the 1787 Edo rice riot, for example, the novelist Takizawa Bakin reported that, "wives, old women, and young girls of the poor mingled with the child beggars to pick up the grain" (Walthall 1986, 146). No other writer noticed their presence, and this description depicts a scene so seemingly natural as to require no comment at all. Yet it suggests that rice riots might have ended not when the last house had been smashed but when the last grain of rice had been collected to feed the poor.

A broader survey of the literature and one that expands the sequence of events to include women discloses that in making demands for food, women sometimes took the lead in creating disturbances.[28] Before the

---

[28] In Iida in 1784, women invaded rice stores and the homes of village headmen to demand alms (Morosawa 1969, 164; Aoki 1980a, 12–13).

Osaka rice riot of 1787, women gathered in groups to ask for charity (Aoki 1980a, 237).[29] That same year, three hundred women marched on the Amagasaki domanial office at Kamikōri village west of Kyoto begging for rice. They claimed that working in the fields kept their menfolk too busy to make appeals (Hyōgo kenshi henshū senmon iinkai 1979, 819). In the neighboring Hayashida domain, an uprising began when women gathered before the home of the senior village headman, the wealthiest commoner in the area, to demand food. Men who had joined the women then ran riot through his house before marching on Hayashida, where they surrounded the castle and held the retainers hostage (Tatsuno shishi hensan senmon iinkai 1980, 516–17, 1981, 253). In these cases it can be argued that the riots were not simply experienced by women but were brought about by them, an argument that recognizes the women's share of the initiative in preparing the stage for acts of violence.[30] In an inversion of the normal hierarchies of gender, women acted, men followed.

Acknowledging a chronology expanded to include the role played by women in instigating rice riots would force a considerable change of emphasis in how these incidents are conceptualized by historians. We have seen how in Hayashida, the women provided the opportunity for the men to riot, a practice followed at the end of the early modern period as well. In 1836, a crowd of some three hundred, mostly women, gathered to demand food for the poor in Kanazawa before men smashed up the rice stores (Aoki 1984, 271). Twenty-two years later, the entire Kaga domain was rocked by a series of incidents called, in one record, "the housewives' riots" (Niigata shishi hensan iinkai 1982, 976). Beginning on the eleventh night of the seventh month of 1858, 2,500 people, many of them women and children, climbed the hill across from the castle where they sobbed and shouted, trying to make themselves heard by the authorities (Wakabayashi 1972, 718). In Hōshōzu, thirty to forty housewives came to wail in front of the rice stores. In Kōrimi, women came to the government office to complain that the high price of rice was starving them to death. The next morning both men and women smashed up houses belonging to the rice merchants. Among those arrested was Sano, a woman who was charged with "outrageous deeds." One disgusted official wrote, "this disturbance was due entirely to foolish women."[31]

The role taken by these "foolish women" in instigating riots suggests that in Japan as in Europe a perceived threat to subsistence might make

[29] After the Edo city riot of 1866, e.g., the poverty-stricken people, young and old, men and women, pushed their way into the homes of the wealthy to demand alms (Tanigawa 1970, 180).

[30] For a discussion of the importance of considering women's and men's shares of initiative, see Knibliehler 1992, 35.

[31] Niigata shishi hensan iinkai 1982, 976. For details see Toyama-ken 1909, 637–40; 1983a, 1085, 1095–96; 1983b, 1065; and Takaoka-shi 1909, 75–88. For a discussion in English of these riots, see McClain 1988, 429, 431–32.

it possible for women not only to appear alongside men in public space but to seize the initiative. According to Olwen Hufton, mothers had a greater right to riot than did fathers when hunger threatened their families. "A bread riot without women is an inherent contradiction" (Hufton 1971, 94–95). This tradition of activism made it seemingly natural that women would participate in reverberating public events. Women marched in France during the October days of 1789. The February revolution of 1917 in Petrograd began with women demanding bread and an end to war.[32] Sian Reynolds has argued that women "are generally welcomed, at least in the early stages of revolution, as proof that the 'the people' . . . are involved, thus profoundly legitimizing revolutionary action" (1987, xiv). Similar uses and deployments of women have occurred throughout the various regions of the world, though of course patterns vary according to country and period.[33] I do not want to impose universalizing categories on the experience of Japanese women that homogenizes them to a single model. Nevertheless, a recognition that women might have reason to participate in some phase of rice riots may lead historians to open their analysis to a wider chronology, one that begins with the initial signs of discontent and ends with pleas for clemency, that includes both feminine and masculine patterns of action, and that incorporates a greater heterogeneity of participants, motives, and deeds.

Given the thousands of peasant uprisings, rice riots, and village disturbances that erupted in various parts of Japan between 1600 and 1868, the number of documents that testify to the participation of women is small indeed and much smaller than in other parts of the world. Historians have assumed that because most issues did not concern women directly, they stayed in their place at home; I wonder, however, if perhaps both men who wrote the documents and historians who analyzed them have overlooked women because the sequence of events for women has been obscured by an overlapping but different sequence dominated by men. Women were more likely to have come forward with their own pleas, to have signed lists of grievances, or to have instigated rice riots in the latter half of the Tokugawa period. Their presence speaks to changes in household composition—an increase in female heads, especially among the poor—and to changes in the composition of the village—the growing social distance between rural entrepreneurs and tenant farmers in a new hierarchy based more on economic criteria than on privilege—as well as to the kind of participation in proto-industrial employment em-

---

[32] Kaplan 1976, 190–92; Perrot 1987, 49; Williams 1987, 68.

[33] For bibliographies on non-Western women that include essays addressing the role of women in riot and revolution see *Journal of Women's History* 2, no. 2 (Fall 1990): 185–211, and 3, no. 1 (Spring 1991): 159–66. Cheryl Johnson-Odin and Margaret Strobel (1988) also discuss this topic in essays covering the various regions of the world.

phasized by Bohstedt. This was also a time when the tendency to litigation and the quantity of documents circulating between authorities and villages was growing. By the nineteenth century, petitions had become much longer, much more detailed, and much more frequent than in the seventeenth century. Social conflict too had increased in scale and frequency. Women participated in both forms of protest at rates impossible to determine from the available evidence, but their participation in and of itself suggests that they were unwilling to accept or were unaware of the conventions of feminine behavior created in the legends of peasant uprisings by the rural elite.

Women who speak for themselves

Underlying the deeds done by women in instigating rice riots, the words attributed to them in petitions, and the depictions of devoted wives in histories of peasant uprisings is the assumption that women were to be defined not as individuals but in relation to others within the household. Thus women who replicated the deeds done by men, acted as surrogates for their men, or demanded justice for their men can be seen as simply reconfirming patriarchal hegemony and the centrality of the patrilineal house (*ie*). As we have seen above, however, it is debatable to what extent a conception of the *ie* as an institution enduring over time had relevance for tenant farmers or the urban poor despite the importance attached to it by the samurai and wealthy members of the commoner class. The women from Hatori most probably wanted their husbands back because they knew that by themselves they could not function as a viable production unit in the here and now. Yet whatever their motives, they, like other women, couched their demands in such a way as to privilege male interests. It would appear that whenever women acted, they did so at least ostensibly on behalf of men.

To disrupt this homogeneous portrayal of self-denying women, let me turn now to a different voice, one in which women speak to their own concerns. Cases that reflect such a voice are few and far between. They come from the nineteenth century, when a commercialized economy had vastly complicated the competition between community members, and they invoke women placed at the double disadvantage of lacking a mate and being poor. The circumstances are extraordinary—corruption at the village level, a threat to a widow's livelihood, and a rape—yet the issues of gender that they expose can expand our understanding of lived experience in family life and relations between it and the community.

The first case involves a woman caught in the complex interplay between political and economic power at the village level. In 1862 Fumi, the wife of the peasant Rokuemon in Fukuse village, went to the Osaka city magistrate because her village headman had tricked her into using her husband's seal. She explained that in 1848, while her husband was absent on a pilgrimage to Mount Kōya, the headman had plied her with sake, said that he was acting on behalf of the entire village, and stamped the seal on a set of papers. Only later did she discover that she had committed her family to stand as a guarantor for a peasant who had pawned his entire estate to the headman. In 1851, the debtor fled the village. The headman ordered Rokuemon to repay the loan; Rokuemon divorced Fumi, saying he could not have a woman in his house who would use his seal without permission. Leaving behind her four children, Fumi tried to return to her natal home, but her relatives refused to take her back. Not knowing what to do, she apologized once again to her husband. If she could retrieve the note she had signed, he said, he would permit her return. This was the gist of, and the reason for, her petition (Izumi shishi hensan iinkai 1968, 193–95).

To make her marital problems the subject of a petition to government officials was an extraordinary step for a woman to take. No woman had the training in official documents to write in that specialized and exacting format, so Fumi must have found a scribe to write it for her.[34] Later events—the headman's resignation and a complaint against a group leader—suggest that some villagers wanted to rid themselves of corrupt officials who took advantage of their position to increase their landholdings. This opposition faction may have encouraged Fumi in her suit, but the grievances listed in her petition centered entirely around her position as a woman. The headman tricked her because she was a woman, her husband divorced her because as a woman she did not have the authority to make decisions that were his prerogative as head of the household, and she found herself without any means of survival once she lost her position as wife and mother. The rhetorical strategies used by Fumi in her petition overwhelmingly supported the patriarchal principle articulated by her husband, but by asserting her presence in official space she at the same time subverted the dictate contained in this principle that women should remain silently at home.

In the second case the issue was not patriarchal authority in the household but the control exercised by a community over its female members. In 1851 the officials of the Karatsu hot springs placed a notice on the official signboard ordering Hisa, a widowed innkeeper, to refrain from doing business for a year because she had been harassing travelers and trying to

---

[34] Somewhere between 10 and 15 percent of women in early nineteenth-century Japan learned to read and write the Japanese syllabary. Those from wealthy families might learn a few hundred Chinese characters. A much smaller number, perhaps no more than one or two hundred at the most, learned to write Chinese poetry. See Walthall 1991a, 46–49; and Fister 1991, 108–9. Petitions, however, required a specialized Sinofied vocabulary and style learned only by those men for whom it was a professional necessity.

force them to stay with her. She tore down the notice and accused the officials of trying to force her out of business permanently. It was a complicated affair with both sides quarreling among themselves and making charges later proved false. Hisa's son was the original defendant, but he quarreled with his mother when he apologized to the officials and promised to obey their decree. He left, never to return, and Hisa went to Edo, where she presented her grievances to one of the shogun's senior councillors. According to the statement she made in her own defense, "I was on pilgrimage to the Buddhist temple in Asakusa when I just happened to meet a stranger to whom I related all my troubles. . . . He then wrote a petition for me." She then claimed she had been sick when her son reached a settlement with the plaintiffs. The settlement had nothing to do with her, nor did any of the misdeeds her son might have committed. Government officials finally forced her to moderate her stance. In the compromise signed by Hisa and the village officials, she agreed to live in harmony with her neighbors, the officials promised not to be unjust, and everyone agreed to observe the local protocols on how to conduct business (Karatsu chōshi hensan iinkai 1976, 640–48).

In the official documents produced by this quarrel, the parties' possible motivations and the harm they may have suffered are carefully couched in socially acceptable language. Stories and legends gave a slightly different picture, one that shifted the blame for Hisa's deeds to the village officials who had made it impossible for her to make a living and ignored the compromise she had accepted. Because the officials had close ties with the local government office, she was forced to appeal to the senior councillors to gain a hearing for her grievances. The councillors were so impressed with her perseverance that they took her petition up for discussion at their next meeting in the shogun's castle. Although she had done wrong in harassing travelers, they agreed that it was more egregious for the village officials to have threatened the livelihood of a widow. Having gotten them officially rebuked and her own punishment reversed, Hisa became exceedingly self-righteous. Thereafter the villagers had to treat her very gingerly indeed (Karatsu chōshi hensan iinkai 1976, 639–40; Hosaka 1989, 7).

By emphasizing her vulnerability as a widow, Hisa managed to transform her social and political marginality into a weapon against the system of domination manifested in the collusion between other innkeepers, all male heads of households, and the village officials. Had her husband been alive, he would have been in a position to abide by the protocols regarding the treatment of travelers, any conflict would have taken place in his name, and he would have been punished for petitioning a senior councillor. Even so, what needed to be explained in the context of village history was how a woman had managed to speak out and hold her own against village officials. In later years, when the mundane details of the negotiations had been forgotten, what stuck in popular memory was her unfeminine audacity in making her appeal and her success in getting the village officials to yield. For that reason her actual failure to have her petition accepted and the loss of her son and heir was ignored while the compromise she was forced to accept took on the aura of victory. Instead of remaining properly subservient to officials, she had forced them to notice her. If only for a moment, she had turned the village order upside down.

The third case also involves a woman marginalized socially and politically by her lack of a husband. In 1819, Tayo from Kubota village in Musashi had a petition written for her because her local officials had done nothing after she was gang-raped by the young men of a neighboring village. "They despise me as a woman," she claimed, but as Nagashima Atsuko has pointed out,they and the rapists probably despised her because her family was vulnerable. A divorcée of thirty-three, she lived with her aged parents and her orphaned nephew. With no able-bodied male to prevent it, the rape represented the worst of the slights and insults she faced regularly in the course of everyday life. She justified her appeal on the grounds that she needed to clear her name through purification rites and a formal apology by the rapists so that she could remarry after her nephew became old enough to succeed her father (Nagashima 1980, 47–50). Tayo's audacity in presenting her petition to the finance magistrate in Edo forced her village headman to take action. He interrogated the young men, whose defense was that they merely had flirted with her while they were drinking. Nevertheless, they agreed to pay all her expenses and to make an apology.[35] This apology needs to be taken seriously, as in the premodern world it meant a vindication at least as satisfying as that of winning financial compensation in a lawsuit today.

Had Tayo been a samurai woman, her accusation would have had more serious consequences. The shogunal government made no distinction between rape and adultery. For both parties, illicit intercourse was punishable by death if the woman was married, by exile if she was not. No respectable samurai woman would ever put herself in a position where she could be raped. She seldom ventured out of doors, and, when she did, she always had an attendant. Divorce was shameful and remarriage unthinkable. Peasants held different attitudes. Even wealthy peasant daughters married repeatedly; in fact, some peasants practiced what might be called serial marriage. As long as the woman remarried, divorce did not carry the stigma it did in Japan's ruling class or in Japan today (Cornell 1990b, 719). In some ways, however, peasant women had less control over their bodies. Especially notorious was the custom of nighttime visits (*yobai*) paid by village youths to young female neighbors in which the

[35] Nagashima 1993, 307–8. Having won her suit, Tayo remarried.

women had little if any right of refusal. Customs change, however, and Seki Tamiko has argued that in the early nineteenth century rape came to be regarded differently. Instead of being simply a violation of a father's or a husband's property rights, it came to be recognized as also a violation of the woman's will (Nagashima 1993, 311). For my purposes here, the point needs to be made that by accepting Tayo's version of events, the ruling authorities inadvertently and briefly acknowledged that peasant women had a voice and might even have a claim on public space.

It is unlikely that Fumi, Hisa, and Tayo were the only women in the entire early modern period who suffered injustices because they were women. It is also unlikely that they were the only ones to raise issues that concerned them as women instead of claiming to speak on behalf of male interests. Yet they cannot be assumed to be simply representative of a much larger group of women who would have liked to speak out or who did assert their presence only to be silenced either by a lack of access to the petitionary format or by pressure from their neighbors and political superiors. Too much should not be made of women who had the luck or courage to say what they thought when most did not or were not heard if they did. The forces of repression, ranging from the structure of the household to the relations within the village to the system of domination imposed on the peasantry by their samurai overlords, were multivalent and powerful. Even protest that subverted the patterns of gendered behavior often confirmed and sealed the status of women as inferior.

Conclusion

Although records that place women at the scene of contention in early modern Japan are much sparser and more fragmentary than for many other periods and parts of the world, a consideration of the methodological issues they raise has implications for both women's history and for the history of resistance to domination. First, it is important to juxtapose different types of records so as to clarify the possibilities and limitations inherent in each. Relying solely on legends leaves the reader with the impression that women did nothing but offer support in the shadows, yet legends also allow us to catch a glimpse of the divisions papered over by assertions of community solidarity and the anguish felt by those who stayed at home. Likewise, petitions for clemency make a case for self-denial that can be disrupted only by individual assertions of female interests, yet they also suggest that conjugal reciprocity meant as much as intergenerational continuity. It is important as well to recognize that women experienced the repertoire of contention differently than did men. Although women may not have been actively involved in the actual acts of destruction, eyewitness accounts of rice riots show that women both took the initiative in creating disorder and followed acts of destruction with practical measures aimed at survival. Thus, regardless of the type of document, the only way to retrieve women's voices is to expand the chronology to incorporate feminine sequences of events that may be incongruous with the masculine.

Yet the implications for recognizing the place of women in conflict go beyond restoring women to the historical record. It is clear that the boundaries of class and status were being challenged in the early nineteenth century by differential commercial opportunities and a fluidity of commoner practices that the ruling class found it impossible to control. What has been less widely recognized is that the social category of gender also was both unsettled and unsettling. Without women willing and able to participate in cottage industries, Japan would not have seen the commercial growth in the eighteenth century that disrupted long-standing relationships between households in the village and transformed the place of women in village affairs. When unruly women asserted that only by making their presence felt in public space could they fulfill the dictates of being devoted wives who loyally supported the patrilineal family—that is, when they spoke in public to defend the domestic sphere—their deeds and statements subverted the very conventions of feminine behavior that they purported to uphold. These women remind us that conflict over taxes or administrative reform is not the only way the social order may be disrupted, as James C. Scott's (1985) work on the everyday forms of resistance has demonstrated. Just as his work has vastly complicated the inquiry into social conflict, a consideration of the methodological issues that arise when actions by women become the subject of analysis can equally challenge theories aimed at explaining the repertoire of contention.

Department of History
University of California, Irvine

References

Addis, Stephen, ed. 1985. *Japanese Ghosts and Demons: Art of the Supernatural.* New York: Braziller.

Aoki, Kōji, ed. 1979. *Hennen hyakushō ikki shiryō shūsei.* Vol. 5. Tokyo: San'ichi Shobō.

——— , ed. 1980a. *Hennen hyakushō ikki shiryō shūsei.* Vol. 6. Tokyo: San'ichi Shobō.

——— , ed. 1980b. *Hennen hyakushō ikki shiryō shūsei.* Vol. 7. Tokyo: San'ichi Shobō.

——— , ed. 1981. *Hennen hyakushō ikki shiryō shūsei.* Vol. 8. Tokyo: San'ichi Shobō.

——— , ed. 1982. *Hennen hyakushō ikki shiryō shūsei.* Vol. 9. Tokyo: San'ichi Shobō.

————, ed. 1983a. *Hennen hyakushō ikki shiryō shūsei.* Vol. 10. Tokyo: San'ichi Shobō.

————, ed. 1983b. *Hennen hyakushō ikki shiryō shūsei.* Vol. 11. Tokyo: San'ichi Shobō.

————, ed. 1984. *Hennen hyakushō ikki shiryō shūsei.* Vol. 13. Tokyo: San'ichi Shobō.

Aoki, Michio. 1981. "Bakumatsu, Ishinki no yonaoshi sōdō." In *Bakuhan-sei kokka no hōkai,* ed. Satō Shigerō and Kawachi Hachirō. Tokyo: Yūzankaku.

Asami, Takashi. 1987. "Ikki to rōjin, kodomo, onnatachi." *Shikan,* no. 116, 68–82.

Bix, Herbert P. 1986. *Peasant Protest in Japan, 1590–1880.* New Haven, Conn.: Yale University Press.

Bohstedt, John. 1988. "Gender, Household and Community Politics: Women in English Riots, 1790–1810." *Past and Present,* no. 120, 88–122.

Canning, Kathleen. 1993. "Comment." *Journal of Women's History* 5(1):102–14.

Chiba-ken, ed. 1962. *Chiba kenshi Meiji hen.* Tokyo: Chiba-ken.

Cornell, Laurel L. 1981. "Peasant Family and Inheritance in a Japanese Community: 1671–1980: An Anthropological Analysis of Local Population Registers." Ph.D. dissertation, Johns Hopkins University.

————. 1983. "Retirement, Inheritance, and Intergenerational Conflict in Preindustrial Japan." *Journal of Family History* 8(1):55–69.

————. 1990a. "The Development of the Concept of the Family in Early Modern Japan." Paper presented at the annual meeting of the Association for Asian Studies, Chicago.

————. 1990b. "Peasant Women and Divorce in Preindustrial Japan." *Signs: Journal of Women in Culture and Society* 15(4):710–32.

Cornell, Laurel L., and Akira Hayami. 1986. "The *Shūmon aratame chō:* Japan's Population Registers." *Journal of Family History* 11(4):311–28.

Davis, Natalie Zemon. 1987. *Fiction in the Archives: Pardon Tales and Their Tellers in Sixteenth-Century France.* Stanford, Calif.: Stanford University Press.

Ehime-ken nōkai, ed. 1943. *Ehime-ken nōgyōshi.* Tokyo: Ehime-ken Nōkai.

Fister, Patricia. 1991. "Female *bunjin:* The Life of Poet-Painter Ema Saikō." In *Recreating Japanese Women, 1600–1945,* ed. Gail Lee Bernstein. Berkeley and Los Angeles: University of California Press.

Fujisawa shishi hensan iinkai, ed. 1973. *Fujisawa shishi.* Vol. 2, *Shiryōhen.* Yokohama: Fujisawa-shi Yakusho.

————, ed. 1974. *Fujisawa shishi.* Vol. 5, *Tsūshi hen.* Yokohama: Fujisawa-shi Yakusho.

Fukaya, Katsumi, and Kawanabe Sadao. 1988. *Edo jidai no morokasegi: Chiiki keizai to nōka keiei.* Tokyo: Nōsan Gyōson Bunka Kyōkai.

Harada, Tomohiko. 1965. *Nihon joseishi.* Tokyo: Kawade Shobō.

Hayami, Akira. 1983. "The Myth of Primogeniture and Impartible Inheritance in Tokugawa Japan." *Journal of Family History* 8(1):3–29.

Hayashi, Reiko. 1977. "Yonaoshi ikki no onna taishō." In *Edo-ki josei no ikikata,* cd. Enchi Fumiko. Tokyo: Sōbisha.

Hosaka, Satoru. 1989. "Ikki, sōdō to josei." *Rekishi hyōron,* no. 467, 1–14.

Howell, David. 1989. "The Capitalist Transformation of the Hokkaidō Fishery, 1672–1935." Ph.D. dissertation, Princeton University.

Hufton, Olwen. 1971. "Women in Revolution, 1789–1796." *Past and Present* no. 53, 90–108.

Hyōgo kenshi henshū senmon iinkai, ed. 1979. *Hyōgo kenshi.* Vol. 4. Kōbe: Hyōgo-ken.

Ihara, Saikaku. 1956. *Five Women Who Loved Love,* trans. William Theodore DeBary. Rutland, Vt.: Tuttle.

Ishii, Ryōsuke, ed. 1974. *Oshioki reiruishū Onna no bu.* Tokyo: Meicho Shuppan.

Izumi shishi hensan iinkai, ed. 1968. *Izumi shishi.* Vol. 2. Izumi-shi: Izumi Shishi Hensan Iinkai.

Johnson-Odin, Cheryl, and Margaret Strobel, eds. 1988. *Restoring Women to History.* Bloomington, Ind.: Organization of American Historians.

Kaplan, Steven L. 1976. *Bread, Politics and Political Economy in the Reign of Louis XV.* The Hague: Nijhoff.

Karatsu chōshi hensan iinkai, ed. 1976. *Karatsu onsenshi.* Gunma-ken, Maebashi-shi: Karatsu-chō Yakusho.

Kashiwa shishi hensan iinkai, ed. 1971. *Kashiwa shishi shiryōhen.* Vol. 5. Kashiwa-shi: Kashiwa-shi Yakusho.

Kelly, William. 1985. *Deference and Defiance in Nineteenth Century Japan.* Princeton, N.J.: Princeton University Press.

Knibliehler, Yvonne. 1992. "Chronology and Women's History." In *Writing Women's History,* ed. Michelle Perrot. Oxford and Cambridge: Blackwell.

Komuro, Shinsuke. (1883) 1957. *Tōyō minken hyakkaden,* ed. Hayashi Motoi. Tokyo: Iwanami Shoten.

Kyonan chōshi hensan iinkai, ed. 1983. *Kyonan chōshi.* Tokyo: Kokusho Kankō-kai, 1983.

Landes, Joan B. 1988. *Woman and the Public Sphere in the Age of the French Revolution.* Ithaca, N.Y.: Cornell University Press.

McClain, James L. 1988. "Failed Expectations: Kaga Domain on the Eve of the Meiji Restoration." *Journal of Japanese Studies* 14(2):403–47.

Matsumoto Hidenobu, ed. 1967. *Ishikawa chōshi.* Fukushima-shi: Ishikawa-chō Kyōiku Iinkai.

Miyako-shi kyōiku iinkai, ed. 1988. *Miyako shishi shiryōshū kinsei.* Vol. 4. Miyako-shi: Miyako-shi.

Moi, Toril. 1985. *Sexual/Textual Politics: Feminist Literary Theory.* New York: Methuen.

Morosawa, Yōko. 1969. *Shinano no onna.* Tokyo: Miraisha.

Nagano-ken kōtōgakkō kyōiku bunka kaigi shakaika kyōiku kenkyūkai, ed. 1989. *Shiryō ga kataru Nagano no rekishi.* Tokyo: Sanseidō.

Nagashima, Atsuko. 1980. "Aru nōson josei no kōdō: Bunsei-ki no gōin deiri kara." *Minshūshi kenkyū,* no. 19, 47–50.

———. 1993. "Kinsei kōki no josei no 'kakekomi' soshō." In *Kinsei-hen,* vol. 5 of *Shinshiten Nihon no rekishi,* ed. Aoki Michio and Hosaka Satoru. Tokyo: Shinjinbutsu Ōraisha.

Ng, Vivien W. 1990. *Madness in Late Imperial China: From Illness to Deviance.* Norman: University of Oklahoma Press.

Niigata shishi hensan iinkai, ed. 1982. *Niigata shishi.* Niigata-shi: Niigata Shishi Hensan Iinkai.

Nomura, Mitsuo. 1932. *Sendai han nōgyōshi kenkyū.* Sendai-shi: Muichi Bunkan Shoten.

Ono, Takeo, ed. 1941. *Nihon nōmin shiryō shūsei.* Vol. 4. Tokyo: Ganshōdō Shoten.

Ōtsuki shishi hensanshitsu, ed. 1976. *Ōtsuki shishi: Shiryōhen.* Ōtsuki-shi: Ōtsuki Shishi Hensan Iinkai.

Perrot, Michelle. 1987. "Women, Power and History: The Case of Nineteenth Century France." In *Women, State and Revolution: Essays on Power and Gender in Europe since 1789,* ed. Sian Reynolds. Amherst: University of Massachusetts Press.

Reynolds, Sian. 1987. "Introduction." In *Women, State and Revolution: Essays on Power and Gender in Europe since 1789,* ed. Sian Reynolds. Amherst: University of Massachusetts Press.

Robertson, Jennifer. 1984. "Japanese Farm Manuals: A Literature of Discovery." *Peasant Studies* 11(3):169–94.

———. 1991. "The Shingaku Woman: Straight from the Heart." In *Recreating Japanese Women, 1600–1945,* ed. Gail Lee Bernstein. Berkeley and Los Angeles: University of California Press.

Saitama kenshi hensan iinkai, ed. 1982. *Saitama kenshi shiryō hen.* Vol. 2. Tokyo: Saitama Ken.

Saitō, Osamu. 1983. "Population and the Peasant Family Economy in Proto-industrial Japan." *Journal of Family History* 8(1):30–54.

Saitō, Yōichi. 1985. "Minshū undō to josei." In *Edo to wa nanika* Vol. 2, ed. Oguchi Yujirō. Tokyo: Shibundō.

Scott, James C. 1985. *Weapons of the Weak: Everyday Forms of Peasant Resistance.* New Haven, Conn.: Yale University Press.

Sekiguchi, Kitaji, ed. 1980. *Iwaizumi chihōshi.* Iwate-ken, Morioka-shi: Iwaizumi Kyōiku Iinkai.

Shōji, Kichinosuke, et al., eds. 1970. *Nihon shisō taikei.* Vol. 58, *Minshū undō no shisō.* Tokyo: Iwanami Shoten.

Sugimoto, Tsutomu. 1985. *Onna no kotoba-shi.* Tokyo: Yūzankaku.

Suzuki, Bokushi. 1986. *Snow Country Tales: Life in the Other Japan,* trans. Jeffrey Hunter, with Rose Lesser. Tokyo: Weatherhill.

Takaoka-shi, ed. 1909. *Takaoka shiryō.* Toyama-shi: Takaoka-shi.

Takatsuki shishi hensan iinkai, ed. 1979. *Takatsuki shishi,* Vol. 4, *Shiryōhen,* pt. 2. Takatsuki-shi: Takatsuki Yakusho.

Tanigawa, Ken'ichi, ed. 1970. *Nihon shomin seikatsu shiryō shūsei.* Vol. 13. Tokyo: San'ichi Shobō.

Tatsuno shishi hensan senmon iinkai, ed. 1980. *Tatsuno shishi.* Vol. 5, *Shiryō hen.* Tatsuno-shi: Tatsuno-shi.

———, ed. 1981. *Tatsuno shishi.* Vol. 2. Tatsuno-shi: Tatsuno-shi.

Toyama-ken, ed. 1909. *Etchū shiryō.* Vol. 3. Toyama-shi: Toyama-ken.

———, ed. 1983a. *Toyama kenshi shiryōhen 4: Kinsei 2.* Toyama-shi: Toyama-ken.

———, ed. 1983b. *Toyama kenshi tsūshi hen 4: Kinsei 2.* Toyama-shi: Toyama-ken.

Uno, Kathleen S. 1991. "Women and Changes in the Household Division of Labor." In *Recreating Japanese Women, 1600–1945,* ed. Gail Lee Bernstein. Berkeley and Los Angeles: University of California Press.

Vlastos, Stephen. 1986. *Peasant Protests and Uprisings in Tokugawa Japan.* Berkeley and Los Angeles: University of California Press.

Wakabayashi, Kisaburō. 1972. *Kaga han nōseishi no kenkyū*. Vol. 2. Tokyo: Yoshikawa Kōbunkan.

Walthall, Anne. 1986. *Social Protest and Popular Culture in Late Eighteenth Century Japan*. Tucson: University of Arizona Press.

———. 1991a. "The Life Cycle of Farm Women in Tokugawa Japan." In *Recreating Japanese Women, 1600–1945*, ed. Gail Lee Bernstein. Berkeley and Los Angeles: University of California Press.

———. 1991b. *Peasant Uprisings in Japan: A Critical Anthology of Peasant Histories*. Chicago: University of Chicago Press.

White, James W. 1992. *The Demography of Sociopolitical Conflict in Japan, 1721–1846*. Berkeley: Center for Japanese Studies.

Williams, Beryl. 1987. "Kollontai and After: Women in the Russian Revolution." In *Women, State and Revolution: Essays on Power and Gender in Europe since 1789*, ed. Sian Reynolds. Amherst: University of Massachusetts Press.

Yamakawa, Kikue. 1992. *Women of the Mito Domain: Recollections of Samurai Family Life*, trans. Kate Wildman Nakai. Tokyo: University of Tokyo Press.

Yamanashi kenritsu toshokan, ed. 1973. *Kōshū bunko shiryō*. Vol. 2. Kōfu-shi: Yamanashi Kenritsu Toshokan.

Yorii-chō kyōiku iinkai chōshi hensan shitsu, ed. 1983. *Yorii chōshi kinsei shiryō-hen*. Tokyo: Saitama-ken Yorii-chō Kyōiku Iinkai.

GENDER AND

THE STATE

Women, the Law, and Cultural Relativism in France: The Case of Excision

Bronwyn   Winter

O NE OF THE DEBATES that has been—I will not say exactly raging, but certainly bubbling away, erupting now and then to return to a threatening simmer at other times— in France over at least the past decade has been the opposition between Enlightenment universalism (the ideological basis of the French Republic) on the one hand and cultural relativism on the other. This extreme polarization not only has kept women out of the picture, except as images to be manipulated, but also has made it virtually impossible to give audible voice to any other ideological or strategic position. This bipolar logic has also to a great extent infiltrated the feminist movement, with the "difference" feminists at one pole and the "universalist" femi- nists at the other. Familiar music, no doubt, to many feminists in the United States and other English-speaking Western countries, where the cultural relativist or "difference" position tends to fall under the umbrella term of *postmodernism.*[1]

However, my major concern here is not the "difference" debate cur- rently in full eruption within the French feminist movement but, rather, some of the legal and political problems that the more general debate has been having for women of non-Western cultural/national origins living in France. As is so often the case, the debate concerning these women is less about the women themselves than about the appropriation of women as political symbols. In other words, it is about the use of women as am- munition in a polemic of central concern to their lives, but where the issue at stake is not the women's own interests but, rather, the consoli- dation of the power of others to define those interests. This became

---

[1] The term *postmodernism* is no longer used in France, the supposed intellectual home of the movement. Jean-François Lyotard's text *La condition postmoderne: Rap- port sur le savoir* (1979) and the philosophy that took the same name have now entered the annals of history, as far as the French are concerned.

[*Signs: Journal of Women in Culture and Society* 1994, vol. 19, no. 4]

painfully apparent in France in 1991, when the excision (clitoridectomy) debate flared up anew, following a much-publicized trial of an *exciseuse* (the woman who performs the operation) and the parents of the *excisées* (the girls having undergone the operation). The trial and the polemic surrounding it threw into sharp relief just how complex and riddled with doublethink the issue of "cultural difference" has become in these "postmodern" times and just how incapable Western legal systems (and in particular the French legal system) are of addressing the problem adequately. The Paris trial further polarized the long-standing debate between a feminist procriminalization position on the one hand and cultural relativism on the other. While the point of departure for many people on both sides of the polemic was a reaction against the abuse of a nondominant class by the dominant class, the procriminalization feminists concentrated on excision as the abuse of female children, whereas the cultural relativists saw criminalization campaigns as the continuing abuse by a hegemonic Western power of peoples it had once colonized.

What has become particularly obvious since the 1991 trials, not the least because of so many cases being heard in rapid succession, is that the history of excision trials in France, far from representing a linear progression toward increasingly harsh sentences and "making the punishment fit the crime" (according to which logic infibulation, with its potentially devastating long-term consequences for women's health, should attract heavier sentences than "mere" clitoridectomy), is more a case of two steps forward, one step back, and even quite a few dodging steps sideways. Certainly, such jolting progress interspersed with often serious setbacks is familiar to French feminists, who have seen other struggles such as those for abortion rights and the criminalization of rape follow a similar pattern.

What makes the history of excision trials stand out, and what makes it particularly problematic, is that we are dealing with a crime which is (*a*) specific, apart from one individual exception, to immigrant communities from former French colonies, (*b*) perpetrated by women against female children, and (*c*) perpetrated within a context of extremely polarized debate around the issues of cultural diversity, respect for minority cultures' customs, and the status of immigrants in France, in terms of citizenship, rights, duties, and equality—or not—before the law. These are difficult issues, and I am not sure there is, for any feminist (whether we are talking African, or Afro-French, or African-American, or white American, or white French) committed to eradicating excision while at the same time maintaining respect for the women who are both the perpetrators and the victims of the practice, one simple solution or one "right" way to go about finding one. For one thing, the answers will vary—as will some of the questions—from one national, cultural, political, social—and legal—context to another. It cannot even be assumed that all French-speaking feminists of African descent will agree; indeed, such an assumption would be both inaccurate and reductionist. The most I can hope to do in the following pages is at least to pinpoint where the contradictions and difficulties lie and comment on what I believe to be some appropriate strategies, at least for the French context.

Some background

First, a brief word on terminology. Terms currently in use in English are *clitoridectomy* (removal of the clitoris), *infibulation* (stitching up of the vaginal opening after clitoridectomy and removal of the labia, leaving only a very small opening for urination), *female genital mutilation* (the generic English term), and *excision* (a term borrowed from French which is usually taken to refer to clitoridectomy and removal of the labia, but not, in general, to infibulation). The term *female circumcision* is totally inappropriate, as it creates a false analogy with the operation performed on infant boys. The removal of the clitoris and also frequently the labia, with or without infibulation, is not only much more serious in medical terms but it also represents a severe physical and psychological mutilation, constituting a direct attack on a woman's sexuality.[2] While the terms *clitoridectomy* and *female genital mutilation* are the most explicit, as they directly describe the nature of the mutilation, I have chosen to use, for the sake of conciseness, the French term *excision* as an approximate synonym for *female genital mutilation,* along with *exciseuse* to refer to the woman who performs the operation and *excisée* to refer to the woman who has undergone it.

Although reasons given for excision vary slightly from one culture to another, the most common justifications include the assumption that not having undergone the operation leaves a girl not only "unclean" but "masculine," in that she retains a vestige of a male sex organ. She is thus

---

[2] This point has been emphatically made by a number of African feminists, among them Lydie Dooh-Bunyah, president of MODEFEN (Mouvement pour la Defense des Femmes Noires), at a number of meetings, interviews, and conferences (among them, a workshop on feminism and racism that I co-organized at the Paris Women's Center for International Women's Day, 1984); Awa Thiam, author of *La parole aux négresses* (1978) and president of CAMS-Internationale (Commission pour l'Abolition des Mutilations Sexuelles); the women of FOWARD, a British-based multiethnic antiexcision group (see, e.g., their brochure, reprinted in *Women Living under Muslim Laws,* 1989, 65–66); the women of GAMS (Groupe pour l'Abolition des Mutilations Sexuelles), an Afro-French antiexcision group based in Paris (see, e.g., their report, 1984a, 45–60). For further discussion of the dangerous consequences of excision and why it is not comparable to male circumcision, see also "Sexual Mutilations: Case Studies Presented at the Workshop: African Women Speak on Female Circumcision" 1989; Sindzingre 1977; Hosken 1979; and Saurel 1985, 115–19.

thought to be sexually aggressive (therefore unlikely to remain a virgin before marriage or faithful within marriage) and otherwise lacking in feminine virtues such as passivity and submission. It is even thought in some cases that she will not be able to undergo pregnancy and childbirth. The overriding fear among mothers is thus that a girl who has not been *excisée* will be unable to find a husband or have children and will consequently end up a social outcast. Even among immigrant communities in France, this social pressure remains, as many families hold on to the idea that one day they will return to the "home country," if only to marry off their daughters there. They also hold on to an image of the "home country" as it was when they left it, so they are often unaware that excision is being challenged as much if not more there than it is in France.[3] (I use the term *immigrant* rather than *minority* as the problem concerns primarily the so-called first generation. The *excisées* who have grown up in France are infinitely less likely to have excisions performed on their own children.)

The forms of excision vary, as does the age of the *excisées,* from as young as two or three months to puberty, even to young womanhood in some cases. It has, however, been noted that there is a growing tendency, particularly among immigrants in European countries, to perform the operation on infant girls "so they won't remember their suffering."[4] One or more of these forms of excision are practiced by some of the different communities within a number of African countries, including Nigeria, Ghana, Mali, Senegal, Burkina Faso, the Ivory Coast, the Gambia, Sudan, Egypt, Kenya, Djibouti, Liberia, Sierra Leone, Togo, Ethiopia, and Eritrea. Most of these countries have passed laws against excision, but to date and to my knowledge, no trial has yet taken place in postcolonial Africa.[5] This is partly because, as Coumba Touré, among others, has pointed out, Western legal concepts of trial and punishment have little meaning within many African communities; prison is often seen as an act of fate rather than an act of justice.[6] Both governments and women's organizations thus put the accent on information and education, a long-term process

---

[3] I thank Coumba Touré (of Malian origin), vice president of the GAMS, and Khadi Koïta (of Senegalese origin), secretary of the GAMS, for confirmation of the reasons given for excision, given during interviews by me at the Paris Women's Center on July 2, 1992, and June 29, 1993, respectively. See also, concerning the justifications given for excision, the influence of male domination and women's response to this: Thiam 1978, 77–117; Hosken 1979; Fainzang 1984; and Gillette-Frénoy 1992, 14–31. For a cultural relativist examination of the reasons given for excision, see Erlich 1986, 173–218.

[4] Koïta interview, 1993.

[5] Colonial rulers, notably Britain, had previously outlawed excision in some of their colonies, such as Kenya (1920s) and Sudan (1940s).

[6] Touré interview, 1992.

that carries meaning for the women concerned, rather than on trial and punishment, an immediate process that is not necessarily completely understood by the women concerned. The immigrant communities where excision is practiced in France are mostly from Western Africa, with the overwhelming majority in purely numerical terms coming from Senegal, Mali, or the Ivory Coast, and the Soninké, Toucouleur, and Bambara ethnic groups being the main ones concerned. In 1983, it was estimated that clitoridectomy was performed, within the country of origin itself, by roughly 80 percent of the Senegalese and Malian populations and by 60 percent of the Ivory Coast population. In France, according to the 1982 census, this would have represented a total of roughly sixty thousand people (men, women, and children combined). Sharp increases in the immigrant populations from these countries over the past decade would bring the total figure to much more. In 1984, the Groupe pour l'Abolition des Mutilations Sexuelles (*le GAMS*) estimated that at least twenty-three thousand little girls overall were at risk in France (GAMS 1984*b*, 77–80).[7]

In Europe, specific laws against excision have been passed in Sweden (1982), Switzerland (1983), and Great Britain (1985), but governments of these countries have been reluctant to enforce them, preferring to prioritize campaigns of information and education within the communities concerned. France is in the unique position of having no specific law but of being nonetheless the only country, at the time of writing, where excision has been the subject of criminal trials. The law that is currently applied in France is Article 312, *Alinéa* 3, of the Penal Code. This law concerns a range of violent acts committed against minors, and the section applied in cases of excision reads as follows: "Whoever beats or otherwise voluntarily inflicts violence upon or assaults a child of under fifteen years of age, excluding minor violence, will be punished as follows: . . . By imprisonment of between ten and twenty years if there has been mutilation, amputation, or deprivation of the use of a limb, blindness, loss of an eye, or other permanent disability or unintentional death" (*Code pénal*, 1983–84, 184).[8]

---

[7] In 1991, it was estimated that this figure had climbed to thirty-six thousand (statistics quoted in the newspaper *Libération* [February 6, 1991]).

[8] "Quiconque aura volontairement porté des coups à un enfant âgé de moins de quinze ans ou aura commis à son encontre des violences ou voies de fait, à l'exclusion des violences légères, sera puni suivant les distinctions ci-après: . . . 3° De la réclusion criminelle à temps de dix à vingt ans s'il en est résulté une mutilation, une amputation ou la privation de l'usage d'un membre, la cécité, la perte d'un œil ou d'autres infirmités permanentes ou la mort sans que l'auteur ait eu l'intention de la donner." (The translations of French quotations appearing in this article are my own, unless otherwise specified; the original French is, as far as possible, given in footnotes for the benefit of those who read the language.)

Excision on trial in France: A brief history

The first trial in France dates back to November 1979, for an excision leading to the death in June 1978 of a little girl of three and one-half months of age. The *exciseuse* received one year's suspended sentence; the parents were not tried. At this time, excision was not considered a criminal offense and was thus tried by a magistrate in a police court (*tribunal correctionnel*). This remained the case until August 20, 1983, when a judgment handed down by the Court of Final Appeal (Cour de Cassation) stated that "the removal of the clitoris constitutes a crime of violence resulting in mutilation as defined by Article 312-3 of the Penal Code" (Gillette-Frénoy 1992, 32–33).[9] This judgment followed two significant events: another death, in July 1982, of a little girl by the name of Bobo, and the police court trial in October of the same year of the father of Bintou Doucara, who in 1980 had been admitted to hospital suffering from a hemorrhage following an excision. At this trial, the defendant once more received a one-year suspended sentence for voluntary assault of a child of under fifteen years of age; even though Article 312 was cited, paragraph 3 was not specifically referred to and excision was still not being judged as a criminal act.[10] However, Bobo's death a few months earlier had caused an outcry and had led a number of feminist organizations to lobby for cases of excision to be tried in the criminal court (Cour d'Assises) under paragraph 3 of Article 312.

The 1983 Court of Final Appeal judgment was in fact handed down in relation to the case of a severely disturbed young white French woman who had mutilated her daughter, but it was also intended to serve as jurisprudence for future cases of excision performed within immigrant communities. The first case to be tried after this judgment, that of the parents of Bobo, nonetheless was again brought before a police court magistrate in 1984. This time, the charge was not even of mutilation of a minor but of "failure to render assistance to a person in danger." This led to a further feminist campaign for the application of the 1983 Court of Final Appeal judgment, which would necessitate trial by jury in a criminal court. At the forefront of this campaign were the associations SOS Femmes Alternatives, CAMS-F (Commission pour l'Abolition des Mutilations Sexuelles, French section), and Enfance et Partage, who also decided to associate themselves with the public prosecutor in an action

---

[9] "L'ablation du clitoris constitue un crime de violence ayant entraîné une mutilation au sens de l'article 312-3 du Code de procédure pénale."

[10] See CAMS Internationale 1990, 18; and Vernier 1990. Much of the information that follows comes from these articles, as well as from two interviews with the lawyer Linda Weil-Curiel, conducted by me in Paris on December 9, 1992, and June 9, 1993, respectively. Weil-Curiel has been at the forefront of the French feminists' ongoing battle in the courts to have excision tried—and sentenced—as a crime.

called *partie civile*.[11] The tribunal ended up declaring itself incompetent to hear the case, which it sent to the criminal court. Bobo's parents appealed, and in spite of a number of drawn-out appeals and reappeals, were never actually brought to trial under Article 312-3.

A second judgment handed down, however, this time by the Court of Appeal (Cour d'Appel) in July 1987, confirmed that excision was a crime in that it was the removal of a healthy and functional organ.[12] This decision upheld the 1986 ruling by a police court magistrate that his court was incompetent to hear a case of excision, as it was a criminal case and thus did not fall under his jurisdiction. (The case in question, that of the Coulibalys and of the *exciseuse* Aramata Keita, finally became the landmark trial of March 1991 that is discussed below.) The first case to be tried in the criminal court followed in May 1988. The parents of Mantessa Baradji, who had died six weeks after an excision, received a three-year suspended sentence for "voluntary assault on a child under fifteen years of age, having led to unintentional death" (CAMS 1990, 18).[13] The second case to be brought before the criminal court, in May 1989, was markedly different in that the child, Assa Traoré, had survived and that only the mother was put on trial, as the father had been at work at the time the excision was performed. Again, a three-year suspended sentence was handed down. Doctors giving evidence asserted that the mother, Dalla Traoré-Fofana, had been informed, both after her daughter's birth and during subsequent consultations at the postnatal clinic, that excision was illegal in France.

Following the Traoré-Fofana case, in June 1990, was the Soumaré case, involving for the first time a so-called mixed marriage, where the mother was French and the father African. The father had arranged the excision without the mother's knowledge, and although the mother pressed charges (which she later withdrew on the grounds that she was afraid of violent reprisals from the father), the examining magistrate (*juge d'instruction*) decided that there was no case against the father, as he had not personally performed the operation. According to the

[11] Under French law any individuals or organizations can associate themselves with the public prosecutor in criminal cases by declaring themselves *partie civile*. A separate lawyer represents the *partie civile* and has the right to present arguments in court. *Partie civile* is thus often if not always used as a means of bringing extra political pressure to bear in criminal courts, and feminist organizations have frequently had recourse to it.

[12] Some explanation is perhaps needed concerning the difference between Cour d'Appel (Court of Appeal) and Cour de Cassation (Court of Final Appeal) (*casser*, "to break"). The former is an ordinary appeals court, where judgments are contested, sometimes on points of law but usually on the evidence. The latter is at the top of the legal hierarchy and thus has the power to override Court of Appeal judgments. It hears cases on points of law only and represents the final resort in the appeals procedure. In this way it bears some resemblance to the Supreme Court of the United States.

[13] For comments on this trial, see Kunstenaar 1988 and Loupiac 1988.

magistrate (who, incidentally, was a woman), he could only be heard as a witness and not as a defendant. The *parties civiles* appealed, and the case was finally heard in Bobigny criminal court. (Bobigny is an inner suburb of Paris.) The father was sentenced to five years (suspended).

The two cases that to date have caused the greatest media stir took place in 1991, the first in March in Paris (the Coulibaly/Keita trial) and the second in June in Bobigny (Keita was once again the *exciseuse* on trial). The Paris trial in particular attracted a great deal of media attention, for a number of reasons. First, the role of the *exciseuse* came under much closer scrutiny than it had in the past (in most previous cases, only the parents or the mother had been tried, and this was in any case the first trial of an *exciseuse* in a criminal court); second, the sentences this time were much heavier; and last, the case became more of a political polemic than a legal trial. This was partly through increasing media interest and therefore public debate around the issue, partly through the efforts of those chosen as "expert" witnesses by the defense (notably the "ethno-psychiatrist" Michel Erlich), and partly through the argumentation of the *parties civiles* that were represented.[14] The Paris trial thus brought many contentious issues to a head and consequently received an enormous amount of adverse publicity from the press. The second trial was held in the Bobigny juvenile court, as one of the defendants had been a minor at the time the excision was performed. It was therefore, as required by law, a closed trial, with no polemic of the sort that had dominated the trial in Paris. Moreover, the white French "experts" who were invited to testify had had closer dealings with the migrant communities concerned than had those who had testified in Paris.[15] Another difference was that at the Bobigny trial, the *exciseuse* acknowledged having performed the operations, whereas in Paris she had denied it; she also benefited in Bobigny from the presence of a Senegalese lawyer who spoke her language. (In Paris, the only part of the proceedings that had been interpreted for the defendants and, indeed, the only part required by law to be interpreted, were the charges made and the questions asked directly of them. Even their own lawyers' closing arguments were not translated.)[16] These differences between the two trials were reflected in the sentences handed

---

[14] These were Enfance et Partage, represented by Catherine Sviloff, Le Planning Familial, represented by Monique Antoine, and SOS Femmes Alternatives, represented by Weil-Curiel.

[15] For example, Catherine Quiminal, who testified at the Bobigny trial, has worked closely for some time with the Soninké community in France. She also works from a feminist perspective; many of the "experts" who testified in Paris were male academics who had had little direct interaction with the women concerned.

[16] Weil-Curiel has pointed out that she had asked the court interpreters to translate her own speech, but they refused, pointing out that they were not required to by law, nor were they paid to do so (interview, 1992).

down: at the Paris trial, Keita (the *exciseuse*) was sentenced to five years' imprisonment and the parents received five years' suspended sentence, whereas at the Bobigny trial Keita received four years (one suspended), three of the parents were acquitted, and the others received one year's suspended sentence. The clemency of the second sentence was somewhat surprising in that, first, Keita had already received a longer sentence and, second, one of the excisions for which Keita was on trial in Bobigny had resulted in the death of the little girl in question.

Notwithstanding this apparent backtracking insofar as the harshness of sentences is concerned, the 1991 trials definitely seem to constitute a turning point in the legal history of excision in France. Although Keita is to date the only *exciseuse* to have been tried in a criminal court (for the simple reason that she is the only one to have been tracked down) and subsequent sentences have been lighter, the publicity given to the two trials has meant that it is now virtually impossible for the government, the courts, the medical profession, or the public to ignore the fact that excisions are being carried out in great numbers in France. Since the 1987 Court of Appeal decision upholding the 1983 judgment, and particularly since the 1991 trials, there has also been greater pressure on medical and social workers to report cases of excision; what had previously been perceived by many as being at the discretion of the professional personnel concerned is now seen as a professional—and indeed, legal—obligation. There is also perhaps a growing movement toward requiring at least some part of sentences to be served, although it has been pointed out that the personality and personal opinions of the presiding judge will have enormous bearing on the outcome of a trial.[17] For example, in January 1993 in Paris (the next case to be tried after the June 1991 case in Bobigny), Teneng Fofana-Jahaté was sentenced to five years (four suspended, one to be served) for the excision of her two daughters, whereas a few days later in Bobigny, Coumba Gréou's sentence was completely suspended, even though this time, for the first time in the history of excision trials in France, there had also been infibulation, performed on a one-month-old baby. The defense, with the help of their favorite "expert" witness, Erlich, created some polemic surrounding the question of whether or not there actually had been an infibulation, maintaining that it could well have been "spontaneous," the labia binding together as part of the scarring process, and in any case there remained no trace of needle marks. The doctor who reported the infibulation countered that spontaneous infibulation would have been impossible, as urination would have forced and kept the labia apart, unless they were deliberately bound and/or sewn together. He further pointed out that on a child of such a

---

[17] Weil-Curiel interview, 1993.

young age, it was unlikely the needle marks would have left a lasting scar. These arguments did not, however, convince the judge, who dismissed the charge of infibulation.

The following trial, which took place the very next month in Paris, represented another first in that the father was sentenced to four years, mostly suspended, but nonetheless with one month required to be served. One month is indeed not what one could call a heavy sentence, but it is the first time a father's criminal responsibility has been clearly acknowledged. One week later, however, another about-face occurred, with two mothers, Doucouré and Traoré-Fofana, being given fully suspended sentences, and both husbands, who had been at work at the time, not even being brought to trial.

The last two trials to have taken place at the time of this writing are the trial of the husband and accomplice of Keita, the *exciseuse* currently serving a prison sentence, who was sentenced in April 1993 to five years (four suspended, one to be served), and the trial of Aïssé Tandian in June 1993, who was sentenced to three years (six months to be served). Tandian's husband, a work colleague of Coulibaly (of the 1991 trial), maintained that he had forbidden his wife to have an excision performed on their daughter. The excision in question had been carried out in 1989, while the father was away in Mali.

One could be forgiven for assuming that this apparently growing number of trials has been a direct consequence of the 1991 trials. Certainly, more cases are being reported and held over for criminal trial, but the glut of trials in 1993 has had as much if not more to do with hiccups and delays in judicial procedure for a number of reasons, with the result that a number of cases were clustered together, although the excisions themselves had been more spread out over time.

La république de la tolérance

The defense in most of the above trials has relied heavily on two interlinked strategies. The first of these is a "these poor illiterate Africans don't know any better" ploy, where lawyers maintain that the immigrant communities concerned have not understood that excision is illegal in France. This strategy is, according to some sources, used not only by lawyers but also by the defendants themselves, who find pleading ignorance a convenient protection against the legal system. One common version of this is professing not to speak French. While limited command of the French language is probably the case for the majority of the mothers concerned, most of the fathers have lived in France for fifteen or twenty years and hold down steady jobs, not all of which are menial. One of them, for example, is a taxi driver; it is impossible to obtain a Parisian taxi license without a reasonable command of spoken and written French.[18]

While it is arguable that it is difficult to determine how much of this role is actually being played by the defendants concerned and how much of it is merely being attributed to them by others, it is certain that when the only role allocated in the first place is that of "the ignorant African," it is somewhat difficult to appear as anything different, since any other reality, any other persona, is denied. Moreover, the "They don't know any better" line certainly has been an extremely successful strategy for the defense; it is therefore plausible that defense lawyers have encouraged the defendants to exhibit such behavior.

Such arguments have enraged both protrial feminists like Linda Weil-Curiel, who sees them as showing singular contempt for the intelligence of African people and as such racist, and antitrial (but also antiexcision) feminists like Khadi Koïta, who is exasperated by the defense lawyers. Says Koïta, "They have unceasingly treated us like idiots, like women who understood nothing, ignorant women, but I can assure them that African women, even those who come from the middle of nowhere, have never been stupid, nor ignorant. . . . It is very hurtful to hear them say, 'These poor cretinous women who turn up in Paris, direct from their bushland.' "[19] Koïta further maintains that even the most illiterate of women is capable of understanding the information she receives, particularly after over ten years of constant work by other African women within their communities, as well as after all the publicity given the trials: practically all African families in France have both a television set and friends who, if necessary, can translate news items concerning them.

Unfortunately, the image of the "ignorant Africans" is further reinforced by the testimony of "expert" witnesses such as the psychiatrists Georges Bitoun and Gilbert Ferrey, who, in their report on Founé Dembelé-Soumaré (who was at the time of writing due to be tried in September 1993), make much of the idea of a "group superego" that controls the actions of the members of the group.[20] This is where a second defense strategy comes in: the perpetrators of excision are acting in accordance with a cultural tradition that in their minds carries the weight of a law that they are bound to obey. The notion of individual

---

[18] Weil-Curiel interview, 1992.

[19] "Ces avocats n'ont pas arrêté de nous traiter d'idiotes, de femmes qui ne comprenaient rien, des ignorantes, mais je peux les assurer que la femme africaine, qu'elle vienne du fond de la brousse, n'a jamais été idiote, ni ignorante. . . . Ça fait très mal de les entendre dire: Ces pauvres femmes connes qui viennent de leur brousse, qui débarquent à Paris" (interview, 1993).

[20] Psychiatric report dated April 24, 1991. My thanks to Weil-Curiel for making this and other documentation available to me.

responsibility in the matter is thus deemed inapplicable. This is not equivalent to a plea of diminished responsibility through temporary or permanent insanity. In fact, the "ethnopsychiatrists" defending the "group superego" theory are practically unanimous in their assurance that the defendant is of sound mind but is entirely subjected to the authority of his or (usually) her cultural traditions. (In the case of women, the "ethnopsychiatrists" occasionally add, as have Bitoun and Ferrey in the case of Soumaré, that they are also completely submissive to their husbands' will.) Article 64 of the French Penal Code is invoked to support the "group superego" line of argumentation. It reads: "There is neither crime nor offense when the accused has been in a state of dementia at the time of the act, or when he [*sic*] has been compelled by a force that he has been unable to resist"(*Code pénal,* 1983–84, 50).[21] The "irresistible force" in this case is thus the weight of tradition. As Tobie Nathan and Marie Rose Moro put it, in the case of Bintou Fofana-Diarra (who was at the time of writing to be tried in October 1993):

> For the *bambaras,* excision is a veritable ritual of initiation that is both systematic and governed by intangible cultural codes. According to tradition, a veritable process of transformation of the child's nature is to be performed, at around the age of eight, so that she may become accepted into the group of women. . . . Whoever has not undergone the ritual cannot be considered to be a fully fledged bambara woman. . . . "Traditional" logic categorically excludes the idea that a child can have a different "nature" to that of her parents. If one wishes to remain within this logic, there is thus no possibility of individual choice in any area of acts of initiation. After having examined her, we can affirm that Ms. Fofana shows no sign of psychiatric or personality disorder. The excision of her daughter must be considered an act beyond her own free will. . . . We can affirm that she was *compelled by a force she was unable to resist, in the sense of Article 64 of the Penal Code.* She can thus not be considered in any case to be responsible . . . for the actions of which she is accused.[22]

[21] "Il n'y a ni crime ni délit, lorsque le prévenu était en état de démence au temps de l'action, ou lorsqu'il a été contraint par une force à laquelle il n'a pu résister."

[22] "Chez les *bambaras,* l'excision est un véritable rituel d'initiation systématique et régi par des codes culturels intangibles. Dans la tradition, il s'agit vers l'âge de huit ans, de procéder à une véritable transformation de la 'nature' de l'enfant pour l'inscrire dans le groupe des femmes. . . . Quiconque n'a pas subi le rituel ne peut être considéré comme une femme bambara à part entière. . . . La logique 'traditionnelle' exclut radicalement l'idée qu'un enfant puisse être d'une autre "nature" que celle de ses parents. Si l'on veut rester dans cette logique, il n'existe donc aucune possibilité de choix individuel pour tout ce qui concerne les actes initiatiques. Après l'avoir examinée, nous pouvons affirmer que Mme Fofana ne présente aucun trouble de nature psychiatrique, aucun désordre de la personnalité. On doit considérer l'excision de sa fille comme un acte échappant à sa

In other words, unlike Westerners who have been brought up on a philosophy of individual rights and the power of reason, Africans are represented as incapable of doing anything but unthinkingly following their traditions. This is where the defense lawyers rely heavily on cultural relativist theories and where they manage to gain a considerable amount of sympathy, as they play on the notion of "respecting cultural diversity," not to mention French postcolonial guilt.

One text, written by a woman, in which the cultural relativist position appears clearly and which received a fair amount of publicity, not the least within feminist circles, is a petition drafted by Martine Lefeuvre and published in 1989 by the Mouvement Anti-Utilitariste dans les Sciences Sociales (MAUSS; Anti-Utilitarian Movement in the Social Sciences), a movement that purports to be both alternative and progressive. An extract reads as follows:

> As scientists, anthropologists, sociologists, philosophers, or psychoanalysts, we believe it to be our duty to bring to the attention [of our readers] the dangers that any attempt to pass off the practice of excision as intrinsically criminal would cause for the spirit of humanity and democracy. . . . Demanding a penal sentence for a custom that does not threaten the republican order and which nothing prevents from being considered as a matter of private choice, as is circumcision, for example, would be tantamount to demonstrating an intolerance which can only create more human dramas than it claims to avoid, and which manifests a singularly narrow conception of democracy. [Lefeuvre 1989, 162–63][23]

It is stupefying, but perhaps not totally surprising, that despite so much proof to the contrary, this assimilation of excision and circumcision is still being made in the minds of many eminent and mostly, although evidently not solely, male practitioners of a number of human sciences,

---

libre volonté. . . . Nous pouvons affirmer qu'elle a été *contrainte par une force à laquelle elle n'a pas résister au sens de l'article 64 du code pénal.* Elle ne peut donc en aucun cas être considérée comme responsable . . . des faits qui lui sont reprochés" (psychiatric report dated July 12, 1992; the emphasis is in the original text).

[23] "En tant que scientifiques, anthropologues, sociologues, philosophes ou psychanalystes, il nous semble de notre devoir d'attirer l'attention sur les dangers que ferait courir à l'esprit d'humanité et de démocratie toute tentative de faire passer les pratiques d'excision pour intrinsèquement criminelles. . . . Exiger la condamnation pénale d'une coutume qui ne menace pas l'ordre républicain et dont rien ne s'oppose à ce que, comme la circoncision par exemple, elle ressortisse à la sphère des choix privés, reviendrait à faire preuve d'une intolérance qui ne peut qu'engendrer plus de drames humains qu'elle ne prétend en éviter, et qui manifesterait une conception singulièrement étriquée de la démocratie." See also Lefeuvre 1988.

such as those who drafted and signed the above petition. What is particularly insidious in this text is its evocation of two related sets of concepts dear to contemporary French minds, the first set being the French republican version of the liberal public/private dichotomy and the second being the idea of "tolerance" (of cultural diversity) in the name of democracy.

The notions of "republican order" and "private choice" are tied in with the symbolism of *La république française*: liberal, democratic, and author and primary defender of the concept of "human rights." As in any liberal capitalist democracy, the "public" and "private" spheres are strongly delineated and demarcated, with a panoply of regulations governing the inevitable incursions of the private sphere into the public and vice versa. The fact that the concept of "human rights" is still archaically known in French as *les droits de l'Homme* ("the rights of Man")—and that hardly anybody in France considers this strange—is in itself particularly illuminating for any discussion of the French concept of "individual rights." In fact, the undeniable progress made in the areas of women's legal rights, along with what in France is called *l'évolution des mœurs* (loosely translated as "the evolution of social norms"), has nonetheless failed to resolve the continuing dichotomy between the "egalitarian" republican view of women as abstract "citizens" and thus fully fledged, independent, "individual" actors in the public sphere and the "fraternal" republican view, where women remain appendages of male citizens, within the latter's inviolable private sphere and thus not fully fledged, independent, individual actors in the public sphere. This is further complicated by the fact that, according to the logic of the French liberal-democratic model, it is impossible to consider the "private" sphere, nonpublic and therefore apolitical by definition, as a domain where political power is exercised by one class of "citizens" over another and thus as a domain open to public scrutiny (except in cases where the greater collective [national] good is deemed to be under threat).

In the French republican tradition, the role of the public sphere in protecting individual rights is particularly strong. So, however, is the notion of individual duty toward the national good through adhering to common values and respecting a common order. Therefore, any defense of "private choice" as unthreatening to the "republican order," as in Lefeuvre's text quoted above, constitutes a particularly persuasive argument. What appears as a flagrant contradiction here is that adherence to a common set of values does not seem to apply, at least not in the opinion of the cultural relativists, where women's bodily integrity is concerned, and particularly not where minority women are concerned. This contradiction is, in my opinion, inherent in the view of women as *citoyennes à part entière* (fully fledged citizens having the same rights and duties as their male counterparts), except when they are defined purely in terms of gender, in which case their social function reverts to what is perceived as their biological role: that of mothers and sexual partners (of men). So any question relating to women's bodies becomes relegated to the "private sphere" only.

So where does this leave women, in legal terms? Basically, it leaves them without any citizenship rights where issues connected to their specificity as women are concerned; it leaves them without a legal concept of gender defined in terms of political power rather than in terms of (socio) biological "difference." To be considered *citoyennes à part entière*, women must leave their bodies in the bedroom and the kitchen and align themselves to the male model.[24] The concrete effects of this are twofold. On the one hand, there is an extremely strong resistance to applying any legislation that would protect or otherwise help women (such as laws against marital rape), as this would mean acknowledging the existence of male power within the "apolitical" private sphere as something other than "natural." On the other hand, coercive legislation abounds (e.g., in the case of restrictions on abortion), usually in the name of "respect for the family and private life."[25] In both cases, women's specificity as women remains firmly defined as a question of "nature" and firmly within the private sphere, thus escaping any political (and thus "public") analysis of gender-based power dynamics.[26]

This "right" to "private family life" was even more staunchly defended following the Paris and Bobigny trials in 1991 by Raymond Verdier, director of the research center Droit et Cultures at the Université de Paris X (Nanterre) and one of the leading lights of cultural relativism. He maintains that "one can measure the extent of the danger of a national penal law which incautiously tries to penetrate the intimacy of families and uncompromisingly imposes our ways of thinking and of living on foreigners who do not necessarily share them" (1991a).[27] Here Verdier not only makes the same links as the MAUSS text had made two years

[24] For a discussion of the failure of the Western liberal-democratic concept of "citizenship" to include a concept of women's specificity and the power dynamics related to this, see Jones 1990. See also Pateman 1988 for an analysis of how the French Republican "social contract" version of liberal democracy positions women, and MacKinnon 1983 for a discussion of the inadequacy of the liberal state to deal with issues specifically affecting women.

[25] Catharine A. MacKinnon has expressed a related idea most succinctly, within the context of a discussion of the "equality versus difference" debates as it pertains to Western and particularly American sex discrimination law (or the absence thereof): "In mainstream doctrine it was sex discrimination to give women what they need because only women need it. It is not sex discrimination *not* to give women what they need because then only women will not get what they need" (1990, 219).

[26] For an analysis of the appropriation of women's bodies within the Western patriarchal order and the concept of "nature" as used to justify male domination of women, see Guillaumin 1978.

[27] "On mesure tout le danger d'un droit pénal national qui voudrait pénétrer sans ménagement dans l'intimité des familles et imposer sans accommodement nos façons de penser et de vivre à des étrangers, qui ne les partagent pas nécessairement."

earlier but spells out in much clearer terms that the right to "private choice" and "family intimacy" is also the right to practice the "customs" of one's own culture without interference from "outside." This has been a persuasive argument; with the collapse of communist Europe and the climate of mounting racism in capitalist Europe, the notions of "tolerance" and "democracy" had become practically the buzzwords of the 1980s, at least in France. Much of the campaigning against racism during that decade had been based on the notion of cultural relativism and its popular and mobilizing equivalent, "tolerance of cultural diversity," which were set up in opposition to the revised form of official French assimilationism, renamed "integration."

Cultural relativists seek support for this notion of "respect for the customs" of cultural minorities within an aspect of French legal philosophy, which gives a particularly privileged place to custom, for, in the absence of a specific legal text, customary practice constitutes the prime reference for the establishment of legal doctrine and jurisprudence, and as such, carries enormous legal weight. This is even provided for, as Geneviève Giudicelli-Delage points out, by Article 327 of the Penal Code, which allows for any practice that is "of a general, continual and obligatory nature" to justify individual behavior (Giudicelli-Delage 1990, 203). Excision is thus defended as fulfilling the criteria for considering a practice customary and therefore more than tolerable from a legal point of view. Moreover, French law also allows for the notions of intention and moral responsibility. That is, for excision to be punished under Article 312-3, it normally has to be proven that there was an intention to commit harm; it further has to be proven, in accordance with Article 64, mentioned above, that the perpetrator acted freely. It is these arguments that are adopted by cultural relativists such as Verdier (who nonetheless professes to be neither cultural relativist nor assimilationist) when he implies that excision, as both a custom of social initiation—not a "mutilative wound"—and a moral obligation with the force of law, does not fall under the provisions of Article 312-3 and is thus not punishable by criminal law.[28] The argument is that what constitutes "mutilation" is a relative notion, determined by cultural conditioning, and that "its legitimacy is always founded in cultural bases that confer a redemptive value" (Erlich 1990, 162).

---

[28] Verdier outlines his supposed "non-cultural-relativist" position as follows: "Cessant de prendre pour point de départ le sujet individuel mais envisageant l'homme comme membre d'une communauté humaine diversifiée, l'approche proposée entend échapper tant à un pur relativisme culturel qui mettrait en pièce l'unité du genre humain qu'à un pseudo-universalisme totalitaire et impérialiste qui méconnaîtrait tout droit à la différence et conduirait à la négation de toute identité culturelle et religieuse, selon la configuration moderne individualiste des valeurs' " (1990, 149).

When is mutilation not mutilation? or, It's all in your head really

Verdier maintains that excision constitutes neither a "mutilation" nor a "marking of inferiority" nor "an affront to equality between the sexes" in African tradition, because, "like circumcision—with which, internationally, it is on a par . . . —it is the sign of the complementarity of the sexes. . . . Excision is an act of social incorporation into the group of women . . . , enabling marriage and motherhood in both a biological and social sense" (Verdier 1991b, 3). These arguments are spurious on a number of counts. The first problem lies with his implication that there exists only one "African tradition" in the matter, as a number of African societies do not practice excision, and those that do, do so in a variety of ways and for a variety of reasons, even if control of women's sexuality is invariably at the root of these traditions. As for the assertions that clitoridectomy is "on a par" with circumcision, that it "enables" marriage and motherhood in a biological sense, that it has nothing to do with "sexual inequality," Verdier, like the authors of the MAUSS petition two years earlier, provides a highly selective interpretation of the facts, while claiming to accurately represent "the" African position. It is likewise illuminating to note that Verdier makes a distinction between infibulation, which he perceives as "incontestably a mark of masculine domination," and clitoridectomy, which he perceives as a gender-neutral "rite of passage" into womanhood. He gives no particular justification for this distinction beyond the fallacious comparison with circumcision.

Verdier goes on to note that excision "is all the more compelling an obligation since to the pre-Islamic tradition has been added the strong pressure of Islam in Africa, which, far from forbidding excision, often recommends it to the faithful; as proof, a good number of accused parents see in it a Muslim custom" (Verdier 1991b, 3).[29] If it is indeed true that some parents perceive the practice as being required by Islamic tradition, it is equally true that none of the *surat* (verses) in the Qur'an, nor any of the major *hadith* (sayings attributed to the Prophet and handed down as tradition), nor the *shari'ah* (Islamic law) contains any mention whatsoever of excision. There is another *hadith* that supposedly accepts the practice of excision but recommends moderation ("reduce but do not destroy"); there is much debate, however, over the religious validity of many of the *hadith*. What can be said for certain is that excision is certainly a pre-Islamic practice that has continued after Islamization— in Egypt, Nigeria, and Senegal, for example—and to which Islam has

---

[29] The original French text reads slightly differently: "Au poids de la tradition ante-islamique vient s'ajouter la pression forte de l'Islam *noir*" (186; my emphasis). "Black Islam" is somewhat more specific than "Islam in Africa," as the African continent also includes the Maghrib and the other Arabic-Berber countries in North Africa.

either adapted or turned a blind eye. In any case, whatever feminist criticisms may be made of Islam, no Islamic text has ever "recommend[ed excision] to the faithful."[30]

Verdier even implies that because excision forms part of a cultural norm, African women "suffer" less from it than a white woman would. Erlich, at the 1991 Paris trial, fed into the myth of African women's "joyful acceptance" of clitoridectomy by explaining to the court that Sémité Coulibaly (the mother of the *excisées*) had told him that her own clitoridectomy had taken place "after a cold bath, painlessly, and with a rather joyful feeling."[31] This is somewhat reminiscent of Western images of the "happy hooker" who "enjoys" her work, or of the women who "enjoy" being Playboy bunnies. In addressing the issue of sexual pleasure, Erlich (1990) also maintained that it was something "very difficult to evaluate according to our own criteria." Certainly, sexuality is defined very differently in different cultures, but the implication that African immigrant women "joyfully accept" clitoridectomy, without its creating any psychological or sexual ill effects whatsoever, is suspect, to say the least. As early as 1978, Awa Thiam had shown that many African women living in Africa did not, even then, perceive excision as a joyful experience, and in 1982 MODEFEN (Mouvement pour la Defense des Droits de la Femme Noire) strongly criticized the relativist position of some academics who maintain that pain is not experienced in the same way in different cultures (in other words, that African women do not suffer as much from excision as Western women would). Moreover, Touré, who has spent many years working closely with adolescent *excisées* in France, has noted that they experience enormous psychosexual problems as a result of genital mutilation (Thiam 1978; MODEFEN 1982).[32]

Erlich has gone even further in his justifications of "acceptable customary practice" by providing examples of culturally admissible so-called ritual mutilation in Western society, such as tonsillectomy and appendectomy. This is by no means a new argument. As far back as 1978, Bakang Tanjé, of Cameroonian origin and at the time practicing medicine in a suburb of Paris, suggested in a radio interview that tonsillectomy and appendectomy, acts of "aesthetic surgery" reimbursed by Social Security,

---

[30] It is possible that in some "black" African countries Islam has been somewhat more accommodating of pre-Islamic traditions; the fact remains, however, that no Islamic text has ever advocated any form of clitoridectomy or infibulation. Moreover, the GAMS (1991, 15) has noted that followers of many other religions in Africa also practice excision.

[31] Maurice Peyrot: in *Le Monde* (March 8, 9, 10, 1991). Translated by the *Guardian Weekly* (March 24, 1991) and reprinted in 1992 in the "Passages" suppl. to *PAS News and Events*, 3:3.

[32] Touré interview, 1992.

were no different from excision.[33] Erlich builds on this argument by maintaining that tonsillectomy and appendectomy can be traumatizing for children, and refers to the work of R. P. Bolande, who asserted in 1969 that tonsillectomy can represent a "secondary castration" (Erlich 1990, 159–60). It is difficult, however, to understand how medical operations that have no demonstrable negative effects on the physical and psychological integrity of children (despite the arguments of Bolande and his disciples) can be considered in the same light as genital mutilation, which does have serious physical and psychological consequences. This is, of course, not to excuse the systematic performing of any medically unnecessary operation, but the issues of power around nonsexualized operations such as tonsillectomy are separate from the issues around the sexual mutilation of women. Any trauma caused by nonsexualized Western operations has much more to do with the power of medical institutions to make decisions on behalf of individuals and with the dehumanizing atmosphere of hospitals than it has to do with the effects of physical mutilation.

Excision is not some innocuous little cut; on the contrary, it is a dangerous operation that has led to death or near death on a number of occasions and that constitutes an attack on women's sexuality comparable, were it to be practiced on boys, not to the removal of the foreskin but to the removal of the penis. A cultural parallel between excision and operations such as tonsillectomy can only be established if one disregards both the question of women's bodily and sexual integrity and the question of men's power to determine what constitutes femaleness.

Erlich, however, takes this medical analogy even further by raising the issue of abortion, which he also describes as a "major mutilation" (he does not specify of whom). According to Erlich, the legalization of abortion at the same time that excision is criminalized constitutes a philosophical and legal paradox in Western society (Erlich 1990, 162). Once again, he is attempting to draw a parallel between two practices that do not have the same social, cultural, and political meaning. Clitoridectomy and infibulation are ritual mutilations, governed and justified by tradition and social pressure, which serve the interests not of women but of the patrilinear and patriarchal society in which they live. Abortion, on the other hand, forms part of a struggle for freedom of reproductive choice that puts women's interests first and that is thus strongly opposed by many Western defenders of patrilinear and patriarchal tradition. Moreover, it is a practice that is subject, in most of the cases where it actually

[33] Interview broadcast by France Culture, December 12, 1978, and quoted in Saurel 1981, 52–53.

is allowed by law, to often severe legal, social, and even financial restrictions, with the result that significant numbers of women still have to wage both a psychological and a political battle to obtain it.

Going a few bounds farther, Jean-Thierry Maertens ties excision in with a Lacanian-style discourse on the separation from the "Motherbody," on women as "Other" and as "Mirror," and on the ritual passage of women into "the symbolic." He also maintains that "in these societies without writing, the body is the only possible surface to print on" (Maertens 1990, 170).[34] He seems here to echo Lefeuvre, who wrote in 1988 that "one is born neither man nor woman, but becomes one through the stylet's inscriptions" (Lefeuvre 1988, 82).[35] It would thus seem that we are no longer dealing with women's bodies but with writing materials. It is indeed difficult to talk of the *mutilation* of a writing surface.

All these attempts by cultural relativists to define mutilation as a culturally loaded term and excision as a practice that thus escapes French jurisdiction are based not only on false analogies but also on a rather bizarre attitude toward the question of male domination. It is true that Western society generally condemns excision, polygamy, and other non-Western misogynist practices while condoning more culturally palatable forms of woman hating (such as pornography, marital rape, or the exploitation and deformation of women's bodies and psyches in advertising, the arts, and fashion). It seems a little paradoxical, however, to use the fact that patriarchy is the dominant form of social organization, and thus a common denominator of sociosexual relations in most societies, as a justification for tolerating "different" expressions of male domination in "other" cultures. In other words, "sameness" ("we" have a patriarchy just like "they" do) is used to justify a "respect" for "difference" ("we" have no right to judge "their" patriarchy). In other words, in the name of "respect" for "other" cultures, a backhanded form of misogynist and racist discourse emerges: "We wouldn't condone or do this to our women because it is not part of our culture. It has no cultural value and thus is indefensible. It does not, however, have the same meaning when it is done to their women: for us it is mutilation; for them it is initiation. It has a cultural value and as such is justifiable within their specific cultural context."

This demand that the legal institutions of "our" patriarchy respect the customs of "their" patriarchy is difficult for the French legal system to respond to, as, despite its professed respect for "custom," it is the epitome of universalist assimilationism. As Giudicelli-Delage points out, French

[34] "En ces sociétés sans écriture, le corps est la seule surface de scription possible."

[35] "On ne naît donc ni homme ni femme, on le devient sous le stylet inscripteur." As Lefeuvre notes herself, she has paraphrased Simone de-Beauvoir's famous sentence, "On ne naît pas femme, on le devient."

respect for customary practice is only valid within the framework of already-established legal principles. For example, "the right of parents to corporally punish their children can be said to derive from [the notion of] parental authority" (Giudicelli-Delage 1990, 203).[36] Excision, as a custom that departs from French cultural and thus "customary" values, is thus, according to Giudicelli-Delage, no more admissible within the French legal system than a foreign law that contradicts French law. Yet here again there are contradictions. France has, for example, signed bilateral conventions with all three Maghrebian countries (Algeria, Morocco, and Tunisia) that allow the marital laws of those countries to prevail in the case of immigrant families, even though the laws in question run contrary to the French law, which is based on the principle of sexual equality. This could be seen to constitute a legal precedent for the respect of "their" patriarchy by "our" patriarchy in the case of excision.

In any case, whatever the degree of its compatibility or incompatibility with the French legal system, the cultural relativist position remains spurious, not the least because it is based on fundamentally flawed logic. In fact, it would seem not merely to contain but to be built upon three paradoxes. First, those who criticize republican universalism in the name of the "respect for cultural difference" nonetheless do so on the basis of the republican—and universalist—notions of "private choice" and "the rights of Man." While the most diehard of the cultural relativists would strongly reject any notion of "universal rights," the fact remains that their defense of cultural difference rests on the assumption—explicit or implicit— that each culture has an intrinsic "right" to exist and to express itself and that members of other cultures do not have a "right" to criticize the forms this "expression" may take. This would seem to be a cross-cultural extrapolation of the classic liberal discourse on the inviolability of the individual's right to "his" inner sanctum that escapes public scrutiny.

The second paradox is that the most zealous defenders of cultural relativism are not from nondominant cultures but are white male intellectuals. It does seem, in fact, that white Western men, and the women who identify with them, are exploiting the ideas coming out of antiracist movements as well as their own collective guilt in order to assume a new position of intellectual and political power, as it is still their voices that are being heard, their position that is being consolidated. Once again, cultural relativists are remaining true to liberal-democratic philosophy in maintaining that Western patriarchal law has no right to interfere in non-Western patriarchal practice, particularly when this practice concerns "family life," that is, control of women and children. This means,

[36] "Le droit de correction manuelle des parents sur leurs enfants dériverait de l'autorité parentale."

of course, that it is ultimately men in general and Western men in particular who benefit from decisions made about the lives of women and female children. I say "Western men in particular," as they manage to obtain the support of minority men in maintaining, first, a strict demarcation between the public and private spheres, thus preserving their own power intact, and second, a cultural and political double standard that perpetuates the ghettoization of the same minority.

This leads me to the third paradox, which is that these white male intellectuals perceive themselves as progressive, left-wing, radical, or avant-garde; the ideology of cultural integrity, however, springs not from revolutionary or avant-garde movements but from the extreme right ideologues and movements of the late nineteenth and early twentieth centuries. While claiming to represent a radical departure from Western universalist enlightenment ideology, the cultural relativists are both feeding from and feeding into extreme right positions of "cultural integrity," where "the respect of difference" is a pretext for the maintenance of segregation and ghettoization.[37]

Feminist positions

While "intention," "responsibility," and the notion of "customary practice" provide possible legal loopholes, the political philosophy embodied in French law is still rooted in a combination of the notion of "public order" (read: national uniformity) with that of "universal human rights" (which are ostensibly the same for all), and it is on this level that excision is perceived as fundamentally incompatible with French law. While the cultural relativists reject this philosophy on the grounds that it is ethnocentric (and therefore racist in this context), preferring to situate their legal arguments exclusively within the technical framework of interpretations and loopholes, protrial feminists, on the contrary, situate their arguments exclusively at the level of the political philosophy of the law. This position creates a whole new set of problems, not the least of which is that protrial feminists are not only perceived as representing "the" feminist position on the subject (which is not the case), but they also are generally misrepresented by cultural relativists as some new brand of white supremacists.

---

[37] The contemporary extreme right "cultural separateness" position is represented by organizations such as the GRECE (Groupe de Recherche et d'Étude pour la Civilisation Européenne) and its journal *Elements pour la civilisation européenne* or the Club de l'Horloge and its journal *Krisis*, and in particular by their main ideologue, Alain de Benoist. For a historical overview of the French extreme right, see Chombart de Lauwe 1986, and for a study of French fascism and of fascist tendencies in the French extreme right, Milza 1987.

The legal representations made by protrial feminists in the form of *partie civile,* especially during the 1991 Paris trial, have provided cultural relativists with an undreamed of opportunity to indulge in some subtle (and some not so subtle) feminist bashing. "The feminists," who of course are all assumed to have the same position and the same strategies, have always been prey to backlashes of all sorts, and in France they currently constitute a prime target for left-leaning intellectuals of varying descriptions, whether the latter fall into the universalist/egalitarian camp that criticizes feminism for insisting on sexual difference as a political issue or the cultural relativist/postmodernist camp that, conversely, criticizes feminism for its inattention to difference, whether it be sexual or cultural. So in France the familiar gap between the reality of feminism, on the one hand, and the fiction of media and academic portrayals of it, on the other, becomes a veritable chasm.[38]

In fact, the positions taken by feminist groups campaigning against excision during the 1980s fall roughly into two camps. First, SOS Femmes Alternatives, CAMS-F, and the other associations mentioned earlier, along with individuals such as the well-known feminist writer Benoîte Groult, support the criminalization of excision in France and are usually represented as *partie civile* during trials (Groult 1991). The position of these protrial feminists is that the only way—certainly the best way—to put an end to excision is to bring legal pressure to bear on those who practice it. This campaign thus ostensibly functions according to similar logic as did the campaign to criminalize rape and the lobby for the imposition of heavier sentences for rapists, the idea being both that the punishment should fit the crime and that heavy sentences will act as a deterrent. The cultural difference argument is perceived as a fudging device used by French men to prevent feminists' speaking out against excision as the exercise of male power over women. Séverine Auffret perhaps best expressed this position in 1982, when she wrote that if there is an argument for nonintervention (at least from the "outside") in the area of cultural customs that do not enter into the political arena, excision is, on the contrary, an exercise of political power over women that calls for "intervention, struggle, and solidarity" (Auffret 1982, 14).[39]

---

[38] It is worth noting that this misrepresentation of French feminism has also been widespread among women's studies practitioners in Western English-speaking countries. "French feminism" has often been equated with "postmodernism" and has been narrowly defined as limited to the work of a few intellectuals such as Luce Irigaray, Hélène Cixous, and Julia Kristeva. Not only are these writers far from representative of French feminist thought and movement, but few of them even identify themselves as feminist. Some, like Kristeva, are actually antifeminist.

[39] "Admettons qu'une coutume ne se juge pas, du moins de l'extérieur. Une politique inversement se juge et se combat. De l' 'extérieur' comme de l' 'intérieur.' La politique est affaire d'intervention, de lutte et de solidarité."

The other camp is that of associations such as the GAMS, which split from the CAMS-F over the issue of criminalization. The position taken by the GAMS is that bringing cases of excision to trial does more harm than good, particularly as it is other women who are being judged and sentenced while the men, who hold the real power of decision, are less and less likely to be brought to trial. The GAMS thus advocates working directly with the families concerned, particularly the mothers, to provide information and support. The position of these organizations, along with that of some feminist intellectuals doing work in the field (such as Catherine Quiminal, who testified at the Bobigny trial), is distinct from that of both the protrial feminists and the cultural relativists. Unfortunately, these groups are less visible to the media and to intellectuals, who are thus often unaware of their existence, with the result that those associations represented as *partie civile* are considered to be the voice of the entire feminist movement.

Certainly, few if any feminists, whether African or white French, would dispute the idea that excision and infibulation, as mutilations of women in the name of femininity, mutilations that have extremely serious and even fatal medical, sexual, and psychological consequences, are indeed an expression of male domination. Few if any would dispute the assertion that the "custom" of excision is built upon a complex mythology that has been elaborated with the primary purpose of controlling women's sexuality for the benefit of men.[40] On the level of fundamental feminist principles, there is thus little to no disagreement between the protrial and antitrial feminists. It is at the levels of strategy, cultural sensitivity, and the dilemma of taking legal action against women in the name, paradoxically, of women's rights that serious divergencies appear.

Western legal systems, based as they are on a concept of the individual that not only excludes women's specific reality as women but also fails to account for differences in social, cultural, and economic conditions that will affect how the system operates, can at the very best provide only a partial solution to what is fundamentally a political and cultural problem. At the same time, these legal systems, along with the political values they represent, inform so much of our lives that they become a primary reference, even for many feminists, who one might have reasonably expected to display a healthy disrespect for patriarchal law. The protrial feminists take the stance that excision is under no circumstances defensible or excusable, for it is a physical, sexual, and psychological mutilation of female children. As such, this mutilation, like any other voluntary mutilation of children, is punishable by French law, which should be the

---

[40] For some of the positions taken by French-speaking African women, see Thiam 1978, 1990; MODEFEN 1984; and Touré 1984.

same for everyone, regardless of sex, class, ethnic origin, and so on. In other words, the notions of women's individual physical integrity and freedom of choice are placed within a global ideological context of "universal rights" and the "indivisibility" of the nation and its laws, which each individual is bound to obey in order to safeguard both national integrity and the principles of universal rights on which the nation is built. These notions, which form the basis of the modern political concept of national sovereignty, are so deeply ingrained in the French collective consciousness that many white French feminists will leap to the defense of the Republic over and above considerations of individual women or groups of women, and with total disregard for issues of cross-cultural context. Groult, for example, makes this stance perfectly clear when she writes: "The immigration of different ethnic groups, the juxtaposition of cultures, should not lead to the breaking up or the renouncement of French law. . . . It is true that the Traorés or other families do not understand what is happening to them. This is unfortunate from an individual point of view, but the law cannot be divided" (Groult 1991, 206–7).[41]

What is particularly "unfortunate" in the case of excision is that the individuals in question are mainly women (in the Traoré-Fofana case of 1989, as noted above, only the mother was found guilty and sentenced) and that these women are often quite isolated from the support networks that most white French women take for granted. The responsibility of their husbands in contributing to this isolation has been stressed by both protrial and antitrial feminists and in particular by the African feminists who work most closely within immigrant communities. For example, few African immigrant women speak French with any degree of fluency—and often not at all—most of them have no independent source of income, and in the case of second wives, their social status is at best vague.[42] This isolation is compounded during legal proceedings, where the mother usually finds herself alone in the dock. Such considerations, however,

[41] "L'immigration de groupes ethniques différents, la juxtaposition des cultures, ne doit pas conduire à morceler ou à répudier le Droit français. . . . Il est vrai que la famille Traoré ou d'autres ne comprennent pas ce qui leur arrive. C'est regrettable sur le plan individuel, mais la loi ne se divise pas."

[42] Koïta, of the GAMS, has pointed out that immigrant women in France have in fact a great deal less autonomy than they had in their country of origin, which is largely due to conditions in which immigrant families arrive and live in France. As in most other cases of large-scale family migration, the husbands arrive long before their wives and children; isolated from community structures and safeguards, the tendency is for African men to take total control, not allowing their wives out, not even to go to literacy classes, controlling all the family finances, including benefits normally paid to mothers, and keeping all official papers. Moreover, contradictions in French immigration law lead to even further isolation of second and subsequent wives, who are, at the time of this writing, recognized for immigration purposes but not recognized by French administrative institutions such as Social Security.

seem to have no place in the preoccupations of Groult and like-minded protrial feminists, whose primary concern is a universal principle of women's and children's rights and the across-the-board application of French law rather than, it would seem, the fate of the particular women who are facing trial.

On the other hand, despite what could be perceived as insensitivity and/or ethnocentricity on the part of some with little understanding of the context in which immigrant African women are operating in France, one would be mistaken in assuming, as do the cultural relativists, that all protrial feminists show a disregard for the complexity of the issues. Apart from the fact that some protrial feminists, such as Thiam, are themselves African, many of the non-African women are well aware of the difficulties and limitations involved in bringing cases of excision to trial. Weil-Curiel, for example, has "always asked the examining magistrate to charge the husbands as well," for given that the wives have no independent income, not to mention their isolation for the reasons outlined above, it is difficult to believe that they arrange and pay for the excisions on their own.[43] Koïta (who does not support criminalization) has further pointed out that African women are brought up to submit to the will of their husbands and maintains that if African men were opposed to excision and expressed their preparedness to marry non-*excisées,* then mothers would stop the practice. However, as the husbands continue to plead their innocence, pointing out that they were at work or even overseas at the time, the wives continue to support their husbands' stories, and both husbands and wives maintain that excision is "women's business" (*une affaire de femmes*); in accordance with cultural tradition (a statement behind which the cultural relativists place all their intellectual weight), the law cannot—or will not—recognize the husbands as accessories to the fact.

One of the greatest problems facing feminists campaigning against excision is, in fact, women's complicity in their own oppression and in that of their children. This is not news; feminists and social scientists working on issues concerning women have observed time and again that if various forms of violence against women and female children are so hard to eradicate, it is precisely because women themselves are propping up the structures that allow such violence to happen. It is women who are the "keepers of tradition," who inculcate in their own daughters the values they have themselves espoused, as it were. As Koïta points out, "All mothers pass on their suffering, their pain, their joy; whether it is white mothers or African mothers, it's the same thing. I think it is uni-

---

[43] Weil-Curiel interview, 1992.

versal for women to pass [such things] on. The women hand down their culture; as for men, they hand down nothing."[44]

This is problematic in the case of excision for protrial and antitrial feminists alike, but many are clear in their assertion that it would be unwise, and indeed disrespectful of the women concerned, to fall into the trap of what the French call *angélisme,* that is, treating oppressed groups as imbued with some sort of saintliness and thus refusing to attribute to them any responsibility either for what they do or for what happens to them. This can in fact become just another variation on the theme of "those poor stupid Africans who don't know any better," as it feeds into the Good Samaritan style of Western discourse where minorities—and particularly minority women—are perceived as passive victims.

For it is impossible to ignore the fact that excisions are indeed carried out by women. The *exciseuses* benefit, in return for their services, from a financial autonomy and social standing accorded few other women in their communities. They are invested with the power to carry on tradition, a power they share to some extent with the mothers. However, many feminists, including African feminists, have difficulty understanding how mothers can impose such suffering on their daughters, particularly when they know firsthand what such suffering entails. Weil-Curiel has put forward the argument that the mothers take some sort of revenge for their own suffering by inflicting the same thing on their daughters, saying to themselves, "Well, I had to go through this; why should my daughter be spared?"[45] Other women find more plausible the argument that the women continue the practice because they are scared that their daughters will not find husbands and will end up as social outcasts with no means of support.[46]

Whatever the reasons given for women's complicity, protrial feminists are adamant, despite the sympathy many feel for the mothers and their wish to see the husbands put on trial as well, that excision is a crime committed not only against women but also by adults against children and that this fact is often ignored or at the very least pushed to the background. As Weil-Curiel puts it, "The reason why associations take action as *partie civile* is that they are, at the present time, the only ones

---

[44] "Toutes les mamans transmettent leur souffrance, leur peine, leur joie, que ce soit les mamans blanches ou africaines, c'est pareil. Je crois que c'est universel que ce soit les femmes qui transmettent. Les femmes transmettent la culture, parce que l'homme ne transmet rien, lui" (Koïta interview, 1993).

[45] "Souvent, une des justifications des mères, c'est de dire: On me l'a fait à moi, ma mère me l'a fait. Il n'y a aucune raison pour que ma fille y échappe" (Weil-Curiel interview, 1992). Camille Lacoste-Dujardin (1985) has made the same observation in her study of the internalization and handing down of oppression among Moroccan women.

[46] Touré interview, 1992; Koïta interview, 1993.

able to speak in the name of the children who are under their parents' authority, the same parents who subject them to excision."[47] For her, excision, as a crime against female children, is to be treated in the same way before the law, whatever the cultural or national origin of the family concerned. "The result, when the clitoris is removed, is the same. Whether it is the clitoris of a little black girl or a little white girl, whether it is a pair of scissors, a razor blade, or a knife, the result is identical. And we should not hand down different judgments according to whether it is a French woman or an African woman. The result is: there has been a crime, whoever has committed it."[48] Putting the mothers on trial, and obtaining prison sentences, as unsatisfactory as this may seem, is seen by protrial feminists as the only way to put a stop to the practice, after more than a decade of campaigning through infant health centers (Centres de Prévention Maternelle et Infantile) or social services and community groups has failed to produce significant results.

A double dead end?

Verdier summed up the general cultural relativist stance concerning the protrial feminists when he wrote: "Our rebuttal proceeds from a recognition of the need for dialogue, not diatribe, and has no other goal in tying together the legal and cultural debates than to re-introduce the contradictory—which is essential to the legal debate—and to emphasize that the political campaign waged by certain associations against sexual inequality has no place in our courts" (Verdier 1991b, 3). Oddly, Verdier criticizes the presence of feminists as *partie civile* and the argumentation of a feminist case in excision trials but has no problem with the other side of the polemic (i.e., the defense of the practice on cultural grounds) being brought into the court. If, as Giudicelli-Delage has noted, "the criminal court is a place where individual behavior is judged and not a place where collective practices are debated" (1990, 208),[49] then it would seem, assuming one respects this function of the law (which Verdier purports to do), that neither the feminist *parties civiles* nor the cultural relativist "experts" have any place in excision trials.

---

[47] "La raison pour laquelle les associations se portent partie civile, c'est parce que elles sont pour le moment les seules à pouvoir prendre la parole au nom des enfants qui sont sous la tutelle des parents, les mêmes parents qui les soumettent à l'excision" (Weil-Curiel interview, 1992).

[48] "La conséquence quand on coupe le clitoris, c'est la même, que ce soit le clitoris d'une petite fille noire ou d'une petite fille blanche, que ce soit une paire de ciseaux, que ce soit une lame de rasoir ou un couteau, la conséquence est identique. Et on ne doit pas juger différemment selon que c'est une Française ou selon que c'est une Africaine. La conséquence: il y a crime, quelle que soit la personne qui l'a commis" (Weil-Curiel interview, 1993).

[49] "Le prétoire pénal est le lieu où l'on juge exclusivement des comportements individuels et non un lieu où l'on débat de pratiques collectives."

This role of the law in judging individual and not collective behavior is, however, exceedingly suspect from a feminist point of view, for individual behavior is in any case not judged from a neutral point of view but within a culturally and politically loaded context—in other words, according to collective criteria. Individual behavior is never the only element brought into play; collective assumptions and political power relationships are always relevant and will have direct bearing on any verdict. Is it then valid for feminists to question this ideological loading, which invariably operates against women (as any rape victim will testify, e.g), by doing everything in their power to unmask the political debate that underlies court procedure? In that case, feminists must also accept that counterarguments will be brought in to weaken their position and the trial will thus inevitably become a political forum of the sort that took over the 1991 Paris trial. Once again, where does this leave the individual women concerned?

It leaves them, at least in this case, in a no-win situation, as what is at stake in court is no longer their lives but a political contest. They are no longer the main actors in the courtroom but symbols manipulated by others who have taken the stage. Does this then mean that no feminist, whether she be plaintiff, defendant, lawyer, witness, jury member, or *partie civile*, has the right to bring into play feminist arguments in order to bend the law as far as possible in women's favor? (I say "bend" and not "challenge," for once the courtroom situation has been accepted as the framework for debate, it is necessary also to accept the limitations imposed by that framework. Otherwise, there is no point in bothering to go to a court of law.) Does it mean that all feminists should shut up and accept whatever interpretation of the law the lawyers, judge, and jury dish out?

Of course not. In the case of excision, however, it is vital to move beyond what Quiminal has called a "double dead end." On the one hand, explains Quiminal, the public prosecutor and the *parties civiles*, "in the name of the principle of fighting against sexual mutilation, are waging an abstract battle without really considering the practical consequences of their action"; on the other hand, the defense "bases its argumentation solely on the 'irresponsibility of these illiterate, impoverished people, who understand nothing of what is happening to them and who are unfamiliar with French law.' . . . No one is interested in the root of the problem, in the social process that is involved. . . . We need to try to find a position that is neither steeped in racism nor in socialworkerism, as were the defense's arguments, nor founded on the respect of all customs, whatever they may be" (Quiminal 1991, 9).[50]

---

[50] "Il faut réfléchir pour sortir de cette double impasse représentée aujourd'hui par la voie choisie par l'accusation et la partie civile qui, au nom du principe de la lutte contre

The problem with bringing excision to trial in the current context is in fact threefold. First, there are limitations to the possibilities of raising issues of political power through a legal system that from the start is in total contradiction with itself. Its whole raison d'être as the third arm of French Republican government is to prop up political power while professing to be outside—or even above—the realm of politics. At the same time, this power system allows the less powerful enough maneuvering room to curb gross—or unfashionable—misuses of power, while at the same time preventing them from becoming too restive. The legal system is thus necessarily, for feminists, both an instrument of oppression and an instrument of, if not liberation, at least emancipation. In the case of excision, the law thus definitely has a role to play. The question is, What role exactly? What laws? What applications?

This brings us to the second problem. If the cultural relativists have so easily been able to obtain mileage out of the Paris trial, it is precisely because there has been little thought given by the prosecutors and the *parties civiles* to the legal ramifications of the emergence of a multicultural society. Of course, many token allusions and gestures have been made to multiculturalism in France as elsewhere, and the predominantly white male cultural relativists have leaped on the bandwagon by indulging the nation's collective guilt toward the ex-colonized. There remains, however, the basic problem of applying a "sole and indivisible law" that is the emanation of a supposedly homogeneous and ethnocentric nation to a society where cultural homogeneity is now neither a social reality nor a politically operative concept, as non-Western minorities, the direct legacy of colonization, represent a significant and increasingly vocal proportion of the mainland French population. In other words, a legal system that is based on universalist principles and thus contains no overall concept of racism or cultural diversity (despite the passage in 1975 of a law against any words or actions that incite "racial hate or violence") has to account for, and be accountable to, the reality of racism and the

---

les mutilations sexuelles, mènent une bataille abstraite sans se préoccuper des conséquences pratiques de leur démarche; l'autre impasse est celle représentée par la défense qui fonde son argumentation uniquement sur 'l'irresponsabilité de ces gens analphabètes, démunis dans la vie, qui ne comprennent rien à ce qui leur arrive et qui ne connaissent pas la loi française.' . . . Personne dans ce cas ne s'intéresse au fond du problème, au processus social qui est en cause. . . . Il faut essayer de trouver une position qui ne soit ni empreinte de racisme, ni de misérabilisme comme l'a été le plaidoyer de la défense, ni fondée sur le respect de toutes les coutumes quelles qu'elles soient." The term *misérabilisme* is extremely difficult to translate. Originally coined to describe an artistic preoccupation with the more sordid aspects of life (associated primarily with poverty but also with other forms of ghettoization), the term is often used to describe a stereotyping of oppressed people as passive victims; this is why I have chosen to coin the term *social-workerism* as a fitting way (I hope) of rendering in English this frequently held attitude of the dominant toward those they feel guilty about dominating.

diversity of cultural contexts within French society. The problem is how to do this coherently, and particularly how to do it without women losing out once again.

For example, a major difficulty in developing actions concerning excision, from both within and outside the legal profession, is that what many doctors and social workers consider to be "adequate and comprehensible information" is not necessarily adequate or comprehensible for the people concerned. In fact, groups and individuals working with African immigrant women have criticized the French government's reluctance to give much attention to information, education, and support programs, both among professionals in health and social services and among the immigrant communities themselves. It could be argued, of course, that it is perhaps just as well that the government does not involve itself overmuch, as it could do more harm than good by instituting culturally insensitive programs, and that it is better to fund community associations working in the area. However, the problem with this argument, in spite of its undoubted validity on some levels, is that total responsibility for the problem is left to individuals and community groups, and the efficiency of any program will thus depend on their number, energy, and motivation.

Whatever the position taken with regard to government intervention within African-French communities, the fact remains that medical personnel working in pre- and postnatal and infant health centers often have a rather peculiar idea of what constitutes meaningful communication. As Isabelle Gillette-Frénoy, administrator of the GAMS, pointed out, there is usually no interpreter present during medical consultations to verify whether information has been understood. For example, the doctor who testified at the Coulibaly/Keita trial in Paris "explained to the mother by using gestures that she mustn't cut," meaning that she must not remove her child's clitoris. (The mother in question spoke no French, and no interpreter was present.) As Gillette-Frénoy points out, "No one is able to say how much the woman understood or did not understand."[51]

The third problem with advocating trials for excision within the current sociocultural, historical, and legal context is that it means addressing an issue of women's rights by putting women on trial; this is vaguely reminiscent of situations where the prostitute is arrested instead of her pimp or her client. It is obvious that excision must be exposed and opposed as both the mutilation of women and female children and the exercise of male power over women. Given, however, that the law does try individual acts and not collective practices or political manipulation,

---

[51] "Dans quelle mesure cette femme a compris ou n'a pas compris l'information, personne ne peut le dire" (interview by me in Paris, June 23, 1992).

it will always, in the case of excision, be the women and not their husbands who are put on trial. In other words, it is the women who not only are the vehicles of their own oppression but also who end up paying for it doubly in the name, paradoxically, of their own "liberation." Moreover, the women being tried are not those who have grown up in France with knowledge of French language, customs, and law but those who have been brought to France (often as a second or third wife, in which case they basically have no social or legal status) and who often are very young, do not speak the language, and have been educated into believing that excision is necessary for their daughters' future psychological, physical, and social development.

Antitrial feminists such as the women of the GAMS have stressed that without even the most basic social or financial autonomy (e.g., access to the main language of communication in the country in which they live), women have little to no intellectual liberty to question the forces that govern their lives. Not on their own, at any rate. This is different from saying that these women are stupid or passive. It is saying that they are acting under severe emotional, social, and financial constraints. Touré has stressed that as long as immigrant women remain without any means of supporting themselves, they will be unable to operate independently in French society. Koïta has added that a significant step toward eradicating the social structures that support excision would be to make it a legal obligation for immigrant men to send their wives to language and literacy classes. "Financial autonomy is all very well, but they first need to be able to express themselves, take the Métro, find their way around, know, when they receive official forms, where they come from and how to keep track of them, or go do their shopping without their husbands' help, and be able to follow their children's schooling, be able at least to communicate basic things to the schoolteachers."[52]

In other words, until immigrant women are able to interact with the society in which they live, they have little hope of obtaining access not only to social and economic survival skills but also to information and debate that will help them make independent decisions about their lives and the lives of their children. It thus seems to me to be unacceptable, from a feminist point of view, to advocate putting these women on trial without prior—and simultaneous—attention both to providing basic health care, information (about both French law and their own rights

---

[52] "C'est bien beau l'autonomie financière mais il faut d'abord qu'elles sachent s'exprimer, qu'elles sachent au moins prendre le métro, au moins se diriger quand elles sortent, au moins aller, savoir que quand elle reçoit tel papier, que ce papier vient de là, classer ses papiers, ranger ses papiers, aller faire ses courses sans l'aide du mari. Et pouvoir suivre ses enfants, la vie scolaire de ses enfants, savoir au moins dire le minimum de choses à la maîtresse, au professeur" (Koïta interview, 1993).

as women), and education (such as language and literacy classes) and to building autonomous women's support networks (which includes campaigning around other issues as well, such as polygamy and child marriages).

Organizations such as MODEFEN and the GAMS have been working in this direction for well over a decade. The GAMS, for example, receives funding from the Fonds d'Action Sociale pour les Travailleurs Immigrés (FAS), which funds a number of minority community organizations, and on a less regular basis from the Women's Rights' Ministry (this source of funding comes and goes, as does the Women's Rights' Ministry, according to which party is in power). Both Koïta and Touré are paid on a part-time basis to work with medical and social personnel, as well as with African women and teenagers (part of Touré's work is in high schools, with adolescent girls now having to come to terms with the fact that they are *excisées*). Other women's organizations have created projects such as NO (Nouvelles Opportunités pour les Femmes), based in the nineteenth arrondissement in Paris (part of the poorer northeast area, where many immigrants live), to provide basic training in language, literacy, and survival skills for the most underprivileged women, the overwhelming majority of whom are African and Maghrebian immigrants, in order to equip them to obtain work as cleaners, garment workers, and so on. While at face value this project may be criticized as traditionalist in that women are being trained to do "female" low-paid, low-valued jobs, it nonetheless corresponds to a social reality: these are the areas where these women are most likely to obtain work and where they can most easily be equipped to do it. Projects such as these may hardly seem revolutionary from an academic feminist standpoint, but it must be remembered that the issues women in this context are dealing with are issues of basic survival in areas that the majority of literate Western women take for granted.[53]

The protrial position is thus inadequate within the present context, in that a set of principles or ideals that, although directly grounded in women's lives and meant to inform feminist activity, remain nonetheless abstract generalizations, is applied, through the operation of a rigid legal system based on fundamentally woman-hating values to a diverse and complex material reality that cannot possibly be accounted for by such a system. The main problem with the criminalization of excision is not that what Françoise Lionnet (1992) has termed feminist "radical individualism"

[53] Kelthoum Bendjouadi, one of the initiators of the NO project, was interviewed by me in Paris on June 28, 1993. She pointed out, for example, that the initial training, during a two-month "introductory" course before women go on to two years' full-time, fully paid training as seamstresses, is often as basic as teaching women to use an iron or to recognize labels on different brands of cleaning products.

(i.e., the feminist ethic that women have a right to physical integrity and sociosexual autonomy) is fundamentally flawed or ethnocentric. The issue is that French law, as designed to serve the interests of a Western liberal democracy, is inadequate to address either the physical, social, and political reality of women's bodies as a vehicle of social organization and control or the fact that the principles of equality and individual rights on which the law is based bear little correspondence to the reality of immigrant women's lives.[54]

The case of excision in France is especially revealing of the need for feminists to maintain a concrete connection with the women on whose behalf they have chosen to act and to develop an understanding of the social, economic, cultural, and political contexts within which these women are having to operate. For while feminism is definitely about establishing and defending principles, these principles become meaningless if they no longer serve the real-life women in whose name they have been elaborated.

Department of French Studies
University of Sydney

References

Auffret, Séverine. 1982. *Des couteaux contre des femmes: De l'excision.* Paris: Des Femmes.

CAMS Internationale (Commission Internationale pour l'Abolition des Mutilations Sexuelles). 1989. "Résolution du colloque international 'Des Violences et Mutilations Sexuelles Infligées aux Fillettes et aux Femmes.' " *Paris féministe* 75/76:45–46.

———. 1990. "L'excision: Dans le monde la blessure. . . ." In "Hommes et libertés: Les violences faites aux femmes," special unnumbered issue of *Revue de la Ligue des Droits de l'Homme,* 14–19.

Chombart de Lauwe, Marie-José. 1986. *Vigilance: Vieilles traditions extrémistes et droites nouvelles.* Paris: Ligue des Droits de l'Homme/Etudes et Documentation Internationales.

Code pénal. 1983–84.

Erlich, Michel. 1986. *La femme blessée: Essai sur les mutilations sexuelles féminines.* Paris: L'Harmattan.

———. 1990. "Notions de mutilation et criminalization de l'excision en France." *Droit et cultures: Revue semestrielle d'anthropologie et d'histoire* 20:151–62.

---

[54] Kathleen B. Jones has shown that the Western liberal/republican concepts of "equality" and "citizenship" posit the individual as an abstract self and the individual body as a possession or "physical container" of this abstract self, whereas many feminists would argue that the body "is a historical object, affected by economic and political structures that mediate its expressiveness. It is also an intrinsic feature of human subjectivity. The body is not a mere container of the self" (1990, 796).

————. 1991. *Les mutilations sexuelles*. Paris: Presses Universitaires de France.

Fainzang, Sylvie. 1984. "L'excision, ici et maintenant: Étude ethnologique." In *Les mutilations du sexe des femmes aujourd'hui en France*. Paris: Tierce.

————. 1985. "Circoncision, excision et rapports de domination." *Anthropologie et sociétés* 9(1):117–27.

————. 1990. "Excision et ordre social." *Droit et cultures: Revue semestrielle d'anthropologie et d'histoire* 29:177–82.

FOWARD. 1989. "Sexual Mutilations: Case Studies Presented at the Workshop 'African Women Speak on Female Circumcision' (Khartoum, October 21–25, 1984)," reprinted in *FOWARD* 1989, 49–64.

GAMS (Groupe pour l'Abolition des Mutilations Sexuelles). 1984a. "Excision et santé publique: Etude médicale." In *Les mutilations du sexe des femmes aujourd'hui en France*, 45–60. Paris: Tierce.

————. 1984b. "Les populations concernées en France." In *Les mutilations du sexe des femmes aujourd'hui en France*, 77–80. Paris: Tierce.

————. 1991. "A minima ou complète: Non à l'excision." *Paris féministe* 128:13–17.

Gillette-Frénoy, Isabelle. 1992. *L'excision et sa présence en France*. Paris: Editions GAMS.

Giudicelli-Delage, Geneviève. 1990. "Excision et droit pénal." *Droit et cultures: Revue semestrielle d'anthropologie et d'histoire* 29:201–11.

Groult, Benoîte. 1991. "Cent fois non à l'appel de Martine Lefeuvre." *Nouvelles questions féministes* 16/17/18:205–8.

Guillaumin, Colette. 1978. "Pratique du pouvoir et idée de Nature (2): Le discours de la nature." *Nouvelles questions féministes* 3:5–28.

Hosken, Fran. 1979. *The Hosken Report: Genital and Sexual Mutilation of Females*. Lexington, Mass.: Women's International Network News Quarterly.

Jones, Kathleen B. 1990. "Citizenship in a Woman-Friendly Polity." *Signs: Journal of Women in Culture and Society* 15(4):781–812.

Kunstenaar, Caroline. 1988. "Excision." *Paris féministe* 66:10–11.

Lacoste-Dujardin, Camille. 1985. *Des mères contre les femmes: Maternité et patriarcat au Maghreb*. Paris: La Découverte.

Lefeuvre, Martine. 1988. "Le devoir de l'excision." *Bulletin du MAUSS*, n.s., 1:65–95.

————. 1989. "Contre la criminalisation de l'excision." *Bulletin du MAUSS*, n.s., 3:162–63.

Lionnet, Françoise. 1992. "Identity, Sexuality and Criminality: 'Universal Rights' and the Debate around the Practice of Female Excision in France." In "Discourses on Sexuality," special issue of *Contemporary French Civilization*.

Loupiac, Marianne. 1988. "La mort de Mantessa." *Paris féministe* 67:12–14.

Lyotard, Jean-François. 1979. *La condition postmoderne: Rapport sur le savoir*. Paris: Editions de Minuit.

MacKinnon, Catharine A. 1983. "Feminism, Marxism, Method, and the State: Toward Feminist Jurisprudence." *Signs* 8(4):635–58.

————. 1990. "Legal Perspectives on Sexual Difference." In *Theoretical Perspectives on Sexual Difference*, ed. Deborah L. Rhode, 213–25. New Haven, Conn.: Yale University Press.

Maertens, Jean-Thierry. 1990. "Les mutilations rituelles en corps et toujours." *Droit et cultures: Revue semestrielle d'anthropologie et d'histoire* 20:163–76.

Milza, Pierre. 1987. *Fascisme français: Passé et présent.* Paris: Flammarion.

MODEFEN (Mouvement pour la Defense des Droits de la Femme Noire). 1982. "Sur l'infibulation et l'excision en Afrique." *Bulletin de l'Association Française des Anthropologues* 9:50–54.

———. 1984. "Au nom de l'identité culturelle." In *Les mutilations de sexe des femmes aujourd'hui en France,* 9–14. Paris, Tierce.

Pateman, Carole. 1988. *The Sexual Contract.* Cambridge: Polity.

Quiminal, Catherine. 1991. "Les procès de l'excision: Leurs effets pervers . . ." [interview with Josette Trat]. *Les cahiers du Féminisme* 57:6–9.

Saurel, Renée. 1981. *L'enterrée vive.* Geneva/Paris: Slatkine.

———. 1985. *Bouches cousues: Les mutilations sexuelles féminines et le milieu médical.* Paris: Tierce.

Sindzingre, Nicole. 1977. "Le plus et le moins: À propos de l'excision." *Cahiers d'etudes africaines* 17(1):65–75.

Thiam, Awa. 1978. *La parole aux négresses.* Paris: Denoël/Gonthier.

———. 1990. "Sauver des millions de vies, c'est possible dès maintenant." In "Hommes et libertés: Les violences faites aux femmes," special unnumbered issue of *Revue de la Ligue des Droits de l'Homme,* 20–21.

Touré, Coumba. 1984. "Des femmes africaines s'expériment." In *Les mutilations du sexe des femmes aujourd'hui en France,* 15–21. Paris: Tierce.

Verdier, Raymond. 1990. "Chercher remède à l'excision: Une nécessaire concertation." *Droit et cultures: Revue semestrielle d'anthropologie et d'histoire* 20:147–50.

———. 1991a. "Excision, du devoir au crime." *Libération,* July 1.

———. 1991b. "L'exciseuse à la cour d'assises: Le procès de Soko Aramata Keita." *Droit et cultures: Revue semestrielle d'anthropologie et d'histoire* 21:184–87. (Translation, 1992. "The *Exciseuse* in Criminal Court: The Trial of Soko Aramata Keita." In "Passages," suppl. to *PAS News and Events* 3:1, 3.)

Vernier, Dominique. 1990. "Le traitement pénal de l'excision en France: historique." *Droit et cultures: Revue semestrielle d'anthropologie et d'histoire* 29:193–99.

Burying Otieno: The Politics of Gender and Ethnicity in Kenya

Patricia Stamp

> Every woman in Kenya should look at this case keenly. There is no need of getting married if this is the way women will be treated when their husbands die. [WAMBUI OTIENO, press conference in Nairobi, January 12, 1987]

Introduction

In 1987 a Kenyan widow was taken to court by her dead husband's family in a sensational contest over the burial of his remains. Wambui Otieno, the wife of a prominent criminal lawyer, S. M. Otieno, became the eye of a storm about customary law, women's rights, and intertribal marriages following the lawyer's death intestate in December 1986. Wambui is a member of the Kikuyu ethnic group; Otieno was a Luo. Otieno's clan, Umira Kager, blocked the widow's plans to bury her husband in Nairobi, the home where he

My thanks and appreciation go to Wambui Otieno for her willingness to meet with me several times in the summer of 1989, to discuss her experiences at length, and to comment upon an earlier draft of this paper. The interpretation of the case is mine alone, however, as are any inaccuracies in the telling.

[*Signs: Journal of Women in Culture and Society* 1991, vol. 16, no. 4]

had lived out his married and professional life and raised fifteen children and where he had asked to be buried. A series of court cases, involving twelve separate court actions and concluding in May 1987 with a Court of Appeal ruling, awarded the custody of Otieno's remains to his clansmen for burial in his birthplace in Western Kenya according to Luo custom.[1]

Wambui's lawyers argued that Otieno had, through his choices of partner, Christian beliefs, life-style, and residence, forsaken tribal custom[2] for a modern life and that customary Luo burial law therefore had no jurisdiction in his case; rather, Kenya's common law applied. Otieno's clan asserted that, on the contrary, Otieno's birth and upbringing as a Luo was paramount. Kenyan legal statutes do not spell out clearly which legal system takes precedence in a clash between common and customary law; the courts chose to come down on the side of "custom" as defined by the clansmen. Their decisions set back women's rights and the development of a national, progressive jurisprudence in Kenya, while fanning the country's ethnic tensions. The funeral in the clan's district was treated as a triumphant homecoming and a vindication of Luo culture and values. Wambui refused to attend the ceremony as custom required of widows; Otieno was thus, ironically, buried as a single man.

During the five months that the burial issue dominated the headlines, Wambui found herself castigated by the presiding High Court judge for her testimony, vilified by national politicians and the press, and rendered a folk villain for over a million Luo Kenyans. How a widow could experience such an ordeal in contemporary Kenya, why there was no effective feminist challenge, and what the case meant for the country's politics are the subject of this article. The study first describes the central characters of the burial saga, Wambui and Otieno, and the marriage that epitomized the nationalist sentiments of a newly independent country. It then recounts the court battles that followed Otieno's death, charting the rise of Wambui's notoriety and the parallel emergence of the Umira

[1] While several of Otieno's female Luo relatives supported Umira Kager's cause and spoke as witnesses for the clan in court, the clan actions were from beginning to end a male initiative, conducted on behalf of a patrilineal structure as part of a patriarchal discourse. (See nn. 11 and 15 below on patriliny and patriarchy, respectively.) The term "clansmen" is therefore used deliberately.

[2] While the term "tribe" has fallen into disrepute among scholars for its connotations of backwardness and has been replaced by "ethnic group," "tribalism" is a word widely used in Kenya to explain and denounce ethnic rivalry. At the same time, however, it is becoming fashionable to be attached to the culture of one's "tribe," as the Wambui case demonstrated. I argue that such concepts are historically constructed in a dynamic ideological process.

Kager clan as the arbiter of Luo custom. How the Kenyan women's movement was silenced in the public debate surrounding the issue is a significant aspect of this narrative. Following an account of the staged drama of Otieno's funeral, the article explores the social, economic, and political implications of the case, focusing on the use of gender relations in clan and ethnic politics. It concludes with reflections on the form of feminist struggle in contemporary Africa as revealed by Wambui's ordeal.

The Otieno burial saga touches on the important question of the relation between women and the state. Analysis of the case displays three themes that illuminate the complexity of this relationship and the subtle ways in which gender relations are implicated in political processes at every level of Kenyan society. Woven through the account that follows, the themes draw upon important findings from several relevant fields of inquiry: the study of African legal systems; the study of precolonial African gender relations and their transformations from the colonial era to the present; and the study of African political economy.

The first theme is the dynamic nature of "custom" and "tradition." Far from being timeless essences called from the precolonial past, they are potent inventions of the present, constructed to serve the interests of protagonists on the modern political stage.[3] The Umira Kager clan manipulated the language of tradition masterfully during the court proceedings; the first to manipulate the idea of tradition, however, had been the colonialists themselves. Customary law, as distinct from precolonial jurisprudence, was introduced in tandem with British common and statutory law in the colonial era as a tool for pacifying and governing the colonized peoples. While elements of precolonial jurisprudence survive in customary law, they have been recruited to serve the needs of the capitalist colonial and postcolonial states. One of the greatest needs was to control and subordinate women, who in many precolonial African societies frequently enjoyed considerable autonomy and political

---

[3] For important anthropological analyses of this process, see David Parkin, *Palms, Wine, and Witnesses: Public Spirit and Private Gain in an African Farming Community* (San Francisco: Chandler, 1972); Jack Glazier, *Land and the Uses of Tradition among the Mbeere of Kenya* (Lanham, Md.: University Press of America, 1985); Martin Chanock, *Law, Custom and Social Order: The Colonial Experience in Malawi and Zambia* (Cambridge: Cambridge University Press, 1985); and Sally Falk Moore, *Social Facts and Fabrications: "Customary" Law on Kilimanjaro, 1880–1980* (Cambridge: Cambridge University Press, 1986). I develop the argument in the context of Kikuyu women's organizations and village gender relations in Patricia Stamp, *Technology, Gender and Power in Africa* (Ottawa: International Development Research Centre, 1989), 100–103.

power.[4] It is for this reason that customary law, as codified by the colonial authorities and later by independent Kenya's lawmakers,[5] ignores or subverts the rights of women that had been enshrined in precolonial jurisprudence.[6] Common law, on the other hand, underpins women's strivings for rights in the contemporary state.[7]

[4] Women's autonomy and political power through much of sub-Saharan Africa in the precolonial era, and their subsequent declining position, have been well documented in a number of historical and anthropological studies. Contributing to this consensus are, e.g., Ifi Amadiume, *Male Daughters, Female Husbands: Gender and Sex in an African Society* (London: Zed Books, 1987); Regina Smith Oboler, *Women, Power and Economic Change: The Nandi of Kenya* (Stanford, Calif.: Stanford University Press, 1985); Karen Sacks, "An Overview of Women and Power in Africa," in *Perspectives on Power: Women in Africa, Asia, and Latin America,* ed. Jean O'Barr (Durham, N.C.: Duke University Center for International Studies, 1982), 1–10; Achola Pala Okeyo, "Daughters of the Lakes and Rivers: Colonization and the Land Rights of Luo Women," in *Women and Colonization: Anthropological Perspectives,* ed. Mona Etienne and Eleanor Leacock (New York: Praeger, 1980), 186–213; Mona Etienne, "Women and Men, Cloth and Colonization: The Transformation of Production-Distribution Relations among the Baule (Ivory Coast)," in Etienne and Leacock, eds., 214–38; Judith Van Allen, " 'Sitting on a Man': Colonialism and the Lost Political Institutions of Igbo Women," *Canadian Journal of African Studies* 6, no. 2 (1972): 165–82.

[5] See Eugene Cotran, *The Law of Marriage and Divorce,* vol. 1, and *The Law of Succession,* vol. 2, of *Restatement of African Law: Kenya* (London: Sweet & Maxwell, 1968, 1969), and *Casebook on Kenya Customary Law* (Abingdon, Oxfordshire: Professional Books; Nairobi: Nairobi University Press, 1989).

[6] This point is made in several of the case studies presented in Margaret Jean Hay and Marcia Wright, eds., *African Women and the Law: Historical Perspectives,* Boston University Papers on Africa, vol. 7 (Boston: Boston University African Studies Center, 1982). See esp. Margaret Jean Hay ("Women as Owners, Occupants, and Managers of Property in Colonial Western Kenya," 110–23), who argues that the dislocations of colonial political economy "provoked a clear conservative backlash from Luo men, and from male elders in particular, and their desires to reestablish control over women influenced the codification of Luo customary law undertaken in the 1950s" (117).

[7] For an important discussion of the social, economic, and legal aspects of widowhood in changing African society, see Betty Potash, ed., *Widows in African Societies: Choices and Constraints* (Stanford, Calif.: Stanford University Press, 1986). The encounter between customary and common law in the Wambui case finds an interesting parallel in the case of a divorced Indian Muslim woman, Shahbano, who sought maintenance from her husband, a case whose complexities and contradictions are explored in an excellent recent article: Zakia Pathak and Rajeswari Sunder Rajan, " 'Shahbano,' " *Signs: Journal of Women in Culture and Society* 14, no. 3 (Spring 1989): 558–82. They argue that codifications of "personal laws" by colonial rulers in India "historically have not benefited women"; rather, they have "reduced the heterogeneity, contextualization, and variety of traditional interpretations, and produced 'consequences of domination' " (576). See Edward Said, *Orientalism* (New York: Vintage, 1979), for an important discussion of the part played by colonially created discourses of tradition in "the enormously systematic discipline" of European rule (3).

The contest between common law and customary law in Wambui's case was a struggle within the state over the definition and control of gender relations. This struggle demonstrates the theoretical point that the state is not a monolithic entity but a contradictory, disunified set of structures, processes, and discourses, the different parts of which often act at cross purposes.[8]

Such a view of the state makes it possible to explore the complex relation between the governing regime and other politically powerful elements of society. This relationship is the second theme raised in analyzing Wambui's case. Characterizing the relationship is a "collaborative hegemony" by which the male-dominated kin group, "that state-within-a-state," is given patriarchal power in the service of the state.[9] The state cannot rule by repression alone, hence ideological domination is one of its most important aims. Such domination relies on the vital link between state power and the realm of culture and family, as political theorists have argued.[10]

In contemporary Africa, significant subnational political structures are drawn into this relationship of collaborative hegemony. Clans and lineages, formerly independent local polities, are now subjected to the political and economic imperatives of the overarching nation-state.[11] Clan and lineage politics are being reconstituted in this national context; indeed, their articulation with national-level political economy gives them a new force. While the ruling regime seeks to control and direct ethnic and kin

---

[8] Nicos Poulantzas, *The Crisis of the Dictatorships* (London: New Left Books, 1976), 82. Poulantzas develops his ideas on the state in an important later work, *State, Power, Socialism* (London: New Left Books, 1978). I review the debate about the nature of the postcolonial African state in Patricia Stamp, "Governing Thika: Dilemmas of Municipal Politics in Kenya" (Ph.D. diss., University of London, 1981). See Peter Anyang' Nyong'o, ed., *Popular Struggles for Democracy in Africa* (London: Zed Books, 1987) for recent analyses of the African postcolonial state.

[9] The quoted material is from Pathak and Rajan, 569.

[10] Gramsci designates this realm as "civil society" (Antonio Gramsci, *Selections from the Prison Notebooks*, ed. and trans. Quintin Hoare and Geoffrey Nowell Smith [New York: International Publishers, 1971], 12–13 and passim). Althusser posits families as "ideological state apparatuses" (Louis Althusser, "Ideology and Ideological State Apparatuses," in his *Lenin and Philosophy and Other Essays*, trans. Ben Brewster [London: New Left Books, 1971], 123–73). The notion of ideological state apparatuses has been much debated by feminists: see Michèle Barrett, *Women's Oppression Today: Problems in Marxist Feminist Analysis* (London: Verso, 1980) for a discussion of feminists' engagement with Althusser's thinking.

[11] A clan is a large kinship group that traces its ancestry to a common founder, through either the male line (patrilineal) or the female line (matrilineal). All Kenyan ethnic groups are patrilineal. A lineage is a smaller group of kin, often a subgroup of a clan, that traces its ancestry by known links to a founder in the more recent past.

politics, it must nevertheless work with the subnational structures to retain its legitimacy.[12]

Gender relations are as central to lineage and clan politics now as they were in the past. Women have always played a vital role as wives of patrilineages,[13] both in creating networks of social and economic ties and in providing certain material and social benefits (it is this role that is recognized and compensated through the institution of bridewealth).[14] Moreover, women have exercised political authority, as sisters of their natal lineage and through their elders' organizations in their marital lineage. Under the increasingly stringent and competitive circumstances of postcolonial capitalism, however, patrilineages are becoming more patriarchal,[15] intensifying control over lineage wives and undermining the power and rights to resources of lineage sisters.[16]

---

[12] Ethnic politics and their relation to class structures have been considered by political scientists, although without much theoretical rigor. Mahmoud Mamdani, *Politics and Class Formation in Uganda* (New York: Monthly Review Press, 1976), probably remains the most insightful case study; see Richard Sandbrook's chapter on "Class, Tribe and Politics," in his *The Politics of Africa's Economic Stagnation* (Cambridge: Cambridge University Press, 1985), 63–82, for an interesting recent argument on the subject. There is silence, however, on the ideology and politics regarding the constituent elements of ethnic groups—lineages and clans.

[13] This is the term by which I designate lineages that trace descent through the male line, i.e., patrilineal descent groups.

[14] Patricia Stamp, "Kikuyu Women's Self Help Groups: Towards an Understanding of the Relation between Sex-Gender System and Mode of Production in Africa," in *Women and Class in Africa*, ed. Claire Robertson and Iris Berger (New York: Holmes & Meier, 1986), 27–46, esp. 32–37. Among the many studies that identify the pivotal position of lineage wives, Jane Guyer's subtle analysis of changing relations among the Beti of Cameroon is pertinent here (see "Beti Widow Inheritance and Marriage Law," in Potash, ed., 193–219). For the structural importance of Luo lineage wives, see Okeyo (n. 4 above), 191–96. See also the studies cited in n. 4 above (Amadiume; Oboler; Sacks, "An Overview of Women and Power in Africa"; Etienne; and Van Allen), all of which also discuss the structural importance of lineage wives.

[15] Agreeing with Rosalynd Coward that the term patriarchy has "a loose currency" (*Patriarchal Precedents: Sexuality and Social Relations* [London: Routledge & Kegan Paul, 1983], 270), I am using the concept "patriarchy" in a precise and restricted sense. Patriarchy is used in this article to denote not a general political system, but an attribute of gender relations in the family and kin group. It involves the control of women and management of gender relations by a male head of household or patrilineal elder. The patriarchal gender system articulates with class relations: it is a necessary mechanism for maintenance and development of an extended family's socioeconomic position in a stratified social system. Those many African societies that were previously unstratified have developed class systems with the incursion of capitalism, and development of the patriarchal tendencies in African gender relations has been a structurally important part of this process.

[16] Karen Sacks, *Sisters and Wives: The Past and Future of Sexual Inequality* (Westport, Conn.: Greenwood, 1979); Fiona MacKenzie, "Gender and Land Rights:

The Umira Kager clan demonstrated through its actions the importance placed on the control of women. It advocated a "customary" funerary procedure and set of behaviors for widows designed to put Otieno's family and resources at the disposition of the patrilineage. The opprobrium Wambui garnered for refusing to play the role cast for her marked the emergence of a virulent patriarchal element in popular discourse. For its part, the ruling regime revealed its collaborative role through its involvement in the court proceedings and in the gender discourse that grew up around the issue.[17]

The third theme central to the analysis of the Wambui case is the concrete significance for late 1980s Kenyan politics of struggles over "tradition" and women's place. At the level of ethnic politics, the burial battle created a legitimate vehicle for the promotion of Luo interests, both within the group and vis-à-vis Kenya's other groups. The proper, "traditional" role of wives, mothers, and widows was safer to champion than more overt claims to political power. At the level of national politics, the case was fraught with implications, revealing the susceptibilities of Daniel arap Moi's presidency. The member of a minor and less educated ethnic group, Moi has had to fight continually for the legitimacy of his leadership. His balancing act has entailed increasing political repression; he has also played against each other Kenya's two chief ethnic adversaries, the Kikuyu and the Luo. Moi's challenge has been to contain the formerly dominant Kikuyu without arousing them to revolt, while maintaining the Luo as quiescent allies, supportive of his regime but not so powerful as to defy it. It was in the regime's interest to see yet another curtailment of Kikuyu potency, especially at the hands of the Luo. Furthermore, Wambui's defeat was part and parcel of Moi's suppression of dissent. Wambui associated her cause explicitly with the radical politics of Kenya's independence struggle; these radical politics are evoked in contemporary democratic struggle against Moi's regime. A victory for her would thus have carried a symbolic importance beyond the immediate issues of the case and could not be allowed.

In short, while Wambui's case is a "women's issue" par excellence, it also displays some of the central preoccupations of Kenyan

---

Murang'a District, Kenya," *Journal of Peasant Studies* 17, no. 4 (July 1990): 609–43. See also Carla Freeman, "Colonialism and the Formation of Gender Hierarchies in Kenya," *Critique of Anthropology* 7, no. 3 (Winter 1987–88): 33–50, for a useful review of works on Kenya that make this argument.

[17] Several informants, including Wambui, indicated that the government intervened directly in the case through instructions to the court. The account below details several instances of pressure exerted on Wambui herself.

politics in the 1980s: the struggle over the place of tradition in a modern nation; the shifting fortunes of Kenya's leading ethnic groups; and increasing repression. The case also reveals the politicization of the judiciary in the context of an ineffective legislative process. Finally, the clan's actions demonstrate the competition for scarce economic resources that is vigorously waged in Kenya's public arenas. The analysis of Wambui's battle to bury Otieno is therefore necessarily an account of contemporary Kenyan political processes and demonstrates the value of combining the tools of feminist and political science scholarship.

Wambui's defense of her rights according to the principles of common law posed a challenge to every level of Kenyan society: family, lineage and clan, ethnic group, and nation. Although her actions occasioned a significant attempt by the state to impose stricter control over gender relations and women and although she lost in court, Wambui's ordeal can be viewed with a measure of optimism. Precisely because it exposed and challenged the increasing oppression of women in postcolonial Kenya, it opened the political space for future resistance. As well, the very act of Wambui's defiance in court and before the media says something important about African women's political agency.[18] Finally, the clan did not succeed in its central aim of controlling Wambui and gaining access to her property: she and her family remain independent.

A "modern" marriage

Wambui Waiyaki and Silvanus Melea Otieno were introduced in the early 1950s by her father, a senior African police officer in the colonial administration who had employed Otieno as a native clerical interpreter in the colonial Supreme Court. They commenced their unusual relationship ten years later, in the heady time before Kenya's independence, marrying in August 1963 under the colonial Marriage Act.

[18] Women have engaged in resistance against the political domination and economic exploitation of African societies since the colonial era, although it has been left to feminist scholars to recognize the existence of these acts. See, e.g., Maud Shimwaayi Muntemba, "Women and Agricultural Change in the Railway Region of Zambia: Dispossession and Counterstrategies, 1930–1970," in *Women in Africa: Studies in Social and Economic Change,* ed. Nancy J. Hafkin and Edna G. Bay (Stanford, Calif.: Stanford University Press, 1976), 83–103; Marjorie Mbilinyi, " 'City' and 'Countryside' in Colonial Tanganyika," *Economic and Political Weekly* 20, no. 43 (October 26, 1985): 88–96, and "Runaway Wives in Colonial Tanganyika: Forced Labour and Forced Marriage in Rungwe District, 1919–1961," *International Journal of the Sociology of Law* 16 (1988): 1–29; Cora Ann Presley, "Labor Unrest among Kikuyu Women in Colonial Kenya," in Robertson and Berger, eds., 255–73.

Great granddaughter of a famous Kikuyu chief who had been buried alive for his opposition to the British, Wambui continued the family tradition of political activism. Born to Presbyterian parents in Kiambu District (southern Kikuyuland) in 1936, she was given a good education and earned a diploma in leadership and community development from a college in Tanganyika. She put this training to work upon her return to Kenya, joining the nationalist movement against colonial rule. According to her testimony in the burial case, her participation in the Mau Mau uprising led to three years' detention by the colonial authorities in the mid-1950s. Upon her release, she joined the more moderate Nairobi People's Convention party, serving it and the subsequently formed national party, Kenya African National Union (KANU), in several official posts. Although she stood unsuccessfully for parliament in the 1969 and 1974 elections, she continued her political involvement and held leadership positions at different times in both of the major umbrella women's groups, Maendeleo ya Wanawake and the National Council of Women of Kenya (NCWK). She was a Kenyan delegate to the 1975 United Nations World Conference on Women in Copenhagen that inaugurated the United Nations Decade for Women and served as the treasurer to the secretariat of Forum '85, the mammoth nongovernmental organizations' conference held in Nairobi in conjunction with the third United Nations World Conference on Women that marked the end of the Decade.

S. M., as he was known, was born in Nyamila village in Nyalgunga Sublocation of Siaya District in 1931, the seventh of twelve children. Following a mission school education, he worked briefly in the law courts before joining the nationalist movement, becoming assistant treasurer of a country branch of the Kenya African Union, precursor of KANU. In 1953 he won a scholarship to study law at the University of Bombay, India. He returned to Kenya in 1960 after receiving his degree and being called to the bar there. In 1961 he was admitted to the bar of the High Court of Kenya and opened a private practice the same year. He gave up his practice for public service between 1963 and 1968, serving as deputy town clerk in the Luo town of Kisumu and later as principal legal assistant to the East African Common Services Organization (the region's short-lived "Common Market"). From the reestablishment of his private practice until his death, Otieno built a reputation as an outstanding criminal lawyer.

In his Indian education, his work and leisure, and his life with Wambui, Otieno remained marginal as a Luo. He visited his ancestral home only a handful of times during his adult life, chiefly for emergencies or family funerals, and established no rural home there as urban Kenyans commonly do. His marriage to Wambui was from the outset a controversial and highly symbolic one. Formed during the time of closest alliance between the Kikuyu and the Luo, it stood for many Kenyans' aspirations to a national rather than ethnic identity; it also displayed the difficulties inherent in realizing these aspirations. Even in Otieno's lifetime, his lineage treated the marriage as an affront to the family and clan; according to Wambui's court testimony, the union was never recognized by Otieno's brother, Joash Ochieng' Ougo, one of the clan's two protagonists in the case. Otieno accepted as his own Wambui's four children born out of wedlock, and he and Wambui had five children of their own (all were baptized with a Christian and either a Kikuyu or a Luo name). In addition, they fostered the six orphaned children of a family friend.

In 1986, according to Wambui, Otieno had premonitions of his death.[19] One of the perplexing aspects of the saga was the failure of one of Kenya's most sophisticated lawyers to draw up a will. Wambui argues that Otieno felt a will would too easily be overturned in a clan contest, which he anticipated. Whether he thought his intestate death was better protection is a matter of speculation: it is worth noting, however, that while the clan was able to win his body, they did not gain possession of his estate, as many of their pronouncements indicated they hoped to do.[20]

Wambui, the courts and the public

S. M. Otieno died of a heart attack December 20, 1986. Soon after, Wambui announced her intention to bury her husband on January 3 according to his verbal wish, at the suburban Nairobi farm not far from his residence.[21] Her intention was immediately challenged by Otieno's eldest surviving brother, Joash Ochieng' Ougo. He and Omolo Siranga, the Nairobi spokesman for the Umira Kager clan, announced competing plans to bury Otieno in Nyamila village and

[19] Wambui Otieno, personal communication, June 1989.

[20] If this was indeed Otieno's opinion about wills, he was not alone in holding it. The final Appeal Court judgment awarding custody of Otieno's body to the clan concluded with the remark that "Parliament may have to consider legislating separately for burial matters covering a deceased's wishes and the position of his widow. . . . It is now clear to us that it is not sufficient to write wills. There are often disputes about burials" (Cotran, *Casebook on Kenya Customary Law* [n. 5 above], 345. See also n. 22 below).

[21] This was not his residential property in the rich Nairobi suburb of Langata, but a small farm within the city limits, a few miles beyond the suburb. The question of whether the house he built on this farm was a "home" in Luo terms, and hence a suitable place for burial, is discussed below.

their intention to claim the body from the mortuary.[22] After mediation by prominent politicians failed, each side hired a lawyer. Wambui filed suit in the High Court to claim her husband's body from the mortuary and received a favorable ruling December 31 from the first judge to be involved in the case. Subsequently refusing the clan's counteraffidavit, he denied the brother and the clan standing on the burial matter. The clan lawyer and the two spokesmen then appealed the ruling to the Court of Appeal (Kenya's highest court), and succeeded in obtaining a reversal of the High Court decision and an injunction against Wambui's burial plans.

On January 13, 1987, the three presiding Appeal Court judges ordered a full High Court trial (an "evidentiary hearing") by a different judge.[23] Furthermore, they made a ruling regarding the applicability of Kenya's written law in the case. Wambui's lawyer John Khaminwa had argued that written law takes precedence over customary law where there are applicable statutes—in this case, the Law of Succession Act, whereby the surviving spouse as next of kin has administrative priority.[24] The Appeal Court dismissed the applicability of the Succession Act and the relevance of the Otieno marriage under the Marriage Act. Instead, the court defined the case in terms of two issues: whether Otieno was subject to Luo customary law, and the nature of that law in the case of burials. In doing so, they placed the court case firmly on the terrain of the clan's claims, excluding from argument Wambui's chief legal

[22] Details of the case are taken from the Kenyan press—specifically, the *Weekly Review* and the *Daily Nation* (see the compilation of articles and court proceedings published by the *Daily Nation*, *S. M. Otieno: Kenya's Unique Burial Saga* [Nairobi: Nation Newspapers Publication, 1988]). Testimony, lawyers' arguments, and court judgments are cited from these sources. As well, references are made to the full text of the Appeal Court ruling in the case of *Otieno v. Ougo and Siranga* (Civil Appeal no. 31 of 1987), published in Cotran, *Casebook on Kenya Customary Law*, 331–45. See John W. Van Doren, "Death African Style: The Case of S. M. Otieno," *American Journal of Comparative Law* 36 (1988): 329–50, esp. 338–42, for a concise summary of the court cases. Although Wambui, as an educated, articulate public figure, is an important contributor to the narrative, I do not intend to burden her with the biography of a "heroine" who is "the origin and repository of her story," to paraphrase Pathak and Rajan's treatment of Shahbano (n. 7 above). Like them, I endeavor instead to interpret the protagonist from "the crises her legal actions produce" (Pathak and Rajan, 570–71).

[23] The court made the technical point that this was not a retrial as no trial had yet taken place.

[24] "The hierarchy of sources of law in Kenya [are] (1) the Constitution, (2) the written laws as applicable including both Kenyan and English statutes . . . , (3) the common law of England subject to qualifications necessitated by local circumstances, if none of the above are applicable, then (4) customary law if one or more parties is subject to it" (Van Doren, 341).

weapon: the precedence of statutory and common law over customary law.

Wambui went back to court to prevent the clan from claiming the body, and Otieno's embalmed body remained in the city mortuary, a magnet for public attention in the ensuing months. The trial began January 22 before Justice S. E. O. Bosire, a Luhya. (The Luhya, like the Kikuyu, belong to the Bantu cultural grouping, but they are situated in Western Kenya adjacent to the Luo, who belong to the unrelated Nilotic cultural grouping. The Luhya have often acted as political brokers between the Kikuyu and the Luo, Kenya's dominant ethnic groups, particularly in the Moi era.) Running for seventeen days, the courtroom drama was a microcosm of the social, legal, and intellectual cross-currents in contemporary Kenyan society, involving an eclectic array of witnesses and authorities, from a Luo grave digger and a German teacher to anthropologists and philosophers, Shakespeare and the Bible. Bosire reiterated the Appeal Court's definition of the case and ruled that the Succession Act did not deal with burial. As there was no common law of burial, Luo custom applied. Bosire asserted, furthermore, that Otieno had intended to be buried at his ancestral home according to that custom. The judge consequently found in favor of the clan.

During the High Court trial, Wambui emerged as an almost mythical figure in the popular imagination. She pleaded her case from a moral position as a mother, wife, Christian, and loyal Kenyan citizen, rather than from overt feminist arguments. In Maxine Molyneux's terms, she focused on the "practical gender issues" of her case (those related to women's responsibilities stemming from the sexual division of labor, such as family welfare) rather than "strategic gender issues" (such as political inequality and institutional discrimination),[25] even though she was no stranger to feminist polemics. She spoke out in court and to the press with spirit and political skill. Claiming the authority of a founder of the nation—"I fought for independence and this judiciary"—she spoke eloquently on behalf of Otieno's standing as a cosmopolitan Kenyan and her rights as a widow. In her refutation of the clan's arguments that Otieno was a loyal clan member, she showed a deep knowledge of both Luo and Kikuyu customs and of Kenyan jurisprudence. The exchanges between her and clan lawyer Richard Otieno Kwach were acerbic and sometimes humorous: they gained her the judge's

[25] Maxine Molyneux, "Mobilization without Emancipation? Women's Interests, the State, and Revolution in Nicaragua," *Feminist Studies* 11, no. 2 (Summer 1985): 227–54, esp. 230–35. Molyneux argues that it is impossible to generalize about "women's interests"; it is to escape from the appearance of "false homogeneity" that she specifies these two categories of gender issues (232).

censure for behavior "unbecoming of a litigant."[26] Following is an example of such an exchange.

> *Kwach.* You said he used to read Shakespeare, did you say Julius Caesar? What else did he read?
> *Wambui.* I said Bernard Shaw, a bit of Perry Mason. . . .
> *Kwach.* You said he watched football on television because of violence at the City Stadium?
> *Wambui.* Yes.
> *Kwach.* And you said because of all these activities he had severed his relationship and contacts with his tribe?
> *Wambui.* You are too much of a Luo.
> *Kwach.* I too read Shakespeare but I am still a Luo.[27]

Wambui noted the Umira Kager clan's propensity to contest wills for financial gain and said this was why Otieno did not write one. She remarked that the clan "is notorious for collecting money purportedly for burial but for spending it." Citing the excessive expenditures on transporting another clan member home for burial, she said, "One would imagine they were going to Egypt or Europe! I don't want to be rude, My Lord, but the clan would have disputed the will."[28]

Once the High Court decision went against her, Wambui startled and titillated the huge audience following the case by declaring that she had been "born again" in her Presbyterian church. Consoled by the church's leaders, she told them that it was God who gave her Otieno, and only He could take away what He had provided. "Tomorrow I will go to court but this time I am going there with Jesus." Her message for the clan: "Go and tell Joash Ochieng' to get saved."[29] In claiming the authority of Jesus, she tapped what is possibly the most important strand of political dissidence inside the country today: Kenya's own "liberation theology," preached against the political repression of the Moi regime from the pulpits of several different faiths.[30]

---

[26] *Weekly Review* (February 20, 1987), 7.

[27] Cross-examination on the third day of the High Court trial (cited in *S. M. Otieno*, 29).

[28] Ibid., 30.

[29] Ibid., 113.

[30] Kenya's priests have increasingly spoken out against political repression in Kenya since the mid-1980s, to the point that by 1990 they constituted, in the eyes of both the Moi regime and ordinary Kenyans, an unofficial opposition in the one-party state (see Patricia Stamp, "The Politics of Dissent in Moi's Kenya," *Current History* 90, no. 556 [May 1991], in press).

Both in and out of court, Wambui thus demonstrated a shrewd understanding of the currents and vehicles of political discourse in Kenya.[31] She initiated a stream of legal actions, protests, commentaries, and press conferences throughout the five-month saga; her refusal to be silent outraged the male protagonists, authorities, and public more than almost any aspect of the affair. As well, she projected a powerful physical presence, with flamboyant displays of grief and anger.[32] It is interesting that the press photographed her endlessly but quoted her sparsely, reserving their newspaper columns for lengthy commentary on clan pronouncements. Meant to be seen but not heard, she nevertheless dramatically conveyed her message to the nation.

Wambui's popularity as a villain was not, however, seriously challenged in any quarter. Ironically, in the country that hosted the United Nations World Conference on Women at the end of the Decade for Women in 1985, women are still all too easily characterized as negative and destructive forces. Umira Kager overtly cast Wambui in this light, claiming that she was "bent on wreaking chaos" for the Luo and for Kenya "for personal and selfish reasons."[33] The judges showed conspicuous bias, as Khaminwa protested vehemently. In his decision in the burial dispute, presiding High Court Judge Bosire portrayed Wambui, the plaintiff, as arrogant and wrong-headed, a bad influence on her sons, and fully responsible for the dispute. "Because of the negative attitude she adopted towards the first defendant [Otieno's brother] and other members from the deceased's ancestral home, soon after the death of her husband meaningful discussions were rendered impossible. I should point out here that the plaintiff was not prepared and still is not prepared to accommodate any other person's views with regard to the place of burial of the deceased."[34] This attitude, according to Bosire, "bordered on contempt of court."[35] The judge made it clear that these were grounds to reject her evidence and render a decision against her. In other words, simply by sticking to the position that propelled her to take court action in the first place,

[31] See Ernesto Laclau and Chantal Mouffe, *Hegemony and Socialist Strategy: Towards a Radical Democratic Politics,* trans. Winston Moore and Paul Cammack (London: Verso, 1985), 127–34 and passim, for an analysis of the way in which different forms of struggle may be united at the symbolic level in democratic discourse.

[32] Wambui recounted the singing of a funeral song in the chief justice's office, much to his displeasure (personal communication, July 1989).

[33] *Weekly Review* (February 20, 1987), 9; see also *Weekly Review* (May 15, 1987), 13.

[34] *S. M. Otieno* (n. 22 above), 112.

[35] Ibid., 110.

Wambui caused the court decision to go against her—a sexist Catch-22 if ever there was one, not to mention a misconception of the function of the court by the judge. Wambui appealed Bosire's judgment and the case went back to the Court of Appeal. Over Khaminwa's objections, the same three judges who had ordered the trial presided. On May 15, 1987, they, too, decided in favor of the clan. In dismissing Wambui's appeal of Bosire's decision, the judges were silent on Khaminwa's charge that the trial judge had "misdirected himself on his finding that the witnesses were arrogant."[36] Their decision, too, was colored by interpretive terminology: the clan's position was cited as fact, while Wambui's version of events was "alleged," "maintained," or "suggested" by the appellant, her lawyer, or her witnesses.[37]

The lack of vigorous public support for Wambui from her own ethnic group is a problematic and complex issue. While Otieno's entire clan became involved in the case, Wambui had to rely on her children and a few close kin for support. Wambui spoke confidently of her own clan: "I am a Muceera in Kikuyu. . . . They should not think I am alone. I can also call my clansmen out to demonstrate in support as [Umira Kager] have been doing."[38] Yet her patrilineage and other Kikuyu were largely silent on the case. Following early protests by two Kikuyu members of parliament who called the situation "bizarre" and a promotion of "tribal chauvinism at the expense of national integration and harmony," little was heard from Kikuyu political leaders.[39] Their reticence could be interpreted as discomfort with her challenge to patriarchal values and practices, which arc by no means restricted to the Luo.

Wambui herself had another interpretation, however. Reflecting on the experience two years later, she asserted that a substantial amount of material and moral support had been covertly given her by Kikuyu politicians and other prominent figures. She argued that the atmosphere of political repression directed against the Kikuyu prevented them from supporting her openly, especially given the interest in an Umira Kager victory shown by the president. Naming many eminent Kenyan politicians including ministers and the vice president, Wambui stated: "I had all the support I needed, but it was difficult for them to come out and show themselves."[40] Wam-

---

[36] Cotran, *Casebook on Kenya Customary Law* (n. 5 above), 333.

[37] See esp. ibid., 335.

[38] *S. M. Otieno*, 16.

[39] *Weekly Review* (February 20, 1987), 9.

[40] Wambui Otieno, personal communication, July 1989. Wambui referred to the many telegrams sent to the president on the matter, copies of which were also sent to her.

bui's explanation is confirmed by the fact that, at the height of the court battle and the public outcry against her in mid-March, a low-profile fundraising drive for her children's education overseas immediately raised over Sh 200,000 (US$10,000).[41] It is worth noting that the Kenyan judiciary has not been independent of the Moi regime for several years. Either it has been careful not to render decisions unpopular with the regime or it has backtracked once presidential displeasure became known. The judges' reasoned and documented arguments for common law's inapplicability in the Otieno case cannot hide the political nature of their decisions.

When a house is not a home: The invention of Luo tradition

The Umira Kager clan's project in court was to reconstruct S. M. Otieno as a Luo whose primary loyalty, in death as in life, was to clan and patrilineage. A major effect of the clan's argument and the court decisions in the Otieno case was thus the reinforcement of the importance of lineages and clans in contemporary Kenyan life. Further, the clan was established as the voice of authority on Luo custom: Otieno's silence in death became a convenient screen on which a new, exclusive lineage ideology and ethnic nationalism could be projected, in the name of his imagined intentions.[42] (While the clan was the corporate entity formally represented in the court case, it is at the level of the lineage that gender relations are mediated, and rights and responsibilities assigned. I use the term "lineage ideology" to designate the discourse of patriarchal familism, promulgated at all levels of Luo society.) Otieno's life was scrutinized for evidence of clan allegiance; incidents such as his attendance at several family funerals were grasped as proof. Much was made of the testimony of an elderly clan witness—a Siaya gravedigger—who claimed that Otieno had paid traditional bridewealth for his son's wife, although the testimony was not corroborated by any other witnesses.

There was a pedantic and lengthy disquisition on the Luo concept of "home." The clansmen's seemingly absurd argument

[41] *Daily Nation* (March 15, 1987). Although the fund was reported in the paper, Wambui said the money was contributed "behind doors—it was a big crowd but we didn't call the press" (personal communication, July 1989).

[42] David W. Cohen provides an insightful discussion of "the broad struggle for control of the interpretation of every conceivable detail of his life" in "The Living Body and Its Intentions, the Dead Body and Its Disposal: The S. M. Otieno Case in Kenya, December 20, 1986–May 23, 1987" (manuscript, forthcoming as a chapter in a book about the burial saga by David W. Cohen and E. S. Atieno Odhiambo).

that Otieno's matrimonial residence in Nairobi was his "house" but not his "home" was in fact a key component of their strategy to construct Otieno posthumously as a dedicated clan member; their case for claiming Otieno's body was based on the need to bury him at his "ancestral home" according to Luo custom. That the courts supported the argument shows that the strategy worked. The Appeal Court upheld Bosire's ruling that Otieno's home was at Nyamila in Nyalgunga Sublocation, Siaya District, even though "he had no house at his home and had no land registered in his name at his home" and seldom went there.[43]

The Appeal Court's factual finding that Nyamila was Otieno's home did more than win the clan its custody battle: it proved that the clan had won in the protagonists' contest to define tradition. In establishing as fact a whole array of Luo customs presented to the court by the clan lawyer and witnesses, Umira Kager succeeded in refurbishing Luo lineage ideology with a wealth of detail about how things were done in the past, giving their rendition the force of truth. That much of this was invented is evidenced, for example, by Kwach's erroneous assertion that Wambui, by marrying Otieno, had "walked out of her tribe and became a Luo."[44] In no African society does marriage cancel a daughter's membership in her patrilineage: rather, the marriage sets up a complex web of relations between the two lineages.[45] The clan told Wambui that she "must take the Luo as she finds them [and] ought not to have rights which other Luo widows could not ask for";[46] what they were really demanding was that she bow to Luo custom as Umira Kager had defined it.

Umira Kager's claim to an authentic Luo voice was in keeping with the ongoing dynamic construction and reconstruction of Luo identity—a process common to many African peoples but particularly marked among the migratory Nilotic grouping to which the Luo belong.[47] David W. Cohen and E. S. Otieno Odhiambo made this point regarding the Siaya subgroup of which Umira Kager is a part—ironically, just prior to the burial saga: "Satisfactions and meanings are sought by Siaya folk that involve the handling and comprehension of materials from many arenas, and from the past. . . . If there is power in custom in Siaya, it is in the way in which

[43] Cotran, *Casebook on Kenya Customary Law*, 335.

[44] *S. M. Otieno* (n. 22 above), 96.

[45] Stamp, "Kikuyu Women's Self Help Groups" (n. 14 above), 32–34; Sacks, *Sisters and Wives* (n. 16 above), 109–23.

[46] Cotran, *Casebook on Kenya Customary Law* (n. 5 above), 335.

[47] See D. W. Cohen, "The River-Lake Nilotes from the Fifteenth to the Nineteenth Century," in *Zamani: A Survey of East African History*, ed. B. A. Ogot (Nairobi: East African Publishing House, 1974), 135–49.

debates over the authenticity and purpose of custom expose custom as an aspect of authority. . . . Such discourses within Siaya work upon the little and often intimate solidarities and oppositions among kin and comrades that give form and direction to Luo culture and society."[48]

Disputes about custom have been the stuff of village litigation at least since the colonial era;[49] the difference in this case is that for the first time they became part of a *national* discourse of tradition, with certain contested elements of gender relations and ethnicity established as traditional "facts," available for any other ethnic group to appropriate in future battles involving gender and ethnicity. Many eminent Kenyans entered the discourse. Henry Odera Oruka, a philosophy professor at Nairobi University who according to his testimony specializes in traditional customs and philosophy, lent the authority of his discipline to lengthy pronouncements about Luo customs and morality.[50] The Appeal Court judgment gave the new ethnic essentialism exemplified by Oruka's testimony the weight of common law: "At present there is no way in which an African citizen of Kenya can divest himself of the association with the tribe of his father if those customs are patrilineal. It is thus clear that Mr. Otieno having been born and bred a Luo remained a member of the Luo tribe and subject to the customary law of the Luo people."[51] Henceforth, the court said, customary law is to carry greater authority. Traditional leaders were implicitly encouraged to participate in the manipulation of custom: "The elders, who are the custodians of African customary law, assisted by the intelligentsia, by the church and other organizations owe it to themselves and to their communities to ensure that customary laws keep abreast of positive modern trends so as to make it possible for courts to be guided by customary laws."[52]

The good Kenyan citizen, promoted in political discourse between independence in 1963 and the 1980s, was the progressive individual who transcended "tribalism." The Otieno presented by Wambui and her lawyer was precisely such a citizen, a man who "lived and died as a Kenyan rather than as a Luo."[53] The new model of the male citizen that emerged from this case, however, is a man who juggles progress with tradition but who fulfills his

[48] David William Cohen and E. S. Atieno Odhiambo, *Siaya: The Historical Anthropology of an African Landscape* (London: James Currey, 1989), 131–32.

[49] See Glazier (n. 3 above); Parkin (n. 3 above); and Chanock (n. 3 above).

[50] *S. M. Otieno*, 79–82.

[51] Cotran, *Casebook on Kenya Customary Law*, 336.

[52] Ibid., 344.

[53] *Weekly Review* (May 15, 1987), 15.

responsibility to the "tribe of his father" above all. In this discourse, the female Kenyan citizen is exemplary only through acquiescence and the submersion of her own interests in those of the patrilineage. The courts made this clear in accepting the clan's argument that "the wishes of a widow and children are relevant if consistent with custom, otherwise they are irrelevant."[54] Kenya's constitution exempts "personal laws," including those governing burial, from the constitutional clause banning discriminatory laws.[55] The Appeal Court's judgment was complacent about this discrimination enshrined in the constitution; further, it dismissed from consideration Wambui's status as a Kikuyu. "The appellant as the deceased's wife has to be considered in the context of all wives married to Luo men irrespective of their lifestyles who become subject to the customary laws. The fact that her marriage was a mixed one would not confer on her any special status under the Luo customary law. Dealing with the argument of discrimination in general we would refer to the [section] of the constitution of Kenya which allows for discriminatory rules respecting burial. At the moment there is no evidence of hardship felt by this particular community."[56]

Not surprisingly, Luo women elders independent of the Umira Kager clan, prominent professional women, and authorities on Luo gender relations such as Achola Pala Okeyo were not called to court to substantiate the Appeal Court's claim that Luo women feel no hardship as a result of the discriminatory laws. Okeyo's work shows that precolonial gender relations, including those of the Luo, were not as unidimensional as the clan's arguments and the court judgments implied.[57] She argues that gender relations were complex and counterbalancing and provided considerable opportunities for women to exercise authority and autonomy. But it was a contradictory complexity:

> While the dominance of a patrilineal ideology is suggested
> by postmarital residence patterns, property rights, and the
> status of children, women occupy an important structural
> position in the Luo lineage system. As mothers and wives

[54] Cotran, *Casebook on Kenya Customary Law*, 344.

[55] Provision S.82(1) of the Constitution of Kenya prevents discrimination in law, except as allowed under sections S.82(4), (5), and (8). Personal laws, as set out in S.82(4), are those which make provision "with respect to adoption, marriage, divorce, burial, devolution of property on death."

[56] Cotran, *Casebook on Kenya Customary Law* (n. 5 above), 343–44.

[57] See, e.g., Kwach's overview of Luo women's passive role in the "disciplined order which has been working since time immemorial" (*S. M. Otieno* [n. 22 above], 96–97).

and to a lesser extent as daughters their productive and reproductive roles are crucial for the continuity of the lineage, a core concept in Luo social structure. While these roles unequivocally testify to the structural importance of women among Joluo they also represent contradictions and conflicts in power relations between men and women as political and economic actors within the context of the lineage system.[58]

It was the contradiction between patrilineal ideology and women's structural importance that opened the door to more patriarchal, sexist interpretations of gender relations in the present, as exemplified by the clan's construction of them in the Otieno case. The court judgments are a striking example of the way in which the historic position of women is shorn of its complexities and contradictions in the construction of customary law, to the detriment of women's standing and rights.

Where was Kenya's women's movement?

It was evident from the outset that Wambui's case was a major feminist issue. The women's movement in Kenya indeed tried to act on Wambui's behalf, but the case precipitated a political crisis among women that rendered the movement ineffective. Individual women politicians or public officials who attempted to intervene in the public debate soon discovered it was political suicide to champion Wambui. Formal feminist organizations in Kenya, as elsewhere in Africa, are weak and easily co-opted, and overt organizing to protect and advance women's human rights faces an uphill road. To use Maxine Molyneux's terminology, "strategic gender issues" derived from women's subordination cannot easily be raised without triggering a backlash from sexist forces in society.[59] The language of Western feminism is easily dismissed as yet another imperialist tool in the oppression of Third World people and a cause espoused by alienated and selfish elite African women. In this discourse, anti-imperialist ideology is articulated with right-wing and sexist political positions in a way that mystifies and discredits feminism and that stymies direct action in the name of women's rights. Any action on behalf of women, whether or not it

[58] Okeyo (n. 4 above), 191. The prefix "jo" designates "the people of" the Kenyan branch of the Luo ethnic group in strict Luo parlance.

[59] Molyneux (n. 25 above), 232–33.

is inspired by Western feminism, is tarred with the feminist brush. High Court Judge Bosire, in the course of discrediting Wambui's testimony and censuring her court behavior, disparaged her lawyer's "support for feministic causes." With feminism a pejorative term, women have a hard time making abstract arguments for their rights.

The dilemma of Kenyan feminists is best captured by the role of Grace Ogot in the burial saga. One of Kenya's two women members of parliament at that time, she is the author of some of the country's most popular novels and the first woman writer in Kenya to articulate a feminist perspective, although, like most women leaders, she has never labeled herself a feminist.[60] She is also a nurse, businesswoman, and doyenne of progressive Luo society in Nairobi. Her husband is the preeminent Kenyan historian B. A. Ogot—one of Africa's most acclaimed scholars. Her first impulse in response to Wambui's dilemma was to come out publicly on the side of progressive gender relations and women's rights. At a funeral in Siaya District several days after Bosire's February 13 judgment against Wambui, Ogot complained about the exclusion of widows from Luo decision making regarding burials. She claimed that women want changes in the traditions and that widows should be respected.[61]

Meanwhile, the National Council of Women of Kenya (NCWK), an umbrella organization for women's groups, was mounting a campaign to correct the flaws in Kenya's statutes pertaining to women's rights. The council had spoken out in the early days of the Otieno case. In a press release on January 16, 1987, following the referral of the case to the High Court for full trial, the NCWK noted numerous similar disputes in the country and deplored the fact that while the Law of Succession Act "gives preference to widows to administer the estate of a husband where the latter has died intestate," it is silent on the question of burial.[62] The council observed that because of this silence, when a dispute arises it is often referred to customary law, which is sometimes unclear and discriminatory against women.[63] The exclusion of widows from burial decisions was, in the council's view, "repugnant and ab-

[60] See, for an example of her feminist writing, her collection of stories, Grace Ogot, *Land without Thunder* (Nairobi: East African Publishing House, 1968).

[61] *Weekly Review* (February 20, 1987), 9.

[62] Ibid. (January 23, 1987), 4. It is telling that the Law of Succession Act, drafted and presented to government by a Law of Succession Commission in 1968 and introduced as a parliamentary bill in 1970, was not passed until 1981, after over a decade of debate and amendment.

[63] Ibid.

surd."[64] The council noted that Kenya was a signatory to the Convention on the Elimination of All Forms of Discrimination against Women adopted by the thirty-fourth session of the United Nations General Assembly.[65]

The NCWK campaign, kicked off after the High Court ruling in mid-February, aimed to collect a million signatures on a petition to be presented to the attorney general and Law Reform Commission; the petition called for legislation to regulate the rights of spouses and next of kin regarding burial. Ogot's speech at the Siaya funeral was just what the NCWK needed to legitimate its campaign: a statement for women's rights by Kenya's most eminent Luo woman leader. Posters with Ogot's picture were displayed in the booths set up across Nairobi to collect signatures. Ogot was outraged at the use of her name in the campaign without her permission, and in her capacity as an assistant minister in the government she ordered police to remove the posters. The police took the matter further, arresting and jailing overnight two young volunteers who were soliciting signatures in the city. The chair of NCWK, Wangari Maathai, apologized to Ogot and denied that the council intended malice toward her as Ogot had angrily claimed. The signature booths were dismantled, and the campaign fizzled out by the end of February after garnering only 4,000 signatures.

Ogot felt it necessary to defend herself publicly against association with the NCWK's position and to qualify the statement she had made at the Siaya funeral. In a letter to the editor published in *Weekly Review,* she said of her funeral statement: "I reminded all married women always to remember that the husbands they loved had a mother, father, sisters and brothers and the extended family who also loved him, and all were entitled to share the joys and sorrows of the family."[66] At Otieno's funeral several months later, she reiterated this position on lineage prerogatives.

Ogot's predicament exposed the contradictions faced by women who make it into formal political office. They are expected to speak for women, and indeed often are appointed to office on this condition (as Ogot was during her first term as a member of parliament).[67] On the other hand, they are expected to serve their political constituencies, and in Kenya this means serving ethnic

---

[64] Ibid. (February 27, 1987), 7 (citing the same press release).

[65] Ibid. (January 23, 1987), 4.

[66] Ibid. (March 6, 1987), 2.

[67] Ogot's appointment to Parliament by President Moi followed a practice widespread in the Third World in which seats in local, provincial, or national legislatures are reserved for representatives of disadvantaged groups (as categorized by the government).

interests. Ogot, now an elected parliament member, was forced to choose between her loyalties to women's issues and those to her Luo constituency. She chose the latter—a rational strategy given her intention to stand again in the upcoming elections. As ethnic politics increasingly rely on more stringently controlled and patriarchal gender relations, it appears impossible for a democratically elected woman to espouse feminist causes.

Ogot's conflict with the NCWK was symptomatic of the problem women's organizations face in taking a stand on strategic gender issues. The ideological resistance in Kenya to an overt feminist stance is well illustrated in the following *Weekly Review* commentary (an editorial in the guise of reportage):

> Many Kenyans from all walks of life are perfectly comfortable with many aspects of customary law, and this includes a large number of women. The NCWK has taken the "women's lib" position which is well-rooted in western society, but which has only taken root in Kenya among a small minority of women, most of whom belong to the educated elite. Many women in Kenya have no time for the western mode of women's liberation. Another question is whether the NCWK has the mandate to speak for all the women of Kenya. . . . The council has further been criticised in the past over the fact that foreign women's organizations, notably the American Women's Association, had great influence within the council.[68]

The difficulties the NCWK faced in mobilizing feminist action during the Otieno case had their roots not only in sexist opposition. The leading women's organizations in Kenya have experienced considerable internecine strife over the years. The first organization, Maendeleo ya Wanawake (Progress of women) was founded in 1952 by a British settler to promote the interests of rural Kenyan women, and it continues today as the largest organization in the country, with thousands of rural branches. At the grassroots it has mobilized women and provided them with the organizational means to promulgate their practical gender issues.[69] Paradoxically, however, the national organization has been the vehicle for elite women's political aspirations.[70] Maendeleo has had close ties with the government from the colonial era to the present, and the organization's leadership has succeeded in promoting neither stra-

[68] *Weekly Review* (January 23, 1987), 4–5.
[69] See Molyneux (n. 25 above).
[70] See Audrey Wipper, "The Maendeleo Ya Wanawake Organization: The Cooptation of Leadership," *African Studies Review* 18, no. 3 (December 1985): 99–120.

tegic nor practical gender issues on behalf of its rural membership. Instead, the organization saw a continual wrangling over the perquisites of office and the disposition of funds among leaders who had not risen from the ranks, but who were prominent political figures, or wives of politicians. In 1986 the Maendeleo chairman [*sic*] was dismissed "amidst allegations of corruption and financial mismanagement," following the report of a government appointed probe committee.[71] The government took the scandal as an opportunity to constrain the organization's autonomy, dissolving the executive committee and placing Maendeleo under the authority of the Ministry of Culture and Social Services. In May 1987 the ruling party KANU decreed that Maendeleo would henceforth be affiliated with the party, revealing the latter's intention to control and direct the women's movement in Kenya. The co-optation was completed in October 1989 when male politicians took over the running of Maendeleo's elections, ensuring that their relatives and allies were nominated for leadership positions.[72]

In spite of the compromised status of its leadership, Maendeleo always maintained that it spoke for the rural membership and justified its hostility toward the NCWK on this basis, maintaining that the umbrella organization was elitist and unrepresentative. In 1981 Maendeleo withdrew from the NCWK, claiming that "the council was infringing on its autonomy," and took a number of smaller women's groups with it.[73] Since then, the NCWK has indeed been more representative of urban than rural women (twenty-seven of thirty-five affiliated member organizations had Nairobi addresses in 1985).[74]

Ironically, however, the NCWK became the champion of the very women Maendeleo and the politicians accused it of ignoring. Founded in 1964 as a voluntary coordinating body for women's organizations in Kenya, the organization attracted intellectual and professional women to its leadership.[75] Precisely because it espoused the most radical and overt feminist position on behalf of ordinary Kenyan women during the burial saga and on other occasions, the NCWK was branded as Western-influenced and

[71] *Weekly Review* (November 3, 1989), 11.

[72] See "Maendeleo Polls—a Male Affair?" *Weekly Review* (November 3, 1989), 4–13, for extensive coverage of this event.

[73] *Weekly Review* (May 8, 1987), 12.

[74] Ibid. (January 23, 1987), 5.

[75] See *A Guide to Women's Organizations and Agencies Serving Women in Kenya,* comp. Mazangira Institute (Nairobi: Mazangira Institute, 1985), for a survey of Kenyan organizations affiliated with the NCWK as well as government and international organizations.

hence elitist—an inauthentic voice for Kenyan women. (The genuinely elitist Maendeleo leadership avoided such censure because it espoused Kenya's conservative development ideology and eschewed feminist rhetoric.) The events surrounding the NCWK's involvement in Wambui's case, including the powerful press censure of the organization, the failure of the women's rights petition, and the Grace Ogot affair, marked a significant hardening of antifeminist sentiment in Kenyan politics, while the NCWK itself suffered a further dramatic decline in credibility. The burial dispute was thus a prominent event in the ideological struggle to define gender relations and women's rights in Kenya. The outcome appeared to represent a defeat for the women's movement, and feminist voices were effectively silenced.

However, the promotion of rigid patriarchal values and practices by leadership at every level from the lineage to the judiciary during the Otieno case is likely to have politicized many Kenyan women.[76] Khaminwa's representation of Wambui was arguably one of the most dramatic feminist polemics ever delivered in a courtroom, and his arguments, published in the *Nation's* compilation of the court proceedings, are widely accessible to literate Kenyan women—even though the *Nation* articles reproduced in the publication implicitly support the Umira Kager position. Khaminwa's court performance must be seen in the context of the fact that the Kenyan legal profession, like the church, is an important locus of opposition to the repressive Moi regime. Khaminwa's feminist arguments thus became linked with the democratic opposition.[77] Beyond the country's borders, Khaminwa was awarded an honorary doctorate by Haverford College in the United States following the case, and invited to participate in a Harvard-sponsored human rights conference in Lesotho; Wambui's cause and Khaminwa's defense of it have been drawn into the ongoing international debate about human rights in Kenya. Throughout Africa, educated women followed the case keenly, finding it pertinent to the circumstances in their own countries and a cautionary tale for their own marital arrangements.

[76] Several young Kenyan women have reported in personal communications (1989, 1990) that it is now common for them to discuss among themselves the advantages and disadvantages of interethnic marriages, potential parental opposition, and the steps they can take to protect themselves against future husbands' families. One woman reported that as she looked like a Kikuyu, she would be accosted on buses during the case as "a Wambui woman."

[77] The Law Society of Kenya, which spearheads this opposition, was the target in 1990 of government censure, and several members were detained without trial. Khaminwa himself was detained in the regime's suppression of the 1990 prodemocracy movement. (See Stamp, "The Politics of Dissent in Moi's Kenya" [n. 30 above], for an analysis of democratic struggle in Kenya up to 1990.)

The Otieno case and the gender issues it raised for public discussion have thus defined a new political and ideological terrain upon which feminist struggle in Kenya (and other African countries) can be waged. As the *Nation* compilation's editor commented: "Let there be no mistake about it. The Otieno case may be closed. But the debate it gave rise to about many issues has only just begun."[78]

The ghost of Otieno

The close of the court case opened another act in the Otieno saga: the carnival around his funeral in Nyalgunga Sublocation on May 23, 1987. The event dramatized the growing tendency for Kenyan burials to become social and political battlegrounds. Funerals have always been important in the life of many African societies, an occasion to affirm kinship ties and reify the social order, which encompasses the living, the dead, and the unborn.[79] The burial site has been a significant part of this affirmation, testifying to the inviolable connection between a lineage and its land. The graves of important lineage elders often acquire the status of shrines over time. Given the dissolution of village-based society in the present, and the scattering of extended families across the country and even across class lines, it is not surprising that burial has become a focus for the conflicts that arise in lineage and gender relations. One type of conflict is the competition between co-wives in polygynous marriages. Settled by their husbands in different homesteads (sometimes in different districts or provinces), they frequently contend for custody of their deceased husband's body. Wangari Maathai, chair of the NCWK, declared that the dead body in such disputes is "like a title deed," possession of which bestows legitimacy when there is a disagreement over inheritance.[80]

Beyond familial disputes, funerals have in the contemporary era become one of the "traditions" manipulated for social and economic gain in the wider political arena.[81] The Umira Kager clan

[78] *S. M. Otieno* (n. 22 above), vii.

[79] See, e.g., John S. Mbiti, *African Religions and Philosophy* (London: Heinemann, 1969), 149–65.

[80] *Weekly Review* (January 23, 1987), 5.

[81] Parkin (n. 3 above) argues that funerals, like bridewealth transactions, have become "spheres of investment" for rich lineage elders (5) and that, among the coastal Giriama, the customs have been increasingly manipulated for economic gain, as well as enhancement of prestige. He goes on to show how "the encapsulating state political structure and inextricable involvement in the international market are providing the conditions for the formation of minor family dynasties" (6). See esp. 77–97.

seized the opportunity of a clansman's intestate death to promulgate its political and economic ends. Following the clan's court triumph, the requiem mass for Otieno in the Anglican cathedral in Kisumu town and the subsequent funeral in Siaya District were occasions for paeans to Luo virtue and custom—rallying points for the most overt expression of Luo nationalism that Kenya had experienced in many years. Attendance at the mass and funeral was de rigueur for Luo political leaders, and massive crowds congregated for the church and homestead rites.[82] The events were also occasions for both ethnic and gender chauvinism: crowds greeting the funeral cortège chanted *wapi Wambui?* (where is Wambui?), taking her absence from the funeral as an affront against Luo custom and proof of the folly of interethnic marriages. Songs were composed and sung about her, and Siranga, the Nairobi spokesman for the clan, told mourners that "though a guinea fowl resembles a chicken and though it lays eggs as chickens do, it can never live with chickens forever."[83] The clan's lawyer Kwach advised young men "not to be content with only their wives-to-be but to look beyond the girls and know their prospective mothers-in-law."[84] The presiding bishop, Henry Okullu, lauded the return of Otieno's body with the aphorism: "Even a bull, no matter how ferocious, is always tethered in the homestead."[85]

The requiem mass was in keeping with the practices of Kenya's elite, for whom large church services are routinely held. Most educated Kenyans are active members in church congregations and the Umira Kager protagonists were not exceptions. No one in the clan saw a contradiction between Christian piety and their attachment to tradition.[86] The clan had requested that the mass be held at the prestigious national cathedral in Nairobi but were turned down by the provost—a Kikuyu—on the grounds that the widow's wishes regarding the funeral were being contravened in violation of Christian principle and that the rite could not be held in her absence.[87] Bishop Okullu took this setback as an opportunity; using

---

[82] Wambui reported that President Moi himself wished to attend but could not in her absence; he sent an aide to persuade her to change her mind (Wambui Otieno, personal communication, July 1989).

[83] *Weekly Review* (May 29, 1987), 13. The comment shows that the clan enjoyed scoring points off Wambui's absence. Indeed, they discouraged her attendance by issuing a warning before the burial that they "could not guarantee Mrs. Otieno any security if she accompanied the body to Nyalgunga" (*S. M. Otieno*, 172).

[84] *Weekly Review* (May 29, 1987), 13.

[85] Ibid., 8.

[86] See *S. M. Otieno*, 58–59, for brother Ochieng's testimony before the High Court regarding the compatibility of Christianity and Luo belief in ghosts.

[87] While it may seem paradoxical that Nairobi was the venue of choice for the clan, a service at the national cathedral would have been a fitting climax to the burial battle, dignifying and politically legitimizing the clan's actions.

the pulpit of the cathedral in Kisumu, the principal Luo town, he presented a pro-Luo diatribe castigating the Nairobi provost for turning "our national cathedral . . . into a tribal ghetto."[88] The congregation in the packed cathedral clapped and cheered the bishop's attack on the few Luo leaders who opposed the clan's position; they clapped as well when the bishop linked Luo concepts of ghosts and spirits to the Bible.[89]

It was the homestead burial that was intended to be the focus for the traditional rites that featured so strongly in the court arguments for a clan burial. (Most important were *tero buru,* a ceremony to chase away spirits, and *magenga,* a funeral fire tended for four days by clan men, who were not allowed indoors during this time.) Ironically, they were not performed. Instead, Otieno was given a Christian burial service. Clan members argued that the widow and children's presence was necessary for the traditional rites and hence the clan could not perform them: Otieno thus had to be buried as an unmarried man. Others close to the family pointed out that in any event Christianity was too firmly entrenched in the village for a return to the old rituals.[90]

The absence of the long-anticipated rites did not dampen enthusiasm at the graveside, however. Clan members and prominent public figures in attendance celebrated the clan protagonists as heroes; members of parliament praised Okullu for highlighting the compatibility of Christianity and African traditions. The minister for education, science, and technology, Peter Oloo Aringo, was among those delivering eulogies at the homestead: "You have done us proud," he said to the clan's spokesmen. Claiming that Luo custom "is part and parcel of Kenya's tradition," he pointed out that a Luo's spirit is immortal and has the power to bless and curse. If Otieno had been buried outside Luoland, "then his ghost would haunt the entire Umira Kager clan."[91] With the tumultuous funeral in Nyalgunga Sublocation, Siaya District, Otieno's ghost had supposedly been put to rest.

The politics of gender and ethnicity

Otieno had a more vivid presence in Kenyan politics and society in death than he did in life. His ghost entered Kenyan politics at an interesting moment in the life of the country. By 1987 the economic as well as political hegemony of the Kikuyu had ended. Indeed, the

[88] *Weekly Review* (May 29, 1987), 10.
[89] Ibid.
[90] Ibid., 11.
[91] Ibid., 8.

steady Kikuyu-led expansion of the middle class that occurred following independence had been halted—by economic recession but also by the economic adventurism of Moi and a small elite close to him.[92] Neither the Luo nor the president's much smaller and less educationally advanced ethnic group, the Kalenjin, have since stepped into the breech en masse to continue the process of petty bourgeois development.[93] In a climate of declining economic fortunes, politics have realigned around ethnic groupings, and intense competition for scarce resources takes place within and between the groupings. Lineages and clans have reemerged as potent political forces for the first time since before colonial conquest.

The burial saga carried considerable economic and political freight in this context. That it was a significant opportunity for the clan was revealed in the extraordinary measures it took to prevail in the dispute. Otieno was a member of the nation's petty bourgeoisie, a successful lawyer who had parlayed his professional remuneration into property and other economic resources as well as the education of his children. In Africa, this class position is a crucial site for redistributing wealth and generating opportunity, particularly in the present recession, which has continued without break in Africa since the late 1970s. Enormous burdens are placed upon a petty bourgeois family to support an ever widening circle of relatives as its fortunes advance. The family that withholds these resources and opportunities and attempts to define itself more narrowly provokes serious tensions in the lineage.

Upon a prominent male elder's death, a Luo lineage would expect the resources of his estate to be redistributed within the lineage and the widow to acquiesce in the decisions of her brothers-in-law and sons (who would, in turn, provide for her needs).[94] Further, the prestige the elder had garnered during his lifetime would upon his death accrue to the lineage—and even to the clan, if he were eminent enough. Finally, the widow herself would be claimed as a resource for the lineage: the Luo still frequently practice the levirate, whereby a brother of the deceased

---

[92] See Michael P. Maren, "Kenya: The Dissolution of Democracy," *Current History* 86, no. 20 (May 1987): 212 and 228, for an account of this adventurism.

[93] The Kalenjin are not a unified ethnic group like the Luo but a loose cluster of subgroups within the Nilotic cultural grouping, including the small Tugen subgroup to which Moi belongs. The Luo are termed the river-lake Nilotes, while the Kalenjin are the highland Nilotes.

[94] In practice today, even the widow's needs are often ignored. Witnesses referred to the "looting" of a widow's house that takes place following the husband's death; Wambui called this practice "brutal" (*S. M. Otieno* [n. 22 above], 30). To protect herself, she maintained a heavy guard upon her Langata house from soon after Otieno's death until well after the court case was over.

marries the widow. This ensures lineage membership of any future children as well as the continued affiliation of existing children.[95]

In Otieno's lifetime, there had been contention within the lineage over his actions and beliefs. By marrying outside his ethnic group and not paying bridewealth, he failed to establish the conventional contract by which his lineage would gain access to the human and material resources he and his wife generated. The court testimony of Wambui and other witnesses affirmed the clan's objection to Otieno's definition of his familial responsibilities (even though he was reportedly generous toward relatives).[96] Their attempt to coerce his support is revealed in a 1985 incident described by Wambui, in which Otieno was forced to pay the entire cost of a brother's funeral after some clan members misappropriated the clan funds designated for that purpose.[97] As Khaminwa put it, "there was no friendship or peace" between Otieno and his clan in Siaya.[98]

Otieno's death represented too important a material opportunity for the lineage to pass up. A significant aspect of the clan's court challenge to Wambui's burial plans was its effort to gain control of Otieno's estate. Umira Kager's challenge to Wambui's appointment as sole executor of the estate was eventually dropped, but the clan's demurral was not the "show of magnanimity" that the press called it.[99] Rather, the patrilineage was prevented from claiming the estate because all property had been registered jointly in Wambui and Otieno's names. Wambui said that when the clan moved to contest her ownership, "the Kikuyu said 'Enough! You can take her husband, but not her property.' "[100] Wambui believed that, thwarted of legal recourse, the clan attempted to punish her covertly: a tax assessment of two million shillings was brought against the estate by a clan member in the revenue department.[101]

In that a direct appropriation of Otieno's estate was impossible, clan members tried another tack: the levirate. Wambui claimed in court that the Umira Kager clan spokesman, Siranga, had proposed marriage to her right after Otieno's death, as had several other clan members.[102] A clan witness in the first High Court hearing stated:

[95] For an interesting discussion of the levirate among the Luo, see Betty Potash, "Wives of the Grave: Widows in a Rural Luo Community," in Potash, ed. (n. 7 above), 44–65. Even Pamela Mboya, cosmopolitan wife of the internationally renowned Kenyan leader Tom Mboya, married her husband's brother following his assassination in 1969.

[96] *S. M. Otieno*, 31.

[97] *Weekly Review* (January 30, 1987), 9.

[98] *S. M. Otieno*, 41.

[99] *Weekly Review* (June 26, 1987), 12.

[100] Wambui Otieno, personal communication, June 1989.

[101] Ibid.

[102] *S. M. Otieno*, 31.

"She is our wife. . . . Her children are our children."[103] Lawyer Kwach suggested that her brother-in-law, Joash Ochieng' Ougo, should set up a home for her in Nyamila, to which Wambui replied: "In what capacity would he do that? Are you trying to suggest that he would take me over? In that case I would tell you to tell him to forget it."[104]

It was the clan spokesman Siranga, rather than Otieno's brother Ochieng', who took a hard line on the human and material resources of Otieno's family. The clan would not allow Wambui to "walk away to her Kikuyu people with Otieno's property."[105] While Siranga pushed for the levirate and took steps to contest Wambui's execution of the estate, Ochieng'—the intended levirate husband— refused to consider marriage with her and renounced claims in Otieno's property, "not even a needle."[106] According to Wambui, Ochieng's more conciliatory stance stemmed from his close knowledge of Otieno and the children.[107] "Personally I think he is a good man but he has been misled by Mr. Siranga," she said in court.[108]

The Umira Kager clan's action can be viewed as an unsuccessful attempt to recapture Otieno's family, his status, and his wealth for the Luo lineage to which Otieno had been born and to control the actions of a wife of the lineage. Wambui blocked the clan's expectations first by being a non-Luo and second by refusing to act as a Luo widow.

Thwarted of economic reward, the clan was more successful in the realm of ethnic politics and ideology. Umira Kager's standing in the wider Luo community and ultimately the Luo's position within the Kenyan polity as a whole became implicated in the burial affair. The case and the clan's actions not only reactivated the longstanding Luo-Kikuyu rivalry but also invoked the old tensions between Left and Right in Kenya. By 1987, President Moi had consolidated his hold on the presidency and had neutralized much of his political opposition, having weathered a plot to prevent his assumption of office in 1978 and a coup attempt in 1982. Any opposition to the regime's policy was labeled as opposition to the values of "Nyayoism," the "philosophy of peace, love and unity" invented by Moi.[109] In this way, Moi's regime was able to coax acquiescence

[103] Ibid., 3.
[104] Ibid., 31.
[105] *Weekly Review* (February 20, 1987), 8.
[106] Ibid.
[107] Wambui Otieno, personal communication, June 1989.
[108] *S. M. Otieno* (n. 22 above), 31.
[109] The term comes from the Swahili word for "footsteps," *nyayo*, and initially referred to the footsteps of Kenya's charismatic first president, Kenyatta. See the

from the populace and to cast a cloak of legitimacy over the escalating repression of his regime.[110] Dissidents were detained without trial and KANU party politics were brought under strict presidential control.

This political climate sent Kenya's leftist forces into full retreat or exile. A prominent Luo member of the Left from the early days of independence was Oginga Odinga, leader of the opposition party Kenya People's Union (KPU) before it was banned by Kenyatta in 1969. Gadfly to both Kenyatta and Moi, Odinga moved in and out of political limbo several times in the following two decades. Although he was generally considered a spent force in 1987, he carried lingering influence, and his vision of a pan-ethnic, socialist Kenya remained a troubling issue in Luo politics. The Otieno burial case provided the Luo with an opportunity to settle old accounts and to establish the ethnic group firmly in the capitalist camp of the Moi regime. At the same time, it allowed them to counter the pan-ethnic tendencies championed by Odinga with a strengthened Luo nationalism. Odinga, an old comrade in arms of left-wing Kikuyu, spoke up for the prerogatives of an interethnic marriage made in the visionary time of Kenya's nationalist struggle, when Kikuyu and Luo were in radical alliance. Almost alone in being unafraid to speak out against the ideological dogmas of the Nyayo era, Odinga railed against the parochial stance of the Umira Kager clan, using Siaya District funerals as his platform.

The Luo leadership rallied around the clan, castigating Odinga. The KANU branch chairman of Siaya District, Peter Oloo Aringo, made the thinly veiled barb, "an elder does not lead us to the dogs."[111] Lawyer Kwach ridiculed him as a "disgraced and slow-punctured politician" and implied that he had put Wambui up to the court action.[112] Anonymous sources told the press that Odinga's plan to bring some Luo witnesses to court to give evidence against the clan were sabotaged.[113] Old leftist skeletons were rattled in their

---

president's formal elaboration of this expediency in Daniel T. arap Moi, *Kenya African Nationalism: Nyayo Philosophy and Principles* (London: Macmillan, 1986).

[110] For discussion and analysis of these events, see Stephen Katz, "The Succession to Power and the Power of Succession: Nyayoism in Kenya," *Journal of African Studies* 12, no. 3 (Fall 1985): 155–61; Kate Currie and Larry Ray, "State and Class in Kenya—Notes on the Cohesion of the Ruling Class," *Journal of Modern African Studies* 22, no. 4 (1984): 559–93; and Patricia Stamp, "Kenya: The Echoing Footsteps," *Current History* 81, no. 473 (March 1982): 115–18, 130, 137–38.

[111] *Weekly Review* (February 20, 1987), 9.

[112] Ibid.

[113] Ibid. (May 22, 1987), 9. The witnesses had traveled from western Kenya to Nairobi but mysteriously failed to appear in court to testify.

cupboards: Wambui's brother Dr. Munyua Waiyaki was a longtime leftist political ally of Odinga. The minister for agriculture, William Odongo Omamo, sought to discredit Odinga by hinting at links to the contemporary dissident movement (led by exiled writer Ngugi wa Thiong'o).[114] Wambui believed herself to be a political target also. At a press conference she called at her home after the final judgment she alluded to the old Left-Right political tensions that surfaced in the case with suggestive remarks about the "political angle."[115]

The Luo leadership was particularly sensitive about the leftist connections given its exclusion from power by both the Kenyatta and Moi regimes and hence its uneasy relationship with both. Leftist challenges by Luos had, over the years, landed a number of them in jail and jeopardized the advancement of the group as a whole in the Kenyan state and economy. Even though these challenges were usually in alliance with radical Kikuyus, it was often the Luos who bore the brunt of government wrath. Odinga's pronouncements in support of Wambui raised old fears among the Luo and had to be neutralized. This was accomplished not only through the public attacks upon Odinga but also through the court case itself. Wambui and all she stood for were discredited. Not far from the surface of the proceedings was an image of Wambui as a symbol of all the evils of Kikuyu domination in the Kenyatta years. Testimony for the clan became the vehicle for anti-Kikuyu sentiments and Luo chauvinism: Luo custom was equated with Kenyan custom, and Kikuyu custom was caricatured and ridiculed.

The Umira Kager clan, by focusing Luo nationalist sentiments on the burial issue and acting on what it perceived to be pan-Luo interests, succeeded both in advancing its standing among the Luo and in promoting Luo interests in Kenya. Observers noted the Umira Kager's emergence as a "warrior clan in the district and a force to be reckoned with in the future politics of the area."[116] The clan's Nairobi spokesman Siranga and its lawyer Kwach were touted as the "embodiment of this warrior spirit" and likely political leaders in the future.[117] In short, the clan brilliantly manipulated gender and lineage ideology as a means to overtly political ends.

[114] Ibid.
[115] Ibid., 8. The press in Kenya censors itself on sensitive political issues to avoid government retribution; the references in the *Daily Nation* and *Weekly Review* to the political dimensions of the case were cryptic.
[116] *Weekly Review* (May 29, 1987), 14.
[117] Ibid.

Reflections on the form of feminist struggle

Analysis of the burial saga supports the key supposition made at the outset: that the contemporary African state and subnational structures have an economic and political interest in the co-optation of gender relations and the control of women. Their actions comprise a strategy of collaborative hegemony, constructing an ideology that manipulates the traditions of motherhood and wifely responsibility. Wambui's fall from wifely virtue becomes a cautionary tale for women about the boundaries they should not cross in the name of progress and modernity.

Yet Wambui's ordeal reveals the powerful political agency possible for Kenyan women. While her attempts to assert her rights as a Kenyan and as a widow met with legal defeat at the hands of the state and her husband's clan, the nation was nonetheless put into turmoil over one woman's insistence on pursuing a practical gender issue. Clan lawyer Kwach dismissed her argument that the clan's burial custom was repugnant to justice with the words: "My lords, one swallow does not make a summer! Wambui is that swallow."[118] But a sensational case such as Wambui's is the visible instance of widespread gender contradictions and inequities. To the extent that Wambui brought these issues to popular attention and generated a whole new discourse articulating women's rights, pan-ethnic nationalism, and progressive social values, her endeavors were profoundly and effectively feminist.

To promulgate her cause, Wambui used the same discourse of wifely responsibility and prerogatives employed by the clan and the courts, but she chose those aspects of the discourse that countered their patriarchal, constraining interpretation of tradition. In doing so, she exemplified the particular form feminist discourse takes in Africa today and charted the political and ideological terrain on which it is carried out. Both on the national stage and in the village, women employ a "combative motherhood" to counter assaults against their rights and against egalitarian gender relations.[119] Their struggle is waged on the terrain of concrete conditions and immediate needs—Molyneux's "practical gender issues."[120] Because women rarely use the language of politics or of feminism (as defined by Western feminists and by the media), the political nature of their struggles often goes unrecognized. Yet

---

[118] S. M. *Otieno* (n. 22 above), 162.

[119] This is another concept of Molyneux's (n. 25 above), whose study on women in the Nicaraguan revolution is useful for its theoretical insights on women, ideology, and the state (228).

[120] Ibid., 230–35.

these struggles can be linked to the nature of the political power women formerly exercised, as linchpins in the organization of lineage affairs. A wide range of social and economic decisions pertaining to village and family life fell within their authority as lineage wives organized into associations of elders.[121] In fighting for practical gender issues today, women are endeavoring to maintain this political role.

Wambui's encounter with her husband's patrilineage and the state, once recognized as a characteristic form of feminist struggle in Africa, prompts certain conclusions about the imperatives of such struggle. More than in the West at present, legal rights are a key strategic women's issue, overarching women's individual struggles for their immediate needs. As a Luo woman lawyer put it: "Many women in Kenya, whether they can read or not, are still ignorant of their legal rights. There are also forms of discrimination that persist despite the laws" because they are "intricately woven into various tribal customs."[122] That gender conflict in Kenya found its most dramatic expression as a legal battle is thus not surprising.

The stakes in the struggle over legal rights are high. As the Otieno case showed, the courts have become a vehicle for the co-optation and control of gender relations. Kenya's legal and political history has made this possible in three ways. First, there is the confusion about the jurisdiction of common law and statutes as opposed to that of customary law; the confusion was used against Wambui to deny a more progressive interpretation of her rights. Second, the discourse of tradition embedded in Kenya's juridical development has reified "custom" and distorted precolonial gender relations in favor of their patriarchal elements. The judges and clan lawyers time and again affirmed a one-sided view of precolonial politics that excluded women's political authority and precluded an argument on customary grounds more favorable to Wambui. Third, this discourse of tradition was engendered by the imperatives of colonial political economy; the resultant patriarchal ideology that suffuses contemporary gender relations continues to serve the interests of the neocolonial state and international political econ-omy.[123] In turn, through its coercion of gender relations and con-

---

[121] See nn. 14 and 58 above.

[122] Rose Adhiambo Arungu-Olende, "Kenya: Not Just Literacy, but Wisdom," in *Sisterhood Is Global*, ed. Robin Morgan (Garden City, N.Y.: Anchor, 1984), 394–98, esp. 397.

[123] See Marjorie Mbilinyi, "Agribusiness and Women Peasants in Tanzania," *Development and Change* 19 (1988): 549–83, for an excellent argument concerning capitalism's interest in controlling African women.

straint of women's authority, the state supports and reinforces the patrilineage system.

Wambui was treated as an individual throughout the case rather than as a member of a group, whether her natal lineage or an association of women (even though the clan acted as a collectivity, referring to her as "our wife").[124] Her experience is symptomatic of a process widespread in Africa: the relegation of women to a private sphere, both in political practice and in imagery. This strategy of privatization supports the co-optation of gender relations and the control of women in the interests of state and patrilineage. Kathleen Staudt examines the colonial strategy that imposed a public/private dichotomy upon African societies: "Public-private distinctions are social creations which seemingly create the proper setting for capitalist transformation and the long-term interests it serves. Much of precolonial Africa, while gender stratified, had no such distinctions. As such, gender issues were political issues, reflected in organizations and authority structures, and both relevant and central to society."[125]

Staudt sees the idealized conception of women as wives and mothers espoused by the elite women's leadership in Kenya as evidence that women have been successfully privatized.[126] Nonetheless, "private" gender matters continue to be public and highly political, as the Otieno case attests.[127] As one prominent women's leader put it to me: "We try not to be too aggressive, or to break the link with the family and even community. We can't expect to break that myth [of men's power as head of the home] right away—it must be gradual. If you want to change it abruptly, you encounter a stronger resistance."[128] The symbol of motherhood is thus a two-

[124] *S. M. Otieno*, 3.

[125] Kathleen Staudt, "Women's Politics, the State, and Capitalist Transformation in Africa," in *Studies in Power and Class in Africa*, ed. Irving Leonard Markovitz (New York: Oxford University Press, 1987), 193–208, esp. 207–8. In this fine study, Staudt also demonstrates the point made above that women's movement politics in Kenya were essentially class politics, promoting the interests of elite women.

[126] Ibid., 203–4.

[127] A more recent case—ironically involving the respected chief justice of Kenya—confirms this. Estranged from his wife in 1985, Chief Justice C. H. E. Miller won custody of their two children. Denied all access until his death in 1989, the mother then attempted to reclaim her children. Briefly reunited with her at Miller's funeral, they were snatched away again by his executors, and the court subsequently denied her either custody or access (*Weekly Review* [December 1, 1989], 20–21). Christine Miller finally won custody of her children in February 1991 (*Weekly Review* [February 8, 1991], 8–9).

[128] Interview, 1981, in Stamp, "Kikuyu Women's Self Help Groups" (n. 14 above), 41.

edged sword: it can be used to legitimize the control of women, but women can also use it to great effect in feminist struggle.

The supposedly private world of the family furnishes other opportunities for feminist struggle besides "combative mother-hood." In that women are the linchpins of the patrilineal system, it follows that the withdrawal of their presence, support, or services are deeply significant political acts. A lineage wife's resistance can be both symbolically damaging and structurally disruptive, whether it be the boycott of formal rituals, such as Wambui's refusal to attend the clan funeral, or the public denouncement of the marital patrilineage, as when Wambui called a press conference after the Appeal Court ruling to announce that she would have no more to do with Nyalgunga and "Nyalgungas" and, henceforth, would be known by her father's name.[129] Jean O'Barr, in her useful categorization of African women's political methods, identifies such withdrawal as one of the indirect methods of resistance that women employ.[130]

Wambui has, without doubt, affected the fortunes of Otieno's lineage. The court triumph can be seen as a Pyrrhic victory for the lineage: while the clan was bathed in symbolic glory, the lineage was denied, by Wambui's actions, Otieno's prestige, children, wife, and estate—the human and material furnishings of a lineage's well-being. Moreover, Wambui showed Kenyan women the possi-bility of defiance. Not many would wish to be defamed as she was, but she proved that women could resist the control of their marital lineage and use the courts to do so. Wambui thus opened the political space for other women's actions and, in this sense, she won.

In conclusion, Wambui's fight to bury Otieno demonstrates the need to integrate theories and analyses of gender relations into contemporary African politics. Such efforts will bring well-deserved prominence to the study of ideological discourse, espe-cially the manipulation of custom and tradition for political and economic ends. Further, the study of ethnicity will gain a new rigor once the centrality of gender relations in the postcolonial state—especially in the subnational political processes of lineage and clan—is recognized. The case also illustrates the importance of incorporating into feminist scholarship concepts and theories from debates in political science if we are to understand the relation between women and the state in Africa.

---

[129] *Weekly Review* (July 22, 1987), 7.

[130] Jean O'Barr, "African Women in Politics," in *African Women South of the Sahara*, ed. Margaret Jean Hay and Sharon Stichter (London: Longman, 1984), 140–55, esp. 140–43.

Finally, the synthesis of feminist and radical political science analysis will serve an important feminist goal: to render visible the agency of women in politics. Especially in the Third World, women have been treated as passive targets of oppressive practices and discriminatory structures. Such a conceptualization, far from contributing to women's emancipation, colludes with sexist ideologies that construct women as naturally inferior, passive, and consigned to a private, apolitical world.[131] We can do far more to counter women's oppression by interpreting Wambui's case in the context of Kenyan politics, explaining what she achieved, than by using her tribulations to demonstrate African women's suffering.

Division of Social Science
York University, Toronto, Canada

[131] For a trenchant critique, see Chandra Mohanty, "Under Western Eyes: Feminist Scholarship and Colonial Discourses," *Feminist Review* 30 (Autumn 1986): 61–88.

Patriarchy, Capitalism, and the Colonial State in Zimbabwe

Elizabeth Schmidt

The process of economic development in the British settler colony of Southern Rhodesia (the modern nation of Zimbabwe) was dominated by the needs of European capitalists who had invested in agriculture and mining.[1] In recent years a functionalist bias has pervaded scholarly accounts of this process. A number of writers have argued that the great need of Southern Rhodesian mining and agricultural capital for large supplies of cheap male labor dictated the colony's reliance on a migratory labor system involving only

I would like to thank Susan Geiger and Margaret Strobel, as well as anonymous *Signs* reviewers, for their helpful comments on earlier drafts of this article.

[1] I use "Southern Rhodesia" to refer to the British colonial period, "Zimbabwe" to refer to the modern nation; in this article I focus on the 1890–1939 period as reflecting the classic years of British colonial rule, before the Second World War and the postwar rise of African nationalism. Capitalists, settlers, and missionaries in Southern Rhodesia came from a number of countries in addition to Britain; my use of the term "European" in this article reflects that reality as well as standard African usage. Documents cited in the footnotes are housed at the National Archives of Zimbabwe (hereafter cited as NAZ), the Jesuit Archives, and the Catholic Archdiocese Archives (all located in Harare, Zimbabwe), and at the Wesleyan Methodist Missionary Society Archives (hereafter cited as WMMS) in London.

[*Signs: Journal of Women in Culture and Society* 1991, vol. 16, no. 4]

men.[2] As a result of state policy, African women and children were forced to stay behind in remote rural reserves, undertaking subsistence cultivation to feed themselves and to subsidize the men's wages. Throughout most of the colonial period, the wages paid, housing provided, and rations issued to African men were based on employers' assumptions about what a single man needed to survive; it was assumed that families left behind could fend for themselves and possibly even supplement the workers' food.

According to the functionalist scenario, the colonial state instituted the migrant labor system because it was functional for capital. Any sense that this particular labor system was the outcome of struggle, and that it might not have been optimal for capital, is marred by the common characterization of the conflict as one between fractions of European capital, or between European capital and African male labor. Such assessments ignore the contest between Africans, specifically between older men and women of all ages at both the household and village levels. Gender struggles within these arenas also shaped capitalist development in the Southern Rhodesian periphery, a reality that has rarely been recognized in the literature.[3]

Several recent works pertaining to other parts of Africa have criticized androcentric functionalism. Claire Robertson and Iris Berger, for instance, contend that African women's unequal access to power and resources does not result exclusively from colonialism and capitalism. The household, as well as the international economy, has been a fundamental locus of gender stratification, and thus

---

[2] See, e.g., Giovanni Arrighi, "Labour Supplies in Historical Perspective: A Study of the Proletarianization of the African Peasantry in Rhodesia," *Journal of Development Studies* 6, no. 3 (April 1970): 218, 223; Charles van Onselen, *Chibaro: African Mine Labour in Southern Rhodesia, 1900–1933* (Johannesburg: Ravan, 1980), 76; Ian Phimister, "Peasant Production and Underdevelopment in Southern Rhodesia, 1890–1914, with Particular Reference to the Victoria District," in *The Roots of Rural Poverty in Central and Southern Africa*, ed. Robin Palmer and Neil Parsons (London: Heinemann, 1977), 265, n. 2.

[3] There are some notable exceptions to this generalization. In her discussion of the development of capitalism in southern Africa as a whole, Belinda Bozzoli states that the outcome of "domestic struggles" may condition and shape the form taken by capitalism in those societies. Similarly, Sharon Stichter notes that the internal dynamics of the domestic modes of production and reproduction set limits on the operation of the capitalist mode. Belinda Bozzoli, "Marxism, Feminism and South African Studies," *Journal of Southern African Studies* 9, no. 2 (April 1983): 147; Sharon Stichter, *Migrant Laborers* (New York: Cambridge University Press, 1985), 58–59. Also see Jane L. Parpart, "The Household and the Mine Shaft: Gender and Class Struggles on the Zambian Copperbelt, 1926–64," *Journal of Southern African Studies* 13, no. 1 (October 1986): 36–56.

of African women's oppression.[4] Similarly, Belinda Bozzoli claims that, while female oppression and capitalism can be mutually interdependent, numerous aspects of female oppression cannot be explained this way. Collapsing female oppression into the capitalist mode of production sidesteps the issue of patriarchy—relations of domination and subordination between men and women that include control over such strategic resources as land, labor, and children, as well as political power.[5] Several recent studies have described African women's struggles against both capitalism and patriarchy in the neighboring British colonies of Nyasaland (now Malawi) and Northern Rhodesia (now Zambia).[6]

Regarding Southern Rhodesia, a functionalist argument might conclude that African women's subordinate position in present-day Zimbabwe is simply the result of colonial land and labor policies, of European intervention in the African social order. And to some extent, that argument would hold true. For as the colonial state undercut peasant agriculture, both to stem African competition with European farmers and to force African men to enter the labor market, the meaning of women's economic contribution to household maintenance changed. And once wage earning surpassed food production as the determining factor in household survival, women's social status deteriorated further.

This article takes a more nuanced view, arguing that African women's subordination is not solely the result of policies imposed by foreign capital and the colonial state. Rather, indigenous and European structures of patriarchal control reinforced and transformed one another, evolving into new structures and forms of domination. The control of women's and children's labor by older African men was central to the establishment and consolidation of colonial rule in Southern Rhodesia. The creation of "native reserves" not only served the interests of capital, by forcing women and children to subsidize male wages through agricultural production. It also served the interests of older African men by facilitating

[4] Claire Robertson and Iris Berger, "Introduction," in Women and Class in Africa, ed. Claire Robertson and Iris Berger (New York: Africana, 1986), 12, 14–15, 22.

[5] Bozzoli, 142.

[6] Martin Chanock, Law, Custom and Social Order: The Colonial Experience in Malawi and Zambia (New York: Cambridge University Press, 1985), esp. chaps. 8–11; Jane L. Parpart, "Class and Gender on the Copperbelt: Women in Northern Rhodesian Copper Mining Communities, 1926–1964," in Robertson and Berger, eds., 141–42, 148–56, and "Sexuality and Power on the Zambian Copperbelt, 1926–1964," in Patriarchy and Class: African Women in the Home and the Workforce, ed. Sharon B. Stichter and Jane L. Parpart (Boulder, Colo.: Westview, 1988), 115–38; Karen Tranberg Hansen, "Negotiating Sex and Gender in Urban Zambia," Journal of Southern African Studies 10, no. 2 (April 1984): 219–38.

their control over women and children. By forcing African women to submit to male authority, the colonial regime both advanced its own project and mollified a potentially powerful opposition force—namely, African men.[7]

Antagonistic as they may have been to other aspects of colonial rule, African chiefs, headmen, and older men in general welcomed the state's efforts to restrict women to the rural areas. For it was women who solidified kinship alliances through their marriages. The bridewealth received for daughters procured wives for the sons, and daughters-in-law produced children for the patrilineage. The labor of women generated food crops and guaranteed continued access to lineage land, for any unused land was returned to the common domain. Because husbands frequently sent a portion of their wages home to their wives, the retention of wives in the rural areas gave senior men some access to those wages, cash income that would otherwise be unavailable to them. For all these reasons, older men struggled to maintain control over women—over their labor, cash, children, and other resources; over their mobility; and over their marriages. This article explores the motivations behind the collaboration of African chiefs, headmen, and other older men with the colonial state, the forms that such collusion took, the resistance of African women to economic and gender oppression, and the dynamics of the struggles that ensued.

European views of African women

European racial and gender prejudices stripped African women of important social, economic, and political roles during the colonial period. While the colonial administrators and missionaries of Southern Rhodesia were not known for their enlightened views of African men, their opinions of African women were even more disparaging. Colonial records are filled with adjectives characterizing African women as indolent, lazy, slothful, immoral, frivolous, savage, and uncivilized. One state official claimed that "to any observer of the native, it is immediately apparent that their women are extraordinarily inferior to the men." While the men were "remarkably receptive of European ideas," he said, women turned a deaf ear, "cling[ing] to the old superstitions, the old customs and the old methods." Furthermore, African women frequently rejected

---

[7] I am indebted to Nancy Folbre for her elaboration on these points. See her article "Patriarchal Social Formations in Zimbabwe," in Stichter and Parpart, eds., 62, 67, 70. Also see Terence Ranger, "Women in the Politics of Makoni District, Zimbabwe, 1890–1980" (University of Manchester, 1981, typescript).

the advice and teachings of European missionaries with the explanation, "We are women."[8] It never occurred to the authorities that African women might resist the imposition of European culture and values because these undermined their own civilization, or that their refusal to work for Europeans was not evidence of their intrinsic "laziness," but a rejection of the European view that African families and fields should take second place to those of white Rhodesian settlers.

Like state officials, European missionaries displayed strong gender prejudices. Describing Chishawasha schoolchildren in the early years of the mission, one Jesuit asserted that the girls were far more difficult to handle than the boys because they were "flighty, lacking in concentration, moody and anxious for notice."[9] Father F. J. Richartz, the Jesuit superior of Chishawasha, pronounced Shona girls "totally devoid of seriousness, both of mind and character."[10] Another Jesuit opposed the employment of African women as teachers or catechists on the grounds that "their characters make such serious occupation impossible. . . . The women are too ignorant, too volatile and feather-headed to allow them to be entrusted with such a charge." Moreover, he maintained, "they would not be listened to with any respect, even by the natives themselves. Their efforts to instruct would only be laughed at."[11]

That such delicately balanced members of the "weaker sex" were engaged in backbreaking agricultural labor horrified the missionaries. Some even decried the plight of African women, whom they described as downtrodden beasts of burden at the beck and call of tyrannical husbands.[12] Colonial officials rarely characterized the women in this way. Instead, they credited African women with having significant power over their husbands and tremendous influence, albeit negative, in societal decision making. Writing in 1924, the native commissioner of Sinoia charged, "The

---

[8] NAZ, Chief Native Commissioner (hereafter cited as CNC) S235/475, Federation of Women's Institutes of Southern Rhodesia, *Report of the Standing Committee on Domestic Service*, July 1930, Testimony of W. S. Bazeley, 22.

[9] Quoted in W. F. Rea, *Loyola Mission, Chishawasha, 1892–1962* (Salisbury: Chishawasha Mission, 1962), 12.

[10] Father F. J. Richartz, S.J., "Twelve Years' Progress at Chishawasha," *Zambesi Mission Record* 2, no. 23 (January 1904): 338.

[11] Father Richard Sykes, S.J., "Women's Work in the Foreign Missions," *Zambesi Mission Record* 4, no. 54 (October 1911): 312.

[12] See, e.g., WMMS, Box 1052, Rev. Latimer P. Hardaker, Epworth Mission, "Letters of the Chairman," March 4, 1924; Jesuit Archives, Box 317, Testimony of witnesses in: Southern Rhodesia, *Report of the Native Affairs Committee of Enquiry, 1910–11* (Salisbury: Government Printer, 1911), par. 6.41.

women, though wielding immense power over the men, are many centuries behind them in civilisation and absolutely unfit to be granted any measure of freedom for the present as their instincts are almost purely animal."[13] Like their missionary counterparts, colonial officials frequently described African women as wanton and immoral. But they were more likely than the missionaries to lay the blame for lascivious tendencies almost exclusively at women's feet. An official from the Charter District could claim in 1923 that "90% of the Mashona women have immoral tendencies, are most irresponsible, readily give vent to their whims and fancies, and are void of all shame." The official concluded by charging that women were responsible for drawing men into temptation and were "the principal offenders" in adulterous liaisons.[14]

Women were judged primarily responsible for the perceived depravity of African society. Missionaries and colonial officials alike blamed African women for adultery, venereal disease, and unhygienic conditions in the home, and for their men's refusal to enter wage employment and to become otherwise "civilized." Native Department officials even claimed that African women's sex drives and overwhelming influence over their men lay at the root of the ever-present labor shortage.[15] Young, able-bodied men were being enticed to stay home to satisfy female sexual desires rather than going to work for the Europeans.[16] State officials were particularly vocal on this subject during the years 1908–11, 1914–20, and 1925–29, when severe labor shortages eroded the profits of European farms and mines.[17]

European men—administrators and missionaries alike—were the product of Victorian society, and did not hold women of any race in particularly high esteem. Their racial bigotry only com-

[13] NAZ, CNC S138/150, Native Commissioner (hereafter cited as NC), Sinoia to Superintendent of Natives, Salisbury, February 23, 1924.

[14] NAZ, N3/17/2, NC, The Range, Charter to Superintendent of Natives, Salisbury, March 14, 1923, no. 88/23.

[15] The Native Department was responsible for matters relating to the indigenous people, including law enforcement, labor recruitment, and tax collection. The European officials in charge of district-level "native" administration bore the title "native commissioner." Because the term "native" was used interchangeably with "savage," "barbarous," or "uncivilized" during the colonial period, it acquired a derogatory connotation. Hence, I use the term only as it appears in official titles.

[16] NAZ, N3/17/2, NC, The Range, Charter to Superintendent of Natives, Salisbury, May 7, 1914, no. 579/500/14.

[17] For data concerning the labor shortage, see Paul Mosley, *The Settler Economies: Studies in the Economic History of Kenya and Southern Rhodesia, 1900–1963* (New York: Cambridge University Press, 1983), 125, 141.

pounded their low opinion of women in general. African women, wrote one state official, were truly "at the bottom of the ladder."[18] The African girl, mused a missionary, "like her black brother [is] naturally idle." Furthermore, "like her white sister, when she has reached her teens and becomes conscious of her fancied or real charms, she is apt to be vain, coquettish, trifling. . . . It will be no easy task," he concluded, "to teach her habits of work, to make her realise the serious character of life and of her duties."[19]

One state official caused an uproar among his colleagues in 1923–24 when he argued for more rights for African women. Native commissioner Posselt suggested that the Native Marriages Ordinance be amended to raise the status of African women, allowing them to possess property in their own right and, under certain circumstances, to retain custody of their children in the event of divorce. Such legislation was necessary, Posselt maintained, because elderly women were often divorced by husbands who no longer wanted to pay taxes for them, and replaced by younger wives. These abandoned women had no independent means of support.[20]

Posselt's colleagues overwhelmingly rejected his proposal, warning that the emancipation of African women would be disastrous. Advocating the retention of laws that condemned African women to perpetual minority status, one native commissioner stressed that African women should remain under the firm control of their fathers, guardians, or husbands for the duration of their lives. "Indeed," he remarked, "until quite recent years, this was the condition among our own race. The native woman of today has not the brain power or civilization of the mothers and grandmothers of the present white generation; her brain is not sufficiently balanced to allow her to think and act in all matters for herself, and I consider the male should be encouraged and assisted to exercise tutelage, within all reasonable bounds, over his womenfolk."[21]

Colonial officials reasoned that African women could best be controlled through economic means. As long as women were totally dependent upon their husbands' access to land and cash income,

[18] NAZ, CNC S138/150, "Native Marriage and the Status of the Native Woman," no name or date (ca. March 1924).

[19] A Visitor, "Some Impressions of Chishawasha," *Zambesi Mission Record* 2, no. 25 (July 1904): 427.

[20] NAZ, CNC S138/150: NC, Marandellas to Superintendent of Natives, Salisbury, November 30, 1923, no. 21/331.

[21] NAZ, CNC S138/150, NC, Hartley to Superintendent of Natives, Salisbury, February 28, 1924. Also see CNC S138/150, NC, Bikita to Superintendent of Natives, Fort Victoria, March 12, 1924, no. 26/24.

their behavior could be kept in line. In the view of one native commissioner, the woman "who submits to the gay life of mining compounds and leaves her lawful husband at the kraal [homestead]" should be forced to "pay the penalty" for her immoral pursuits. When "old age overtakes her and she no longer attracts the opposite sex," she should not be rewarded for her behavior by judicial leniency. By no means should she be given custody of her children. Raising the status of the African woman by permitting her to own property would only encourage in her "a state of independence and lead her to dishonour and ruin."[22] A corollary of this argument, of course, was that economically dependent women would continue to subsidize male wages through subsistence production in the rural areas. Thus, the ideological basis for the domestication of African women masked the broader economic objectives of colonial capital and the state.

Women were thus in a double bind. A "good mother" stayed at home with her children and thus could not earn money to support them. Without independent access to land, and ineligible for most forms of wage employment, most women were considered unsuitable guardians for their own children. On the other hand, if they had access to cash, they were presumed to have obtained it through "immoral means," such as prostitution or beer brewing. Consequently, they were deemed unfit mothers and unsuitable guardians. Either way, women stood to lose.[23]

Economic motives for controlling African women

As the self-appointed trustees of African "advancement" and moral welfare, state officials considered it their duty to punish the "moral laxity" of African women.[24] For example, the Natives Adultery Punishment Ordinance, ratified in 1916, rendered adultery between African men and married African women a criminal offense punishable by a fine of 100 pounds or one year's imprisonment with hard labor. Both partners in crime were subject to the penalty.[25]

[22] NAZ, CNC S138/150, NC, Zaka to Superintendent of Natives, Fort Victoria, March 4, 1924, no. 45/24.
[23] NAZ, CNC S138/150, NC, Gwanda, February 27, 1924.
[24] NAZ, N3/17/2, Acting NC, Wankie to Superintendent of Natives, Bulawayo, May 7, 1914, no. N174/14.
[25] NAZ, N3/17/2, NC, Hartley to Superintendent of Natives, Salisbury, March 13, 1923; CNC S235/429–31, Alfred Drew, "Drew's Articles on Native Affairs, Southern Rhodesia, Part II, No. 26: The Black and White Cohabitation Problem," 10, 13. For discussions of the criminalization of adultery elsewhere in Africa, see Parpart,

Signing the bill into law at the height of a labor crisis on European farms and mines, state officials exposed an interesting intersection of moral prescription and economic objectives. In the course of the debate that preceded enactment, the native commissioner of Mtoko wrote, "Adultery is becoming more and more frequent amongst Natives, and in almost all cases the women concerned are the wives of absentees at work."[26] Rather than attributing the increase in adultery to the migratory labor system's disruption of family life, the official asserted that the problem lay in the fact that too few men were going out to work. The "more vicious and debauched characters" who spent "their lives in idleness in their kraals" were committing adultery with the wives left behind by the migrant laborers. Fear that they would lose their wives made African men hesitant to seek wage employment. The official concluded, however, that if adultery were made a criminal offense, and if men could be assured of their wives' fidelity in their absence, "there would be a marked improvement in the number of males turning out to work."[27] In the view of the state, the financial well-being of the colony required that African women's sexual practices be firmly controlled.

Although many mine owners opposed the criminalization of adultery, fearing it would drive away workers who were forced to come to the mines without their wives, the native commissioner of Chilimanzi maintained that the proposed law would have the opposite effect. He argued that the criminalization of adultery would compel African men from other territories to obtain women "through legitimate means." That is, if they wanted to have sexual relations with local women, they would have to marry them—and pay bridewealth to the women's families. This would force "regular mine boys," most of whom came from other territories, to work for longer periods and "save their wages to pay for wives." Thus an important consequence of the adultery ordinance would be the

---

"Sexuality and Power" (n. 6 above), 119–20; Chanock, *Law, Custom and Social Order* (n. 6 above), 192–201; Martin Chanock, "Making Customary Law: Men, Women, and Courts in Colonial Northern Rhodesia," in *African Women and the Law: Historical Perspectives,* Boston University Papers on Africa, no. 7, ed. Margaret Jean Hay and Marcia Wright (Boston: Boston University, 1982), 60–65.

[26] NAZ, N3/17/2, Acting NC, Mtoko to Superintendent of Natives, Salisbury, May 12, 1914, no. C68/14.

[27] Ibid. For similar statements in support of criminalization, see N3/17/2, C. H. Tredgold, Attorney General, "Minute by Mr. Tredgold, Attorney General of Southern Rhodesia," August 27, 1914; N3/17/4/1, CNC, Salisbury to Secretary, Department of the Administrator, May 9, 1913, no. 25/1121/13.

tying down of foreign workers, "keeping them in the country and ... secur[ing] their services for good."[28]

Women who could not be categorized as adulteresses or prostitutes fared little better in the eyes of the colonial state. Even loving mothers who conformed to the Victorian ideal were held to be accountable for the shortage of African male workers. When a serious labor shortage threatened the nascent European agricultural sector in 1908–11, the state appointed a committee to investigate the matter. According to the report of the Native Affairs Committee of Enquiry (1910–11), "Women frequently adversely affect the labour supply, as they refuse to allow their sons to proceed to work lest they should die or be injured in the course of their employment." Such women, the report concluded, were known to force their husbands to sell cattle in order to pay hut taxes for their sons, even though the sons were fully capable of earning the tax themselves through wage labor.[29] The Committee of Enquiry and its government supporters did not consider the possibility that such women were consciously resisting colonial intrusion into their lives.

The maintenance of law and order

In addition to economic objectives, state officials had important political reasons for attempting to control African women's behavior. Having based their system of colonial administration on the manipulation of indigenous authority structures, colonial officials could not afford to let those structures be undermined. The refusal of women to marry their appointed partners, their persistence in entering into adulterous liaisons, and their flight to missions, mines, farms, and urban areas posed a serious threat to African male authority and, consequently, to the entire system of indirect rule.[30]

[28] NAZ, N3/17/2, NC, Chilimanzi to Superintendent of Natives, Victoria, May 8, 1914, no. 2/331/14.

[29] Jesuit Archives, Box 317, Southern Rhodesia, *Native Affairs Committee of Enquiry* (n. 12 above), par. 6.41. Also see Mosley (n. 17 above), 130–31; NAZ, N9/1/17, Annual Report, Gutu District, 1914, 50–51; Agnes Sloan, "The Black Woman," *NADA [Native Affairs Department Annual]* 1 (1923): 64.

[30] Folbre (n. 7 above), 67–68; Ranger, "Women in the Politics" (n. 7 above), 10–11. Briefly, " indirect rule" refers to a British pattern of keeping indigenous authorities (like chiefs and headmen) in place and then using them to help carry out colonial policy. Colonial officials elsewhere in Africa also understood the relationship between patriarchal control over women and the survival of the system of indirect rule. See Parpart, "Class and Gender" (n. 6 above), 143, and "Sexuality and

One native commissioner provided the following example: if a woman deserted her husband "without just cause" and was ordered to return, the native commissioner must be able to make her comply. If he had no legal means to enforce his order, the woman would see that she was capable of disobeying "recognized authority, thus undermining all law and order."[31] A colleague claimed that, if adultery continued unchecked, African men would begin to resent "the inability of the white government to deal properly with adulterers." Ultimately, he concluded, the problem "threatens to upset the peace of the native races under our control." Unless the government supported African men in exercising "their rights over the wives," not only the family "but the whole existence of a nation" could be placed in jeopardy as well.[32]

British regard for the maintenance of law and order was rivaled only by their respect for private property. Not surprisingly, the severe punishment of adulterers found its ultimate justification in English property law. Basing his case on a misrepresentation of African custom, the native commissioner of Ndanga noted that because an African man had paid bridewealth for his wife, she was his property.[33] Adultery, therefore, was "a serious breach of the

---

Power" (n. 6 above), 115, 119–20; Chanock, *Law, Custom and Social Order*, 111–24, 207–8; George Chauncey, Jr., "The Locus of Reproduction: Women's Labour in the Zambian Copperbelt, 1927–1953," *Journal of Southern African Studies* 7, no. 2 (April 1981): 136, 153; Marjorie Mbilinyi, "Runaway Wives in Colonial Tanganyika: Forced Labour and Forced Marriage in Rungwe District, 1919–1961," *International Journal of the Sociology of Law*, no. 16 (1988), 3, 11–12, 25.

[31] NAZ, N3/17/2, Acting NC, Wankie to Superintendent of Natives, Bulawayo, May 7, 1914, no. N174/14.

[32] NAZ, N3/17/2, Assistant NC (hereafter referred to as ANC), Umtali to Superintendent of Natives, Umtali, May 12, 1914, no. J960. Also see CNC S138/150, NC, Gwanda, February 27, 1924.

[33] Prior to colonial rule, the transfer of bridewealth payments from the husband's to the wife's kin represented the creation of a social bond between two lineages, and the transfer of the woman's productive and reproductive capacities from her kin to her husband and his kin. The transfer of marriage gifts, which could include blankets, baskets of grain, hoes, goats, or cattle, constituted a symbolic social act. Yet it was also a means of petty accumulation involving the exchange of subordinate women and material goods. With the introduction of a cash economy, bridewealth became increasingly commoditized. Now used as beasts of burden, cattle gained in productive value. As young men entered wage employment, fathers began to demand dramatically inflated bridewealth payments composed primarily of cattle and cash. Gradually, bridewealth degenerated into a fundamentally commercial transaction in which wealth was transferred between generations of males, and women were the bartered goods. Most important, bridewealth became one of the few ways in which older men could gain access to the cash wages of younger ones. The practice, which European observers described as "bride buying," was thus the

rights of property only comparable with the more serious kinds of theft." He advocated that "the court should be authorised to assess damages," just as it did in the case of stock theft. However, here the analogy ended. While the native commissioner called for the punishment of both partners—as "in many cases [the woman] is the more guilty of the two"—he did not go so far as to blame the milch cow for enticing the cattle thief.[34]

Like their English counterparts, African women were considered the "principal offenders" in cases of adultery and were held responsible for the growing rate of marital disintegration.[35] This trend was of particular concern to the government because the migratory labor system was predicated upon family stability. The official view of African women was that they were fickle and irresponsible, ensnaring and deserting men at will. In the words of one native commissioner, many "marry men of their own choice and within a few months change their affections and refuse to live with their husbands."[36] Colonial officials accused women of taking advantage of the "freedom of choice bestowed on them by the Native Marriage[s] Ordinance." Whereas the administration had been attempting to prevent the marriage of African girls against their will, the girls had taken "this freedom [as] a cloak for licence." Young women did not have the freedom, officials insisted, "to change their husbands as often as they please."[37]

Colonial courts frequently charged women with having left their husbands "without just cause or reason," although precisely what

---

product of both African custom and European intervention in African society. For a discussion of the social and symbolic significance of bridewealth and inflating bridewealth demands, see J. F. Holleman, *Shona Customary Law: With Reference to Kinship, Marriage, the Family and the Estate* (Manchester: Manchester University Press, 1952), 33, 148–56, 161–65. For evidence that bridewealth became a means by which elderly men consciously acquired cash from younger wage earners, see CNC S138/47, ANC, Goromonzi to NC, Salisbury, February 10, 1932, no. 14/10/32. For a discussion of the degeneration of bridewealth into a commercial transaction, see Jesuit Archives, Box 32, Father Henry Quin, S.J., St. Joseph's Mission, Umvuma, "Letters and Documents," October 27, 1924.

[34] NAZ, N3/17/2, NC, Ndanga to Superintendent of Natives, Fort Victoria, May 18, 1914, no. C527/14.

[35] NAZ, N3/17/2, NC, The Range, Charter to Superintendent of Natives, Salisbury, March 14, 1923, no. 88/23. Also see N9/1/21, Annual Report, Mrewa District, 1918, 86. For a discussion of adultery in England during the same period, see Annette Lawson, *Adultery: An Analysis of Love and Betrayal* (New York: Basic, 1988), 41–45.

[36] NAZ, N3/17/2, NC, The Range, Charter to Superintendent of Natives, Salisbury, March 14, 1923, no. 88/23.

[37] NAZ, N3/17/2, ANC, Umtali to Superintendent of Natives, Umtali, May 12, 1914, no. J960.

the state considered "just" was never specified.[38] Veronica Chigomo, who was born at Chishawasha Mission in 1916, claimed that many women who ran away did so when their husbands married other wives. Alice Chidamahiya indicated that young girls who were pledged to marry against their will also resisted by fleeing their husbands' homes.[39] Despite such testimony, the native commissioner of Goromonzi was confident that "in the majority of divorce cases the wife is in the wrong." Often she was merely—and he implies wrongly—jealous "on account of the husband being married to a younger wife."[40] Taking this argument to its logical conclusion, the native commissioner of Wankie recommended that if the court determined that a woman had left her husband or guardian "without some lawful or just cause," she should be imprisoned if she refused to return to him. "Without a doubt," he proclaimed, "the most effective punishment of the women would be by birching [whipping] them publicly."[41]

State officials were especially irked by wives' growing disregard for the orders of their husbands. According to one irate official, "For some time, and in recent years in particular, I have noticed that the women assume a very arrogant, independent and indifferent attitude towards their husbands and take exception to any genuine

[38] NAZ, N3/17/2, Acting NC, Wankie to Superintendent of Natives, Bulawayo, May 7, 1914, no. N174/14. Of the 345 civil cases heard by the native commissioner of the Goromonzi District between October 1899 and February 1905, ninety-five involved girls who refused to marry men who had paid bridewealth for them, and sixty-five concerned runaway wives. In this district adjacent to the capital, nearly half the civil cases heard by the state were brought by men attempting to obtain the return of recalcitrant wives. Although it was customary for a husband to accept the return of an errant wife, European officials found the practice morally offensive and encouraged African men to divorce wives who had been unfaithful to them. By the 1930s African men were seeking dissolution of their marriages, along with damage payments, return of bridewealth, and child custody. Thus, the vast majority of cases heard by the Goromonzi native commissioner during the 1930s involved divorce petitions by abandoned husbands. Of the 171 cases heard between July 1931 and July 1939, 128 (or 75 percent) were petitions for divorce, most brought by husbands who accused their wives of prostitution, adultery, or refusing to have sex with them. In only fourteen cases did husbands plead for the return of their runaway wives. NAZ, NSL 1/1/1, Civil Cases, Goromonzi District, October 1899–February 1905; S370, Civil Cases, Goromonzi District, July 1931–July 1939; N3/17/2, NC, Rusapi to Superintendent of Natives, Umtali, March 13, 1923, no. 218/21/23.

[39] Interviews with Veronica Chigomo, Chishawasha Mission, December 21, 1985; Alice Chidamahiya, Chihota Communal Lands, February 15, 1986. Also see NAZ NSL 1/1/1: Mandaza vs. Marira, December 12, 1899; Madzima vs. Shikwana, May 7, 1900; Kaduku vs. Zewere, May 4, 1900; Gabaza vs. Tshapangara, January 28, 1901.

[40] NAZ, CNC S138/150, NC, Goromonzi to Superintendent of Natives, Salisbury, March 7, 1924, no. 130/24.

[41] NAZ, N3/17/2, Acting NC, Wankie to Superintendent of Natives, Bulawayo, May 7, 1914, no. N174/14.

remonstration which he may make and this is very often pounced upon as an excuse for deserting him."[42] In fact, women who ran away from their husbands frequently did so as a result of physical abuse. Flight was often the only form of resistance available to them. In 1900, for instance, Tshenjeni was called before the native commissioner's court in Goromonzi. She had run away from her husband, who was suing for her return. "I don't want to go back to my husband," she told the court. "He always ties me up. At the present time he has ropes ready to tie me up. . . . He is always beating me." Despite the woman's pleas, the native commissioner ordered her return to her husband.[43] Some three decades later, Terise ran away from her husband because he beat her constantly and accused her of being a prostitute. "He accused me of prostitution, but never produces or tries to produce proof," Terise told the court. "I refuse to endure this."[44] Clearly African women and European men held very different opinions regarding the limits of a husband's prerogatives.

Wives also ran away because their husbands married other women, were sterile, provided them with insufficient food or clothing, refused to work for their families, or spent too much time and money on beer.[45] Ariyenyanwi left her husband in 1931 "because he would not plough lands" for her.[46] Raaoodzi, a junior co-wife, ran away from her husband, a migrant laborer, in 1902 "because he had neglected [her] for a long time." Explaining her actions to the Goromonzi native commissioner, Raaoodzi said, "My husband has always made me build my own huts and do all my own work," reneging on the assistance that he as a husband was traditionally bound to provide.[47]

[42] NAZ, CNC S138/150, "Native Marriage and the Status of the Native Woman," no name or date (ca. March 1924).
[43] NAZ NSL 1/1/1, Tshigumbi vs. Muza, March 10, 1900. In most cases judicial records contain only "first names" for the Africans involved.
[44] NAZ S370, Case 17/34, Terise vs. Musiwa, July 11, 1934. Also see S370: Case 15/36, Motsi vs. Marumbidza, May 22, 1936; Case 18/36, Zinyemba vs. Maria, June 12, 1936; Case 13/37, Mandaza vs. Mandiwadza, March 9, 1937; interviews with: Musodzi Bvumbwe, Nyadire Resettlement Area, March 31, 1986; Handina Makonyonga, Chihota Communal Lands, February 15, 1986.
[45] Interviews with: Lawrence Vambe, Harare, August 20, 1985; Veronica Chigomo, Chishawasha Mission, December 21, 1985; Musodzi Bvumbwe, Nyadire Resettlement Area, March 31, 1986; Handina Makonyonga, Chihota Communal Lands, February 15, 1986; NAZ NSL 1/1/1, M'fanyana vs. Munenzo, May 5, 1902; S370, Case 16/36, Nemara vs. Pango, May 22, 1936.
[46] NAZ S370, Case 31/33, Ariyenyanwi vs. Chaka, November 1, 1933.
[47] NAZ NSL 1/1/1, Mataranyeka vs. Goradema, September 9, 1902. Also see S370, Case 24/36, Maronje vs. Semnis, November 26, 1936.

New lives for women: Missions, mines, and towns

Despite limited alternatives, women whose domestic situations had become intolerable resisted as best as they could. As legal minors without independent access to land, housing, or wage employment, they were usually forced to find new male patrons. A woman's options were few: she could run away with a lover who would become her new husband; she could seek refuge at a mission station, exchanging the patriarchal control of her father or husband for that of the European missionaries; or she could flee to the towns, mines, or farming compounds. There she would most likely form an informal, often temporary, liaison with a male worker, providing him with domestic and sexual services in exchange for shelter. Her own means of acquiring cash were few; a woman of independent means earned money primarily through the sale of beer or through prostitution.[48]

Prostitutes in the towns and mining compounds often earned enough to live relatively comfortably, and women who formed temporary liaisons frequently did so with an eye to upward mobility. In 1925, a government commission contended that the presence of large numbers of migrant laborers, "separated from their own womenfolk," made prostitution "easy and profitable." The commission further observed that "in some locations and compounds some of the best huts are occupied by women who, if not exactly prostitutes, form irregular, short alliances, and are constantly changing husbands."[49]

Lawrence Vambe, who grew up on Chishawasha Mission during the 1920s, had a similar impression. During the late 1920s or early 1930s, Vambe recalled, a woman named Misi left their village, a dozen miles to the east of Salisbury, and became a prostitute in the capital city. Before she left home, Misi had struggled to support her

---

[48] Lawrence Vambe, *From Rhodesia to Zimbabwe* (London: Heinemann, 1976), 185; NAZ, N3/17/2, Assistant Magistrate, Shabani to Secretary, Law Department, February 21, 1923; CNC S138/150, NC Marandellas, March 13, 1924. For a similar analysis pertaining to Kenya, see Luise White, *The Comforts of Home: Prostitution in Colonial Nairobi* (Chicago: University of Chicago Press, 1990), "Prostitution, Identity, and Class Consciousness in Nairobi during World War II," *Signs: Journal of Women in Culture and Society* 11, no. 2 (Winter 1986): 255–73, and "Domestic Labor in a Colonial City: Prostitution in Nairobi, 1900–1952," in Stichter and Parpart, eds. (n. 6 above), 139–60; Janet M. Bujra, "Women 'Entrepreneurs' of Early Nairobi," *Canadian Journal of African Studies* 9, no. 2 (1975): 213–34; Margaret Strobel, *Muslim Women in Mombasa, 1890–1975* (New Haven, Conn.: Yale University Press, 1979), 135–47.

[49] Jesuit Archives, Box 305, Southern Rhodesia, *Report of the Commission Appointed to Enquire into the Matter of Native Education in All Its Bearings on the Colony of Southern Rhodesia* (Salisbury: Government Printer, 1925), 666, 668.

children with little assistance from her husband, a migrant laborer who worked "very far away from [the village], and . . . could only come and see his family very rarely."[50] Once she became a prostitute, Misi's situation changed dramatically. "As a young boy," Vambe remembered, "I used to see her from time to time when she returned from her travels. . . . She came to her parents' home loaded with gifts and the impression she gave to everybody was that she was doing a very lucrative trade." "Respectable" village women purported to "despise" her, but in Vambe's opinion, "they admired her, not only for her courage, but for the fact that she was so well off materially."[51]

Likewise, female beer brewers frequently earned substantial sums, far more than the average mine laborer. In 1927, for instance, an unskilled underground mine worker earned an average of thirty shillings per month, plus rations valued at six and a half shillings. The same year, the Southern Rhodesia Criminal Investigation Department (CID) reported that a beer brewer could earn as much as fifty pounds in a single weekend. The wife of a "police boy" from one mine "left for Nyasaland with over 900 [pounds] in her possession," the CID claimed, adding that another woman had "evidence to show she had deposited 800 [pounds] with a European. Practically the whole of these amounts had been obtained by the sale of kaffir [African] beer."[52]

In their efforts to escape unhappy marriages and the general adversities of rural life, women sought men who could provide them with something better. Migrant laborers from other territories, who by force of Rhodesian law had left their own wives at home, were particularly attractive to local women. Having entered wage employment at an earlier date, they earned much higher wages than their local counterparts.[53] Native commissioners frequently commented that married women in the vicinity of industrial areas were enticed by "the advantages offered them by natives in employment at mines and other places where they can get plenty of food and clothing and on the whole more pleasure and less hard

[50] Interview with Lawrence Vambe, Harare, August 20, 1985.

[51] Ibid.; Lawrence Vambe, *An Ill-fated People: Zimbabwe Before and After Rhodes* (Pittsburgh: University of Pittsburgh Press, 1972), 200.

[52] Mosley (n. 17 above), 159; NAZ, CNC S138/53, Extracts, C.I.D. Report, April 29, 1927. For similar trends on the Northern Rhodesian Copperbelt, see Chauncey (n. 30 above), 145; Parpart, "The Household and the Mineshaft" (n. 3 above), 41.

[53] N3/17/2, NC, Gutu to Superintendent of Natives, Victoria, May 12, 1914, no. D.G. 7/150/14; N3/17/2, NC, Chilimanzi to Superintendent of Natives, Victoria, May 8, 1914, no. 2/331/14.

work than they have at the kraals."[54] Even colonial officials had to admit that foreign mine workers generally offered local women better living conditions than their own husbands were able to provide.[55]

African women and girls also ran away to European mission stations, submitting to the strict disciplinary codes of puritanical Christians rather than enduring even less tolerable circumstances at home. Missionaries intervened in the most intimate aspects of their daily lives, monitoring their sexual and marital practices. Jesuit and Wesleyan Methodist missionaries, for instance, required that newcomers agree to monogamous Christian marriages. They banned premarital sex and the custom of elopement, which would have entailed sexual relations before a church wedding. Any woman who became pregnant out of wedlock, who married according to local custom rather than Christian rite, or who ran away with a man who was not her husband was summarily expelled from the mission.[56]

Life on the mission stations was not easy. Chishawasha women made and maintained mission roads. They weeded and harvested crops on the mission farm, as well as taking care of their own fields and families after they married.[57] Nonetheless, many women preferred such a life to the one they had abandoned. They could go to school, they would not be forced to marry against their will, and they could choose a husband without the consent of their guardians.[58]

From the early days of European occupation, women who had been mistreated by their husbands and the junior wives of polygynous men were frequently among those who fled to mission stations.[59] In the 1910s, Dominican sisters at Chishawasha reported

[54] N3/17/2, NC, Selukwe to Superintendent of Natives, Gwelo, May 14, 1914, no. D.221/218/14.

[55] N3/17/2, NC, Gutu to Superintendent of Natives, Victoria, May 12, 1914, no. D.G.7/150/14.

[56] Vambe, An Ill-fated People, 3–14; interviews at Chishawasha Mission (Jesuit) on December 12, 1985: Sophia Chitia; Evangelista Mazhindu; interviews at Epworth Mission (Wesleyan Methodist): Elijah Marwodzi and Rhoda Maruva, January 27, 1986.

[57] Interviews at Chishawasha Mission: Elizabeth Mbofana, January 4, 1986; Eve Dembetembe, November 23, 1985.

[58] W. R. Peaden, Missionary Attitudes to Shona Culture, 1890–1923, Local Series, no. 27 (Salisbury: Central African Historical Association, 1970), 22; Ranger, "Women in the Politics" (n. 7 above), 15.

[59] Jesuit Archives, Box 100/1, "African Visitors etc. at Chishawasha, 1892–3," from Father Rea's manuscript notes; Peaden, 25–27.

harboring the sixth wife of a local elder.[60] This woman brought her five children with her, an unusual step that undoubtedly incensed male authorities because child custody was normally awarded to the father by virtue of the bridewealth payment. In 1924, Chief Seki refused to let the Wesleyan Methodists establish a mission school near his village, charging that the missionaries interfered with his authority. "When I beat my wives they will run to the teacher for protection," he told the missionaries.[61]

Missionary and colonial records are replete with cases of girls seeking refuge at missions to avoid forced marriages, and occasionally to further their education.[62] Emelda Madamombe, who was born in 1918 in Chief Seki's reserve on the outskirts of Salisbury, ran away to Chishawasha after her eldest brother refused to let her continue her schooling. He had pledged her in marriage to an old man and was anxious to collect the bridewealth. Having learned from local villagers that the government had outlawed the pledging of young girls, Madamombe absconded to the mission school, both to free herself from an unwanted marriage and to continue her education. "That is the reason I ran away to Chishawasha and refused to marry the man he had chosen for me," she explained.[63]

Some women repudiated all suitors, choosing instead to become "brides of Christ." During the 1920s and 1930s, unmarried girls and widows who refused to be "inherited" as wives by their husbands' kin fled to Catholic mission stations, where they declared their intention of becoming nuns.[64] "Long back lots of [girls] came to be sisters because their parents wanted to give them to old men," Veronica Chigomo claimed.[65]

[60] A Dominican Sister, *In God's White-robed Army: The Chronicle of the Dominican Sisters in Rhodesia, 1890–1934* (Cape Town: Maskew Miller, n.d., ca. 1947), 189.

[61] WMMS, Box 828, Rev. Latimer P. Hardaker, Epworth to Miss Bradford, March 4, 1924.

[62] A Dominican Sister, 215, 232–33; "Chishawasha Notes," *Zambesi Mission Record* 1, no. 4 (May 1899): 118; NAZ, CNC S138/47, NC, Rusapi to CNC, Salisbury, February 5, 1927, no. 317; interviews with: Elizabeth Sande, Chishawasha Mission, December 18, 1985; Elijah Marwodzi, Epworth Mission, January 27, 1986; Hamundidi Mhindurwa, Seke Communal Lands, January 26, 1986.

[63] Interview with Emelda Madamombe, Seke Communal Lands, January 26, 1986.

[64] Ranger, "Women in the Politics," 14–16; interview with Elijah Marwodzi, Epworth Mission, January 27, 1986; interview with Francis C. Barr, S.J., Emerald Hill Orphanage, Harare, February 5, 1986; A. J. Dachs and W. F. Rea, *The Catholic Church and Zimbabwe, 1879–1979* (Gwelo: Mambo Press, 1979), 139. Leviratic marriage was common in this region, as in many other parts of the world.

[65] Interviews with Veronica Chigomo, Chishawasha Mission, December 21, 1985; Dambudzo Nengari, Seke Communal Lands, February 1, 1986; NAZ, CNC

According to state law, missions could not accept the girls without their guardians' consent.[66] But many guardians would not acquiesce unless they were paid the equivalent of the bridewealth they would have received upon their daughters' marriage. If their daughters were the "brides of Christ," the guardians contended, then Christ should pay their bridewealth.[67] Since the church was not prepared to accept this burden, "the priests let the girls work so they could pay their own bridewealth," Veronica Chigomo recalled. "Even my sister, Mary, who was a nun, worked in town to get bridewealth to pay my brother." Employed as a nanny, Mary was able to earn the requisite eighteen pounds after two years of hard work. Other girls worked for up to four years to satisfy their guardians' demands.[68]

The creation of "customary" law

The colonial state tried to coerce women into staying with their husbands through a variety of mechanisms it attempted to legitimate by referring to "native custom." Seeking versions of Shona and Ndebele customs that promoted their agenda, state officials consulted an array of "legal experts," invariably chiefs, headmen, and elders—men who had a stake in reasserting control over women.[69] Senior men took advantage of this opportunity to bolster old bases of power and to establish new ones. According to these African "experts," women's claims in court cases of abuse or neglect were contrary to "tradition" and thus not worthy of consideration.[70]

S235/376, "Affidavits of Emma Chikaidzo and Hilda Chihodziwa," presented to NC, Umvuma, March 6, 1931.

[66] Francis C. Barr, S.J., *Archbishop Aston Chichester, 1879–1962, a Memoir* (Gwelo: Mambo Press, 1978), 23; Ranger, "Women in the Politics," 16; A Dominican Sister, 243.

[67] Archdiocese Archives, Box 545, NC, Salisbury to Father Burbridge, S.J., Vicar Delegate, Salisbury, June 17, 1940; interviews with Sr. Clara, LCBL, Makumbi Mission, December 30, 1985; Sr. Immaculata, LCBL, Chichester Convent, Harare, November 27, 1985.

[68] Interview with Veronica Chigomo, Chishawasha Mission, December 21, 1985. Similar examples are cited in interview with Sr. Anna, O.P., House of Adoration, Harare, November 26, 1985; Dachs and Rea, 141; A Dominican Sister, 243; Barr, 23.

[69] See, e.g., Holleman (n. 33 above), x. The Shona and Ndebele were the two major ethnic groups in colonial Southern Rhodesia.

[70] Martin Chanock, who pioneered recent investigations into the creation of "customary" law in colonial Africa, described a similar process of law making in Northern Rhodesia: "The lengthy process of taking evidence and cross-examining chiefs and elders . . . led to a stating, defining, clarifying, a regularizing of customary

While custom had been both flexible and sensitive to extenuating circumstances, "customary law," now written in stone, was not.[71] This transformation was particularly striking in child custody cases, where colonial authorities attempted to control women by using their children as bait. According to Shona and Ndebele custom, bridewealth payments conferred upon men rights over their children. Thus, fathers were usually awarded custody in the event of marital breakdown. Occasionally, however, mothers and their kin might be considered the preferred guardians, particularly if the fathers' kin could not adequately support the children.[72] Colonial officials refused any such flexibility. Intent upon applying hard-and-fast rules based upon immutable principles, they invariably favored fathers over mothers, husbands over wives—all in the name of "respect for native custom."

Through the rigid application of the father-right principle, native commissioners' courts frequently coerced women into remaining with abusive or disinterested husbands, under threat of losing their children. According to one official, "The knowledge that she will be deprived of her children if she misbehaves or leaves her husband is a gentle stimulus to keep her in the path of virtue."[73] Numerous cases reveal that women who rebelled were, indeed, forced to relinquish their children. Such judgments, the state maintained, instilled in women obedience and respect for their husbands' authority. In 1938, for instance, Tembenawo sought to divorce his wife, Makawana, on grounds of desertion. Presenting her case to the native commissioner, Makawana said, "I have lived

---

practices (both real and manufactured) in a way which was designed to turn fluid accounts of relationships at work into rules. It must be seen . . . not as part of the process of discovering the rules of customary law but as a vital part of the rule-making process. . . . The rules would reflect the current anxieties and aims of the witnesses, and if these coincided with the moral predilections and administrative purposes of the officials, a 'customary law' might become established." Chanock, "Making Customary Law" (n. 25 above), 65, 66–67. Also see Chanock, *Law, Custom and Social Order* (n. 6 above), 4, 8, 146, 149; Terence Ranger, "The Invention of Tradition in Colonial Africa," in *The Invention of Tradition,* ed. Eric Hobsbawn and Terence Ranger (New York: Cambridge University Press, 1983), 212, 247–58.

[71] For a similar critique of "customary" law as it was applied to the Shona, see M. F. C. Bourdillon, "Is 'Customary Law' Customary?" *NADA* 11, no. 2 (1975): 142–43, 147.

[72] Interviews with Lawrence Vambe, Harare, August 20, 1985; Chikowore Chivhunga, Seke Communal Lands, January 18, 1986; Mirika Makoni, Chihota Communal Lands, March 1, 1986.

[73] NAZ, CNC S138/150, Superintendent of Natives, Fort Victoria, March 11, 1924. Also see NC, Zaka to Superintendent of Natives, Fort Victoria, March 4, 1924, no. 45/24; ANC, Mtetengwe to NC, Gwanda, March 5, 1924, no. 128/182/24.

with [Tembenawo] many years—more years than I know. I refuse to return to him. He always beats me." Despite these circumstances, the native commissioner granted Tembenawo a divorce and custody of the two children.[74] Similarly, Chimbuya ran away from her husband, Mujambi, after successive beatings, the last of which had caused her to be hospitalized. After hearing the case, the native commissioner granted Mujambi a divorce on grounds of desertion and awarded him custody of the five children. Despite the evidence of his brutality, the plaintiff was considered a more fit guardian for the children.[75]

Bridewealth was another device used to keep African women in line. Prior to the colonial period, a deserted husband was much more likely to petition for his wife's return—even over the course of several years—than attempt to get his bridewealth back. Generally, he had no interest in severing the ties between his wife's lineage and his own, which the return of bridewealth was bound to do. If a husband had been brutal, a woman's family was unlikely to force her to return, relying instead on time to heal the wounds and resolve the conflict. But when native commissioners began to prescribe divorce and the return of bridewealth as a remedy for women's desertion or adultery, families began pressuring their daughters to remain in potentially life-threatening situations.[76]

Although some officials warned that bride "prices" were inflating far beyond the means of most young men, creating a potential for social unrest, others felt that the higher bridewealth payments had positive ramifications. One official described bridewealth as "the only corrective to a woman's tendency to go wrong." If a woman deserted her husband, colonial courts would order her guardian to return the substantial bridewealth, which could cause severe financial distress to the woman's relations.[77] Older men, who had long since paid their own bridewealth and now looked forward to receiving an even greater amount for their daughters, tended to concur. At a Native Board meeting held at Goromonzi in 1932, a number of them indicated that "nowadays women were fickle enough anyhow, but . . . if [bridewealth] was reduced to a small amount there would be even less hold on them, as there was no doubt that the average girl, if tempted to leave her

[74] NAZ S370, Case 20/38, Tembenawo vs. Makawana, July 2, 1938.

[75] NAZ S370, Case 32/37, Mujambi vs. Chimbuya, November 26, 1937.

[76] Chanock, "Making Customary Law," 56–58, 64–65; see, e.g., NAZ S370, Case 26/37, Tigere vs. Mukweru, May 28, 1937.

[77] NAZ, CNC S235/475, Federation of Women's Institutes of Southern Rhodesia, *Report of the Standing Committee on Domestic Service*, July 1930, Testimony of E. R. Morkel, 48.

husband for no real cause, was at the moment influenced to a certain extent by the fact that her father had received a large amount of [bridewealth] for her which he would find difficult to refund."[78]

Patriarchal control: An unholy alliance

Colonial officials justified their crackdown on African women by claiming that a "mandate" had been bestowed upon them by African men. According to attorney general C. H. Tredgold, the criminalization of adultery was recommended almost unanimously by officials and "natives" who had testified before the Southern Rhodesia Native Affairs Committee of Enquiry in 1910–11.[79] "Natives," of course, referred only to African men, specifically older men of the highest social and political strata. In 1913, the chief native commissioner in Salisbury wrote of the elders' dissatisfaction throughout Mashonaland: "At almost every meeting of Chiefs held by me the chief topic of conversation is in regard to their wives and the way they run off with other men (chiefly aliens on mines) with impunity. The Chiefs are very bitter on the subject and would welcome an amendment to the [Native Marriages] Ordinance placing some restraint on their wives running away as they do."[80] Another official referred to the "continual outcry" for the criminalization of adultery from "the more influential portion of the community." He maintained that the present law "does not meet the most urgent claims of the older and middle aged men"—the primary constituents of the Native Department, and those whose discontent was to be most assiduously avoided.[81] The adultery ordinance was finally enacted in 1916 as a "result of continuous representations made by Chiefs, Headmen, Heads of Kraals and responsible natives throughout the country."[82]

In spite of the passage of the Natives Adultery Punishment Ordinance, the situation did not improve insofar as African men

[78] NAZ, CNC S138/47, ANC, Goromonzi to NC, Salisbury, February 10, 1932, no. 14/10/32.

[79] NAZ, N3/17/2, C. H. Tredgold, Attorney General, "Minute by Mr. Tredgold, Attorney General of Southern Rhodesia," August 27, 1914.

[80] NAZ, N/17/4/1, CNC, Salisbury to Secretary, Department of the Administrator, May 9, 1913, no. 25/1121/13.

[81] NAZ, N3/17/2, NC, Gutu to Superintendent of Natives, Fort Victoria, May 12, 1914, no. D.G.7/150/14.

[82] NAZ, N3/17/2, NC, Mtoko to Superintendent of Natives, Salisbury, March 12, 1923, no. 26/23.

were concerned. Nearly two decades after the passage of the act, African men were still complaining to the government that their women were out of control. These complaints took on a special urgency during the 1930s, a period when African men and women migrated to the cities in rapidly growing numbers.[83] All-male Native Boards, instituted during the 1930s as safety valves for African discontent, were popular forums for the airing of grievances concerning wayward women. In 1933, a member of the Native Board in the Goromonzi District spoke for many of his colleagues when he called upon the administration to "arrest unmarried women in [urban] locations . . . also on farms and mining compounds." This sort of action, he claimed, would make them return to their fathers and guardians.[84]

Senior African men and colonial officials agreed that they would have more leverage over women if corporal punishment were inflicted for adultery, desertion, and other offenses. In 1931, a chief in the Goromonzi District suggested that the government impose such punishment on women "who made frivolous complaints" against their husbands. Endorsing the chief's recommendation, the native commissioner noted that "the same views were held in England not many generations ago" and queried, "Are we wiser than our forebears?"[85] A few years later, the members of the Goromonzi Native Board requested that the native commissioner inflict corporal punishment on girls who refused to return to their parents after having been found in the town locations.[86]

Restrictions on women's mobility

From the 1910s through 1930s, both African and European men registered numerous complaints concerning the mobility of African women. In 1913, several Manyika men working in Salisbury complained to the native commissioner of Umtali about the behavior of three Manyika girls in the town location. As the girls were purportedly committing "all sorts of evil, going from one man to another," the complainants asked that the girls be forced to return to their fathers' homesteads. Further, the men wrote, "we wish [there were] a law that shall never allow a Manica [Manyika] girl to come

[83] See Mosley (n. 17 above), 168.

[84] NAZ, S1542/N2 (E-G), "Minutes of the Fourth Session of the Native Advisory Board of Salisbury District," held at Goromonzi on October 12, 1933, 71.

[85] NAZ, S1542/N2 (E-G), Acting NC, Goromonzi to CNC, Salisbury, July 2, 1931, no. 196/264/31.

[86] NAZ, S1542/N2 (E-G), ANC, Goromonzi to NC, Salisbury, April 25, 1934, no. 63/224/34.

here and not let any of them ride the train from Umtali or from any of the stations and sidings, such as Odzi, Rusape, etc." Although he doubted the writers' claim to authority over the girls, the chief native commissioner found the girls at the bidding of his Umtali subordinate and forcibly sent them home.[87]

Numerous sources criticized the facility with which African girls and women gained access to "motor lorries" and trains. In 1927, several chiefs called for a pass system for women, in an effort to limit the number who "escaped" by taking trains to the urban centers. According to one native commissioner, it was far too easy for women to abscond: "If a woman has a grievance against anybody—if she has been smacked by her husband for not cooking properly—she is off by the next train."[88] A few years later a chief in the Goromonzi District complained that girls and women went out "to farms and townships and mines" as prostitutes: "Our daughters go about everywhere because they are helped to travel by motor lorries. Also whenever a man punishes his daughter by beating for going away without the father's permission, they complain to the police and the father is prosecuted."[89] Because the native commissioner himself encouraged parents to inflict "corporal punishment in mild form" on their errant daughters, the veracity of the latter statement is somewhat in doubt.[90]

While European administrators and senior African men agreed that African women should be prevented from "travel[ing] unchecked from one end of the country to the other," the ideal method for restricting their movement continued to be a matter of debate.[91] In 1933, the native commissioner of Salisbury proposed that African women be issued travel passes.[92] In this way, the marital status and guardianship of every woman could easily be established. A few years later, the same official indicated that female visitors to the city would "receive no pass unless the consent of their husbands or

[87] Quoted in Ranger, "Women in the Politics" (n. 7 above), 13. Tswana men exercised similar prerogatives over unrelated women of their ethnic group who had made their way to Cape Town in the 1920s and 1930s. Sheila Tlou, remark at the annual meeting of the National Women's Studies Association, Minneapolis, Minnesota, June 25, 1988, and personal communication, October 30, 1988.
[88] Quoted in Kersten England, "A Political Economy of Black Female Labour in Zimbabwe, 1900–1980" (B.A. thesis, University of Manchester, 1982), 53.
[89] NAZ, S1542/N2 (E-G), "Minutes of the Fourth Session," October 12, 1933, 5.
[90] NAZ, S1542/N2 (E-G), ANC, Goromonzi to NC, Salisbury, April 25, 1934, no. 63/224/34; "Minutes of the Fifth Session of the Native Advisory Board of Salisbury District," held at Goromonzi on April 24, 1934, 45.
[91] NAZ, CNC S235/475, Federation of Women's Institutes of Southern Rhodesia, *Report of the Standing Committee on Domestic Service,* July 1930, Testimony of F. Hulley, 43.
[92] NAZ, S1542/N2 (E-G), "Minutes of the Fourth Session," October 12, 1933, 6.

guardians has been obtained."[93] Members of the Goromonzi Native Board proposed that marriage registration certificates serve as a form of pass document; no woman should be allowed to stay on European farms, in mining compounds, or in town locations unless she could produce one.[94] Unmarried women, or at least those whose unions were not recognized under the Native Marriages Ordinance, could thus be identified—and forced to return to the rural areas.

Conclusion

During the colonial era in Southern Rhodesia, African chiefs, headmen, and other senior men; European capitalists; and state officials collaborated in their efforts to control the behavior of African women. While African men sought to reassert their waning authority over women, their services, and their offspring, European men had a different agenda. In the economic realm, they were concerned with obtaining cheap African male labor. If it took the regulation of African women's sexual practices to achieve this objective, the state was prepared to pass laws to that effect. In the political sphere, the colonial administration was intent upon maintaining law, order, and respect for authority, both African and European. While European officials were expected to keep order at the state level, African chiefs, headmen, village elders, and male heads of households were expected to maintain tight control in the villages and homes. Rather than destroying African male authority in toto, the colonial state intended to harness it for its own ends.

If colonial officials were worried by African women's disregard for authority, they also feared the anger of the African men who had lost control over their women. Having blamed European rulers for their predicament, older African men were at once seething with resentment and pleading for colonial intervention. With its own authority at stake, the colonial state sought to mollify male discontent by helping the men regain control. For unless patriarchal authority was in some measure restored, the growing disenchantment of older men and their female charges could throw into jeopardy the whole colonial enterprise.

Department of History
Loyola College, Baltimore

[93] NAZ, S235/517, Annual Report, Salisbury District, 1939, 11.
[94] NAZ, S1542/N2 (E-G), "Resolutions Passed at Meeting of Native Board of Salisbury Native District," held at Goromonzi on May 5, 1933.

The "Woman Question" in Cuba: An Analysis of Material Constraints on Its Solution

Muriel Nazzari

At the turn of the century European socialists believed that the advent of a socialist society would solve what they called the "woman question." Women would gain equality before the law; they would enter socially useful production on a par with men; private domestic economy would be transformed into a public enterprise through the socialization of housework and child care; and the personal subjection of women to men would end.[1] The Soviet Union, the Eastern European nations, and the People's Republic of China have all proclaimed these goals, yet they have fallen short of fully realizing them.[2]

Participants in the Cuban Revolution shared the belief that socialism would bring about complete equality between the sexes. As early as 1959, Fidel Castro spoke about the need to free women from domestic slavery so that they could participate widely in production to the benefit of women themselves and the Revolution.[3] Over the next twenty years the government increased women's educational opportunities and labor force participation while providing more and more services to lighten domestic chores for those who worked outside the home. In the early seventies it went one step farther than any other socialist nation by

I wish to thank Emilia da Costa, Silvia Arrom, David Montgomery, Peter Winn, Frank Roosevelt, and the Women's History Study Group of the Institute for Research in History for comments on earlier drafts of this essay.

1. *The Woman Question: Selections from the Writings of Karl Marx, Frederick Engels, V. I. Lenin, Joseph Stalin* (New York: International Publishers Co., 1951).

2. Gail W. Lapidus, *Women in Soviet Society: Equality, Development and Social Change* (Berkeley and Los Angeles: University of California Press, 1978); Batya Weinbaum, "Women in Transition to Socialism: Perspectives on the Chinese Case," *Review of Radical Political Economics* 8, no. 1 (Spring 1976): 34–58.

3. Fidel Castro, "Speech to the Women" (Havana, 1959), p. 9.

[*Signs: Journal of Women in Culture and Society* 1983, vol. 9, no. 2]

enacting the Cuban Family Code, which makes husband and wife equally responsible for housework and child care.[4]

Despite these positive developments, the consensus in Cuba today is that full equality for women has yet to be achieved. A factor frequently invoked to explain this state of affairs is the persistence of prejudice and machismo in Cuban society. According to one scholar, these attitudes remain because of the inevitable time lag between structural and ideological change.[5] Important though ideological change may be for achieving women's equality, this paper concentrates instead on the material constraints that prevent Cuban society from attaining this goal. The changing position of women will be analyzed in the context of the larger struggle surrounding the economic strategies adopted during Cuba's transition from capitalism to socialism. I will argue that the Cuban Revolution's full adoption in the early seventies of a system of distribution based on material incentives and the requirement that enterprises show a profit perpetuates women's inequality in the home and in the work force.

My argument rests on the fact that child rearing requires both labor and resources. Marxist-feminist theory has stressed the social importance of women's labor for reproducing the work force, both generationally (through biological reproduction and the socialization of children) and on a day-to-day basis (through housework and emotional nurturance).[6] If we assume that the labor involved in the daily care of a worker (housework) is a given in any society and could conceivably be performed by workers for themselves, then the variable that determines women's position in the home and society is generational reproduction, that is, childbearing and child rearing. This follows the trend of current feminist thought, which recognizes that reproductive labor is implicated in women's oppression.

I take this argument one step further, however. Women's position is determined not only by the institutional arrangements that apportion the labor of child rearing to women but also by the institutions that determine how children gain access to means of subsistence. In developed industrial societies, both capitalist and socialist, most children receive their means of subsistence from the wages of one or both parents. Wage labor, however, cannot usually be performed simultaneously with the labor necessary to raise children. The resulting contradiction historically led to a specific division of labor within the family, the father working outside the home for a wage, the mother doing housework.

4. Marjorie King, "Cuba's Attack on Women's Second Shift, 1974–1976," in *Women in Latin America: An Anthology from Latin American Perspectives,* ed. Eleanor Leacock et al. (Riverside, Calif.: Latin American Perspectives, 1979).

5. Lourdes Casal, "Revolution and Conciencia: Women in Cuba," in *Women, War and Revolution,* ed. Carol Berkin and Clara M. Lovett (New York: Holmes & Meier, 1980).

6. For example, see Isabel Larguia and John Dumoulin, "Aspects of the Condition of Women's Labor," *N.A.C.L.A.'s Latin America Empire Report* 9, no. 6 (September 1975): 2–13.

The theoretical socialist answer to the woman question was to change this division of labor by socializing child care and housework so that married women and mothers could engage in production on an equal basis with men.[7] In practice, socialist countries have thus far found it impossible to eliminate all aspects of privatized household and family maintenance. Cuba has sought to compensate for this shortcoming by passing a law requiring men to share housework and child care.

My analysis of the Cuban case makes it seem evident that both socialist strategies (the socialization of domestic chores and child care and the equal apportionment of the remaining tasks between husband and wife) are necessary but not sufficient conditions for achieving full equality between women and men. Although both address the issue of the allocation of labor for child rearing, neither considers the implications of the fact that raising children also requires access to resources. A full solution to the woman question must therefore address the issue not only of the labor needed to raise children but also of the income needed to raise children. Power relations within the family can be affected by whether that income comes from the father, the mother, both parents, or society as a whole. The issue of systems of distribution therefore has a direct impact on Cuba's attempts to solve the woman question.

The Choice of Systems of Distribution in Cuba

The Cuban Revolution moved quickly toward the implementation of a socialist society. In the early sixties it effected a general redistribution of income by raising wages while lowering rents and prices. Meanwhile, it nationalized all means of production except for small peasant holdings and small businesses. To manage the nationalized productive units, the new government had to develop and institute nationwide systems of management and choose a system of distribution of goods, services, and income. Because the Revolution was committed to guaranteed employment for all, it also had to design a system of work incentives to replace the fear of unemployment that motivates workers in capitalist economies.

The problem of work incentives in a socialist society is linked to the choice of a system of distribution. In capitalist economies, income distribution is carried out principally through the wage and through the profit that accrues from ownership of the means of production. In socialist economies, private ownership of the means of production is largely abolished, and private profit disappears as a source of income.

7. A review of the problems socialist countries have encountered trying to implement this solution can be found in Elisabeth J. Croll, "Women in Rural Production and Reproduction in the Soviet Union, China, Cuba and Tanzania: Socialist Development Experiences," *Signs: Journal of Women in Culture and Society* 7, no. 2 (Winter 1981): 361–74.

When Marx envisioned this ideal society he proposed that distribution be carried out by the formula: "From each according to his ability, to each according to his need." He called this the communist system of distribution. Under this system people would be expected to work to contribute to society, but not for wages, because goods and services would not be bought or sold, and needs would be met as they arose. Marx believed it would be impossible to implement a communist system of distribution during the transitional stage from capitalism to socialism. For a time, distribution would have to follow a different formula: "From each according to his ability, to each according to his work." This formula is called the socialist system of distribution, and under it needs would primarily be met through remuneration for work, that is, through the wage.[8] After the triumph of the Cuban Revolution, the question was whether it would be possible to use a combination of both the socialist and the communist systems of distribution.

During the early sixties there were ideological struggles within the Cuban Communist party over this issue as well as the related issue of incentives—a problem embedded in the formula of distribution according to need.[9] In all historical eras people have worked to satisfy their needs, either directly through access to the means of production or indirectly through wage labor. But if a socialist society satisfies needs independently from work, what will induce people to labor? The Cuban Revolution never completely abandoned the wage as a system of distribution or a work incentive. Nevertheless, throughout the sixties the Revolution emphasized moral over material incentives and promoted nonwage volunteer labor.

During that period Castro expressed the belief that Cuba could utilize both systems of distribution simultaneously. In 1966 he declared that as soon as possible society must use its resources to provide for all essential needs, including health, housing, adequate nutrition, physical and mental education, and cultural development. The Revolution was already providing free education, health care, sports, recreation, and meals in schools and workplaces. He added that the government intended to supply housing and day care without charge as soon as possible.

In the same speech Castro discussed the problem of family dependents. Should the earning power of a son determine how an elderly parent lives, or would it not be preferable for society as a whole to ensure that the old have all they require? In the case of children, he contended that the "shoes and clothing they receive, as well as their toys, should not

8. Castro explained both systems to the Thirteenth Congress of the Confederation of Cuban Workers. See "XIII CTC Congress: A History Making Event," *Cuba Review* 4, no. 1 (July 1974): 15–25.

9. See Bertram Silverman, *Man and Socialism in Cuba* (New York: Atheneum Publishers, 1971).

depend on whether the mother has ten children and can do little work, but rather on the needs of the child as a human being."[10]

These statements indicate that Castro envisioned a society in which the means to satisfy basic needs would be freely available to everyone and children and old people would receive their subsistence from society itself rather than depend on relatives' wages for support. Although this ideal solution was never fully implemented in Cuba, much of the initial redistribution after the Revolution was evidently carried out according to need, unrelated to recipients' work in production.

Initial Effects of the Cuban Revolution on Women

Many Cuban women have claimed that women were the greatest beneficiaries of the Revolution. Are they right in their assessment? Did women gain more from the Revolution than men?

Differences in the ways women and men were affected by the Revolution can be traced to their traditional roles. Most Cuban women were housewives, not wage workers. The initial measures of redistribution brought about a change in their living and working conditions, but the class lines that divided Cuban women caused them to experience these changes in very different ways.

Middle- and upper-class women experienced a loss, since they shared with their male relatives a reduction of income. The nationalization of productive enterprises and banks abolished dividends at the same time as lower rents decreased landlords' profits. Many emigrated, but of those who remained in Cuba, women experienced greater hardships than men. Men from these classes retained their status because their skills as entrepreneurs and professionals were valuable to the Revolution. In contrast, the status of middle- and upper-class women (except for those who were themselves professionals) had formerly been defined by the large amount of leisure they enjoyed, which was a function of their ability to avoid performing menial labor by hiring others to do domestic chores. After the Revolution, these women lost servants, chauffeurs, and nurses.

Conditions for lower-class housewives, on the other hand, improved dramatically during the first five years. All the initial measures of redistribution resulted in positive changes within the lower-class home, with the most spectacular differences evident in rural areas where pre-revolutionary poverty had been greatest. The Agrarian Reform eliminated rural rents and evictions by giving tenants, sharecroppers, and squatters free title to the land they were farming. All large estates were

10. Martin Kenner and James Petras, eds., *Fidel Castro Speaks* (New York: Grove Press, 1969), p. 213.

nationalized and transformed into collective farms to be worked by landless agricultural workers, resulting in permanent incomes and adequate housing for the remaining rural families.[11] The Urban Reform slashed rents and electricity and telephone rates by half. These redistributive measures meant a 15–30 percent rise in wages, which increased the purchasing power of the poor at the same time that prices for other essentials were being lowered.[12]

Lower-class housewives could feed and clothe their families better. Consumption of the foods that a majority of Cubans had rarely eaten before, such as milk, eggs, and meat, soared. Until production could be increased to meet the expanded purchasing power, rationing was instituted to guarantee everyone a certain amount of these products. At the same time, better clothing became available through a program that brought young women to Havana from all over Cuba to learn to sew. The first thousand took free sewing machines back to their rural homes; each committed herself to teach at least ten other women how to cut and stitch.[13]

During this early period housing was also upgraded. Urban housing was redistributed by transforming large old residences abandoned by their former owners into apartments. New buildings were constructed for the agricultural collectives, latrines were added to existing rural dwellings, cement replaced dirt floors, and many people had running water and electricity for the first time. New roads in rural areas made buses available to previously isolated families.[14]

The most spectacular accomplishments of the Cuban Revolution—the literacy campaign and the institution of free education and health care for all—also had an effect on the working conditions of lower-class housewives. Education revolutionized both immediate opportunities and future expectations for them and their children. Free health care combined with lessons in hygiene and an improved standard of living to yield a decline in the infant mortality rate from 43.6 per one thousand live births in 1962 to 19.4 in 1979.[15] By the early seventies, 98 percent of all childbirths were medically attended.[16] Polio, diphtheria, and malaria were eradicated, and life expectancy rose to seventy years. Since women were the ones who traditionally cared for the ill, they especially benefited from these improvements in health.

11. Edward Boorstein, *The Economic Transformation of Cuba* (New York: Monthly Review Press, 1968), pp. 42–54, 78–79.

12. Archibald R. M. Ritter, *The Economic Development of Revolutionary Cuba* (New York: Praeger Publishers, 1974), p. 107.

13. Laurette Séjourné, ed., *La mujer cubana en el quehacer de la historia* (Mexico, D.F.: Siglo Veintiuno, 1980), pp. 124–33.

14. Ibid., pp. 121, 128.

15. Fidel Castro in *Granma Review* (March 16, 1980).

16. *Economia y desarrollo*, September–October 1974, p. 198.

Much of the early redistribution in Cuba was undoubtedly effected through the formula "to each according to his need." Rural inhabitants were not given cement floors because they had money to pay for them, nor were they allocated housing because their individual jobs were important. Rather, people learned to sew and read and received health care solely because they needed these skills and services. Yet not all distribution was carried out according to this formula. During the same period, a large portion of people's needs was still met through the wage. The improved purchasing power of the wage, however, was not due to wage earners' efforts or productivity but to deliberate policies framed by the Revolution in accordance with the formula of distribution according to need.

This lavish initial redistribution was only made possible by drawing on existing reserves such as nationalized land and capital, formerly unused resources in equipment and land, and underutilized sectors of the labor force like women and the unemployed.[17] But these reserves were not inexhaustible. To achieve economic growth, hard work and increased productivity became necessary.

Economic Growth and Work Incentives

To meet these economic imperatives, in the mid-sixties the Revolution adopted a mixture of moral and material incentives and experimented with different strategies for growth. One strategy involved industrialization through import substitution and agricultural diversification. By 1963 a crisis in the balance of payments prompted a shift in economic policy. From 1964 to 1970, the government returned to sugar production as the principal source of foreign exchange, stressing investment in production for export and the acquisition of capital goods at the expense of the production of consumer goods.[18] Meanwhile, services such as education, health care, public telephones, sports, and child care continued to be furnished at no cost. The income gap between workers with the highest wages and those with the lowest narrowed, as did the gap between urban and rural incomes.[19]

By the end of the decade the combination of ample wages and free services with rationing and the restricted production of consumer goods put money in people's pockets but gave them nowhere to spend it. The wage no longer functioned as an incentive to work when there was not enough to buy and many goods and services were provided at no cost. Absenteeism at work reached a high point.

17. Boorstein, pp. 81–83.
18. Ritter, pp. 128–270.
19. Jorge I. Dominguez, *Cuba: Order and Revolution* (Cambridge, Mass.: Harvard University Press, Belknap Press, 1978), pp. 227–28.

At the same time, economic problems were multiplying, leading to an increased awareness of general inefficiency and low productivity. In response to these problems, massive readjustments of Cuba's social, economic, and political structures took place after 1970, culminating in 1975 with the First Congress of the Communist Party. This restructuring addressed several areas of concern. A deflationary monetary policy corrected the imbalance between money in circulation and the amount of available consumer goods. A reorganization of the managerial system and the substitution of material for moral incentives responded to the problems of low productivity and inefficiency. Union reforms, moves to strengthen and broaden the Communist Party, and the creation of People's Power (the new government administrative system) sought to structure channels for carrying negative feedback to the central planning bodies.[20]

All these measures increased the efficiency of Cuba's planned socialist society, but the first two (the monetary policy and the new system of management) involved a change from a commitment to carry out as much distribution as possible according to need to an ever greater reliance on the socialist formula. Distribution became principally tied to the wage, and enterprises were expected to show a profit. Since the wage, material incentives, and production for exchange are also the mainstays of capitalist societies, these measures represented a decision not to go as far in revolutionizing society as initially planned.

This was a conscious decision. The Thirteenth Congress of the Confederation of Cuban Workers, which took place in 1973, extensively debated the two systems of distribution and the issue of moral versus material incentives. Castro maintained that the development of productive forces had been hindered because Cuba had been too idealistic in the use of moral incentives and distribution according to need. The Congress concluded that Cuba must adopt distribution according to work, since the productive forces would have to develop much further to reach the stage in which all distribution could successfully be carried out according to need.[21]

In order to analyze the effects of these policy decisions on the condition of women in Cuba, we will compare the situation of women in the labor force and the home before and after the shift in systems of distribution.

Women in the Work Force, 1959–69

Because the Batista regime left a legacy of seven hundred thousand unemployed and three hundred thousand underemployed men, one of

20. Ritter, p. 250; Dominguez, pp. 243–49, 271–79, 306–40.
21. Castro (n. 8 above).

the first goals of the Revolution became full male employment. By 1964 this goal had been achieved, and it affected not only the men involved but also the women and children who depended on the men's wages.

Despite the priority placed on achieving full male employment during the first five years, the Revolution did not entirely ignore the issue of women's participation in the work force. Instead, it concentrated on women who were already working by providing child care and other services to assist them. Night schools and boarding schools were set up for the large number of women who had been domestic servants or prostitutes at the time of the Revolution. These institutions functioned until the women learned new jobs, becoming typists, secretaries, bank tellers, and bus drivers.[22]

Though the Revolution did not immediately incorporate all women into paid work, it created the Federation of Cuban Women to mobilize them for building the new society. The federation organized day-care centers and started schools to train day-care workers, formed sanitary brigades to supplement professional medical care, and became the backbone of the campaign to eliminate illiteracy.[23]

Women's participation in voluntary organizations required their liberation from the patriarchal norms that had traditionally confined them to the home. Individual men often resented this change. One woman recalled, "It was husbands who were most limiting, and the rest of the family, too, because they were used to seeing woman as the center of the home, the one who solved all problems, and they didn't understand that women could solve problems outside the home, too."[24] Going from the home to the street, from solving the problems of a family to resolving issues in the larger community, profoundly altered women's lives and perceptions of themselves.

As soon as full male employment was achieved, a demand for women in the work force developed. In May 1966, Castro called for the addition of a million women to the labor force, remarking that, if each woman created a thousand pesos of value per year, a billion pesos of wealth would be produced by women annually. And he indicated that the government was building more and more nurseries and school cafeterias to make it easier for women to work outside the home.[25]

Yet only nine months later, Castro's emphasis had shifted. Women were still needed in production, but the Revolution was finding it difficult to provide the thousands of facilities that would make it possible for a million women to work. He pointed out that, to liberate women from all the activities hindering their incorporation into the work force,

22. Ramiro Pavon, "El empleo femenino en Cuba," *Universidad de Santiago*, December 1975, p. 123.

23. Ministerio de Justicia, *La mujer en Cuba socialista* (Havana: Editorial Orbe, 1977), pp. 20–42.

24. Séjourné, ed. (n. 13 above), p. 193, my translation.

25. Kenner and Petras, eds. (n. 10 above), p. 207.

society had to create a material base. In other words, Cuba had to develop economically.

This means that, at the same time Castro was asking women to work, he was also informing them of material constraints that prevented the government from providing the costly social services that would free them for wage labor. When government planners had to decide between alternative investments, day-care centers frequently came in second. Castro noted that the establishment of day-care centers was slowest in regions where the greatest amount of road and building construction was underway. Nevertheless, this speech was a rousing call to women. In it Castro claimed that the most revolutionary aspect of Cuba's transformation was the revolution taking place in Cuban women.[26]

During the rest of the decade the Federation of Cuban Women responded valiantly to his appeal. It mobilized thousands of women for volunteer work, especially in agriculture, culminating in the 41 million hours of volunteer labor women contributed to the sugarcane harvest of 1970. Meanwhile, the federation continued to pursue its objective of incorporating one hundred thousand women per year into the paid work force and conducted a search for women to run the countless small businesses nationalized in 1968.

By the early seventies, however, it was obvious that recruiting women into wage work was an uphill effort. Seventy-six percent of the women who joined the labor force in 1969 left their jobs before the year was out.[27] As the Cuban Revolution modified its policies to address inefficiency and low productivity, analysts began to explore the causes behind women's impermanent tenure in paid occupations.

Diagnoses and Solutions

In 1974 the Federation of Cuban Women reported that high turnover among women workers could be attributed largely to "the pressure from housework and family members; the lack of economic incentive; and the need for better services to aid working women."[28] The federation also organized a survey to investigate why there were so few women leaders in government. In the trial run of People's Power held in the province of Matanzas, women constituted only 7.6 percent of the candidates and 3 percent of those elected. Both male and female respondents to the survey believed that if women had not been nominated, had

26. *Bohemia* (December 16, 1966). Day-care centers continued to be built, providing three meals a day and laundering clothes worn at the center. There were 433 centers in 1970 and 782 in 1978 (Federation of Cuban Women, *La mujer cubana, 1975–1979* [Federation of Cuban Women, Havana, n.d., mimeographed], p. 10).

27. Ministerio de Justicia (n. 23 above), pp. 252–57.

28. Ibid., p. 252, my translation.

refused nomination, or simply were not elected, it was due to family responsibilities.[29]

These disturbing trends at the national level posed the question of whether the problems that prevented women from participating in government were the same as those that kept women from joining or remaining in the labor force. Another study was conducted comparing the free time available to working women with that available to working men and nonworking women. It found that housework occupied nine hours and fourteen minutes of the daily time budget for housewives, four hours and forty-four minutes for working women, but only thirty-eight minutes for working men. In the words of the study's authors, "The time society and especially women dedicate to housework is at the center of all discussion having to do with the struggle toward women's full equality."[30]

I would argue, in contrast, that the issue in the struggle for women's equality is not housework per se but child care and the additional housework the presence of children requires. In this respect the research mentioned above has a serious defect, since it averages time spent performing housework and child care without establishing how many women in the sample had children. A survey of mothers alone, as opposed to women in general, would have revealed much less free time. Thus the "family problems" cited to explain why few women were nominated or elected to People's Power in Matanzas must have referred not to housework, which can usually be postponed, but to child care, which cannot.

In response to these and other studies, the federation made many suggestions that were later implemented to help correct the problems women experienced. Day care was restricted to children of working mothers. Those children were also given priority access to boarding schools and to day schools that served meals. Stores lengthened their business hours so women could shop after work, and a plan was devised to give working women precedence at food markets. Employed women received better laundry services, some provided at the workplace.[31] These measures helped, but they did not eliminate women's double work shift. The conclusion ultimately reached by Cubans was that men and women must share housework and child care. As one woman worker argued in one of the many popular debates about the Family Code, "If they're going to incorporate us into the work force, they're

29. Primer Congreso del Partido Comunista, *Sobre el pleno ejercicio de la igualdad de la mujer,* 3d thesis, p. 5.

30. Marta Trigo Marabotto, ed., *Investigaciones científicas de la demanda en Cuba* (Havana: Editorial Orbe, 1979), pp. 96–101, esp. p. 101, my translation.

31. Carollee Benglesdorf and Alice Hageman, "Emerging from Underdevelopment," in *Capitalist Patriarchy and the Case for Socialist Feminism,* ed. Zillah Eisenstein (New York: Monthly Review Press, 1979).

going to have to incorporate themselves into the home, and that's all there is to it."[32] In 1975 this belief was made law with the adoption of the Family Code that gave women and men equal rights and responsibilities within the family.

This law can be seen as a change in the locus of the solution to the woman question. The solution first attempted, socializing child care and housework, tried to move women toward equality by transferring their family duties to social institutions without disturbing men's lives or roles.[33] Cuban economists calculated that for every three women who joined the work force, a fourth must be employed in institutions supplying supportive services to facilitate their incorporation.[34] The great cost of this solution meant that it had to compete with other investment needs in the national budget, especially those that would more obviously aid economic development. The Family Code, on the other hand, provided a solution to the woman question that did not need to come out of the national budget. It would take place within the home without affecting the rest of society. It did, nevertheless, require a change in individual men's lives, and men resisted.[35] However, as we shall see, other factors operating in the Cuban context indicate that the difficulties encountered in achieving equality between men and women within the family cannot be attributed solely to men's recalcitrance.

Inequality within the Home

To discover what factors make the equality proclaimed by the Family Code difficult to achieve, we must analyze the situation of wives and mothers. Housewives constituted three-fifths of the adult women outside the work force in 1972, and married women were only 18 percent of women employed.[36] A possible conclusion to draw from this data would be that housework and child care discouraged married women from taking paid employment. Yet the same set of data shows that the largest category in the female labor force was divorced women (43 percent, followed by single women, 30 percent, and ending with widows, 9 percent). Since divorced women are just as likely as married women to have children to care for, the variable determining their incorporation into the work force must have been divorce itself. Conversely, the variable permitting married women to remain outside the work force must have been access to a husband's wage. Under a system of distribution accord-

32. Margaret Randall, *Afterword* (Toronto: Women's Press, 1974).

33. As suggested by Edmund Dahlstrom, *The Changing Roles of Men and Women* (Boston: Beacon Press, 1971), p. 175.

34. Pavon (n. 22 above), p. 115.

35. Megaly Sanchez, "Rights and Duties Go Together," *Cuba Review* 4, no. 2:13–14.

36. Juceplan, *Aspectos demográficos de la fuerza laboral femenina en Cuba* (Havana, 1974), pp. 32, 44.

ing to work, the needs of the wageless housewife are met only through her husband's labor, reinforcing his power and her dependence.

The dependence of children and the elderly also continued under the socialist system of distribution. The Family Code held parents rather than society responsible for the support of minors.[37] This section of the new law provoked no objection when the code was debated throughout Cuba, possibly because similar statutes prevail in most modern nations. But tying the fulfillment of children's needs to the wages of their parents directly contradicted Castro's 1966 statement that a child's subsistence should be determined solely by the "needs of the child as a human being." The Family Code also established the responsibility of workers to support parents or siblings in need, contrary to Castro's suggestion that the income of the elderly should not depend on the earning power of relatives.[38] In this sense the Family Code itself was a step away from distribution according to need toward distribution according to work.

While the Family Code was being elaborated and discussed in the early seventies, the Cuban Revolution was making important economic changes related to the full implementation of the socialist formula for distribution. The government instituted price increases that were explicitly intended to reduce the amount of money in circulation and to act as an incentive to individual productivity.[39] The goal of abolishing house rents was postponed indefinitely. Prices for long-distance transportation, cigarettes, beer, rum, restaurant meals, cinemas, and consumer durables rose. Free public telephones were abolished, and people were now charged for canteen meals, water, and electricity.[40] By 1977 day care was no longer free, forcing mothers to bear part of the cost of providing the conditions that enabled them to work.

In the face of higher prices and fewer free services, the nonworking mother's increasing dependence on her husband's wage might lead her to avoid pressing him to share housework and child care. Whether the working mother would do so would depend on the degree of parity between her wage and her spouse's. If the husband's income were much greater, making the well-being of the children more heavily dependent on the father's wage than the mother's, a woman might perform the extra labor associated with child care so as not to hinder her husband's productivity. This would allow him to work overtime, join the Communist Party, or be elected to People's Power as ways to augment his earning capacity. Unless the wages of husband and wife were equal, we would therefore expect a system of distribution tied to the wage to

37. Ministry of Justice, *Family Code* (Havana: Editorial Orbe, 1975), articles 33, 122.
38. Ibid., articles 122, 123.
39. Dominguez (n. 19 above), p. 170.
40. Carmelo Mesa-Lago, *Cuba in the 1970's* (Albuquerque: University of New Mexico Press, 1974), pp. 42–48.

exacerbate inequalities between men and women in the home. What is the current situation in Cuba?

Women in the Work Force, 1970–80

It is not at all evident whether there is a gap between the national average wages of male and female workers in Cuba. Cuban law establishes that men and women must be paid an equal wage for equal work, and no statistics are compiled comparing men's and women's earnings. Yet the General Wage Reform of April 1980 shows a difference between the minimum wage set for office and service employees, $85 per month, and that of industrial workers, $93.39 per month.[41] In 1979 only 21.9 percent of the female work force held industrial jobs, while 66.5 percent were in service occupations.[42] We can conclude that, at least at the level of minimum wage work, women's average wage is lower than men's due to the concentration of female labor in the service sector. This is partially confirmed by data on day-care workers, an exclusively female occupational group, who were the lowest-paid workers in 1973, receiving only 77 percent of the national average wage.[43]

Yet the fact that women are overrepresented in the service sector does not necessarily mean that women as a whole earn less than men, since there are also many female professionals. For example, in 1977, 66 percent of the employees at the Ministry of Public Health were women. Professionals were 39 percent of all workers in that ministry, and of these, 75 percent were women. Women constituted 5 percent of the superior personnel who formulate overall plans and policies for public health, 20 percent of upper-level administrators, 33 percent of the doctors, 95 percent of the nurses, 82 percent of the paramedics, and 75 percent of community assistants.[44] In 1979 professionals and technicians constituted 27 percent of the entire female work force. If we add the 4.7 percent who were managerial personnel, we find that over 30 percent of all women employed in Cuba are technicians, professionals, or managers.[45] This high proportion of women in better-paid positions means there may not be a gap between the national average wages of men and women.

There is, however, a general inequality between Cuban men and women that proceeds from the way the constitutional principle of guaranteed employment has been interpreted. In practice, only males

41. *Granma Review* (April 6, 1980).

42. Calculated from a table in *La mujer cubana, 1975–1979* (n. 26 above), p. 9.

43. Dominguez (n. 19 above), p. 501.

44. Federation of Cuban Women (n. 26 above), pp. 16–17.

45. Statistics presented to the Third Congress of the Federation of Cuban Women (see *Direct from Cuba,* March 15, 1980).

and female heads of household are guaranteed jobs. The antiloafing law, passed in the early seventies, makes work compulsory for all males (but not females) over seventeen who are not students or military personnel. As a result of these policies, women in Cuba are used as a labor reserve.

Categorization as a labor reserve has had different effects for women under each system of distribution. During the sixties when Cuban women provided much unpaid voluntary labor, the lack of a wage was not such a disadvantage because a large number of needs were met at no cost. In contrast, once the satisfaction of needs became principally tied to the wage, to go without a wage for volunteer work or to have difficulty finding employment had more serious consequences.

Being part of the labor reserve results in lower wages for some working women in Cuba. This is certainly the case for female cyclical contract workers in agriculture. Although contracts protect these women from uncertain employment, and the women also receive full maternity benefits even when childbirth occurs outside the work period,[46] their wage and pension rights are apportioned according to work accomplished.[47] Because they work only part of the year as seasonal laborers, their annual income and pension rights will necessarily be smaller than those of male counterparts who work year-round.

There are also indications of a lack of sufficient employment for Cuban women. An important function of the Federation of Cuban Women is to coordinate information about job vacancies for female applicants. In 1980, even women trained as technicians were reported to be having difficulty finding jobs.[48]

When full male employment is viewed against the shortage of jobs for women, it appears that women are hired only as needed. This is confirmed by Vilma Espin, who notes that the proportion of women in the work force grew from 23 percent in 1974 to 30 percent in 1979 but adds that expansion of the female labor force will not be able to continue at this pace because women's participation in employment depends on the "requirements of the economic development of the nation."[49] Linking women's job opportunities to national economic needs adds an insecurity to the lives of Cuban women that Cuban men, with guaranteed employment, do not experience.

There are also negative consequences for women that follow from the new system of management adopted in the seventies, which established that enterprises must show a profit by producing over and above inputs. This profit is different from profit in capitalist societies, which goes to shareholders and owners. In Cuba, since all enterprises belong to the state, the largest share of the profit goes to the national

46. Ministerio de Justicia (n. 23 above), p. 130.
47. Vilma Espin in *Granma Review* (March 7, 1980).
48. Ibid.
49. Ibid., my translation.

budget by way of a large circulation tax. The remaining profit is distributed by the workers' collective of each enterprise for three purposes: (1) to improve the technical and productive capacity of the enterprise; (2) to improve the sociocultural level of employees; and (3) to provide material and monetary rewards to individual workers, including management, in proportion to results achieved.[50] But an emphasis on profit includes a concern with cost. Under the new system of economic management, any extra expense entailed in the employment of women would logically result in prejudice against hiring them. There is evidence of both the cost and the discrimination.

The first expenditure enterprises employing women encounter is tied to the maternity law. This excellent law provides that pregnant women receive a fully paid leave of six weeks before and twelve weeks following childbirth. However, the employing enterprise must underwrite the total cost of this leave.[51] It is safe to assume that, given the choice between hiring women who might become pregnant and hiring men, any enterprise required to show a profit would prefer to hire men.

The most constant cost of employing women workers lies in their higher absentee rate, which is due to family obligations. In his 1980 speech to the Federation of Cuban Women, Castro remarked that a certain amount of absenteeism has now practically been legalized so that women can perform duties they cannot carry out after hours, such as taking children to the doctor.[52] Castro's comments confirm that, despite the Family Code, men have not assumed family responsibilities that interfere with their wage labor. This may be partly due to resistance in the workplace. If we accept the existence of a cost to the enterprise in women's conflicting duties at work and at home, it becomes evident that it would require major readjustments in the workplace if males, 70 percent of the work force, were to perform an equal share of domestic tasks. These conflicting responsibilities continue to be identified as "women's problems."

In the early seventies the Revolution created the Feminine Front to provide an "organized channel through which women workers' needs are made known to the entire workplace, to be solved by the entire workplace."[53] But having women workers' needs addressed by the workplace signifies yet another cost to the enterprise. In practice, we would expect to find a tendency for businesses to avoid or reduce the extra expenses inherent in solving the "problems" of women workers. This reality may have prompted the Federation of Cuban Women to

50. Fidel Castro, *Report of the Central Committee of the Communist Party of Cuba to the First Party Congress* (Havana, 1977), p. 159; Raul Martell, *La empresa socialista* (Havana: Editorial Orbe, 1978).

51. Ministerio de Justicia (n. 23 above), pp. 120–32.

52. Castro (n. 15 above).

53. *Cuba Review* 4, no. 2 (September 1974): 27–28.

recommend in 1975 that enterprises employing women hire sufficient personnel to compensate for absences caused by maternity leaves, vacations, and illnesses of the worker or her family; otherwise, female co-workers end up absorbing the added work load.[54] Attempts to put this recommendation into practice would certainly conflict with the need to lower costs and show a profit under the system of management now in effect.

There is ample evidence of ongoing discrimination against hiring women. For example, a report to the Second Congress of the Federation in 1974 reads, "Managers sometimes refuse to employ female labor, because this forces them to increase the number of substitutes with the consequent growth of the staff, which affects the evaluation of productivity."[55] Another account describes the prejudice that leads managers to choose men to occupy jobs instead of women and documents how women are denied political and administrative promotions to avoid subsequent difficulties related to their family responsibilities.[56] In 1980, Vilma Espin denounced the persistence of this prejudice.[57] But denunciations alone cannot be effective as long as such prejudice has a material basis in the actual cost to the enterprise of finding solutions to the "problems" of women workers.

Conclusion

Material constraints to the solution of the woman question in Cuba originate in the drive for socialist accumulation and the development of the country's productive forces. These concerns have led the Revolution to make policy decisions that preserve women's inequality in the labor force, perpetuate the personal dependence of women on men, and thus work against the equal sharing of housework and child care decreed by the Family Code.

The Cuban constitutional guarantee of employment for all has, in practice, been transformed into guaranteed male employment, backed by a law making work compulsory for men. Underlying these measures is the assumption that adult women will be supported by their husbands or other male relatives. In accordance with this premise, the government feels free to use women for seasonal agricultural labor and as a labor reserve. Though efficient at the national level, at the individual level these practices reinforce male power at women's expense.

The Cuban Revolution's current endorsement of the socialist system

54. Primer Congreso del Partido Comunista (n. 29 above), p. 7.
55. *Memories: Second Congress of the Cuban Women's Federation* (Havana: Editorial Orbe, 1975), p. 4.
56. Primer Congreso del Partido Comunista (n. 29 above), p. 5.
57. Vilma Espin (n. 47 above).

of distribution and material incentives also contributes to women's continued subordination. Distribution through the wage, combined with higher prices and fewer free goods or services, makes wageless or lower-paid wives more dependent on their husbands than they were during the period when distribution according to need was also in effect. For mothers this dependence is compounded by concern for the well-being of their children. The requirement that enterprises show a profit contributes to discrimination in hiring because women's needs increase operating expenses. Since they constitute a labor reserve and cannot always find employment, individual women who realize they may not be economically self-sufficient all their lives will rely primarily on relationships with men for financial support. The degree to which women's access to resources is more limited than men's in an economy where distribution is tied to the wage and children rely on parental support thus constitutes a material barrier to any final solution of the woman question.

Because the socialist formula for distribution based on material incentives has had negative effects for women in Cuba, women would seem to have an even greater stake than men in the eventual implementation of a communist system of distribution. Such a system would allow people to work according to their abilities and reward them on the basis of their needs. Household maintenance and child care would be counted as work. Inequalities would disappear between manual and intellectual labor, between service providers and industrial workers, between individuals who raise children and those who do not, and between women and men. This ideal society appears to be far in the future.

In the meantime the Cuban national budget could subsidize maternity leaves and other expenses related to women's employment in the paid labor force. At a national level, plans could be made to restructure enterprises so that men can assume their share of family responsibilities. Lessening the individual mother's dependence on her husband's wage would also involve carrying out what Fidel Castro envisioned in 1966: society as a whole must provide the means of subsistence for children, so that not only parents but all workers share in their support.

Department of History
Yale University

"The Teachers, They All Had Their Pets": Concepts of Gender, Knowledge, and Power

Wendy Luttrell

Tell me what you remember about being in school.

What I remember most about school was that if you were poor you got no respect and no encouragement. I mean if you didn't have cute ringlets, an ironed new uniform, starched shirts, and a mother and father who gave money to the church, you weren't a teacher's pet and that meant you weren't encouraged.

What I didn't like about school, the teachers they had their own pet. If you were a pet you had it made, but if you weren't they didn't take up no attention with you. Everybody knew that the teachers treated the kids who were dressed nice and all better—the teachers all had their pets.

Introduction

THIS ARTICLE is about what two groups of women remember about being in school and what their stories tell us about the twisted relations of gender, knowledge, and power. It is part of a larger research project that illuminates the ways in which gender, race, and class together shape the knowledge that women define

I would like to acknowledge the women who shared their school memories with me, especially those who read and responded to portions of my manuscript. I am indebted to many others who have read versions of this paper; special thanks to Mary Hawkesworth, Nancy Hewitt, Dorothy Holland, Naomi Quinn, Robert Shreefter, Jean Stockard, and John Wilson for their insightful and critical comments. Finally, I would like to thank the *Signs* editors and anonymous reviewers for their help revising the manuscript.

[*Signs: Journal of Women in Culture and Society* 1993, vol. 18, no. 3]

and claim for themselves. My goal in the project is to draw new bound-aries for the by-now familiar discussion of "women's ways of knowing" that will allow us to move between more theoretical discussions about women as knowers and more empirically grounded discussions about how social differences make a difference in women's knowing and, in so doing, to revitalize discussion about how to improve women's education.

Since the pathbreaking work of Nancy Chodorow (1978) and Carol Gilligan (1982), many compelling yet incomplete claims have been made about how women construct and value knowledge in ways that are re-lational, oriented more toward sustaining connection than achieving au-tonomy, and governed by interests to attend to others' needs.[1] Similarly, some feminist accounts have invested women with distinctive intuitive and/or emotional capabilities, citing women's exclusion from other ways of acquiring knowledge under patriarchy and locating women's knowl-edge in the "body," or female sexuality.[2] Still others have written about women's epistemic advantage in viewing the world more wholistically based on their particular "standpoint."[3] In contrast, men's ways of knowing have been associated with instrumental reason and abstract rules, oriented toward gaining mastery over nature, and governed by interests in dominating others; by this account, men's social position intrudes on their ability to see the world accurately.[4] The dangers of this gender symbolism within feminist discussions of epistemology have been noted by several scholars, one of whom warns against claims that un-wittingly reproduce "patriarchal stereotypes of men and women—flirting with essentialism, distorting the diverse dimensions of human knowing, and falsifying the historical record of women's manifold uses of reasons in daily life" (Hawkesworth 1989, 547).[5] These theoretical speculations and debates notwithstanding, however, very little empirical work has been done that either maps out women's diversity as knowers or describes the varied and changing conditions under which different women claim and construct knowledge.[6]

---

[1] There is an ongoing dialogue about how gender shapes what and how women know. This debate has spanned the disciplines, including philosophy, psychology, sociol-ogy, and education (Chodorow 1978; Gilligan 1982, 1988, 1990; McMillan 1982; Har-ding and Hintikka 1983; Lloyd 1984; Martin 1985; Belenky et al. 1986; Smith 1987; Levesque-Lopman 1988; Bordo and Jaggar 1989; Ruddick 1989; Collins 1990).

[2] See Daly 1973, 1978; Cixous 1976, 1981; Griffin 1980; Irigaray 1985; Trask 1986.

[3] O'Brien 1981; Jaggar 1983; Rose 1983; Hartsock 1985; Smith 1987; and Collins 1990 represent the range of feminist "standpoint" theorists.

[4] See Gilligan 1982; Keller 1984; Bordo 1986; Harding 1986; Tronto 1989.

[5] See also Harding and Hintikka 1983; Grant 1987; and Heckman 1987.

[6] *Women's Ways of Knowing* (Belenky et al. 1986) is a noteworthy example of re-search that considers the different contexts within which women claim and/or deny knowledge (as children in abusive relationships, as female students in school, as new

My research seeks to fill this gap in the scholarship by juxtaposing the views, values, and schooling experiences of two groups of women who have been underrepresented and misrepresented in the literature: learners in adult basic education classes. I was interested in exploring what skills and knowledge these women learners claimed, dismissed, denied, and minimized in themselves and what skills and knowledge they sought to acquire by returning to school. School was by no means the only site where these women defined, valued, and/or claimed knowledge.[7] Through their past and present schooling experiences, however, they had developed certain views about themselves and others as authoritative or deficient knowers that I sought to untangle.[8]

I was particularly concerned about how the women saw themselves as knowers, as the literature characterizes them as "dropouts" who had been damaged by or failed at school and as individuals seeking a "second chance" by participating in adult basic education. My experience as an educator of adults made me question this oversimplified characterization. Instead, I had heard adult basic education learners, particularly women, define their relationship to schooling in ambivalent, sometimes oppositional, and often contradictory ways. Moreover, I had heard adult learners talk about the gaps between "schoolwise" and "commonsense" knowledge and knowing, and I wondered about the consequences of these distinctions for adult literacy learning and teaching (Luttrell 1989). Through extensive classroom observation and in-depth interviews, I sought to provide a more complicated and rich account of women's paradoxical relationship to schooling, knowledge, and power.

Research process

My research can best be described as a comparative ethnography of two adult basic education programs: the first a community-based pro-

---

mothers raising children, e.g.). The conclusions they draw, however, have more to do with developmental stages of knowing than with the historical, political, or ideological conditions that shape women's knowing.

[7] I have been influenced by Mary Hawkesworth's suggestion that feminist theories of knowledge would be improved if we focused more on the process of knowing than on the knowers themselves. She defines knowledge or a way of knowing as a "convention rooted in the practical judgments of a community of fallible inquirers who struggle to resolve theory-dependent problems under specific historical conditions" (1989, 549). I am interested in how the women came to define themselves as a "community of fallible inquirers" with specific problems and in how these communities and problems are shaped by gender, race, and class.

[8] Indeed, as several black feminist scholars have noted, school may not be the best site for exploring African-American women's claims to knowledge. Instead, black churches and/or black community organizations serve as more informative contexts for how African-American women develop their authority and knowledge. See Grant 1982; Giddings 1984; Gilkes 1985, 1988; Collins 1990.

gram in Philadelphia and the second a workplace literacy program at a North Carolina state university. I interviewed three hundred women about their reasons for returning to school, observed several classes in each program, and selected fifteen women from each program to interview in depth about their school, family, and work lives.

In 1980 I began collecting data from the community-based program in Philadelphia that I had helped organize in 1976 as part of a larger program serving the needs of local women as they faced changes in the community. Once stable and vibrant, this historically white, ethnic (mostly Irish and Polish), and working-class neighborhood had lost its industrial base, suffering economic decline and rising unemployment. In addition, the community had long been ignored by public institutions. Local residents complained about poor health services, nonexistent childcare facilities, a lack of recreational facilities, increased rates of drug and alcohol abuse, environmental hazards, and a rising crime rate. In the face of city, state, and federal cutbacks, neighborhood women were taking on new or additional burdens to make ends meet. Some women were entering the labor force for the first time, while others were seeking more lucrative employment so they could support their families. For everyone, the integrity and quality of community life was being called into question. This questioning included a profound shift in what had traditionally been expected from women residents. In response to these changes, the Women's Program offered a wide range of educational opportunities, counseling services, on-site child care, vocational training, and a battered women's hotline.

In developing new adult education curriculum materials for the program, during 1980–83 I interviewed 180 women who had grown up in the neighborhood and had participated in the program. These interviews were loosely structured to elicit discussion about the women's views about community needs and why they had returned to school.[9] At the same time I observed several classes noting student-student and teacher-student interactions and student responses to the coursework and its demands. After a year of observation I conducted three in-depth interviews over a year's time with selected women in their homes. In the course of these interviews, I met family members and friends, observing the women in an environment outside of school that enabled me to better elicit and

---

[9] The purpose of these interviews was to develop a curriculum guide for adult basic learners that identified certain "generative" themes. The concept of generative theme is drawn from the work of Brazilian educator and political activist Paulo Freire 1970, 1973, 1987. The two most talked-about concerns that emerged in these interviews were parenting and unemployment. The curriculum guides that I wrote based on these generative themes are titled *Women in the Community: A Curriculum Guide for Students and Teachers* (Luttrell 1981) and *Building Multi-Cultural Awareness: A Teaching Approach for Learner-centered Education* (Luttrell 1982).

contextualize the women's educational experiences, views, and values. I tape-recorded and then transcribed each interview.[10]

My stratified, selective sample represented the basic demographic profile of women in the community, including marital status, occupation, income, educational level, religion, and race. The sample also reflected the basic profile of program participants in terms of age, family situation, past attendance and type of school, academic achievement, and level of participation in the classroom, program, or community. In addition to these sampling guidelines, all the women I interviewed were mothers with children still living at home. This decision was based on the results of the unstructured interviews with program participants and/or graduates in which the overwhelming response to the question, "why are you returning to school," was the general statement, "to better myself." Upon further probing about what it meant to "better" oneself, 80 percent of the women volunteered that they were returning to school to become "better mothers." Less than half of these same women explained that they were in school to secure "better jobs" and roughly a third mentioned that a high school diploma would increase their willingness and confidence to converse with family members, particularly husbands. I wanted to explore these findings more fully in the in-depth interviews.[11]

The Philadelphia interviewees were all white and had been raised in the neighborhood. Most still lived within blocks of where they had been born and where extended family members still resided. They had all attended neighborhood schools during the 1940s, 1950s, and early 1960s. One-third had gone to parochial school, and two-thirds had gone to public school.[12] Five of the fifteen women had graduated from high school, and the rest had dropped out either before or during their sophomore year of high school. They had all moved in and out of the work force as factory hands, clerical workers, waitresses, or hospital or teachers' aides. Two-thirds of the women were married at the time of the

[10] The focus of each in-depth interview was loosely defined and depended on how each woman responded to the opening question. In the first interview I asked the women to tell me what they remembered about being in school; in the second interview I asked them to describe themselves as learners; and in the third interview I asked about why they were returning to school. As we talked about their schooling experiences, the women offered detailed accounts of their work and family histories as well.

[11] I elaborate elsewhere on the range and thematic content of the reasons that the women gave for returning to school (Luttrell 1992). Briefly stated, my argument is that the women's shared reasons for attending adult basic education programs illuminate the hidden structure of schools that are organized around women's work as mothers and the ideology of maternal omnipotence.

[12] The Philadelphia women's school careers varied. While a third had at one point attended Catholic coeducational grammar school, only two of these had attended Catholic all-girl high schools. Of the women who had attended public coeducational grammar and high schools, two had attended the public girls' high school before it had become coed.

interviews, although over the course of the study half of these became divorced single mothers. (Of the unmarried women, only two had never been married.)

In 1985, I began the second case study in which I followed the same research protocol as in the first. Again I entered the field as a teacher, curriculum-development specialist, and researcher. The second program was considerably smaller than the first and offered only literacy and high school equivalency classes to selected members of the university's maintenance staff. This program had served approximately two hundred people over a ten-year period, including janitors, housekeepers, painters, electricians, landscapers, and members of the motor pool. The majority, however, were black female housekeepers. I interviewed fifty women participants, and a year later selected fifteen women to interview in depth.

The North Carolina women were all black and had been raised in southern rural communities, although they now resided in communities close to the university. Most had grown up on tenant farms, and all but two had tended tobacco and picked cotton in their youths. All had attended segregated rural grammar schools, often in one-room schoolhouses, and reported sporadic school attendance for reasons I will discuss later. All were employed as housekeepers at the university and shared similar work histories that included domestic work in white people's homes. Throughout the interviews they offered accounts of the tremendous social and political changes in the South that had fundamentally challenged their expectations and roles as black women.

In responding to the question about why they were returning to school, the North Carolina women also replied that school would help them to "better themselves." Upon further inquiry, 85 percent of them mentioned their desire to become "better mothers"; half explained that while it was unlikely, perhaps a high school diploma would translate into a better job; and slightly more than half said they had always meant to finish school but that extenuating circumstances had made this impossible. To elaborate on these findings, my sample included only women who were mothers with at least one child living at home.

There were significant differences in the two samples of women. While equal numbers had gotten pregnant as teenagers, a higher proportion of the Philadelphia women had gotten married as a result. Whereas two-thirds of the Philadelphia women were or had been married, two-thirds of the North Carolina women had been single heads of households for most of their lives. Because of life cycle differences, several of the North Carolina women but none of the Philadelphia women were grandmothers raising school-age grandchildren.

While the two groups of women attended school during the same historical period, their schooling experiences were quite different, as I will elaborate later in the article. While a third of the North Carolina women had changed grammar schools several times during their childhood, only one Philadelphia woman had experienced such transitions. Although most of the North Carolina women had attended rural high schools, there were three who had attended small city public high schools, with two of them graduating. One of these women had attended an all-black college for one year. None of the Philadelphia women had attended college. Worth noting is that the educational skills of both groups of women ranged from roughly third grade to ninth grade level.

Finally, whereas none of the North Carolina women had spent any time out of the labor force since becoming mothers, roughly half of the Philadelphia women had been out of the paid labor force when raising children under school age. The North Carolina women on average earned less than the Philadelphia women, but all the women's family incomes had fluctuated considerably over the past fifteen years.

Interpretive methodology

My intention in contrasting the accounts of both groups of women is to shed light on the problem of interpretation rather than to generalize about either group. I share Gilligan's interest in "the interaction of experience and thought, in different voices and the dialogues to which they give rise" rather than in the "origins of the differences described or their distribution in a wider population, across cultures, or through time" (1982, 2). Indeed, there are many layers of contrast in the life experiences of the women I interviewed, including race, region, ethnicity, religion, schooling, levels of economic deprivation, and political participation, to name just a few, and all of these variations give rise to the different voices and dialogues.

Documenting, describing, and analyzing these variations has demanded tedious and systematic coding procedures that treat each woman's interview as its own text while also looking for themes and patterns that emerge across all the women's interviews. The coding procedure I developed to address inter- and intragroup patterns was two-pronged. First I examined *what* the women said—specifically, what they identified as difficult or problematic in their schooling and how they had sought to resolve these problems. Second, I examined *how* they narrated their recollections of the past—specifically, who they identified as primary actors and the events that defined for them the problems they encountered in school, how they ordered their stories, and what themes tied the stories together.

To interpret what I have come to call the women's schooling narratives, I have drawn on the traditions of cultural studies and narrative analysis.[13] My analytical task has been to discern both the meanings and the conditions that shaped the stories that the women told (Johnson 1986/87). I have tried to write about their stories in ways that the women would recognize, but also in ways that reveal underlying assumptions or structural relations that they may not recognize or agree with.[14]

Deciding how to label the two groups of women has been yet another problem of interpretation. Worth noting is that there was no single way that each group of women referred to themselves and their family backgrounds. For example, while the North Carolina women consistently referred to themselves and their family members as "black," the Philadelphia women never once referred to themselves as "white." The North Carolina women most often referred to their families as having been "poor" and/or having "country ways." Most of the Philadelphia women described their family background in religious (Catholic), ethnic (Irish or Polish), and/or class (such as "working class," "blue collar," or "union") terms, yet some simply referred to themselves as being "working" or "neighborhood" women.

Critics warn us that labels such as any of those mentioned above can fix our understandings of how gender, race, and class shape our identities, perspectives, and histories.[15] With this in mind, I have chosen to refer to the groups by locality, as the Philadelphia women and the North Carolina women, and to focus on the similarities and differences in how they made sense of and negotiated gender, race, and class relations. Having said all this, I also want to emphasize that these schooling narratives should not be understood as static. The women's stories are reconstructed and retrospective—a way that each woman has made sense of her past in light of the present. Also, what each woman wanted me to know about herself and her schooling influenced what she said and how she organized her narrative. Thus, the narratives are dependent on numerous personal, social, and political factors, not the least of these being

---

[13] By cultural studies I am referring to the work of the Birmingham Centre for Contemporary Cultural Studies such as that of Willis 1977, Hebdige 1979, and Hall 1986; historians Williams 1961, 1965, 1976 and Thompson 1963; Connell 1982, 1985 and the feminist critics of or contributors to cultural studies, including McRobbie 1978, 1984, 1991; McCabe 1981; Radway 1984; Long 1986; Roman 1987, 1988; and Holland and Eisenhart 1990, to name a few. The narrative analysts include Labov 1972; Mishler 1986; and Personal Narratives Group 1989.

[14] See Smith 1987 for a discussion of her collaborative research project with Alison Griffith on women's work as mothers in relation to schooling. She refers to her attempt to bridge between women's experiences and social organizations of power as "institutional ethnography" and warns feminists against establishing a feminist version of reality that supersedes those whose experiences are being investigated. I have tried to be sensitive to this warning by making it clear when I am presenting the women's experiences and interpretations and when I am presenting my own.

[15] Such critical works include, but are not limited to Hall 1986; Flax 1987; Steedman 1987; Alcoff 1988; hooks 1990; Williams 1991; and Higginbotham 1992.

how they viewed me as an educated, white, middle-class woman who had been their teacher.[16] Moreover, my request for a history of schooling and my underlying assumption that there must be a story as to why these women who had perceived themselves as school failures decided to pursue education as adults also shaped both the telling of the stories and my own interpretation.[17] This, coupled with the women's own desire to tell their life stories (made most evident by the frequent comment "I could write a book about my life"), converged to produce the schooling narratives on which this article is built.

In reviewing the literature I found very little research documenting how adult literacy learners reflected on their past schooling experiences, a curious gap given the conventional wisdom that says past schooling experiences are determining factors in current educational pursuits.[18] Most relevant for interpreting the schooling narratives was the work of sociolinguist Charlotte Linde in which she observes that people "seem to take enormous zest in discussing their experiences in school, however horrific the stories they tell about it" (n.d., chap. 2, p. 4). She attributes this to the fact that American culture places little emphasis on class as a legitimate explanation for why people end up in the particular social position that they do; instead, there seems to be an unspoken assumption that important life decisions are made in schools, decisions for which people feel compelled to account. Richard Sennett and Jonathan Cobb (1972) echo this viewpoint in their discussion of white working-class men's "defensive" accounts about school that the authors attribute to the hidden injury of class. Lillian Rubin (1976) refers to this phenomenon in

[16] I have been influenced by the work of several feminist scholars writing about the problems and possibilities of feminist research methods, including McRobbie 1982; Stanley and Wise 1983; Strathern 1987; Stacey 1988; and Devault 1990. For an excellent discussion of the theoretical and political underpinnings of this issue of self-reflexivity in ethnographic research and writing, see Mascia-Lees, Sharpe, and Cohen 1989.

[17] In her paper "Interpreting Women's Narratives: Towards an Alternative Methodology," Susan Chase makes a similar point about her interviews with women about their career histories. "The request for a career history is essentially this: in a world in which so few women have highly paid, prestigious, leadership positions, there must be a story about how you acquired one of those jobs. The nature of the interaction surrounding the request and the telling—the smoothness of both the asking and the response, the ease with which the career history is formulated and told—show that women shared this assumption with us" (1991, 17).

[18] There are no studies of how adult literacy learners view their skills, knowledge, or competencies except for the work of Arlene Fingeret 1983a, 1983b, which ignores the issue of how social differences affect these views. With the notable exception of Kathleen Rockhill's 1987 study of Hispanic women literacy learners, there are no ethnographies of adult basic education programs and/or classrooms. Nor are there any studies of school culture or student resistance like those of Ogbu 1974; Willis 1977; McRobbie 1978, 1991; Weis 1985, 1988; Holland and Eisenhart 1990; or Fine 1991 that examine adult basic education learners and their compliance and/or resistance to school.

her discussion of the "ambivalent" educational views and values of white working-class respondents. Although my research confirms such observations, I will suggest that class is not the only unspoken or unrecognized explanation as to why people end up in the social positions they do. Indeed, the women's stories reveal a much more complicated web of gender, race, and class relations for which they feel compelled to account.

One of the themes around which the women narrated their schooling experiences is that of teachers' pets. In the following sections I discuss the teacher's pet theme as an illustration of the women's shared view of schooling as a struggle over identities, values, and the acquisition of schoolwise knowledge. This struggle pits middle-class teachers against working-class students, "good" girls against "bad" girls, and light-skinned blacks against dark-skinned blacks as symbolic antagonists in the struggle for knowledge and power. I then examine how each group of women differently identified the problems and conditions of this struggle, leading to distinct versions of the teacher's pet theme. The Philadelphia women consistently framed their schooling struggles around issues of discipline and resistance; the North Carolina women framed theirs around issues of access and ability. In both cases, however, the women's understanding of teachers' pets ultimately served to undermine their claims to knowledge and power. The article concludes by considering the pedagogical implications of this embattled view of schooling.

Teachers' pets: How social differences make a difference in school

While each woman had her own unique story to tell, none of the women interviewed had felt comfortable in school. This shared discomfort, while expressed differently by the two groups of women, was attributed primarily to the fact that there were important differences between teachers and students and among certain students. Indeed, the women's feelings and thoughts about teachers' pets crystallized in story form how the women understood and acted on these social differences.[19] In these stories the women describe who and how teachers chose certain students as pets; what the women thought about these "pets"; how they felt about having or not having been chosen as a pet; and how this had affected their success and failure in school.

For both groups of women the most frequent difference that characterized uncomfortable teacher-student relationships was class. Cora, one of the North Carolina women, began her schooling narrative with the following remark, which might be called the "abstract" of her experience

[19] The concept of teacher's pet parallels the concept of common sense that I discuss in Luttrell 1989.

in school:[20] "Back a long time ago when I was going to school, and I can remember just as good as elementary school—if your parents wasn't a doctor, a lawyer, or a teacher, or someone you know, high, then the teachers would look down on you. That's right. And they wouldn't, they just wouldn't, you know, well, they would class you as nobody." Being "classed as nobody," "looked down upon," treated with "no respect and no encouragement" because of class differences figured prominently in all the women's narratives. These class differences not only were related to what their parents did for a living but also served to distinguish students from each other and from their teachers in terms of knowledge and power. Mary's discussion was typical of the conversations I had with the Philadelphia women about their teachers (which sometimes included me and my difference as well):

> The teachers were always different from us. They lived in different neighborhoods—they just weren't like the rest of us.
>
> *How would you describe how the teachers were different?*
>
> I don't know, as my superiors I guess. I always saw them as more intelligent. I never saw them as equal.
>
> *You said that they lived in different neighborhoods. Where did your teachers live?*
>
> They didn't live in our neighborhood, but then there were a couple who did in grade school. That surprised me when I found out.
>
> *Why?*
>
> Because I always thought of them (I guess I should say you) as being real rich. I just didn't think they were like us. They were from a higher class and must have been real smart to go to college in the first place. I just never felt very comfortable with them.

Regardless of whether the women liked or disliked a particular teacher, they viewed them as different from themselves, which (as Mary's words above illustrate) was often expressed in geographic terms. The Philadelphia women most often explained that teachers were not like students or parents because teachers came from other neighborhoods, most specifically from the suburbs.

The Philadelphia women believed that the suburbs fostered different kinds of relationships between people, particularly family members and neighbors. As Eileen remarked, the suburbs produced people who "just

[20] "Abstract" is Labov's term (1972, 363).

don't know about certain things. You know, when I grew up everybody in the neighborhood knew everything about me, who my mother was, what my father did, what we were doing on a Friday night. I had relatives everywhere and they kept me and my sisters in line; we couldn't do anything without everybody knowing about it. The teachers, they didn't know. I guess you could say I liked that about them, but then again, they didn't care to know much about us." The Philadelphia women viewed their teachers as outsiders to their communities. Moreover, teachers had different concerns, life-styles, activities, and opportunities, not all of which the women thought were beneficial to family or community life. Doris characterized teachers' concerns in the following way: "You know teachers are married to lawyers and doctors. They're worried about different things, things like nice clothes and what country club they're going to belong to. They have children, it isn't like they didn't know about children, but their children are different, like they assume their children are going to college, but they don't expect our kids are going to college. Then again, there's a lot that goes on in college that isn't so great for kids."[21]

While the Philadelphia women drew suburban-urban distinctions, the North Carolina women drew urban-rural distinctions to talk about class. Thirteen of the fifteen North Carolina women interviewed recalled that their teachers were different because they "came from the city." More than half told stories about how their parents were reluctant to deal with teachers or take part in school activities because of their own "country ways" or an inability to read or write. Cora gave the following account of a childhood incident that she continues to have strong feelings about as an adult:

> Cause I was going to say that my parents, they was well, decent people. But they couldn't read and write, you know what I mean. And they was clean peoples, they never got in no trouble. They never did nobody no harm or nothing. But they just couldn't read and write and they was honest and hard working. And when they would go to PTA meetings, well naturally I would have to go along to try to explain to them what's going on so they could, you know, and they tried their best to do whatever was right. And them teachers said things that, but just because they had no profession they looked down on them and they looked down on me too. You know and then back then wearing home-made dresses and things, I wasn't

---

[21] Rubin 1976 notes that the working-class parents she interviewed expressed concern that by attending college their children might be exposed not only to views that conflict with their family and community values but also to views that devalue and dismiss a working-class way of life that these parents have worked hard to achieve.

dirty or raggedy but I just wore home-made clothes that my mother would make for me because they only made but so much you know. And like if I want to participate in a play the teacher would pick all over me and get somebody else.

How did the teachers do that exactly?

Well, you see we would be sitting in the classroom in elementary school and the teacher would say, "We're going to have a play." And she would read out the parts. If you raised your hand and somebody else behind you or either on the other side of the classroom that's mother or father was in professional business, well they got the part that they raised their hand for. If you were the only person that raised your hand, in fact I was the only person to raise my hand for a part, then the teacher would probably give it to me. But then she would tell me after school, "Be sure you get that, learn this part, be sure to get the right costume." And you know, everything like that. She would tell me so much so that I would be hating that I raised my hand for the part. And I'd have to go home and talk to my momma and see if they can squeeze out enough money for the costume. And then one time my momma went to ask the teacher for if she could kind of describe a little bit the way that the costume she wanted me to have so she could make it. And the teacher was kind of rude to her, so much so that it kind of hurt my feelings. Then my momma told me, "If you really want to be in that play okay, but I wouldn't even bother." But I didn't really understand. I was only in the third or fourth grade. I didn't quite understand what my momma said, "If you really wants to be then I will go back to her again and get some understanding about it." It gave me sort of an inferiority complex cause I saw how the teacher was talking to my momma. I loved her and I just didn't want nobody to be hurting her feelings.

Cora's story captures how social differences between teachers, parents, and students were lived out, felt, and interpreted. Cora's perception that the teacher was anxious that she might not learn her lines or that her mother would not provide the right costume confirmed not only her sense of difference but also her sense of deficiency as a learner and performer. For Cora, school—but particularly the teacher—had actively undermined the efficacy, dignity, mastery, and cultural inheritance of her background.

It is notable that while the Philadelphia women most often described their teachers as outsiders with different concerns and values, the North Carolina women described themselves and their parents as being the outsiders. As outsiders, they had "come up with country ways" of living for which they were made to feel ashamed and rejected. I will return to this point and its significance later. At this point, my emphasis is on how the theme of teachers' pets illustrated the women's shared awareness of class divisions and struggles through which they learned to view their place in school and to project their futures. As Jeanne, a Philadelphia woman remembers, "I wasn't encouraged much in school, mostly the teachers didn't think much of me. They didn't think much of my background, I guess you could say. I wasn't the teacher's pet type, you know the kind that got picked to stand in front of the line or to pass out paper or pencils. I suppose the teachers didn't think I had promise or was going anywhere."

Being a "teacher's pet type" also referred to how different students understood and acted on their femininities. Both groups of women offered examples of how teachers favored girls over boys in school, yet through this preference the women noted that traditional constraints were being put on girls to be "pretty," "cute," and "good." Said one, "The teachers liked the girls better. But then I think it was easier for my brothers in school because nobody expected them to be quiet. But I couldn't keep my mouth shut, talking all the time and I was loud too, so the teacher, she didn't care too much for me." In the words of another, "I was Miss 'Tough Girl.' I was a real bully and a troublemaker. A lot of us played tough, but you couldn't be too tough or you would stand out in class. The teachers didn't treat the girls as rough as the boys—I guess because girls aren't supposed to be as bad as boys—but anyway I was pretty bad."

To be chosen as a female pet, girls had to comply to traditional, middle-class femininity, which for some women was either unrealistic or simply impossible: "Life was rough on the streets. You couldn't go around being Miss Priss and stay alive. So I got tough and the teachers didn't like me." "I didn't have no frilly dresses with lace and skirts and all. I was worried about soles on my shoes. There were lots of days I didn't go to school because I was just too ashamed of my clothes." Both groups of women believed that teachers preferred not only smart but *good* girls as well. As Sallie, a Philadelphia woman, explained, "I remember Miss Fulton and her sister. They lived in this really beautiful house and would invite all their goodies to their house. The goodies were smart kids—they liked smart girls. But you also had to behave and act like a lady if you were going to get invited to their place."

Considerable research documents teachers' differential behaviors toward boys and girls and its negative effect on girls' school achievement.[22]

<hr />

[22] For examples, see Martin 1972; Serbin et al. 1973; Brophy and Goode 1974; Stacey, Bereaud, and Daniels 1974; Dweck et al. 1978; Best 1983; Stockard 1985; Sadker and Sadker 1986; Jones 1989.

While this research confirms the women's perceptions that teachers be-
haved differently toward boys and girls, it simplifies the social learning
that goes on in the classroom. Despite the fact that most education theory
and practice implicitly assumes that teachers direct gender socialization
in the classroom, we know little about how teachers react to boys and
girls who do not fit into expected gender roles. Moreover, we know little
about how students interpret teachers' different attitudes and behaviors
toward boys and girls or what students do to get teachers to respond to
them in specific ways. More important in this case, we do not know how
girls from different classes, races, or ethnic backgrounds interpret their
interactions with teachers.

What we learn from these women's schooling narratives is that girls do
not all have the same opportunities to look, act, and be treated as "feminine" or as "teachers' pets." Indeed, the women's stories illustrate the
complexities of gender relations in the classroom—how female socialization is problematic rather than given. Most important, these narratives
illustrate that the two groups of women differed in how they perceived
these complexities and problems and as a result developed different views
about the connection between gender, knowledge, and power.

There were striking similarities within each group of women as they
recalled their roles in and responses to teachers' pets. The Philadelphia
women described themselves as having made choices about whether they
would pursue being a teacher's pet. As Debra explained, "I remember
one girl used to act in a real cutsie way and the teacher would be so
impressed. I didn't like the teacher and I didn't like the girls who acted
like that. I just wouldn't be cutsie like that—not even if it did impress the
teacher." Debra reasoned that if the teacher chose you to be a pet, you
risked losing friends; other kids would be jealous. And even if you did
choose to act "cutsie" and "sit like a lady," you knew it was an "act"
rather than the real thing. Helen talked about this dilemma:

> I was a teacher's pet so I got by pretty well. [Laughing.]
>
> *A couple of other women have laughed just like you when they
> describe themselves as teacher's pet, can you explain this?*
>
> Because you know you are and it's uncomfortable. I mean either
> they like you or they don't, but when I was a kid I guess I was a
> smooth talker. I was real cute and learned how to bat my eyes, look
> cute, sit like a lady, and boy the teachers really ate that stuff up. I
> guess I felt bad because I felt like I had conned them.

The choice to become a teacher's pet, to represent oneself falsely in order
to win the teacher's approval, was not a happy one. Those Philadelphia

women who did get chosen as pets and were successful in school described their achievements with guilt or discomfort. As Helen continued, "I used to feel so bad for my sister. I mean, I didn't even have to study and I got A's. The teachers liked me cause I knew how to win them over with my smile. But my sister, she worked so hard and didn't get anywhere. I couldn't feel too good about how I was doing when she was having such a hard time." At the same time, others who did not get chosen or saw themselves rejecting the opportunity to be teacher's pet also suffered (eleven of the fifteen Philadelphia women interviewed).

The North Carolina women, however, did not talk about their choices about being teacher's pets. These women, who were all dark-skinned, saw themselves as noncontenders in the contest to win the teacher's approval. They did, however, observe lighter-skinned students making this choice. As Gloria explained, there were always some girls "putting on the dog" in order to attract the teacher's attention. Integrally woven into the North Carolina women's accounts of school was the persistent memory that teachers favored light-skinned children over dark-skinned children. Bessie recalled: "What I didn't like about school, the teachers they had their own pets. Like if you were light skinned, you had it made. But if you were *Black,* they didn't take up no attention with you." Not just one, but all the North Carolina women referred to the role of skin color, emphasizing that teachers' pets were cute, good, smart, higher class, and "what we used to call 'yeller,' back then." They described how teachers "passed right over," "looked straight through," or "looked over the top of" darker-skinned children. As Gladys added, "I suspect it was 'cause them teachers were yeller too."

Mary Helen Washington (1982, 208–17) claims that this "intimidation of color" surfaces as a recurring theme in the lives and literature of black women. In the introduction to her anthology *Black-Eyed Susans* she writes: "In almost every novel or autobiography written by a black woman, there is at least one incident [of] the dark-skinned girl who wishes to be either white or light-skinned with 'good hair' " (1975, xv). One such example, *Lemon Swamps and Other Places,* the life history of Mamie Garvin Fields (1983), highlights the complexities of the color line. Her story suggests that distinctions made on the basis of color cannot be explained simply as class differences. She describes how members of the same family with lighter skin color were awarded greater recognition, resources, and success in school. Growing up in a middle-class black community in Charleston, South Carolina, in the early 1900s, she recalls:

When I was a little girl, I recognized that there was a difference, because my brother Herbert used to tease me and call me black— "blakymo"—although he was as black as I was. It used to make me so mad I would almost fight him. He would say, "Well, we are the black ones and they [their siblings] are the light ones. They can do this and that." We used to joke this way, but it wasn't all joke either. One reason why I didn't go to our private school for Negroes in Charleston was that, back then, honors were always given to mulatto children, light-skinned half-sisters and brothers, grands and great-grands of white people. It didn't matter what you did if you were dark. Used to leading my class up through elementary school, I hated this idea, so I began to say I wanted to go somewhere else. [Fields 1983, 47]

For the North Carolina women interviewed, lighter skin meant having more opportunities to learn because the teachers would "take up more attention with the lighter-skinned kids." Bessie remembered Dorothy, a light-skinned girl, who Bessie resents to this day:

You know, if you come to school dressed real nice, you know with one of them ruffle dresses, little bows and stuff on your hair, looking real neat, the teacher would take up time with you. Something that she would tell her, she probably wouldn't tell me. Like this girl, her name was Dorothy. She was the teacher's pet. She had light skin, pretty black hair, she came from a wealthy family, you know.

What was it that made her the teacher's pet?

I believe it was her lighter skin. And then the clothes she would wear. And the teacher would have PTA meetings, and my mom she never went to no PTA meeting or nothing like that. I reckon that showed the teacher you wasn't interested in your child. So that was that and the teacher wouldn't take up no time. But she took up time with Dorothy with her light skin and pretty black hair.

These differences did not exist simply in the realm of attitudes within the black community or in the society at large, but got lived out daily in the lives of black students as part of acquiring school knowledge and basic skills. Embedded in the North Carolina women's perceptions of themselves as learners was a legacy of being ignored by their black teachers who reinforced the message of dominant white society—that black children need not be educated.[23]

Both groups of women organized their schooling narratives around the theme of teachers' pets as a cautionary tale about how social differ-

[23] It would be important, of course, to know how the "Dorothys" felt about their approval from the teacher in order to fill out the picture of black students' experiences and interpretations of power relations in the classroom.

ence makes a difference in school. The moral of their tale is that school divides students against each other and against themselves along the fault lines of gender, race, and class in the struggle for schoolwise knowledge. Yet the two groups of women negotiated these divisions differently, and thus each presented a distinct version of what was at stake.

Discipline, resistance, and the struggle to be heard

The Philadelphia women most often framed their struggles in school around the issue of discipline and resistance.[24] This emphasis emerged most clearly as they described school as "boring," "routine," or a "farce." They attributed their problems in school to teachers who were more interested in order and discipline than in teaching anything of interest: "Everything was just like routine. Everyday we did the same thing over and over. The teachers weren't interested in teaching us; they were there to keep order."

The Philadelphia women's version of school is linked to their view of authority relations, specifically their memories of the arbitrary rules and harsh disciplinary behavior of nuns and teachers. Without any prompting, all fifteen provided detailed examples of what they considered to be unfair or unnecessary restrictions on both their person and their learning. Their frustration was captured by the repeated phrase that teachers had "treated us like children, to be seen but not heard." They saw teachers being overattentive and/or restrictive in terms of student behavior and personal style (clothing, hairdo, makeup) while at the same time "ignoring" students needs or concerns, as explained by the following two women:

> Well, I was used to making money, being on my own. But they treated me like a child. The rules were ridiculous. You had to read what they wanted you to read. Your dress couldn't be too short, you couldn't wear too much makeup, your bangs couldn't be too long—there were rules for everything. Things were very regimented and rigid—they treated us like children.

[24] This same observation is made by Lois Weis (1983, 235–61) in her comparative study of black community college students in a large northeastern U.S. city with students in two other accounts (Willis 1977; London 1978). These authors identified distinctly negative attitudes toward authority and school knowledge among white, working-class students, which they argue is based on a working-class rejection of mental labor. In contrast, I will argue that the women's attitude toward authority stems from what they perceive is the school's dismissal of working-class women's labor. Paralleling my findings, Weis observed that black students did not reject the authority of teachers or question the legitimacy of their knowledge. Instead, they resented teachers for what they perceived were racist motives in ignoring or dismissing black students (1983, 244).

I like going to school as an adult. In my classes you can talk person to person, not child to adult like in school. When I went to school you wouldn't have dreamed of telling a teacher how to do something or making a suggestion about anything. The teachers just didn't respect kids and their ideas. They bothered you about talking in class or being a problem in class, but they couldn't be bothered if you had a problem, like you didn't understand something or you couldn't concentrate.

The importance of order and discipline extended beyond the classroom, as Peggy and Doreen described:

What the nun said was rule. If a nun hit you, then you deserved it. In some families if you told your parents that a nun hit you, then you got hit at home because obviously the nuns were always right. But in my family if I told them a nun hit me they could understand why I was upset, but they would never challenge it.

I had an attitude towards authority even when I knew I would get in trouble in school and then again at home. In those days the teacher called your parents and you got it twice—once at school and then again at home. Parents didn't think to challenge the teachers. There was no discussion about why you were in trouble, if the teacher said it was so, it was so.

Teachers' authority and discipline was a backdrop against which the Philadelphia women either claimed a voice or were silenced. Indeed, the metaphor of voice persisted throughout their schooling narratives as they told stories about their struggles to "control my mouth," "speak my mind," and "tell the teacher off."[25] This struggle, or "attitude towards authority" as twelve of the fifteen Philadelphia women called it, was described as a character trait that had interfered with their school success. It explained why they were not chosen as or had rejected being teachers' pets and why they were not the "teacher's pet type" or "suited" for school. Those women who described themselves as good students dealt with what they considered arbitrary or unnecessary discipline through silence: "I learned at a young age to button my lip. You couldn't win with the teachers; they hated fresh mouthed kids, so . . . [long pause].

[25] I also found that in response to the question about why they were returning to school, two-thirds of the Philadelphia women surveyed gave examples that drew on their desire to be able to "speak up" and "voice" their opinions and be heard by family members, social service agents, and school or city officials. See also Belenky et al. 1986 for their observations about women's silence and voice in the educational process.

My sister couldn't put up with it and she didn't do well, I guess you could say it was more my style to take it, so I did real well in school."

There are several ways to interpret the Philadelphia women's discussion of teacher's authority and discipline. On one level, it could be argued that their preoccupation with discipline and resistance was based on unresolved childhood images and expectations of what power and authority should be. Perhaps their resentment about being "treated like children" and about others being teachers' pets is a projection of their feelings about parent-child and sibling relations onto teacher-student relations in the classroom.[26] But on another level, their complaints about "being treated like children" and their quest for a voice reveals their implicit critique of schooling. Sounding much like the low-income high school girls (white, black, and Hispanic) in Michelle Fine's study (1991), the Philadelphia women felt at best muted and at worst silenced by schooling practices that ignored the exigencies of poor and working-class families and communities, particularly for young women in their roles as caretakers. Teachers' middle-class conceptions of childhood simply did not correspond to the demands placed on working-class girls, as the following quotations illuminate:

I had a lot of responsibility for my younger brothers and sisters. I accepted it at the time. I used to babysit at the age of ten, but now that I think of it, I was really young to be doing all that. In the first grade I had to wake my mother up to let her know I was ready to go to school. Everyone I knew came from big families—we were all used to a lot of responsibility.

I remember going shopping for clothes for my brother and sister when I was twelve. My mother just didn't have the time 'cause she was working hard to support all of us by herself.

The Philadelphia women had worked hard to keep themselves and often their families together, taking care of siblings, preparing meals, shopping, cleaning, and often managing a job after school as well. Yet, despite its centrality and importance in their everyday lives, school undermined the knowledge, value, and authority invested in caretaking. Joanne explained that she never expected school to encourage or validate her, but had her own views about the value of caretaking when she dropped out of school at sixteen: "My mother worked as a waitress for sixty-five cents an hour and raised three children without any assistance.

---

[26] This kind of interpretation follows from the Frankfurt school, specifically Adorno et. al's 1950 study of the authoritarian personality. See Waller 1932 and Sennett 1980 for discussion of the fear and illusion of authority.

She just really didn't have any time to encourage us much. But I also worked since I was fifteen—I was very independent and I didn't expect to get any encouragement, especially from the teachers. I had to be very responsible, not like a child in school. When my mother died my sister was only thirteen and I took care of her. I'm very proud that she made it through school and graduated, even if I didn't." Joanne's story was not uncommon in that she took pride in and valued her mother's and her own ability to independently support themselves and others. Yet she didn't expect to get validated for her caretaking skills or knowledge in school. Instead, school penalized working-class girls for their commitments and responsibilities at home and rewarded "good girl" behavior and traditional middle-class femininity, an image of women as domestic, tranquil, attractive, and dependent on others for economic support.[27] School denied the reality and legitimacy of working-class femininity, an image of women as hardworking, responsible caregivers.

There was much at stake in the Philadelphia women's view of their schooling as embattled, especially in light of the school "choices" for which they felt compelled to account. Debra described herself weighing the following choices:

> I didn't really want to be a smart kid in school. I don't know—maybe it was the friends I hung with. If I did something too good, they would look at me funny. They thought why are you doing that? You don't have to do that to get through.

> *So you didn't want to look like you were trying?*

> Mostly I didn't want to try too hard for the teachers.[28]

Debra's distinguishing between the demands of "the girls she hung with" and the demands of teachers or school is similar to Ann's distinguishing between school and work in her account of why she chose the "commercial" rather than the "academic" track:

> I wasn't interested in the academic track. I didn't know why I needed to study history and all. I was interested in learning what I

---

[27] This dominant image of femininity or the "cult of true womanhood," a term coined by Welter 1978, emerged during the mid-nineteenth century as part of the consolidation of the American middle class. Polite and proper middle-class manners, styles, and values were associated with "feminized" traits and were important for class mobility.

[28] Debra's reference to "the friends I hung with" emerges in contrast to the "teacher's pet" types. The contrast between these two groups of girls is notable throughout the Philadelphia women's narratives as a set of embattled relationships that characterized school.

needed for a job like typing, bookkeeping, and the commercial courses. I couldn't wait to get out of school where I could be on my own, where I could be myself and do what I wanted to do. Some of it was to have my own money so I could buy what I wanted for myself, but we all, all the girls I hung with, all of us were in commercial and we knew what we wanted. We knew what we needed to do to, you know, about life, we knew about life even if we didn't know what they were teaching us about in school.

These accounts are reminiscent of Helen's pondering the pros and cons of being the "teacher's pet" and Peggy's concerns about the costs and benefits of her "mouthing off" toward teachers. Such inner dialogues about "choice" persisted throughout the Philadelphia women's narratives as they accounted for not only their school decisions but also their claims to "schoolwise" knowledge that they posed in opposition to their own "streetwise" or "commonsense" knowledge.[29] As Debra explained:

It was crazy the way they treated us as if we were children. We did everything adults do and we had a lot of experience under our belts. It was as if we were supposed to pretend like we had nothing to do except come to school everyday and be good little girls. I guess we also thought we knew more than they did so we didn't have to do the school work. The girls I hung with, we all thought we had one up on the teachers.

What did you know more about?

Getting by in life. We knew how to get over on the teachers. We all thought we were so smart. Now that I look back at it, we were all wrong.

Tina's account of having dropped out of school serves as a good example of the Philadelphia women's antagonistic and paradoxical relationship to school:

I didn't even consider going back to school when I found out I was pregnant. All those restrictions and all those hang-ups, I thought I'm having a baby and I'm going to not go to school and be a kid anymore. It was like my adult statement.

So you wanted the baby?

Well, the baby wasn't planned. But I wasn't going back to school. No way. I took the books and dumped them in a corner some place.

[29] See Luttrell 1989 for elaboration of this point.

Tina resisted the discipline of school and asserted her autonomy and independence by making what she calls her "adult statement." While she admits that her pregnancy was not intended, her decision to drop out of school was, and thus served as a way for Tina simultaneously to oppose school authorities and to stake a claim to her own values, interests, and knowledge. From Tina's perspective, her pregnancy was not the problem; school was. Pregnancy and motherhood offered her an opportunity to escape the disciplining force of school (as does Ann's view of work as a way to escape from the disciplinary force of school). Nevertheless, Tina's resistance to school had its own cost in that it drew on dominant gender ideologies, including the familiar but false dichotomy between "good" and "bad" girls that characterizes female sexuality and power. On the one hand, Tina's "problem with authority," her "mouth," and ultimately her sexual activity defined her as a "bad" girl. Yet, at the same time, her impending marriage and motherhood defined her not only as a "good" girl but also as the envy of the "girls she hung with":[30] "I remember in the beginning that my friends used to come visit after school and talk about how much fun it must be, taking care of the baby, buying cute clothes and all. We lived with his mother then and it wasn't so easy, but they didn't know about that part of it. Still, it was better than being in school."

Ironically, Tina's decision to drop out of school was a "statement" (again the metaphor of voice) in which she resisted one "regime" of discipline and authority (school and teachers) only to accept a different "regime" (family, husband, mother-in-law).[31] It is not that Tina would have made a different choice if she were to do it again but, rather, as she explains regarding her current participation in school, that "I don't want my daughters making the same mistake I did. Part of why I'm in school now is to show them that they have options and that they need to finish school before they decide to get married and have kids."

In the end, the Philadelphia women's view of schooling kept them from acknowledging the full range of their abilities. The false yet clear division of what they "knew" from what school wanted them to know ultimately served to limit their claims to knowledge and power. Regrettably, in order to resist the discipline of school and class-based ideologies

---

[30] McRobbie 1978 argues that fashion, beauty, and female sexuality all contribute to working-class feminine antischool culture, which paradoxically pushes girls into compliance with stereotypical female roles. McRobbie observed that working-class girls asserted their sexualities within the classroom as part of their counterschool culture. The girls' corollary fascination with marriage (partly because it was the only legitimate means through which their sexualities could be expressed) was also part of their counterschool culture that ultimately worked to insure their complicity in dominant gender and class relations.

[31] This notion of regimes of discipline and authority is borrowed from Foucault 1977, 1979.

about knowledge and the value of upward mobility, the Philadelphia wom en were forced to borrow on gender-based ideologies that located their source of knowledge, power, and resistance in traditionally defined female domains and concerns such as marriage, motherhood, and female sexuality. Thus, as part of a "choice" to assert their female working-class interests, concerns, and knowledge, the Philadelphia women's abilities and desires for intellectual or academic mastery were minimized, denied, or repressed.

Access, ability, and the struggle to be seen

The North Carolina women framed their struggles in school around the issues of access and ability. This emphasis emerged most clearly through their stories about difficulties attending school, inequities in school resources, and their anxieties about "falling behind" that persisted throughout their narratives. In contrast to the Philadelphia women's characterization of school as routine or boring, the North Carolina women most often described it as a luxury, something they enjoyed when able to attend. As Ola explained, "We loved going to school. We enjoyed it, it was all we had to enjoy sometimes." Or as Lois emphasized, school was reserved for rainy days when they were not needed on the farm: "Most times we were working on the farm and we wouldn't go to school nothing but rainy days, no way. Sometimes daddy would let my younger brothers and sisters go, but not me, I was the oldest."

The North Carolina women's narratives focused on the problems encountered by both teachers and children in rural segregated schools. Their stories highlighted the difficulties black teachers faced in one-room schoolhouses with little or no heat or supplies where they were expected to manage forty to fifty children ranging in age and grade level. Similarly, the North Carolina women offered accounts of long and sometimes dangerous walks to school, bad weather, and irregular attendance that made it hard to keep up with the demands of school. For example, Ella started school at nine years of age when her younger brother was old enough to walk the five miles to school with her. Louise explained that she didn't attend school until she was eight years old when her teacher offered to pick her up in the mornings. And Jackie remembered that by the time she and her siblings got to school their hands were so cold that it took them half the morning to warm up. Lilly explained that she and her sister were required to help their mother with the wash in the morning and most days "we just never made it."

Unlike the Philadelphia women, these women never mentioned being "treated like children." If anything, they saw school as a welcomed opportunity to get out of adult responsibilities at home, such as taking care of siblings, farming, or washing. Moreover, they did not focus on the discipline or demands of school but rather on the demands of rural poverty. Louise illuminates this recurring concern among the North Carolina women: "What I remember most was being tired. By the time we got to school, there was no bus long and then for black childrens, the morning was half over. We be missing how the teacher told us to do the work, or were just too tired to think."

Teacher-student relationships were profoundly affected by rural poverty as well. Perhaps most striking were the North Carolina women's descriptions of teachers that focused more on their caretaking rather than on their disciplining characteristics. They recalled with great fondness the "good" teachers who "took special care," fixed hot food, bought them clothes, and acknowledged their particular family/work responsibilities and demands. Not surprisingly, these descriptions echo the writings of black teachers of the time who found ways to pass on schoolwise knowledge despite untenable conditions.[32] School practices could not so easily separate out the daily survival needs of black children from their intellectual needs. Teachers who showed concern about poverty, lack of transportation, and the harshness of farm work inspired students to persist despite overwhelming odds.[33]

Linked to the issue of poverty was the all-pervasive reality of racism that shaped schooling practices. Throughout their narratives, the North Carolina women drew on metaphors of vision rather than voice to narrate their experiences in school.[34] Their narratives were charged with memories of painful events that had made them feel invisible both within the classroom as darker-skinned children and outside the classroom as

[32] See Fields 1983; Giddings 1984; Stuckey 1988; and Collins 1990.

[33] I learned firsthand about what was at stake for the North Carolina women when they placed themselves into a teacher's "care" and immersed themselves in the traditions of schooling. It has always been my practice to call students at home if they miss several classes. During the first month of teaching in the workplace literacy program I called one student who had been absent to find out what was keeping her out of class and to offer my assistance if needed. As it happened, she was waiting until payday so that she could buy a new pair of glasses. She was getting headaches from reading and had not yet been able to afford the new prescription. I offered to loan her the money so that she would not have to miss two more weeks of class. She did not take me up on the offer, but she returned to class the next day. Later, during the end-of-the-year evaluation meeting, she commented on her motivation for continuing in the program: "I figured if you cared enough to call me at home then you must really think that I can do the work. Then too if you cared enough to call me and to loan me the money, then I should care enough about myself to be in class everyday and not give up on myself. I just never had a teacher to call me like that."

[34] See Williams 1988, where the author starts out her essay "on being invisible" as a way to narrate her own place in history.

blacks attending segregated schools. Ola's story is but one example of being "passed by" by white society in both literal and symbolic terms:

> When we were little there was no bus for black children. Everyday we be walking to school and watch that big yellow bus drive by. It would stop right up in front of us to pick up the white childrens. And when we were little, this is the truth. A white person, if you were riding on the road, you know down the highway, and you was in front of them, that white person would run you off of that road to get in front of you. They didn't care. And then one time daddy had all his little childrens in the car, I don't know where we was going. Anyway, a white man come up, and daddy had to pull over and if he hadn't a went like that, the white man probably a killed us all. My daddy just pulled over to the side and let him go right on by. I remember we used to stand over on the side and watch all the white childrens pass right on by to school.

Lilly described how the teachers "looked over the top" of dark-skinned children:

> We really had a hard time in school cause if we know something, like if I go home and do my homework and really learn something and really get into it, we go back to school the next day. Then the teacher start asking about the lesson, getting us to go to the board and asking questions, we sitting and raising our hands and they would just look over the top of us. Now, all the little dark-skinned childrens, the teachers didn't take up no time with them. All the little light-skinned kids, teachers would take up time with them. And I got, [pause] I had went so far I just got tired. I had got to the place where I didn't care if I learned anything or not.

And Geraldine talked about black students' invisibility within the entire system of education: "Long and then nobody cared if black children went to school. There were no officers coming around to see if you was in school." Struggling to make themselves "seen" was draining and left the North Carolina women with little if any energy for their own creative, intellectual, and emotional development in schools.

Coupled with their sense of having been rejected was a sense of humiliation and shame. Repeatedly, the North Carolina women said they had felt "ashamed" because of their clothes or appearance, their size in relation to the other children, their inability to keep up in class, or their parents who had "country ways." (All fifteen of the women interviewed described an event in which they had been shamed in school.) Most often, they recounted that children "picked" on them and that teachers added flame to the fires.[35]

> The kids picked at us so much about our clothes, they picked about me carrying a brown bag and eating biscuits for lunch. I got to where I would go behind the gym or go behind the building or go to a classroom where nobody else was around and eat my lunch. It would never have gotten out except for my biology teacher. He happened to see me one day going into a classroom. I thought I was in there by myself and I pulled out the jelly biscuit. He was standing at the door looking at me and I didn't know he was cause he was looking through the glass on the door. And getting back to biology class, we was dissecting a frog and I couldn't quite get it cause I was so fat. I was fat and my fingers were clumsy. He spoke up right there in front of the class, everybody was listening to him and he says, "Doyle, you could dissect that frog if you would leave off eating all those biscuits. And you wouldn't be so big and fat." And everybody in class laughed and I tell you, I hated to go into class after that. And sometimes I would tell my mother that I had forgot my lunch, but I wouldn't forget, I was just too ashamed to carry it, the brown bag. If he had never told them about me carrying biscuits, but they [the teachers] looked down on me.

Fond memories of teachers who had taken "special care" paralleled with equal frequency such memories of teachers calling attention to students' deficiencies, both social and intellectual. Whereas the Philadelphia women provided stories in which they were angry with or shamed by teachers' extreme punishment (tying students to chairs, locking students in closets, hitting students with rulers, etc.), the North Carolina women shared stories in which they had been shamed by a teachers' cruel or arbitrary verbal abuse, as this one of Geraldine's: "In the classroom I got along most of the time, I knew the lesson and stuff like that. But she [her teacher] would always be saying that was I dumb or something like that. Maybe that come from me having kind of a stutter, and she said from that. In front of the whole class she would talk about me." In such stories, some women recalled being shamed by their teachers for things related to being poor (having inadequate clothes or no shoes), having "country ways" (bringing brown bags with biscuits), or not being able to attend school regularly. Indeed, Beverly explains that she dropped out of school

[35] Like the Philadelphia women, some of the North Carolina women referred to the girls they hung with, their "friend girls" in contrast to the "teacher's pet" types, but more often they talked about children who "picked" on them. These were the embattled relationships that organized their schooling narratives.

to insure that her new baby could one day attend school without shame: "And when I had my son I said, I don't want him to come up poor, go to school half ragged and everything. And then at that time white people liked for you to work in their houses so I told momma I ain't going back to school cause I want my son to wear nice clothes, you know and all to school too."

Others, like Geraldine, recalled having suffered public humiliation for what was most often referred to as being a "slow learner." Most telling was the finding that all the North Carolina women chronicled their school narratives according to whether they were passed onto the next grade or were kept behind. In light of the fact that they attended one-room schoolhouses or schools with only a few rooms, I asked how they knew what "grade" level they were in. Even without age-graded class-rooms, standardized tests, or formalized report cards, the North Carolina women perceived that they had been judged by some set of rational, performance-based set of standards that did not correspond with their abilities or opportunities to perform. Nevertheless, they internalized these standards and explained the moral behind their failure: they had been "slow learners." Gloria sums up what more than half the North Carolina women said about their problem in school: "My problem was that I was a slow learner. I didn't catch on the way the other childrens did. I was always behind trying to catch up; the teachers didn't take up no time with me. Except in third grade with Miss Johnson. She was a good teacher and she made sure that I stayed up with the class."

Despite images of themselves as invisible and as slow learners, the North Carolina women also agreed that school held little promise for them. It did not offer upward mobility and, as Ola explains, schoolwise knowledge was not perceived as necessary for their work as women in their families: "Long back at that time we didn't have nothing to go to school for. All of us, like a bunch of girls would get together, they'd say, 'What good is going to school? We's out here on the farm so we ain't going to do nothing but stay out here on the farm and have babies, farm, and keep house.' You can do that, you can learn that from momma and daddy. You don't need to go to school for that, to stay out on the farm or to babysit and clean house for white peoples." Or as Beverly further explained why she had dropped out of school, "I decided I'm just going to give up my education so [my son] could get his. Cause education didn't mean nothing to me back them, it didn't lead to nothing. Now I see that we both should probably have went on to school, but I just made sure that he went to school and graduated."

Whether they attributed their problem in school to one of limited access, ability, or promise, the North Carolina women did not view school as posing a set of conflicting choices for them. Ironically, despite the fact that school held no promise for them, the North Carolina women were more free to immerse themselves in school values, styles, and authority. They were not concerned over who knew more, teachers or students, but rather who was allowed to know or who was capable of knowing, who was encouraged and who was passed over. It was not the authority or legitimacy of schoolwise knowledge that was at stake in the North Carolina women's school struggles but, rather, their own legitimacy as school students.

Effects of school organization and mission

How do we account for the women's different versions of school and what do these versions tell us about the twisted relations of gender, knowledge, and power? In this section I will consider the effects of school organization and mission on the women's different versions of school. My argument is that the two school contexts—one rural-community and the other urban-comprehensive—organized the relationship between gender, knowledge, and power differently and thus generated different views among the women about these twisted relations.

Writing about how gender relations operate differently according to school organization, Elisabeth Hansot and David Tyack (1988) characterize the rural-community and the urban-comprehensive school in the following ways. In the rural-community school, age and cognitive proficiency organized instruction, whereas in the urban-comprehensive school, gender organized the curriculum. In the 1920s, "progressive" school reform sought to design the curriculum to address the so-called different needs of boys and girls. Educational reformers worried about the way high schools were differentiating students by class, yet these same reformers tended to see differentiation by gender as natural and desirable. Whereas the explicit goal of the urban comprehensive school was to prepare students for adult occupations, fashioned primarily around the needs of industry, the implicit effect was to replicate in the school the same sexual division of labor that students would be expected to accommodate as adults. Thus, according to Hansot and Tyack, gender gained greater "institutional salience" in the urban public schools, even as school practices worked to obscure this salience. Moreover, gender gained greater, if not hidden, salience in the urban public school because of the rigid institutional boundaries that separated family, work, and school. In rural communities, these boundaries were more fluid, viewed by students as "part of a seamless web of community contexts, each interwoven with and legitimating the other" (1988, 752). In contrast, the urban school system was large and bureaucratic, no longer analogous in either structure or operation to families, churches, or community life.

Thus, school was viewed by students as set apart from, rather than integral to, other institutions that prepared them for their future roles and responsibilities. Furthermore, because gender relations varied from one institution to the other, students in urban-comprehensive schools were forced to negotiate different gender expectations. For example, a young girl might find that in school she did the same work as boys and was rewarded in the same way for her efforts. But when she entered the work force and found that her opportunities were limited and that she was not rewarded in the same way as her male counterparts, she was forced to somehow make sense of the discrepancy. How she made sense of and negotiated changing gender practices and meanings was not simply the result of personal insight but was also governed by historical, cultural, ideological, and institutional forces.

In this light, let us consider how each school context generated a different set of gender practices and problems for the women to negotiate. Consider the Philadelphia women's view of school as both stemming from and answering to the urban-comprehensive school's organization and mission.[36] Organized around the requirements of industry, the urban-comprehensive school emphasized the obedience and discipline required in working-class jobs as it prepared students to enter a sex-segregated labor force (Bowles and Gintis 1976). The "commercial track" and the "kitchen practice" (the latter referred to by one Philadelphia woman as "where they put the real low life in the school") were part of this preparation where girls learned clerical or waitressing skills while boys learned a skilled trade in "shop" classes. I would argue that the Philadelphia women made sense of this school organization in class rather than gender terms. For example, to explain why they chose the commercial track, the women drew on class-based antagonisms between teachers and students and between schoolwise and streetwise knowledge to account for their "choices." Their explanations pit their middle-class teachers, for whom they did not want to "work too hard" and with whom they did not share the same life concerns or values, against their peers, with whom they shared common interests, knowledge, and authority about how to "get by in life."[37] Similarly, the Philadelphia women

[36] There were in fact three school contexts, including Catholic school. I discuss the particular effects of Catholic School on the women's aspirations in Luttrell 1992. However, in terms of framing their school "problems," there was no difference between those Philadelphia women who attended public and those who attended parochial school. This may be due to the small number of women who attended Catholic school in the sample. Future research might yield important contrasts.

[37] Such antagonistic relationships are reminiscent of how Thompson 1963 accounts for the development of class consciousness, as a process that happens when people articulate and identify their interests, capabilities, or concerns as being common to others like themselves and against those whose interests are different from (and usually opposed to) theirs.

made sense of the separation between schools, families, and workplaces and of the discrepant gender expectations of each in class terms. Recall how the women resented their middle-class teachers for refusing to acknowledge the multiple responsibilities of working-class girlhood and thus rejected schools as a way to claim a voice (i.e., knowledge and authority) about family life and its demands. Yet regrettably, these class-based understandings of school worked against the Philadelphia women's abilities to see the implicit gender inequalities organizing school, families, and workplaces, as in the case of Tina who opted for marriage and motherhood, which she viewed as natural and desirable, over school.

Then, in contrast, consider the North Carolina women's views of school as both stemming from and answering to the organization and mission of the rural-community school. Organized as part of a seamless web of family, work, church, and community contexts, each woven with and legitimating the other, the rural segregated school context produced a different set of gender practices and problems for the women to negotiate. The rural school did not track students according to gender, nor were the gender practices in school so different from those on the farm, in families, or in church. Through their daily caretaking efforts, black teachers in rural schools promoted the value of what is traditionally defined as "women's work" to sustain family life. In this seamless web of caretaking institutions (school, families, church), black female teachers implicitly, if not explicitly, promoted the knowledge and authority of black women in their efforts to preserve black communities. In contrast to the female teachers in urban-comprehensive schools who were supervised by male principals, these black teachers in rural schools also exercised more autonomous authority, especially in isolated one-room schools. Thus through their affiliation with black female teachers, the North Carolina women were encouraged to claim rather than to deny their knowledge as women as part of their schooling.

Regrettably, however, the affiliation was made problematic by the "racial uplift" mission of the black rural-community school. At the time when the North Carolina women attended school, black middle-class female teachers who had been assigned to rural schools were committed to racial uplift that "equated normality with conformity to white, middle-class models of gender roles and sexuality" (Higginbotham 1992, 271). Exposed to the domestic science movement as a way to promote the moral uplifting of rural blacks, these teachers sought to correct black country ways, including speech, appearance, behavior, dress, and etiquette, that were viewed as impediments to social mobility not only within black communities but also within white society.[38] This model

---

[38] Fields 1983, 88–90, refers to this influence in her teacher training.

contrasted sharply with the vocational model and thus generated different relationships between female teachers and students. We can recall that the North Carolina women spoke about the school's mission to correct country ways with shame and humiliation. Moreover, they interpreted the school's mission in race and class-based terms, citing in anger all the ways in which teachers invoked the "intimidation of color" as they "passed over" groups of darker-skinned students or neglected to encourage students whose parents were not professionals. Less recognized was the way in which teachers invoked traditional, middle-class styles of femininity as part of their uplift mission. Instead, the North Carolina women remembered with fondness those teachers who had made them "feel special" by attending to their daily needs. Yet by buying bows and dresses for those girls who because of poverty could not attain a traditionally feminine image, these teachers unwittingly promoted split images of femininity.

Yet, whatever their goals, the efforts of black, middle-class teachers were undermined by the racism and segregation that signaled to rural black children living in poverty that they were worth less than white children. Whatever schoolwise knowledge black students might claim would not be recognized by the larger white society, nor would it provide them occupational mobility, regardless of gender. Organizing instruction around age and cognitive proficiency, when regular school attendance was sporadic if not impossible for girls as well as boys, also served to promote the view that individual ability more than anything else accounted for school success. Admittedly, such organization was not intended to undermine black students' beliefs in their academic abilities. Yet the North Carolina women's narratives speak to the unintended consequences of institutional practices that, when joined with racist ideologies about blacks' inferior intelligence, converged to support their perceptions of themselves as slow learners.

Thus each group of women understood and negotiated the twisted relations of gender, knowledge, and power differently according to school organization and mission. I do not offer this explanation as a complete account but, rather, as a corrective to essentialist accounts that ignore the varied and changing contexts within and against which women construct and claim knowledge. In the next section I want to broaden the scope of our understanding of these contexts and obstacles by considering the ideological dimensions of the women's view of school as a battleground, and particularly of the teacher's pet theme.

Another version of the teacher's pet theme

While both groups of women viewed teachers' pets as having knowledge and power, on closer scrutiny we can see that this is a distortion, if not an illusion. Despite their distinct versions of school and teachers' pets, both groups of women shared contradictory insights about the process of schoolwise knowing. On the one hand, the women believed that the acquisition of schoolwise knowledge was not haphazard, random, or idiosyncratic. It was not Dorothy as an individual, that is, but Dorothy as a light-skinned, middle-class, traditionally feminine black girl that made her the teacher's pet and enabled her success in school. It was not Helen as an individual, but feminine, cute, and obedient Helen as a "type" that accounted for her school achievements. Whether defined in race, class, or gender terms, both groups of women believed that teachers chose pets and passed on schoolwise knowledge according to interests that were in conflict with the students' own. The women's experience of teachers' pets served to corroborate what they already knew about social divisions. Moreover, these relationships served as a way to express their affiliation with and opposition to certain collective identities, interests, values, and knowledge. Yet at the same time, the women also shared the belief that teachers acted on personal prejudices and preferences rather than on structural imperatives of either the educational system or the society at large when they chose their pets. Put another way, the theme of teachers' pets offered the women an individual and psychologized explanation of knowledge and power for what is in fact a structural and political relationship.

The women's shared view of school was based on gender ideologies that pitted good girls against bad girls in the struggle for schoolwise knowledge. This good girl/bad girl dichotomy falsified gender relations in the classroom. Likewise, the light skin/dark skin dichotomy falsified race relations, making it appear as if it was a teacher's individual prejudice rather than institutional racism that undermined black students' success. Lighter-skinned blacks were sanctioned as smart and as successful learners at the expense of darker-skinned blacks, thereby dividing black students against each other and undermining their collective knowledge and power. At the same time, the light skin/dark skin dichotomy also falsified gender relations, making it appear that it was only the color line rather than patriarchal impositions that colluded in dividing the black rural female students against each other.

Furthermore, the women understood the relationship between teachers and their pets as a form of patronage whereby teachers chose individual students to be theirs or to "own." The pet's ability to succeed thus was dependent on her patron, the teacher. According to the terms of this relationship, the patron promised support, encouragement, and praise in exchange for the pet's productivity and achievement. Additionally, this relationship was understood as a unique, one-to-one relationship between a particular teacher and a particular student (your pet cannot also be my pet). As a result, the women learned to view the nature of knowledge and power as personalized and individual rather than collective or social. Moreover, this personalized image of the teacher's pet connoted an affective bond. Being someone's pet suggested an emotional or even erotically tinged relationship between pets and their owners (as in the common expression, "petting"). In this individual, personal, emotional, and perhaps erotically tinged relationship between teachers and pets, a process of deception and objectification took place. Girls who participated in such relationships were seen or saw themselves as presenting a false self to attract the teacher's attention. Because the pet's achievements and school knowledge was gained through such deception, it was at once false and suspect. Thus the women came simultaneously to long for and to distrust the pet's recognition, attention, and power. Last but not least, the concept of teacher's pet implied that a student was less than a teacher, the human pet being an infantilized person. Thus the pet's power was based on diminution and was ultimately self-negating.[39]

In all these cases, the pet and her power could never be autonomous from the realm of the teacher. Ironically, then, the concept of teacher's pet makes it appear that those who are not teachers' pets have no knowledge or power. The view of teachers' pets or good girls as powerful based on their ability to get approval of those in power masked the real threat to patriarchal power: those who chose not to be or are not chosen to be pets, the bad girls.

I would argue that the women's shared views about teachers' pets exposes the force of patriarchal impositions, particularly how split images of femininity undermine women's knowing. These split images, invoked by the women as symbolic antagonists in the teacher's pet theme, served to locate the source of their power in female attractiveness, desirability, and submission rather than in intellectual capabilities or in collective identities and interests.

Implications for feminist education research and reform

The varied contexts within and against which women construct, value, and claim knowledge and power have profound implications for how we think about improving women's education. The contextualized account of women's ways of knowing that I have developed here suggests that we must acknowledge the politics of being female when we consider how schools shortchange girls, moving beyond analyses based simply on female socialization or gender identity development.

---

[39] I am indebted to John Wilson for starting me thinking about the ideological nature of the pet's power.

There is still much to know about the politics of women's knowing—how different women understand and negotiate gender, race, and class relations across institutional contexts and within different schools—before we can develop pedagogical practices that address the multivaried ways that women claim and deny knowledge. I believe that comparative ethnographic research holds the most promise toward this end. The task for feminist educators, as I see it, is to become ethnographers, in the broadest and best sense of the word, actively and systematically observing what students are doing, listening to what they are saying, and probing what they are feeling despite school practices that conspire to distort, mute, or silence what they know and have to say about themselves and the world around them.[40]

When we listen and take seriously what the women in this study have to say about school, especially in their shared theme of teacher's pet, we gain critical insight into how schools shortchange girls and what is to be done. I will briefly sketch two implications about how to improve women's education that I draw from their accounts.

Revising school mission and organization

The teacher's pet theme reminds us that what is most memorable about schooling is not what is learned, but how we learn. By viewing school in terms of embattled relationships, the women held teachers and students accountable for what school organization and mission ignores or dismisses: the knowledge and ethics of care.

Educational philosopher Jane Roland Martin (1985) has argued that the explicit mission of schooling in this century has been to prepare students for what she calls "productive" processes that focus primarily on the workplace and the public/political spheres of life, spheres that until recent history have been associated with men. Missing from such models are discussions about society's "reproductive" processes, including all those activities that define and maintain communities, families, and private life, spheres that continue to be associated with women. As a result, schools promote a narrow view of citizenship, one that privileges the ethics of work and public life over the ethic of care. Whereas schools introduce students to such values as property, justice, freedom, and equality that support political and economic development, what goes unacknowledged are values such as empathy, nurturance, and sensitivity that support personal growth and development. Evaded in the curriculum are the skills, knowledge, and values that have to do with "taking care": everything from knowing about and caring for human bodies, to

---

[40] Gilligan 1990 and Fine 1991 both write about how schools actively silence what girls already know about the world. This silencing drives girls' knowledge "underground" or causes them to develop a split consciousness.

knowing about and attending to human feelings and relationships.[41] Moreover, these skills and knowledge, passed down within families and communities, are not viewed with the same reverence or value as those skills and knowledge that are passed down in schools. While we may pay lip service to the values and ethics of caretaking, we have yet to incorporate them into our educational practices and policies. Thus, schools fail to prepare students for citizenship in the broadest sense, as agents of social justice infused with an ethic of care.

The women's schooling narratives highlight the shortcomings of this narrow mission and separation of productive from reproductive skills and knowledge. While being careful not to reify these separate spheres, it is important to note that school policies and practices that enforce rigid boundaries between these two spheres of activity have particularly damaging effects on poor and working-class girls who may be major contributors to family survival. The failure of schools to broaden their mission and organization not only compromises poor and working-class girls' success in school but also, more fundamentally, threatens to disenfranchise them as citizens lacking either visibility or a voice.

Rethinking school success

The women's stories about teachers' pets speaks to the fact that attending to the ethics and politics of relationships is what makes a difference in women's (and, for that matter, men's) education. Their charged memories about being or not being a pet force us to consider what Frederick Erikson (1987) calls the "politics of legitimacy, trust and assent" as key factors that affect school success. The women's distinct version of teachers' pets illustrates the varied ways in which schools can betray girls' trust and legitimacy as they are played out in school mission, organization, curriculum, pedagogical practice, and student-teacher relationships (including but not limited to the teacher's pet phenomenon). For when school practices and policies acknowledge and validate some students over others, certain students will experience school as a no-win situation where they risk feeling unconnected and unknown, either betrayed by school or feeling as if they have betrayed themselves and others. Indeed, that was what had bothered the women about teachers' pets—that these relationships had allowed some students to "feel special" at the expense of others. Thus from their vantage point, school had violated the rules and ethics of relationships. Teachers' pets had enhanced the hold of teachers and certain students on the privilege of their social

---

[41] See the American Association of University Women's report *How Schools Shortchange Girls* (Wellesley College for Research on Women 1992) for an excellent discussion of the formal, hidden, and evaded curriculum and its effects on the education of girls.

difference (whether gender-, race-, or class-based), and thus served as a ritual celebration of social injustice.

Perhaps the women's view of school as a set of embattled relationships of power and care helps to resolve the seeming paradox about why women who did not see themselves as successful students nevertheless sought education as adults. Ironically, what had propelled the women out of school as girls is also what had propelled them back to school as adult women: their desire to be viewed as legitimate, to connect and be known, and to remake their relationship to self and others through adult basic education. As feminist educators we should take heed of women's paradoxical relationship to schooling by working to transform the material and ideological conditions under which students and teachers enter into relationships of knowledge, power, and care.

Department of Sociology
Duke University

References

Adorno, Theodor, et al. 1950. *The Authoritarian Personality.* New York: Harper & Brothers.

Alcoff, Linda. 1988. "Cultural Feminism versus Post-Structuralism: The Identity Crisis in Feminist Theory." *Signs: Journal of Women in Culture and Society* 13(3):405–36.

Belenky, Mary Field, Blythe McVicker Clinchy, Nancy Rule Goldberger, and Jill Mattuck Tarule. 1986. *Women's Ways of Knowing: The Development of Self, Voice, and Mind.* New York: Basic.

Best, Raphaela. 1983. *We've All Got Scars: What Boys and Girls Learn in Elementary School.* Bloomington: Indiana University Press.

Bordo, Susan. 1986. "The Cartesian Masculinization of Thought." *Signs* 11(3):439–56.

Bordo, Susan, and Alison Jaggar, eds. 1989. *Gender, Body, Knowledge: Feminist Reconstructions of Being and Knowing.* New Brunswick, N.J.: Rutgers University Press.

Bowles, Samuel, and Herbert Gintis. 1976. *Schooling in Capitalist America.* New York: Basic.

Brophy, Jere, and Thomas Goode. 1974. *Teacher-Student Relationships: Causes and Consequences.* New York: Holt, Rinehart, & Winston.

Chase, Susan. 1991. "Interpreting Women's Narratives: Towards an Alternative Methodology." Paper presented at the Southern Sociological Society Meetings, Atlanta, Georgia, April 6.

Chodorow, Nancy. 1978. *The Reproduction of Mothering: Psychoanalysis and the Sociology of Gender.* Berkeley and Los Angeles: University of California Press.

Cixous, Hélène. 1976. "The Laugh of the Medusa." *Signs* 1(4):875–93.

———. 1981. "Castration or Decapitation?" *Signs* 7(1):41–55.

Collins, Patricia Hill. 1990. *Black Feminist Thought: Knowledge, Consciousness, and the Politics of Empowerment.* London: HarperCollins Academic.

Connell, R. W. 1985. *Teachers' Work.* Sydney: George Allen & Unwin.

Connell, R. W., et al. 1982. *Making the Difference: Schools, Families and Social Division.* Sydney: George Allen & Unwin.

Daly, Mary. 1973. *Beyond God the Father.* Boston: Beacon.

―――. 1978. *Gyn/Ecology: The Metaethics of Radical Feminism.* Boston: Beacon.

Devault, Marjorie. 1990. "Talking and Listening from Women's Standpoint: Feminist Strategies for Interviewing and Analysis." *Social Problems* 37(1):96–116.

Dweck, Carol S., William Davidson, Sharon Nelson, and Bradley Enna. 1978. "Sex Differences in Learned Helplessness: II. The Contingencies of Evaluation Feedback in the Classroom. III. An Experimental Analysis." *Developmental Psychology* 14:268–76.

Erickson, Frederick. 1987. "Transformation and School Success: The Politics and Culture of Educational Achievement." *Anthropology and Education Quarterly,* 18(4):335–56.

Fields, Mamie Garvin, with Karen Fields. 1983. *Lemon Swamp and Other Places.* New York: Free Press.

Fine, Michelle. 1991. *Framing Dropouts: Notes on the Politics of an Urban Public High School.* Albany: State University of New York Press.

Fingeret, Arlene. 1983a. "Social Network: A New Perspective on Independence and Illiterate Adults." *Adult Education Quarterly* 33(3):133–46.

―――. 1983b. "Common Sense and Book Learning: Culture Clash?" *Lifelong Learning* 6(8):22–24.

Flax, Jane. 1987. "Postmodernism and Gender Relations in Feminist Theory." *Signs* 12(4):621–43.

Foucault, Michel. 1977. *Discipline and Punish: The Birth of the Prison.* New York: Pantheon.

―――. 1979. *The History of Sexuality,* vol. 1: *An Introduction,* trans. Robert Hurley. London: Allen Lane.

Freire, Paulo. 1970. *Pedagogy of the Oppressed.* New York: Seabury.

―――. 1973. *Education for Critical Consciousness.* New York: Continuum.

―――. 1987. *Literacy: Reading the Word and the World.* South Hadley, Mass.: Bergin & Garvey.

Giddings, Paula. 1984. *When and Where I Enter: The Impact of Black Women on Race and Sex in America.* New York: Bantam.

Gilkes, Cheryl Townsend. 1985. " 'Together and in Harness': Women's Traditions in the Sanctified Church." *Signs* 10(4):678–99.

―――. 1988. "Building in Many Places: Multiple Commitments and Ideologies in Black Women's Community Work." In *Women and the Politics of Empowerment,* ed. Ann Bookman and Sandra Morgen, 53–76. Philadelphia: Temple University Press.

Gilligan, Carol. 1982. *In a Different Voice: Psychological Theory and Women's Development.* Cambridge, Mass.: Harvard University Press.

————. 1988. *Mapping the Moral Domain: A Contribution of Women's Thinking to Psychological Theory and Education.* Cambridge, Mass.: Harvard University Press.

————. 1990. *Making Connections: The Relational Worlds of Adolescent Girls at Emma Willard School.* Cambridge, Mass.: Harvard University Press.

Grant, Jacquelyn. 1982. "Black Women and the Church." In *But Some of Us Are Brave,* ed. Gloria T. Hull, Patricia Bell Scott, and Barbara Smith, 141–52. Old Westbury, N.Y.: Feminist Press.

Grant, Judith. 1987. "I Feel Therefore I Am: A Critique of Female Experience as a Basis for Feminist Epistemology." *Women and Politics* 7(3):99–114.

Griffin, Susan. 1980. *Woman and Nature: The Roaring Inside Her.* New York: Harper Colophon.

Hall, Stuart. 1986. "Gramsci's Relevance to the Analysis of Racism and Ethnicity." *Communication Inquiry* 10:5–27.

Hansot, Elisabeth, and David Tyack. 1988. "Gender in American Public Schools: Thinking Institutionally." *Signs* 13(4):741–60.

Harding, Sandra. 1986. *The Science Question in Feminism.* Ithaca, N.Y.: Cornell University Press.

Harding, Sandra, and Merrill Hintikka, eds. 1983. *Discovering Reality: Feminist Perspectives on Epistemology, Metaphysics, and Philosophy of Science* Dordrecht: Reidel.

Hartsock, Nancy. 1985. *Money, Sex and Power: Towards a Feminist Historical Materialism.* Boston: Northeastern University Press.

Hawkesworth, Mary E. 1989. "Knowers, Knowing, Known: Feminist Theory and Claims of Truth." *Signs* 14(3):533–57.

Hebdige, Dick. 1979. *Subculture: The Meaning of Style.* New York: Methuen.

Heckman, Susan. 1987. "The Feminization of Epistemology: Gender and the Social Sciences." *Women and Politics* 7(3):65–83.

Higginbotham, Evelyn Brooks. 1992. "African-American Women's History and the Metalanguage of Race." *Signs* 17(2):251–74.

Holland, Dorothy, and Margaret Eisenhart. 1990. *Educated in Romance: Women, Achievement and College Culture.* Chicago: University of Chicago Press.

hooks, bell. 1990. *Yearning: Race, Gender, and Cultural Politics.* Boston: South End Press.

Irigaray, Luce. 1985. *Speculum of the Other Woman,* trans. Gillian Gill. Ithaca, N.Y.: Cornell University Press.

Jaggar, Alison. 1983. *Feminist Politics and Human Nature.* Totowa, N.J.: Rowman & Allanheld.

Johnson, Richard. 1986/87. "What Is Cultural Studies Anyway?" *Social Text: Theory, Culture, Ideology* 16:38–40.

Jones, M. Gail. 1989. "Gender Bias in Classroom Interactions." *Contemporary Education* 60(4):218–22.

Keller, Evelyn Fox. 1984. *Reflections on Gender and Science.* New Haven, Conn.: Yale University Press.

Labov, William. 1972. *Language in the Inner City: Studies in the Black English Vernacular.* Philadelphia: University of Pennsylvania Press.

Levesque-Lopman, Louise. 1988. *Claiming Reality: Phenomenology and Women's Experience.* Totowa, N.J.: Rowman & Littlefield.

Linde, Charlotte. n.d. "Life Stories: The Creation of Coherency." Institute for Research on Learning, Palo Alto, Calif.

Lloyd, Genevieve. 1984. *The Man of Reason: Male and Female in Western Philosophy.* London: Methuen.

London, Howard B. 1978. *The Culture of a Community College.* New York: Praeger.

Long, Elizabeth. 1986. "Women, Reading, and Cultural Authority: Some Implications of the Audience Perspective in Cultural Studies." *American Quarterly* 38(4):591–612.

Luttrell, Wendy. 1981. *Women in the Community: A Curriculum Guide for Students and Teachers.* Harrisburg: Pennsylvania State Department of Education.

———. 1982. *Building Multi-Cultural Awareness: A Teaching Approach for Learner-centered Education.* Harrisburg: Pennsylvania State Department of Education.

———. 1989. "Working-Class Women's Ways of Knowing: Effects of Gender, Race, and Class." *Sociology of Education* 62:33–46.

———. 1992. "Claiming Authority, Claiming Self Worth: Women's Narratives of 'Schoolwise' Knowledge and Power." Unpublished manuscript, Duke University.

McCabe, Toni. 1981. "Schools and Careers: For Girls Who Do Want to Wear the Trousers." In *Feminism for Girls: An Adventure Story,* ed. Angela McRobbie and Toni McCabe, 57–79. London: Routledge & Kegan Paul.

McMillan, Carol. 1982. *Women, Reason and Nature.* Oxford: Basic Blackwell.

McRobbie, Angela. 1978. "Working Class Girls and the Culture of Femininity." In *Women Take Issue: Aspects of Women's Subordination,* ed. Women Studies Group CCCS, 96–108. London: Hutchinson.

———. 1982. "The Politics of Feminist Research: Between Talk, Text and Action." *Feminist Review,* no. 12, 46–57.

———. 1984. *Gender and Generation.* London: Macmillan.

———. 1991. *Feminism and Youth Culture: From "Jackie" to "Just Seventeen."* Boston: Unwin Hyman.

Martin, Jane Roland. 1985. *Reclaiming a Conversation.* New Haven, Conn.: Yale University Press.

Martin, Roy. 1972. "Student Sex and Behavior as Determinants of the Type and Frequency of Teacher-Student Contact." *Journal of School Psychology* 10(4):339–44.

Mascia-Lees, Frances, Patricia Sharpe, and Colleen Ballerino Cohen. 1989. "The Postmodern Turn in Anthropology: Cautions from a Feminist Perspective." *Signs* 15(1):7–33.

Mishler, Elliot. 1986. *Research Interviewing: Context and Narrative.* Cambridge, Mass.: Harvard University Press.

O'Brien, Mary. 1981. *The Politics of Reproduction.* London: Routledge & Kegan Paul.

Ogbu, John. 1974. *The Next Generation: An Ethnography of Education in an Urban Neighborhood.* New York and London: Academic Press.

Personal Narratives Group. 1989. *Interpreting Women's Lives: Feminist Theory and Personal Narratives*. Bloomington: Indiana University Press.

Radway, Janice. 1984. *Reading the Romance: Women, Patriarchy and Popular Culture*. Chapel Hill: University of North Carolina Press.

Rockhill, Kathleen. 1987. "Literacy as Threat/Desire: Longing to Be Somebody." In *Women and Education: A Canadian Perspective*, ed. Jane Gaskell and A. T. McLaren, 315–33. Calgary: Detselig Enterprises.

Roman, Leslie. 1987. "Punk Femininity: The Formation of Young Women's Gender Identities and Class Relations in the Extramural Curriculum within a Contemporary Subculture." Ph.D. dissertation, University of Wisconsin Madison.

———. 1988. "Intimacy, Labor, and Class: Ideologies of Feminine Sexuality in the Punk Slam Dance." In *Becoming Feminine: The Politics of Popular Culture*, ed. Leslie Roman, Linda Christian-Smith, and Elizabeth Ellsworth, 143–84. London: Falmer.

Rose, Hilary. 1983. "Hand, Brain and Heart: A Feminist Epistemology for the Natural Sciences." *Signs* 9(10):73–90.

Rubin, Lillian. 1976. *Worlds of Pain: Life in the Working-Class Family*. New York: Basic.

Ruddick, Sara. 1989. *Maternal Thinking: Toward a Politics of Peace*. Boston: Beacon.

Sadker, Myra, and David Sadker. 1986. "Sexism in the Classroom: From Grade School to Graduate School." *Phi Delta Kappan* 68:512.

Sennett, Richard. 1980. *Authority*. New York: Vintage.

Sennett, Richard, and Jonathan Cobb. 1972. *The Hidden Injuries of Class*. New York: Knopf.

Serbin, Lisa, K. Daniel O'Leary, Ronald Kent, and Illene Tonick. 1973. "A Comparison of Teacher Response to the Preacademic and Problem Behavior of Boys and Girls." **Child Development** 44(4):796–804.

Smith, Dorothy. 1987. *The Everyday World as Problematic: A Feminist Sociology*. Boston: Northeastern University Press.

Stacey, Judith. 1988. "Can There Be a Feminist Ethnography?" *Women's Studies International Forum* 11(1):21–27.

Stacey, Judith, Susan Bereaud, and Joan Daniels, eds. 1974. *And Jill Came Tumbling After: Sexism in American Education*. New York: Dell.

Stanley, Liz, and Sue Wise. 1983. *Breaking Out: Feminist Consciousness and Feminist Research*. London: Routledge & Kegan Paul.

Steedman, Carolyn. 1987. *Landscape for a Good Woman*. New Brunswick, N.J.: Rutgers University Press.

Stockard, Jean. 1985. "Education and Gender Equality: A Critical View." In *Research in Sociology of Education and Socialization*, ed. Alan C. Kerckhoff, 5:293–321. Greenwich, Conn.: JAI.

Strathern, Marilyn. 1987. "An Awkward Relationship: The Case of Feminism and Anthropology." *Signs* 12(2):276–92.

Stuckey, Elspeth. 1988. "Invisible Women: The Black Female Educator in the Segregated South." Paper presented at the Southeastern Women Studies Association Annual Meeting, University of North Carolina, Chapel Hill.

Thompson, Edward P. 1963. *The Making of the English Working-Class*. New York: Vintage.

Trask, Haunani-Kay 1986. *Eros and Power: The Promise of Feminist Theory*. Philadelphia: University of Pennsylvania Press.

Tronto, Joan. 1989. "Women and Caring: What Can Feminists Learn about Morality from Caring?" In Bordo and Jaggar, eds.

Waller, Willard. 1932. *Sociology of Teaching*. New York: Wiley.

Washington, Mary Helen. 1982. "Teaching Black-Eyed Susans: An Approach to the Study of Black Women Writers." In *All the Women Are White and All the Blacks Are Men, But Some of Us Are Brave*, ed. G. Hull, P. B. Scott, and B. Smith, 208–17. Old Westbury, N.Y.: Feminist Press.

Washington, Mary Helen, ed. 1975. *Black-Eyed Susans*. New York: Anchor/Doubleday.

Weis, Lois. 1983. "Schooling and Cultural Production: A Comparison of Black and White Lived Culture." In *Ideology and Practice in Schooling*, ed. Michael Apple and Lois Weis. Philadelphia: Temple University Press.

———. 1985. *Between Two Worlds: Black Students in an Urban Community College*. Boston: Routledge & Kegan Paul.

———. 1988. *Class, Race, and Gender in American Education*. Albany: State University of New York Press.

Wellesley College Center for Research on Women. 1992. *How Schools Shortchange Girls: A Study of Major Findings on Girls and Education*. Washington, D.C.: American Association of University Women.

Welter, Barbara. 1978. "The Cult of True Womanhood: 1820–1860." In *The American Family in Social-Historical Perspective*, ed. Michael Gordon, 313–33. New York: St. Martin's Press.

Williams, Patricia. 1988. "On the Object of Property." *Signs* 14(1):5–24.

———. 1991. *The Alchemy of Race and Rights: Diary of a Law Professor*. Cambridge, Mass.: Harvard University Press.

Williams, Raymond. 1961. *Culture and Society*. New York: Penguin.

———. 1965. *The Long Revolution*. New York: Penguin.

———. 1976. *Keywords: A Vocabulary of Culture and Society*. New York: Oxford University Press.

Willis, Paul. 1977. *Learning to Labour: How Working-Class Kids Get Working-Class Jobs*. Westmead: Saxon House, Teakfield.

SONIA E. ALVAREZ is assistant professor of politics at the University of California, Santa Cruz. She has published articles on Latin American social movements and on contemporary gender politics in Brazil and the Southern Cone. She is author of *Engendering Democracy in Brazil: Women's Movements in Transition Politics* (Princeton, N.J.: Princeton University Press, 1990) and is coeditor, with Arturo Escobar, of *The Making of Social Movements in Contemporary Latin America* (Boulder, Colo.: Westview Press, 1992). She is working on a book about popular movements, urban regimes, and democratic consolidation in Brazil.

YEŞIM ARAT is associate professor of politics at Boğaziçi University, Istanbul, Turkey. She has worked primarily on women in politics, including the politics of Islamic women in Turkey. She is author of *Patriarchal Paradox: Women Politicians in Turkey* (Cranbury, N.J.: Fairleigh Dickinson University Press, 1989). Her current work is on feminist activism in the 1980s in Turkey.

RUTH H. BLOCH is on the faculty of the history department at University of California, Los Angeles, where she teaches courses on American women's history, American intellectual history, and colonial/revolutionary American history. Her historical interests have been centered on early American religion, women, popular culture, and political ideology and the intersections between them. Her book *Visionary Republic* (Cambridge: Cambridge University Press, 1985) and several related essays examine religious ideas in the American revolutionary movement. In addition to the one reprinted here, she has written several other articles on women and gender definitions in the colonial and revolutionary periods.

JOHANNA BRENNER is professor of sociology and women's studies and coordinator of the women's studies program at Portland State University. She has published work on feminist theory and politics, most recently "The Best of Times, The Worst of Times: U.S. Feminism Today," *New Left Review* (1993).

PATRICIA CHUCHRYK is associate professor and chair of the department of sociology at the University of Lethbridge, Alberta. She has published articles on feminism and the women's movement in Latin America, including "Women in the Revolution," in *Revolution and Counterrevo-*

lution in Nicaragua: 1979–1990, ed. Thomas Walker (Boulder, Colo.: Westview Press, 1991), and "Feminist Antiauthoritarian Politics: The Role of Women's Organizations in the Chilean transition to Democracy," in *The Women's Movement in Latin America: Feminism and the Transition to Democracy,* ed. Jane S. Jaquette (Boston: Unwin Hymen, 1989). Her research interests include the career paths of academic women, feminist pedagogy, and Latin American women and women's movements. She has recently completed a project on First Nations women of Canada and is working on a book about the Chilean women's movement and the transition to democracy.

TRISHA FRANZEN is director of the Anna Howard Shaw Center for women's studies and programs at Albion College, Albion, Michigan. She received her Ph.D. in American studies from the University of New Mexico and has been active in women's studies and the women's movement for eighteen years. Her book, *Spinsters and Lesbians: Resisting and Surviving as Independent Women, 1890–1920 and 1950–1980* (New York: New York University Press), is forthcoming. She lives in Albion with her partner and daughter.

NANCY FRASER is professor of philosophy and faculty fellow of the Center for Urban Affairs and Policy Research at Northwestern University, where she is also an affiliate of the women's studies program. She is the author of *Unruly Practices: Power, Discourse and Gender in Contemporary Social Theory* (Minneapolis: University of Minnesota Press, 1989), coauthor of *Feminist Contentions: A Philosophical Exchange* (New York: Routledge, 1994), and coeditor with Sandra Lee Bartky of *Revaluing French Feminism: Critical Essays on Difference, Agency, and Culture* (Bloomington: Indiana University Press, 1992). Her research interests include feminist theory and social and political theory.

LINDA GORDON is Florence Kelley Professor of history and women's studies at the University of Wisconsin—Madison. She is the author of *Woman's Body, Woman's Right: A History of Birth Control in America,* 2d ed. (New York: Penguin, 1990), and *Heroes of Their Own Lives: The Politics and History of Family Violence* (New York: Viking Press, 1988). Her work on welfare includes *Pitied But Not Entitled: Single Mothers and the History of Welfare* (New York: Free Press, 1994), and she is editor of *Women, the State, and Welfare* (Madison: University of Wisconsin Press, 1990). With Ros Baxandall, she has just completed a second edition of *America's Working Women: A Documentary History* (New York: Norton, 1995), and they are beginning to put together a multivolume collection of documents from the women's liberation movement.

SAMIRA HAJ is assistant professor of history at New York University. Her major area of specialty is the modern Middle East; she is at work on a book about the agrarian roots of the 1958 National Revolution in Iraq and is planning a future research project on the construction of gender in the Arab Moslem world.

TEMMA KAPLAN is professor of women's studies and history at the State University of New York at Stony Brook. She is concerned with the gendered bias of women's resistance movements and how new strategies develop in the course of struggle. She is the author of *Anarchists of Andaulsai, 1868–1903* (Princeton, N.J.: Princeton University Press, 1977), winner that year of the Berkshire Society Prize, and of *Red City, Blue Period: Social Movements in Picasso's Barcelona* (Berkeley: University of California Press, 1992). She is currently completing a volume titled *Making Spectacles of Themselves: Grass-Root Movements of Women.*

SONIA KRUKS is the Robert S. Danforth Professor of politics and member of the women's studies program at Oberlin College, where she teaches political philosophy and feminist theory. She is the author of *The Political Philosophy of Merleau-Ponty* (Atlantic Highlands, N.J.: Humanities Press, 1981) and *Situation and Human Existence: Freedom, Subjectivity and Society* (Boston: Unwin Hymen, 1990). She is also co-editor with Rayna Rapp and Marilyn B. Young of *Promissory Notes: Women in the Transition to Socialism* (New York: Monthly Review Press, 1989).

BARBARA LASLETT is professor of sociology at the University of Minnesota and editor (with Ruth-Ellen B. Joeres) of *Signs*. She is the former editor of *Contemporary Sociology* and president of the Social Science History Association. Her scholarly work has focused primarily on the historical sociology of gender relations, social change and the family, and social reproduction. Recently she has also applied a feminist perspective to the history of American sociology.

WENDY LUTTRELL is assistant professor in cultural anthropology and assistant director of the Center for Teaching and Learning at Duke University. She writes about how gender, race, class, and sexual identities are formed and transformed as part of the schooling process. She is author of *Schoolwise and Motherwise: An Ethnography of Women's Learning* (New York: Routledge, in press), which compares two groups of women literacy learners and their educational views, values, and experiences. She has translated much of her research findings into adult basic education curriculum materials. Currently she is conducting ethnographic research about pregnant teens and teen mother's views about parenthood, sexuality, and schooling.

ARLENE ELOWE MACLEOD is assistant professor of political science at Bates College, where she teaches comparative politics and participates in the women's studies program. Her research centers on forms of resistance and women's agency in power relations, particularly in the Middle East. She is author of *Accommodating Protest: Working Women, the New Veiling and Change in Cairo* (New York: Columbia University Press, 1991).

MARYSA NAVARRO-ARANGUREN is professor of history at Dartmouth College. She has written on the mothers of Plaza de Mayo, authored a political biography of Evita (*Evita* [Buenos Aires: Corregidor, 1981]), and is writing a book about Argentine women during the 1976–83 military dictatorship in Argentina. She has been an international correspondent for *Signs* since it began its second volume in 1976.

MURIEL NAZZARI is associate professor of history at Indiana University. She has published *Disappearance of the Dowry: Women, Families, and Social Change in San Paulo, Brazil (1600–1900)* (Palo Alto, Calif.: Stanford University Press, 1991). She is currently studying the intersections of gender and race within concubinage and the process of miscegenation in colonial Brazil.

ELIZABETH SCHMIDT is assistant professor of history at Loyola College in Maryland. Her 1992 book, *Peasants, Traders, and Wives: Shona Women in the History of Zimbabwe, 1870–1939)* (Portsmouth, N.H.: Heinmann, 1992), examines the impact of colonial land and labor policies and gender ideology on women in Zimbabwe. Her most recent manuscript, "Mobilizing the Masses: Gender, Ethnicity, and Class in the Guinean Nationalist Movement, 1946–1958," focuses on the role played by market women and trade unionists in the Guinean independence struggle.

GAY W. SEIDMAN is assistant professor of sociology at the University of Wisconsin—Madison. Her recent book, *Manufacturing Militance* (Berkeley: University of California Press, 1994), compares the emergence of radical workers' movements in Brazil and South Africa. Her current research is on women's organizations and changing gender ideologies during democratic transitions.

PATRICIA STAMP is associate professor of social science at York University, Toronto. She is affiliated with the graduate programs in social and political thought, women's studies, and political science and teaches courses on African politics and society and Third World gender relations. The author of *Technology, Gender, and Power in Africa* (Ottawa: International Development Research Center, 1989), she recently founded the Development Studies Resource Center at York University, designed to offer researchers "the view from below" in development initiatives.

NANCY SAPORTA STERNBACH   is associate professor of Spanish and women's studies at Smith College, where she teaches Latina and Latin American literature and women's studies. She is currently working on an anthology of Latina playwrights tentatively titled "Stages of Life: Latinas in Teatro." Her interests and recent publications also include research on Latin American women essayists. She has published widely on Latina and Latin American women writers.

LOUISE A. TILLY   is Michael E. Gellert Professor of History and Sociology at the New School for Social Research. Her current project is a historical narrative and analysis of family and gender relations in the process of cotton textile industrialization across the world, but she continues to investigate and write about French women tobacco workers at the turn of the twentieth century.

ANNE WALTHALL   is professor of history at the University of California, Irvine, and director of the Tokyo Study Center for the University of California Education Abroad Program. Her publications include *Peasant Uprisings in Japan: A Critical Anthology of Peasant Histories* (Chicago: University of Chicago Press, 1991) and "The Family Ideology of the Rural Entrepreneurs in Nineteenth Century Japan," *Journal of Social History* 23, no. 3 (Spring 1990): 463–83. She is working on a biography of Matsuo Taseko (1811–94), a peasant woman whose dedication to the imperial cause in the 1860s brought her posthumous court rank and a reputation as a right-wing ultranationalist but also led to the preservation of her diaries, letters, and poems.

BRONWYN WINTER   teaches French studies at the University of Sydney, where she is completing her Ph.D. dissertation on Maghrebian women, nationalist/identity discourses, and feminist responses in contemporary France. Recent publications include "La 'communaute lesbienne' et l'ideologie heteropatriarcle: Les pieges de liberalisme," *Resources for Feminist Research/Documentation sur la Recherche Feministe* 19, nos. 3/4 (September/December 1990): 49–53, of which a revised form appeared in English as "Western Liberalism and Lesbian Politics, or a Guide to Dyke Doublethink," *Journal of Australian Lesbian Feminist Studies* 1, no. 2 (December 1990): 35–54. She also recently gave a paper titled

"(Mis)representations: What French Feminism *Isn't*" at the Australian Women's Studies Association national conference in Geelong, Victoria (December 4–6, 1994).

IRIS MARION YOUNG   teaches ethics and political theory in the graduate school of public and international affairs at the University of Pittsburgh. She is the author of *Justice and the Politics of Difference* (Princeton, N.J.: Princeton University Press, 1990) and *Throwing Like a Girl and Other Essays in Feminist Philosophy and Social Theory* (Bloomington: Indiana University Press, 1990). She is currently working on a book on democracy and communication.

Index

Abortion, 215, 228

Accommodating protest, 4, 186, 203–9

AFDC (Aid to Families with Dependent Children), 35, 45–7, 51–4

African women: in France, 315–50; in Kenya, 351–88; in South Africa, 210–39; in Zimbabwe (Southern Rhodesia), 389–413

Albuquerque: lesbian community in, 61–76

America, Revolutionary: gendered notions of virtue in, 11–32

American women: See U.S. Women

Androcentric functionalism: in studies of African development, 389–91

Backlash: in response to strategic gender issues, 370–1

Bandita: Linda Singer on feminist philosopher as, 109

Barcelona: female consciousness and collective action in, 145–166

Beauvoir, Simone de: and dialectical realism, 95–6; and feminism, 82–3, 85, 95–6; and postmodernism, 95; and Jean-Paul Sartre, 83–91, 94–5; and situated gender subjectivity, 77–98; works: *Ethics of Ambiguity, The*, 88–9; *Prime of Life, The*, 86; *Pyrrus et Cinéas*, 87–9, 93; *Second Sex, The*, 83–4, 88–92

Bordo, Susan, 107

Butler, Judith, 89, 93–4, 101–2, 108, 120

Cairo: and the new veiling in, 185–209

Calvinism, 12, 22–3

Capitalism: development of and gender conflict in Zimbabwe, 389–413; and income distribution, 416; lineage and transition to, 379; and oppression of women in Latin America, 256, 259; as reinforcing patriarchy, 173; *See also* Industrialization and women; Proletarianization; Welfare state

Caraway, Nancie, 107–8

Caregiving: and citizenship, 466–7; failure of schools to value, 451–2, 466–7; by teachers in schools, 456; *See also* Family roles of women as grounds for protest

Catholic church, 11

Chodorow, Nancy, 86n16, 199–20, 433

Circumcision. *See* Female circumcision

Citizenship: emergence of modern notions of, 2; and independence, 39; schools' narrow view of, 466–7

Class: debates over in Latin American *Encuentros*, 258–60; and female virtue, 32; and women's school experiences, 432–73

Classical republicanism. *See* Republicanism

Classic patriarchy: defined, 168–9; *See also* Patriarchy

Cliteridectomy, 317, 331, 333; *See also* Excision

Collaborative hegemony: defined, 355; in Kenya, 355–7, 384; in Zimbabwe, 391–2, 413

Collaborative patriarchy. *See* Collaborative hegemony

Collective action: conditions under which working-class women most likely to engage in, 142–4; defined, 129; forms engaged in by working-class women in France, 133–44

Combative motherhood: as feminist strategy in Kenya, 384–5

Consent: Antonio Gramsci on, 196–7; need for complex notion of, 196–7; Joan Scott on, 197n28

Cuba: material constraints on solution of the "woman question" in, 414–31

Cuban Family Code, 415, 426–9

Cuban Revolution: effects on women, 418–9

Cultural relativism: as defense in excision trials, 325–36; and tradition, 325–7; versus Enlightenment universalism, 315–50

Customary law: creation and manipulation of to subordinate women, 352–8, 407–11; manipulation of for social and economic gain in Kenya, 376–8; role of in Kenyan law and politics, 352–7

Dependency: and Dependent Personality Disorder, 50; as feminized, 49–50; genealogy of, 33–60; and the housewife, 42; in industrial usage, 38–43; as keyword of U.S. welfare state, 33–60; and the native/slave, 41; and opposition to negative imagery, 53–5; as pathology, 49; and the pauper, 40–1; in preindustrial usage, 36–8; principal icons of, 40–3; as racialized, 50–1; registers of, 36; in welfare state usage, 43–57

Dialectical realism, 95–6

Dichotomies: between autonomy and double militancy, 255–7, 260, 279–80; between dependence and independence, 33–60; between Enlightenment universalism and cultural relativism, 315–50; between ethic of care and ethic of work and public life, 466–7; between male/public and female/private, 287; between modernization and patriarchal "tradition," 358–70; between victimization and acceptance, 186; between women's equality and national unity, 210–1, 249

"Difference" feminism: and postmodernism, 315

Distribution systems: impact on Cuban women, 416–7

Division of labor. *See* Sexual division of labor

Domestication of women: ideological and economic bases for in Africa, 396

"Double day," women's: 7; in Cuba, 425–6; and economic policy decisions, 414–31; in South Africa, 220

Double militancy: problem of for Latin American feminists, 255–7, 260, 279–80

Dual demands: on women elected to political office, 372–3

Educational systems: and gender relations, 460–68; as state institutions, 7

Edwards, Jonathan: 22–3, 25

Egyptian women. *See* Cairo

Encuentros, 242–281: in Bogota, Columbia (1981), 252–7; in Lima, Peru (1983), 257–60; in Bertioga, Brazil (1985), 260–4; in Taxco, Mexico (1987), 264–73; in San Bernardo, Argentina (1990), 273–9

Enlightenment universalism: masculinity embedded in, 15–9, 29–30; versus cultural relativism, 315–50

Essentialism: of women and problems with, 119

Ethnicity: and politics in Kenya, 378–88

Excision: in Africa, 318–9; defense of in French trials, 324–36; defined, 317; in Europe, 319; justifications given for, 317–8; and trials in French courts, 320–4

Family Code. *See* Cuban Family Code

Family roles of women as grounds for protest: in Barcelona, 145–66; in Japan, 286–289; in Kenya, 362–4; in Latin America, 248; in occupied territories, 178

Family wage: and definition of dependency, 42–3, 48

Federalist Papers, The, 28–9

Female consciousness: 145–8, 150; and community solidarity, 150–1; and female solidarity, 147–51; and feminist theory and politics, 165–6; and gossip, 148; and sexual division of labor, 145–66; and social welfare, 164–6

Female circumcision, 317, 327–8, 331; *See also* Excision

Female genital mutilation, 317; *See also* Excision

Female labor: exploitation of in occupied territories, 172–7; *See also* Sexual division of labor; Work force participation by women

Female life cycle: and gender identity in Palestinian family, 169–70

Female sexuality. *See* Sexuality

Feminism: African rejection of as Western, 370, 373; Simone de Beauvoir on, 82–3, 85, 95–6; and "French feminism," 337; in Latin America, 240–281; need for more diverse definitions, 183, 240–4; and Otieno case, 351–388; and Palestinian women, 183–4

Feminisms in Latin America: and authoritarian patriarchy, 244–47; genesis of, 244–52; and *movimientos de mujeres* (women's movement), 248–50; and New Left, 247–8

Feminist consciousness: compared to female consciousness, 146–7; generational differences in, 181–3; of Palestinian women, 181–88; in Palestinian women's movement, 183–4

Feminist politics: and female consciousness, 165–6; in Kenya, 370–6; in Latin America, 240–81; and seriality, 123–4

Feminist theory: and category of woman, 100–5; and essentializing category of woman, 103; as Eurocentric and ethnocentric, 168; and female consciousness, 165–6; and identity politics, 107–8; and multiple genders, 105; and need for more inclusive definition, 184; and practice as source of conflict in Albuquerque lesbian community, 74–5; and problem of women's complicity in own oppression, 186–90, 203–9; and postmodernism, 77–80

Feminists: and anti-excision movement in France, 336–48; and conflict with *movimientos de mujures* (women's movement), 257–60, 280–1; and demands within ANC, 231–4; and Otieno case, 370–6; and sexuality debates, 62, 73–4; and struggle against imperialism in Latin America, 250

Ferguson, Ann, 105–6

Foucault, Michel: 34, 81–2, 91, 93, 94, 185–9

France: African women in, 316–50; excision trials in, 316, 319, 320–48; proletarianization and women's collective action in, 127–44

"French feminism": and postmodernism, 337

Fuss, Diana, 107

Gender: and economic development in South Africa, 235; inequality in Zimbabwe, 390–1; and migrant streams in South Africa, 213–6; and lineage and clan politics in Kenya, 356–8; representations of, 1–2; as seriality, 99–114; and women's schooling, 432–73

Gender bias: in South African courts, 364–5

Gender conflict: and capitalist development in colonial Zimbabwe, 389–413

Gender division of labor. *See* Sexual division of labor

Gender identity: and female life cycle, 169–70; and feminist struggle, 107–8; as multiple, 105–7; problems inherent in, 119–20; theories of, 100–3

Gender issues: incorporation into national agenda, 234–5; practical vs. strategic, 362–4, 370–1, 384–5; as Western and bourgeois, 216

Gender politics: and ethnicity in Kenya, 378–83

Gender relations: in Cairo, 185–209; in Cuba, 414–31; in Kenya, 351–88; in occupied territories, 167–84; in South Africa, 210–39; in Zimbabwe, 389–413

Gender resistance. *See* Women's resistance

Genital mutilation. *See* Female genital mutilation

Gilligan, Carol, 86n16, 433
Gossip: and female consciousness, 148
Gramsci, Antonio, 186, 196–7, 205, 208
Group: in contrast to series, 109–110

Hegel, G. W. F., 146
Hegemony: 186–8, 207–8; *See also* Collaborative hegemony
Heterosexism, 100, 102: and enforced heterosexuality, 115
Household: and change in relations with village in early modern Japan, 283; and gender inequality in Cuba, 425–7
Housewives: and dependency, 42–4, 46, 48–50, 55–7
Housework and working women: in Cairo, 200; in Cuba, 423–4; in South Africa, 220

Identity. *See* Gender identity
Industrialization and women: in France, 128–132; in Japan, 290–1, 295–6, 303, 308; in South Africa, 211–2, 216–7
Infibulation, 317, 323–4
International feminism: polemics of, 189; role in South African activism, 229–30
Intifada: women in, 178–84
Israel: impact of colonization policies on Palestinian gender relations, 171–8

Japan: and invisibility of women in history of social protest, 282–312

Kandiyoti, Deniz, 168–9, 173n16
Kenya: politics of gender and ethnicity in, 351–88
Keyword: defined, 34; *dependency* as, in U.S. welfare state, 33–60

Labor shortages: blaming women for, 397–8; using women to fill, 428
Latin America: feminisms in, 240–81
Latinas: and participation in *encuentros*, 266
Legal system: as instrument of both oppression and emancipation in France, 344; political pressures on in Kenya, 366
Legends: women in Japanese, 283, 285–91, 307–8
Lesbians: and community in Albuquerque, 61–76; and participation in *encuentros*, 259, 264
Liberation theology, 363
Locke, John, 23–4

Machiavelli, Niccolò, 17
Martin, Jane Roland, 466
Marx, Karl, 146–7

Material constraints: on attendance at *encuentros*, 258, 261–2, 265–6, 274n38; on solution of "woman problem" in Cuba, 410–31

Maternal roles and responsibilities. *See* Family roles of women as grounds for protest; Motherhood

Middle East: gender relations in, 167–84, 185–209

Mobility: control of women's, 411–13

Mobilization: of women in South Africa, 210–39

Mohanty, Chandra, 101

Molyneux, Maxine, 362, 370

Motherhood: combative, 384–5; and women's schooling, 436–7, 439n14; and women's struggle for equality, 386–7; *See also* Family roles of women as grounds for protest

Moynihan, Daniel P., 33

Muslim custom: and excision, 331–2; and oppression of women, 170n8; and veiling, 190–1; and women's working, 202

New veiling, the. *See* Veiling

Otieno case, 351–88; and appeal to practical gender issues, 362–4; and lack of public support for Wambui, 364–5; and politicizing of women, 375–6

Palestinian women: and patriarchal relations in occupied territories, 167–84

Patriarchal familism, 366

Patriarchal relations: erosion of during Intifada, 183n37; in occupied territories, 167–84; role of liberation movement in defiance of, 183

Patriarchy: classic, 168–9; and privatization of women, 286, 386–7; and "tradition," 367–70; variation in, 168; *See also* Collaborative hegemony

Patrilineal family form: and women, 169–70

Political protest. *See* Women's resistance

Political resistance. *See* Women's resistance

Postmodernism: Simone de Beauvoir and, 95; as difference feminism, 315; and Enlightenment thought, 77–82; and feminism, 77–8; and feminist theory, 77–80; in French usage, 315n1

Poverty: and dependency, 33–4, 40–1, 44–6; and schooling practices, 455–60

Practical gender issues: versus strategic gender issues, 362–4, 370–1

Pragmatic theorizing, 103–4

Protest. *See* Women's resistance

Prejudice: of Europeans against African women, 392–6

Privatization: of role of women in Japan, 286; as strategy in controlling women in Africa, 386–7
Proletarianization: defined, 129; in occupied territories, 167; and women in France, 129–42
Protestantism, 12, 14–6, 22, 24, 39–40

Qur'an. *See* Muslim custom

Race: and dependency, 41–3, 46, 50–1, 55; as issue at *encuentros*, 259–60, 263; and women's schooling, 432–73
Racial uplift movement: paradoxical effect on black women's schooling, 462–3
Rape, 226, 306–7
Reproduction: need to value women's role in processes of, 466–7; as variable in women's social position, 415
Rice riots: women as participants in, 299–303
Richardson, Samuel, 26
Representation: of women's concerns in Japanese legends, 286–91
Republicanism: classical, 13–6, 24
Resistance. *See* Women's resistance
Rhodesia. *See* Zimbabwe

Sartre, Jean-Paul: 81–2; and Simone de Beauvoir's thought, 83–91, 94–5; on race, 117–8; on serial collectivity, 100, 109–14, 116n2, 117–8; works: *Being and Nothingness*, 82, 84, 86–8; *Critique of Dialectical Reason*, 82, 84, 109–19
Schools: as sites of political conflict and social action, 432–73; *See also* Women's schooling
Serial collectivity: as constraint, 112; and practico-inert reality, 111–2; and relation between series and groups, 109–10, 121; and serialized action, 112; *See also* Seriality
Seriality: as constraint and experience of Otherness, 111, 117; defined, 114; gender as 114–7, 119–22; as level of social existence, 114; as milieu of action, 112; race or nationality, 117–9; as structural relation to material objects, 114
Sexual division of labor: and economic policy decisions on in Cuba, 414–31; and female consciousness, 145–66; and school organization, 460–62; and sex segregation in work force in Cairo, 213–6; as structuring gender, 116
Sexual harassment: and female consciousness and solidarity, 152; and mobilization in South Africa, 276; and new veiling, 204; and political intimidation in occupied territories, 177

Sexuality: debates, 62, 73–4; male control over women's, 170–1, 338, 396–400, 405; as problematic basis for political solidarity among women, 73–5; *See also* Heterosexism; Lesbian

Singer, Linda, 109

Situated subjectivity: Simone de Beauvoir on, 77–98

Socialism: and distribution of resources in Cuba, 414–8, 430–1; and feminism in Latin America, 247–9, 256–7

Social Security, 46

South Africa: mobilization and gender in, 210–39

Spain: female consciousness and collective action in Barcelona, 145–66

Spelman, Elizabeth, 100–1, 105, 120

Spivak, Gayati, 115

Strategic gender issues: backlash against, 370–1; versus practical gender issues, 362–4

Subject, the: Simone de Beauvoir on, 80, 83–96; and inherence in the body, 93–5; and intersubjectivity of, 91–2

Tax, Meredith, 121–2

Teacher's pets: 441–9, 463–5, 467–8

Theory: defined, 103; *See also* Feminist theory; Pragmatic theorizing

Tradition. *See* Cultural relativism; Customary law

Trials: and excision cases in France, 320–4; and Otieno case in Kenya, 360–70, 375–6; as political contests, 343

U.S. Women: 11–32, 33–60, 61–76, 432–73

Veiling: and cooption, 208; and economic pressures on Egyptian women, 199; as message of protest and accommodation, 188; as mode of political struggle; as movement, 193; symbolic nature of, 187–92, 201–3; Western views of, 189–90

Violence against women: in Latin America, 246; in South Africa, 215, 227; *See also* Sexual harassment; Rape

Virtue: and American political thought, 27–32; gendered notions of in Revolutionary America, 11–32; and literary sentimentalism, 25–7; and psychological theories, 23–4; and religious ideas, 22–3

Welfare dependency. *See* Dependency

Welfare state: dependency as keyword of in U.S., 33–60; in Egypt, 187–8

Western stereotypes: of Mid-Eastern women as oppressed, 167–8, 186–7

Williams, Raymond, 34

"Woman question" in Cuba, 414–31

Women: in Africa, 210–39, 351–413; in Barcelona, 145–66; and collective action, 99–100, 105, 122–4, 127–44, 145–66; and complicity in own oppression, 186–90, 203–9, 340–1; in Cuba, 414–31; and "double day," 414–31; as elected office holders with dual demands upon, 372–3; in France, 127–44, 315–50; in Japan, 282–312; in Kenya, 351–88; as knowers, 433; in Latin America, 240–81; in Middle East, 167–209; Palestinian in occupied territories, 167–84; as social collective, 99–124; in South Africa, 210–39; in United States, 11–76, 432–73; in Zimbabwe, 389–413

Women's activism: in Barcelona, 151–66; in France, 336–42; in Kenya, 370–6; in Latin America, 210–39; and seriality, 123–4; in South Africa, 221–34; See also Women's movement; Women's resistance

Women's movement: and Albuquerque lesbian community, 62, 68–72, 74; in France, 336–42; in Kenya, 370–6; in Latin America, 240–81; in South Africa, 223

Women's resistance: adultery and running away as, 398–407; and capitalism and patriarchy, 391; and collective action, 145–66; and domestic abuse, 400–7; dropping out of school as, 449–55; and imperialism, 358n18, 359; in Japanese legends about peasant uprisings, 283, 285–91, 307–8; and mobilization in South Africa, 221–34; need for more expansive definition of, 5, 202–5, 282–311; Otieno case as example of, 387–8; by Palestinian women, 177–84; in rice riots, 299–303; and state repression and economic exploitation, 244–51; veiling as, 185–209; See also Family roles of women as grounds for protest

Women's schooling: 432–73

Women's subjectivity: as both active and dominated, 186; under domination, 185–207; See also Situated subjectivity; Subject, the

Work force participation by women: in Cuba, 421–3, 427–30; in occupied territories, 172–6; in South Africa, 212, 216–21; See also "Double day," women's; Female labor

Zimbabwe: patriarchy and capitalism in the colonial state, 389–413

Tues:
Honig & Hershatter – Personal Voices
Intro + 3 out of 9 Chapters

Thurs:
article by Rey Chow in Mohanty book
The Joy Luck Club

Tues ⎰ Scott   + personal
     ⎨ Jones   essay
     ⎱ Kamuf